F. C. WEAVER

MANAGERIAL MARKETING:

PERSPECTIVES AND VIEWPOINTS

MANAGERIAL MARKETING:

PERSPECTIVES AND VIEWPOINTS

A Source Book

EUGENE J. KELLEY, Ph.D.

Research Professor of Business Administration, College of Business Administration, The Pennsylvania State University

WILLIAM LAZER, Ph.D.

Professor of Marketing, Graduate School of Business Administration, Michigan State University

1967: *THIRD EDITION*

RICHARD D. IRWIN, INC.

HOMEWOOD, ILLINOIS

Third Edition

First Printing, June, 1967
Second Printing, February, 1968

Library of Congress Catalog Card No. 67–15846

PRINTED IN THE UNITED STATES OF AMERICA

To Dorothy and Joyce

PREFACE

This book is designed for use either as a primary source book in marketing management courses or in conjunction with standard textbooks and casebooks in advanced undergraduate and graduate marketing courses. This third edition, as did the first two editions, features the managerial approach to the study of marketing. The managerial approach to marketing is receiving increasing attention in universities; the marketing concept has been widely accepted as a necessary focus for business survival and growth in the dynamic American economy.

We are grateful that the two previous editions of this book were well received and used widely as teaching vehicles in marketing management courses, seminars, and executive development programs. The articles included in this edition, as in the previous two, were selected for their fundamental contributions, forward-looking insights, and effectiveness in stimulating marketing thought and understanding. Several manuscripts were developed especially for this volume by leading marketing authorities. The coverage of this edition has been extended to give more emphasis to emerging marketing topics. The majority of the articles in this edition are new to the book.

Four major topics are receiving greater coverage in this edition. First, the systems approach to the study of marketing is featured. The systems approach was identified as a promising area in the first edition. It now receives increased emphasis. Second, the international dimension of marketing is dealt with in a separate section, containing coverage of both its impact on the multi-national firm and its contribution to economic development. Third, greater emphasis is given to the decision-making developments—including mathematical models and computers—and the new technology that is shaping marketing strategy. Fourth, attention is directed to the societal dimensions of marketing—the area of marketing beyond the profit motive. The public policy area will be receiving increasing attention by marketing scholars and practitioners.

This third edition extends, clarifies, and readjusts, rather than alters, the fundamental focus, approach, and objectives of the first edition. The selections emphasize the dynamic aspects of marketing management, including developments in marketing theory that underlie and ultimately influence the practice of marketing. Consideration of behavioral science-based marketing contributions, the interdisciplinary focus, and the macro dimensions in marketing are featured. We are grateful that the first two volumes had an impact on curricula, course structures, and literature development.

The selections in this revision are intended to be used in educating students and administrators to analyze problems in an environment of increasing business and social change. The thrust of the selections is toward the frontiers of marketing knowledge. The action and strategic dimensions of marketing, including public policy considerations, are stressed, and descriptive and technical materials are de-emphasized.

The objective of developing competence in theory construction will probably not become important for most students. Nevertheless, we believe students should be introduced to the role of theory at an early point in their marketing education. Marketing dynamics requires considerable appreciation and utilization of both theoretical and problem-solving approaches. Marketing theory and problem solving are intimately related. Therefore, considerable emphasis is again directed to the role of marketing theory.

Many of the selections in this book may invite more careful study and rigorous analysis than is required by other supplementary readings. However, understanding a discipline which proposes to explain and predict human action in the modern marketplace requires substantial intellectual effort. It requires a desire and capacity to continue learning. It is to those with such desire and capacity that this book is addressed.

We are greatly indebted to many groups of people in preparing this revision. In particular, we wish to thank the authors and publishers who gave us permission to reproduce their articles and the authors who prepared original contributions for this volume. Without their cooperation this book would not have been possible. This third edition has become a reality because of the complete cooperation of contributors and publishers.

We owe a deep debt of thanks to the teachers and students who used the book in its first two editions and whose acceptance made this revision possible. Many of them offered extremely valuable guidance. Their ideas and suggestions are incorporated in this volume.

We are grateful to our wives for their encouragement and assistance during the preparation of this third edition. We also wish to acknowledge the assistance of several graduate students for their valuable aid in the technical preparation of the manuscript. We are particularly indebted to Roy Nicely and Robert Witt for their contributions during several stages of manuscript development. Others who contributed to the preparation of the book include Marvin Borgelt, Margo Calkin, Warren French, Edward Mayo, Douglas White, and Arch Woodside. We also wish to thank Mrs. Irene Giessl for her many secretarial contributions to the development of the manuscript.

We shall feel well rewarded if this revision brings further clarity to the marketing management approach, and if it can convey some of the challenge and excitement of marketing to the university classroom and to executive development programs.

EUGENE J. KELLEY
WILLIAM LAZER

TABLE OF CONTENTS

INDEXES

I. THE MARKETING MANAGEMENT APPROACH

A. An Overview of Managerial Marketing: Perspectives and Viewpoints

This introductory section outlines the structure and organization of the book, the major topics covered in managerial marketing, and the nature of interrelationships among diverse aspects of marketing management. Among the areas discussed are: the systems approach to marketing, marketing management, the role of consumers and consumer behavior, the managerial functions of marketing, decision strategies and techniques, and the marketing mix. Some new broader dimensions influencing the marketing manager's job are also presented, including recent developments in international marketing and management's increasing concern with the social responsibility of the firm. These marketing developments are receiving increased consideration because their effect on marketing success is now more widely recognized.

Marketing as a field of study is generally categorized as being part of the broader field of business administration. However, marketing also involves considerations that extend beyond these boundaries. Marketing decisions are shaped by and influence the external environments of the firm. Marketing, therefore, has social, economic, legal, international, and political dimensions in addition to its managerial focus. Profitable solutions to marketing problems can only be realized if the significance of environmental change on the firm and its customers is recognized. These external forces which affect consumer behavior and business action must be reflected in marketing policies, plans, programs, and decisions.

The student of marketing must develop a facility for integrating useful contributions from many disciplines. He must also understand the functional purpose of each component in a marketing action system. Illustration I depicts a total marketing system and serves as a model for the study of marketing management. The conceptual relationships portrayed are developed in subsequent illustrations and readings. This marketing system model is presented in the spirit of the following passage from Konrad Lorenz:[1]

> I am aware that the task I have set myself makes excessive demands upon my pen. It is almost impossible to portray in words the functioning of a system in which every part is related to every other in such a way that each has a causal influence on the others. Even if one is only trying to explain a gasoline engine it is hard to know where to begin, because the person to whom one seeks to explain it can only understand the nature of the crankshaft if he has first grasped that of the connecting rods, the pistons, the valves, the camshaft, and so on. Unless one understands the elements of a complete system as a whole, one cannot understand them at all. The more complex the structure of a system is, the greater this difficulty becomes—and it must be surmounted both in one's research and in one's teaching. Unfortunately the working structure of the instinctive and culturally acquired patterns of behavior which make up the social life of man seems to be one of the most complicated systems we know on this earth.

THE EXTERNAL ENVIRONMENTS OF MARKETING

Marketing managers, by the nature of their problems, are environmentalists. They give attention to the implications of environmental changes for marketing policies and practices. Illustration I shows the external environment in which the systemic functions of marketing are managed. These environments and interactions affect marketing opportunities, customer behavior and satisfaction, and the degree of success achieved by the business.

In this model, the major external environmental influences on business actions are categorized as: scientific and technological forces; life style and life space forces; ethical, legal, and social forces; and both domestic and international economic and political forces. Each of these forces interacts with the corporate system. Their impact on marketing management is investigated in Chapter II.

The marketing manager needs to appreciate the pervasive influence of these forces on consumer attitudes and behavior. While the activities of any single business cannot appreciably alter any of the external forces, the converse relationship exists—any one force can affect business outcome. Customers react to and help shape their environments, and market opportunities or problems result from changed customer attitudes toward products and services.

Three linkage levels involved in the analysis of marketing systems are shown in the model.

1. Marketing activities are linked through the corporate enterprise system to the various public and private agencies external to the firm. Examples of

---

[1] Konrad Lorenz, *On Aggression* (New York: Harcourt, Brace & World, Inc., 1966), p. xi.

these agencies, which are not depicted in the model, include: suppliers; advertising firms and media; financial institutions; governmental and private research organizations; federal, state, and local governmental commissions; transportation companies; and the various publics.

2. Linkages exist between marketing and the other business functions that comprise the corporate enterprise system. These other areas are represented by the firm's human, physical, and financial resources, its competitive structure, and its goals. Because the purpose of this model is depiction of a marketing action system, other functional areas of the business have not been explicitly differentiated. Similar models could be constructed for production, finance, and other functions of an enterprise.

3. The systemic functions of marketing are linked to produce an effective marketing-customer satisfactions mix. Three submixes—product-services, communications, and distribution—are combined to achieve marketing objectives. The objective of the marketing mix is to balance marketing effort with marketing opportunity in order to provide optimal marketing support of stated corporate goals.

Illustration I indicates the nature of marketing operations within the corporate enterprise system, and emphasizes that corporate goals are achieved by concentrating on defined areas of market opportunity or, more precisely, on customers in particular market segments. Corporate goal setting is recognized today as a complex process for conglomerate, multinational, multiplant firms.

THE CONSUMER

Chapter III deals with the consumer, the focal point of marketing effort. The consumer, by his decision to buy or not buy a product, holds veto power over the firm's entire marketing and business effort. Many of the elements that influence consumer behavior and satisfaction are considered in this chapter.

Like the others, Chapter III is future-oriented. One purpose of analyzing the articles in the book is to enable the reader to better understand and ultimately meet the problems consumers will have in the future. For example, understanding of consumer behavior is increased by studying trends in life style and life space forces. In Chapter III, some of these trends are identified, and their impact on marketing programs are treated in detail.

Market segmentation provides one way of identifying marketing opportunities that have arisen because of changing life styles. Broad potential markets are broken down into many smaller segments, each with its own tastes, preferences, values, and needs.

The market segmentation concept is the basis of a marketing strategy directed toward consumers with particular life styles and needs. It has been based primarily on demographic variables, such as population, age composition, geographic concentration, sex, marital status, education, and income. While demographic methods are basic, other criteria for market segmentation are also useful. Examples of newer methods of segmentation analysis include the determination of differences in buyer attitudes, motivations, values, patterns of usage, and aesthetic preferences.

Consumer motivation is a function of the extent to which human needs are satisfied. One theory of human motivation holds that needs are arranged on a continuum that ranges from basic physiological needs to those of self-actualization.[2] An appreciable measure of satisfaction of lower needs is a precondition for emergence of higher ones. The marketing manager's task is to assemble a market offer that promises gratification of at least one level in this hierarchy of needs.

Consumer behavior is influenced by the life style and life space forces discussed in this book. Many marketing efforts of American business and many of the changes taking place in consumption cannot be understood unless life style trends are considered.

There seems to be an increasing worldwide interest in personal achievement, social goals, and a better way of life. This has been described as the "revolution of rising expectations" and seems to be worldwide. For example, throughout the world there is an upward mobility thrust toward more education and more real income. The above trends are especially evident in the United States. Trends toward home entertainment and family-centered enjoyment are related to increasing discretionary time and mobility. Changes in the geographic distribution of the population are reflected in a redistribution of the labor force and purchasing power.

Tomorrow's customers may have problems that are quite unlike the buying and consumption problems prevalent today. Future consumers will generally be better educated, have greater mobility, possess more discretionary income, and have more time to spend that income. Hopefully, new communication and distribution patterns will lead to increasingly informed decisions and prompt satisfaction of consumer wants.

DECISION MAKING IN MARKETING

The articles in Chapter IV deal with marketing as a prime focus of managerial decision making. Marketing management is becoming increasingly analytical as models and techniques for information gathering and problem solving are developed, and as new marketing applications of existing scientific methods are discovered. Scientific and technological developments are having a continuing impact on the advancement of science in marketing. For example, the computer is exerting a significant influence on such areas as marketing planning, the evaluation of pro-

---

[2] A. H. Maslow, *Motivation and Personality* (New York: Harper & Row, Publishers, 1954), pp. 80–106.

motional alternatives, and distribution systems. Some authorities see marketing as the great growth area of computer applications in business. The rapid accumulation of new knowledge is resulting in widespread application of mathematical, statistical, economic, psychological, and sociological techniques to marketing problems. These interdisciplinary contributions to marketing promise better understanding of complex consumer needs and of other marketing problems.

MARKETING MANAGEMENT FUNCTIONS

The functions of marketing management identified in the upper center of Illustration I are discussed in Chapter V. The functions are marketing opportunity assessment, marketing planning and programming, marketing organization and leadership, and evaluating and adjusting marketing effort. The marketing management team must perform these four entrepreneurial functions if the firm is to develop an efficient corporate marketing system in a changing environment.

Marketing opportunity assessment centers on the delineation of actual and potential customers and their wants and needs. Market opportunity exists when a business either possesses or can develop capabilities that enable it to profitably satisfy the wants of potential customers. The business must continually develop marketing strategies that will enable it to cultivate these market opportunities.

Research and development activities of business, government, and educational institutions are resulting in increasing numbers of new consumer and industrial products. Similarly, increased productivity resulting from automation and other forces has resulted in production capacity that enables most manufacturing firms to produce more than they can sell. The mass production capability of American industry is predicated on the discovery of new markets and the expansion of existing ones. This is one of the factors underlying the marketing orientation of American business.

Planning is essential to the organization, operation, and control of a business. Planning also provides a basis for an integrated systems orientation and a coordinated marketing strategy. The development of new products and new markets raises organizational and leadership problems for marketing management. The interaction that occurs between an organization and its environment illustrates the dynamics of the systems approach and reflects the demands being placed on the marketing organization and its leadership.

Evaluating and adjusting the marketing effort enables the firm to react to changes occurring in the environment. The process of change—and the ability to cope with it—is a major challenge to marketing management. Financial and integrative controls are used to keep the marketing effort keyed to areas of profitable market opportunity.

MANAGING THE MARKETING MIX

Chapter VI includes discussions of many of the multiple factors involved in managing a marketing-customer satisfactions mix. The lower central section of Illustration I and all of Illustration V provide an overview of the dimensions and complexities of developing and managing a marketing mix. Preparing an effective marketing mix that furthers attainment of corporate objectives is the marketing manager's responsibility.

A marketing mix consists of three submixes—the product and service mix, the communications mix, and the distribution mix. The product and services mix is composed of elements that form the set of utilities a customer buys. Examples of utility set contents include the product, price, services, container, brand, label information, conditions of sale, and warranty. A communications mix consists of the firm's efforts to disseminate information about its market offer to the potential buyers. The elements of a communications mix are advertising, sales promotion, personal selling, merchandising, and special sales aids. The distribution mix is formed of two major components—channels of distribution through which goods and titles to goods flow from the firm to the ultimate purchasers, and physical distribution, which is concerned with loading, transporting, storing, and delivering the product.

The marketing manager's responsibility for formulating an effective mix and for putting it into practice does not culminate with the sale of the product or service. He must not neglect the posttransactional ingredients of his marketing mix if the firm's long-range marketing strategy is to be successful.

INTERNATIONAL MARKETING

The external environmental areas of Illustration I include both domestic and international economic and political forces. The evolution of international markets is one of the most significant trends in contemporary marketing. Chapter VII presents an international view of marketing and the development of the multinational firm.

Many of the forces described in the book are related to the United States market. However, their impact in the United States portends changes of a similar nature in many countries throughout the world. For example, the knowledge explosion, particularly in science and technology, is influencing nearly all cultures. New marketing opportunities are presented by widespread rising consumption expectations and increased interest in personal achievement and social gains. Political unrest in newly formed nations around the world reflects, at least in part, dissatisfaction with present living standards. These people want, and intend to obtain for themselves, those goods now enjoyed by consumers in more advanced economies. Similarly, some nations with controlled economies seem to be moving from a production to a partial consumer orientation. The marketing knowledge and ability possessed by multinational firms can aid immensely in the development of balanced economies in both new and changing political-economic systems. Marketing managers must recognize, analyze, and adjust to the marketing systems of each international market. Attempts to improve the efficiency of these marketing systems must be based on a thorough evaluation of the system's sociopolitical environment.

Marketing plays a key role in the economic growth of developing countries. To the extent that the socioeconomic growth of a nation is related to the marketing process, marketing can be a critical element in the development process. Marketing is not only an economic tool, but a political and social tool as well. Ultimately, marketing's most important social role may lie in its contribution to the stimulation and facilitation of world peace.

SOCIETAL AND INTERDISCIPLINARY DIMENSIONS OF MARKETING

Marketing practitioners and academicians realize that various ethical, legal, social, economic, and political forces are becoming increasingly important for marketing. Illustration I identifies these forces as major influences on markets. Their effects on marketing thought and action are discussed in Chapter VIII.

The socioeconomic dimensions of marketing account, in part, for the growing concern of business and marketing leaders with public and private views of social responsibility in business. The continuing emphasis on the need for businesses to increase their efforts to fulfill their assigned citizenship roles reflects an expanding concept of business' social responsibility.

In order to fully understand marketing's dynamics and the changes in marketing described in this book, students and managers must not only understand problem-solving techniques, they must also understand the theory underlying these techniques and practices. Some developments that influence marketing as a discipline, the interdisciplinary approach to marketing, and the contributions of theory to marketing management are explored in Chapter VIII.

The articles included in the book were chosen for their contribution to an understanding of managerial marketing. The perspective throughout is that marketing managers must equip themselves to better understand the problems of potential customers and, ultimately, to help customers satisfy their requirements in a manner that meets the needs not only of customer and firm but also of society.

B. The Marketing Management Concept

Peter Drucker has written that it is marketing that distinguishes business from other forms of organization. This statement is based on his view that the purpose of a business is to create a customer. A firm that sees its basic purpose in such terms inevitably recognizes the importance of marketing. Decisions concerning marketing questions frequently go well beyond the functional limits of an organization's marketing system. This is why many of the topics in this book are of interest to nonmarketing executives. Marketing activities interact with research and development, production, finance, procurement, and personnel functions. Decisions in one area often influence one or more other functions of the firm.

MARKETING MANAGEMENT AND BUSINESS POLICY

Marketing is such an integral part of the study and practice of business administration that it cannot be logically separated from the basic questions of business strategy and policy. This is the underlying rationale for the systems approach to marketing management, which will be explained in the next section. As a result, one of the interesting trends in policymaking today is top management's recognition that the study of broad business policy issues cannot be fruitfully pursued without an understanding of the close relationship between marketing considerations and corporate policy.

From a social point of view, the future development of a free society depends in substantial measure on progress in the marketing area. In the United States economy, mass distribution faces the challenge of matching the technical excellence of mass production. Economies cannot enjoy the benefits of mass production without efficient marketing systems. This is as true in Russia as it is in the United States. An automated economy produces only filled warehouses and clogged pipelines unless marketing progress is made. The problem of facilitating distribution progress now confronts marketing managers. It can be met only if the pivotal role of modern marketing in our economy is understood and appreciated and marketing factors are related directly to company decisions.

When the marketing concept is accepted as a matter of corporate philosophy, marketing becomes the basis for designing total systems of business action. Fundamental strategies of the business are conceived and implemented on the basis of market needs, forces, and opportunities. Marketing then becomes a way of corporate life and a philosophy of business organization and operation, with the ultimate purpose of helping consumers solve diverse consumption problems in ways compatible with the profit position and objectives of the firm.[1]

A major marketing management task is that of adapting to market opportunity through planned innovation. Planned innovation is a basic characteristic of the modern marketing concept. Innovation based on programmed research and development is now standard competitive procedure; in fact, it has become a necessity if a firm is to survive and grow. Planned marketing involves both adjusting to the innovations of competitors and providing creative counterinnovation by the firm.

It is likely that in the future more firms will accept the point of view that innovation and change are fundamental considerations in formulating marketing policy. In a dynamic marketing climate, the marketing manager must take on, as a first order of business, the task of developing and implementing strategy that will overcome resistance to change. As this occurs, research and development will become more integral parts of the marketing function.

Fred Borch, president of General Electric Company, pointed out that understanding modern marketing rests on two key fundamentals—the "dual-core" job of marketing and the profit, rather than the volume, concept. These two key fundamentals are described below.[2]

Dual-Core Marketing Job

The initial part of the dual-core job is that marketing management must focus business effort on the customer's needs and desires, including those needs and desires the customer is *not* aware of, as well as those he recognizes. Only after identification of these needs can marketing people guide the firm in determining what each function of the business should do to provide the necessary products and services to satisfy customers. The other half of the dual-core job of marketing is a more familiar one—namely, the need to persuade the prospective customer, through all the arts of selling and advertising, to purchase the products and services that have been developed.

[1] For a discussion of some of the changing parameters of marketing management, see William Lazer, "Changing Dimensions in Marketing," *The Business Quarterly*, Spring, 1959, pp. 24–27.

[2] See Fred J. Borch, "The Marketing Philosophy as a Way of Business Life," *Marketing Series No. 99,* American Management Association, 1957.

The Profit Concept

The second fundamental on which the modern marketing philosophy rests, according to Borch, is the profit concept, not the volume concept. Volume is not eliminated as a rewarding way of obtaining profits; rather, Borch is referring to the profitless volume or volume-for-the-sake-of-volume-alone concept.

His position, which has been accepted widely, is that marketing is essentially a philosophy of business operation and not merely a function of business. Basic to this philosophy is the acceptance of a customer-oriented way of doing business. "Under marketing, the customer becomes the fulcrum, the pivot point about which the business moves in operating for the balanced best interests of all concerned."

This is not to suggest that marketing is necessarily more important as a business function than production or finance. Manufacturing, marketing, and other business functions are complementary components of the total business process. But, it is now recognized that marketing factors must be considered before physical production begins. In an advanced economy such as that of the United States, where consumer considerations are dominant, producing a market is at least of equal significance to producing a product. As Drury has pointed out: "The making and the marketing of goods are becoming so interwoven they are being recognized and practiced for what they have always been in theory—complementary parts of the productive process. Engineering know-how produces the workable know-how; marketing know-how produces a salable product." [3]

In short, ample justification exists for acceptance of the marketing management concept. The essence of this justification is contained in three points noted by Wroe Alderson:

> 1. The American Economy is a market-oriented economy.
> 2. It is essential that the top management of successful companies consist of market-oriented executives.
> 3. Top management executives who accept the marketing concept must rely on marketing executives who are knowing and skillful users of marketing techniques, analyses and planning. . . .[4]

These three points are still basic; the question is how best to implement them. In summary, the relationship of the marketing concept to the corporate enterprise system and to responsible executive action as shown in Illustration II (page 15) involves:

---

[3] See James G. Drury, "Is Your Problem Overproduction—or Underproduction of Markets?" *Printers' Ink,* July 5, 1957, pp. 19–22, 58.

[4] See Wroe Alderson, "Advancing Marketing Efficiency," from the *Proceedings of the 41st National Conference of the American Marketing Association,* December, 1958.

1. Establishment of the firm's market offerings in accordance with actual and potential consumer demand.
2. Continuous monitoring of market offerings to relate them more adequately to customer wants and needs.
3. Continuous feedback of marketing intelligence to determine existing or predicted imbalances and thus delineate market opportunities for managerial consideration.
4. The integration and coordination of resources to achieve a total system of action.

MARKETING MANAGEMENT AND THE CONSUMER

The two essential missions of marketing management in a firm are: (1) to mobilize and direct market-related resources of the enterprise to capitalize on market opportunities by serving consumer wants and needs; (2) to help imbue company management and employees with the consumer orientation to business action. The consumer is thus the focal point around which marketing, and ultimately all business activity, revolves. The consumer orientation to business decision making is fundamental to the marketing concept. It is the key to understanding the marketing management concepts presented in this book.

In practice, marketing problems are often considered from the point of view of an industry, a manufacturer, a middleman, or a governmental unit. As a result, they are viewed from the wrong problem-solving perspective, because the primacy of the consumer is misunderstood. With a consumer orientation to business, market-related problems are appraised as customer and consumer problems rather than as corporate or functional problems.

In essence, the business enterprise is governed largely by consumer sovereignty rather than by authoritarianism of either corporate management or the government. Accepting the point of view that the consumer is king implies a recognition of the freedom of consumer choice and the voluntary action that underlies achievement of market goals. A consumer-oriented company is one in which the total resources of the firm are attuned to existing and potential areas of profitable market opportunity. Since the concept of consumer satisfaction is so important to the marketing philosophy, the scientific study of consumers is central to the development of marketing strategy.

A research-based method of solving marketing problems is a cornerstone of the marketing management concept. Up-to-date information about consumers and consumer behavior is pivotal to the effective mobilization of marketing resources. A growing recognition of the importance of investigating and understanding the complexities of consumer behavior is evidenced in contemporary research projects and the growing use of the interdisciplinary approach in solving marketing problems.

With the application of automation and the resulting increase in rate of

ILLUSTRATION II

Marketing Action System—Corporate Enterprise Elements

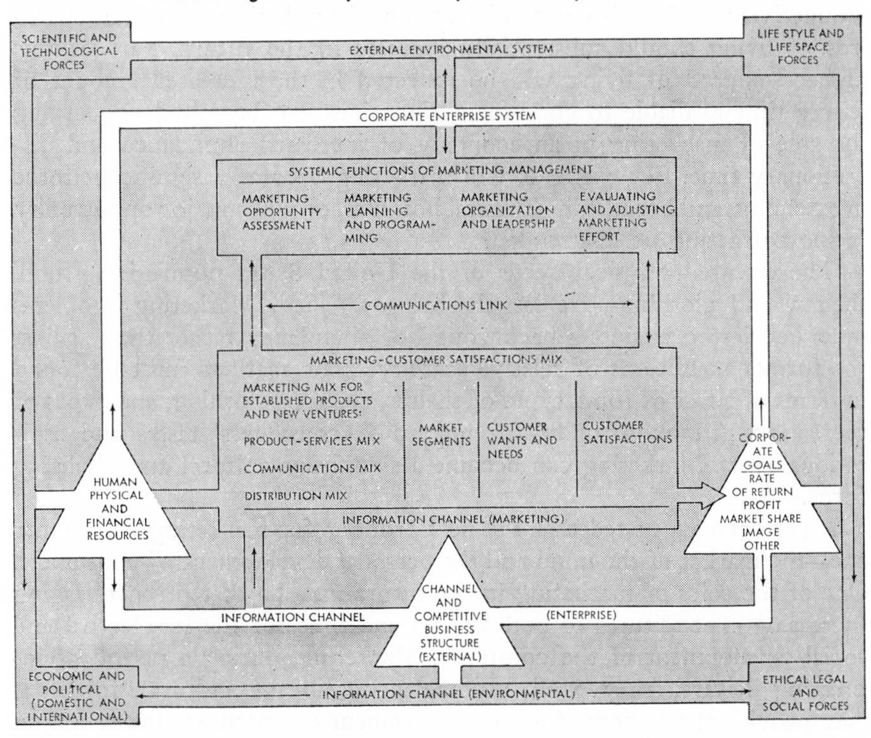
SCIENTIFIC AND TECHNOLOGICAL FORCES
EXTERNAL ENVIRONMENTAL SYSTEM
LIFE STYLE AND LIFE SPACE FORCES
CORPORATE ENTERPRISE SYSTEM
SYSTEMIC FUNCTIONS OF MARKETING MANAGEMENT
MARKETING OPPORTUNITY ASSESSMENT
MARKETING PLANNING AND PROGRAM-MING
MARKETING ORGANIZATION AND LEADERSHIP
EVALUATING AND ADJUSTING MARKETING EFFORT
COMMUNICATIONS LINK
MARKETING-CUSTOMER SATISFACTIONS MIX
MARKETING MIX FOR ESTABLISHED PRODUCTS AND NEW VENTURES:
PRODUCT-SERVICES MIX
COMMUNICATIONS MIX
DISTRIBUTION MIX
MARKET SEGMENTS
CUSTOMER WANTS AND NEEDS
CUSTOMER SATISFACTIONS
HUMAN PHYSICAL AND FINANCIAL RESOURCES
CORPOR-ATE GOALS
RATE OF RETURN
PROFIT
MARKET SHARE
IMAGE
OTHER
INFORMATION CHANNEL (MARKETING)
CHANNEL AND COMPETITIVE BUSINESS STRUCTURE (EXTERNAL)
INFORMATION CHANNEL
(ENTERPRISE)
ECONOMIC AND POLITICAL (DOMESTIC AND INTERNATIONAL)
INFORMATION CHANNEL (ENVIRONMENTAL)
ETHICAL LEGAL AND SOCIAL FORCES

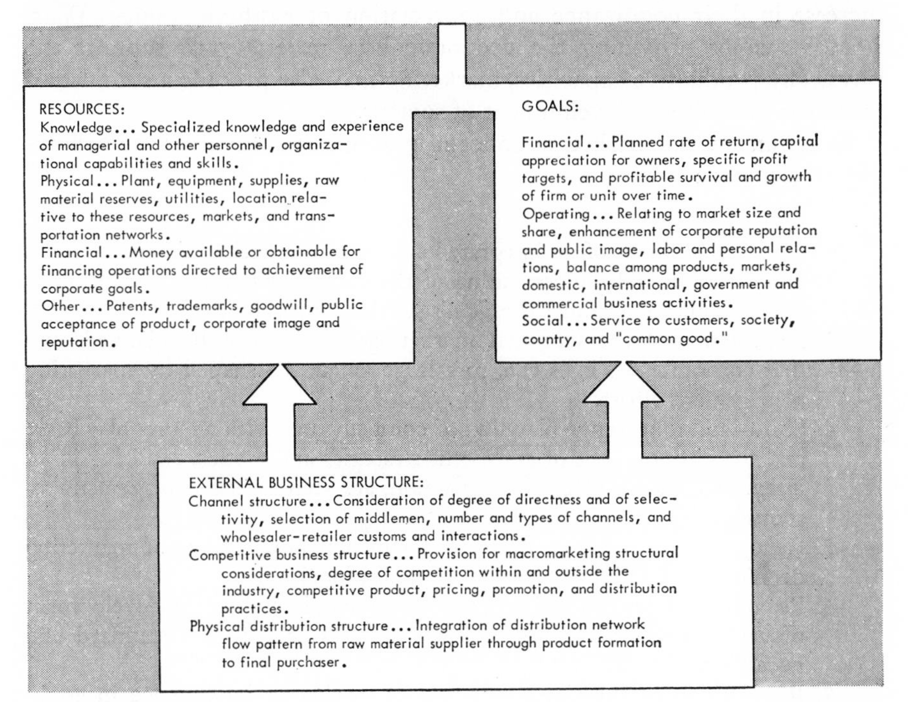
RESOURCES:
Knowledge... Specialized knowledge and experience of managerial and other personnel, organizational capabilities and skills.
Physical... Plant, equipment, supplies, raw material reserves, utilities, location relative to these resources, markets, and transportation networks.
Financial... Money available or obtainable for financing operations directed to achievement of corporate goals.
Other... Patents, trademarks, goodwill, public acceptance of product, corporate image and reputation.
GOALS:
Financial... Planned rate of return, capital appreciation for owners, specific profit targets, and profitable survival and growth of firm or unit over time.
Operating... Relating to market size and share, enhancement of corporate reputation and public image, labor and personal relations, balance among products, markets, domestic, international, government and commercial business activities.
Social... Service to customers, society, country, and "common good."
EXTERNAL BUSINESS STRUCTURE:
Channel structure... Consideration of degree of directness and of selectivity, selection of middlemen, number and types of channels, and wholesaler-retailer customs and interactions.
Competitive business structure... Provision for macromarketing structural considerations, degree of competition within and outside the industry, competitive product, pricing, promotion, and distribution practices.
Physical distribution structure... Integration of distribution network flow pattern from raw material supplier through product formation to final purchaser.

productivity, and with more efficient use of marketing resources, standards of living should substantially increase in the future. Part of this higher standard of living will be reflected in the increased amount of leisure time available to consumers. Questions can be raised concerning the role of marketing in an economy of increased abundance and discretionary time. For example, will marketing become a significant force in extending and broadening cultural horizons, or will a major opportunity facing marketing be unattended?

The essential physical needs of the United States population—food, shelter, and clothing—are largely being satisfied. Marketing problems must be viewed against a background of abundance rather than against the former conditions of relative scarcity. New markets must be found in terms of types of food, types of shelter, types of clothing, and types of recreation. An opportunity for upgrading consumers' tastes and aspirations exists. Marketing can become a significant cultural and civilizing force.

It has been suggested that the next frontier for marketing is an inner one—the market of the mind and the personal development of consumers. One of the roles of marketing in the future may be that of encouraging increasing expenditures of both dollars and time for the intellectual and social development of the consumer. Marketing, during a period of increasing leisure, may well become a significant cultural force. It may provide the impetus for an improvement of consumer tastes and an increase in their cognizance and appreciation of aesthetic values. Thus, besides merely providing the economic base necessary to support the physically productive capacities, marketing may also provide a stimulating force for the cultural development of society.

In summary, the marketing concept in application involves the following 10 elements:

1. The development of an integrated system of marketing action.
2. Appreciation and understanding of the consumer's strategic position as it shapes and determines the firm's survival and growth.
3. Acceptance of the fact that marketing activity can be planned, and that corporate destinies can, to a large extent, be shaped by marketing management effort.
4. Short- and long-range planning of company activities on a regular basis, and the development of consistent strategies and tactics, resulting in an integrated system of marketing action, are seen as key management responsibilities.
5. Recognition of intra- and interdepartmental implications of marketing decisions and actions of various organizational units.
6. Programmed process and product innovation, including the development of a climate that encourages innovation, is accepted as standard and necessary.
7. Recognition of the significant role of marketing intelligence in estab-

lishing goals and targets. Market potentials become guides to corporate action.

8. Emphasis on new-product development and its impact on company profits and posture.
9. The adoption of a marketing focus in coordinating company effort, and in establishing corporate and departmental objectives consistent with achieving the firm's profit goals.
10. Reshaping company products, services, and activities to more effectively meet the demands and opportunities of the marketplace.

Some of the problems and difficulties of applying the above elements are considered in the selections in this book.[5]

---

[5] For a discussion of the relationship between the marketing concept and the managerial functions of marketing, see Eugene J. Kelley, *Marketing: Strategies and Functions*. (Englewood Cliffs, N.J.: Prentice-Hall, Inc., 1965).

C. The Systems Approach to Marketing*

MARKETING SYSTEMS DEFINED

The marketing management philosophy is based on a systems perspective of decision making. The systems approach to marketing has already had a substantial impact on the development of marketing thought and the management of marketing activity. This approach provides a conceptual framework for market planning, determination of the marketing mix, physical distribution, and the use of operations research techniques in marketing. Systems thinking recognizes the interrelations and interconnections among the components of a marketing system.

The systems approach is based on the work of Von Bertalanffy, who is credited with coining the phrase "general systems theory." He defined a system as a set of objects together with the relationships among them and their attributes.[1]

As Illustration I indicates, marketing institutions and operations can be perceived as complex, large-scale systems. For analytical purposes, any group of marketing elements and activities that can be physically or conceptually delineated is a marketing system. A system is a collection of entities that can be understood as forming a coherent group. The fact that the entities can be defined as a coherent group is what differentiates a system from a meaningless collection of parts.[2]

In marketing systems, there are flows of products, services, money, equipment, and information. It is these flows that largely determine the survival and growth capacities of a firm. The systems approach places great emphasis on the analysis of flows and communications. It stresses the

---

* This section is based on an article by William Lazer and Eugene J. Kelley that appeared in the second edition of this book.

[1] See Arthur D. Hall, "A Methodology for Systems Engineering," (Toronto, Canada: Van Nostrand, 1962), p. 60.

[2] Stafford Beer, "What Has Cybernetics To Do With Operational Research?" *Operational Research Quarterly*, Vol. X, No. 1 (March, 1959), p. 3.

development of communication systems for transmitting information about changing market environments and subsequent adjustments of marketing policies and strategies.

ELEMENTS OF MARKETING SYSTEMS

Marketing systems include the following components:

1. A set of functionally interdependent marketing relationships among people and institutions in the system—manufacturers, wholesalers, retailers, facilitating agencies, and consumers.
2. Interaction between individuals and firms to maintain relationships, and facilitate adjustment to change, innovation, cooperation, and competition.
3. Establishment of objectives, goals, targets, beliefs, symbols, and sentiments that evolve from and reinforce the interaction, thus producing realistic marketing objectives and programs, and creating favorable images, attitudes, and opinions.
4. A consumer-oriented environment within which interactions take place, subject to the constraints of a competitive market economy, the legal and socioeconomic environment, and the evolving relationships and methods of marketing entities.
5. Technology of marketing, including communications media, credit facilities, standardization and grading, marketing research, and physical distribution.

KINDS OF MARKETING SYSTEMS

The operational delineation of a system depends, in part, on the dominant activity being described, i.e., whether it is a sales management system, a manufacturer–dealer system, a physical distribution system or a corporate communications system. But the systems perspective is a useful one regardless of the kind of system being delineated, since it directs analysis to the actions and reactions of the firm as it operates within its many environments.

Marketing systems may be of two types—conceptual or physical. Most marketing systems are conceptual. However, some systems, such as physical distribution systems, are physical entities. Also, the parts of a marketing system may be within or outside the formal boundaries of the firm. Many of them extend beyond the firm. For example, a manufacturer's marketing system may well include wholesalers, retailers, financial institutions, and advertising agencies.

A marketing system as an assemblage or combination of activities, institutions, and operations is composed of subsystems. Any marketing component can be explained in terms of various systems. Hierarchies of subsystems exist. Marketing systems are linked to larger formal systems. The advertising department can be viewed as a system, as can the marketing department, the business enterprise, or the totality of a number of business enterprises.

Marketing systems may be perceived of as small systems, middle-range systems, and large systems.[3] Small systems are concerned with marketing within the firm. The marketing mix or the physical distribution system are examples. The middle-range systems are those concerned with marketing's linkage to other functional activities, such as finance and production. A good example is the credit system. The large system or macrosystem is concerned with marketing's linkages among manufacturers, or manufacturers, wholesalers, and retailers. Voluntary cooperatives are large systems.

A question can be raised about the appropriate structural forms that marketing systems should take. The true test is survival and effectiveness. Certain forms and system structures are more suitable at one period of time in a market than at another. Over time, the elements of the system that are approved by the marketplace are the most appropriate.

Systems thinking—the integration and coordination of marketing activities—is providing a new perspective for solving marketing problems. Systems have become powerful interpretative marketing tools. The systems approach to marketing turns on the central theme that reality occurs in systems. "It is in systems that all forms of activity manifest themselves. Therefore, any form of activity may be produced by a suitable system."[4] This implies that the system is the master model for marketing activity.

The mathematical theory of systems analysis, based on electrical engineering, conceives of systems in terms of two complementary variables—propensities and flows. These variables apply to the understanding of systems in general.[5] The way in which they relate to different systems is indicated in Chart 1.

THE SYSTEMS APPROACH

The systems approach provides a master model for marketing activity. Like other models, it is imperfect. It has the advantage of focusing attention on issues broader than those usually contained in any single aspect of marketing. It places emphasis on the inputs to the system and the outputs produced. It greatly aids in the formulation of overall marketing and corporate objectives, and the development of marketing programs and the total marketing mix. However, the systems model of marketing activity makes no attempt to predict or understand human behavior. It

---

[3] For a discussion of this classification, see Wroe Alderson, *Dynamic Marketing Behavior* (Homewood, Ill.: Richard D. Irwin, Inc., 1965), chap. 1.

[4] J. L. Henderson, *The Order of Nature* (Cambridge, Mass.: Harvard University Press, 1917), p. 172.

[5] Adapted from Herman E. Koenig, "Theory of Modeling Socio-Economic Systems," mimeographed paper. Department of Electrical Engineering, Michigan State University, p. 12.

focuses on the components of the marketing systems in terms of performance rather than understanding.[6]

CHART I

Kinds of Systems

Systems Variable	*Mechanical Systems*	*Hydraulic Systems*	*Electrical Systems*	*Traffic Systems*	*Marketing Systems*
Propensity	Velocity	Pressure	Voltage	Density	Cost or price per unit of marketing effort
Flow	Force	Flow rate	Current	Current	Sales or profit per unit

What are the benefits of adopting a systems perspective? First, it provides a good basis for the logical, orderly, and coherent analysis of marketing activity. This viewpoint stresses marketing linkages inside and outside the firm. It emphasizes inputs and relates them to outputs. Systems thinking furnishes information about adaptations of systems, emphasizes changing environments, and provides a conceptual framework for control.

To a large extent, the effectiveness of marketing systems depends on having and using the right information. Markets can be understood only through the study of information—communications and messages. Systems must be adjusted to markets. Thus, the information base of a system is critical to its survival and effectiveness.

SYSTEMS AND MARKETING MANAGEMENT

The marketing management concept, with its emphasis on integration, implies a systems approach to the management of marketing effort. Marketing management includes a recognition of the interrelation and interconnection between marketing and other business elements. It adopts a systems approach as the basis for the solution of marketing problems; it is concerned with integrated and coordinated use of marketing resources to achieve predetermined and realistic objectives in an effective manner.

In accepting total responsibility for all marketing activities, and in striving for the effective use of total resources, the marketing manager must be able to see the interrelationships between various parts of the system. This perspective is suggested by Forrester. In referring to the systems view of perceiving the firm as a dynamic whole, he states, "The company will come to be recognized not as a collection of separate functions, but as a system in which the flows of information, materials,

---

[6] W. M. A. Brooker, "The Total Systems Myth," *Systems and Procedures Journal* (July–August, 1965), p. 29.

manpower, capital equipment, and money set up forces that determine the basic tendencies toward growth, fluctuation, and decline."[7]

SYSTEMS CONCEPTS

Four groups of concepts in general systems theory have significance for marketing systems: descriptive factors, regulation and maintenance factors, factors concerning dynamics and change, and factors related to the decline and breakdown of systems.[8]

Descriptive factors are those concepts that make important distinctions in the classification of systems, structures, elements, and processes. For example, there are open and closed systems, input—output systems, boundaries and environments, orders of interaction, interdependence and independence.

Regulation and maintenance concepts deal with the control, stabilization, and regulation of systems. They are concerned with systems stability, systems equilibrium, systems feedback, homeostasis and regulation, steady-state maintenance, and communication.

Dynamics and change are internally generated factors that deal with the response of systems to environmental conditions. They include such concepts as adaptation of a system, plasticity and elasticity of systems, learning and growth, change, dynamism and dynamics.

Decline and breakdown concepts are concerned with the disruption or breakdown of a system. Included are such factors as overload, stress, disturbance, decay, and decline.

If the integration of marketing activities is not recognized organizationally, a marketing system is not complete. However, the system need not be rigidly controlled from a central point. The components of the system can be guided by common purpose and policy without rigid control.

Two concepts are important in understanding the integrated character of the systems approach. First is the concept of synthesizing the elements and subsystems into a whole. It is concerned with integrating the above-mentioned component parts into a system. Second is the concept of linkages. Linkages are the paths of connection that integrate two or more separate and distinct major or minor subsystems, each of which can function independently, to create a higher order system.

Application of the systems approach requires analysis of the elements and their functions and interactions from the point of view of individual contributions to the total system. It reflects the philosophy of the operations researcher and his perception of business as a total system of action.

---

[7] Jay W. Forrester, "Industrial Dynamics," *Harvard Business Review,* Vol. XXXVI, No. 4 (July–August, 1958), p. 52.

[8] O. R. Young, "A Survey of General Systems Theory," *General Systems,* Vol. IX (1964), pp. 61–62.

CONFLICTING GOAL ORIENTATION

To function effectively as a system, a marketing organization should be goal directed. Unfortunately, however, the goals or objectives of marketing systems and subsystems are not always clearly specified or even compatible. It is difficult for the marketing manager to precisely define the objectives of his particular unit. To the extent that a marketing organization does not clearly specify its objectives, and is not able to co-ordinate various marketing subsystems to achieve goal-directed action, a complete systems approach has not been achieved.

In trying to achieve common goals, every business system operates through subsystems that have their own respective goals. As a result, there are usually conflicts in any business system, and a goal tradeoff between subsystems becomes important in order to achieve greater efficiency of the overall system. Given existing or likely marketing constraints, determination of the one marketing program that promises an optimal total marketing position becomes the major objective of a systems approach to marketing. Intrasystem concessions must occur if major marketing and corporate goals are to be achieved.

SYSTEMS AND GOAL MODELS

There is a basic difference between systems and goal models—largely a difference of focus and emphasis. The goal model starts with a task to be achieved and focuses directly on the use of company resources to achieve it. It implies that output is directly related to input. Doubling resources is usually equated with doubling output. The goal model, therefore, may lead to segmented perspectives and may not be the most effective model of total marketing operations.

The systems model is based on the assumption that all marketing system elements function together to achieve the objectives of the overall system, rather than the objectives of a subsystem. The starting point in the systems model is not a goal but the model of the total functioning unit. A system model is a more realistic representation of an ongoing marketing entity capable of achieving multiple goals. The systems model recognizes the multifunctional and multidimensional units involved in reaching marketing goals. It emphasizes that some resources must be allocated to nongoal-directed effort. Resources are allocated to functions involved in maintaining the marketing organization itself. These functions include supporting marketing services and action that permits the use of effective marketing striking power. Such functions are not always directly goal-oriented.

Two inherent dangers must be recognized in using a goal model. (1) The danger that in solving problems management will adopt the perspective of one subgroup in the organization. This is especially true when pressure exists from action-oriented marketing groups. For example, marketing managers are likely to be sales-oriented, since most marketing goals are achieved through sales. (2) The administrative, facilitating, and control functions of the marketing system may be neglected. Management must allocate resources and perform functions necessary for the maintenance of the marketing system itself.

SCOPE AND COMPLEXITY OF MARKETING SYSTEMS

Marketing systems are often large and complex. For example, consider the dollar and physical volume of goods handled, the number of people employed, the number and variety of components of an advertising campaign, or the components of a sales promotion campaign in any major business concern today. Other additional considerations include the alternative methods of selling, distribution, or advertising, the number and types of functions performed, the possible combination of marketing inputs, and the dimensions of absolute marketing costs and revenue.

Marketing systems contain a wide variety of components, elements, and interrelationships that have infinite gradations. In addition, there is incomplete information concerning each element, so that marketing management always deals with systems under conditions of uncertainty. The complexity of the marketing decision problem is compounded by the large number of variables that are generated by the dynamic nature of the marketing process.

Large and complex marketing systems contain not only harmonious but also discordant or dysfunctional elements. For example, tension, strains, and conflict are intrinsic to marketing systems when one considers what is best for the wholesaler versus the retailer versus the manufacturer in a total system. The best course of action for the wholesaler may be the worst for the manufacturer.

OPEN SYSTEMS

Conceptually, marketing systems may be either open or closed; however, most marketing systems are open. An automatic vending machine is an example of a closed system. Known inputs (money) are put into the machine, and known outputs are obtained from it (provided the machine is working properly). Thus, the vending machine represents a highly predictable, deterministic system.

Uncertainty plays an important role in most marketing decisions. Results vary from those predicted because of changes in inputs and unpredicted variances in the states of the environment. Such systems are indeterminate and are frequently referred to as probabilistic systems. They present a more difficult planning and operating environment than does a closed system.

INTELLIGENCE NETWORKS AND SYSTEM ADJUSTMENT

An important characteristic of a marketing system is the existence of complex intelligence networks. The intelligence network includes multiple feedback and forecast loops. Normally, marketing management feedback loops are thought of in terms of various marketing research, sales management, and distribution cost accounting activities, which provide management with information about events that have already occurred. Forecast loops may be viewed as providing future information derived through predictive processes, such as sales forecasting and simulations. The availability of pertinent past and future information is essential to system control and integration.

Marketing management has a prime responsibility for creative adaptation to change. Marketing systems must be constantly adjusted to changes in the marketplace. Information systems are necessary for recognition of new developments and management of marketing change. Despite the existence of complex intelligence networks, marketing systems do not automatically adjust to changing market conditions. The use of existing automatic control systems will not insure automatic adjustment of the marketing system. The present state of the art in information management has not produced a device similar to the servomechanism, which has widespread application in engineering.

Automatic control mechanisms cannot be instituted in most areas of marketing, although it is sometimes possible to set up an automatic control system for certain routine inventory decisions. Marketing activity is at a stage of development where human beings are involved in controlling the direction of company activity to a considerable extent.

Continuing advances in electronic data processing technology and in systems and procedures applications will improve marketing intelligence. Marketing managers will be provided with more timely, pertinent, dependable information on which to base decisions. Marketing activities generate huge quantities of data, from which essential information can probably be best assembled and communicated through computer processing. Improved control and more rapid adjustment of marketing systems should result from new and increased computer applications to marketing problems. For example, market simulation computer problems now provide strategic information that is not available through any other means.

COMPETITION AND CHANGE

A characteristic of most marketing systems in free enterprise and mixed economies is that they are competitive. Each competitor faces opponents who constantly seek to promote their individual advantages. Competitors can be expected to react to offensive strategies with either a defensive strategy or a new offensive effort. Thus, marketing managers are faced with the problem of evaluating the probable effects of not only their own decisions but also their competitors' reactions. Maintenance of market position and growth of the firm require a willingness and ability to change.

The marketing system is characterized as a system constantly adjusting its elements and focus. The interaction of changing technology, research and development, shifting consumer attitudes and opinions, together with competition, necessitate continuous system adjustment. The marketing manager must plan for change and accept it as an integral part of the systems approach to marketing.

Bibliography—Chapter I

BAKKE, E. WRIGHT. "Concept of the Social Organization," *General Systems*, Vol. IV (1959), pp. 95–121.

BARACH, ARNOLD B. "U.S.A. and Its Economic Future," *Twentieth Century Fund Report*. New York: Macmillan Co., 1964.

BAUMOL, WILLIAM J. *Business Behavior, Value and Growth*. New York: Macmillan Co., 1959.

CHANDLER, ALFRED D., JR. *Strategy and Structure*. Cambridge, Mass.: M.I.T. Press, 1962.

KATONA, GEORGE. "Rational Behavior and Economic Behavior," *Psychological Review*, Vol. LX, No. 5 (September, 1953), pp. 307–18.

KELLEY, EUGENE J. *Marketing: Strategy and Functions*. Englewood Cliffs, N.J.: Prentice-Hall, Inc., 1965.

KELLEY, EUGENE J.; LAZO, HECTOR; CORBIN, ARNOLD; AND KAHN, EDWARD. *Marketing Management: An Annotated Bibliography*. Chicago: American Marketing Association, 1963.

SIMONDS, ROLLIN H.; BALL, RICHARD E.; AND KELLEY, EUGENE J. *Business Administration: Problems and Functions*. Boston: Allyn and Bacon, Inc., 1962.

TARPLEY, LAWRENCE X. "Marketing Research and the Behavioral Sciences," *Business Topics*, Vol. XIII, No. 1 (Winter, 1965), pp. 61–67.

YOUNG, O. R. "A Survey of General Systems Theory," *General Systems*, Vol. IX (1964), pp. 61–80.

ILLUSTRATION III

Marketing Action System—External Environments

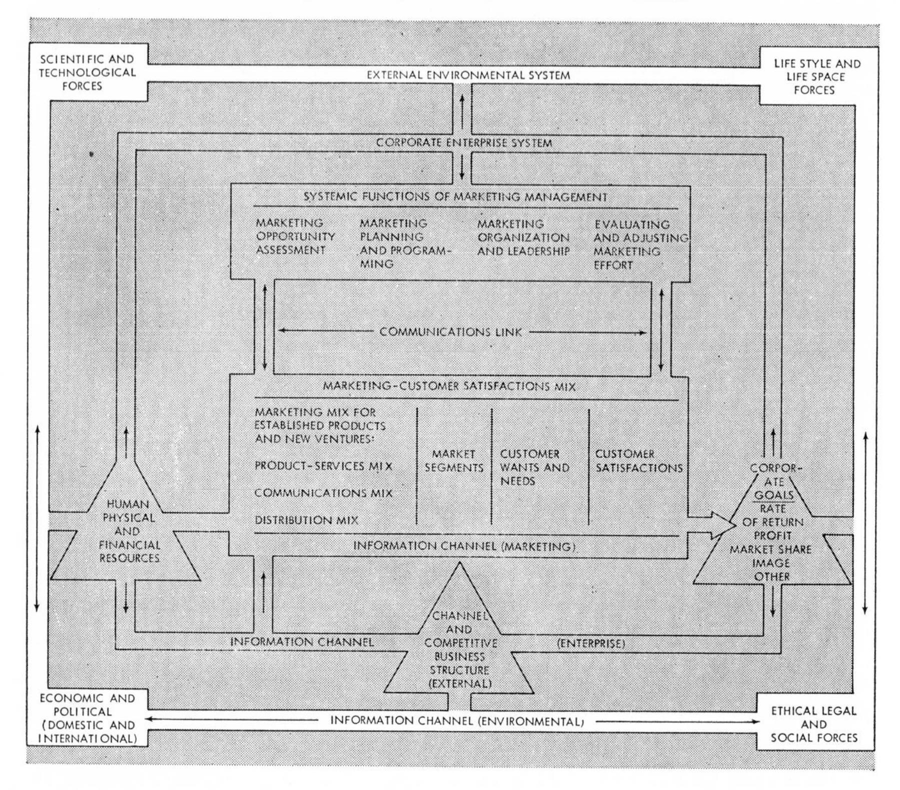

SCIENTIFIC AND TECHNOLOGICAL FORCES

A. Increasing governmental, institutional, and corporate commitments to exploration, research, and development in fields of human interest and concern.
B. Increasing productivity through automation and growing mechanization of industrial processes.
C. Increasing communications capability through automation and electronic data processing.
D. Increasing capability in transportation modes.
E. Advances in control of energy, extension of man's sensory capabilities, and in managing technological innovation.

LIFE STYLE AND LIFE SPACE FORCES

A. World-wide interest in personal achievement and social gains.
B. Upward mobility thrust in education and income.
C. Trends toward home- and family-centered enjoyment of increasing discretionary time and mobility.
D. Changes in geographic distribution of the population, labor force composition, age distribution and family composition.
E. Increasing market segmentation and competitive efforts to upgrade consumer concepts of living standards and ways of life.

ECONOMIC AND POLITICAL FORCES
(Domestic and International)

A. Rising world-wide levels of individual and societal aspirations and consumption.
B. Recognition and acceptance of mass consumption economies and world-wide drive toward economic development.
C. Increasing internationalization of business.
D. Increasing domestic and international competition.

ETHICAL, LEGAL, AND SOCIAL FORCES

A. Improved corporate citizenship attitudes both domestic and international.
B. Increased moral orientation to business problems.
C. Increased societal expectations of professionalism in business.
D. Broadened concepts of business responsibility beyond the profit motive.
E. Increased business-government sharing of social and economic concerns.
F. Broadened role and influence of government at all levels as evidenced in monetary and fiscal policies, employment practices and labor legislation.

II. THE EXTERNAL ENVIRONMENTS OF MARKETING SYSTEMS

Marketing managers must be environmentalists, for external and internal environmental change is often the dominant factor in marketing decisions. The rate and magnitude of change and its effect on the firm in the form of innovations, flow of new products, and new competitive pressure are fundamental influences on marketing managers who are attempting to match customer needs and wants with corporate capabilities and resources.

Illustration III portrays the external environmental system surrounding the firm; it indicates the basic environmental forces that influence marketing strategy and performance. These forces are classified as: (1) scientific and technological, (2) life style and life space, (3) economic and political, and (4) ethical, legal, and social. Management's skill in meeting and adjusting to these forces is a significant determinant of the firm's profitability and growth. The articles in this chapter discuss the impact of these environmental forces on such important marketing variables as the consumer, corporate planning, and marketing strategy.

As technology and value systems change, new business problems and opportunities are created by a "society in motion." Consumption patterns, for example, are continually modified and altered by life style forces. These changing patterns are exemplified in the higher aspiration levels and goals of consumers. Constantly evolving consumer attitudes toward products and services create a need for new marketing tactics. The study of life style forces contributes to the marketing manager's awareness and understanding of the complexity of consumer behavior, and ultimately to more efficient marketing by the firm.

Technological change may be the major environmental force for many firms. We live in a period when 90 per cent of all the scientists in the world's history are alive, and the majority of man's store of scientific literature has been published in the last decade. Thus, it is not difficult to appreciate why marketing management must become increasingly aware of technological developments if they are to focus the firm's resources on the needs of today's dynamic markets. Environmental forces interact, as indicated in Illustration III, to create marketing problems and opportunities. For example, technology and changing life styles can interact to create a major force for change, as Marshall McLuhan has noted in his evaluation of the impact of television and other communications media on society. Developments in communications technology are shrinking distances and time scales, and the scope of marketing and market concepts must be adjusted accordingly.

Marketing problems should be solved and marketing opportunities developed in light of existing political, economic, and institutional forces. Consideration of these forces is contributing to a broader view of the firm's responsibility to society. Public policy decisions have significant effects on marketing decisions. Marketing decisions, in turn, influence public policy. Marketing managers and public policymakers can make a significant contribution to the process of constructive innovation and to society through the integration of private and public objectives. An effective marketing system is essential to economic growth, not only for a developing nation, but also for a mature economy.

Ethical considerations constitute another environmental force acting on the marketing decision maker. Because marketing is a logical focal point for ethical evaluations of business, marketing managers should integrate ethical values and scientific marketing procedures. Present-day marketing cannot be understood without recognition of both domestic and international economic and political forces. The emergence of multinational enterprises is one development arising from and contributing to such forces. Competitive pressures in the American economy, together with other environmental forces, create the necessity for a market orientation in which the consumer becomes the focal point of all corporate activity.

Formulation of a marketing strategy requires determination of an optimal customer-satisfactions mix. Marketing resources and procedures are combined with market segmentation factors and focused on customer needs and satisfactions. The degree of success in blending these elements into a workable strategy is determined by management's skills in planning and establishing corporate goals, and in the coordinating of marketing management's systemic functions. These functions and their relationships are depicted in Illustration IV on page 90. Achievement of the firm's goal and marketing objectives depends on customer response to its marketing mix.

A. Marketing Action and the External Environments

Life style is an important concept for marketers, because marketing is both a product and a determinant of life style. Life style facilitates the understanding, explanation and prediction of consumer behavior. It also influences economic activity.

1. LIFE STYLE CONCEPTS AND MARKETING*

William Lazer†

A general concept, referred to vaguely as "life style," is being used by behavioral scientists, especially sociologists. The precise nature and scope of the concept is not clear. However, in interviews about life style, several behavioral scientists revealed that they understood its general meaning and its significance for research purposes. They were also willing to discuss relevant life-style research projects and to recommend a body of literature that reflected a life-style orientation. They did not, however, define the concept specifically, and none of the recommended literature contained a definition.

THE LIFE STYLE CONCEPT

What is life style? Life style is a systems concept. It refers to the distinctive or characteristic mode of living, in its aggregative and broadest sense, of a whole society or segment thereof. It is concerned with

* Reprinted from "Life Style Concepts and Marketing," *Proceedings of the Winter Conference of the American Marketing Association*, 1963, pp. 130–39.

† Michigan State University.

those unique ingredients or qualities which describe the style of life of some culture or group, and distinguish it from others. It embodies the patterns that develop and emerge from the dynamics of living in a society.

Life style, therefore, is the result of such forces as culture, values, resources, symbols, license, and sanction. From one perspective, the aggregate of consumer purchases, and the manner in which they are consumed, reflect a society's life style.

Following this definition it is logical to speak of the American life style, our family life styles, consumer life styles, the life style of various social strata, and the life style of specific groups in different stages of the life cycle.

In marketing we have been particularly interested in consumer life styles in terms of the way people individualize, and identify themselves as members of various groups, and the resulting patterns of living. For example, we have gathered and analyzed data on consumer incomes, age groups, and expenditure patterns for decades. The goal is not one of assembling statistics for the sake of statistical information. Rather it is one of translating statistical findings about consumers into models of consumer life styles that will permit us to understand and predict various dimensions of consumer behavior, particularly purchase behavior.

A life style hierarchy may be charted consisting of:

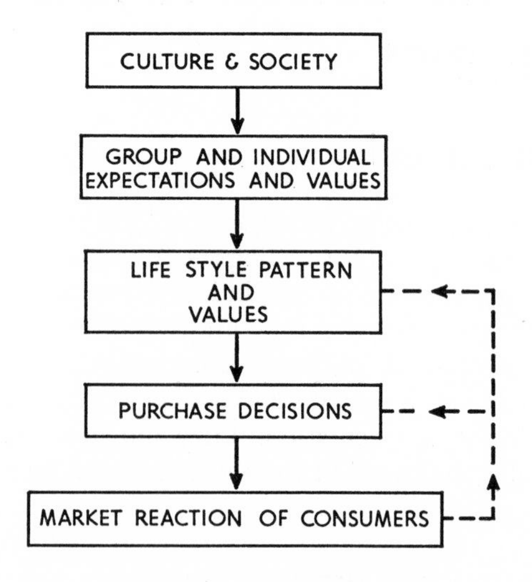

Life style, therefore, is a major behavioral concept for understanding, explaining, and predicting consumer and business behavior. It is a more generalized concept than existing concepts of consumer behavior that have been advanced in marketing. Such topics as mobility, leisure, social class, life cycle, status, conformity, mass, and the family as a consuming unit are all part of the life-style fabric. As a result, life-style studies could foster the unification of findings and theories related to consumer behavior. In fact, life style is a point of interdisciplinary convergence among marketing and such subject-matter areas as sociology, social and cultural anthropology, psychology, demography, and social psychology.

Economists and marketing people seem to have a different perspective on the value of life style concepts and findings. In most economic studies the life style of a society is usually assumed or ignored. It is part of the "state of the art" and "other things being equal," statements. (One striking exception is Veblen who developed such concepts as vicarious consumption and vicarious leisure.)

By contrast, in marketing, *life-style factors are viewed as among the most important forces influencing and shaping economic activity.* They are the very focus of a major part of marketing. Foote, for instance, has suggested that in essence marketers are becoming taste counselors.[1] If this is the case, marketing and life style are surely intertwined.

Since ours is a materialistic, acquisitive, thing-minded, abundant economy, marketing becomes one of the cores for understanding life styles. Therefore, marketing is in a position to make a significant contribution to a number of life-style oriented disciplines. Moreover, since our life style is being emulated in other parts of the world, such as Europe, Japan and Latin America, a better understanding of our life style may also enhance economic development theory.

MARKETING AND THE LIFE STYLE OF ABUNDANCE

When we think of abundance, we usually perceive of the physical capabilities and potentialities of a society. Abundance, however, is also a result of the culture itself since it stems partly from physical factors and partly from cultural forces. In large measure, our economic abundance results from certain institutions in our society which affect our pattern of living.

Potter maintains that advertising is the institution identified with abundance, particularly American abundance.[2] However, the institution that is brought into being by abundance without previous emphasis or existence in the same form is the institution of marketing. It is marketing expressed not only in advertising forms, but in such forms as the emphasis upon consumption in our society, marketing research, marketing planning, the marketing concept, new approaches to product development, credit, the management of innovation, the utilization of effective merchandising

---

[1] Nelson Foote, "The Anatomy of the Consumer," in Lincoln H. Clark, ed. *Consumer Behavior, The Dynamics of Consumer Reaction,* New York University Press, pp. 21–24.

[2] David M. Potter, *People of Plenty,* The University of Chicago Press, Chicago, 1954, p. 167.

techniques, and the cultivation of mass markets: that is the institution of abundance.

Ours is a business-dominated society. Hence, business influences our life styles as profoundly as any other force. One of the unique characteristics of American business, however, is the distinctive approach it adopts to marketing. Marketing has reached its most mature form and has had its greatest impact on life styles in the American economy.

Other cultures have made significant contributions to business thought and practice in such areas as business law, ethics, accounting, finance, production systems, and organization theory. By contrast, marketing progress to date is uniquely attributable to the American life style, and it is being studied and emulated in other parts of the world. Such institutions and techniques as self service, supermarkets, discount houses, marketing research, credit plans, and packaging are spreading part of the American life style in many parts of the world.

In a life-style sense, marketing is an institution of social control. It is an institution of social control in the same sense the school and the home are. It exerts an extensive influence on our life style which I maintain is for the betterment of our social and economic life. Moreover, since marketing is responsible to a very large extent for our standard of living it is impossible to understand our culture fully, and hence our life style, without some comprehension of marketing.

The impact of marketing on our patterns of living, particularly advertising, has not been ignored. Advertising has been criticized pointedly. Toynbee, for example, writes that if it were demonstrated to be true "that personal consumption stimulated by advertising is essential for growth and full employment in an economy of abundance . . . it would also demonstrate to my mind that an economy of abundance is a spiritually unhealthy way of life, and that the sooner we reform it the better . . . The moral that I draw is that a way of life based on personal consumption, stimulated by advertising, needs changing."[3] These are strong indictments of unfavorable marketing influences on our life style and are reinforced by the writings of such people as Warne, Galbraith, and Schlesinger.

When abundance prevails, however, the limitations and constraints upon business and other parts of our life style shift. Potter writes: "The most critical point in the functioning of society shifts from production to consumption . . . the culture must be reoriented to convert the producer's into a consumer's culture . . . and the society must be adjusted to a new set of drives and values of which consumption is paramount."[4] This becomes the challenge of marketing in altering life styles in an abundant

---

[3] "Toynbee vs. Bernbach: Is Advertising Morally Defensible?" *Yale Daily News*, Special Issue, 1963, p. 2.

[4] Potter, *op. cit.*, p. 173.

economy. *Marketing becomes an instrument for changing production-oriented value into consumption-oriented norms.*

Marketing and Values

Our basic value system determines the nature and significance of various social institutions. These fundamental values, moreover, are not merely the result of the whims of marketers. It is true that we live in a sensate culture, one which stresses sensory enjoyment, materialism and utilitarianism.[5] Consumers desire and can own those items and symbols that are associated with status, achievement, and accomplishment. Material values have become important. Marketing responds to, and reinforces, such values in our abundant culture, and in so doing appeals to the senses and emphasizes materialism.

The life-style question still to be answered, however, is one concerning the relative desirability of our life style with such emphases as contrasted with other life styles. Great materialistic stress and accomplishment is not inherently sinful and bad. Moral values are not vitiated as many critics seem to think by substantial material acquisitions. In reality the improvement of material situations can lead to a greater recognition of intrinsic values, the lifting of general tastes, the enhancement of a moral climate and the direction of more attention to the appreciation of art and esthetics.

This I would suggest is occurring today. It has also been the pattern of the past. In history great artistic and cultural advancements are at least accompanied, if not shaped, by periods of flourishing trade and commerce.

The next marketing frontier may well be an inner one—the market of the mind and the personal development of consumers.[6] Marketing in the future may be geared to filling the needs of this inner frontier. One of its roles may be that of encouraging increasing expenditures by consumers, of both dollars and time, to develop themselves intellectually, socially, and morally. This has already been accomplished to a limited degree: witness the increasing demand for classical records, good books, the attendance at symphony concerts, the purchase of good oil paintings through mail order catalogues, and the support for the arts in general. Social critics, while prone to point out the undesirable impact of marketing on our life styles, have neglected to indicate the progress and contributions that have been made.

---

[5] See Pitirim A. Sorokin, *The Crisis of Our Age*, New York, E. P. Dutton & Co., Inc., 1946, especially Chapter III.

[6] For a discussion of this point see William Lazer & Eugene J. Kelley, "Editorial Postscript," *Managerial Marketing: Perspectives & Viewpoints* (rev. ed.; Homewood, Ill.: Richard D. Irwin, Inc., 1963), p. 683.

LIFE STYLE AND CONSUMER EXPECTATIONS

Part of the American life style may be referred to as the American Dream. A big difference exists between the American Dream with its expectations and the dreams and expectations of other countries. The gap, however, is narrowing.

The American Dream as a life style concept includes a belief in equality of opportunity to obtain a good standard of living, to acquire status and success in a community through individual initiative, determination, sacrifice and skill. It involves the contradictory concepts of equality for all and the rank and status orderings that result in the social ladders so characteristic of the functioning of our complex society. It requires the maintenance of an open society with opportunity for upward economic and social movement and the availability of education which is a root for social achievement, occupational advancement, and higher incomes on a widespread basis. These aspects of the Dream are reflected in our life style.

In general, American consumers, especially younger consumers, in living out the Dream exude optimism for the future. They feel sure that tomorrow will be better than today. American consumers believe that they can continue to expand their consumption and increase their relative amount of pleasure rather than merely limit desires. They feel sure they can continue increasing the area of purchasing power under their control.

One result of this optimistic outlook is that American consumers see virtue not so much in curbing desires, but rather in realizing oneself by acquiring the necessary goods and symbols. This optimistic life style has a historical root, for as Kraus has pointed out, unlike the European who only hoped that tomorrow would be no worse than today, Americans felt cheated if tomorrow were not better than today.[7] This orientation is supported and reflected in such marketing concepts and techniques as programmed innovation and product development, installment credit, advertising, sales promotion and merchandising activities.

Life Style and Change

In our life style we do not accept institutions, techniques, and products as permanent. Our society contains a rich tradition of expecting and anticipating change. This anticipation results from a conscious belief that changes are normal, useful, helpful, and good. We seem to accept what appears to be good today and anticipate that it will be superseded by items that are superior tomorrow. The rather trite expression "innovate or

[7] See Michael Kraus, "The United States to 1865," The University of Michigan Press, Ann Arbor, Michigan, 1959.

perish" has rich meaning for businesses trying to meet the demands of our pattern of life.

Such an attitude is one of the foundations of aggressive marketing. Girod has written that in our culture, "Innovation, change, mobility, and movement are permanent traits," and that, "In stressing the need for innovation, Americans are fighting for the maintenance of this aspect of their way of life for permanency of the one thing to which they are attached."[8]

By contrast, some other cultures which are more restrictive in their anticipations do not expect, hope for, or plan for any great change in their environment. They strive to maintain the status quo. In these cultures which are resolute against the suggestion of new ideas, new products, and new processes, marketing tends to play but a minor role.

To date, technological changes have had the greatest effect on our life styles. Changing methods of marketing are, however, very significant. Consider the effect on our life style, and the life style of other cultures, of supermarkets, self-service, discount houses, shopping centers, automatic vending machines, credit plans, new products, packages, and new communications techniques. Such process and service innovations will have an even greater effect in the future.

CONSUMERS, CONSUMPTION, AND LIFE STYLE

In the scheme of our life style, because of a previous production orientation, the relative significance of consumers and consumption as economic determinants has been under-emphasized. The importance of maintaining physical production is, of course, widely recognized. Only limited reference, however, is made to the corresponding necessity of maintaining consumption. *The critical nature of consumption in an abundant economy demands that consumption should not be considered as a happenstance activity*. We must establish the necessary conditions for consumption to proceed on an adequate and orderly basis.

Until recently, even the relative significance of consumer investment in our economy was greatly under-emphasized. Business investment, which is certainly a most significant factor in influencing business conditions, received almost all the attention. Katona points out, however, that "growth and expansion of the American economy are dependent on consumer investment as well as business investment . . . business investment and consumer investment are equally important forces which either stimulate or retard the economy."[9]

---

[8] Roger Girod, "Comment on Consumer Reaction to Innovation," in Lincoln H. Clark, ed. *Consumer Behavior, Research on Consumer Reactions,* Harper & Brothers, New York, 1958, p. 10.

[9] George Katona, *Michigan Business Review,* July 1961, pp. 17–20.

What must also be recognized is the important fact that consumer investments are not merely the function of increased income. They stem from and reflect life styles.

A distorted picture has been presented of consumers and the purchase and consumption process. Consumers have been portrayed in much of the non-marketing literature as emotional, irrational, uninformed beings, manipulated at will through marketing devices. It is held that conformity, followership, waste, ostentation, and meaningless style changes have been foisted upon consumers by marketers. Rokeach points out, however, that marketers have been using the wrong psychological theory. He emphasizes that the theory that consumers are irrational creatures who must be appealed to only on an emotional level is outmoded. Modern psychological theories view man as "not only a rationalizing creature but also a rational creature curious, exploratory and receptive to new ideas."[10]

Competition as Part of Our Life Style

Essentially, competition is directly related to and can be defined only in terms of the culture and nature of the environment that surrounds it. Competition has its fullest meaning in the marketing environment of a consumeristic economy rather than in a controlled, planned, or cooperative environment such as exists in many other countries.

In thinking about competition, however, we tend to be retrospective and do not relate it to current life styles. In interpreting laws and in our economic analysis we often cling to past or previous models of competition and competitive situations. For example, we often conceptualize competition in terms of an emerging industrial society rather than a maturing industrial society, in terms of price competition neglecting convenience and service competition, in terms of an economy of scarcity with relatively low consumer purchasing power rather than an economy of abundance with widespread discretionary purchasing power; in terms of manufacturers and distributors controlling and dominating the market place rather than an economy governed (or at least influenced to a large extent) by customer sovereignty; and in terms of intra-industry competition rather than inter-industry competition.

In particular, there is a misplaced emphasis, stemming from past economic models, on *price* as the key competitive weapon. This does not mean that price competition is no longer important in our mode of living. Certainly it is. It does mean, however, that ours is a competitive situation in which *price obscurity* and not price clarity seems to be the rule and in which other variables including convenience and service are very important.[11]

[10] *New York Times*, November 7, 1963, p. 60, "Advertising: A Wrong Psychological Limb?"

[11] See Eugene J. Kelley, "The Importance of Convenience in Consumer Purchasing," *Journal of Marketing*, July 1958. (Also reprinted in this book, pp. 155–62.)

We seem to take competition for granted as one of the inherent aspects of our life style. J. M. Clark points out, however, that "There can be no certainty that competition will remain vigorous in American business," and that "The necessary conditions are a fascinating subject for speculation." The necessary and sufficient condition for the existence of keen, vigorous competition, however, is clear. *It is aggressive marketing.* Changes in price, advertising, products, and channels of distribution tend to keep things stirred up and prevent competition from lapsing into routine passivity.[12]

CONCLUSION

To a large extent our marketing technology sets us apart from other cultures. It is a motivating force behind our competitive system and characterizes our life style. Marketing in the future must be recognized as a major institution in our way of life as well as a force that can contribute greatly to the influence of international life styles.

Yet analysts of our culture and life styles have virtually ignored marketing. It is often regarded as but a minor type of activity which is not important enough to be investigated. It has been neglected by psychologists, sociologists, social and cultural anthropologists, economists, and historians. It is treated as though it were a side issue in our economic activity, when in essence, it is one of the core or focal points.

Marketing is one of the longstanding institutions in our society. Its impact reverberates throughout our culture. It has shaped our life styles and has affected everyone of us significantly. The inextricable intertwinement of marketing and our life style was emphasized by a theologian who wrote, "The saintly cannot be separated from the market place for it is in the market place that man's future is being decided, they must be schooled in the arts of the market place as in the discipline of saintliness itself."[13]

---

[12] J. M. Clark, "Competition: Static Models and Dynamic Aspects," *American Economic Review,* Vol. XLV, No. 2, May 1955, p. 462.

[13] Louis Finkelstein in Conference On The American Character, *Bulletin, Center For The Study of Democratic Institutions,* October 1961, p. 6.

Significant issues concerning consumer behavior and satisfaction arise during life style analysis of the values and objectives of individuals in their normal social settings. Information resulting from the study of such issues may be vital to efficient marketing decision making. Life style forces and technology interact with each other and the firm to create marketing problems and opportunities. Several researchable questions are posed within the framework of the life style concept.

2. COMMENTARY ON LIFE STYLE*

Eugene J. Kelley†

Marketing in its broadest sense is the medium through which the material goods and culture of a society are transmitted to its members. As the style of living of members of a society—consumers—changes, the media of distribution and the products and services marketed must also change, or be replaced. All social institutions face the threat of obsolescence in a period of rapid change. Life style analysis can help marketing institutions both to minimize the risk of lagging behind cultural needs and to render more effective consumer services profitably.

Marketing's concern with the satisfaction of consumer needs explains why concepts, insights, or tools useful in understanding consumer satisfactions and behavior should receive the thoughtful consideration of all marketing people. . . .

The idea of product symbolism has been accepted for some time. But to think of a consumer life as a symbol, or as a family living a patterned way of life, living a family theme and image, opens several research possibilities for academic marketers and marketing research practitioners. A manufacturer, for instance, could ask such questions as:

- What are the firm's concepts about consumers and their ways of living?
- What assumptions about consumer life styles underlie the advertising and marketing decisions made recently in the firm?
- How do these assumptions check out with the realities of consumer life style patterns?

---

* Reprinted from "Discussion," *Proceedings of the Winter Conference of the American Marketing Association*, 1963, pp. 164–71.

† The Pennsylvania State University.

- How can our concepts of consumer behavior be sharpened through life style analysis?

Life style analysis reminds us that the consumer is indeed a complex person operating in a complex world. The approach forces an examination of the values and objectives of individuals under social settings in which consumers live. Perhaps one of the great values of life style analysis is that it raises certain questions about consumers and that it can bring information about such questions into marketing decision making.

Two of the greatest forces for change in the world today have life style dimensions. The movement to full citizenship of the American Negro is basically an ethical and social matter. But a movement which directly involves one tenth of our population is also bound to affect the style of living of the remainder. The revolution of rising expectations among people of the developing nations also represents life style movements just as basic to marketing men and to society as technological change. Less dramatic than these revolutionary social changes in the domestic and international markets are the changes in life styles of nearly all Americans. These changes will have a major impact on established institutions and firms, particularly those who do not develop and distribute consumer-satisfying products and services appropriate to changing technologies and modes of living. . . .

The gap between technology and modes of living seems to be widening. The problem is becoming both more complex and important because of the tremendous advances in technology which have taken place in recent years and the growing complexity of internal business operations within the firm. Management has a difficult task keeping up with technological changes and coping with complex internal problems resulting from the increasing scale of operation. When to this is added the rapid obsolescence of existing engineering, management, and marketing knowledge, we can see why management's attention had been diverted from studying changes in the style of living of consumers toward the problems of changes in the style of management of business.

The marketing concept suggests that this may well be the wrong emphasis. Marketing minded firms might do well to begin with the life style needs of consumers and then attempt to integrate their technological research and development with these life style needs rather than the other way around. . . .

The essence of marketing today is innovation, and life style analysis suggests many areas of profitable innovistic opportunity. In some cases, a study of consumption patterns in life style terms may suggest a substantial departure from traditional methods of marketing and doing business.

The implications are clear for a seller whose marketing thinking is geared to meeting the needs of old life styles. Until quite recently many department stores resisted the new needs of a suburban population and continued to gear operations to their image of apartment dwelling consumers completely oriented to the central business district. American automobile manufacturers were quite slow to move to the compact car because they did not understand the new life style needs of an important market segment. . . .

Life style translates into symbols so the symbolic meaning of products and services is something to be examined constantly by marketing people. Symbols are not merely status symbols, but symbols of a style of life. In an affluent society, the use to which people put products takes on more and more symbolic value. Professor Levy has earlier suggested the importance of symbols in the marketing world, particularly in regard to age, sex, and social class. As indicated earlier, *marketers are not selling isolated products which can be viewed as symbols; they are selling, or consumers are buying, a style of life or pieces of a larger symbol.*

The consumer can be perceived as following a system of living, a family style. The job of marketing then becomes one of providing consumers with models of styles of living and the ingredients in which they, if they are so minded, can compose their own style of living, to reach their own inner frontiers as they satisfy material needs.

The question of applications of life style research is of interest. The prime value may be in the insights and perspectives the authors have stimulated. One of the greatest needs in marketing is for new concepts, and this concept seems most promising.

Life style analysis is valuable not only in terms of product development and adjustment, but once understood can be very effective in terms of the communications mix. Many marketing communication efforts are wasted because they emerge from an assessment of the style of living of consumers which misses reality.

How well do advertising and marketing men understand the nature of changing patterns of life style? Undoubtedly a great deal is known about consumers. Whether the right questions are asked is another subject in itself. Many advertisements seem to fly in the face of an elementary understanding of life style needs. The people in the ads are unreal, and the way in which they live is unreal. Browse through any consumer magazine and you can see the advertisers have a standard American life style in mind. They visualize, or seem to, their market as made up of beautiful and handsome people with several idealized children in an award-winning suburban setting. Happily such families are numerous in America today. But, *consider how many people are not living this style of life or do not aspire to it.* Where are the minority groups? Where are the poor people? Where are the senior citizens? Where are the non-Hollywood types? Where are the working wives? Where are the housewives who don't look as though they have two-car garages, all-electric kitchens, and white collar husbands?[1]

---

[1] For some examples indicating areas of advertising ignorance of the consumer, see Marya Mannes, "How Well Do Advertisers Know the Consuming Public?" Proceedings, Thirty-Fifth Annual Boston Conference on Distribution, 1963, pp. 75–81.

Life style approaches make it a little easier to take a new and longer special look at consumer behavior. Focusing on the future to anticipate the nature of life style changes over a five or ten year period can bring a new dimension to marketing planning. The study of life style patterns can help sophisticated sellers see consumers as they exist today and are likely to look tomorrow. The danger of the kind of advertising mentioned is that it is self-deceptive to advertisers and marketers. We begin to believe it ourselves after a while and, therefore, to sell to consumers as we believe them to be.

Nelson Foote has suggested a question about how marketing fits into the changing life style of consumers. He asked whether we are correct in thinking that the consumer is an individual with constantly expanding needs, and that the job of marketing is just to move more goods and services, to build more shopping centers, stuff more homes, to keep turning out the goods which clog the closets, attics, and basements of America as well as its living rooms.[2] As one speculation, is it possible that before the year 2000 the life style of consumers may not be as product oriented as it is today? It is possible, as Foote suggested, that we are seeing a pattern develop in which the consumer is devoting more of his attention to the satisfaction of wants that do not require consumption or production or distribution in the ordinary sense, but to inner satisfactions of a variety of kinds. He also pointed out that the customer of 2000 will experience as his first constraint not income, but time; as a second constraint, learning. Our very term "consumer" is a seller-defined term. People are not as likely to see themselves as consumers in the future, but as something else—perhaps as individuals creating their own style of living by using the services of business.

Several researchable questions suggested by David G. Moore are paraphrased below.[3] Such questions may be heard in consumer marketing research more often in the future.

1. What are the life problems and challenges perceived by various market segments in different life cycle stages as they relate to the product mission and opportunities of the firm?
2. How are these life problems and challenges likely to change over the next five to ten years for various market segments as defined in both economic and social terms?
3. How do our present and programmed products and services help consumers deal with these challenges and problems? How can our products be improved in life style terms during the next five to ten year product-planning period?

---

[2] Nelson N. Foote, "The Image of the Consumer in the Year 2000," Proceedings, Thirty-Fifth Annual Boston Conference on Distribution, 1963, pp. 13–18.

[3] See David G. Moore, "Life Styles in Mobile Suburbia," *Proceedings of the Spring Conference of the American Marketing Association,* 1963, pp. 151–63.

4. How do customers use the products now available to them in their daily routines, as tools of activity, in their personal, social, and recreational lives, and as symbolic expressions of their desires and interests?

Such questions may challenge some marketers to do more work in defining consumer groups in life style and systems terms, establishing the goals of various market segments, and doing a more effective job of generating products and services which will help consumers deal with their most important problems. By moving in such directions, marketing can continue to fulfill its promise as an important social discipline concerned with the advancement of economic and social life.

The task of business leadership in understanding and serving changing consumer needs is made more complex because society is entering a new era. According to the author, society is in transition from a "ritualistic-absolutistic" to a "relativistic" era. This implies new dimensions of business activity and consumer behavior. Consumer goals, such as asset ownership, are being replaced by use value, and the relative importance of time desirability over product desirability is moving up the consumer's scale of values.

3. A UNIVERSE-IN-MOTION APPROACH TO MARKETING*

Ferdinand F. Mauser†

Significant marketing literature of the last half of the present century often relates marketing to relativity. This is because the tempo and inventive audacity of the times calls for a universe-in-motion approach to marketing. Nothing is static, all is ever changing and at a faster and faster pace. With the new marketing emphasis, for example, the term *principles* becomes old hat because it suggests the static; the term *marketing concept* is fashionable because it suggests progressiveness and change orientation.

The new approach suggests endlessness and fluidity. A business should be defined in terms of process rather than product (Theodore Levitt[1]), a

* Not previously published.

† Wayne State University.

[1] Theodore Levitt, "Marketing Myopia," *Harvard Business Review,* July–August, 1960.

market is made up of shifting segments (Wendell Smith[2]), family buying units pass through life cycles (William H. Whyte, Jr.[3]).

The universe-in-motion characteristic abounds at this point in history for immensely significant reasons. The marketing manager must acutely be conscious of how the marketing environment relates to the pervading spacetime dimension. To cope with the fast-moving future, he must be change oriented for maximum effectiveness. This means he must ask if the way he looked at things in the past is appropriate for facing the future. Our present point in history especially, as this discussion will demonstrate, calls for a rethinking of fundamental concepts. New concepts must be developed to assist in bridging today's yawning gap between what was and what is to be.

Creatively conceived concepts and theories must evolve before the world's vast new unknowns can be tackled if problems are to be faced in a methodical fashion.

Concepts, theory, and philosophy serve practical purposes for they enhance efficiency of the thought process. They provide a needed reference framework so men, equipped with mental apparatus of limited scope, can assess new problems as they arise, make predictions, and pursue courses of action without constantly rethinking the premises involved.

THE THREE WORLD THOUGHT ERAS AFFECTING MANKIND

A look into history reveals a pattern of thought development that is most useful in formulating new thought frameworks for facing the future. Paleontologists estimate that man, at his present level of sophistication, has inhabited the earth for approximately 250,000 years. During this span of time, the intellectuality of man has been dominated by what may be called three major thought eras. Most of man's time on earth has been spent living during World Era I, or what could be called the Age of Ritualism, which extended back from Greece's Golden Age (450–300 B.C.) into the darkness of prehistory. During World Era I, man explained that things happened because the gods deemed them so. Man attempted to control and shape his destiny by appeasing the gods. The most sophisticated civilizations of the ritualistic ages, the ancient Egyptians in Africa, the Aztecs in Central America, and the peoples of India, developed highly ritualistic societies—as characterized by pompous religious pyramids and temples, ceremonial burial methods, rigid caste stratifications of society, and stylized art forms.

The ritualistic World Era prevailed until the coming of Aristotle. This Greek genius, who lived from 384 to 321 B.C., ushered in World Era II, or

---

[2] Wendell R. Smith, "Product Differentiation and Market Segmentation as Alternative Marketing Strategies," *Journal of Marketing*, July, 1956, p. 3.

[3] William H. Whyte, Jr., "Budgetism: Opiate of the Middle Class," *Fortune*, May, 1956.

what may be called the Age of Absolutism. Aristotle opened the flood gates of scientific inquiry for he taught the revolutionary idea of cause and effect. Aristotle introduced logic and divided intellectual inquiry into disciplines—mathematics, philosophy, astronomy, and so on. Thus, scholars could specialize in their pursuit of knowledge, record and store it so it could accumulate, be built upon, and passed on from generation to generation.

Aristotle's ideas prevailed until the coming of World Era III, or the Age of Relativity. Today's most sophisticated thinkers feel that absolutism is no longer appropriate to the times. Aristotle's ideas of logic and truth are now viewed as useful semantic means that make scientific inquiry and communication possible. Dr. Niels Bohr, Nobel Prize Winner and colleague of Einstein, writes:

> Indeed, the general theory of relativity, by which Einstein in renouncing all ideas of absolute space and time gave our world picture a unity and harmony surpassing any previous dreams, offered an instructive lesson as regards the consistency and scope of plain language. The extension of physical experience in our days has . . . necessitated a radical revision of the foundation for the unambiguous use of our most elementary concepts, and has changed our attitude to the aim of physical science. Indeed, from our present standpoint physics is to be regarded not so much as the study of something *a priori* given, but rather as the development of methods for ordering and surveying human experience.[4]

Since the coming of Albert Einstein and his Law of Relativity, we know that nothing has a beginning or end. All is flow, process, and rhythm. Truth, then, is not fixed for eternity; it becomes, rather, the ability to predict accurately. Indeed, Heraclitus, a contemporary of Aristotle's, even at the dawn of the Age of Absolutism foresaw the Age of Relativity when he said, "You cannot step twice into the same river for fresh waters are ever flowing in upon you." What better advice can there be for the modern marketer than to suggest that he think in terms of the fresh aspects that flow into his environment, or in other words, that he make his decisions only after looking into the future in terms of ever-changing variables?

MOST OF MAN'S INSTITUTIONS ARE OBSOLETE

What bearing, then, has knowledge of the three World Eras on marketing? The marketing manager must know the cause of change so that he may manage it, capitalize on the opportunity it presents, and avoid the pitfalls it creates. Viewed in terms of modern man's 250,000 years on

---

[4] From the essay *The Unity of Human Knowledge;* in *Essays 1958–1962 on Atomic Physics and Human Knowledge,* by Niels Bohr, Interscience Publishers, New York, 1963.

earth, the Age of Relativity is but a speck in time. It must be realized that the institutions man developed to cope with his environment have evolved from earlier ritualistic and absolutistic periods. It can be said that the institutions of family, religion, political organization, economic system, legal code and so on, are all under challenge because they are ritualistic-absolutistic and are not appropriate to the times of relativism. Today's review of its ancient tenets by the major Christian Church, the state's questioning of the appropriateness of absolutistic legal procedures (divorce laws, penal codes, etc.), and the challenge of absolutistic forms of government, all provide examples of revolt or evolution away from our ritualistic-absolutistic heritage.

Not only man's institutions but also his art forms tie themselves to the three World Era concept. Dance, under the first World Era, was ritualistic, under the second absolutistic—dance steps were fixed—the minuet, waltz, etc. In the Age of Relativity, the dancer responds to whatever is felt to be appropriate to the immediate point in space and time—the Frug, Watusi, what-have-you. Art, under the Egyptians and Aztecs, was ritualistic-stylistic. A form of artistic representation was ritualistically fixed and was passed on from generation to generation. With the coming of Aristotle, art sought the truth—to paint and sculpt as realistically as possible—Rembrandt and Michelangelo represented the acme of this quest. Today, under relativity, art represents a feeling in space and time—surrealism, abstractionism and so on.

In the theater, the ancient Japanese No plays, largely incomprehensible to the modern Western mind, represent ritualistic theater. Shakespeare, and the Greek drama, where plays seek the truth about the nature of man and follow a true-to-life plot, demonstrate the peak of absolutistic theater. Today's non-plot Theater of the Absurd portends the theater art form of the Age of Relativity. In all areas of culture, the trio of the World Eras persists—in poetry it is the chant handed down from generation to generation (ritualism) versus the fixed verse forms of Shelley and Keats (absolutism) versus the free verse of today (relativism).

RELATIVITY RELATES TO MARKETING

Now how does this all relate to what is ahead in marketing? One example will alert the marketer as to how the switch from ritual-absolutism to relativity explains a present-day phenomenon directly related to marketing. The example is money. Under ritual-absolutism the ideal was to attain money that represented ritual symbolism and maintained absolute value. The history of economics offers endless examples of the search for the perfect money—embossed gold came closest to fulfilling the ideal. Today it can readily be seen that money in the ritual-absolutistic sense is obsolete. The flexibility of checks and the adaptability of credit cards both point to the development of monetary media designed to meet changing conditions in keeping with the Age of Relativity. This convincing example of how the concept of money has altered to meet the needs of the three World Eras points up why it is important to think through the meaning of the coming of the Age of Relativity in terms of marketing. The concluding sections of this discussion analyze certain influences behind the times and relate them to marketing.

OWNERSHIP IS AN ANACHRONISM[5]

Since the Garden of Eden, civilization's institutions and precepts have been based on two assumptions: that there is always a scarcity of material things, and that for the masses of people work is inevitable. But today these two assumptions are becoming less and less valid. For, as man comes to emphasize consumption, many of the precepts at the very base of his society must change. One key change lies in the attitudes he takes toward ownership. Such changes are already taking place. In the new world of technological affluence, the principle of ownership of material possessions by individuals is fast becoming an anachronism.

Through the ages, people placed value on ownership because there were not enough goods to go around. They were willing to accept ownership responsibilities to assure themselves of supplies of scarcities.

Reflect for a moment. How many people actually want to own an automobile, take home a "handy six-bottle carrying case" of soft drinks, or have a drawer full of shirts they can call their own? In the final analysis, not many.

In reality, what they want is a car in the model of their choice, well maintained, kept in excellent mechanical condition, and at their disposal when they want it. Cars get bumps and scratches, brakes need relining, and all must be pampered into running and retaining their resale value. As for soft drinks, a person wants to have a cold drink in his hand when he wants it. "Handy" carrying cases imply returning bottles, lugging, and storing.

A man holds little affection for shirts as such. What he wants is a freshly laundered shirt with all buttons in place, in a weight and style to meet the seasonal and social situation he intends to face. Thus, people in a busy, rapidly moving, affluent society increasingly realize that they are not interested in things per se, but rather in their use in a convenient and worry-free manner.

THE GROWING IMPORTANCE OF TIME

The implication is clear. The affluent citizen of the next century will be oriented to *buying time rather than product*. He will take the myriad of sophisticated products at his disposal for granted. His chief concern

[5] The concluding portions of this article, slightly altered, appeared in the *Harvard Business Review*, November–December, 1963.

will be to provide himself with free time in which he can conveniently use products that function to conserve time for leisure and pleasure. It is scarcity which creates value. Hence, *as scarcity of product disappears, the scarcity of time ascends the value scale.*

Since time grows more valuable as people grow in affluence, service expenditures increase proportionally as incomes rise. In the past, when domestic and service personnel were available, wealthy segments of society spent large proportions of income for service manpower (for housemaids, butlers, grooms, gardeners, game keepers, and so on). These helpers made time available so the wealthy could conveniently and pleasantly use their owned properties and possessions.

The affluent masses of today also seek to free time. However, because the personal service of domestics and service staffs is not available, the factory is expected to produce the wherewithal for freeing time. Throwaway goods; leasing communally owned facilities (where maintenance and servicing responsibilities are assumed at centrally located places that are staffed by experts); highly processed goods such as frozen foods, instant coffee, and the like (which provide a sort of built-in maid service)—all of these developments help to free time. In essence, citizens provide themselves with time by shedding themselves of ownership responsibilities.

GROWTH OF USE VALUES FOSTERS ECONOMIC STABILITY

The realization by consumers that they prefer to spend their incomes for *time-oriented use values* rather than *product-oriented asset ownership* has enormous implications that are largely unrecognized. Use-value is realistic, for it relates to change; asset-ownership is absolutistic-ritualistic, for it is fixed and inflexible. An enticing aspect of the impending switch in consumer attitudes is that it holds a key to solving one of capitalism's basic problems, namely, the instability of employment.

Unemployment is a perpetual erosion which undermines the foundations of capitalism. During the first part of the twentieth century the idea emerged that modern capitalism's survival depended on its ability to provide continual production expansion. In the latter part of the twentieth century, two essential corollaries must be added to the goal of production expansion: (1) production must be steady, and (2) increased convenience must regularly be provided for products in order to facilitate their consumption. Most hopefully, the use-value doctrine can contribute to achieving these goals for stabilizing capitalistic economies. It is ironic that automation, which is roundly accused of causing unemployment, provides the affluence which will in the long run stabilize and expand employment.

Stabilization involves getting at one symptom of business cycles, namely, fluctuation in the rates at which individuals, industry, and government spend money. Fluctuations in spending reflect directly on production scheduling. Production must be steady, for this is the only means of assuring steady incomes for those who produce. Furthermore, efficiencies of automated production can only be fully realized when output is even and regular. Expansion or curtailment of automated manufacturing is so costly that its advantages are quickly lost when production fluctuates.

Stabilized production is also a necessary adjunct to introducing a still shorter workweek. The shorter workweek compounds problems in manufacturing and selling in feast-or-famine industries.

MARKETING AS A SOCIAL FORCE

Elimination of fluctuations in spending requires that businessmen must increasingly apply their marketing ingenuity to secure regularly committed amounts from each individual's income.

The privilege of individuals doling out their incomes at any rate of speed or schedule they please will be a luxury which will have to be curtailed (not by fiat, but by persuasion) if we are to fully reap the material benefits of an automated world. The question is: Can we take advantage of the time-oriented use value to secure this effect?

If the goals of economic stability and full employment are to be achieved, marketing must be viewed as a social force. The public in general, and business leaders in particular, must better understand the place of marketing in the new society, for it is the force which will shape economic destiny by expanding and stabilizing consumption.

Methods for forcing consumption must be expanded and widely accepted as a permanent part of our social convention. The tempo of continuous consumption must be accelerated. Puritanical (absolutistic) attitudes (mothered all these centuries by scarcity) that view excessive consumption as immoral must be discarded. For example, the question of whether we basically need or even wish the goods that are produced is beside the point. Thinking in terms of conservation of replaceable resources will not solve the problems of the Age of Relativity.

The complexity of the problems involved in the social and economic adjustments which will be necessary to stabilize and increase the rate at which the private citizen spends his money staggers the imagination. However, the problems must and can be grasped with purposeful vigor. The largest roles in overcoming this Garguantuan challenge will be played by marketing men. In their hands lie the keys to selling merchandise so the family income is doled out in committed amounts, without interruption, and at accelerating rates. How this can be done is not so far-fetched as to evade the imagination.

MERCHANDISING NON-OWNERSHIP

One of the more promising approaches to spending family income in committed amounts is either to lease merchandise or to sell it on a replenishment contract basis.

Many steps in the direction of contractual selling and leasing are already in evidence. As instances:

A large appliance manufacturer has announced the renting of home appliances to apartment-house owners. Not only will refrigerators, air conditioners, dishwashers, freezers, washers, and dryers be rented, but they will also be serviced and replaced by newer models.

Auto rental companies are already among the fastest expanding in our economy. One of the largest auto rental companies plans to extend a New York experiment with cars garaged directly in luxury apartments.

Department stores are promoting their own rental services. A leading store in Washington advertises availability of hundreds of items for rent, among them dishwashers, public address systems, linens, china, power tools, baby bassinettes, and wheelchairs.

Even further steps are possible. Under a contract selling plan, which is a method for getting people used to leasing what they traditionally owned, automobile contracts could stipulate, for example, that a manufacturer will provide the family with a new automobile every three years. The amount paid each month would be fixed, and the all-important delivery date would be left to the discretion of the manufacturer.

Let us look at a hypothetical sales contract embellished with merchandising gimmicks. For customers entering into a contract for two, three, or four cars delivered at three-, six-, and nine-year intervals, the inducement might be a completed-contract "dividend" at the end of each three-year period which would make the next car 10% to 15% cheaper than one bought in the present manner.

Indeed, such savings dividends would be wholly practical since renewal sales costs would be small. Costs also would be reduced because the buyer under contract would be asked to indicate the model of car he wants perhaps six months in advance of delivery date. The buyer would choose his car by visiting a centrally located showroom where a complete range of the latest models would be displayed.

This method of advance ordering would create the ideal situation manufacturers have dreamed about since the beginning of mass production, for it enables the manufacturer to plan production on a long-range basis. Certainly greater facility in planning ahead would lead to cost reductions that could be passed on to consumers. The promise-to-buy provision in the contract might be for a minimum of two cars with a right to cancel at the end of any three-year period, the penalty for canceling a contract being the loss of the 10% to 15% renewal dividend.

The selling format of the Book-of-the-Month Club, which has been widely adapted for selling things other than books, provides us with a precedent for this kind of selling. The method has already demonstrated that such contracts force sales, for it has sold many books that would otherwise never have been sold. It is also able to sell books the year round, doing much to compensate for Christmas and vacation sales peaks. Use of contractual selling means that competition would be as vigorous as ever, just as it is now among the book and record clubs.

Variations of contractual arrangements, such as those mentioned for automobiles, could be worked out for many lines of goods. For example, shoes could be provided at the rate of four pairs each year, for $5 per month; three suits a year, at $10 a month; and so on. This is actually not a far cry from the monthly payment of installment selling which is already well entrenched. Indeed, it seems that the British may have intuitively seen sales contracts and leasing coming, for they use the term "hire-purchase plan" when referring to selling on the installment basis.

Another convincing piece of evidence that contract selling is on the way is the extension by the automobile companies of service warranties, which have increased from 10,000 up to 100,000 miles in a short time. The warranty, in essence, is recognition that the customer prefers buying use-value and is not interested in ownership responsibility. Long warranties serve to stabilize the repair business, which illustrates in part how contractual selling serves to stabilize the economy as a whole. When a customer has a warranty, he brings his car in for repairs at the time the repair is needed. He is less inclined to postpone a repair for seasonal reasons, nor does he wait until the economic climate is right. Manufacturers benefit by being able to forecast parts and service requirements more accurately. Long-range planning can be entered into, the benefits of which can be passed along from supplier to supplier for end benefits to the company as a whole.

Two additional areas for expanding and stabilizing expenditures hold attractive potential. One area may be called throw-away consumption. This is the new world of disposable tableware such as plates, cups, tablecloths; single-use medical supplies such as needles, sheets, and dabbers; and portable and switchable building decor items such as curtains, partitions, and lighting fixtures. Expansion possibilities for disposables are unlimited. Consumer purchases of disposable items are continuous and regular and relate closely to use patterns.

The other area for steadying spending lies in the provision of centralized facilities for communal living. People living in apartment houses and suburban areas increasingly provide themselves with communal recreational and service facilities. Swimming pools and tennis courts, guest and reading rooms, and laundry and hobbyshop facilities will increasingly be provided privately for smaller and smaller groups of people. Payment for such facilities becomes an adjunct to the monthly rent, a steady claim on income which is economically desirable.

By all these means, the increasing inclination of consumers to spend income for use-value instead of asset ownership can be capitalized on. This will help stabilize the economy to the extent that people thus are involved in long-term commitments that are paid for at regular intervals.

In addition, people also tend to use up what they lease or contract more quickly since they do not take care of things as well. In this way, consumption also would be stepped up. Furthermore, requests for replacements for worn-out, obsolete, or otherwise unsuitable merchandise would be made as the need occurs; thus, the psychology of needing to make a decision to buy, that upsets economic stability, is bypassed.

THE MARKETER WILL BE THE LEADER IN A SILENT REVOLUTION

A review of emerging consumption-forcing methods which seek to expand and stabilize spending makes it clear that most of them (leasing, contract selling, consumption of disposables, communal facilities) do indeed relieve the citizen of property ownership responsibilities. Use-value rather than individual ownership implications dominate.

This silent revolution—which substitutes use-value for asset-ownership and raises the relative importance of time desirability over product desirability on the consumer's scale of values—has fantastically important implications for the business leader. Businessmen must be counted on to provide the leadership which will gain the silent revolution victories in the marketplace.

The challenge to the businessman is two-dimensional. First, there is the social and economic dimension and the preservation and strengthening of capitalism. The business leader has to be aware of the magnitude of the silent revolution and understand the significance of how his role as the marketing leader and policy-maker is tied to production expansion and stabilized spending. Second, there is the business operational dimension. Here the silent revolution must be understood so that management decisions are geared to seizing the real business opportunities the Age of Relativity presents.

The change from the Ritualistic-Absolutistic to a Relativistic society implies that enlightened business leadership must increasingly understand and cater to the many needs and desires of a society in transition. Consumers, on the one hand, must be given to feel that their property-owning and conservation standards of the past are not violated. On the other hand, they must be made to feel comfortable about a future which will be more rootless, yet will have the modern advantages of providing free time for leisure, pleasure, convenience, mobility.

Correct business decisions will be made most frequently by leaders who understand these conflicting needs on the part of the consumer of the future. Furthermore, tomorrow's executives will have to be fast on their feet. Use-value emphasis will most certainly produce a market which reacts more quickly to various influences. An economy with no ownership can more rapidly embrace change and improvements, for there are no property franchises to disentrench or dispose of.

"Buy use, not ownership" is the rallying cry of the Age of Relativity.

The idea is not so radical as a first-blush consideration of it may suggest. As has been shown, installment selling, extended warranties, and growth of leasing have already led us far along the road to divorcing the U.S. public from ownership. Further evidence that indicates trends leading to contractual spending are found in growth of prepaid medical service, payment of utilities and heating costs in 12 identical payments spread over a year, and rental of works of art by local art museums.

Provision for steady spending of the major portion of all incomes is the last link in the chain after mechanization, mass selling, mass credit, and automation. Provision for steady spending will forge the greatest material well-being the world has ever seen. By promoting the goals of committed and expanded spending of incomes, the marketer's ingenuity can reduce business-cycle fluctuations and ensure prosperity. Theirs is the moral obligation to do this even if in the process they may be damned and misunderstood.

The process of innovation involves more than finding a need and creating a product, process, or service to satisfy it. Managing technological change or innovation requires consideration of several complex variables that are frequently difficult to isolate and measure. This article examines the problems and opportunities associated with the management of technological change.

4. MARKETING AND THE MANAGEMENT OF TECHNOLOGICAL CHANGE*

Robert D. Bruce†

Since the marketing concept has become so well accepted, at least by marketing men, the role of marketing in managing technological change

* Reprinted from "Marketing and the Management of Technological Change," *Proceedings of the Fall Conference of the American Marketing Association,* 1966, pp. 33–43. See Robert L. Clewett, "Market Opportunity and Corporate Management," in *Marketing and Economic Development,* Peter D. Bennett (ed.), American Marketing Association Proceedings of Fall Conference, September, 1965, pp. 187–99, for a definition of the market opportunity concept. For a discussion that focuses

would seem to be fairly obvious. If satisfaction of consumer or customer needs is the dominating force in directing a business, it would appear that technological innovations should logically derive from the same source. I take no argument with this thesis except to say that it doesn't always work that way. There are other forces that stimulate technological change and the process of innovation is more complex than simply finding a need and building a product, process, or service to satisfy it.

For one thing, the task of finding new consumer needs is somewhat difficult, because it is necessary to anticipate needs five or ten years hence. True technological innovation requires relatively long lead times; to produce a new product that will not satisfy requirements of future consumers is a useless exercise and a waste of money. For another, the process of managing technological change or innovation requires consideration of a number of variables that are not always easy to isolate and measure. Finally, some of the strongest forces stimulating innovation are not consumer requirements, but business competition, making adequate use of available capital, and the sheer desire of the innovator to innovate.

FORCES OF CHANGE IN BUSINESS

Let's look at some of the forces in our business society that will tend to be dominating pressures on business leaders and that will affect the rate of future technological innovation.

The rapid growth of corporate funds is making it increasingly difficult for top management of companies to find good investment outlets. Internal sources of corporate funds have increased from about $11 billion in 1946 to around $38 billion in 1963. At the same time, external sources of funds—both long and short term—have hovered around the $10 billion mark. As a percentage of the total, internal sources have increased from about 50% to 61% or 62% today. The main reasons for this increase are the accrual of funds for tax and dividend payments; the buildup of cash flow, primarily because of growing depreciation allowances; and the adoption of better cash management techniques.

Retained cash flow of 120 corporations in a Stanford Research Institute sample of manufacturing corporations increased from $3.3 billion in 1947 to $13.2 billion in 1965. This is an increase of 400%. In spite of the present disharmonies in the money market with record high interest rates, the long term outlook is for growing generation of internal capital.

The result is that many companies in the United States today have idle

attention on the entrepreneurial aspects of translating scientific and technological knowledge into profitable want-satisfying products and services, both from the societal and business enterprise points of view, see Robert L. Clewett, "Integrating Science, Technology, and Marketing: An Overview," in *Science, Technology, and Marketing*, Raymond M. Haas (ed.), American Marketing Association Proceedings of National Fall Conference, August 31–September 1–2, 1966, pp. 3–20.

† Stanford Research Institute.

cash or are getting a marginal return on part of their funds. Many a board room echoes with semi-hushed question, "What are we going to do with all that money?" For lurking in the shadows is the spectre of the government (federal, state, and local), which might feel the money could be put to better use to benefit society. Virtually half of the firms that come to Stanford Research Institute seeking research assistance in planning and corporate strategy are faced with the problem of new investment for idle funds.

Attempts to solve this growing problem will probably take many forms in the coming decade—all of which have implications for marketing men. The first of these is a growing channeling of funds toward overseas investment in the industrialized nations. Capital expenditures abroad have been advancing strongly since 1957. In spite of current efforts on the part of the United States and some foreign governments to retard additional U.S. investment abroad, the coming decade will see an increase in this kind of outlay. Most European nations do not have enough capital to finance their long term industrial development, and the U.S. balance of payments problem may well be alleviated within the next three to four years. We will also see more investment in the underdeveloped nations and in Australia and Japan. . . .

A second outlet for excess cash will be a diversification by many companies into financial operations. A number of companies that produce consumer products have set up captive finance companies. Others have established subsidiaries to finance dealers or other businesses. Although the amount of capital that may be absorbed in this manner may not be great, the advantages of financial subsidiaries are substantial, and the number of captive finance companies will grow over the next ten years. Marketing men have an obvious stake in this sort of development. If anything, such activities will make product acquisition by the customer easier. Competition in financing terms is likely to grow, and, if you aren't now, you soon may be selling the payments—not the product.

A third use of corporate funds will probably have profound long term effects on the economy and marketing—more profound perhaps than any of the others. This is the channeling of more money into innovation—to research on products, processes, and services. Research expenditures in the United States have been rising at stupendous rates since World War II, but a large percentage of the money spent has come from the federal government. Today, about 70% of the more than $20 billion spent on research and development in the United States is federal funds. But industry now has the wherewithal to finance research, some of which has been begging for funding.

This form of channeling funds will be aided by another phenomenon in the business society. Mounting cash flow and the need to find profitable investment opportunities for these funds have contributed to the growth of mergers, acquisitions, and diversification in U.S. industry. Over the next decade, however, antitrust considerations will make it increasingly difficult for large corporations and even some medium-sized ones to find suitable candidates for merger or acquisition. . . .

Now, this is somewhat of an old song. But this time the old song has a new verse—and even the harmonics are different. Enormous quantities of capital will be needed by industry for expansion, and that capital is available. Increasing shares of this capital will be used for research on new products, processes, and services, and for developing new markets. The markets are big and they are getting bigger. But the number of products to satiate the markets is even greater. The new products and services will satisfy old needs better than ever, and will awaken new needs that we didn't know existed. They will be more sophisticated, more utilitarian, and of greater value than their counterparts today.

The burgeoning availability of capital and the need for new outlets will create new opportunities and problems for those associated with the marketing process. The need for technological innovation does not automatically imply that there will be wise investment in innovation. Indeed, one of the major false assumptions of our age is that change, by definition, is good. However, lest there be some confusion about my attitude, I firmly believe in change—that is, change for the better. And the best way to achieve good technological change (or any other kind) is to manage it.

MANAGING CHANGE

The fact that men seek to manage change is a unique characteristic of modern industrial life. Men are increasingly confident that they can shape their environment rather than be its creatures. This attitude has evolved gradually in Western society, but has been strikingly emphasized in the past few decades. That people who have lived for centuries in static societies have suddenly been caught up in a "revolution of rising expectations" is testimony to the validity of the concept. All men seek to grow, and growth is enhanced if the environment can be adapted to conditions that foster growth.

To foster growth, men plan. Men have always thought about the future. They have wished about it and daydreamed about it. Some have made attempts to shape it by planning about it. The new thing about planning is not that it exists, but that it is being done in a rigorous, formalized manner.

Planning is the process of thinking ahead and making a predetermination about a course of action. That business firms have begun to do this systematically, using standard procedures, has been occasioned by the growing size and complexity of business enterprise as well as by the increasing rapidity of changes in the business environment. Planning is an attempt to do more than respond to the environment. It is an effort to think ahead, to select a course of action, and to manage the environment so that events can be anticipated.

MANAGING INNOVATION

One of the key factors in the process of technological change is the management of innovation. Industrial firms must master the process of innovation rather than being buffeted by it, if they wish to grow and prosper. Mastering innovation does not imply resorting to instant invention—that is, just hiring a team of scientists, adding money, and hoping for automatic results. Innovation is more complex and comprehensive than that.

Genuine innovation covers much more than technology. It includes innovation in production, finance, administration, marketing, and all other functions of business. Seeking technological innovation without considering improvement in the other elements of the enterprise is comparable to putting a modern jet engine in a DC-3 airframe.

Successful technological innovation occurs when it is considered in a broad context, embracing all of the environments in which the business firm operates. It isn't a question of *whether* to integrate science, technology, and marketing management, for it is done in some manner by some mechanism. The question is how to integrate these factors most efficiently to enhance the opportunities for technological and marketing success.

Knowledge of the Environments

To manage technological change, it is vital to have a knowledge of the environments—business, technological, political, and social. Every company has knowledge about itself. And, if the company is astute, it has reasonably accurate intelligence about the industry in which it operates. Knowledge of the company and its industry constitute partial knowledge of its environments. These particular environments are either friendly or hostile, and by knowing about them the company has some degree of control or response to changes within them. But equally important is the requirement for knowledge of what is occurring in the vast areas outside the company's immediate periphery. In large part, this wide environment is unknown, and in order to grow, innovate, and manage change, a business must convert its unknown environment to a known (and hopefully, friendly) one. If the environment is friendly, it presents an opportunity for innovation. If it is hostile, it presents a threat to the continued success of the enterprise, and some form of innovation is required to respond to the challenge. . . .

Inputs to Innovation

Matched against the need for a knowledge of the various environments is the need for an understanding of the inputs to innovation or certain criteria that must be examined and met if an innovation is to be successful. There are five major criteria: the needs of the market or user, the product concept, the state of the art, competition, and timing. I have not listed cost and price as criteria because they underlie and are the result of all of the others.

Genuine innovation stems from a requirement to satisfy the needs of people. Today, needs are not as obvious or as simple as they once were, and relatively complex goods and services are required to meet them. The prudent supplier of goods is faced with a prudent buyer; in addition, he is faced with a plethora of trends and countertrends, all of which augur an accelerating rate of change.

By identifying trends in the business, technological, political, and social environments, we can begin to get some idea of the needs of people. Some trends reinforce each other. Consider, for example, the trends of growing disposable income, increased leisure time, lengthened life spans, increasing educational attainment, growing job boredom among white collar workers, and an increasing "professionalization" among business people. This combination creates a receptive environment for products and services to fulfill a growing desire for education and recreation. In another instance, the growth of population, the increase in government activity, the expanding size of businesses, the increasing complexity of business enterprise, and the inadequacy of data for decision-making indicate a need for improved communication and information systems. The real focus in this kind of trend analysis is to identify the needs of tomorrow's customers, not today's. Through observing the environmental trends and identifying where and how these trends reinforce each other, organizations can obtain some insight into the needs of users five and ten years hence.

The product concept is the set of ideas describing a product, process, or service that will meet a user or market need. The path we are following has a sign on it which says, "Necessity is the mother of invention." Product concepts are usually developed from an analysis of user needs. If people could just say what they need, the problem would be simple; but, unfortunately, they usually don't know. The trick is to look at things in a different perspective so that imperfections in the present order of things can be identified. By doing this, new needs can be generated, and new product concepts can be identified to fulfill those needs.

Most often, product concepts will require determining whether the current state of the art is sufficiently advanced to fulfill their specifications. This can frequently be done with existing technology, but sometimes it calls for new and improved technology. Occasionally, it demands new scientific understanding. Such was the case in the development of the transistor. In his efforts to obtain a solid-state device that would amplify, Dr. Shockley obtained some unexpected results from his experiments. These results demanded new theory. The new theory necessitated additional experiments to verify it. Additional unexpected results led to the junction transistor, which is the basis for the industry as we know it today. The results also led to a far better understanding of solid-state physics, the effects of which will be felt for many years.

The examination of the state of the art should not be limited to technology, but should ask questions concerning marketing and distribution, production, finance, manpower, administration—in other words, all of the major business functions.

Consideration of competitive conditions should embrace more than traditional competition for markets. Competition for funds, manpower, and physical resources, as well as competition with substitutes and governmental bodies, should be reviewed. It is important to analyze competition thoroughly within and among technologies as they apply to the projected innovation.

As marketing men readily recognize, timing is supremely important in the introduction of innovations. All four other criteria for a successful innovation may be favorable, but poor timing can ruin the entire undertaking. Timing may be too early as well as too late. Remember the Airflow Chrysler? The need was identified, the product concept of a streamlined automobile was sound, the state of the art was such that it could be built, and Chrysler was far ahead of the competition. But the timing was off. The auto was in advance of its time, was not readily accepted, and the innovation floundered, leaving a scar on that company that took years to overcome.

The Role of Marketing in Managing Innovation

Given all the environments that stimulate or impede innovation and the factors that must be considered in the innovative process, what then is the role of marketing in managing innovation?

To examine this role, let us array the various environments—business, technological, political, and social—in a matrix with the criteria for innovation. By examining the interfaces or squares and the kinds of problems involved in each, we can estimate the role of marketing in managing innovation. Figure 1 indicates the major and moderate roles that marketing plays in each instance.

It is important to note that marketing plays a role in all sectors of the matrix. It is not confined to an examination of the needs of the market or to a look at the social environment.

As shown in Figure 1, marketing's strongest roles are in establishing the needs of the market and in determining whether the product concept

FIGURE 1

Role of Marketing in Managing Innovation

ENVIRONMENTS / CRITERIA	BUSINESS	TECHNOLOGICAL	POLITICAL	SOCIAL
NEEDS OF MARKET	●	▲	●	●
PRODUCT CONCEPT	●	●	▲	●
STATE OF THE ART	▲	▲	●	●
COMPETITION	●	▲	▲	●
TIMING	●	▲	▲	●

● MAJOR ROLE ▲ MODERATE ROLE

meets those needs. There are lesser but important inputs to be made in considering the state of the art, competition, and timing.

In establishing the needs of the market, marketing has the responsibility of examining consumer income trends, changes in the population mix, households, age and education patterns, and the like within the business environment. Similarly, it has a major role to play in identifying political encouragement or impedance within the political environment. The role of marketing in the social environment is obviously that of examining and detecting the values and attitudes of consumers or industrial users, the desire for product improvement, or such things as trends in consumer living patterns. It is primarily the function of R&D to examine the needs of the market in terms of the technological environment, but marketing has a moderate role to play in determining whether the market or users need and can accept an advanced and sophisticated technology or whether they require one that is less revolutionary.

In determining the product concept, marketing plays a strong role in the business, technological, and social environments. Does the product concept meet the needs of the user in terms of the business environment? Questions to be answered include those such as: Is the product concept oriented to the right population segments or age groups? Will rising personal income in European countries enable the product to be marketed there? Will inflation make a difference? Within the social environment, marketing is responsible for determining whether the product concept meets user requirements or falls short of the mark. In the technological area, marketing's role is to help determine whether the technology makes the product overly complicated. It is also important that marketing ensure that the technology is being applied to the correct problem. In recent years, a host of companies rushed into the business of building teaching machines, only to find that the problem was less one of designing an efficient device than of obtaining or developing the proper learning programs. The product concept must also be suitable to the political environment; it must be acceptable in terms of government regulations, and in line with government interests. In the beginning, the supersonic transport was primarily conceived to meet public and international policy needs rather than a burgeoning market. In California, vehicle exhaust control devices have had to meet specifications established by the state.

Examination of the state of the art is largely concerned with determining whether existing technology can do the job, or whether new technology needs to be developed. However, marketing has a moderate role to play in this instance by ensuring that the proposed technology (existing or new) will produce a product that is priced right, will sell, and is economically feasible. Within the social environment, marketing men need to examine the state of their own art and determine whether present marketing methods are appropriate to marketing the innovation or whether new ones need to be developed. For example, if service requirements for the product are unique or frequent, a new service organization may have to be established. If the product is high priced, replacement parts might be better supplied by air freight than by establishing complete stocks in regional warehouses.

In examining competition within the social environment, marketing's role need not be belabored. It is primarily a question of determining whether any competitor is offering a comparable product, and, if so, how the one contemplated can be superior. Marketing also has a major role to play in determining competition within the business environment, in terms of competition for salesmen, use of competitive advertising media, competition in financing, and the like. Marketing's role in assessing technological competition is fairly limited. Within the political environment the regulation of competition is an important factor for marketing to consider. As aerospace men can readily testify, marketing to government agencies is fraught with competition.

I have previously mentioned the importance of timing in terms of consumer acceptance of a new innovation. Less apparent perhaps is the role of marketing in ensuring introduction of a product at the correct time in the business cycle or in relation to other general business conditions. Marketing men may also lend a hand to those most concerned with technology in determining whether or not the product using the technology will be acceptable. For example, renovated sewage for drinking water may be technologically (and even economically) feasible, but it may take a bit of consumer education before the timing is right.

SUMMARY

The forces of change in business auger for a continuation and increase in the rate of technological innovation. The demand for new products to meet competition, utilize economic wealth, and satisfy the needs of increasingly independent and affluent consumers will channel more funds into technological innovation and create more technological change.

The role of marketing in managing technological change involves more than transmitting the needs of the market to those who develop new products. Rather, it is a multi-faceted role of examining the forces of change and the various environments in which it exists, and of relating them to the factors involved in the process of innovation. By isolating these factors and relating them to the environment in which business operates, marketing men can make a distinct contribution in the wise application of effort to technological development.

An effective general market system is mandatory for nations that want to maintain a private enterprise base and free choice among genuine market alternatives. This article evaluates the market system of the United States and the impact of governmental policies and regulations on the rule of competition and private decision making in marketing. The drift away from competition as our national policy is examined.

5. MARKETING AND PUBLIC POLICY*

E. T. Grether†

Character and Capacities of an Acceptable General Market System

. . . A competitive general market system in a country such as the United States should not be conceptualized in terms of the economics of perfect competition. Hence, the market system is not synonomous with the functioning of the economy. Similarly, it is a mistake to conceptualize the market system or even market economy as synonomous with capitalism. Instead, the character and capacities of the market system must be conceptualized in terms of the historical background and drift, traditions, legal system and social and political goals and values of a nation or society.

If a nation or society wishes to (a) maintain a strong, widespread, and varied private enterprise base along with (b) free consumer-buyer choices among genuine alternatives and (c) "the rule of competition" in some acceptable degree, then the general market system must have the following interrelated capacities:

* Reprinted from *Proceedings of the Fall Conference of the American Marketing Association*, 1965, pp. 533–57. These excerpts constitute approximately 45 percent of the complete text of Dean Grether's commissioned commemorative paper presented at the conference.

† University of California, Berkeley.

1. To respond to and aid the free choices of buyers at all levels, especially the choices of consumer-buyers, as a mechanism of communication, coordination and organization.
2. To respond to and interact with general and specific *external* environmental influences, forces and conditions (i.e., the system must be open ended).
3. To interact among the elements of the system *internally*, as an input-output system, including particularly the adjustment and shifting of resources from lesser advantaged uses to products, services, or geographical areas of greater advantage.
4. To allocate acceptably that portion of economic resources not allocated by government outside the market system.
5. To "regulate" in the sense of placing the participants under strong competitive compulsions for both (a) the efficient use of resources in production and in marketing, and (b) the effective fulfillment of the economic wants and desires of the members of the society. . . .

DUAL IMPACTS OF GOVERNMENTAL POLICIES AND COMPETITION UPON MARKETING AND GROWTH DECISIONS OF PRIVATE ENTERPRISE

We turn now to a brief interpretive appraisal of the dual impacts of competition under the market system and of governmental policies and regulations upon the basic market decisions and actions of private enterprise.

Commodity versus Enterprise Competition

It is of high importance at this point to distinguish between two broad types of competition, which may be labelled "commodity" and "enterprise" competition. Always, of course, business enterprises are the producing and marketing entities. But in the case of so-called "commodity competition," prices are definitely established for the enterprise's homogeneous products by the impersonal supply and demand forces of the market. The problem of the enterprise is to collect, combine and use productive resources so efficiently as to make profits and allow survival under the prices registered by a great macro-supply and demand cash register.

But in the case of "enterprise competition" the enterprise is in an environment, or creates one, in which profits and survival are not so clearly related to and determined by a simple price factor. The enterprise competes not only in the use of resources in production, but also in marketing and in "selling." In a sense in this situation, the enterprise has its own micro-cash register which is still linked, however, with those of other enterprises (the macro-cash register) in a series of processes similar to those of modern computers linked together and also interacting with multiple remote control operators.

One test of the economic drift or trend of an economic society is the extent to which enterprises may be classified as under "commodity" or "enterprise-type" competition. Clearly, this distinction, too, has significance for both the nature and functioning of the market system and appropriate public policy.

The discussion to follow is oriented primarily in terms of marketing decisions under the conditions of "enterprise competition"[1] as now the more characteristic one in the United States.

Product Policies

On the whole product innovation, development and diversification are the bright spots under "enterprise competition" in the United States. The combined effects of governmental and private research and development and encouragement in a general environment of rapid scientific and technological change have given private enterprise an enormous dynamic, innovative thrust. On the whole, governmental policies and programs are favorable, although there are unsettled issues concerning patent rights under governmentally sponsored Research and Development in some industries and of the new products in the food and drug industries.

Promotion Policies

In the main, too, the environment in the United States is favorable to the use of personal and impersonal instruments and media for selling and promotion. This observation is of high importance because product innovation and development and promotion are parts of integrated processes. Time and again, we would not obtain the benefits of invention and innovation at all or as rapidly without effective promotion.

Product differentiation and promotion are supported by strong legal trademark and copyright protections. The chief thrust of public regulation is towards the protection of buyers, especially consumer-buyers, from deceit, falsehood and misrepresentation and to maintain conditions of fair competition among enterprises. On the whole, there is relatively little public oversight of the use of personal selling, except through some local licensing. The focus of public regulation is upon impersonal selling or advertising in its various guises. Although such conjoined federal, state and local regulation often is onerous, the net effects on the whole usually are to support and channelize the competitive compulsion of the market system.

The chief burden of the public regulation of advertising is the protection of buyers, especially consumers, both with respect to quantity

---

[1] For a more detailed, but not entirely similar analysis see Michwitz, G., *Marketing and Competition: The Various Forms of Competition at the Successive Stages of Production and Distribution* (Helsingfors, 1959).

(weights and measures) and quality, and safety in use. Current public issues involve packaging (Hart Bill)[2] and consumer credit sales (Douglas Bill),[3] and additional safeguards for users in fields in which health and safety[4] bulk high, as food and drugs and motor vehicles. In these and other instances, the problem of public regulation is to provide the requisite protection to buyers without encumbering business enterprises with unduly, detailed positive requirements.

Public issues in the field of promotion, important though they may be, appear to be much less important and much more likely of reasonable mutual solution than in some other areas of business decision making. The chief ultimate risks could arise out of unnecessarily detailed prescriptions over business promotional behavior. Promotional policies and practices should be, and for the most part are, amenable to reasonable regulation under a combination of private, individual and cooperative efforts and public oversight. In addition, legally recognized "puffing" provides some latitude and flexibility in sales promotion even in the face of stringent, positive regulations.

Pricing Policies and Practices

Public policy and regulation, like economic analysis, focuses strongly upon prices and pricing. Pricing is the holy of holies of antitrust enforcement with its *per se* prohibition of price conspiracies and strong suspicion of the conscious parallelism and price leadership of oligopolistic competition and of so-called administered pricing.

Public policies affecting pricing bring into sharp contrast the differences in market circumstances and compulsions affecting "commodity" and "enterprise" competition. On the one hand, there is a strong tendency to support prices artificially when under the pressures of severe commodity competition. On the other, aggressive price cutting by enterprisers is under suspicion as "price chiselling" and unfair competition. There tends to be a contradictory interaction as between the efforts of antitrust to break down price conspiracies and to enhance competition and special federal and state legislation directed at the aggressive use of price cutting by individual enterprises.

Much of the controversy and issues in public regulation is centered about so-called "administered pricing," and what to do about it. In all of this there tends to be an inherent and basic contradiction between public policies and regulations conceptualized in terms of traditional commodity

[2] *Packaging and Labeling Practices,* 87th Congress, 1st, 2nd Sessions, 1961, 1962; *Packaging and Labeling Legislation* (3 parts), 88th Congress, 1st Session, 1963.

[3] *Truth in Lending Bill,* 87th Congress, 1st, 2nd Sessions, 1961, 1962.

[4] At the time of writing, a Congressional Subcommittee was questioning top executives of the auto industry concerning safety devices and features and air pollution. *Business Week,* July 17, 1965.

competition and the complex, totality of business-getting variables, of which "net price" is but one, in enterprise competition.

The conflicts and issues affecting pricing are focused on three broad bodies of special regulation (1) under the Robinson-Patman Act addressed to price discrimination, (2) geographical, delivered pricing and (3) the resale price maintenance of branded goods. In not one of these broad, important areas of pricing has public policy achieved a reasonable, balanced relationship with the forces and compulsions of competition in the market. In all three areas, there tends to be a general impact towards uniformity in pricing quite contrary to the accepted, *per se* prohibition of price agreements. The so-called "Fair Trade" laws allow manufacturers of trade-marked goods to impose uniform price structures upon the distributive trades when such action would be unlawful by their dealers themselves. Authorities[5] agree that the net impacts of the enforcement of the Robinson-Patman Act probably have been towards restraint in pricing and a form of direct regulation contrary to the purposes of antitrust.

Oversight over geographical pricing has established clearly that organized, disciplined geographical, delivered price structures are unlawful in accordance with the general *per se* prohibition of price agreements. But there is a large zone of uncertainty and difference of attitudes and, in fact, a basic dilemma in enforcement under the conditions of "enterprise competition." On the one hand, systematic enforced delivered pricing structures on the part of business could subvert or even stifle the normal competitive forces and surplus and deficit adjustments of geographical competition in our great internal free trade market. On the other, simple enforcement solutions of the *per se* species on the part of enforcement agencies, if they run counter to basic market structural factors, could either be meaningless, or could produce a type of artificial, geographical price uniformity.[6]

Marketing Organization of Individual Enterprises

Individual enterprises enjoy a great deal of freedom for choice among organizational alternatives to achieve marketing objectives, ranging from ownership and operation through vertical integration, through partial vertical integration, to a variety of exclusive and selective contractual and franchising arrangements. None of these forms of organization are illegal

---

[5] See especially, Edwards, C. D., *The Price Discrimination Law: A Review of Experience* (Brookings Institution, 1959); Rowe, F. M., *Price Discrimination Under the Robinson-Patman Act* (Boston, 1962); Sawyer, A. E., *Business Aspects of Pricing Under the Robinson-Patman Act* (Boston, 1963); *Report of the Attorney-General's National Committee to Study the Antitrust Laws* (Washington, D.C., 1955).

[6] Cf. Clark, J. M., *Competition as a Dynamic Process* (Brookings Institution, 1961); Machlup, F., *The Basing Point System* (Blakiston, 1949); *Report of the Attorney General's National Committee to Study the Antitrust Laws* (Washington, D.C. 1955).

per se, but some are very nearly so. Thus, the acquisition of a competitor by a large firm raises legal risks so serious that most firms, especially large ones, would not wish to assume them. Thus, also, exclusive dealer or exclusive territorial arrangements are almost *per se* illegal for large enterprises with substantial volumes of sales. Similarly, franchise agreements by powerful manufacturers must be drawn carefully in relation to a strong presumption of unilateral control comparable to vertical integration without all of its risks. The recent and current boom in franchise arrangements raises a host of unsettled legal issues.

In most public policy issues concerning organizational arrangements, legal determination requires the analysis and appraisal of the special circumstances of the case in terms of the actual and probable effects upon competition. The spectrum of legal risks ranges from horizontal acquisition to vertical downstream integration, to vertical upstream integration, to the variety of exclusive and selective contractual arrangements. In general small and local enterprises enjoy greater relative freedom than large established national firms. The doctrine seems to be emerging that arrangements that would be restrictive of competition by large firms may aid and strengthen competition when employed by smaller firms.

Conclusion Concerning Conjoined Impacts of Governmental Policies and Competition upon Private Decision Making

It appears that private enterprise decisions and practices in product innovation, development and promotion, on the whole are in both a favorable competitive and public policy environment (with notable exceptions, of course). Public policy affecting pricing starts out bravely with its *per se* prohibition of price agreement but falters and to some extent reverses itself under the Robinson-Patman and Fair Trade Laws and shows signs of internal contradiction in geographical pricing. The broad drift of public policy affecting organizational arrangements seems increasingly to be oriented against restrictionism and in opposition to growth in size, market share and vertical ownership and control, especially downstream and less so upstream. On the whole, the total net impact of governmental policies affecting private decision making, except in some strategic aspects of pricing, tend to support the internal competitive compulsions of the market system. The debits on the side of pricing may be more than offset by the credits on the side of product development and promotion.

Growth Policies and Market Structure

In recent years there has been an enormous interest in problems of economic growth in this country and even more so in the so-called undeveloped or underdeveloped countries. In the United States the discussion of National policies affecting economic growth have often been interlinked with discussions of the control of inflation and the maintenance of price stability. Obviously, in a society with a private enterprise base, therefore, the impact of total national economic policies and of law and regulation upon growth incentives, opportunities and the patterns of growth of business firms is of highest importance. We shall omit from our discussion at this point national policies aimed at influencing aggregate demand by spending programs, tax reduction and the like. Clearly, of course, these affect the marketing opportunities of private business. Insofar as such programs can be timed appropriately and not used to weaken normal competitive forces, they can improve the environment of private opportunity. Our concern is more definitely with the effects of governmental regulations, including antitrust, upon incentives and policies for expansion and growth by individual firms.

First, in general, the intent of our national economic policies and regulations is not to inhibit growth of individual enterprises, except in one major respect to be discussed below, but to channelize it within the rules of the game. These rules comprise the great body of the law and regulations of unfair competition, abusive and predatory practices and behavior and endeavors to monopolize. Such laws and regulations govern relations with competitors and suppliers and customers, i.e., all aspects of production and marketing.

Second, growth by internal expansion within the rules of the game is now looked upon much more favorably than growth by acquisitions and mergers, especially in antitrust enforcement. In general, it is believed that growth through ploughing back earnings and through gradual increase in the patronage of satisfied customers is more solid and substantial than by the acquisition of or merger with established firms. From the point of view of antitrust it is held that growth internally expands investment and production and hence increases competition, while growth by merger and acquisition in some sense removes a competitor or a supplier or a customer from the market. In any event, there is no necessary increase in net investment or of production.

This view, when stated so simply, of course, disregards the new investments and expansion of output that might be and often are made following a merger. Even so, it cannot be defined that if this same investment had been made in developing entirely new facilities in addition to the existing ones, total investment and hence competition would most likely be greater. Much will depend upon the special circumstances and especially upon the longer run trends, including the likelihood that the acquired firm would have failed in any event. Thus, it is currently alleged that mergers that would maintain or enhance local employment against a threat of unemployment are looked upon with favor under the antipoverty program.[7] At issue, of course, also is not only the degree of competition but also the cost and efficiency factors about which it is difficult to generalize.

Third, the most critical issue affecting the growth of corporations in the United States is the trend of enforcement under the 1950 revision of Sec. 7 of the Clayton Act. As of the time of writing, the number and character of cases adjudicated and in process, and the weight of opinions by the Supreme Court of the United States in the small number of cases adjudicated,[8] indicate that almost any merger or acquisition can be questioned, and a large proportion most likely negated. There is almost no large American corporation that does not now face one of the following problems: (1) the possibility that acquisitions made earlier may be questioned under "the backward bite" of antitrust, (2) whether to invest heavily in the improvement of recent acquisitions that might be questioned, or (3) whether to move forward with acquisitions under consideration.

American business now finds itself in a new environment so far as growth by mergers and acquisitions is concerned. Under the present portents, it may well turn out that we have witnessed the last great merger movement in American history. If this be true, it could be of tremendous importance because many great American corporations were built to a considerable extent through the processes of merger. To state this is not to deny the tremendous forces of internal expansion separately or together with mergers.

Perhaps the most significant factor of all in terms of the maintenance and promotion of competition is that the entire force of action under Section 7 is to change market structure. But if existing and new firms are denied growth by acquisition, then powerful established corporations to some extent receive protection in growth through internal expansion. The successful, established firms whose growth by acquisition is most likely to be questioned are also the firms best equipped in terms of resources for growth through building new facilities. It would seem almost inevitable, therefore, that strong enforcement under revised Section 7 would at some stage involve an increasing interest in Big Cases under Section 2 of the Sherman Act. In other words, bigness and giantism, and concentration of market and economic power, would come to the front in antitrust policy both with respect to growth by internal expansion and growth by acquisition.

---

[7] *Wall Street Journal*, June 16, 1965.

[8] As, for example, the *Brown Shoe* and the *Philadelphia Bank* cases already mentioned. *Brown Shoe Co.* v. *United States*, 370 U.S. 326 (1962); *United States* v. *Philadelphia National Bank*, 374 U.S. 326 (1963); *United States* v. *Aluminum Co. of America*, 377, U.S. 271 (1964); *United States* v. *First National Bank & Trust Co. of Lexington*, 376, U.S. 665; *United States* v. *Penn-Olin Chemical Co.*, 378 U.S. 158 (1964); *United States* v. *Continental Can Co.*, 378 U.S. 441 (1964).

Very likely, the issues and drift on this score will be clarified somewhat when further cases involving conglomerate acquisitions are adjudicated, for these, in a very direct sense, focus upon *Bigness, per se*, or economic concentration as opposed to market concentration. But the cases adjudicated or now moving forward to the Supreme Court most likely will touch only upon peripheral issues. The determination of public policy on this issue probably will be in the political arena and not through the application of economic and marketing analysis in antitrust cases. Hopefully, economics and marketing will not be disregarded entirely, however, in the political moves. The character of the testimony at recent hearings is an optimistic omen.[9]

In public policy it was widely believed (with some dissident views) that investment diversification and growth by conglomerate acquisitions were relatively acceptable in contrast with horizontal and vertical integration and acquisitions.[10] Horizontal expansion, especially by acquisitions, reduced competition on the same level. Vertical expansion, and especially acquisition, reduced competition presumably by removing or weakening a supplier or customer. But conglomerate diversification, broadly conceived, was held to increase competition by the entrance of established firms into new areas. In such moves, broad inter-industry forces of competition could be promoted and presumably competition increased. But in recent years, a view has been arising that broad nonfunctional diversification, especially by the acquisition of established firms, is one of the greatest threats to competition through the exercise of "conglomerate power,"[11] allegedly a new, insidious type of monopoly power.

As of now, it is impossible to reconcile these two views either in economic and managerial theory or in law and regulation. Again, we are forced to revert to the legal processes of case by case analysis and determination. Undoubtedly, conglomerate diversification at times strengthens the competitive compulsions of the market system, and sometimes such overlapping of large corporations may be the only feasible means of doing so. Undoubtedly, too, the reverse does, or could occur, especially when large, powerful firms enter areas occupied by small local and regional enterprises. Undoubtedly, too, in public policy, some bounds must be provided to protect the market system from large indigestible globs that could become almost global in competitive outreach.

Very likely, too, in many situations, the character of the use of what-

---

[9] *Economic Concentration*, Part 1, "Overall and Conglomerate Aspects," Subcommittee on Antitrust and Monopoly, 88th Congress, 2nd Session, 1964.

[10] A specialized exception was the Public Utility Holding Act of 1935 which imposed a limitation on the size of utility holding companies which bore no relationship to operating economies or integration.

[11] This viewpoint was clearly expressed by some of the proponents of revised Sec. 7 in Congressional Hearings. See the unpublished Ph.D. thesis of John C. Narver, *Conglomerate Mergers and Market Competition*, Graduate School of Business Administration, University of California, Berkeley, 1965.

ever "conglomerate power" may have been achieved, could be subject to control under either (1) Section 5 of the Federal Trade Commission Act governing unfair methods and practices or of (2) Sec. 1 of the Sherman Act governing the restraint of trade, without structural change. In this manner, the enhanced competitive impacts might be preserved but within the rules of the competitive game. Both persons and business enterprises can be expected to show restraint in the exercise of abilities and capacities. To make the mere possession of power to act the basis of action pushes regulation towards structural adjustments intended to enhance the impersonal compulsions of the market system. Whether this makes sense depends upon the actual and potential market structural and behavioral circumstances of each situation and cannot be answered in general terms.

Above all, it is a mistake to assume that the character and effectiveness of competition bear a simple, direct relationship to the number of competitors alone. Consequently, it could be a grievous error to take action based upon the mere presence of ability to act when (1) market structure adjustments would not in fact negate such power and (2) the beneficial aspects of enhanced competition could be preserved without abuse. . . .

Appraisal in Terms of the Required Capacities of an Acceptable Market System

We are in a position now to generalize concerning the extent to which the general market system in the United States is able to exercise the five types of capacities suggested as essential for the maintenance of an acceptable, viable market system.

1. *Response to and facilitation of buyer choices, especially of consumer buyers:* In the main, the conclusion here is favorable, although many, including some top professional economists, will disagree. There is a widespread view that consumer sovereignty is a wasting, perhaps already wasted asset—that consumer choices are determined largely by a conjoined group behaviorism and Madison Avenue.[12] No one, of course, is able to prove or disprove a generalization so sweeping and so subjective, and running so counter to the marketing experience of even the most powerful corporations. It would seem much more sensible for purposes of public policy in a democracy to accept the fact of consumer choice among genuine alternatives as given and then to continue to try to guarantee that the choices can be made from among genuine, honest, competitive alternates. The same conclusion would seem even more reasonable and easier to enforce at the other levels of buying choice. The lack of opportunity for choice among independent alternatives might well be a major criterion in the selection of antitrust cases. Such opportunity, for

[12] For a provocative statement see Mason, E. S., "The Apologetics of Managerialism," *Journal of Business*, University of Chicago, January 1958.

choice, if at all possible, should be available at all levels and for all offerings in the market system.

2. *Interaction to external environmental influences:* Our market system is not a mechanical closed system but is open-ended and is responding to innumerable external pressures and influences including governmental regulations and intervention. There is no guarantee, however, that the net results of the interventions are beneficial in terms of maintaining a viable effective market system adequate for a society with a private enterprise base. It would be an enormous contribution to make an objective considered estimate of the net effects and the general drift and tendencies.

3. *Internal interaction within the system:* The interactions within the market system are focused most sharply on product (output) markets instead of at the level of factor inputs. Increasingly, the prices of factor inputs are being removed from determination by the market system or placed under the shared rule of governmental regulations and the market. This observation applies for example to labor, energy, freight, some raw materials, some services, and some communication inputs which are outside the market bargain, more or less. The Robinson-Patman Act tends also to place restraints over the input price level. A consequence of the constraints at the input levels is to line up competitors at the same starting blocks or at handicapped, predetermined starting points. A consequence is to accentuate tendencies towards upstream vertical integration.

So far as the shifting of resources within the system from lesser advantaged to more profitable areas is concerned, these are through the continuing processes of innovative and of imitative competition. On the whole, the American marketing system displays enormous internal vitality in terms of the innovative, adaptive and imitative use of resources in "enterprise competition." When this does not occur, because of barriers to entry or agreement among competitors, then antitrust authorities should be interested and take the appropriate steps. The largest such area in terms of economic analysis, of course, is allegedly the short term or long term strength of market position engendered by the successful product differentiation and brand promotion as noted earlier.[13]

In this area, however, public policy must tread softly and deftly, because much of the high strategy and dynamism of American enterprise competition is found here, and must be so in the presence of a strong anticartel policy, let alone the magnitude of the potential gains of success in our rich national market amplified by multi-national opportunities. Furthermore, opportunity for differential gain along these lines must be held out to enterprises, in order to encourage and support the costs and risks of product innovation and development.

---

[13] The classic study is Bain, J. S., *Barriers to New Competition: Their Character and Consequences in Manufacturing Industries*, Cambridge, Harvard University Press, 1956.

4. *Ability to act as an allocating medium for resources not allocated by government outside the market system:* To some extent, the allocating responsibility was discussed in the preceding section in terms of the internal interactions of the system. It remains to be noted, however, that in all societies, governments take some direct responsibility for the allocation of much or all of the land, raw material and capital resources. In some underdeveloped countries the allocations of the market system are either not trusted or are considered too slow for the purposes of economic development, and, in communist and socialist societies, the primary means of control under the Central Plan is through the allocation of basic resources.

But even in the United States, a large portion of resource allocation is outside the market system, through public ownership and employment, the public services, defense and military programs, and tax collections and disbursements. It would be enormously helpful to have a solid estimate of the extent to which resource allocation occurs through the market mechanism in the United States, or is under a planned sharing of governmental regulation and the market.

In this connection there is a well publicized view that the market can or should have a decreasing role in a society of abundance, as in the United States. In other words, we should look forward to a broad expansion of the public services outside and in lieu of the market system.[14] This view reflects to some extent (1) the belief that consumer sovereignty through the market has wasted away and (2) a higher degree of confidence in voting through the ballot box than through cash registers.

5. *To regulate; i.e., to enforce the discipline of the "rule of competition":* In the United States, the "rule of competition" is relied upon chiefly in the final, manufactured product markets and in the distributive trades. Insofar as market discipline has been removed from factor-input markets, its remaining impact is chiefly towards the efficient use of resources in production and in marketing in final product markets and in the effective fulfillment of given buyer choices or in market innovation. Obviously, this is a large important and strategic responsibility for the market system, especially because it is the medium for serving and influencing the ultimate consumers. This is also the accepted area of active antitrust enforcement, although recent indications suggest that antitrust, under new interpretations of areas of primary jurisdiction, may tend to become more effective in some of the factor-input markets than has been assumed traditionally, unless restrained by new special legislation. It is in this area, too, that the chips as they fall, indicate the type of society or position on the spectrum between a full command society or a full market society. And finally, it is here and in the trend of the allocation of basic resources, including capital resources, that the broad economic, political drift of a society can best be observed. . . .

[14] Galbraith, J. K., *The Affluent Society* (Boston, 1958).

EDITORS' NOTE

Marketing managers are not expected to be experts in the field of antitrust law. However, they are expected to have some understanding of the legal environment in which the firm operates. A condensed and simplified description of the major federal antitrust restraints affecting marketing strategy is presented in the following table:

THE FEDERAL ANTITRUST LAWS AND THEIR PRINCIPAL EFFECTS UPON MARKETING STRATEGY

	Strategy Affected			
Act	*Pricing*	*Channel*	*Promotional*	*Product*
Sherman	Bans collusion with competitors	Bans some vertical agreements with dealers		Bans monopolization of a product or its distribution
Clayton	Bans some primary line price discrimination	Bans most tie-in sales and some exclusive dealing arrangements		
Federal Trade Commission	Bans deceptive pricing and some pricing systems	Bans all "unfair" channel strategy	Bans false advertising	
Robinson-Patman*	Bans some secondary line price discrimination	Regulates certain brokerage payments	Regulates certain promotional aids and allowances	
Celler-Kefauver*		Bans acquisition of some distributors		Bans acquisition of some products

* Strictly speaking, both of these bills are amendments to the Clayton Act.

SOURCE: Kenneth Elzinga, Assistant Professor of Economics, University of Virginia, in an unpublished paper, 1966.

Ethical considerations are a dynamic environmental force influencing marketing decisions. Marketing is a logical focal point for ethical evaluations of business. Cultural evolution is the dynamic determinant of ethical attitudes toward management methods and objectives. Marketing managers must integrate current ethical values and scientific marketing approaches. To be successful, a firm's view of the societal responsibilities of marketing must equate with those currently held by society.

6. ETHICS AND SCIENCE IN MARKETING*

Eugene J. Kelley†

The challenge, as I see it, is that we have to be as dynamic, imaginative, and research-minded in the ethical field as we have been in the scientific and materialistic fields. We must accept this new world as a new opportunity for being ethical. The case is far from hopeless.[1]

Research methodology and decisions in marketing are influenced by the interacting cultural approaches of the "manager," the "scientist," and the "humanist." These approaches are considered in this excerpt as they relate to ethics and science in marketing and to the social functions of marketing. The purpose of this excerpt is to raise some questions about the philosophical dimension of ethics as it relates to marketing. This is a relatively new area of marketing inquiry. The thoughts presented are

---

* Reprinted from *Science in Marketing,* (ed.) George Schwartz (New York: John Wiley & Sons, Inc., 1965) pp. 465–83. Implementation of the marketing management concept parallels the emerging concern about ethical aspects of marketing action. In a world of accelerating change, marketers must consider the extent to which ultimate values should be related to the practice of marketing. See, also, Eugene J. Kelley "Marketing and Moral Values in An Acquisitive Society," in Martin L. Bell (ed.), *Marketing: A Maturing Discipline* (Proceedings of the Winter Conference of the American Marketing Association, 1961), pp. 195–203.

† The Pennsylvania State University.

[1] James W. Culliton, "The Problem of Ethics in Business," in *Ethics in Business,* Robert Bartels (ed.), Bureau of Business Research, Columbus, Ohio, 1963, p. 9. A comprehensive forty-three page annotated bibliography on the general subject of ethics in business is included in this book.

designed to stimulate independent and intelligent thought about the ethical issues inherent in the practice of marketing.

In this excerpt, some marketing questions with ethical dimensions are identified, and the various factors involved in these questions are defined. The questions focus on the moral responsibilities of marketing decision makers. The social functions of marketing, including survival, profit-making, and social responsibility, are discussed, and the ethical stages of a discipline are indicated. Meta-marketing is presented as the vehicle by which marketing science and social responsibility can be integrated in meeting the challenges of the scientific revolution.

SOME MARKETING ETHICS QUESTIONS

Some marketing questions with ethical dimensions include the following:

1. Are marketing scientists and individual contributors to marketing morally responsible for the marketing decisions to which they contribute their talents?

This is not a new issue in business. For instance, in marketing the question of moral responsibility has arisen to confront advertising executives. Are executives in advertising agencies "morally responsible for the advertising they create," and "are media executives morally responsible for the advertising contents their media carry?"[2] A common position of advertising people in the face of such questions traditionally has been that the advertising agency is a technical service group with the job of creating and placing advertisements. Responsibility belongs with the client according to this view. Whether an agency is or is not morally responsible for client's claims or is or is not acting simply as a technician is a question being discussed in advertising today.

2. As an example, does the marketing scientist concerned with developing media allocation models have any responsibility for the messages carried in those media? Or is he only concerned with the techniques involved, not with the messages sent to sell products of which he might not personally approve—cigarettes, liquor, or anything else?

3. Is a marketing scientist concerned with the ethics of persuading people to do something which might not be in their long-term interest? What are the responsibilities, ethically, of the motivation researcher and the manager who uses his findings? The ultimate objective of much research in marketing is to influence or manipulate purchase behavior through probing into the consciousness of individual consumers. The question of the use to which the work of marketing scientists and individual contributors to marketing is put is a difficult one. Scientists in other fields have faced it. One conclusion of interest is that:

[2] *New York Times* (February 16, 1964).

It is inevitable that in the long run researchers as a group will have to be concerned with the applications of their work, in the same way that atomic scientists formed a federation so that as citizens they would have a voice in determining the utilization of what they had developed as technicians.[3]

4. Is the marketing scientist concerned with the ethical problems involved in programs of planned product obsolescence? Many product programs can be seen as efforts to make a product obsolete before it is completely worn out. Many projects in which marketing science studies are undertaken are done with the direct objective of rendering present products obsolete even though a measure of utility remains.

5. Is the marketing scientist concerned with any aspect of marketing other than the efficient movement of goods on a profitable basis? Does a marketing scientist have responsibility for developing standards for measuring contributions other than efficiency—perhaps by contributing to the development of "ethical science"?

6. There is some evidence that profits are taking on a subsidiary role in many business problems. Questions of economic and social stability, public relations, and a fear of government intervention have proved strong influences on executive decisions in the past. These factors have modified the traditional view of the profit maximization objective to the extent that profit maximization rules provide limited guidance for business executives. Are there ethical implications of significance to marketing science in the development of the "corporate conscience" and the social responsibility view of business? There is a danger of becoming concerned for the sake of ethics alone. It has been suggested that an attitude of this kind can prove harmful and even undermine that enterprise system. Levitt has said, "In the end business has two responsibilities—to obey the canons of everyday face-to-face civility, (honesty, good faith and so on), and to seek material gain and to seize profit. Anything beyond this gets very complicated."[4]

Such questions can be answered on two levels. One is the level of facts. This is the area in which scientists deal or at least prefer to deal. Another is the ethical level. This level requires that standards for approval or disapproval be used.

Disagreements about the place of ethical issues in business sometimes reflect the fact that the conception and definition of ethics is often a highly personal matter. A set of definitions is offered here in the hope that it might facilitate discussion and further exploration of the questions raised in this chapter.

---

[3] Robert Ferber, Donald F. Blankertz, and Sidney Hollander, Jr., *Marketing Research,* Ronald Press, New York, 1964, p. 602.

[4] Theodore Levitt, "Dangers of Social Responsibility," *Harvard Business Review,* Vol. XXXVI (September 1958), pp. 41–60.

DEFINITIONS

Marketing

Marketing can be perceived as a field of management practice, as a social discipline, or as a developing science. As a field of business practice, marketing consists of the activities involved in the generation of markets and customers and in the development and distribution of customer-satisfying goods and services. As a socio-management activity, marketing includes all the tasks involved in the development and delivery of a flow of goods and services from production to consumption. As a social discipline, marketing is the study of the economic and social instrumentality through which a standard of living is delivered to consumers.

Marketing Science

Marketing science is the application of scientific method to marketing problems. One aspect of this science is the use of quantitative approaches to problem solving and decision making. The computer is one important tool of management science; more important is the scientific approach, which involves the use of reliable research methods to unearth valid marketing knowledge and the use of such knowledge in order to better attain marketing objectives. The task of the marketing scientist is to provide decision makers who have the responsibility of committing corporate resources with the scientific and technical input required to reduce or eliminate the areas of uncertainty in marketing problem solving.

Ethics

Ethics as used in this chapter refers to the philosophy of moral values or moral norms, that is, normative ethics. As used here, ethics does not belong to empirical science, but to a division of philosophy—the study and philosophy of human conduct with emphasis on the determination of right and wrong. By definition, it is concerned with good and evil, what is right and what is wrong, that should be, rather than what exists. As White stated, "The purpose of philosophical, or normative, ethics is to state norms for human action or judgments about moral values."[5]

Moral Values

Moral values refer to the degree of conformity to right conduct. This involves questions of the sense of good, the true and right. History is

---

[5] Morton White, *The Age of Analysis,* The New American Library, New York, 1955, p. 217.

replete with examples of men being actuated by a sense of good, true and right procedures to accomplish dubious or even satanic ends. Ethics refers to the rules of human behavior considered right and proper by a society at a specified time. Moral becomes a descriptive adjective denoting a study of standard ethical behavior.

Marketing Ethics

Marketing ethics is the area of marketing study and thought concerned with defining norms for judgments about the moral consequences of marketing actions. In practice, marketing ethics is concerned with standards of adequate behavior in terms of marketing policies and practices within legal and social constraints at a point in time. The concern of the theorist is with what is acceptable behavior in terms of right and wrong in a culture at a point in time so that decision making can be more successful.

Ethics are not linked to any narrow part of life. It can be argued that there are no "marketing ethics," that there may or may not be any "business ethics," and ethics are only a matter for individuals concerned with marketing or any other activity. Thus it is held there are no marketing ethics, medical ethics, or legal ethics, and ethics are considered as being concerned with all rational behavior. Accordingly, criticisms of marketing activity are really criticisms of the level of ethics of a business system or of a society. The criticism of marketing comes about, in this view, primarily because marketing is by nature more visible and conspicuous than other areas of business practice. The point of view of this chapter is that for analytical purposes it is at times useful to think of a level of ethics in business and marketing as it exists at a point in decision time and place.

Meta-Marketing

Meta-marketing (beyond marketing) as in metaphysics, metapsychology, or in other disciplines, is used to designate a new, although related, discipline which deals critically with marketing as a discipline. All concerned with marketing can contribute to what may be this promising direction. Marketing is a discipline offering multiple opportunities for speculations on the interrelationships of mental and physical processes to supplement the facts and empirical regularities of marketing science. Kane, in discussing the need for new approaches to planning methodology in national security planning, suggested the term "meta-planning" to seek to bring in the whole of experience and of the human personality to bear on planning.[6] The concern of meta-marketing is similar—to bring the

[6] Francis X. Kane, "Security Is Too Important to be Left to Computers," *Fortune*, Vol. LXIX, No. 4 (April 1964), p. 147.

whole of scientific, social, ethical, and managerial experience to bear on marketing.

The fact that disagreement exists about these terms reflects the fact that marketing is a field of study and a business activity with significant economic, social, and administrative dimensions. It is not surprising that an economist, mathematician, sociologist, or a manager would tend to define terms differently and that different approaches to definitions, and to research, produce different results. As Bartels said:

> . . . research findings are dependent not only upon the hypotheses, data, methodology, etc. which comprise scientific research practice, but also upon subjective factors such as the researcher's area and intensity of interest, economic opportunism, social affiliations, personality, background, concepts and the like.[7]

An example is that some scientists are reluctant to raise ethical questions which involve moral judgments because such considerations do not advance the body of the science with which they are concerned. However, the interdisciplinary approach to marketing is proving to be of sufficient value so that some students are willing to explore the possible contributions of hybrid disciplines such as marketing ethics. Marketing science itself is essentially a "multisexual" discipline, to use a term from Boulding,[8] and a natural area of convergence for the interdisciplinary approach to business administration.

One indication that marketing is a natural focal point of ethical problems and considerations in business is that much government regulation is designed to govern marketing activities. Presumably, some regulation developed because of the feeling that businessmen were failing to regulate themselves according to the proper ethical standards. There is a continuing dialogue between business and government on the question of regulation of business. The legal conflicts can be settled by legislation and the courts. The conflict discussed here between ethical concepts and marketing practice is philosophical. It exists because philosophers concerned with ethical issues are concerned with an ideal in which absolute ethical values and concepts are superimposed on the culture according to the highest moral values. But the standards of ethical behavior in business which influence the areas in which management scientists operate are taken from the prevailing culture of the time. The standards may be far from the philosophic ideal. So, by definition, ethics is a subject which is not related

---

[7] Robert Bartels, "A Methodological Framework for Comparative Marketing Study," in *Toward Scientific Marketing*, Stephen A. Greyser (ed.), Proceedings of the 1963 Winter Conference of the American Marketing Association, Chicago, 1964, p. 383.

[8] Kenneth E. Boulding, "General Systems Theory—The Skeleton of Science," *Management Science* (April 1956). See also the discussion in William Lazer and Eugene J. Kelley, *Interdisciplinary Contributions to Marketing Management*, Bureau of Business Research, E. Lansing, Michigan, 1959, pp. 1–31.

primarily to business practices but rather to the promise and potential of a higher climate. Discussions of marketing issues with ethical dimensions can help to develop an appreciation of the relations between existing business practices and ethical concepts and standards.

While marketing scientists can abstract ethical and moral decisions from many problems, and students of marketing ethics can choose not to communicate with management scientists, management must face the task of integration. Management decision making inevitably involves the balancing of ethical and moral issues with scientific approaches. A manager rarely has to contend with a problem which is exclusively a marketing science or a marketing ethics problem any more than he has to contend with problems which are exclusively economic in nature. He deals routinely with complex, multidisciplinary problems.

One academic viewpoint is that problems of ethics and morality in business need not be discussed in any formal way in the business schools. (This attitude may be one reason why there are relatively few business ethics courses.) Those holding this view, who think ethical questions should be discussed at all, feel that each teacher should handle ethical problems of business in his own course, just as each businessman should handle such problems in his own firm. Some marketing practitioners have also expressed doubt that fields called "Marketing Science" or "Marketing Theory" can be identified. Others accept the existence of these fields but see them as unrelated. Probably most readers of this chapter are willing to grant the existence of an area called marketing science. Perhaps not so many would be as tolerant of marketing ethics.

Managers are not usually concerned with whether they are "marketing scientists" or "ethical scientists." Their position is they are practicing executives attempting to manage the efforts of an organization to accomplish corporate objectives. Even though staff advice inside the business tends to come from men committed to one or another basic position, the manager does not normally expect the marketing scientist to integrate ethical considerations in the body of his science. Managers have long accepted the notion of division of labor; managers are prepared to integrate where their specialized staff and professional personnel are unwilling or unable to integrate. However, managers are usually pleased to find technicians who have the ability to do relational thinking. This ability is one measure of a person's ability to change roles from marketing scientist or social marketer to marketing management.

It may be that the survival of the enterprise system depends on the manager's ability to integrate the contributions of the scientist and of the ethical scientist or social philosopher. In a university the marketing teacher might well have to consider the extent to which he should attempt the integration of the sometimes polarized forces of quantifiable goals and moral values.

The integrating task of management is no easier than the task of the social historian, political scientist, or economist who attempts to bridge cultures. One reason the integration problem for managers is complex, is that management theory and practice are in a transitional stage, and the manager is confronted with several diverse approaches to the problem of integrating ethics and science. . . .

SOCIAL FUNCTIONS OF MARKETING

Ethical issues are necessarily involved in any discussion of the social functions of marketing. Business, and specifically marketing, includes many social institutions which are important influences on the value of society. Because marketing is so significant to society, the question of social goals and social responsibility inevitably must be faced. If business does not establish its own social goals and design programs to achieve those social goals, it is a certainty that society will fill the void. There inevitably are social functions of business in contemporary society. Eells and Walton have suggested four social functions.[9] These are functions which concern marketing management and which should be considered by marketing scientists. Each function has marketing overtones; the functions can be perceived as the social functions of marketing.

Survival

This may be the basic and the ultimate goal of a business and the prime measure of marketing activity. Profits are both a prerequisite for survival and a test of survivability; service is the road to customer satisfactions and, therefore, to survival in a competitive economic climate. Social responsibility is probably a necessary condition of survival over the long run. Many marketing strategies can be designed to achieve the survival goal. Questions about the strategies of growth, institutional survival, subsidies, and institutional and enterprise abandonment, are in part ethical questions.

Profit Making

A business is the only human organization whose existence depends on profit. As Eells and Walton point out, governments can tax, churches can call on members for support, and the family can survive without profits. But a business requires profits to justify its existence. Profit making is a basic goal of business and the profit concept underlies marketing. Profit goals are achieved in the marketplace, and the basic task of the marketing manager is to serve consumer needs profitably in a way which will be consistent with long-range survival goals.

---

[9] Richard Eells and Clarence Walton, *Conceptual Foundations of Business*, Richard D. Irwin, Inc., Homewood, Ill., 1961, pp. 432–33.

There are many ethical aspects to questions about business goals, such as the following:

Growth of the firm, of a division, a product line or a product.
Short-term profit maximization.
Profit maximization over the long run.
Service to the country, society, and the common good.
Service to customers.
Enlargement of size of market.
Maintenance or increase in share of market.
Establishment of an image for the firm, division or product.
Diversification of corporate activity.
Achievement of industry leadership.
Development of reputation and stature of management.
Employee welfare and satisfactions.
Securing a balance between government and domestic business.
Securing a balance between domestic and foreign business.
Making the firm a satisfying one for employees and managers.
Maintaining employment at certain levels in particular plants.
Minimizing risk of government antitrust enforcement activities.

The length of the list may suggest that goal setting is not a simple matter or that it can be undertaken on purely factual terms.

Service

Business has service functions to perform in addition to profit making. Timothy E. Shea, Vice President in Charge of Engineering of Western Electric Company, has said, "Business is a vehicle through which man serves society." Such a view of service and profits requires a balancing of functions by managers. Customer service is one of the keys to survival and profit. The serving of customer needs profitably is the basic concern of marketing executives. Service to customers and to society concepts rests on an ethical view of business practice.

Social Responsibility

Another social function of business is the obligation of a firm to meet its social responsibilities to its employees, the community, and the public, as well as to its owners and customers. Social responsibilities are those of corporate good citizenship in a society. Sometimes social and economic goals and the functions required to perform them may be in conflict. More often, in the long run, enlightened self-interest and the corporate sense of social responsibility coincide. When they do not, managers acting as both businessmen and citizens attempt to reconcile conflicts knowing that failure to do so may mean additional government regulation.

Business itself is a social instrumentality of society designed to facilitate the achievement of given ends. Marketing, or any business function, is a corporate activity designed to achieve given objectives. The genius of American business is that through the marketing system consumers are offered an infinite variety of goods and services from which they can choose those which will best enable free individuals to approach fulfilling their own view of the good life. Critics of marketing frequently neglect the point that the pursuit of the good life may be largely an individual matter and that restrictions on selling effort almost always result in restrictions on the buyers' freedom to choose and act.

A business manager is, of course, concerned with the social view of business problems just as he is concerned with the economic environment in which the firm operates. But the operating manager is primarily concerned with other problems, such as managing marketing activity in order to achieve particular corporate goals in a market society. As such, he tends to see social and economic areas not as ends in themselves but as environmental restraints on corporate activity or as areas of marketing opportunity. However, top management does have as one of its major challenges the job of answering the question whether a free market economy can provide social welfare with individual freedom as it meets the material needs of free consumers. This is a difficult and complex question; the degree of success of business executives in answering it will, to a large extent, determine the future of the free enterprise system.

Business executives are aware that strategies to fulfill these social functions have varying levels of ethical acceptability. It is interesting to consider the relationship between the acceptability level and profit returns. Simon has suggested that ethical considerations can be introduced into computer programmed business games and that the higher the acceptability level, the less the profit return to the alternative.[10] There does not seem to be any computer business game which at present has built into it a set of strategies, opportunities, and tactics that would have varying degrees of moral acceptability as judged by our business society. It is possible to build into a game strategies or varying degrees of moral acceptability which would have payoffs attached corresponding to the payoffs they might produce in the real world. Simon suggests such acts as "gouging customers in an emergency, moving out of a small town precipitately, cutting off established dealers, and using unfair sources of information." Players in such a game could be told that they would be judged as both profit makers and as ethical businessmen. As Simon put it, they would not necessarily be told what calculus, if any, is used to make ethics

---

[10] J. L. Simon, "How Do Beliefs Affect Business Performance?" (Unpublished manuscript, Urbana, Illinois, 1963, p. 36.) For a report on an empirical study of business ethics see Raymond C. Baumhart, "How Ethical Are Businessmen?" *Harvard Business Review,* Vol. XXXIX (July–August 1961), p. 6.

and profits commensurable. The real world does not offer any such calculus as an accurate guide to ethical costs. Possibly players will be told that not only their scores but their particular ethical acts would be publicized to the other players in the game. An interesting line of experimentation is opened up by such suggestions.

On a pragmatic basis it is possible to relate the level of ethical expectations of a society to the negative control of government regulation of business. In a complex industrial society it is government which sets the legal boundaries and enforces the rules of business conduct. Their rules do much to mold the environment of business and the climate in which marketing decisions are made. In marketing terms it can be said that the consumer is the controller of a firm's destiny. But on a broader scale, it is the government, representing public consensus, which exercises the ultimate control over business. In some societies the government is more important than the market as the dominating mechanism of society. A prime function of decision makers then becomes the management of policies and conditions which will minimize public demands for regulation of business. But the ultimate case for ethical behavior does not rest on these grounds, although such might be an acceptable form of corporate rationalization of efforts to better ethical levels. Efforts to still or neutralize the voices of protest are not the reasons. Perhaps it is that the business of business is to serve society—and that this is difficult, if not impossible, unless the ethical norms of society are understood and fulfilled, and over the long run, perhaps exceeded.

INTEGRATING ETHICS AND SCIENCE IN MARKETING

The anticipation of tomorrow is one of the major concerns of managers, and a function of marketing scientists is to help marketing managers anticipate the future. Thus marketing scientists are concerned with the subject of changing moral values of society. All concerned with advancing science in marketing must understand the nature of the rising standards of ethical expectations of business on the part of the public. To ignore these would be as unwise as to ignore changing educational, income or other levels of consumer expectations or behavior. The integration of science and ethics can today be questioned on the grounds that it means a mix of rational scientific information (facts) with moral judgments. However, the trends of history seem to indicate the promise of a greater degree of integration between these two cultural approaches to the problems of meeting man's material needs. The hope is not inconsistent with scientific method.

One step toward science-ethics-management integration is to be aware of the problem of relating moral and ethical considerations to marketing practice. Another step is to ponder, study, and research the area of ethical and marketing science relationships. Perhaps what is called for is experimentation with new approaches which will enable us to overcome existing barriers to communication and understanding between cultural representatives. This is a hoped-for outcome of the meta-marketing approach as it might fuse marketing science and theory, management policy, and social philosophy to meet the challenges of the scientific revolution.

ILLUSTRATION IV

Marketing Action System—Marketing Management Functions

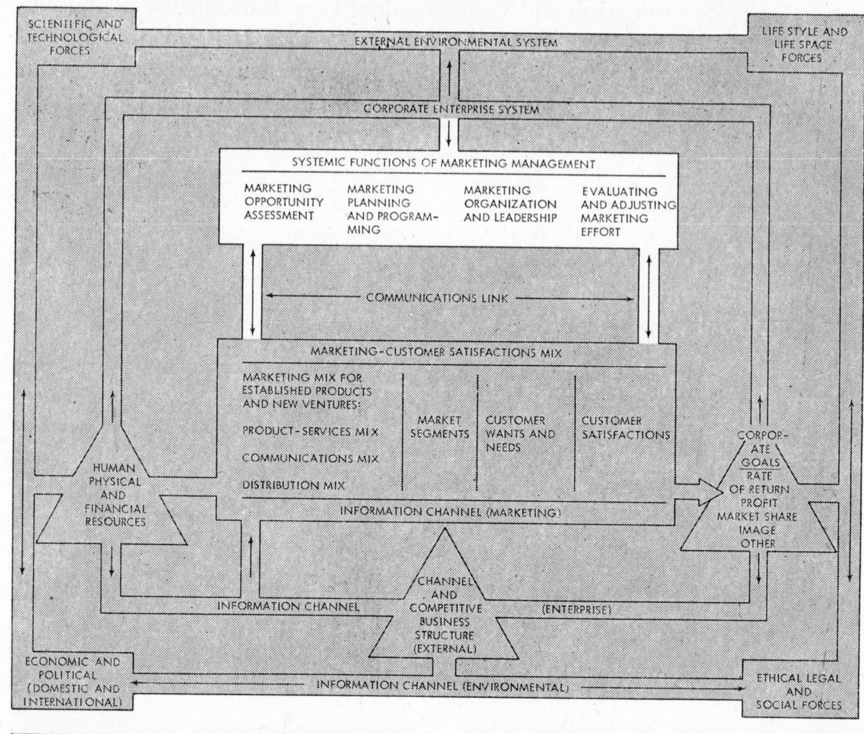

SYSTEMIC FUNCTIONS OF MARKETING

MARKETING OPPORTUNITY ASSESSMENT

A. Corporate goals, resources and capabilities evaluation.
B. Customer (actual-potential) delimitation.
C. Innovistic orientation to long-term planning and growth.
D. Scientific sales forecasting.
E. Identification and selection of profitable marketing opportunities.

MARKETING PLANNING AND PROGRAMMING

A. Analysis of research-based information.
B. Designation of financial, operational, and time priorities.
C. Provision of requirements and characteristics of long-range planning; identification of major and specific new-knowledge content.
D. Responsibility-authority assignments for planning.
E. Development and review of marketing plans.
F. Program development and implementation.

MARKETING ORGANIZATION AND LEADERSHIP

Desirable conditions and characteristics:

A. Top management market-oriented philosophy.
B. Total enterprise systems orientation.
C. Coordinated-integrated communications patterns.
D. Definitively stated scopes of responsibility and authority.
E. Maximization of leadership abilities and human relations skills.
F. Marketing-oriented staffing policies and practices.

EVALUATING AND ADJUSTING MARKETING EFFORT

The Marketing Audit:

A. Distinguishing characteristic--re-examination and evaluation of objectives, policies and practices.
B. Purpose--search for opportunities and malfunctions.
C. Timing--planned continual program reappraisals
D. Problems - 1. Defining standards and criteria; 2. Funding; 3. Selecting auditors; 4. Scheduling; 5. Minimizing impact on personnel.

B. Managing Marketing Effort

Competitive pressures compel a firm to become a market-oriented mechanism. Three fundamental concepts are offered as a foundation for a marketing viewpoint. First, all thinking about the firm should begin with the market—actual and potential. Second, the future of a firm is more important than the present, for it is the future that presents the opportunity for innovation. Third, commitment to adaptive change is the key to profit optimization. A comparison of marketing and production viewpoints is presented.

7. HEAR THE MESSAGE OF THE MARKET PLACE*

Melvin Anshen†

For the past several years, the "marketing point of view" has probably been the most popular recurring topic at professional, trade association and company meetings. As a result, many companies and their managers have accepted a superficial commitment to market-minded thinking. They often lack, however, a clear understanding of what is involved for their organizations. In time, they are likely to become discouraged with results,

---

† Columbia University.

and they may even abandon what could be the most profitable administrative change their firms could introduce.

It is important, therefore, to ask what is meant by the term "marketing viewpoint." What is its proper role in management planning and action? How can it be introduced and put to work effectively? What benefits should be anticipated?

The place to start answering these questions is not the office of the marketing vice president. Rather, it is the office of the president, the man responsible for formulating and executing the general management function in his business.

The general management function is the brain of a business—the guiding control. It determines principal goals and organizes the resources to achieve them. It designs the policies that define a firm's character and the strategies and tactics that follow. Inevitably, therefore, the way a general manager views his business must have a strong influence on how that business is run and how it performs.

The significance of this point has not been clearly grasped in many proposals to give the marketing function greater attention. To say that marketing needs more emphasis is superficial. What managers really need is a new way of looking at their organization, an ability to see in the familiar business a wholly different character than they formerly observed and perhaps took for granted.

This is the kind of fresh viewpoint that in the 1920's saw the opportunity to launch the Sears, Roebuck and the Montgomery Ward mail-order firms into general merchandise retailing on a national scale. It is the viewpoint that in the 1930's grasped the potential of self-service grocery stores and proceeded to revolutionize the retailing of food. The same innovative outlook is now beginning to use the grocery supermarket for distributing a variety of non-food items. Another example is offered by the successful attack of the discount houses in the 1950's on the traditional high markup, full-service retailing of household appliances.

This is the kind of management imagination that sees in the computer not simply a high-powered clerical machine but an information-processing tool that can change techniques of decision-making and help to displace management art and hunch with a rational, quantitative approach to the solution of complex problems.

We can best see the significance of this revolution in management thinking if we contrast two basic ways of looking at a business.

The first—which dominated management thinking through the initial phase of the industrial revolution—sees the firm primarily as a producing organism.

Management attention is focused on engineering and manufacturing problems. The drive for efficiency identifies production as the place to reduce costs. It presses to simplify product design, substitute cheaper materials, mechanize work operations, replace batch with continuous-flow processes. Most recently, the thrust is to automate manufacturing activities. In this setting, efforts to innovate are directed principally toward improving existing products and processes. In short, management sees a direct relation between cost cutting and profits, and acts accordingly.

Marketing is not, of course, ignored in this management view. But the sales function is treated largely as an effort to find customers for the output of the plant. Marketing costs are regarded as a necessary evil—as expenses rather than investment. They are dealt with as if they were passive influences in the total array of business activities. One common result of this attitude is that marketing budgets tend to be established in relation to revenue, usually as a predetermined percentage of present or forecast sales.

A contrasting way of looking at a business sees the firm primarily as a marketing organism.

QUESTIONS TO ANSWER

Here, management's view looks outward toward the customer. The important questions to be answered before making policy or investment decisions are: Who are the present and potential customers? Where do they live and buy? What are their purchase habits and preferences, and why? What needs are served by the company's products and services? What important needs are not adequately served? What is the state of competition? The market share? The trends? The prospects? What sales potentials are suggested by evolving economic and social developments? Out of the answers to these questions come the data for investment, research, engineering and production decisions, as well as the design of marketing programs.

Production and engineering are not ignored in this management view. But it treats the manufacturing function and everything related to it as resources to be used in designing and delivering the most profitable responses to the challenges and opportunities of the market. Expenditures for marketing activities are seen as investments. They are determined flexibly in relation to profit potentials, rather than rigidly as ratios of costs to sales.

The history of the introduction of scientific management techniques clearly reveals the dominance of the production-centered view in management thinking throughout the first half of this century. What we call scientific management was designed for the control of manufacturing. Time and motion study, cost analysis, budgeting, mathematical rules for decision-making, in fact every advance from art to science in administration occurred initially in production. Scientific management in marketing has lagged by at least one generation. It is only since about 1950 that any lively interest has appeared in applying the new management techniques to marketing.

A PERVASIVE INFLUENCE

The marketing-centered view of a business influences every aspect of management.

Consider, for example, the policies that govern decisions about variety in a product line. In contrast to the simplicity urged by the production view, the marketing view recommends diversity to meet the full range of customers' wants and needs. The production manager's concept of an ideal world is one in which a single product—one design, one size, one color—moves uninterruptedly down the manufacturing line. This minimizes all product costs: tooling, set-up, instruction and supervision of workers, scheduling of work flow, ordering of raw materials, investment in inventories. The marketing manager's contrasting concept is one in which no customer ever has to be told he cannot have what he wants.

The historical dominance of the production view has been assisted by solid evidence (in accounting records) of costs attributable to product variety. Marketing has been weakened by the inability to trace an identifiable cost to an order unfilled or a shipment delayed because of a narrow product line or a thin inventory.

The production view presses for retaining old products for which tooling, materials and knowledge are established. The marketing view presses for discarding old products in favor of improved models, or designing new products to serve customers' needs more precisely, or gaining an advance on competitors.

The production view, in short, is cost-oriented. The marketing view is revenue-oriented.

The production view cherishes stability. The marketing view welcomes and encourages change and innovation.

The production view approaches pricing decisions from the expense side. The marketing view approaches them from the revenue side.

The production view asks: "How much will it cost to make this?" The marketing view asks: "How much will we make if we sell this?"

The production view sees the future through the eyes of the present. The marketing view sees the present through the eyes of the future.

At the general management level the two views must, of course, be brought into balance and tested against the profit criterion. A total surrender to the marketing view could lead to a galloping case of profitless growth. Nevertheless, the dynamic competitive pressures of our economy increasingly compel an approach to the profit balance by way of the marketing viewpoint. This amounts to a prescription to look at a business first as a market-oriented mechanism. Production considerations can be surveyed later on the way to a summary assessment of investment, cost, risk and profit.

This changed viewpoint can be brought about even in a long-established industry, like railroading. The Southern Pacific, for example, has long been acclaimed for defining its business mission as the provision of transportation, not only railroad services. Another road, the Southern, has recently been applauded by observers for its creative, revenue-and-profit-conscious attack on the complex problems of freight rates.

A comparable change is being accomplished in some equipment manufacturing companies that have broadened their operations from selling individual machines to designing and marketing integrated materials handling and processing *systems*, under automated control.

When the marketing view takes precedence in top management thinking, the business is often seen in a new way. One of the most dramatic examples of this fresh view is the recognition that research and development can be applied in marketing as usefully and as profitably as in production. A retail chain may use one unit as an experimental laboratory for studying layout, traffic flow, merchandise display or prices. A manufacturing company with national distribution may use one territory as a research area in which experiments are conducted on marketing methods, sales promotion techniques or customer services. New types of advertising, new copy slants or a new package are tested on "guinea pig" audiences before major investment commitments are made.

In this way, the information required for a profitable approach to servicing dynamic consumer demand can become the first input to management thinking about every aspect of the business. Out of such studies come guidelines for engineering and product research. Out of these studies, too, come ideas for innovation in distribution techniques. Products may be profitably sold in retail stores or through industrial middlemen previously not in the marketing stream. Novel packaging ideas, such as containers with secondary household uses, may be evolved. New services or financing arrangements may be developed. Research on competitive practices and consumer demand may throw light on pricing decisions and encourage managers to break the shackles of cost-plus pricing.

MORE INNOVATION

The primacy of a marketing viewpoint is likely to be felt in other areas, as well. It may lead to greater variety in product line and more frequent innovation. It encourages planning and locating inventories to meet customer requirements rather than production convenience. It favors scheduling manufacturing to serve customers' needs. It induces budgeting around a profit rather than a cost criterion.

Above all, leadership from the marketing viewpoint sees the future as a source of profitable opportunities ready for exploitation by imaginative management. In contrast, a dominant production view is likely to see the future as largely a source of risk. It fears the changing circumstances that threaten investment in manufacturing facilities which may be obsolete before their useful life has been exhausted.

How can the marketing viewpoint be brought into a position of dominance in general management thinking?

There is no single, simple answer to this question. Installing an experienced marketing manager as chief executive officer will not be effective if his principal associates in research, production and finance do not change the way they look at the business. Redesigning the organization chart to bring more marketing managers into the policy-making arena may encourage divisive factionalism and delay in planning and executing programs.

What is required is no less than a comprehensive turn-around of the thinking, of the total mental set of *all* top-level managers. Such a transformation will do more than affect the shaping of policy at the organization's peak. It will also help to thrust the new ideas down through the layers of the line organization.

The head of one large corporation attacked the problem by hiring an outside consultant to study the company's weak market position in one part of its diversified product line and recommend a new approach. He then used the consultant's radical marketing proposals as a target for interdepartmental study by working groups at several levels, from vice presidents down to middle managers in the line organization, with an assignment to examine every implication of the recommended program for engineering, production and finance. The outcome was an amended program to which all functions were committed. The new marketing approach was then put into operation. Its successful performance in revenues, profits and strengthened competitive position led to queries about the possibility of studying other parts of the product line in the same way. In the president's view, the evolving experience, building step by step, is demonstrably encouraging an active interest in marketing potentials and requirements throughout his management group.

Another company is trying a different route toward the same objective. Outstanding divisional managers in every part of the business are being assigned planned tours of duty in the marketing department. Here they work not as observers but as responsible line executives. Early results make the president confident that the value of a marketing viewpoint is being properly appreciated in all parts of the management team.

Whatever the approach, the job must be viewed as a comprehensive educational effort. What we know about the educational process tells us that it is slow, that it builds strength through reinforcement of theory in practice, that it needs both precept and example. No simple policy pronouncement of the "we have entered a new era" variety can do more than delude the gullible and inflame the naïve within a management group.

First, top management must understand the necessity for reorienting its own thinking.

Second, it has to put that understanding to work in tackling its own jobs.

Third, it has to teach managers at lower levels the need for and the meaning of the new approach to the administration of the business.

Fourth, it has to reinforce its teaching with practice.

Finally, it has to supervise and control management performance to assure consistency and continuity in making progress toward the new goals.

THREE SIMPLE CONCEPTS

Three simple concepts are the key to building the requisite fundamental understanding:

One is the proposition that all thinking about a business should begin with study of the market—actual and potential.

The second is the proposition that the future of a business is more important than the present because only the future is open for creative design.

The third is the proposition that a commitment to adaptive change is the most profitable way to manage a firm in our dynamic society.

Whatever the difficulties may be in moving toward this new management outlook, there is one powerful reason for attacking them vigorously: This is the fact that precisely because marketing has lagged as a target for rational management study, it is the area where efficiency and productivity are low. It is therefore the area where the returns for imaginative investment are likely to be highest.

This is not counsel to abandon the hard test of profitable investment. This is not a recommendation to expand marketing budgets blindly or to pursue for its own sake a program of headlong innovation. Rather, this is a proposal to businessmen to manage in such a way that they fully exploit the great opportunities for revenue and growth that face business.

If business management is to become more scientific, the firm's objectives must first be clearly stated. This is essential, since formulating marketing strategy involves the definition of the firm's broad objectives and the translation of these into marketing objectives. After this has been done, marketing targets must be set, and the appropriate marketing mix to achieve these targets must be selected.

8. THE FORMULATION OF A MARKET STRATEGY*

Alfred R. Oxenfeldt†

I. INTRODUCTION

Business management has been called many things: it commonly is described as an art; some describe it as a guessing game. Perhaps the height of wisdom on this subject is contained in the phrase, "business is business," for business is not like anything else. Clearly, success as a business executive requires what some people describe as "artistry" and intuition—though these probably are far less vital than just plain luck. In addition, as this paper endeavors to prove, successful business management demands careful and maximum application of the scientific method.

The scientific method obviously needs no defense; only an eccentric will maintain that guesses are more valid bases for decision than careful observation and experimentation. However, the phases of business management that *are* amenable to scientific methods are far from obvious.

II. IS THERE A SCIENCE OF BUSINESS MANAGEMENT?

Little is to be gained by pointing a finger at businessmen for having left managerial decision-making in a relatively primitive state until recently while production men applied the fruits of science to achieve miracles in the factory. The very large number of business failures and high turnover

---

* This article first appeared in the revised edition of this book.

† Columbia University.

among business executives have been punishment enough. However, the contrast between the methods by which managerial and production decisions are made deserves emphasis, for there exists an influential body of executives—and some academicians—who find the main ingredient of business success to be "good judgment and practice of the managerial art." These phrases are question-begging unless one is able to define what is meant by good judgment and the managerial art. Moreover, such a view deprecates the importance of fact-gathering, rigorous reasoning, hypothesis-testing—and all elements of the scientific method that can be applied to many of the problems faced by businessmen.

It may appear pretentious to link business management with the scientific method. When one speaks of "scientific management" or "scientific marketing" he simply means that business decisions should have the maximum benefit of factual support, close rigorous reasoning, and empirical test; also, that every conclusion reached should be open to challenge and be capable of rational defense. There is no room in this concept for bowing to authority, deference to the intuitions or "experience" of older men or persons associated with the business for a longer time; it requires that decisions be made on the basis of facts and logical argument rather than by appeal to authority.

No one familiar with business dreams that it will become an "exact science" which rests upon a body of proved principles analogous to what has been produced by the chemist and physicist. Everyone knows that duplicatable experiments cannot be the main technique employed for arriving at generalizations applicable to business. The methods available to business executives for solving concrete problems are, at best, relatively crude, unreliable and unproved by the standards of most physical sciences. However, they are vastly more reliable than reliance on hunch, intuitions, feel and guess, or appeal to authority.

The scientific method, or the most scientific techniques applicable to business—however one prefers to express it—is not to be confused with the use of the conference or committee method of decision-making. All too often, these methods are applied in a manner that brings several uninformed people together to pool their thoughts and hammer out a common agreement. A "bull session," no matter by what elegant title it may be dignified, will not produce valuable results unless at least some participants are very well informed. Once maximum use is made of observation and experimentation, discussion will generally prove very valuable; however, it certainly cannot substitute for the collection and analysis of facts.

Practitioners in most fields—especially those who practice for a fee—understandably are anxious to persuade others that their fields of specialization are sciences. Only recently, however, have some persons specializing in business fields claimed to be "applied" scientists. To understand what they claim, one must also know what they disavow. Almost all admit their inability to remotely approach the accuracy, predictability and even objectivity of most physical sciences. But they maintain that there do exist data, methods of data collection, experimental and testing procedures, and methods of analyzing and testing findings whose application to business would greatly increase the proportion of correct managerial decisions. Rather than *great* accuracy in absolute terms, these people claim to be relatively accurate in a field where attempts at systematic and rigorous answers to problems remain exceptional.

III. HOW CAN BUSINESS MANAGEMENT BE MADE MORE SCIENTIFIC?

To make business management into an applied science, executives must first clarify their firm's objectives. Although the selection of *ultimate* business objectives is necessarily unscientific, for they express the fundamental values of individuals who establish broad policy, operating objectives stated fully, clearly, and concretely are indispensable if one is to make managerial decision-making amenable to the scientific method. Once objectives are known, the *selection of means* becomes the task of appraising, by the best means available, the relative effectiveness of alternatives.

A. *Statement of a Firm's Broad Objectives.* Business objectives can be stated on a variety of levels; one must begin with the ultimate—the broadest and most general—and work back to the more narrow and specific ends that they imply. The two most widely expressed ultimate objectives of corporate managements these days are: first, to make maximum profits for the firm over the life of the enterprise and strictly within the limits of the law; and, second, to conduct operations in a manner that gives equal weight to the claims of: stockholders, labor, consumers and government. Both of these broad objectives must be translated into more specific market goals if they are to be very helpful to executives responsible for making concrete business decisions.

B. *Statement of Market Objectives.* In pursuit of maximum profits, for example, management might set its operating objectives at: a maximum of dollar or unit sales; a maximum share of total or of particular geographic markets; maximum profit figured as a percentage of net worth or of sales; it might set itself the objective of a steadily increasing return on sales or profits; or the goal of an increasing market share. But even if narrowed this far, the objectives are not as helpful as they can be made. It is possible to state market objectives in a form that facilitates an application of the scientific method.

Market objectives are best expressed as customer types—narrowly defined—whose patronage the business will try especially to win. (Of course, it will not turn away others desiring to buy.) Once objectives have been refined to this point, management is in a position to formulate more specific problems in a manner that makes it readily amenable to solution by the scientific method.

A determination of the types of customers the firm should try to serve in particular does not flow simply and logically from a firm's ultimate objectives. A careful consideration of alternative markets must underlie the selection of those markets to be cultivated intensively.

IV. CONCEPT OF A "MARKET STRATEGY"

Put differently, use of "scientific" methods for making marketing decisions calls for what is here termed a "market strategy." The main purpose of this paper is to explain what a market strategy consists of and how it can serve as a potent organizing tool for the decisions of business executives. It may well assist students of marketing by giving a central structure to various facets of the study of business.

A market strategy consists of two parts: (1) the definition of market targets—selecting the types of customers whose patronage will be sought; and (2) the "composition of a marketing mix"—picking a combination of sales promotion devices that will be employed. Market targets represent the operating objectives (which are subject to change of course) of top management; the marketing mix represents a combination of instruments by which these objectives are pursued.

The scientific method finds its greatest potential application to marketing by calling for a rigorous appraisal of the relative effectiveness of alternative means of winning the patronage of particular types of potential customers. The scientific marketer must assemble the best evidence available, determine what additional evidence should be gathered, subject all information collected to rigorous analysis, formulate and test hypotheses regarding the effect on unit sales of such things as: price changes, changes in the quality of the product, advertising outlays, number of salesmen, margins offered retailers, number of retail outlets, etc.

It will be acknowledged at the outset that no generalizations about these matters can be applied to all or even to many products. Answers to specific marketing problems probably differ for each individual business—and will not even be stable for it over long periods of time. Thus, top management must reconcile itself to an unending study of the relative effectiveness of sales promotion devices. Management's success in achieving the market targets it sets itself will, it is maintained here, depend upon the scientific rigor with which it conducts this endless study—rather than upon the artistry and intuition of its top executives.

The steps involved in the formulation of a market strategy will be discussed in broad general terms in this paper. First, the determination of market targets will be taken up; thereupon, the composition of a marketing mix will be discussed.

A. *Definition of Market Targets.* No one can hope to please everybody! Persons who attempt to win the friendship of everyone are likely to have few friends, for they will lack individuality and basic personality.

Many will doubt their sincerity and almost everyone will get an uneasy feeling in their presence and think that there is something "fishy" about them. Businesses who try to sell to everybody risk a similar fate. If they attempt to convince their prestige conscious customers that their product represents the highest possible quality and the brand that customers buy if they do not have to worry about cost, they may repel potential customers who are extremely concerned about economy. But, if they claim that the product represents both the highest possible quality and the lowest price, they will be believed by almost no one.

No business needs to sell to *all* potential customers. A fraction of the total market is all any firm need hope for—and the Department of Justice frowns on those with more ambitious hopes. It is almost always wise for a management to select consciously the types of customers it will try to win as their firm's main patrons; in so doing, management can mobilize the full resources of the firm to a clearly defined task. To make such a selection, management should first divide the total potential market into its "significant" segments.

Potential customers must be divided into groups that have some significance *from the standpoint of what management can and should do about them.* The most important criteria for segmenting the market for any product are: (1) strength of their need or desire for the product; (2) channels (media, distribution outlets, etc.) through which they can be reached; (3) "appeals" (lines of argument) to which they are responsive; (4) degrees of responsiveness to particular types of sales appeal (that is, their ability to be influenced by price considerations, availability of credit, sales talk of salesmen, etc.); and (5) physical location.

The most significant market segments vary widely from product to product. Customers must be classified according to the many special features of the product in question and of the circumstances under which it is sold. In almost every case, however, there are two types of criteria that should be employed: the first are the features traditionally used by market analysts. These generally can be measured and include such things as: incomes, marital status, size of family, religion, age, size of community, whether or not the product is already owned, the age and condition of the product owned, etc. The second are social and psychological characteristics that almost always are unmeasurable and apply particularly to the product in question. For example, one might divide potential customers of most products into: the self-confident and those who are unsure of themselves; the adventurous and those craving the familiar; the ostentatious and the modest, etc. In addition, particular attitudes are confronted in the marketing of some products but have no bearing upon others. For example, it seems to have been established that the use of instant coffee is associated in the minds of many housewives with neglect of a wife's proper duties. This attitude is not likely to have any bearing upon the sale of women's hats, however.

As already indicated, the criteria by which potential customers are divided should meet two tests: (1) they should reflect differences which indicate or affect the actions that businessmen should take in trying to win their patronage; and (2) they should apply to the particular product in the specific markets in which they are being sold. In classifying potential customers, one should err, if at all, in the direction of dividing them into too many rather than too few groups. Both measurable and unmeasurable characteristics should be combined into one scheme of classification. It is likely that one will end up with many scores of market segments; as stated, the more the better.

Those segments should then be scrutinized carefully to determine: (1) which ones are least adequately served at present; (2) those which the particular firm is best qualified to attract—because of its product, personnel, tradition, reputation, standing in the customer's mind, etc.; and (3) those that management would like to make the core of the business over the future, simply on grounds of personal taste.

By scrutinizing the total potential market broken down into segments possessing significance for action, a management may well find that several parts of the market had gone relatively uncovered. If so, it may profit by cultivating those particular markets, using measures especially effective in winning their patronage.

Management should also select the market segments to cultivate intensively by matching its own resources against what is needed to "sell" particular types of prospective customers. Special qualities about a firm's management, location, past performance, design of product, company tradition, etc. may make it particularly effective in serving certain market segments. To match the firm against market segments involves a realistic appraisal of the firm's strengths and weaknesses and of the factors that influence the purchase of each potential customer group. Often a firm will find itself especially suited to win patronage from particular types of customers—which may also be actively cultivated by some of its competitors. Not infrequently, there is a conflict between market targets that are uncovered and those for which the firm has special talent. A choice must be made, and often it will not be an easy one.

Businessmen are people! They have likes and dislikes that do and should influence their decisions. The most profitable markets may be found in regions which require location in uncomfortable climates or uncongenial social environments. In part, a selection of market segments for intensive cultivation must be influenced by such considerations. However, management cannot long follow its inclinations if they would result in persistent losses.

To summarize what has been said up to this point, a scientific market strategy first requires that a business formulate general and broad objectives. These must then be translated into operating objectives, by specifying the particular market segments the firm will cultivate most intensively.

To make such a decision, which is among the most crucial that management must make, requires an exhaustive division of all potential customers into segments which possess marketing significance—that is, they are best cultivated in different ways. The selection of the particular segments that the firm should cultivate intensively should be made on grounds of the extent to which they are being neglected at present, the special qualifications that the firm possesses to serve them, and the taste of the business owners.

B. *Composition of the Marketing Mix.* Once the firm's market targets have been specified, management faces the task of selecting measures most likely to achieve them. In modern marketing parlance, we must discuss the "marketing mix."

The "marketing mix" is composed of a large battery of devices which might be employed to induce customers to buy a particular product. The same devices are involved whether one is thinking of inducing altogether new buyers to purchase the product or of shifting customers from rival brands to one's own. These devices are here termed "sales promotion devices" and include a wide variety of instruments. It is wise to list separately those which are at the disposal of the manufacturers and those which may be employed by distributors and dealers.

Sales promotion devices that might be used by manufacturers to induce customers to buy their products include such things as: quality of product, special product features, amount of advertising outlays, lines of advertising appeals employed, types of advertising media used, number of personal salesmen employed, quality of salesmen, distributive channels employed, quality of distributors used, number of distributors, location of sales effort (geographically), product guarantees, servicing arrangements, credit and accommodations supplied.

Distributors and dealers might use the following instruments to induce customers to patronize them: price inducements, advertising, number and quality of salesmen, location, air conditioning, location of merchandise departments in the store, breadth of selection offered customers, width of aisles, hours of operation, return privileges, credit accommodation, delivery service, etc.

Even though the foregoing lists of sales promotion devices are far from complete, they are long. And, what is especially significant, managements must make decisions regarding almost every one of them. Either consciously or by default, a management decides whether or not to employ each device and in what form and to what degree.

Although a firm may concentrate on one particular sales promotion device, it almost invariably employs many of them to some degree. Even firms which rely primarily upon the appeal of low price must do some advertising; if they were not to do so, their low price offerings might not be noticed by many customers. Moreover, they are generally compelled to give some assurance of acceptable quality (by guarantees or return privileges). The point urged here is that each firm must employ a combination of sales promotion devices, rather than only one, and that the overriding task of marketing management consists in selecting the optimum combination. The formulation of a combination of sales promotion devices is sometimes described as the "composition of a marketing mix" for an actual firm.

1. The selection of a marketing mix must be made very explicitly in terms of the particular market segments whose patronage is to be sought most intensively.
2. To a considerable degree, the individual sales promotion devices are substitutes for one another. One could spend more on advertising or to hire personal salesmen of higher quality, or to build more quality into the product, etc.
3. Almost every one of the possible sales promotion devices must be employed in some form and to some degree. No single line of appeal for patronage will suffice.
4. In deciding how much to rely upon each sales promotion device, the following general rules should be applied:
   a) Never expend sums for sales promotion unless you anticipate that they will produce enough additional revenue to cover all of the costs incurred to obtain that revenue—including the sales promotion outlay. (One must take account of the effect of a sales promotion outlay on future sales as well as their immediate impact.)
   b) Compare alternative sales promotion devices that might be employed to obtain any specified increase in sales volume and employ that one which involves least cost.

V. CONNECTION BETWEEN "SCIENTIFIC MARKETING" AND MARKET STRATEGY

Executives with responsibility in the marketing area will find maximum opportunity to apply the scientific method if they consciously endeavor to formulate a concrete market strategy. Preferably, this formulation will take a written form, and be quite explicit and detailed. A market strategy combines explicit ends and the means selected to achieve them; the scientific method can be employed to a considerable degree to assess the effectiveness of alternative measures for attaining any given objective.

Specifically, top marketing executives will be entitled to regard themselves as "scientific" if they carry out the following steps:

1. Formulate each problem clearly and sharply, and in a form that lends itself to maximum verification by the use of evidence.
2. Gather available evidence bearing on the problem.
3. Arrange for the collection of additional information that would contribute to a solution to the problem—within the financial means of the firm.

4. Organize and analyze the information gathered in a manner that will shed maximum light on the solution to the original problem.
5. Formulate conclusions suggested by the evidence into hypotheses, each of which implies a potential solution to the original problem.
6. Test the hypotheses to the fullest extent possible.
7. Make a list of alternative solutions to the problem that has been discarded in favor of the one selected.

VI. HISTORICAL ANTECEDENTS OF THE MARKETING STRATEGY CONCEPT

When a new concept stands by itself, its meaning and significance often are unclear. If contrasted with other views and seen as part of a general progression of ideas, it generally can be understood and appraised rather easily. Accordingly, the notions which preceded the marketing strategy concept will be described very briefly. Historians recording the process of intellectual discovery invariably conclude that thought develops in an orderly, step-by-step method. Whether this view is valid or is the creation of the historians themselves sometimes is unclear. Consequently, the following sketch of the marketing strategy concept's development may not describe how individuals came by their ideas; it does, however, describe the state of thinking at successive points in time.

The marketing strategy concept attempts to organize the factors that determine the sales of individual products. We must therefore seek its antecedents among the writings of men who were interested in explaining or actually influencing the volume of sales. The earliest probably would be the merchants of ancient times and the early Greek philosophers who occasionally wrote about commercial affairs. Given the modest purposes at hand, this review will pass over the early writings and will start with the "Classical" economists.

Although they doubtless knew that they were oversimplifying the matter, classical economists based their explanations of sales solely on the effect of price. (All other possible influences were held constant and left unexplored.) They offered a simple and monolithic view of the determination of sales that was later incorporated into the demand schedule. In their view, sales varied inversely with price—at any given time and with all other things remaining equal; later economists summarized the relationship between sales and price in the "Law of Demand."

The second stage in the attempts of professional economists to explain the determinants of sales might be dated from the publication of Edward Chamberlin's "Theory of Monopolistic Competition."[1] It was during this stage that academic economists first took explicit account of nonprice influences on sales. Professor Chamberlin explored the effects of advertising on sales and explained this factor in the traditional manner common to

[1] Harvard University Press, Cambridge, Massachusetts, 1933.

formal economics. Despite the fact that the "Theory of Monopolistic Competition" was written over a quarter of a century ago, many academic discussions of sales still proceed as if price were the overwhelmingly important determinant of sales. Little attention is devoted even now to nonprice influences on sales by economists, although several books have been written by academic economists on the subject of individual nonprice influences on sales.

At this stage, the development of concepts to explain product sales reached a fork in the road. One prong continued the application of traditional techniques to take account of a larger number of influences on sales. An important step in this direction was taken in 1941 when Professor Kenneth Boulding[2] treated sales efforts and costs in the same way that theorists had handled production costs; this theoretical framework contained the implicit analogy between the top marketing executive and the engineer. Economists have not built on this major breakthrough, however. An article by P. J. Verdoorn in 1956[3] represents perhaps the high point of this line of development, which is characterized by the use of geometric tools of analysis.

Further developments along this traditional route are in the hands of persons with a mathematical orientation. The field of operations research known as "programming" handles many sales promotion activities without serious difficulty, because mathematics is vastly more powerful than geometry. Programming of sales activity is not being explored by formal economics but represents the contribution of marketing specialists in the main.

The second fork in the road reached after the writing of the "Theory of Monopolistic Competition" might be termed the checklist approach to the sales problem. It was along this road that the term "marketing mix" was introduced for the first time by Professor Neil Borden in approximately 1953.[4] Writers who have followed this route were concerned with two major factors: first, they sought to itemize the large number of influences upon sales that marketing executives must take into account; second, they were interested in facilitating practical application of the concept to concrete operating problems. Foremost among the writers who adopted this approach were Professors Neil Borden and Albert Frey.[5] The latter attempted to relate the marketing mix concept directly to the development of marketing programs in his publication, which carries the subtitle, "Programming for Optimum Results."

[2] See his *Economic Analysis*, Harpers, 1941.

[3] See his "Marketing from the Producer's Point of View," *Journal of Marketing*, January 1956.

[4] Professor Borden first introduced the concept in his presidential address to the American Marketing Association in 1953.

[5] Professor Frey dealt with the subject in a pamphlet entitled, "The Effective Marketing Mix," and published by the Amos Tuck School of Business Administration in 1956.

With the development of the checklist approach, the enormity of the problem confronting the top marketing executive became apparent. The task of balancing a very large number of variables (even if one ignores their interdependence) clearly is huge. Paucity of evidence about the productivity of individual sales promotion devices, and the difference between present and future markets inevitably makes the task of the chief marketing executive overwhelming, if not impossible. The inability to set down a workable method of composing a marketing mix is not a failing of the concept itself; the concept *does* describe what the top marketing executive should attempt to do. It certainly represents a substantial improvement over earlier views that took explicit account of only a few factors influencing sales. The complexity of the sales function is real and not a figment of the imagination of the concept builders.

Doctrine discussing determinants of sales had reached this state when the concept of marketing strategy was first set down in 1957. This concept differs from earlier thought on the subject by relating customer targets directly to the marketing mix. (It may be regarded as another step down the road from the checklist approach to the sales problem.) It emphasizes that an effective marketing mix requires top management to be explicit about the kinds of customers to whom the business is trying to sell because specific sales promotion devices that appeal to some customers will bore others and even repel some.

The addition of customer targets to the concept of the marketing mix partly overcomes the difficulties in implementing the concept caused by a lack of information. When a marketing specialist is explicit about his target customers and informs himself thoroughly about their needs, desires, perceptions, habits, attitudes, assumptions, economic situation, etc., he can guess more confidently about the productivity of different sales promotion devices than if he thinks in terms of so unrealistic an abstraction as "the average customer."

The marketing strategy concept also directed attention to a major omission in the thinking of many business executives. When the marketing strategy concept was reduced to writing, even as today, the greatest marketing errors resulted from the failure of sellers to be explicit and selective about customer targets.

The concept of marketing strategy certainly does not represent the pinnacle of thought about the determinants of sales. It is intended primarily for businessmen who must make operating decisions—rather than for mathematicians or econometricians. Superior methods of formulating the sales problem are certain to be developed. Nevertheless, this view of sales determination may explain the sales and marketing function more clearly and suggest how to deal with it more effectively than did earlier views.

A marketing mix is the unique combination of marketing procedures and policies used by a firm. The marketing mix evolves from the firm's strategy and tactics, its resources, and market forces. An optimizing marketing mix must blend empirical information with an assessment of future market trends. Understanding an application of the marketing mix is a step forward in the development of scientific marketing.

9. THE CONCEPT OF THE MARKETING MIX*

Neil H. Borden†

I have always found it interesting to observe how an apt or colorful term may catch on, gain wide usage, and help to further understanding of a concept that has already been expressed in less appealing and communicative terms. Such has been true of the phrase "marketing mix," which I began to use in my teaching and writing some 15 years ago. In a relatively short time it has come to have wide usage. This note tells of the evolution of the marketing mix concept.

The phrase was suggested to me by a paragraph in a research bulletin on the management of marketing costs, written by my associate, Professor James Culliton (1948). In this study of manufacturers' marketing costs he described the business executive as a

> "decider," and "artist"—a "mixer of ingredients," who sometimes follows a recipe prepared by others, sometimes prepares his own recipe as he goes along, sometimes adapts a recipe to the ingredients immediately available, and sometimes experiments with or invents ingredients no one else has tried.

I liked his idea of calling a marketing executive a "mixer of ingredients," one who is constantly engaged in fashioning creatively a mix of

---

* Reprinted from "The Concept of the Marketing Mix," *Journal of Advertising Research*, Vol. IV, No. 2 (June, 1964), pp. 2–7. This article also appeared as a chapter in *Science in Marketing*, ed. George Schwartz (New York: John Wiley & Sons, Inc., 1964). For a different approach to the marketing mix, see the treatment of quantitative and spatial dimensions of the mix and the discussion of methods of constructing marketing mixes in Alfred R. Oxenfeldt, *Executive Action in Marketing* (Belmont, Calif.: Wadsworth Publishing Co., 1966), chap. 24, pp. 759–80.

† Harvard University.

marketing procedures and policies in his efforts to produce a profitable enterprise.

For many years previous to Culliton's cost study the wide variations in the procedures and policies employed by managements of manufacturing firms in their marketing programs and the correspondingly wide variation in the costs of these marketing functions, which Culliton aptly ascribed to the varied "mixing of ingredients," had become increasingly evident as we had gathered marketing cases at the Harvard Business School. The marked differences in the patterns or formulae of the marketing programs not only were evident through facts disclosed in case histories, but also were reflected clearly in the figures of a cost study of food manufacturers made by the Harvard Bureau of Business Research in 1929. The primary objective of this study was to determine common figures of expenses for various marketing functions among food manufacturing companies, similar to the common cost figures which had been determined in previous years for various kinds of retail and wholesale businesses. In this manufacturer's study we were unable, however, with the data gathered to determine common expense figures that had much significance as standards by which to guide management, such as had been possible in the studies of retail and wholesale trades, where the methods of operation tended toward uniformity. Instead, among food manufacturers the ratios of sales devoted to the various functions of marketing such as advertising, personal selling, packaging, and so on, were found to be widely divergent, no matter how we grouped our respondents. Each respondent gave data that tended to uniqueness.

Culliton's study of marketing costs in 1947–48 was a second effort to find out, among other objectives, whether a bigger sample and a more careful classification of companies would produce evidence of operating uniformities that would give helpful common expense figures. But the result was the same as in our early study: there was wide diversity in cost ratios among any classifications of firms which were set up, and no common figures were found that had much value. This was true whether companies were grouped according to similarity in product lines, amount of sales, territorial extent of operations, or other bases of classification.

Relatively early in my study of advertising, it had become evident that understanding of advertising usage by manufacturers in any case had to come from an analysis of advertising's place as one element in the total marketing program of the firm. I came to realize that it is essential always to ask: what overall marketing strategy has been or might be employed to bring about a profitable operation in light of the circumstances faced by the management? What combination of marketing procedures and policies has been or might be adopted to bring about desired behavior of trade and consumers at costs that will permit a profit? Specifically, how can advertising, personal selling, pricing, packaging, channels, warehousing, and the other elements of a marketing program be manipulated and fitted together in a way that will give a profitable operation? In short, I saw that every advertising management case called for a consideration of the strategy to be adopted for the total marketing program, with advertising recognized as only one element whose form and extent depended on its careful adjustment to the other parts of the program.

The soundness of this viewpoint was supported by case histories throughout my volume, *The Economic Effects of Advertising* (Borden, 1942). In the chapters devoted to the utilization of advertising by business, I had pointed out the innumerable combinations of marketing methods and policies that might be adopted by a manager in arriving at a marketing plan. For instance, in the area of branding, he might elect to adopt an individualized brand or a family brand. Or he might decide to sell his product unbranded or under private label. Any decision in the area of brand policy in turn has immediate implications that bear on his selection of channels of distribution, sales force methods, packaging, promotional procedure, and advertising. Throughout the volume the case materials cited show that the way in which any marketing function is designed and the burden placed upon the function are determined largely by the overall marketing strategy adopted by managements to meet the market conditions under which they operate. The forces met by different firms vary widely. Accordingly, the programs fashioned differ widely.

Regarding advertising, which was the function under focus in the economic effects volume, I said at one point:

> In all the above illustrative situations it should be recognized that advertising is not an operating method to be considered as something apart, as something whose profit value is to be judged alone. An able management does not ask, "Shall we use or not use advertising," without consideration of the product and of other management procedures to be employed. Rather the question is always one of finding a management formula giving advertising its due place in the combination of manufacturing methods, product form, pricing, promotion and selling methods, and distribution methods. As previously pointed out different formulae, i.e., different combinations of methods, may be profitably employed by competing manufacturers.

From the above it can be seen why Culliton's description of a marketing manager as a "mixer of ingredients" immediately appealed to me as an apt and easily understandable phrase, far better than my previous references to the marketing man as an empiricist seeking in any situation to devise a profitable "pattern" or "formula" of marketing operations from among the many procedures and policies that were open to him. If he was a "mixer of ingredients," what he designed was a "marketing mix."

It was logical to proceed from a realization of the existence of a variety of "marketing mixes" to the development of a concept that would comprehend not only this variety, but also the market forces that cause managements to produce a variety of mixes. It is the problems raised by these forces that lead marketing managers to exercise their wits in devising mixes or programs which they hope will give a profitable business operation.

To portray this broadened concept in a visual presentation requires merely:

1) a list of the important elements or ingredients that make up marketing programs;
2) a list of the forces that bear on the marketing operation of a firm and to which the marketing manager must adjust in his search for a mix or program that can be successful.

The list of elements of the marketing mix in such a visual presentation can be long or short, depending on how far one wishes to go in his classification and subclassification of the marketing procedures and policies with which marketing managements deal when devising marketing programs. The list of elements which I have employed in my teaching and consulting work covers the principal areas of marketing activities which call for management decisions as revealed by case histories. I realize others might build a different list. Mine is as follows:

ELEMENTS OF THE MARKETING MIX OF MANUFACTURERS

1. *Product Planning*—policies and procedures relating to:
   a) Product lines to be offered—qualities, design, etc.
   b) Markets to sell: whom, where, when, and in what quantity.
   c) New product policy—research and development program.
2. *Pricing*—policies and procedures relating to:
   a) Price level to adopt.
   b) Specific prices to adopt (odd-even, etc.).
   c) Price policy, e.g., one-price or varying price, price maintenance, use of list prices, etc.
   d) Margins to adopt—for company; for the trade.
3. *Branding*—policies and procedures relating to:
   a) Selection of trade marks.
   b) Brand policy—individualized or family brand.
   c) Sale under private label or unbranded.
4. *Channels of Distribution*—policies and procedures relating to:
   a) Channels to use between plant and consumer.
   b) Degree of selectivity among wholesalers and retailers.
   c) Efforts to gain cooperation of the trade.
5. *Personal Selling*—policies and procedures relating to:
   a) Burden to be placed on personal selling and the methods to be employed in:
      1. Manufacturer's organization.
      2. Wholesale segment of the trade.
      3. Retail segment of the trade.
6. *Advertising*—policies and procedures relating to:
   a) Amount to spend—i.e., the burden to be placed on advertising.
   b) Copy platform to adopt:

1. Product image desired.
2. Corporate image desired.

c) Mix of advertising: to the trade; through the trade; to consumers.

7. *Promotions*—policies and procedures relating to:
    a) Burden to place on special selling plans or devices directed at or through the trade.
    b) Form of these devices for consumer promotions, for trade promotions.
8. *Packaging*—policies and procedures relating to:
    a) Formulation of package and label.
9. *Display*—policies and procedures relating to:
    a) Burden to be put on display to help effect sale.
    b) Methods to adopt to secure display.
10. *Servicing*—policies and procedures relating to:
    a) Providing service needed.
11. *Physical Handling*—policies and procedures relating to:
    a) Warehousing.
    b) Transportation.
    c) Inventories.
12. *Fact Finding and Analysis*—policies and procedures relating to:
    a) Securing, analysis, and use of facts in marketing operations.

Also if one were to make a list of all the forces which managements weigh at one time or another when formulating their marketing mixes, it would be very long indeed, for the behavior of individuals and groups in all spheres of life have a bearing, first, on what goods and services are produced and consumed, and, second, on the procedures that may be employed in bringing about exchange of these goods and services. However, the important forces which bear on marketers, all arising from the behavior of individuals or groups, may readily be listed under four heads, namely the behavior of consumers, the trade, competitors, and government.

The outline below contains these four behavioral forces with notations of some of the important behavioral determinants within each force. These must be studied and understood by the marketer, if his marketing mix is to be successful. The great quest of marketing management is to understand the behavior of humans in response to the stimuli to which they are subjected. The skillful marketer is one who is a perceptive and practical psychologist and sociologist, who has keen insight into individual and group behavior, who can foresee changes in behavior that develop in a dynamic world, who has creative ability for building well-knit programs because he has the capacity to visualize the probable response of consumers, trade, and competitors to his moves. His skill in forecasting response to his marketing moves should well be supplemented by a further skill in devising and using tests and measurements to check consumer or trade response to his program or parts thereof, for no marketer has so much prescience that he can proceed without empirical check.

Below, then, is the suggested outline of forces which govern the mixing of marketing elements. This list and that of the elements taken together provide a visual presentation of the concept of the marketing mix.

MARKET FORCES BEARING ON THE MARKETING MIX

1. *Consumers' Buying Behavior*, as determined by their:
   a) Motivation in purchasing.
   b) Buying habits.
   c) Living habits.
   d) Environment (present and future, as revealed by trends, for environment influences consumers' attitudes toward products and their use of them).
   e) Buying power.
   f) Number (i.e., how many).
2. *The Trade's Behavior*—wholesalers' and retailers' behavior, as influenced by:
   a) Their motivations.
   b) Their structure, practices, and attitudes.
   c) Trends in structure and procedures that portend change.
3. *Competitors' Position and Behavior*, as influenced by:
   a) Industry structure and the firm's relation thereto.
      1. Size and strength of competitors.
      2. Number of competitors and degree of industry concentration.
      3. Indirect competition—i.e., from other products.
   b) Relation of supply to demand—oversupply or undersupply.
   c) Product choices offered consumers by the industry—i.e., quality, price, service.
   d) Degree to which competitors compete on price vs. nonprice bases.
   e) Competitors' motivations and attitudes—their likely response to the actions of other firms.
   f) Trends, technological and social, portending change in supply and demand.
4. *Governmental Behavior—Controls over Marketing:*
   a) Regulations over products.
   b) Regulations over pricing.
   c) Regulations over competitive practices.
   d) Regulations over advertising and promotion.

When building a marketing program to fit the needs of his firm, the marketing manager has to weigh the behavioral forces and then juggle marketing elements in his mix with a keen eye on the resources with which he has to work. His firm is but one small organism in a large universe of complex forces. His firm is only a part of an industry that is competing with many other industries. What does the firm have in terms of money, product line, organization, and reputation with which to work? The manager must devise a mix of procedures that fit these resources. If his firm is small, he must judge the response of consumers, trade, and competition in light of his position and resources and the influence that he can exert in the market. He must look for special opportunities in product or method of operation. The small firm cannot employ the procedures of the big firm. Though he may sell the same kind of product as the big firm, his marketing strategy is likely to be widely different in many respects. Innumerable instances of this fact might be cited. For example, in the industrial goods field, small firms often seek to build sales on a limited and highly specialized line, whereas industry leaders seek patronage for full lines. Small firms often elect to go in for regional sales rather than attempt the national distribution practiced by larger companies. Again, the company of limited resources often elects to limit its production and sales to products whose potential is too small to attract the big fellows. Still again, companies with small resources in the cosmetic field not infrequently have set up introductory marketing programs employing aggressive personal selling and a "push" strategy with distribution limited to leading department stores. Their initially small advertising funds have been directed through these selected retail outlets, with the offering of the products and their story told over the signatures of the stores. The strategy has been to borrow kudos for their products from the leading stores' reputations and to gain a gradual radiation of distribution to smaller stores in all types of channels, such as often comes from the trade's follow-the-leader behavior. Only after resources have grown from mounting sales has a dense retail distribution been aggressively sought and a shift made to place the selling burden more and more on company-signed advertising.

The above strategy was employed for Toni products and Stoppette deodorant in their early marketing stages when the resources of their producers were limited (cf. case of Jules Montenier, Inc. in Borden and Marshall, 1959, pp. 498–518). In contrast, cosmetic manufacturers with large resources have generally followed a "pull" strategy for the introduction of new products, relying on heavy campaigns of advertising in a rapid succession of area introductions to induce a hoped-for, complete retail coverage from the start (cf. case of Bristol-Myers Company in Borden and Marshall, 1959, pp. 519–533). These introductory campaigns have been undertaken only after careful programs of product development and test marketing have given assurance that product and selling plans had high promise of success.

Many additional instances of the varying strategy employed by small versus large enterprises might be cited. But those given serve to illustrate the point that managements must fashion their mixes to fit their resources. Their objectives must be realistic.

LONG VERSUS SHORT TERM ASPECTS OF MARKETING MIX

The marketing mix of a firm in large part is the product of the evolution that comes from day-to-day marketing. At any time the mix represents the program that a management has evolved to meet the problems with which it is constantly faced in an ever changing, ever challenging market. There are continuous tactical maneuvers: a new product, aggressive promotion, or price change initiated by a competitor must be considered and met; the failure of the trade to provide adequate market coverage or display must be remedied; a faltering sales force must be reorganized and stimulated; a decline in sales share must be diagnosed and remedied; an advertising approach that has lost effectiveness must be replaced; a general business decline must be countered. All such problems call for a management's maintaining effective channels of information relative to its own operations and to the day-to-day behavior of consumers, competitors, and the trade. Thus, we may observe that short range forces play a large part in the fashioning of the mix to be used at any time and in determining the allocation of expenditures among the various functional accounts of the operating statement.

But the overall strategy employed in a marketing mix is the product of longer range plans and procedures dictated in part by past empiricism and in part, if the management is a good one, by management foresight as to what needs to be done to keep the firm successful in a changing world. As the world has become more and more dynamic, blessed is that corporation which has managers who have foresight, who can study trends of all kinds—natural, economic, social, and technological—and, guided by these, devise long-range plans that give promise of keeping their corporations afloat and successful in the turbulent sea of market change. Accordingly, when we think of the marketing mix, we need to give particular heed today to devising a mix based on long-range planning that promises to fit the world of five or ten or more years hence. Provision for effective long-range planning in corporate organization and procedure has become more and more recognized as the earmark of good management in a world that has become increasingly subject to rapid change.

To cite an instance among American marketing organizations which has shown foresight in adjusting the marketing mix to meet social and economic change, I look upon Sears Roebuck and Company as an outstanding example. After building an unusually successful mail order business to meet the needs of a rural America, Sears management foresaw the need to depart from its marketing pattern as a mail order company catering primarily to farmers. The trend from a rural to an urban United States was going on apace. The automobile and good roads promised to make town and city stores increasingly available to those who continued to be farmers. Relatively early, Sears launched a chain of stores across the land, each easily accessible by highway to both farmer and city resident, and with adequate parking space for customers. In time there followed the remarkable telephone and mail order plan directed at urban residents to make buying easy for Americans when congested city streets and highways made shopping increasingly distasteful. Similarly, in the areas of planning products which would meet the desires of consumers in a fast changing world, of shaping its servicing to meet the needs of a wide variety of mechanical products, of pricing procedures to meet the challenging competition that came with the advent of discount retailers, the Sears organization has shown a foresight, adaptability, and creative ability worthy of emulation. The amazing growth and profitability of the company attest to the foresight and skill of its management. Its history shows the wisdom of careful attention to market forces and their impending change in devising marketing mixes that may assure growth.

USE OF THE MARKETING MIX CONCEPT

Like many concepts, the marketing mix concept seems relatively simple, once it has been expressed. I know that before they were ever tagged with the nomenclature of "concept," the ideas involved were widely understood among marketers as a result of the growing knowledge about marketing and marketing procedures that came during the preceding half century. But I have found for myself that once the ideas were reduced to a formal statement with an accompanying visual presentation, the concept of the mix has proved a helpful devise in teaching, in business problem solving, and, generally, as an aid to thinking about marketing. First of all, it is helpful in giving an answer to the question often raised as to "what is marketing?" A chart which shows the elements of the mix and the forces that bear on the mix helps to bring understanding of what marketing is. It helps to explain why in our dynamic world the thinking of management in all its functional areas must be oriented to the market.

In recent years I have kept an abbreviated chart showing the elements and the forces of the marketing mix in front of my classes at all times. In case discussion it has proved a handy device by which to raise queries as to whether the student has recognized the implications of any recommendation he might have made in the areas of the several elements of the mix. Or, referring to the forces, we can question whether all the pertinent market forces have been given due consideration. Continual reference to the mix chart leads me to feel that the students' understanding of "what marketing is" is strengthened. The constant presence and use of the chart leaves a deeper understanding that marketing is the devising of programs that successfully meet the forces of the market.

In problem solving the marketing mix chart is a constant reminder of:

1) The fact that a problem seemingly lying in one segment of the mix must be deliberated with constant thought regarding the effect of any change in that sector on the other areas of marketing operations. The necessity of integration in marketing thinking is ever present.

2) The need of careful study of the market forces as they might bear on problems in hand.

In short, the mix chart provides an ever ready checklist as to areas into which to guide thinking when considering marketing questions or dealing with marketing problems.

MARKETING: SCIENCE OR ART?

The quest for a "science of marketing" is hard upon us. If science is in part a systematic formulation and arrangement of facts in a way to help understanding, then the concept of the marketing mix may possibly be considered a small contribution in the search for a science of marketing. If we think of a marketing science as involving the observation and classification of facts and the establishment of verifiable laws that can be used by the marketer as a guide to action with assurance that predicted results will ensue, then we cannot be said to have gotten far toward establishing a science. The concept of the mix lays out the areas in which facts should be assembled, these to serve as a guide to management judgment in building marketing mixes. In the last few decades American marketers have made substantial progress in adopting the scientific method in assembling facts. They have sharpened the tools of fact finding—both those arising within the business and those external to it. Aided by these facts and by the skills developed through careful observation and experience, marketers are better fitted to practice the art of designing marketing mixes than would be the case had not the techniques of gathering facts been advanced as they have been in recent decades. Moreover, marketers have made progress in the use of the scientific method in designing tests whereby the results from mixes or parts of mixes can be measured. Thereby marketers have been learning how to subject the hypotheses of their mix artists to empirical check.

With continued improvement in the search for and the recording of facts pertinent to marketing, with further application of the controlled experiment, and with an extension and careful recording of case histories, we may hope for a gradual formulation of clearly defined and helpful marketing laws. Until then, and even then, marketing and the building of marketing mixes will largely lie in the realm of art.

REFERENCES

Borden, Neil H. *The Economic Effects of Advertising.* Homewood, Ill.: Richard D. Irwin, 1942.

Borden, Neil H., and M. V. Marshall. *Advertising Management: Text and Cases.* Homewood, Ill.: Richard D. Irwin, 1959.

Culliton, James W. *The Management of Marketing Costs.* Boston: Division of Research, Graduate School of Business Administration, Harvard University, 1948.

The achievement of corporate marketing objectives depends on customer response to the firm's marketing mix. Demand, demand elasticity, and the marketing mix are critical elements in the firm's efforts to reach marketing objectives. "Customer appeals mix" describes customer perception of the total satisfaction associated with a particular offering of the firm. There is a significant difference between the customer appeals mix concept and the marketing mix concept. A marketing program is a synthesis of marketing mix elements created to influence the customer-appeals mix.

10. FROM PRICE ELASTICITY TO THE MARKETING MIX—AND BEYOND*

Alfred R. Oxenfeldt†

Marketing executives are concerned, perhaps, beyond all else, with customers' responses to their sales efforts. This paper accordingly traces the development of that stream of ideas which relates to demand—that is, to the effects of sellers' actions upon customer behavior. It starts with the demand curve and the related concept of demand elasticity and then discusses the marketing mix concept. Thereupon, it introduces two somewhat new notions: "marketing programs" and "the customer appeals mix." These notions are designed mainly to eliminate ambiguities in the marketing mix concept.

THE DEMAND CURVE AND PRICE ELASTICITY

As developed by classical and neo-classical economists, the demand curve summarizes all that a price-setter needs to know about his customers. It indicates how many units they would buy at different prices. Properly constructed, it would take account of the following factors: 1) customers' responses; 2) competitors' responses; 3) the effects of reaching

* Reprinted from *The Business Quarterly*, Vol. XXX, No. 4 (Winter, 1965), pp. 23–26.

† Columbia University.

a given price by an increase as opposed to reaching that price by a decrease (this point related to the reversibility of the demand curve). In addition, the demand curve "takes account of" other sales devices than price by holding them constant. (No account is taken, it should be noted of the possibility that the slope of a demand curve might differ markedly according to the amount of other sales devices that are held constant).

Neoclassical theorists developed the concept of price elasticity of demand, to describe variations in the sensitivity of unit sales to changes in price. One can describe, by an elasticity measure, the response of customers as a whole to varying price changes. (Here again, economists simplified matters a good bit by assuming that customers' responses would be much the same at all levels of price).

With the writings of Edward Chamberlin, one other sales device was considered explicitly in demand theory. Specifically, promotional efforts were discussed frontally, and the concept of "promotional elasticity of demand" made its appearance. Not much later, the concept of income elasticity of demand was formulated. Demand theory at the present time largely revolves about three determinants of unit sales: price, promotional outlays and level of national income.

THE MARKETING MIX CONCEPT

Marketing specialists have pushed ahead in a different direction since World War II. Their contributions started in 1947 when Professor Neil Borden coined the phrase "marketing mix." Although as originally stated, this concept was simply a long list of the marketing activities in which many businesses engage in order to win customers, the "marketing mix" became the focal point of a significant extension of demand theory. The greatest single advance can be credited to the very interesting article published by Professor P. J. Verdoorn early in 1956.[1] He established the parallel between the marketing mix and production theory. (He made other contributions as well, especially by placing the concept of the marketing mix—as he came to use it—within the structure of decision theory).

The marketing mix concept makes explicit the fact that top management consciously or unconsciously allocates resources among alternative and partially-substitute marketing activities. One consequence is the recognition that a firm would gain by bringing together under a single intelligence all of the activities that relate to the customer—the main organizational result of the "new marketing concept." Also, the marketing mix concept provided "room" for any and *all* marketing activities and broke the bounds that limited discussion of sales determinants to price, promotion and income.

---

[1] See P. J. Verdoorn, "Marketing from the Producer's Point of View," *Journal of Marketing*, January 1956, pp. 221–235.

The marketing mix concept has fairly grave limitations, however. Even in 1965, as one examines it closely, he finds very great fuzziness. The measurement of any company's marketing mix poses very great difficulties which will only be intimated here. First, it does not explain what proportion of product costs should be charged to marketing—or how to draw a line between say, packaging and delivery costs that are marketing and those that are non-marketing costs. Second, it does not show how one might assign a cost to price—which clearly is one and a major element of the marketing mix. This factor involves no direct monetary outlay and must, somehow, be measured indirectly. Third, it fails to relate a firm's marketing efforts to specific types of customers. Clearly, a firm can select among alternative marketing programs only if it is conscious of the kinds of customers to whom it is trying to appeal. Fourth, it calls for horrendous efforts if one is to measure or estimate the payoff of alternative marketing efforts.[2]

Perhaps the greatest fuzziness in the marketing mix concept results from the shifting perspectives that it invites. As usually interpreted, the marketing mix denotes a firm's total expenditures for marketing and the proportions of that total that are devoted to different uses. The term also is used sometimes to refer to the way that customers are affected by these expenditures. That is, advertising expenditures are taken to be directly related to the strength of a company's advertising appeals; a firm's "outlays" *for products* are taken to be proportional to the *product appeal* that customers receive. In other words, most writings imply a direct equivalence between marketing outlays on one hand and the benefits or attractions offered to customers on the other.

A little reflection shows that there need be no direct connection between a firm's outlays and its customers' perceptions of that firm's offerings. In the first place, the attractions that customers perceive in a firm's offering at any time more often reflect its past expenditures than those of the present. A firm's reputation and the other intangible values inhering in its brand name often are mainly a residue of past advertising and past customer experience with that brand; current advertising expenditures may contribute relatively little. Conversely, some heavy advertisers still are perceived to offer negative intangible values because of past product failures or a poor service record.

In the second place, marketing efforts vary widely in their perceptual impact. One firm's expenditures of one million dollars on advertising might do far more to create customer readiness to buy than a similar expenditure by its competitors. Indeed, the same company might get far

---

[2] This concept was first published in Kelley and Lazer, *Managerial Marketing: Perspectives and Viewpoints* in 1958 though it had been mimeographed and distributed to students in 1956. See A. R. Oxenfeldt, The Formulation of a Market Strategy, Lazer & Kelley, *Managerial Marketing: Perspectives and Viewpoints* (Homewood, Ill.: Richard D. Irwin, 1962), pp. 34–44.

more customer impact from a given expenditure now than from the same outlay last year.

Third, some marketing outlays by firms are not intended to create a customer appeal. Included among such outlays are purchases of equipment for handling, storage and delivery of product; the outlays required to open up new territories; the cost of adding and dropping distributors, etc. Instead, their purpose may be to reduce future marketing costs or to expand the scope of the firm's efforts.

Since marketing outlays are not correlated closely with customers' perceptions, another concept is clearly needed. This concept, termed the "customer appeals mix," means what the words imply; it denotes the benefits that the firm's target customers *perceive* in the firm's total offering. Rather than being measured in dollars spent by the firm, it is measured by its target customers' perceptions of the firm's offering. Obviously, individual customers' perceptions of the benefits offered by any brand will vary. Usually a firm benefits from grouping prospective customers into customer "types" or segments, each of which is fairly similar in the benefits perceived and desired in the product.

"CUSTOMER APPEALS MIX"

This concept possesses several difficulties, even if it satisfies an obvious need. First, one must expect substantial differences in customers' perceptions of any offerings; therefore, one must find a way of describing "*the*" customer appeal mixes. Second, one must find some technique by which one can describe these appeals accurately and quantitatively. Third, one must develop a method of identifying customer appeals in a way that is lacking at present. Since the first two points are self-evident, though extremely difficult, we shall confine our attention to the third.

The marketing mix is generally broken down into such things as price, advertising, personal selling, product, customer service, marketing research, distributor development and the like. Customer appeals, on the other hand, are best described in very different terms and doubtless vary widely from product to product. Among the more obvious customer appeals are the following: convenience in purchase, convenience in the use of the product, distinctiveness, a "feeling of luxury," reliability, confidence, freedom from interrupted usage, speedy repair and the like.

Two points follow from the foregoing list: first, the terms used to define the marketing mix do not readily apply to the elements in the customer appeals mix. Second, and more important, a combination of marketing mix elements usually is required to create a particular customer appeal. For example, a firm may redesign its product, change its package, carry out certain types of advertising, indoctrinate retail salesmen, etc., in order to convey a customer appeal of luxuriousness. This example illustrates that four marketing mix elements can be combined effectively to create one customer appeal.

Important consequences follow from this last conclusion: Namely, marketing expenditures probably should *not* be regarded as marketing mix components. More specifically, a marketing executive might be unwise to conceptualize his outlays in terms of price, advertising, personal sales, etc. Instead, he might conceptualize them in terms of the customer appeals that they are intended to create. He will try to put together in a single package—which we shall call a "marketing program"—all of the elements that combine to create customer appeals by the most efficient methods available to him.

THE MARKETING PROGRAM

As indicated, many firms do not think of marketing efforts as consisting of isolated activities like pricing, advertising, etc. Instead, they fashion what we call "marketing programs" which represent a bundle of marketing efforts which have an explicit goal. That goal usually is to create a particular customer appeal; though it could aim to reduce marketing costs also.

The chief distinguishing features of marketing programs are: First, they have explicit objectives—are not designed simply to raise profits. Second, they consist of a combination of marketing expenditures rather than a single one. These fit together, ordinarily in a manner that reinforces the effects of each one. Third, marketing programs, unlike elements in the marketing mix, are also distinguished by their originality and uniqueness. One does not simply vary the proportions of different types of marketing efforts to find that combination which gives greatest total impact. Rather, one conceives of a particular approach—possibly a unique customer appeal—and then puts together the measures that will bring it into existence.

The relationship among the chief concepts discussed here is perhaps best expressed in a few simple statements:

1. Firms' marketing efforts are designed to achieve a hierarchy of business objectives. Two key intervening objectives are: 1) Target customer segments; and 2) A customer appeals mix.

2. In developing and selecting among alternative marketing actions, marketing managers should start with a description of their existing customer appeals mix—that is, they should know how potential target customers perceive their offerings.

3. They will want to develop a bundle of marketing programs that would bring them closer to their "*target* customer appeals mix"—taking account of relative cost and effectiveness of their alternatives. The target customer appeals mix is the one that management seeks to establish and may be very different from the one that prevails.

4. The marketing expenditures that result from these marketing programs

may be described as the firm's marketing mix. A marketing mix largely reflects a firm's efforts to move from its current customer appeals mix to its target customer appeals mix.

SUMMARY AND CONCLUSIONS

This article sketches the development of ideas that deal with customers' reactions to measures taken by businesses to sell their products. It shows that economic theory contributes the demand curve which, with embellishments, develops into the price, promotional and income elasticities of demand. It further reviews the marketing specialist's contributions and finds that they take the form of the marketing mix concept.

An analysis of the marketing mix shows it to be deficient on several scores. To rectify these deficiencies and to supplement it, two additional notions are set forth: the customer appeals mix and the marketing program. Both of these notions have a conceptual value in themselves. Moreover, they sharpen ideas that are only set forth in a hazy manner in the market mix concept.

Bibliography—Chapter II

DEMOS, RAPHAEL. "Business and the Good Society," *Harvard Business Review*, Vol. XXXIII, No. 4 (July–August, 1955), pp. 33–44.

EDWARDS, CORWIN D. *Maintaining Competition: Requisites of a Governmental Policy*. New York: McGraw-Hill Book Co., Inc., 1949.

EELLS, RICHARD, AND WALTON, CLARENCE. *Conceptual Foundations of Business*. Homewood, Ill.: Richard D. Irwin, Inc., 1961.

FELLNER, WILLIAM J. *Competition Among the Few: Oligopoly and Similar Market Structures*. New York: Alfred A. Knopf, Inc., 1949.

GRETHER, E. T. *Marketing and Public Policy*. Englewood Cliffs, N.J.: Prentice-Hall, Inc., 1966.

HOLLOWAY, ROBERT J., and HANCOCK, ROBERT S. (eds.). *The Environment of Marketing Behavior*. New York: John Wiley & Sons, Inc., 1964.

THORELLI, HANS B. *The Federal Antitrust Policy: Origination of an American Tradition*. Baltimore: The Johns Hopkins Press, 1955.

TUCKER, W. T. *The Social Context of Economic Behavior*. New York: Holt, Rinehart & Winston, Inc., 1964.

ILLUSTRATION V

Marketing—Customer Satisfactions Mix

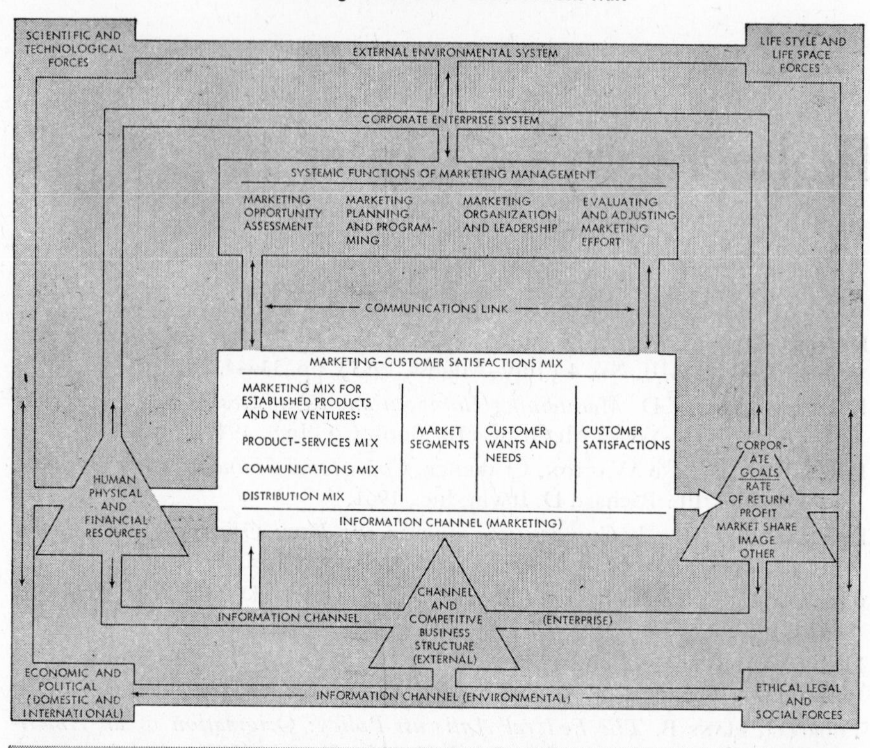

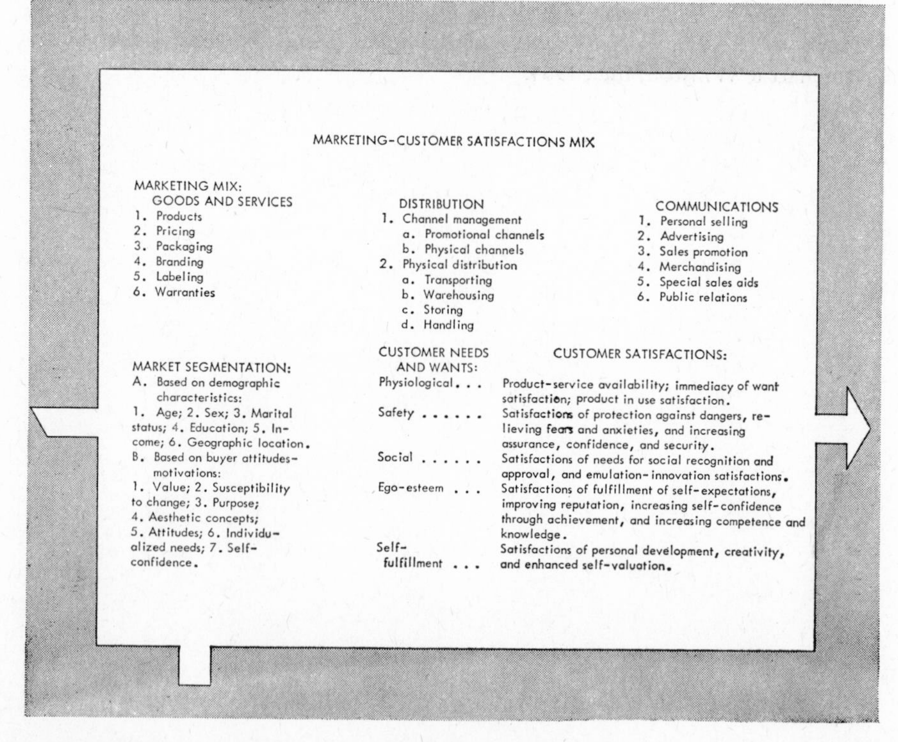

MARKETING-CUSTOMER SATISFACTIONS MIX
MARKETING MIX:
GOODS AND SERVICES
1. Products
2. Pricing
3. Packaging
4. Branding
5. Labeling
6. Warranties
DISTRIBUTION
1. Channel management
a. Promotional channels
b. Physical channels
2. Physical distribution
a. Transporting
b. Warehousing
c. Storing
d. Handling
COMMUNICATIONS
1. Personal selling
2. Advertising
3. Sales promotion
4. Merchandising
5. Special sales aids
6. Public relations
MARKET SEGMENTATION:
A. Based on demographic characteristics:
1. Age; 2. Sex; 3. Marital status; 4. Education; 5. Income; 6. Geographic location.
B. Based on buyer attitudes-motivations:
1. Value; 2. Susceptibility to change; 3. Purpose; 4. Aesthetic concepts; 5. Attitudes; 6. Individualized needs; 7. Self-confidence.
CUSTOMER NEEDS AND WANTS:
CUSTOMER SATISFACTIONS:
Physiological. . . Product-service availability; immediacy of want satisfaction; product in use satisfaction.
Safety . . . . . . Satisfactions of protection against dangers, relieving fears and anxieties, and increasing assurance, confidence, and security.
Social . . . . . . Satisfactions of needs for social recognition and approval, and emulation-innovation satisfactions.
Ego-esteem . . . Satisfactions of fulfillment of self-expectations, improving reputation, increasing self-confidence through achievement, and increasing competence and knowledge.
Self-fulfillment . . . Satisfactions of personal development, creativity, and enhanced self-valuation.

III. THE CONSUMER

All activities of the business must be focused on the consumer. This is an essential viewpoint in firms that operate under the marketing management concept. Any business unable to provide goods and services that fulfill the needs and satisfy the wants of consumers has lost its prime reason for existence; it will not long survive in a competitive environment. Consumers judge business performance and determine business destinies by the manner in which they, consumers, exercise their purchasing power. Thus, whether a business is rewarded or penalized in the marketplace is determined to a large extent by how well the needs and wants of its customers are understood and fulfilled.

Consumer reactions to market offerings result from a myriad of influences. Marketing managers must endeavor to understand the complexities of consumer behavior and give due weight to what they believe to be the more important forces acting on the consumer. Before marketing opportunities can be recognized and marketing strategies adopted, customer traits or characteristics that permit target market identification or segmentation must be studied. Selections in this chapter were chosen for their potential contribution to an understanding and appreciation of consumer behavior and the forces underlying that behavior.

An interdisciplinary approach to marketing integrates potentially useful findings from other disciplines. Psychology, social psychology, sociology, cultural anthropology, and economics are among the areas that provide useful insights into consumer behavior.

Changing life styles for consumption and spending units have introduced important considerations for managers who must evaluate marketing opportunities. Discretionary time, mobility, and purchasing power have helped to create a more discerning customer who in purchase decisions may assign greater significance to convenience costs than to commodity cost. Similarly, social class and demographic methods of market segmentation, although still important, need to be combined with newer tools of marketing analysis. Illustration V (p. 126) indicates the interrelated elements of the marketing-customer satisfactions mix. The satisfaction of customers and the attainment of marketing objectives result from successful integration of these elements.

Governmental agencies and other distinctive groups constitute special markets that present unique marketing problems and opportunities. These markets must be analyzed in depth if their potentials are to be capitalized.

A. Consumer Behavior Analysis

Sound marketing decisions are based on a knowledge of consumer motivations. Man is characterized as a wanting animal with a hierarchy of needs. Behavior should be looked at as a channel through which multiple needs are expressed and satisfied.

11. A THEORY OF HUMAN MOTIVATION*

A. H. Maslow†

INTRODUCTION

In a previous paper various propositions were presented which would have to be included in any theory of human motivation that could lay claim to being definitive. These conclusions may be briefly summarized as follows:

1. The integrated wholeness of the organism must be one of the foundation stones of motivation theory.

2. The hunger drive (or any other physiological drive) was rejected as a

---

* Reprinted from "A Theory of Human Motivation," *Psychological Review*, L, No. 4 (July, 1943), pp. 370–96. For a later, comprehensive treatment of human motivation, see A. H. Maslow, *Motivation and Personality* (New York: Harper & Row, Publishers, 1954), pp. 80–106. The Customer Needs and Wants element in Illustration V, "Marketing Action System: Marketing–Customer Satisfactions Mix," is based on Maslow's hierarchy of needs. For a discussion of psychological theories and their relevance to the study of consumer behavior, see James A. Bayton, "Motivation, Cognition, Learning—Basic Factors in Consumer Behavior," *Journal of Marketing*, January, 1958, pp. 282–89.

† Brandeis University.

centering point or model for a definitive theory of motivation. Any drive that is somatically based and localizable was shown to be atypical rather than typical in human motivation.

3. Such a theory should stress and center itself upon ultimate or basic goals rather than partial or superficial ones, upon ends rather than means to these ends. Such a stress would imply a more central place for unconscious than for conscious motivations.

4. There are usually available various cultural paths to the same goal. Therefore conscious, specific, local-cultural desires are not as fundamental in motivation theory as the more basic, unconscious goals.

5. Any motivated behavior, either preparatory or consummatory, must be understood to be a channel through which many basic needs may be simultaneously expressed or satisfied. Typically an act has *more* than one motivation.

6. Practically all organismic states are to be understood as motivated and as motivating.

7. Human needs arrange themselves in hierarchies of prepotency. That is to say, the appearance of one need usually rests on the prior satisfaction of another, more prepotent need. Man is a perpetually wanting animal. Also no need or drive can be treated as if it were isolated or discrete; every drive is related to the state of satisfaction or dissatisfaction of other drives.

8. *Lists* of drives will get us nowhere for various theoretical and practical reasons. Furthermore, any classification of motivations must deal with the problem of levels of specificity or generalization of the motives to be classified.

9. Classifications of motivations must be based upon goals rather than upon instigating drives or motivated behavior.

10. Motivation theory should be human-centered rather than animal-centered.

11. The situation or the field in which the organism reacts must be taken into account, but the field alone can rarely serve as an exclusive explanation for behavior. Furthermore, the field itself must be interpreted in terms of the organism. Field theory cannot be a substitute for motivation theory.

12. Not only the integration of the organism must be taken into account, but also the possibility of isolated, specific, partial or segmental reactions.

It has since become necessary to add to these another affirmation.

13. Motivation theory is not synonymous with behavior theory. The motivations are only one class of determinants of behavior. While behavior is almost always motivated, it is also almost always biologically, culturally and situationally determined as well. . . .

SUMMARY

1. There are at least five sets of goals, which we may call basic needs. These are briefly physiological, safety, love, esteem, and self-actualization. In addition, we are motivated by the desire to achieve or maintain the various conditions upon which these basic satisfactions rest and by certain more intellectual desires.

2. These basic goals are related to each other, being arranged in a hierarchy of prepotency. This means that the most prepotent goal will monopolize consciousness and will tend of itself to organize the recruitment of the various capacities of the organism. The less prepotent needs are minimized, even forgotten or denied. But when a need is fairly well satisfied, the next prepotent ("higher") need emerges, in turn to dominate the conscious life and to serve as the center of organization of behavior, since gratified needs are not active motivators.

Thus man is a perpetually wanting animal. Ordinarily the satisfaction of these wants is not altogether mutually exclusive, but only tends to be. The average member of our society is most often partially satisfied and partially unsatisfied in all of his wants. The hierarchy principle is usually empirically observed in terms of increasing percentages of non-satisfaction as we go up the hierarchy. Reversals of the average order of the hierarchy are sometimes observed. Also it has been observed that an individual may permanently lose the higher wants in the hierarchy under special conditions. There are not only ordinarily multiple motivations for usual behavior, but in addition many determinants other than motives.

3. Any thwarting or possibility of thwarting of these basic human goals, or danger to the defenses which protect them, or to the conditions upon which they rest, is considered to be a psychological threat. With a few exceptions, all psychopathology may be partially traced to such threats. A basically thwarted man may actually be defined as a "sick" man, if we wish.

4. It is such basic threats which bring about the general emergency reactions.

5. Certain other basic problems have not been dealt with because of limitations of space. Among these are (*a*) the problem of values in any definitive motivation theory, (*b*) the relation between appetites, desires, needs and what is "good" for the organism, (*c*) the etiology of the basic needs and their possible derivation in early childhood, (*d*) redefinition of motivational concepts, *i.e.*, drive, desire, wish, need, goal, (*e*) implication of our theory for hedonistic theory, (*f*) the nature of the uncompleted act, of success and failure, and of aspiration-level, (*g*) the role of association, habit and conditioning, (*h*) relation to the theory of interpersonal relations, (*i*) implications for psychotherapy, (*j*) implication for theory of society, (*k*) the theory of selfishness, (*l*) the relation between needs and cultural patterns, (*m*) the relation between this theory and Allport's theory of functional autonomy. These as well as certain other less important questions must be considered as motivation theory attempts to become definitive.

Marketing decisions are based upon assumptions concerning consumer behavior. A consumer's overt purchasing behavior is a function of several factors, all processed by his psyche. Five "partial" behavioral models are presented, and their underlying theories are evaluated.

12. BEHAVIORAL MODELS FOR ANALYZING BUYERS*

Philip Kotler†

In times past, management could arrive at a fair understanding of its buyers through the daily experience of selling to them. But the growth in the size of firms and markets has removed many decision-makers from direct contact with buyers. Increasingly, decision-makers have had to turn to summary statistics and to behavioral theory, and are spending more money today than ever before to try to understand their buyers.

Who buys? How do they buy? And why? The first two questions relate to relatively overt aspects of buyer behavior, and can be learned about through direct observation and interviewing.

But uncovering *why* people buy is an extremely difficult task. The answer will tend to vary with the investigator's behavioral frame of reference.

The buyer is subject to many influences which trace a complex course through his psyche and lead eventually to overt purchasing responses. This conception of the buying process is illustrated in Figure 1. Various influences and their modes of transmission are shown at the left. At the right are the buyer's responses in choice of product, brand, dealer, quantities, and frequency. In the center stands the buyer and his mysterious

---

* Reprinted from "Behavioral Models for Analyzing Buyers," *Journal of Marketing*, XXIX, No. 4 (October, 1965), pp. 37–45. For a comprehensive collection of readings and articles on behavioral models, see *Marketing Models Quantitative and Behavioral*, ed. Ralph L. Day (Scranton, Pa.: International Textbook Co., 1964), Parts I and II, p. 3–268. For a view that relates consumer decision strategies and risk reduction techniques to the concepts of brand loyalty, personal influence, and prepurchase deliberation, see Raymond A. Bauer, "Consumer Behavior as Risk Taking," *Proceedings of the Summer Conference of the American Marketing Association*, 1960, pp. 389–98.

† Northwestern University.

psychological processes. The buyer's psyche is a "black box" whose workings can be only partially deduced. The marketing strategist's challenge to the behavioral scientist is to construct a more specific model of the mechanism in the black box.

Unfortunately no generally accepted model of the mechanism exists. The human mind, the only entity in nature with deep powers of understanding, still remains the least understood. Scientists can explain planetary motion, genetic determination, and molecular behavior. Yet they have only partial, and often partisan, models of *human* behavior.

Nevertheless, the marketing strategist should recognize the potential interpretative contributions of different partial models for explaining buyer behavior. Depending upon the product, different variables and behavioral mechanisms may assume particular importance. A psychoanalytic behavioral model might throw much light on the factors operating in cigarette demand, while an economic behavioral model might be useful in explaining machine-tool purchasing. Sometimes alternative models may shed light on different demand aspects of the same product.

FIGURE 1
The Buying Process Conceived as a System of Inputs and Outputs

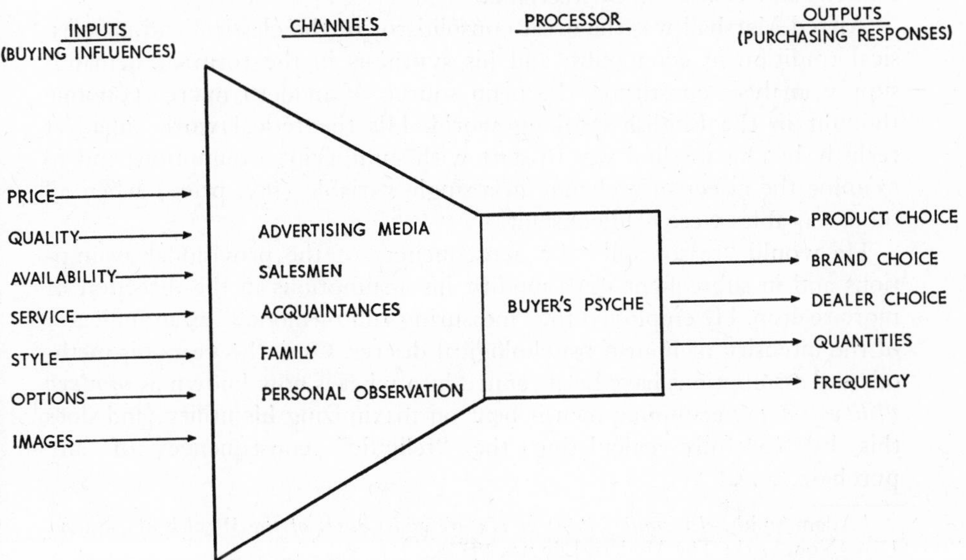

What are the most useful behavioral models for interpreting the transformation of buying influences into purchasing responses? Five different models of the buyer's "black box" are presented in the present article, along with their respective marketing applications: (1) the Marshallian model, stressing economic motivations; (2) the Pavlovian model, learning; (3) the Freudian model, psychoanalytic motivations; (4) the Veblenian model, social-psychological factors; and (5) the Hobbesian model, organizational factors. These models represent radically different conceptions of the mainsprings of human behavior.

THE MARSHALLIAN ECONOMIC MODEL

Economists were the first professional group to construct a specific theory of buyer behavior. The theory holds that purchasing decisions are the result of largely "rational" and conscious economic calculations. The individual buyer seeks to spend his income on those goods that will deliver the most utility (satisfaction) according to his tastes and relative prices.

The antecedents for this view trace back to the writings of Adam Smith and Jeremy Bentham. Smith set the tone by developing a doctrine of economic growth based on the principle that man is motivated by self-interest in all his actions.[1] Bentham refined this view and saw man as finely calculating and weighing the expected pleasures and pains of every contemplated action.[2]

Bentham's "felicific calculus" was not applied to consumer behavior (as opposed to entrepreneurial behavior) until the late 19th century. Then, the "marginal-utility" theory of value was formulated independently and almost simultaneously by Jevons[3] and Marshall[4] in England, Menger[5] in Austria, and Walras[6] in Switzerland.

Alfred Marshall was the great consolidator of the classical and neoclassical tradition in economics; and his synthesis in the form of demand-supply analysis constitutes the main source of modern micro-economic thought in the English-speaking world. His theoretical work aimed at realism, but his method was to start with simplifying assumptions and to examine the effect of a change in a single variable (say, price) when all other variables were held constant.

He would "reason out" the consequences of the provisional assumptions and in subsequent steps modify his assumptions in the direction of more realism. He employed the "measuring rod of money" as an indicator of the intensity of human psychological desires. Over the years his methods and assumptions have been refined into what is now known as *modern utility theory:* economic man is bent on maximizing his utility, and does this by carefully calculating the "felicific" consequences of any purchase. . . .

---

[1] Adam Smith, *An Inquiry into the Nature and Causes of the Wealth of Nations,* 1776 (New York: The Modern Library, 1937).

[2] Jeremy Bentham, *An Introduction to the Principles of Morals and Legislation,* 1780 (Oxford, England: Clarendon Press, 1907).

[3] William S. Jevons, *The Theory of Political Economy* (New York: The Macmillan Company, 1871).

[4] Alfred Marshall, *Principles of Economics,* 1890 (London: The Macmillan Company, 1927).

[5] Karl Menger, *Principles of Economics,* 1871 (Glencoe, Illinois: Free Press, 1950).

[6] Leon Walras, *Elements of Pure Economics,* 1874 (Homewood, Illinois: Richard D. Irwin, Inc., 1954).

Marketing Applications of Marshallian Model

From one point of view the Marshallian model is tautological and therefore neither true nor false. The model holds that the buyer acts in the light of his best "interest." But this is not very informative.

A second view is that this is a *normative* rather than a *descriptive* model of behavior. The model provides logical norms for buyers who want to be "rational." Although the consumer is not likely to employ economic analysis to decide between a box of Kleenex and Scotties, he may apply economic analysis in deciding whether to buy a new car. Industrial buyers even more clearly would want an economic calculus for making good decisions.

A third view is that economic factors operate to a greater or lesser extent in all markets, and, therefore, must be included in any comprehensive description of buyer behavior.

Furthermore, the model suggests useful behavioral hypotheses such as: (a) The lower the price of the product, the higher the sales. (b) The lower the price of substitute products, the lower the sales of this product; and the lower the price of complementary products, the higher the sales of this product. (c) The higher the real income, the higher the sales of this product, provided that it is not an "inferior" good. (d) The higher the promotional expenditures, the higher the sales.

The validity of these hypotheses does not rest on whether *all* individuals act as economic calculating machines in making their purchasing decisions. For example, some individuals may buy *less* of a product when its price is reduced. They may think that the quality has gone down, or that ownership has less status value. If a majority of buyers view price reductions negatively, then sales may fall, contrary to the first hypothesis.

But for most goods a price reduction increases the relative value of the goods in many buyers' minds and leads to increased sales. This and the other hypotheses are intended to describe average effects.

The impact of economic factors in actual buying situations is studied through experimental design or statistical analyses of past data. Demand equations have been fitted to a wide variety of products—including beer, refrigerators, and chemical fertilizers.[7] More recently, the impact of economic variables on the fortunes of different brands has been pursued with significant results, particularly in the case of coffee, frozen orange juice, and margarine.[8]

[7] See Erwin E. Nemmers, *Managerial Economics* (New York: John Wiley & Sons, Inc., 1962), Part II.

[8] See Lester G. Telser, "The Demand for Branded Goods as Estimated from Consumer Panel Data," *Review of Economics and Statistics,* Vol. 44 (August, 1962), pp. 300–324; and William F. Massy and Ronald E. Frank, "Short Term Price and Dealing Effects in Selected Market Segments," *Journal of Marketing Research,* Vol. 2 (May, 1965), pp. 171–185.

But economic factors alone cannot explain all the variations in sales. The Marshallian model ignores the fundamental question of how product and brand preferences are formed. It represents a useful frame of reference for analyzing only one small corner of the "black box."

THE PAVLOVIAN LEARNING MODEL

The designation of a Pavlovian learning model has its origin in the experiments of the Russian psychologist Pavlov, who rang a bell each time before feeding a dog. Soon he was able to induce the dog to salivate by ringing the bell whether or not food was supplied. Pavlov concluded that learning was largely an associative process and that a large component of behavior was conditioned in this way. . . .

The model has been refined over the years, and today is based on four central concepts—those of *drive*, *cue*, *response*, and *reinforcement*.[9]

Drive. Also called needs or motives, drive refers to strong stimuli internal to the individual which impels action. Psychologists draw a distinction between primary physiological drives—such as hunger, thirst, cold, pain, and sex—and learned drives which are derived socially—such as cooperation, fear, and acquisitiveness.

Cue. A drive is very general and impels a particular response only in relation to a particular configuration of cues. Cues are weaker stimuli in the environment and/or in the individual which determine when, where, and how the subject responds. . . .

Response. The response is the organism's reaction to the configuration of cues. Yet the same configuration of cues will not necessarily produce the same response in the individual. This depends on the degree to which the experience was rewarding, that is, drive-reducing.

Reinforcement. If the experience is rewarding, a particular response is reinforced; that is, it is strengthened and there is a tendency for it to be repeated when the same configuration of cues appears again. . . .

Forgetting, in contrast to extinction, is the tendency for learned associations to weaken, not because of the lack of reinforcement but because of nonuse.

Cue configurations are constantly changing. The housewife sees a new brand of coffee next to her habitual brand, or notes a special price deal on a rival brand. Experimental psychologists have found that the same learned response will be elicited by similar patterns of cues; that is, learned responses are *generalized*. . . .

A counter-tendency to generalization is *discrimination*. When a housewife tries two similar brands and finds one more rewarding, her ability to discriminate between similar cue configurations improves. Discrimination increases the specificity of the cue-response connection, while generalization decreases the specificity.

[9] See John Dollard and Neal E. Miller, *Personality and Psychotherapy* (New York: McGraw-Hill Book Company, Inc., 1950), Chapter III.

Marketing Applications of Pavlovian Model

The modern version of the Pavlovian model makes no claim to provide a complete theory of behavior—indeed, such important phenomena as perception, the subconscious, and interpersonal influence are inadequately treated. Yet the model does offer a substantial number of insights about some aspects of behavior of considerable interest to marketers. . . .[10]

Light introductory advertising is a weak cue compared with distributing free samples. Strong cues, although costing more, may be necessary in markets characterized by strong brand loyalties. For example, Folger went into the coffee market by distributing over a million pounds of free coffee.

To build a brand habit, it helps to provide for an extended period of introductory dealing. Furthermore, sufficient quality must be built into the brand so that the experience is reinforcing. Since buyers are more likely to transfer allegiance to similar brands than dissimilar brands (generalization), the company should also investigate what cues in the leading brands have been most effective. Although outright imitation would not necessarily effect the most transference, the question of providing enough similarity should be considered.

The Pavlovian model also provides guide lines in the area of advertising strategy. The American behaviorist, John B. Watson, was a great exponent of repetitive stimuli; in his writings man is viewed as a creature who can be conditioned through repetition and reinforcement to respond in particular ways.[11] The Pavlovian model emphasizes the desirability of repetition in advertising. A single exposure is likely to be a very weak cue, hardly able to penetrate the individual's consciousness sufficiently to excite his drives above the threshold level.

Repetition in advertising has two desirable effects. It "fights" forgetting, the tendency for learned responses to weaken in the absence of practice. It provides reinforcement, because after the purchase the consumer becomes selectively exposed to advertisements of the product.

The model also provides guide lines for copy strategy. To be effective as a cue, an advertisement must arouse strong drives in the person. The strongest product-related drives must be identified. . . .

THE FREUDIAN PSYCHOANALYTIC MODEL

The Freudian model of man is well known, so profound has been its impact on 20th century thought. It is the latest of a series of philosophical "blows" to which man has been exposed in the last 500 years. . . .

---

[10] The most consistent application of learning-theory concepts to marketing situations is found in John A. Howard, *Marketing Management: Analysis and Planning* (Homewood, Illinois: Richard D. Irwin, Inc., revised edition, 1963).

[11] John B. Watson, *Behaviorism* (New York: The People's Institute Publishing Company, 1925).

According to Freud, the child enters the world driven by instinctual needs which he cannot gratify by himself. Very quickly and painfully he realizes his separateness from the rest of the world and yet his dependence on it.

He tries to get others to gratify his needs through a variety of blatant means, including intimidation and supplication. Continual frustration leads him to perfect more subtle mechanisms for gratifying his instincts.

As he grows, his psyche becomes increasingly complex. A part of his psyche—the id—remains the reservoir of his strong drives and urges. Another part—the ego—becomes his conscious planning center for finding outlets for his drives. And a third part—his super-ego—channels his instinctive drives into socially approved outlets to avoid the pain of guilt or shame.

The guilt or shame which man feels toward some of his urges—especially his sexual urges—causes him to repress them from his consciousness. Through such defense mechanisms as rationalization and sublimation, these urges are denied or become transmuted into socially approved expressions. Yet these urges are never eliminated or under perfect control. . . .

The individual's behavior, therefore, is never simple. His motivational wellsprings are not obvious to a casual observer nor deeply understood by the individual himself. If he is asked why he purchased an expensive foreign sports-car, he may reply that he likes its maneuverability and its looks. At a deeper level he may have purchased the car to impress others, or to feel young again. At a still deeper level, he may be purchasing the sports-car to achieve substitute gratification for unsatisfied sexual strivings.

Many refinements and changes in emphasis have occurred in this model since the time of Freud. The instinct concept has been replaced by a more careful delineation of basic drives; the three parts of the psyche are regarded now as theoretical concepts rather than actual entities; and the behavioral perspective has been extended to include cultural as well as biological mechanisms. . . .

Marketing Applications of Freudian Model

Perhaps the most important marketing implication of this model is that buyers are motivated by *symbolic* as well as *economic-functional* product concerns. The change of a bar of soap from a square to a round shape may be more important in its sexual than its functional connotations. A cake mix that is advertised as involving practically no labor may alienate housewives because the easy life may evoke a sense of guilt.

Motivational research has produced some interesting and occasionally some bizarre hypotheses about what may be in the buyer's mind regarding certain purchases. Thus, it has been suggested at one time or another that

Many a businessman doesn't fly because of a fear of posthumous guilt—if he crashed, his wife would think of him as stupid for not taking a train.

Men want their cigars to be odoriferous, in order to prove that they (the men) are masculine.

A woman is very serious when she bakes a cake because unconsciously she is going through the symbolic act of giving birth.

A man buys a convertible as a substitute "mistress."

Consumers prefer vegetable shortening because animal fats stimulate a sense of sin.

Men who wear suspenders are reacting to an unresolved castration complex.

There are admitted difficulties of proving these assertions. Two prominent motivational researchers, Ernest Dichter and James Vicary, were employed independently by two separate groups in the prune industry to determine why so many people dislike prunes. Dichter found, among other things, that the prune aroused feelings of old age and insecurity in people, whereas Vicary's main finding was that Americans had an emotional block about prunes' laxative qualities.[12] Which is the more valid interpretation? Or if they are both operative, which motive is found with greater statistical frequency in the population?

Unfortunately the usual survey techniques—direct observation and interviewing—can be used to establish the representativeness of more superficial characteristics—age and family size, for example—but are not feasible for establishing the frequency of mental states which are presumed to be deeply "buried" within each individual.

Motivational researchers have to employ time-consuming projective techniques in the hope of throwing individual "egos" off guard. When carefully administered and interpreted, techniques such as word association, sentence completion, picture interpretation, and role-playing can provide some insights into the minds of the small group of examined individuals; but a "leap of faith" is sometimes necessary to generalize these findings to the population.

Nevertheless, motivation research can lead to useful insights and provide inspiration to creative men in the advertising and packaging world. Appeals aimed at the buyer's private world of hopes, dreams, and fears can often be as effective in stimulating purchase as more rationally-directed appeals.

THE VEBLENIAN SOCIAL-PSYCHOLOGICAL MODEL

While most economists have been content to interpret buyer behavior in Marshallian terms, Thorstein Veblen struck out in different directions.

---

[12] L. Edward Scriven, "Rationality and Irrationality in Motivation Research," in Robert Ferber and Hugh G. Wales, editors, *Motivation and Marketing Behavior* (Homewood, Illinois: Richard D. Irwin, Inc., 1958), pp. 69–70.

Veblen was trained as an orthodox economist, but evolved into a social thinker greatly influenced by the new science of social anthropology. He saw man as primarily a *social animal*—conforming to the general forms and norms of his larger culture and to the more specific standards of the subcultures and face-to-face groupings to which his life is bound. His wants and behavior are largely molded by his present group-memberships and his aspired group-memberships.

Veblen's best-known example of this is in his description of the leisure class.[13] His hypothesis is that much of economic consumption is motivated not by intrinsic needs or satisfaction so much as by prestige-seeking. He emphasized the strong emulative factors operating in the choice of conspicuous goods like clothes, cars, and houses.

Some of his points, however, seem overstated by today's perspective. The leisure class does not serve as everyone's reference group; many persons aspire to the social patterns of the class immediately above it. And important segments of the affluent class practice conspicuous underconsumption rather than overconsumption. There are many people in all classes who are more anxious to "fit in" than to "stand out." As an example, William H. Whyte found that many families avoided buying air conditioners and other appliances before their neighbors did.[14] . . .

Marketing Applications of Veblenian Model

The various streams of thought crystallized into the modern social sciences of sociology, cultural anthropology, and social psychology. Basic to them is the view that man's attitudes and behavior are influenced by several levels of society—culture, subcultures, social classes, reference groups, and face-to-face groups. The challenge to the marketer is to determine which of these social levels are the most important in influencing the demand for his product.

Culture

The most enduring influences are from culture. Man tends to assimilate his culture's mores and folkways, and to believe in their absolute rightness until deviants appear within his culture or until he confronts members of another culture.

Subcultures

A culture tends to lose its homogeneity as its population increases. When people no longer are able to maintain face-to-face relationships

---

[13] Thorstein Veblen, *The Theory of the Leisure Class* (New York: The Macmillan Company, 1899).

[14] William H. Whyte, Jr., "The Web of Word of Mouth," *Fortune*, Vol. 50 (November, 1954), pp. 140 ff.

with more than a small proportion of other members of a culture, smaller units or subcultures develop, which help to satisfy the individual's needs for more specific identity.

The subcultures are often regional entities, because the people of a region, as a result of more frequent interactions, tend to think and act alike. But subcultures also take the form of religions, nationalities, fraternal orders, and other institutional complexes which provide a broad identification for people who may otherwise be strangers. The subcultures of a person play a large role in his attitude formation and become another important predictor of certain values he is likely to hold.

Social Class

People become differentiated not only horizontally but also vertically through a division of labor. The society becomes stratified socially on the basis of wealth, skill, and power. Sometimes castes develop in which the members are reared for certain roles, or social classes develop in which the members feel empathy with others sharing similar values and economic circumstances.

Because social class involves different attitudinal configurations, it becomes a useful independent variable for segmenting markets and predicting reactions. Significant differences have been found among different social classes with respect to magazine readership, leisure activities, food imagery, fashion interests, and acceptance of innovations. . . .

Reference Groups

There are groups in which the individual has no membership but with which he identifies and may aspire to—reference groups. Many young boys identify with big-league baseball players or astronauts, and many young girls identify with Hollywood stars. The activities of these popular heroes are carefully watched and frequently imitated. These reference figures become important transmitters of influence, although more along lines of taste and hobby than basic attitudes.

Face-to-face Groups

Groups that have the most immediate influence on a person's tastes and opinions are face-to-face groups. This includes all the small "societies" with which he comes into frequent contact: his family, close friends, neighbors, fellow workers, fraternal associates, and so forth. His informal group memberships are influenced largely by his occupation, residence, and stage in the life cycle.

The powerful influence of small groups on individual attitudes has been demonstrated in a number of social psychological experiments.[15] There is also evidence that this influence may be growing. David Riesman and his coauthors have pointed to signs which indicate a growing amount of *other-direction*, that is, a tendency for individuals to be increasingly influenced by their peers in the definition of their values rather than by their parents and elders.[16]

For the marketer, this means that brand choice may increasingly be influenced by one's peers. For such products as cigarettes and automobiles, the influence of peers is unmistakable.

The role of face-to-face groups has been recognized in recent industry campaigns attempting to change basic product attitudes. For years the milk industry has been trying to overcome the image of milk as a "sissified" drink by portraying its use in social and active situations. The men's-wear industry is trying to increase male interest in clothes by advertisements indicating that business associates judge a man by how well he dresses.

Of all face-to-face groups, the person's family undoubtedly plays the largest and most enduring role in basic attitude formation. From them he acquires a mental set not only toward religion and politics, but also toward thrift, chastity, food, human relations, and so forth. Although he often rebels against parental values in his teens, he often accepts these values eventually. Their formative influence on his eventual attitudes is undeniably great.

Family members differ in the types of product messages they carry to other family members. Most of what parents know about cereals, candy, and toys comes from their children. The wife stimulates family consideration of household appliances, furniture, and vacations. The husband tends to stimulate the fewest purchase ideas, with the exception of the automobile and perhaps the home.

The marketer must be alert to what attitudinal configurations dominate in different types of families, and also to how these change over time. For example, the parent's conception of the child's rights and privileges has undergone a radical shift in the last 30 years. The child has become the center of attention and orientation in a great number of households, leading some writers to label the modern family a "filiarchy." This has important implications not only for how to market to today's family, but also on how to market to tomorrow's family when the indulged child of today becomes the parent.

---

[15] See, for example, Solomon E. Asch, "Effects of Group Pressure Upon the Modification & Distortion of Judgments," in Dorwin Cartwright and Alvin Zander, *Group Dynamics* (Evanston, Illinois: Row, Peterson & Co., 1953), pp. 151–162; and Kurt Lewin, "Group Decision and Social Change," in Theodore M. Newcomb and Eugene L. Hartley, editors, *Readings in Social Psychology* (New York: Henry Holt Co., 1952).

[16] David Riesman, Reuel Denney, and Nathan Glazer, *The Lonely Crowd* (New Haven, Connecticut: Yale University Press, 1950).

The Person

Social influences determine much but not all of the behavioral variations in people. Two individuals subject to the same influences are not likely to have identical attitudes, although these attitudes will probably converge at more points than those of two strangers selected at random. Attitudes are really the product of social forces interacting with the individual's unique temperament and abilities.

Furthermore, attitudes do not automatically guarantee certain types of behavior. Attitudes are predispositions felt by buyers before they enter the buying process. The buying process itself is a learning experience and can lead to a change in attitudes.

Alfred Politz noted at one time that women stated a clear preference for G.E. refrigerators over Frigidaire, but that Frigidaire continued to outsell G.E.[17] The answer to this paradox was that preference was only one factor entering into behavior. When the consumer preferring G.E. actually undertook to purchase a new refrigerator, her curiosity led her to examine the other brands. Her perception was sensitized to refrigerator advertisements, sales arguments, and different product features. This led to learning and a change in attitudes.

THE HOBBESIAN ORGANIZATIONAL-FACTORS MODEL

The foregoing models throw light mainly on the behavior of family buyers.

But what of the large number of people who are organizational buyers? They are engaged in the purchase of goods not for the sake of consumption, but for further production or distribution. Their common denominator is the fact that they (1) are paid to make purchases for others and (2) operate within an organizational environment.

How do organizational buyers make their decisions? There seem to be two competing views. Many marketing writers have emphasized the predominance of rational motives in organizational buying.[18] Organizational buyers are represented as being most impressed by cost, quality, dependability, and service factors. They are portrayed as dedicated servants of the organization, seeking to secure the best terms. This view has led to an emphasis on performance and use characteristics in much industrial advertising.

Other writers have emphasized personal motives in organizational buyer behavior. The purchasing agent's interest to do the best for his company is tempered by his interest to do the best for himself. He may be

---

[17] Alfred Politz, "Motivation Research—Opportunity or Dilemma?", in Ferber and Wales, same reference as footnote 12, at pp. 57–58.

[18] See Melvin T. Copeland, *Principles of Merchandising* (New York: McGraw-Hill Book Co., Inc., 1924).

tempted to choose among salesmen according to the extent they entertain or offer gifts. He may choose a particular vendor because this will ingratiate him with certain company officers. He may shortcut his study of alternative suppliers to make his work day easier.

In truth, the buyer is guided by both personal and group goals; and this is the essential point. The political model of Thomas Hobbes comes closest of any model to suggesting the relationship between the two goals.[19] Hobbes held that man is "instinctively" oriented toward preserving and enhancing his own well-being. But this would produce a "war of every man against every man." This fear leads men to unite with others in a corporate body. The corporate man tries to steer a careful course between satisfying his own needs and those of the organization.

Marketing Applications of Hobbesian Model

The import of the Hobbesian model is that organizational buyers can be appealed to on both personal and organizational grounds. The buyer has his private aims, and yet he tries to do a satisfactory job for his corporation. He will respond to persuasive salesmen and he will respond to rational product arguments. However, the best "mix" of the two is not a fixed quantity; it varies with the nature of the product, the type of organization, and the relative strength of the two drives in the particular buyer.

Where there is substantial similarity in what suppliers offer in the way of products, price, and service, the purchasing agent has less basis for rational choice. Since he can satisfy his organizational obligations with any one of a number of suppliers, he can be swayed by personal motives. On the other hand, where there are pronounced differences among the competing vendors' products, the purchasing agent is held more accountable for his choice and probably pays more attention to rational factors. Short-run personal gain becomes less motivating than the long-run gain which comes from serving the organization with distinction.

The marketing strategist must appreciate these goal conflicts of the organizational buyer. Behind all the ferment of purchasing agents to develop standards and employ value analysis lies their desire to avoid being thought of as order-clerks, and to develop better skills in reconciling personal and organizational objectives.[20]

SUMMARY

Think back over the five different behavioral models of how the buyer translates buying influences into purchasing responses.

---

[19] Thomas Hobbes, *Leviathan*, 1651 (London: G. Routledge and Sons, 1887).

[20] For an insightful account, see George Strauss, "Tactics of Lateral Relationship: The Purchasing Agent," *Administrative Science Quarterly*, Vol. 7 (September, 1962), pp. 161–186.

Marshallian man is concerned chiefly with economic cues—prices and income—and makes a fresh utility calculation before each purchase.

Pavlovian man behaves in a largely habitual rather than thoughtful way; certain configurations of cues will set off the same behavior because of rewarded learning in the past.

Freudian man's choices are influenced strongly by motives and fantasies which take place deep within his private world.

Veblenian man acts in a way which is shaped largely by past and present social groups.

And finally, Hobbesian man seeks to reconcile individual gain with organizational gain.

Thus, it turns out that the "black box" of the buyer is not so black after all. Light is thrown in various corners by these models. Yet no one has succeeded in putting all these pieces of truth together into one coherent instrument for behavioral analysis. This, of course, is the goal of behavioral science.

The impact of consumer discretionary time, mobility, and purchasing power on the American economy is growing. Technological advances, widespread automobile ownership, and an expanding highway network provide the consumer with increasing discretionary time and mobility. An understanding of these discretionary influences is essential to an understanding of consumer attitudes and behavior. Products and services must be developed to meet the need for non-productive-nonessential time-consuming activities. The concepts of "multiple" and "concurrent" consumption are presented.

13. DISCRETIONARY TIME AND DISCRETIONARY MOBILITY*

John M. Rathmell†

Labor saving devices in the home, longer weekends, shorter working days, and almost universal vacations with pay add up to one fact: more time. But more time for what? The answer to this question is of interest to

* Not previously published.

† Cornell University.

all marketing people. We see the housewife save time with a washing machine and spend it in the garden or at the sewing machine. Her husband spends less time producing for pay and more time producing for fun in his basement workshop. Changing consumption patterns have forced revisions of the consumer price index to reflect greater expenditures for time-consuming goods and services. Alert businessmen are also reacting to new consumer interests—witness the ubiquitous brazier, the indoor-outdoor living fashion, the range of do-it-yourself merchandise.

Discretionary purchasing power plus free time spells consumer mobility—mobility in consumption and mobility in buying. Consumers on the move buy different things and tend to spend more freely and certainly do not recognize trading areas designed to reflect a stationary consumer market. Recognition of this mobility is reflected in merchandise offerings which facilitate mobility, in market analysis to determine new shopping patterns, and in a reappraisal of advertising media.

Sellers are challenged to perform this experiment. Plot unit sales curves for the years since World War II for merchandise which requires a perceived expenditure of time by the consumer in its consumption. This class of merchandise includes sporting equipment, records and record playing machines, books, home workshop gear, hobby materials, house and garden equipment. It is the contention of this paper that sales of goods in this category have increased at a greater rate than that of merchandise whose consumption is not a function of time: furniture and furnishings, clothing, jewelry, and the like. The same sort of experiment may be performed for merchandise associated with travel; luggage and camping equipment are examples. Finally, the seller is urged to analyze the location of his customers through a statistical sampling of charge accounts. It is likely that he will not find the compact geographical patterns of an earlier period. The combination of discretionary purchasing power, time, and mobility, has resulted in "scrambled markets."

Free time and opportunities for travel have been increasing gradually since the turn of the century, but the general recognition of these two conditions (combined with widespread diffusion of discretionary purchasing power) has been of recent origin. The impact of this recognition on the market place may well be an explosive one since it is not likely that we have yet reached the end of work-week contraction nor is there any doubt concerning greater flexibility in movement during the coming years.

The implication is clear: the seller must recognize the effects of discretionary time and mobility on modes of living and adapt his product mix, promotion themes, and media selection to these changes. People have the time to *do* new things and the transportation facilities to *go* in new directions—to achieve a greater degree of self-actualization; these new frontiers will be translated into action in the market place in terms of *what* is bought and *where* (geographically) it is bought.

Until recent years any consideration of the utilization of time by consumers was largely in the realm of conjecture. Today, the bulk of the world's population still finds little choice: labor and the basic maintenance of life are its lot. However, in the United States and a few other technologically advanced countries, increasing productivity has provided the average consumer with some free choice in the utilization of a measurable portion of his time.

Similarly, our antecedents did not concern themselves with mobility simply because there was no choice; they were destined to be born, to produce, to consume, and to die in one place. Today the almost universal ownership of the private automobile in the United States has changed all this; the average consumer is no longer confined to animal locomotion or even mass transportation with its imposed directions and schedules. He is free to determine his own destination and route within the limits of time and pocketbook.

In short, the average American has acquired two new freedoms, *discretionary time* and *discretionary mobility*.

As in the case of all new opportunities to choose, patterns of choice are not self-evident but emerge from the interplay of psychological, social, economic, and political forces. Many interests and agencies are cognizant of these two new freedoms and are seeking to appraise their significance and influence their directions. None has a greater stake in discretionary time and discretionary mobility than the marketing institution since both areas of choice will have profound effects on consumer attitudes and wants as well as buying practices.

It should be emphasized that discretionary time and mobility assumed significance concurrently and part-and-parcel with the expansion and diffusion of discretionary purchasing power. It is the amalgam of these three areas of choice which is contributing much to the profile of the "new" American consumer. (Note that it is the concurrent emergence of the three areas of choice for the average consumer that is distinctively twentieth century and American.)

Consumer discretionary time and mobility on a significant scale are neither new nor future phenomena but have been growing in significance over several decades. Such diverse elements as increased productivity, unionization, the private automobile, and the paved highway have contributed. The fragmentary and overdue recognition and analysis of consumer time and mobility as contrasted with that bestowed upon purchasing power may be attributed in large part to the economist's inclination toward dollar figures and the but recently partially bridged gulf existing between economics and the other social sciences. It is the purpose of this article to offer a theoretical framework from which to advance and to explore some of the significant implications for management deriving from consumer time utilization and mobility.

DISCRETIONARY TIME

Since the late fifties economists and behavioral scientists have directed their attention to trends in the division of time between work and leisure and to the use of the increasing amount of leisure time, respectively. That hourly employees and many segments of the salaried group are spending less time at work is generally known. How people spend their free time is not yet clear. Cultural and moral questions are raised. Some observers have stressed the need for education in the use of leisure time. Studies of the purchasing patterns of different market segments give some indication of the use of non-productive time.

The increase in free time results from a number of changes. First, there is a later entrance into and an earlier retirement from the work force than was true only a few years ago. Second, for those members of the population who are producers, both work-days and work-weeks have been shortened; there are more holiday shut-downs and longer vacations. Third, there has been a tremendous increase in labor-saving devices in the home together with a shift from the household to industry and trade in the preparation for consumption of food, clothing, and shelter. These trends have occurred throughout the whole population (with some variations, of course) regardless of location, occupation, and income and they have occurred without any impairment of purchasing power: shorter work periods have been accompanied by higher rates of income; holidays and vacations "are on company time." The one major movement tending to decrease free time has been the increasing flow of women into the work force. However, it could be argued that this development has been more of a shift from non-economic work in the home to economically productive work in industry rather than an absolute decrease in free time. Interestingly, there seems to be a desire on the part of many to utilize freed time in activities that were once considered essential to life: cooking outdoors; home work-shops; do-it-yourself painting; and the manufacture of clothing in the home, for example.

The use of the term "leisure time" in current literature beclouds the real significance of free time. More appropriately, these non-working time periods might be called *discretionary time*, that is, time available for use at the individual's discretion and *essential time*, that is, time required for the maintenance of life: sleeping, eating (and the preparation of food), the act of clothing (and the production of clothing), and sheltering. Thus, an individual's time span might be divided into: (1) productive time (in the economic sense); (2) essential time (productive but in a non-economic sense); and (3) discretionary time.

So long as personal income for the bulk of the population was sufficient only to provide for the necessities of life, marketing was largely a process of physical distribution. It was with the advent of the discretionary purchasing power that marketing took on its dynamic character. However, discretionary purchasing power without discretionary time would have resulted in far different patterns of consumption and contributing marketing structures than those which exist today. Given a prosperous society but with workers on the job 10 hours a day, six days a week, with minimal holidays and no vacation period, consumption would be confined largely to up-graded food, clothing, and shelter. In other words, consumption would be limited to goods and services perceived by the consumer not to be related directly to the passage of time. This assumes that the family unit's pattern of living would be geared to that of the breadwinner(s), a point which might or might not be argued. However, because increased productivity has resulted in discretionary purchasing power *and* discretionary time the consumer has both time and money with which to harvest (or dissipate) the rewards of labor. The producer and his family have the time to travel, to enjoy, to learn, to create. Results in terms of marketing are evident on every hand: increasing gasoline consumption; the rise of boating as a recreation; stereo; home workshops; outdoor-living; television; renaissance in serious reading. Add to this the myriad of derived products and services and one gets some notion of the effect of discretionary time on buying and consumption patterns.

It should be noted that affluent Americans seem to spend their discretionary time consuming more than one product at a time—a concept of multiple consumption or concurrent consumption, if you will. If one goes to the theater, reading matter, food, and drink are mandatory. Many Americans could not possibly work in the yard without a radio and television or recordings provide an accompaniment for indoor discretionary time activities. Snack food sales have outrun population growth and food sales in general.[1] Perhaps this practice of concurrent consumption is one answer to the fear of limited or satiated demand!

Expansion has occurred in goods and services, the consumption of which is recognized by the consumer to be a function of time.

Of course, a significant proportion of discretionary purchasing power will be directed toward the acquisition of more exotic foods, better shelter facilities, more extensive wardrobes, no matter how great the discretionary time available. But it takes no more time to eat steak than it does to eat hamburger and the consumption of a $50,000 home takes no more time than does a $5,000 home. Conceivably, an individual might save all income above that needed to maintain a bare subsistence or devote all of it to bigger and better food, clothing, and shelter or divide it in some proportion between saving and up-graded necessities.[2] If any of these alternatives

---

[1] "Leisure Stirs Rush to Snacks," *Business Week*, February 26, 1966, p. 102.

[2] In this connection, care should be taken to distinguish between more of the same on the one hand and food, clothing, and shelter whose demand is derived from

were adopted, the individual's discretionary time would be given over to meditation. Except for the very aged, this is not likely; people will be doing and consuming something with discretionary time.

Thus time, as well as income, is a dimension of demand and consumption. An abundance of free time without purchasing power would result in a primitive civilization indeed. An abundance of purchasing power without free time existed to a degree in this country during World War II. The modern communist-dominated consumer has neither, while the American consumer has a relatively large measure of both. The existence of these two discretionary dimensions contributes to the unique character of the American market.

DISCRETIONARY MOBILITY

But to purchasing power and time, marketing people must add *mobility*. The marketing significance of consumer mobility goes far beyond the currently widely-held impression that travel is just another means of using up time.

Kelley points out that purchasing patterns may not necessarily be limited to a single metropolitan area in the future.[3] Russell's study of the relationship (or lack of relationship) between income and retail sales in local areas clearly exposes the effect of discretionary mobility on a number of preconceived notions regarding trading areas.[4] Paranka explores the trend toward interurban development, traces a profile of the interurban consumer, and enumerates some of the marketing implications, especially for retailing and advertising, in interurbia.[5] *Printers' Ink* cites specific cases of interurban competition:[6]

1) Madison *vs.* Chicago's northwest suburbs
2) Trenton *vs.* New York City and Philadelphia
3) Kentucky communities *vs.* Memphis, Cincinnati, and Nashville
4) Toledo *vs.* Detroit and Cleveland
5) Fort Worth *vs.* Dallas
6) Colorado Springs *vs.* Denver

---

time-consuming interests. Discretionary time activities have influenced the growth in demand for casual wear and the already cited snack foods, for example. Both have far outstripped trends in the demand for "conventional" clothing and food. Similar shifts have occurred in housing and furniture.

[3] Eugene J. Kelley, "Convenience in Consumer Purchasing," *Journal of Marketing*, Vol. 23, No. 1 (July, 1958), pp. 32–38.

[4] Vera Kilduff Russell, "The Relationship Between Income and Retail Sales," *Journal of Marketing*, Vol. XXI, No. 3 (January, 1957), pp. 329–32.

[5] Stephen Paranka, *Marketing Implications of Interurban Development* (Atlanta: Bureau of Business and Economic Research, School of Business Administration, Georgia State College of Business Administration, 1958), pp. 1–39.

[6] "The Frantic Competition to Lure More Shoppers Is Reaching Inter-City Stage," *Printers' Ink*, Vol. 265, No. 12 (December 19, 1958), pp. 7–9.

The significance of more extensive consumer mobility in terms of time and space can be inferred from a report prepared by the American Automobile Association which indicates that 23 states plus the District of Columbia rank travel among their three most important industries.[7] Many publishers have surveyed the travel characteristics of their readers, and state governments have been notably active in analyzing the inflow of travelers. A travel survey made by the Bureau of the Census during the first 15 weeks of 1957 produced the following data: (1) During the average winter day two million persons were away from home on trips.[8] (2) The American public took about forty-eight million round trips averaging 4.3 days per round trip during the first 15 weeks of 1957.[9] (3) Fifty-six per cent of the trips originated within standard metropolitan areas whereas forty-four per cent of the trips originated outside standard metropolitan areas.[10] (4) Fifty per cent of those making trips were in the labor force.[11] (5) Approximately two-thirds of those traveling were between the ages of 25 and 64; twenty-five per cent were in the age bracket up to 24 years of age and the remainder were 65 years of age and over.[12]

The figures in Table 1 show that Americans are an increasingly mobile society. Figure 1 reinforces the concept of mobility.

Two factors contributing to consumer mobility stand out: the private automobile and improved (and improving) highways. Advertising media have also advanced mobility significantly through their ability to penetrate beyond the immediate trading area and to inform and enthuse consumers about new experiences "beyond the horizon" but not beyond their means. To these facilitating and persuasive factors, the widespread existence of discretionary purchasing power and discretionary time should be added. These are fundamental or primary. Their actuality throughout the population makes consumer mobility possible and gives it marketing significance. Without discretionary purchasing power, the means of mobility and the reasons for mobility would be lacking. Without discretionary time, consumers would be stationary rather than mobile in terms of buying and consumption in the sense that consumers were stationary in past generations.

Consumer mobility is more than "travel," "shopping," and "tourism"—terms that are in common usage. More properly, the moving about which characterizes the "new" consumer might be termed *discretionary mobility*, a form of travel in which the individual is free to select des-

---

[7] *Americans on the Highway* (Washington, D.C.: American Automobile Association, 1956), p. 11.

[8] *Preliminary Report for 1957 Travel Survey* (Washington, D.C.: Transportation Division, Bureau of the Census, 1957), p. 2.

[9] *Ibid.*

[10] *Ibid.*, p. 29.

[11] *Ibid.*, p. 33.

[12] *Ibid.*, p. 41.

TABLE 1

POPULATION GROWTH AND TRAVEL GROWTH COMPARED

	Population		*Intercity Passenger Miles Traveled**	
Year	*Total (Millions)*	*% Change From 1929*	*Total (Billions)*	*% Change From 1929*
1929	122	—	216	—
1930	123	.8	220	1.9
1931	124	1.6	223	3.2
1932	125	2.5	203	−6.0
1933	126	3.3	203	−6.0
1934	126	3.3	219	1.4
1935	127	4.1	232	7.4
1936	128	4.9	259	19.9
1937	129	5.7	279	29.2
1938	130	6.6	277	28.2
1939	131	7.4	291	34.7
1940	132	8.2	309	43.1
1941	133	9.0	348	61.1
1942	135	10.7	306	41.7
1943	137	12.3	283	31.0
1944	138	13.1	298	38.0
1945	140	14.8	331	53.2
1946	141	15.6	403	86.6
1947	144	18.0	403	86.6
1948	147	20.5	414	91.7
1949	149	22.1	449	107.9
1950	152	24.6	473	119.0
1951	154	26.2	533	146.8
1952	157	28.7	573	165.3
1953	160	31.1	610	182.4
1954	162	32.8	625	189.4
1955	165	35.2	665	207.9
1956	168	37.7	697	222.7
1957	171	40.2	695	221.8
1958	174	42.6	705	226.4
1959	177	45.1	736	240.7
1960	180	47.5	759	251.4
1961	183	50.0	769	256.0
1962	186	52.5	802	271.3
1963	189	54.9	834	286.1
1964	191	56.6	876	305.6

* Figures are for *all* forms of transportation and reflect absolute changes, not shifts from one form of transportation to another.

SOURCES: Population Totals: *Statistical Abstract of the United States, 1965.* (Washington, D.C.: U.S. Department of Commerce, Bureau of the Census, *1965*), p. 5.

Passenger Mile Totals: *Bus Facts*, 1965 ed. (Washington, D.C.: National Association of Motor Bus Owners, 1965), p. 8.

tination and route. This is in contrast to *essential mobility*, that which is essential to the acquisition of the minimal essentials of existence. Thus, an individual's movements can be assigned to three categories: (1) productive mobility, that is, travel related to work as by salesmen, truck drivers, and executive travel; (2) essential mobility, that is, travel necessary to get to and from work and minimal travel necessary to acquire food, clothing, and shelter; (3) discretionary mobility, that is, travel that the individual is free to embark upon for personal satisfaction: pleasure, creative activity, hobbies, and distant ventures in shopping, for example.

It is, of course, true that some consumers, at their discretion or out of necessity, choose not to travel for purposes other than productive and essential. They may lack discretionary purchasing power or discretionary time or they may be committed to a habitual pattern of living inherited from an earlier generation. They do, however, represent a small and declining class and therefore do not typify today's and tomorrow's consumer.

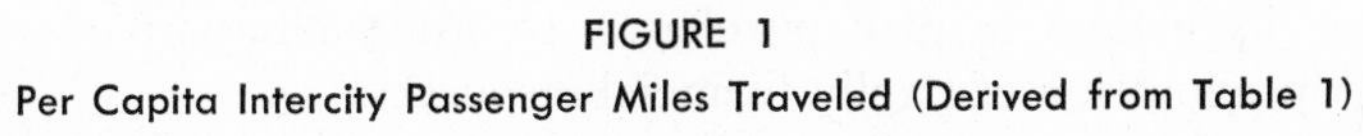

FIGURE 1

Per Capita Intercity Passenger Miles Traveled (Derived from Table 1)

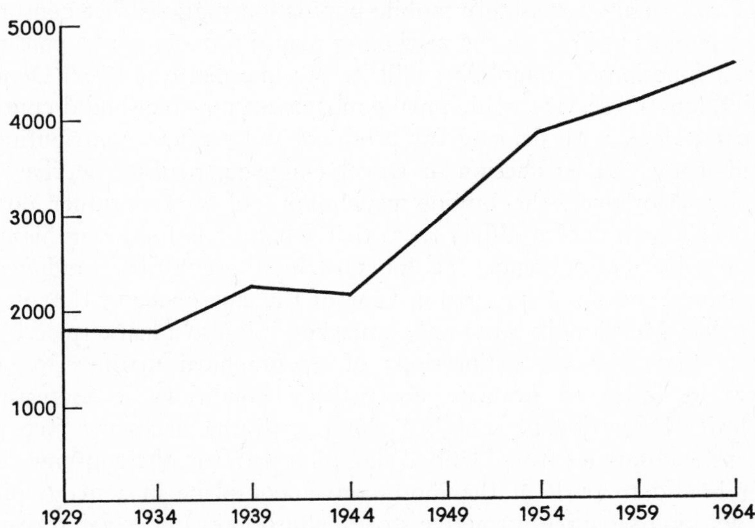

To describe an economy with widely diffused discretionary purchasing power and time, but without the means or inclination to travel borders on the ridiculous. It is essential then, that the discretionary dimensions of demand and consumption be expanded to three: purchasing power, time, and mobility. Recognizing the concurrent and pervading impact of the three dimensions on the American economy suggests a theoretical starting point toward an understanding of the buying and consuming interests of the American consumer.

IMPLICATIONS FOR MARKETING MANAGEMENT

As consumers become more aware of the uncommitted time at their disposal and as more such time becomes available to them, if current projections of working hours are accepted, they will be more inclined to acquire goods and utilize services whose consumption is perceived to be a function of time or whose demand is derived from time-consuming activities. Managers should be aware of this time dimension in appraising their line of products or services. Do the products or services release more time? Do they require time in their consumption? Implicit here is the assumption that products or services shorten the time required for effort conceived to be drudgery or use up time in activities which contribute to enjoyment, satisfaction, creation, and advancement. The moral and social implications for management are significant. In addition to products and services offered, managers will also want to consider time utilization as an appeal to be included in promotional efforts. Not bluntly, of course, but through market analysis of the use of discretionary time. In addition, consumers have time to plan purchases, to study alternatives, to think through the allocation of family financial resources.

The fact of an increasingly mobile population suggests that consumers are not points but lines on the marketing map. Products whose consumption is a function of immobility will be at some disadvantage.[13] Demand for products and services which make movement possible should continue to expand along with demand for products and services contributing to the efficiency and satisfaction of travel (luggage, roadside services, for example). Moreover, the buying psychology of the consumer on the move at his own choice differs from that when he is following his more habitual pattern of existence; the "purse-strings" are untied. Trading area concepts may need a reappraisal in view of the emergence of the interurban market. Megalopolis is not only a market; it is also a marketplace. This suggests that arbitrary delineations of geographical markets by antitrusters in order to evaluate competitive conditions is increasingly unrealistic. Discretionary mobility along with the necessary free time releases the consumer from habitual shopping patterns; the consumer is no longer bound to trade at the most convenient place in a geographical sense. Parking facilities, attractive stores, and opportunities for relaxation and pleasure take on added stature as competitive weapons in inter-center and inter-city competition. The consumer is tending to classify the process of buying as a satisfying, enjoyable activity, an adventure, a break in routine rather than a household chore. Finally, a more mobile market adds to the complexities of media selection: the advertiser must consider the point of departure, the route, and the destination in deciding where and when to advertise.

Discretionary purchasing power, time, and mobility exist today throughout the American market. Given a peace-time economy, it is reasonable to assume that the discretionary share of purchasing power, time, and mobility will expand rather than contract. These three discretionary dimensions of demand and consumption have implications

---

[13] For example, the Stanford Research Institute foresees the day when rental furnishings and homes may be more convenient than ownership. See: "Home Furnishings Head Toward a New Design," *Business Week*, August 14, 1965, p. 45.

for management with regard to product line, promotional appeals, media selection, and location.

Both product and convenience costs influence consumer purchasing behavior. The increased importance consumers are attaching to convenience offers a key to understanding consumer shopping behavior and is a major opportunity for marketers. Consumer valuation of several forms of convenience is discussed, with special attention devoted to place convenience.

14. THE IMPORTANCE OF CONVENIENCE IN CONSUMER PURCHASING*

Eugene J. Kelley†

CONVENIENCE FORMS AND MARKETING THEORY

Two factors are of utmost importance in understanding consumer shopping behavior. First, consumers making shopping decisions achieve an equilibrium between commodity costs and convenience costs. Second, convenience costs are assuming more importance as patronage determinants.

Commodity costs are defined as the monetary price paid the seller to obtain possession of goods and services. Convenience costs are incurred through the expenditure of time, physical and nervous energy, and money required to overcome the frictions of space and time, and to obtain possession of goods and services. For instance, a consumer shopping in the central business district spends time, energy, and frequently carfare or parking fees, in addition to commodity expenditures. Such costs have always been involved in trading decisions. The new emphasis on convenience does not necessarily mean that consumers are less price conscious than formerly; rather, insistence on convenience cost minimization has

* A 1967 revision of "The Importance of Convenience in Consumer Purchasing," *Journal of Marketing*, Vol. XXIII, No. 3 (July, 1958), pp. 32–38.

† The Pennsylvania State University.

been superimposed on the desire for economically favorable commodity transactions.

Shopping Costs

The question of consumer time expenditures for shopping is an interesting one. It has been estimated that there is a minimum of five billion adult leisure hours each week in the United States. This reflects in part a population consensus to accept a substantial share of the benefits of the production and marketing revolutions in increased leisure. Paradoxically, the increase in leisure time has been accompanied by a reaction against spending much of that leisure shopping. The modern family is confronted with too many more attractive possible uses of time.

Many forces favor higher consumer valuations of leisure and other convenience considerations. The suburban population movement with its living habit changes and broader family interests is one such force. In urban areas also, fundamental social forces are operating which have resulted in families functioning more as a group than as individuals in certain activities, even to the extent of buying together. Such forces favoring higher convenience cost valuations include the large numbers of working housewives, the age group imbalance within the population, and higher educational levels.

Consumer estimates of purchasing costs are determined by their evaluations of alternative trading and social opportunities. Purchase decisions are made at the point where the total of commodity and convenience costs are considered minimal.

On the supply side sellers are operating in what seems to be an increasingly standardized production and legal matrix which is tending to limit price competition. The relatively narrow price spread among most retailers carrying identical nationally advertised merchandise suggests a new importance for convenience costs in the strategy determination of sellers. It appears reasonable to speculate that the range of competitive advantage based on commodity costs will narrow. In this setting, it is probable that convenience considerations will assume more importance as determinants of purchase behavior and seller strategy, and that more of the competition of the future will focus on convenience considerations.

Ten Convenience Forms

The importance of convenience as a determinant of consumer acceptance of products and services can be observed in an increasingly wide range of convenience features built into new products and in new convenience forms appearing in the marketing system. Charles G. Mortimer, President of the General Foods Corporation, has described ten forms of convenience which the American consumer now expects almost as a matter of course.[1]

1. *Form Convenience*—cigarettes in various sizes and tips, and vest-pocket radios.
2. *Time Convenience*—typified by evening hours, and fresh fruits and vegetables out of season.
3. *Place Convenience*—life insurance in airline terminals, drive-it-yourself automobile rental services; and the planned shopping center.
4. *Quantity or Unit Convenience*—aspirin in tins of 12, or bottles of 500; and smaller pianos for the smaller home.
5. *Packaging Convenience*—disposable and utility packages; and the packaged vacation plan. The packaged home is already on the market.
6. *Readiness Convenience*—instant coffee; pre-cooked foods; and *The Reader's Digest.*
7. *Combination Convenience*—do it yourself kits; and combination and matched sets.
8. *Automatic Operations Convenience*—automatic kitchen equipment; power steering and brakes on automobiles; and automation in many fields.
9. *Selection Convenience*—the new variety of dairy products; and automobile color combinations.
10. *Credit Convenience*—cars; homes; vacation cruises; and education on credit.

Four Aspects of Place Convenience

Sellers should study all ten convenience forms to find areas in which consumer convenience costs may be reduced. This article is concerned specifically with place convenience. In maximizing place convenience advantages, sellers have related decisions at four levels to make about the spatial positions that products ideally should occupy in the market.

(1) The geographic area or areas in which the goods or services are to be offered must be selected. In these areas or markets are found the consumers of the goods. This seller decision usually is not of concern to the shopper who may choose from the offerings of many sellers of substitute products.

The shopping mobility of consumers has tended to be limited to one metropolitan area, but this may not be the case in the future. Perhaps some larger scale retailers may become concerned about competition between metropolitan areas as well as with competition within a metropolitan area. For instance, it may represent the same expenditure of convenience costs for a West Hartford resident to order by mail from Hartford, or even to make the trip to downtown Hartford. Conceivably, a Hartford department store could become concerned about the drawing

[1] Charles J. Mortimer, *Two Keys to Modern Marketing* (Scarsdale, New York: The Updegraff Press, Ltd., 1955), pp. 7–17.

power of New York, Boston, and Providence department stores, as well as competition from suburban Hartford stores.

On the other hand, as metropolitan areas grow together to form urban regions, the primate cities of New York, Chicago, and Los Angeles are likely to lose some of their retail leadership to burgeoning regional and provincial metropolitan areas. This may occur in the same fashion, and for much the same reasons, that the central business district has lost ground to suburban elements in the retail structure.

(2) The most satisfactory positions within the market must be selected from those offered by distributors and retailers selling space in the market. Channel-of-distribution decisions are involved. The one-stop shopping tendency of consumers has made channel selection more difficult for sellers in today's fluid market.

(3) Choices must be made among competing retail and wholesale institutions offering access to the customer. Should a full service wholesaler be utilized, or would a limited function wholesaler represent a better channel choice? Are urban or suburban positions preferred? What is the role of the shopping center?

The planned shopping center movement can be rationalized with some justification in terms of consumer convenience. At the same time, planned centers are more than devices for convenient shopping or mechanisms for retail sales expansion in suburban areas. Planned shopping centers are a basic part of the restructuring of metropolitan communities. Their long-term importance to the economy is based on a continuing reassessment by consumers of shopping and social activities. Consumer convenience is still probably the basis of the shopping center movement. But the social, economic, and architectural concepts underlying planned centers are geared to a new kind of social pattern and to what may be an eruption into a new American social dimension in which consumer desires will require new patterns of marketing.

(4) Problems of positioning of goods within outlets must be settled. Display and layout decisions are involved at this level. An experiment by Alfred Politz suggests the importance of convenience within the store. In studying the anatomy of the sale, he purchased and operated a large hardware store in Tampa, Florida. He found that if a product is sufficiently well known to get consumer acceptance and is conveniently located, the consumer will buy it in preference to a better known product. While the customer will not select a product he has not heard about, "the least little bit of inconvenience wipes out the impressiveness of even the best known brands."[2]

Conflicting Cost Considerations

A dominant characteristic of consumer goods marketing at present is the state of flux of consumer valuations of commodity and convenience

[2] Alfred Politz, "Politz Studies Store Customers." *Tide* Vol. 21 (September 28, 1956), pp. 20–21, from p. 21.

costs. While such developments as the discount house reflect strong consumer interest in the reduction of commodity costs, it is quite possible that convenience costs will increase in importance as patronage determinants for more low dollar value items. This will pose anew one of the most challenging problems facing retailers in our complex distribution system: offering the right mix of convenience and economy to customers. Rich rewards may go to merchants able to do this successfully. A wedding of the shopping center concept and the discount house idea represents one promising approach.

Convenience cost pressures are likely to affect more marketing agencies in the future. Some of the possible impacts on planned shopping centers and established business districts are suggested below.

CONVENIENCE FORCES AND THE RETAIL STRUCTURE

Planned Center Increase

The shopping center movement is so new that currently two-thirds of existing centers are less than five years old. This fact, together with the predicted center expansion, indicates that the full impact of the movement has yet to be felt. A fundamental change in the retail structure of metropolitan communities seems certain, as a result of shopping center growth. Over 10,000 planned shopping centers are now in operation. Estimates have been made that by 1975, 17,500 of them will be operating. This means a planned shopping center for each 14,000 of a projected 1975 population of 245 million. This expansion is not expected to be uninterrupted. Many poorly planned intermediate centers are particularly vulnerable to new competition.

Individual stores and shopping centers are tending to be larger. Department store branches of 300,000 square feet, and super markets of 50,000 square feet have already appeared. A minimum site for regional centers used to be considered fifty acres. Regional center developers are now thinking in terms of one hundred acres as a minimum site. Tracts of this size are extremely expensive, especially if they are in or near large cities. The increasing size of regional centers may mean that in the future such centers will be located farther from large population concentrations, and nearer the suburban periphery.

Consumer convenience considerations also set a limit to the growth of individual stores and centers. For instance, it is generally agreed that shoppers resist walking more than 600 feet from their parked cars to the nearest center store. With planned centers, this suggests a limit for the maximum parking distance that can be used before the planned center loses its advantages over unplanned shopping districts.

The Distance Concept and Convenience

The distance concept involves time-cost elements rather than a purely spatial one. High speed roads enabling consumers to travel farther from home on shopping trips are changing consumer views on distance. In our society of automobile-borne suburbanites, distance between metropolitan points will increasingly be judged on a time basis, not a mileage basis. The impact of this on established retail patterns is already evident. Downtown retailers have had to compete aggressively for suburban business in order to hold a satisfactory market position. Effective downtown competition for suburban trade is still possible. Indeed, a pattern for the rehabilitation of central business districts has developed. It includes improving access, traffic, and parking conditions; modernizing physical facilities; conducting imaginative promotions; and strengthening mass transportation. In short, it means restoring some of the lost convenience aspects to central business district shopping.

Changing Functions in the Metropolitan Retail Structure

The central business district and suburban shopping center provide essential but different services to the community.[3] Retail functions within the central business district and the other elements of the metropolitan retail structure are being modified. Store locations are shifting in the inner core, inner belt, and outer belt of the central business district and main business thoroughfares. Similarly, retailers in planned and unplanned secondary commercial sub-districts, neighborhood business streets, small store clusters, and planned regional shopping centers are modifying functions to adapt to the needs of consumers living and shopping over a wider area. The downtown area may respond by becoming more of a business, service, and recreational center and less of a mercantile one. Opinions on this vary widely. Frank Lloyd Wright visualizes the city of the future without a central shopping district. Others anticipate a downtown renaissance stimulated in part by shopping center competition, which will force more downtown property owners and merchants into rehabilitation and redesign programs.

Other Dimensions of Convenience

In addition to spatial and temporal aspects, convenience has social and esthetic dimensions. This is one reason shopping centers are likely to play an increasingly important role in community social life. All shopping centers are likely to benefit by following a policy of community identification, although the benefits are particularly apparent with the larger community and regional centers. Auditoriums, meeting rooms, restaurants, and other facilities making shopping more convenient are found in more planned centers. As more planned centers include such amenities, shopping centers may come to resemble earlier market places, which served social as well as trading functions.

---

[3] Eugene J. Kelley, "Retail Structure of Urban Economy," *Traffic Quarterly*, Vol. 9, No. 3 (July, 1955), pp. 411–430, from p. 411.

Consumers favor centers in which merchandise is presented conveniently, informally, and interestingly. Shopping-center planning, therefore, extends logically to promotions and events calculated to restore some of the excitement and pleasure to shopping. The modified bazaar concept of the center is likely to gain favor as weather-controlled centers without window displays and partitions come into being. For instance, Southdale, the new regional center outside Minneapolis, has a glass enclosed mall connecting the various stores in the center.

Convenience and New Retail Types

New store types are likely to appear in planned centers. Since shopping centers are located on choice, relatively low cost land compared to downtown stores, one floor retailing operations are possible to an extent not practical downtown. This may mean a reduction in handling costs and in the number of people needed to conduct and supervise operations. Some specialty stores in planned centers should be in a position to offer more variety in prices and styles than downtown specialty stores operating in less space.

Convenience pressures may provide a stimulus for other retailing developments offering lower convenience costs to consumers. Among these may be increased direct-to-consumer selling, catalogue and telephone selling, perhaps a combination of television and telephone selling, and automatic vending machines. Improved vending equipment selling an increasingly broad variety of merchandise could turn some planned centers and store clusters into round-the-clock merchandising machines.

Implications for Decision Making

The success of convenience based innovations, such as planned shopping centers, raises questions about the role of spatial and other convenience considerations in marketing. The shopping center movement is distinguished by its spatial differentiation from other elements in the metropolitan retail structure. Essentially, consumers have attempted to overcome friction of space; and sellers have responded by offering a spatially or convenience-differentiated product. The results have been outstanding. Yet many sellers have ignored the lessons implicit in shopping center success. In most retailing operations the major concentration of managerial attention is still focused on the product and the promotion of the product, while the convenience conditions, surrounding the sale of the product receive little study. But the retailing process exists in space over time; and retailers are concerned with the creation of place and time as well as possession utilities. Indeed, the very art of marketing is based on the skillful manipulation of spatial, temporal, and ownership forces in the market to achieve that objective.

Understanding of the current state of the art requires acceptance of change itself as the dominant characteristic of marketing. If understanding of the process of market change, the forces producing change, and, therefore, ability to develop policies under accelerated change conditions is to be increased, more attention to the convenience aspects of marketing seems justified.

Measurement of convenience costs, while difficult, is not impossible. Reilly's Law represents one approach to quantifying some convenience costs. Reilly discovered from a three-year national study of retailing dynamics, which began in 1927, that retail business gravitated from smaller cities and towns in accordance with a definite law. Reilly based his law of retail gravitation on two rules. The first is that, the larger the city, the more outside trade it will draw. The second rule is that a city draws more trade from nearby towns than distant ones.

Reilly's contribution was in providing a quantitative measure of the rate that trade increases as the population of a city increases. His law of retail gravitation follows: Two cities attract retail trade from any intermediate city or town in the vicinity of the breaking point approximately in direct proportion to the population of the two cities and in inverse proportion to the square of the distances (via most direct improved automobile highway) from these two cities to the intermediate town.[4]

The law can be supplemented by discounts based on surveys, and observations to obtain approximations of convenience cost considerations in trade areas. Factors such as time expenditures, distance (including distances to the store and within the store), and intervening shopping opportunities can be isolated in individual experiments. Development of a consumer-distance concept to measure the costs of various locations is possible. This could be based on the number of consumers within an area multiplied by driving time minutes from a location. But the core of convenience analysis lies in the areas of consumer psychology and sociology. This means that marketers will have to absorb more of what these and other disciplines, in addition to economics, have to contribute to marketing theory.

More goods and services will be distributed at the price in convenience and commodity costs that consumers are willing to pay, as more sellers develop convenience based policies. It seems probable that sellers reacting ponderously to the new consumer assessment of convenience costs will suffer. On the other hand, sellers creatively alert to the importance of convenience costs to contemporary consumers, and who adjust strategy accordingly, should strengthen their market position. These sellers will also contribute to producing the volume of transactions necessary to maintain and expand the American economy.

---

[4] William J. Reilly, *The Law of Retail Gravitation* (New York: Pilsbury Publishers, Inc., 2nd ed.), 1953, p. 9.

Social class frequently exerts a significant influence on consumer purchasing behavior. Differences as well as similarities exist within each social class. The concept of under- and overprivileged families is introduced as an example of an intraclass difference. In some situations, social class, like income, may not be a relevant factor in explaining market behavior.

15. THE SIGNIFICANCE OF SOCIAL STRATIFICATION IN SELLING*

Richard P. Coleman†

Dating back to the late 1940's, advertisers and marketers have alternately flirted with and cooled on the notion that W. Lloyd Warner's social class concept[1] is an important analytic tool for their profession. The Warnerian idea that six social classes constitute the basic division of American Society has offered many attractions to marketing analysts when they have grown dissatisfied with simple income categories or census-type occupational categories and felt a need for more meaningful classifications, for categorizations of the citizenry which could prove more relevant to advertising and marketing problems. However, in the course of their attempts to apply the class concept, marketers have not always found it immediately and obviously relevant. Sometimes it has seemed to shed light on advertising and merchandising problems and at other times it hasn't—with the result that many analysts have gone away disenchanted, deciding that social classes are not much more useful than income categories and procedurally far more difficult to employ.

It is the thesis of this writer that the role of social class has too often been misunderstood or oversimplified, and that if the concept is applied in a more sophisticated and realistic fashion, it will shed light on a great many problems to which, at first glance, it has not seemed particularly relevant. What we propose to do here, then, is discuss and illustrate a few

---

* Reprinted from "The Significance of Social Stratification in Selling," *Proceedings of the Winter Conference of the American Marketing Association*, 1960, pp. 171–84.

† Social Research, Inc.

[1] See W. Lloyd Warner, Marchia Meeker, Kenneth Eells, *Social Class in America* (Chicago: Science Research Associates, 1949).

of these more subtle, more refined and (it must be acknowledged) more complicated ways of applying social class analyses to marketing and advertising problems. In other words, the purpose of this paper is to clarify *when* and *in what ways* social class concepts are significant in selling, and to suggest when they might not be as significant as other concepts, or at least need to be used in concert with other analytic categories.

THE WARNERIAN SOCIAL CLASSES

The six social classes which are referred to in this paper are those which W. Lloyd Warner and his associates have observed in their analyses of such diverse communities as Newburyport, Massachusetts,[2] Natchez, Mississippi,[3] Morris, Illinois,[4] Kansas City, Missouri,[5] and Chicago. These social classes are groups of people who are more or less equal to one another in prestige and community status; they are people who readily and regularly interact among themselves in both formal and informal ways; they form a "class" also to the extent that they share the same goals and ways of looking at life. It is this latter fact about social classes which makes them significant to marketers and advertisers.

Briefly characterized, the six classes are as follows, starting from the highest one and going down.[6]

1. The Upper-Upper or "Social Register" Class is composed of locally prominent families, usually with at least second or third generation wealth. Almost inevitably, this is the smallest of the six classes—with probably no more than one-half of one per cent of the population able to claim membership in this class. The basic values of these people might be summarized in these phrases: living graciously, upholding the family reputation, reflecting the excellence of one's breeding, and displaying a sense of community responsibility.

2. The Lower-Upper or "Nouveau Riche" Class is made up of the more recently arrived and never-quite-accepted wealthy families. Included in this class are members of each city's "executive elite," as well as founders of large businesses and the newly well-to-do doctors and law-

[2] See W. Lloyd Warner and Paul Lunt, *The Social Life of a Modern Community* (New Haven: Yale University Press, 1941).

[3] See Allison Davis, Burleigh B. Gardner and Mary R. Gardner, *Deep South* (Chicago: University of Chicago Press, 1941).

[4] See W. Lloyd Warner and Associates, *Democracy in Jonesville* (New York: Harper & Brothers, 1949).

[5] The writer's observation on the Kansas City social class system will be included in a forthcoming volume on middle age in Kansas City, currently being prepared for publication by the Committee on Human Development of the University of Chicago.

[6] Some of the phrases and ideas in this characterization have been borrowed from Joseph A. Kahl's excellent synthesizing textbook, *The American Class Structure* (New York: Rinehart & Company, Inc., 1957).

yers. At best only one and one-half per cent of Americans rank at this level—so that all told, no more than 2 per cent of the population can be counted as belonging to one layer or the other of our Upper Class. The goals of people at this particular level are a blend of the Upper-Upper pursuit of gracious living and the Upper-Middle Class's drive for success.

3. In the Upper-Middle Class are moderately successful professional men and women, owners of medium-sized businesses and "organization men" at the managerial level; also included are those younger people in their twenties or very early thirties who are expected to arrive at this occupational status level—and possibly higher—by their middle or late thirties (that is, they are today's "junior executives" and "apprentice professionals" who grew up in such families and/or went to the "better" colleges). Ten per cent of Americans are part of this social class and the great majority of them are college educated. . . .

4. At the top of the "Average Man World" is the Lower-Middle Class. Approximately 30 per cent or 35 per cent of our citizenry can be considered members of this social class. For the most part they are drawn from the ranks of non-managerial office workers, small business owners, and those highly-paid blue-collar families who are concerned with being accepted and respected in white-collar dominated clubs, churches, and neighborhoods. The key word in understanding the motivations and goals of this class is Respectability, and a second important word is Striving. The men of this class are continually striving, within their limitations, to "do a good job" at their work, and both men and women are determined to be judged "respectable" in their personal behavior by their fellow citizens. Being "respectable" means that they live in well-maintained homes, neatly furnished, in neighborhoods which are more-or-less on the "right side of town." It also means that they will clothe themselves in coats, suits, and dresses from "nice stores" and save for a college education for their children.

5. At the lower half of the "Average Man World" is the Upper-Lower Class, sometimes referred to as "The Ordinary Working Class." Nearly 40 per cent of all Americans are in this class, making it the biggest. The proto-typical member of this class is a semi-skilled worker on one of the nation's assembly lines. Many of these "Ordinary Working Class" people make very good money, but do not bother with using it to become "respectable" in a middle-class way. Whether they just "get by" at work, or moonlight to make extra, Upper-Lowers are oriented more toward enjoying life and living well from day to day than saving for the future or caring what the middle class world thinks of them. They try to "keep in step with the times" (indeed, one might say the "times" are more important than the "Joneses" to this class), because they want to be at least Modern, if not Middle Class. That is, they try to take advantage of progress to live more comfortably and they work hard enough to keep themselves safely away from a slum level of existence.

6. The Lower-Lower Class of unskilled workers, unassimilated ethnics, and the sporadically employed comprises about 15 per cent of the population, but this class has less than 7 or 8 per cent of the purchasing power, and will not concern us further here. Apathy, fatalism, and a point of view which justifies "getting your kicks whenever you can" characterize the approach toward life, and toward spending money, found among the people of this class.

Now, we do not mean to imply by these characterizations that the members of each class are always homogeneous in behavior. To suggest such would be to exaggerate greatly the meaning of social classes. To properly understand them, it must be recognized that there is a considerable variation in the way individual members of a class realize these class goals and express these values. . . .

All of this is by way of indicating that the millions of individuals who compose each social class are not necessarily similar or identical in their consumption patterns, even though they are of equal status socially and share a set of goals and points of view which are class-wide. Thus far, the literature on social class in both marketing journals and sociological publications has emphasized the similarities of people within classes and rarely pointed out these variations. This has been necessary, of course, in order to properly introduce the concept and educate social scientists and marketers to its utility, but it has led on occasion to naive misuse of the concept and ultimate disillusion. In my view, it has come time for us to advance into a more sophisticated application of social class to marketing problems, which involves awareness of the differences as well as similarities within each class.

SOCIAL CLASS VERSUS INCOME

Let us proceed now to stating the basic significance of this class concept for people in the selling field. In the first place, it explains why income categories or divisions of Americans are quite often irrelevant in analyzing product markets, consumers' shopping habits and store preferences, and media consumption. For example, if you take three families, all earning around $8,000 a year, but each from a different social class, a radical difference in their ways of spending money will be observed.

An Upper-Middle Class family in this income bracket, which in this case might be a young lawyer and his wife or perhaps a college professor, is apt to be found spending a relatively large share of its resources on housing (in a "prestige" neighborhood), on rather expensive pieces of furniture, on clothing from quality stores, and on cultural amusements or club memberships. Meanwhile, the Lower-Middle Class family—headed, we will say, by an insurance salesman or a fairly successful grocery store owner, perhaps even a Diesel engineer—probably has a better house, but in not so fancy a neighborhood; it is apt to have as full a wardrobe though not so expensive, and probably more furniture though none by name designers. These people almost certainly have a much bigger savings account in the bank.

Finally, the Working Class family—with a cross-country truck driver or a highly-paid welder as its chief wage-earner—is apt to have less house and less neighborhood than the Lower-Middle or Upper-Middle family; but it will have a bigger, later model car, plus more expensive appliances in its kitchen and a bigger TV set in its living room. This family will spend less on clothing and furniture, but more on food if the number of children is greater, as is likely. One further difference: the man of the house probably spends much more on sports, attending baseball games (for example), going hunting and bowling, and perhaps owning a boat of some description.

The wives in these three families will be quite noticeably different in the kind of department stores they patronize, in the magazines they read, and in the advertising to which they pay attention. The clothing and furniture they select for themselves and their families will differ accordingly, and also because they are seeking quite different goals. This has become very clear in studies Social Research, Inc., has done for the *Chicago Tribune* on the clothing tastes of Chicagoland women, for the Kroehler Company on the place of furniture in American homes, and for MacFadden Publications on the purchasing patterns and motivations of their romance magazines' Working Class readers.[7] (These have been contrasted in turn with the motivations of Middle Class women who read service magazines.) . . .

Up to now, we've been talking about product areas—clothing, furniture, and residential neighborhoods—where the relationship between social class and quality of goods purchased is highest. In these things the so-called "Quality Market" and the Upper-Middle (and higher) markets coincide. That is, the purchasers of highest quality clothing and highest quality furniture are more nearly from the Upper-Middle and Upper social classes than from the highest income categories, and so on it goes down the hierarchy. The correlation between price of goods purchased and social class is relatively quite high in these product areas while the correlation between price paid and annual income is lower than one might expect. . . .

THE "OVERPRIVILEGED" AS "QUALITY MARKET"

Within each social class group there are families and individuals whose incomes are above average for their class. The Upper-Lower family with an income above $7,000 a year—sometimes a product of both husband

[7] This study has been published under the name *Workingman's Wife* (Oceana Press: New York City, 1959) by Lee Rainwater, Richard P. Coleman, and Gerald Handel.

and wife working, and sometimes not—is an example of this. So, too, is the Lower-Middle Class business owner or salesman who makes more than $10,000 a year, but has no interest in either the concerts or country clubs of Upper-Middledom and hence is still Lower-Middle Class. The Upper-Middle Class couple with more than $25,000 a year at its disposal but no desire to play the "society game" of subscription balls or private schools is also in this category. These are what might be called the "overprivileged" segments of each class. They are not "overprivileged" in the absolute sense, of course; they are "overprivileged," however, relative to what is required or needed by families in their class. After they have met the basic expectations and standards of their group in the housing, food, furnishing, and clothing areas, they have quite a bit of money left over which is their equivalent of "discretionary income."

In much the same way, each class has its "underprivileged" members; in the Upper-Middle Class these are the younger couples who haven't made the managerial ranks yet, the college professors, the genteel professionals, and a few downwardly mobile people from high-status backgrounds who are trying to hang on to what fragments of status they have left—for the most part these people are below the $12,000-a-year mark and they can barely meet some of the basic requirements of Upper-Middle life, much less experience any of its little luxuries; in the Lower-Middle Class these are the poorly paid bank tellers, the rows of bookkeepers in railroad offices, the school teachers with considerably more status aspiration than income; and in the Upper-Lower Class it is almost any family earning less than $4,500 or $5,000 a year, at today's rates of pay in metropolitan areas.

In the middle of each class's income range are its "average" members, families who are neither underprivileged nor overprivileged by the standards of their class. You might think of this as the Upper-Middle Class family between $12,000 and $20,000 a year, the Lower-Middle family in the $7,000–$9,000 range, and the Upper-Lower family near $6,000 per annum. However, this word of caution is necessary: a lot of people in the middle income range of their class see themselves as underprivileged because they are aspiring to become one of the "overprivileged" in their class or to move on up the ladder to a higher class. . . .

In summary, today's market for quality goods and quality brands is not necessarily drawn from what has historically been described as the "Quality Market" of Upper-Middle and Upper-Class people, nor even necessarily from the highest income categories. Rather, in many instances, it is drawn from those people within each social level who have the most discretionary income available for enjoying life's little extras above and beyond the requirements of their class. Every merchandiser and advertiser ought to take a good hard look at what he is selling and ask himself if it bears this particular relationship to the class and income picture. If his product does, and if his brand is one of the more expensive, then he should merchandise it not as if it were just for social climbers or for the upper classes, but rather as part of the Better Life, U.S.A. If, on the other hand, his brand is one of the least expensive, then he is not just selling to the poor, but rather to those in all classes who feel it is only sensible on their part to settle for a brand such as his and save the difference for other things which are more important in their statement of social class aspiration and identity.

SOCIAL CLASS ISN'T ALWAYS IMPORTANT

Now, to make the picture complete, it must be pointed out that Social Research, Inc., has found some products in which the income factor is all-important and the social class variable is relevant only to the extent that it is correlated with income. Perhaps the most perfect example of this is the market for air conditioners in the Southwestern cities. There, everybody—except the sickly and the extremely old-fashioned—agrees that air conditioning one's home is imperative if summer is to be survived with any degree of comfort. Consequently the expensiveness of a family's air conditioning equipment—whether centrally installed, or window units to the number of four, three, two, or one—is directly correlated with family income. It is not merely a function of discretionary income—as in our example about purchase of medium-priced cars; it is instead almost completely a function of total annual income. If more Upper-Middles than Upper-Lowers are fully air-conditioned it is only because more of them can afford to be; it is not because Upper-Middles as a group are placing higher priority on the air-conditioned existence.

Undoubtedly air conditioners are not alone in being classless—so that one more thing the marketer who uses social class in a truly sophisticated way needs to understand is that there can be occasions when it is an irrelevant variable. Realizing this, he will not become disenchanted with social class when he finds a marketing problem where it does not shed light or where it does not seem pertinent. Of course, he will want to make sure that in advertising such a product there is indeed no need to take class into account. After all, some apparently classless products are properly sold to the market in a segmental approach, appealing first on one ground to one class, then on other grounds to another.

There are other products—and probably air conditioning is one of them and children's play clothes may be another—where this is not necessary. For such products some factor, such as physical comfort (in the one case) or simple durability (in the other), is so basic in the consumer's consideration that all other motivations pale into insignificance beside it. There are even products, like beer, where the democratic approach—that is, a tone of "let's-all-be-good-fellows-together" is exactly right and segmental appeals or snob stories are all wrong.

Another aspect to the sophisticated employment of social class refers back to the point made earlier that social class groups are not always homogeneous. It must be recognized that at times a product's market is formed by "highbrows" from the Upper-Upper Class on down to the Lower-Middle, or by "suburbanites" and suburban-minded people of all classes—in which case the social class variable may confuse a market analysis more than clarify it.

Particularly must merchandisers and market analysts beware of equating "Class" with "Brow"; for they are not synonymous. For example, the Upper-Middle Class and those above it are mainly middlebrow in taste (veering toward an all-American lower-middlebrow level of preferences in television shows and advertising messages) even though the majority of highbrows are found at this level. At times advertisers have made the mistake of assuming that the Upper-Middle Class should be appealed to in a highly sophisticated fashion—and though this is just fine if the product itself is likely to appeal primarily to the Manhattanized type of Upper-Middle, it is not correct if it is expected to sell to the kind of doctor in Dubuque who enjoys a visit to New York every now and then but would never want to live there.

In short, not only must the sophisticated marketer abandon social class in favor of income categories on occasion in his analysis and interpretation of a market, he must recognize that at times both income and class are superseded in importance by divisions of the public into brow levels, by divisions into "high mobiles" and "low mobiles," innovators and non-innovators, inner-directed and other-directed, urbanites, suburbanites, ex-urbanites, ruralites, and Floridians, or what have you. Usually, of course, fullest understanding of a market will require that social class be linked in with whichever sub-categorization proves pertinent from among those in the catalogue just recited, much as income and class were linked together for fullest comprehension of the car market.

As a final point, let it be noted that the way of life and the goals of people in each social class are in perpetual flux. Neither the "who" of each class nor "what motivates them" are constants to be assumed without continual re-evaluation. Right now, particularly, it is very clear that our society is changing. Every year the collar-color line is breaking down further. More blue-collar workers are becoming Middle-Class as well as middle income and Modern, and a white-collar position is less and less a guarantee of Lower-Middle status. As a consequence of this, the Lower-Middle Class is perhaps somewhat more "materialistic" in outlook and slightly less "respectability" conscious than it was 25 years ago, or even 8. Meanwhile, for men and women to achieve Upper-Middle status without college backgrounds is becoming more and more difficult, so that this class is turning much more worldly-wise and well-read, much less conventionally bourgeois than it was in the zenith of Babbitt's day.

In short, the form of our society and its division into social classes is not fixed as of Yankee City in 1931, Jonesville in 1944, Kansas City in 1952, or St. Louis in 1960. We won't be able to say exactly the same things about either the classes themselves or their relationships to specific markets by next year at this time. This fact about the American class structure, that it is not static, that it is in the process of change, is in itself important to merchandisers, to advertisers, to anyone in selling. Among other things, it means that undoubtedly they have played a part in past changes and can play a leading role in directing future changes. But of more direct concern here, to the marketing analyst it means that if he allows his stratification concept to become dated, his use of it will cease as of that moment to be sophisticated.

B. Market Segmentation and Consumer Behavior

In addition to the number of consumers and their incomes, the distribution of consumers over space is important to marketers. Changes in population distribution are producing important economic, social, and marketing consequences. Interurbia is defined as "an agglomeration of cities and surrounding, densely populated, nonfarm counties." Marketers have a vital interest in the commercial impact of interurbia, and in the problems and opportunities created by this new population distribution pattern. Interurbian psychology and advertising media factors are discussed.

16. INTERURBIA: THE CHANGING FACE OF AMERICA*

NOTE: This article summarizes a presentation dealing with the rapid evolution of the now-familiar phenomenon of *suburbia* into an infinitely more complex social pattern. The presentation developed from a partnership involving the J. Walter Thompson Company and the School of Architecture and Design of Yale University. William H. Whyte, sociologist, an editor of *Fortune* and author of "The Organization Man," cooperated in developing some of the implications of the cooperative study.

BACKGROUND

As a nation, we did not reckon with the *pace* of our growth.

The quickened pace of our population growth has caused the Census

* Memo of the J. Walter Thompson Company, May 10, 1960.

Bureau to increase its forecast for 1965 by four million . . . its 1970 forecast by over 7 million.

The dimensions of the automobile boom were not foreseen either. In 1953, hard-boiled automotive economists forecast 50 million cars on the road by 1959. The fact is that 58,591,000 cars were registered in 1959. This forecasting error of approximately 8.6 million cars represents about half the passenger cars in Western Europe.

We failed to anticipate many factors that affect housing. By the late nineteen-forties, we did include playgrounds in city apartments built for young families. But we did not foresee the number of cars they would buy. And we did not reckon with the demand for television sets, automatic washing machines, and air conditioners that made these buildings electrically obsolete while they were still new. Most serious of all, most city apartments do not have enough bedrooms for the baby crop. So the young families move out to the suburbs.

But they aren't much better off in the suburbs either. There aren't enough bedrooms for babies in the typical two-bedroom house built in the '40's. And many lack garages and carports. Young owners invest millions trying to expand their little homes. Many give up and move out. Thanks to the automobile and the rise in real income, they can move still further from town, to find more space in the far suburbs in new homes they soon outgrow once again.

Business planners in the suburbs also failed to anticipate our growth. Many post-war shopping centers allowed only two square feet of parking space for every square foot of selling space. But today often a ratio of five square feet to one square foot is required.

As a result . . .

The 600-mile city arrives unheralded.

One of the main characteristics of this dynamic growth is the rapid evolution of the now-familiar phenomenon known as *Suburbia* into an infinitely more complex social pattern now known as INTERURBIA.

The most graphic demonstration of this evolution is in New York City. There, as elsewhere, it is no longer quite realistic to speak of a city and its suburbs. The New York metropolitan area has long been a conglomeration of many cities and many suburbs. In terms of population and physical plant, the "city" goes beyond the already obsolete limits of the New York metropolitan area. Indeed, it is no longer a Greater New York, or a Greater Boston, Philadelphia, Baltimore or Washington. It is virtually one 600-mile city from Maine to Virginia. Actually, there are only two stretches in this 600-mile city—one of 2 miles, the other of 17 miles, which are not part of metropolitan areas. And while this 600-mile "city" comprises less than 2 per cent of its nation's land area, it represents 24 per cent of its retail sales. (See Figure I.)

Interurbia, by definition, has these characteristics: it contains two or more adjacent metropolitan areas with either two cities of 100,000 or

FIGURE 1

Core Cities (in Black) with Today's Adjacent Densely Populated Areas (in Gray)

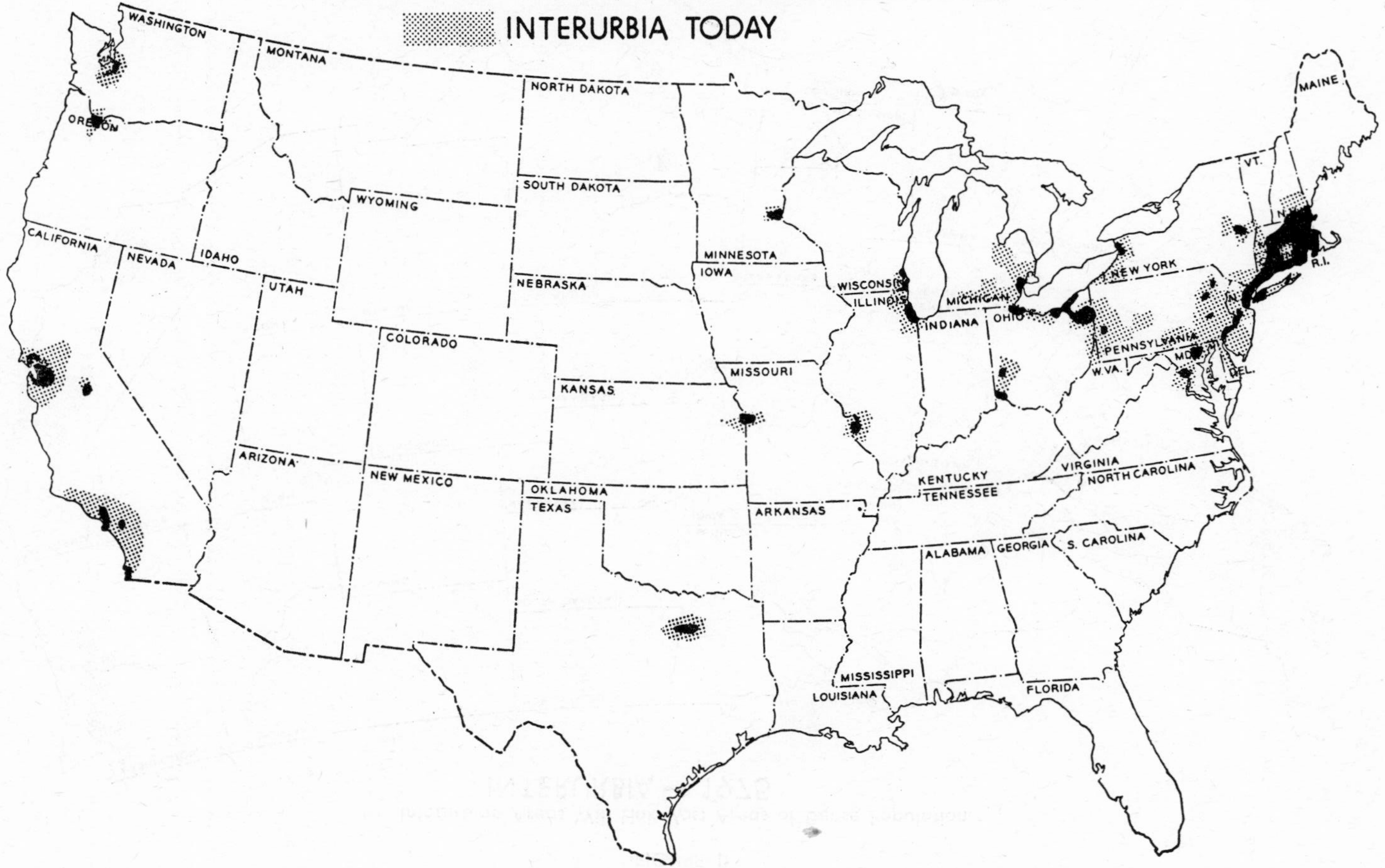

INTERURBIA TODAY

WASHINGTON
MONTANA
NORTH DAKOTA
OREGON
SOUTH DAKOTA
WYOMING
CALIFORNIA
NEVADA
IDAHO
MINNESOTA
IOWA
NEBRASKA
UTAH
COLORADO
KANSAS
MISSOURI
WISCONSIN
ILLINOIS
MICHIGAN
INDIANA
OHIO
NEW YORK
PENNSYLVANIA
W.VA.
MD.
DEL.
VT.
MAINE
R.I.
ARIZONA
NEW MEXICO
OKLAHOMA
TEXAS
ARKANSAS
KENTUCKY
TENNESSEE
VIRGINIA
NORTH CAROLINA
ALABAMA
GEORGIA
S. CAROLINA
MISSISSIPPI
LOUISIANA
FLORIDA

FIGURE II

Interurbian Areas Will Link Vast Areas of Dense Population

INTERURBIA — 1975

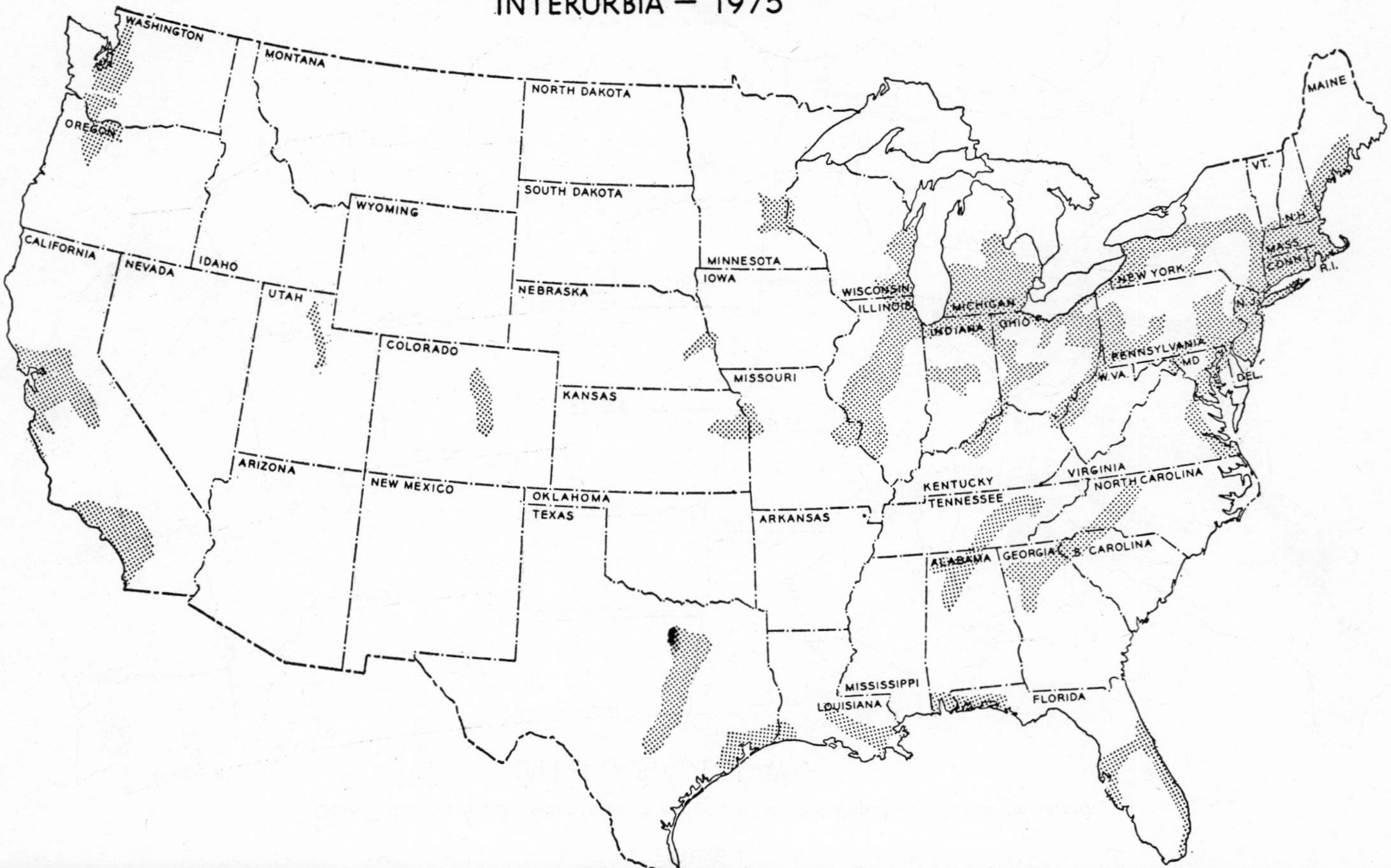

more, or one city of 100,000 and 3 cities of 25,000 or more, plus adjacent counties with less than 25 per cent farm population and more than 100 people per square mile.

There are now 14 of these Interurbias in the U.S. based on the last Census—plus two Interurbias in the making in the Southwest. They dot the landscape of the Eastern Seaboard, Midwest, Southwest and Pacific Coast. Together they account for almost half of the country's population of 178 million and for more than half of its retail sales, yet they stand on less than 4 per cent of the country's total land. Within these fourteen Interurbias, an average of 620 people live in every square mile—over 12 times as many people per square mile as there are in the rest of the country. (See map—Figure II.)

There are also some areas that did not at the last census quite fit the definition of an Interurbia, but that almost certainly will fit it soon.

One of these is along the Florida coast and across the middle of the peninsula. North of Miami the coastal strip is already filled in for many miles. A big Interurbian growth is now under way south of Tampa and is beginning to touch the Fort Myers area. By 1965, this Interurbia will probably account for two thirds of the population of Florida.

Another potential Interurbia is to be found in the Piedmont area. So far this long chain of cities has reflected only the first stage of urbanization. Cities have grown faster than surrounding country. And there are long gaps of open country between many of the cities. But the area is growing faster than the states it lies in and shows signs of becoming an Interurbia in the near future.

WHAT HAS CAUSED OUR CITIES TO MERGE

The explanation is quite simple, although the results are incredibly complicated. What has happened is that homes and jobs, at one time closely tied to each other and firmly fixed in their places, have both been made movable—as though at the end of increasingly long ropes.

The central fact which distinguishes Interurbia from Suburbia is that the labor force does not move in a steady one-way stream, but more in a series of cross currents. Westport, Connecticut, in Northeastern Interurbia serves as an example.

Most people commuting from Westport move southwesterly to New York, but a significant percentage commute to Bridgeport, and New Haven. And Westport itself also receives part of its own labor force from lower Connecticut, nearby New York and the surrounding countryside. Thus the interchangeable day and night populations which used to be so exclusively a feature of the central city are now typical of Interurbia's satellite cities as well.

The emergence of Interurbia from the now out-dated concept of city, suburb and country has been stimulated more by the growth of satellite cities than it has from the big central city. The Interurbia in the Chicago and Milwaukee area or strip serves to illustrate this fact.

Between 1930 and 1959 the population in the suburban areas between Chicago and Milwaukee proper has increased 95 per cent while the cities themselves have increased 17 per cent. The same is true of the retail sales. In the areas between Chicago-Milwaukee, retail sales in 1959 were 460 per cent greater than in 1930, while in the two cities themselves, retail sales had increased 167 per cent.

What is true in the suburban areas in the Chicago-Milwaukee strip, appears to be true of the entire country. In 1958, dollar sales per capita in the Interurbian suburbs were, on the average, 68 per cent higher than in the other suburbs of the country.

INTERURBIA IN 1975

As we look to the future, we can with some confidence, predict that the day is not too far distant when most of our people will be encompassed within Interurbia—as most of our sales now are. In 1975, it is

FIGURE III

600-Mile City Stretches along Coast from Maine to Virginia, Represents 21% of U.S. Population, 24% of All Retail Sales

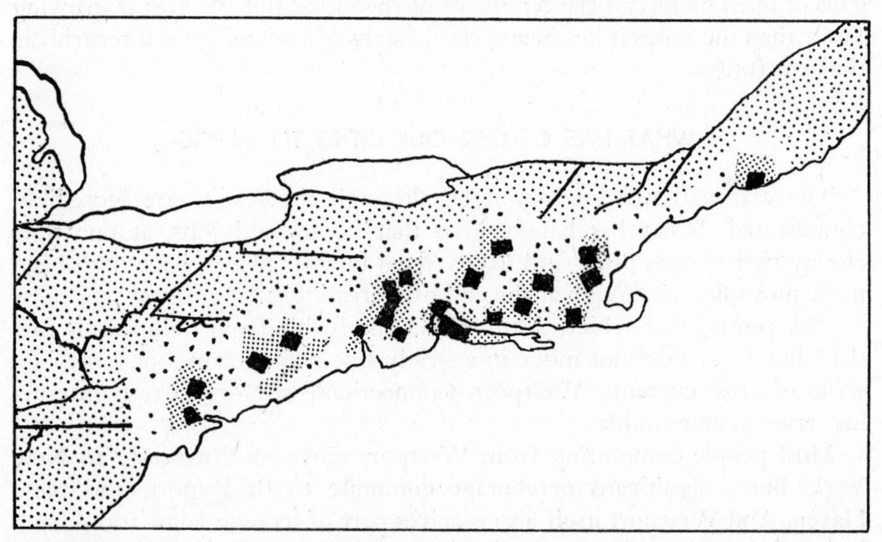

estimated that Interurbia will represent 60 per cent of our population and 70 per cent of retail sales. (See map—Figure III.)

Our 600-mile city in the Northeast may well grow toward the Piedmont. Its arm now creeping up the Hudson, will in all probability link with Cleveland, Detroit, and Chicago, and stretch down Illinois to St.

Louis. That would be an Interurbia about twice the length of the Atlantic strip—a city more than 1,200 miles long.

On the West Coast, the future holds the distinct possibility of an urban strip stretching northward from San Diego and connecting somewhere in the California Valley with the southward movement from San Francisco and the Bay area.

In the South, Dallas and Fort Worth extend in one direction down to Houston and Galveston, and in another, through Waco and Austin to San Antonio.

People will, as in the past, settle close to waterways, whether they be ocean, lake, river, or canal; but there will be other motivations, too—climate, the need for land and, as always, the desire for better living.

HOW INTERURBIA MAY AFFECT OUR WAY OF LIVING

Beneath the shell of uniform mass housing there most likely will be a series of different communities each catering to a different age and income group. The trend toward physical uniformity is creating a counterdesire to be socially different. And this desire to be different is already apparent in some of the ostensibly homogeneous suburbs such as the Levittowns in the East and in Park Forest, south of Chicago.

Families are on the move. More and more people are leaving the old home town—in a series of moves—from home town to college, from college to a great organization, and then from one provincial outpost to another, until finally comes the day when the man is summoned home to Rome.

The old home town may look pretty much the same. Yet if you check the leadership in the traditional town, you will find that the sons of the "early" families have more often than not left to join the transient life. Someone else, very much like them, is now sitting in the place they might have had in the Junior Chamber of Commerce, the Community Chest, or on the Greens Committee of the Country Club.

Then there is the more familiar kind of mobility—the great exodus from the city to the country. Familiar, yes, except that the exodus does not necessarily consist of just one jump—from city to suburbs.

To illustrate: since the war, there has been a tremendous growth in new row-house developments in Northeast Philadelphia. Socially, however, for many of these people there is still another transition to be made. For all their boasting about what a wonderful place the "5600" block is, the unspoken goal is to move out of the city. If the husband gets that raise, the "For Sale" sign goes up.

Mobility breeds more mobility. Once a person has learned to change environment it becomes easier to adapt to another. The good transient is quite professional about this. He has learned how to keep his bags packed—mentally.

Another aspect of this mobility is the tremendous upgrading urge it produces. One of the most characteristic complaints to be found in the new villages of Interurbia is about the quality of goods they have in the stores. The complaint usually takes the lines of "who-do-they-think-we-are-anyway?"

The most interesting thing about this upgrading urge is how very much it is conditioned by the immediate group in which a couple find themselves.

It is the group in Interurbia that determines when a luxury becomes a necessity. Take something like an automatic dryer. When only a few housewives in a block have one, other housewives can take it or leave it. As more and more housewives follow suit, it soon becomes an almost unsocial act not to own one. Finally only the most resolute can hold out.

This urge to improve one's own status has caused the developer of one of the new suburbs to suggest somewhat facetiously building a "life cycle suburb." You would live in one court as a child, a two bedroom apartment as a newlywed: then a ranch house; finally, then you're old and gray, and your children are scattered to the four winds, you would move back to a court to serve out your term as a baby sitter.

INTERURBIAN PSYCHOLOGY

Do the psychological needs of the people living in Interurbia differ from those in the rest of the country? They do most decidedly. Here, from a special study of several thousand people, are the principal drives of these Interurbian people, and some idea as to how they may differ from the rest of the population.

The Interurbian man is significantly above the national average in his expressed desire for achievement—his desire to rival and surpass others—to do his best—to achieve prestige and acclaim. He has an equally pronounced need to dominate other people. He wants to be a leader and influence others. The Interurbian man is more willing to talk about sex and less strict in his attitudes.

Our Interurbian man likes also to be the center of attention—to have others notice him—to make an impression on others. In short, vanity and self-dramatization are stronger needs in him than they are in the man living elsewhere in our land. Change he doesn't mind. In fact, our Interurbian man likes to do new and different things . . . to change his daily routine. He likes variety and novelty. Possibly this is a key as to why he accepts the need for mobility with such calm.

Our Interurbian woman is also an interesting creature. Her attitudes toward sex also differ from the rest of the country. She is more willing to talk about the subject. If this doesn't strike you as news, rest assured that this trait is more highly developed within Interurbia than it is elsewhere.

She, too, likes to be the center of attention—to have others notice her

. . . she is long on vanity. Out beyond Interurbia, this quality hasn't quite reached the same high point.

She, too, likes to do new and different things—change her daily routine. Variety is her spice of life. Perhaps that's why we find her in Interurbia.

It is a fact of great significance in the development of future advertising appeals that the characteristics which are most highly developed in the men and women of Interurbia are those on which so many great advertising success stories have been built and will be built. The people of Interurbia might be said to represent a pre-conditioned audience for the skillful advertising of many products and services to a greater degree than the people outside Interurbia.

HOW INTERURBIA STIMULATES AND STABILIZES OUR ECONOMY

Interurbia will push us toward a national economy that certainly will be bigger, and probably more stable. The stability will be due to the changing pattern of ownership and consumption Interurbia imposes. Except for a little furniture and a closet full of clothes, most Interurbia city dwellers have no possessions. New York City, for example, accounts for only three per cent of the nation's automobiles, but represents 15 per cent of the country's restaurant sales.

By contrast, the Interurbanite who has left the big city is forced to become a man of property. His ownership of a house creates a hunger for hard goods that inevitably drives him into hard work more relentlessly than the metropolitan dweller.

For example, one large builder found that the purchase of every new home automatically created 17 other purchases, such as furniture, appliances, curtains, garden tools, a new car—even a second car.

The stabilizing influence of Interurbia also arises from the huge spending program on the part of businesses, utilities and public authorities that Interurbia demands. And Interurbia's need for new highways alone is accelerating the need for housing in a brutally direct fashion. The present highway construction program calls for the destruction or removal of about 90,000 houses a year—just to build roads!

Still another stabilizing influence lies in the increased opportunity for workers to maintain employment by being more mobile. When the Bloomfield, New Jersey, plant of one of America's largest corporations closed in 1959, workers employed in the plant were able to climb in their cars and find employment in the nearby towns of West Caldwell, Newark and East Orange.

The compactness of Interurbia provided employment opportunities which the workers were able to seize by virtue of their rubber-tired mobility. This resilience is in striking contrast to the days when such a closing would have caused tragic economic and human consequences.

While the automobile has become the symbol of many Interurbian problems, it fills a basic need. The phenomenon of Interurbia is based on the mobility supplied by the private car to drive miles to shopping center, school, church and job. If anything, the need for this mobility will grow, as business and homes spread further out.

But the growing use of the automobile is outstripping the ability of the central city to cope with it. In fact, the congestion has become so overpowering that some planners are persuaded that the means taken to open the choked downtown arteries are mere expedients. Some are bold enough to predict a not-too-distant day when the private car is barred altogether from the metropolitan city, as an improved intra-city transit system takes on the job of moving people about faster than they are now moving.

NEW MARKETING PROBLEMS

The marketing problems created by Interurbia will be no less complex. With 31,000,000 changes of residence every year, the retailer worrying about new locations will have to keep a close watch on consumer movements.

The friendly neighborhood dealer may lose some of his old sales punch, as he sees new faces among his customers more often than before.

The manufacturer may find that the Central Cities in Interurbia are no longer the focus of marketing, but somewhere in between. Test marketing may be expanded to Interurbian strips, instead of individual markets. The same may be true of product research.

Sales organizations may grow smaller, as they concentrate more on retail service. The two-thousand-man sales force may become a thing of the past.

Executives in charge of areas with traditional designations such as New England, Middle Atlantic, may be re-assigned to supervise a particular Interurbian strip.

New stores, service stations, and discount houses will expose customers to brands they've never seen before. As New York and Boston push toward each other in the nation's largest Interurbia, they carry with them certain brands that New London, Connecticut, had never heard of. The same may apply to prices. Discount houses will introduce some cut prices hitherto unknown to various communities along the way.

The Interurbian shopper for a refrigerator or other hard goods may soon be shopping in a retail store which carries no stock except that needed for demonstration or display. The retailer will simply phone in the order to a warehouse, and the model ordered will be on the truck and delivered to the customer's house within a matter of hours.

This new convenience for the retail shopper within Interurbia will be made possible through a mammoth warehouse system handling many brands and a variety of products. It is conceivable, for example, that the hard-goods' needs of Northeast Interurbia alone could be efficiently supplied by four or five such warehouses.

The Interurbian influence can already be detected in the marketing procedures of many important food chains. The central city is no longer the sole location for their warehousing and buying. Rather their nerve centers have either moved out from the metropolitan area, or they are being duplicated out in the growing Interurbian territory.

Even today, in major chains like Kroger and Colonial stores, we find some warehouse buying headquarters outside the central city with well-developed "spokes" that are completely independent of any historic city or political boundaries.

As we change from the old concept of a metropolitan marketing area to a new Interurbian marketing area, perhaps we should re-examine the traditional methods by which we separate and study our markets.

Perhaps it may not be too early for market research firms to break down their findings on the basis of Interurbia versus non-Interurbia.

ADVERTISING MEDIA IN INTERURBIA

Concentration of population has virtually always meant lower advertising costs. The bigger the mass of circulation an advertiser buys, the lower the relative cost to him.

Today the space an advertiser buys in a country weekly can cost him ten times as much per unit of circulation as the space in a large daily. As Interurbia develops, this discrepancy may be narrowed—with increased efficiency in advertising expenditure.

In the new Interurbia, the metropolitan daily may, of necessity, become less and less identified with the central city of Interurbia, and more with Interurbia as a whole. One way of accomplishing this is to publish more zoned editions, as some large dailies are already doing.

The smaller dailies and weeklies may stand to benefit from the Interurbian development in two ways: first, they are in the happy position of having their readers come to them; secondly, the pattern of marketing is changing so fast that major chain stores are becoming less and less identified with the central city, as they develop new spokes in their marketing wheel.

Interurbia also presents a challenge to Sunday supplements, whose substantial post-war growth has been based on their ability to provide intensive coverage of the large metropolitan centers. More and more, the supplements may find it beneficial to buttress their circulation in the medium-size cities between their present major metropolitan markets. This would enable them to provide the same intensive coverage of the Interurbian areas that they now provide in central cities.

Today some 70 national magazines representing 71% of all audited magazine circulation accept advertising for circulation covering individual regions or markets. This trend of magazines toward regional advertising may gain further momentum as more advertisers begin to look at circulations for whole Interurbias, and not just their metropolitan segments. In so doing, they will find in many cases that the traditionally broad-base magazines can cover as many or more families within an Interurbia as some of the individual local media that they have used traditionally.

TV set ownership throughout Interurbia will increase to something close to the 90 per cent that now exists in metropolitan areas. But TV network structures still lag behind the Interurbian development due to their historical tie to individual markets. Thus an advertiser seeking saturation coverage of Northeastern Interurbia would have to supplement his ten network stations with several spot stations. Future network requirements for "must-buy" TV stations may be related more directly to Interurbias.

Radio's future welfare in Interurbia may rest in part on it becoming more and more a vehicle for news and music—an economical type of programming which could help keep costs competitive with TV. The degree to which smaller local stations within Interurbia are used will depend, as in the case of small dailies and weeklies, on the saturation required in the new areas which retailers are cultivating.

In closing . . .

We are at the foothills of a way of life which will require a more intensive study than we have ever given it before . . . a study of people's motivations and desires . . . of how they live and why they live as they do. And we must learn all this before it is too late.

Of one thing we are certain as we enter this new way of life: that Interurbia will produce fundamental changes. And as it does, probably no one of us will be able to do business as we have been doing it. No one will find paradise in Interurbia. Paradise will always be just around the corner. And that for all of us may be our greatest opportunity.

Current demographic and economic information is essential to effective marketing management. Changes in demography not only affect the structure of market demand, but also have far-reaching implications for such marketing decisions as product design and media selection. A review of important socioeconomic characteristics at various stages of the family life cycle is presented.

17. CONSUMER MARKETS: FAMILIES BY AGE, I: CHARACTERISTICS*

Fabian Linden†

A striking 90% of the growth in the nation's family population expected during the Sixties will be accounted for by the relatively young and the relatively old—by families under 30 and those over 55. In the preceding 10-year span these age groups represented only two fifths of the total growth.

As these simple statistics suggest, the age composition of our population is being significantly altered. Two major demographic tremors have been working their way through the nation's population structure over the past 30 years. The first shock wave was triggered by the sharp drop in births during the Depression Thirties, the second by the postwar birth boom.

The changing age structure of our population is, of course, of special interest to marketers. Clearly, it is not only affecting the structure of demand, but it also has far-reaching implications for such merchandising decisions as product design and media selection. This article, the first of two, reviews the most current available demographic and economic information on families by age of head. A second story will be concerned with the purchasing patterns of families at various stages of the life cycle.

FAMILY HEAD UNDER 25

Households under 25 account for about 5% of the nation's families, but only 3% of all consumer demand. Last year the median earnings of

---

* Reprinted from National Industrial Conference Board, "A Graphic Guide to Consumer Markets," *Monthly Supplement* (April, 1964).

† Consumer Economics Department, National Industrial Conference Board.

these families came to roughly $4,300, or about 25% below the all-country figure. Three out of every five young couples earned less than $5,000, and barely 15% had over $7,000.

The birth rate at this stage of the family's life cycle is at a peak level. Thus, although they constitute only 5% of the family population, these households had 28% of all children born last year. Two thirds of all under-25-year-old homes include children and about 30% have more than one. Nevertheless, well over half of all wives work all or part of the year. A third of all young families live in the central cities of metropolitan areas, and about 20% own their own homes.

Three out of every five family heads of his age have earned high school diplomas, a level of education well above the all-country average. However, fewer youngsters in this age bracket have finished college than in next-oldest grouping. Youngsters who remain in school longer generally marry later.

FAMILY HEAD 25–34

A fifth of all households and about the same share of the country's spending power are to be found in this age bracket. The median annual income is about normal, and at this age a full third of all families earn more than $7,000. But indebtedness as well as income has increased: two thirds of these families owe money.

Although the birth rate has slowed appreciably at this age level, to about one new arrival in every four homes annually, over half of all children born last year were to parents in this bracket. Close to 90% of these households include children, and two thirds of them more than one.

As would be expected under these circumstances, relatively fewer wives now work; of those that do, about three in five work the year round. The proportion of families living in the suburbs is far greater than that for the under-25 group. The frequency of home ownership has also increased substantially, although it is still under the all-family rate.

This age group is better educated than any other. Close to 15% of the household heads have completed college, and an additional 43% have high school diplomas. Roughly one quarter of all males are employed in professional-technical occupations or are managers and officials. Craftsmen account for an additional fifth, operatives for another quarter.

FAMILY HEAD 35–44

The largest proportion of total family spending power—an estimated 27%—is in the hands of this age group, which accounts for a quarter of all households. The median family earns well above the norm: close to half of these homes are in the over-$7,000 bracket. The frequency of indebtedness continues in the neighborhood of two thirds, but the size of outstanding obligations appears to have declined in this bracket.

A very large proportion of these families have children living at home, but fewer households include youngsters under six. Nevertheless, over two fifths of our entire child population is accounted for by the 35–44 age bracket.

The ratio of working wives in this group is near the average. The family now appears to be fully rooted, and barely 15% change their residence in the course of a year. The rate of home ownership has increased sharply: two thirds of these families own their homes.

The level of educational achievement is well above average, with one out of every two household heads having completed high school. This is a slightly smaller fraction than in the 25–34 age bracket, as each upcoming generation in recent years has been staying somewhat longer in school than the one preceding.

FAMILY HEAD 45–54

This the most affluent of all the age groups. Earning capacity at this stage of the life cycle is at its peak. Last year the median income of these families exceeded $7,000. More than a quarter of all homes in this age category have incomes in excess of $10,000. All in all, this group accounts for a fifth of all families but a quarter of all spending power. Only one out of every two of these households is in debt.

The proportion of families with children has dipped below 60%. Actually, many of the offspring of these families have by now reached 18 and hence are no longer classified as children in government statistics.

As would be expected, there is a sharp increase at this age level in the proportion of wives who work, and an even greater rise in the number working all year.

The educational level of this age category is substantially below that of the one preceding. Most of the family heads in this group were of school age during the depression years of the Thirties. All in all, fewer than two fifths of them achieved a high school diploma.

The occupational mix of this category more or less parallels the national pattern, except that there are slightly fewer professional and technical persons and somewhat more managers and officials.

FAMILY HEAD 55–64

The income pattern in this age bracket reflects the presence of some retired and semiretired families. There is clustering at both ends of the income scale. Nearly 40% of these families—a substantially larger proportion than found in the 45–54 group—earn below $5,000. At the other end of the scale, one fifth of all households, a better than average proportion, have annual incomes exceeding $10,000. On balance, median earnings are still above par. Indebtedness has dropped sharply, to only about one third of these families.

Only one out of every five of these households includes children. Family size has now declined to 3.0, as compared to an all-family average of 3.7. Also, there are relatively fewer working wives in this group than among younger families. And there apparently has been some moving back into town from the suburbs.

Only slightly better than a quarter of these family heads have completed high school, while a third failed to go the full course in elementary school. Some decline in the ownership of durable goods is in evidence at this stage of the life cycle, sharpest of all in cars. However, three fourths of these families still operate automobiles, and one in five has two or more vehicles.

FAMILY HEAD 65 AND OVER

This is the age of the retired. Median income for this group last year was $3,200, or only slightly better than half the all-family figure. About 70% of these households have less than $5,000 a year to spend, while only about one in ten have over $10,000. In the neighborhood of 10% of total demand originates with this age bracket, which includes about 15% of all our citizens.

Few of these families still have youngsters living at home. As a matter of fact, there has been a rather substantial change in family composition—fewer husband and wife units, more cases of a man or a woman living with a relative. Close to one fifth of all wives, however, are still working.

A relatively large proportion of families reside outside the urbanized areas, which probably explains the continued high level of home ownership.

The general educational achievement of this group is lower than that of any other: only one out of every five family heads has completed high school. More than two out of every five have failed to complete elementary school. This generation was born in an era in which less emphasis was put on formal training.

A relatively high proportion of this group (20% as compared to a national average of only 8%) work on farms. This may reflect the fact that while persons employed in industry tend to retire upon coming of age, farmers are more likely to continue working on a reduced schedule. Also, in the recent migration away from the land, younger families left in relatively large numbers.

There is a further contraction in the proportion of families owning durable goods in this age bracket. Cars are now maintained by less than half of all households.

Selected Family Characteristics by Age Groups

	All Families	Under 25	25–34	35–44	45–54	55–64	65 & Over
Families:							
Millions	47.0	2.5	9.1	11.4	9.9	7.3	6.8
Distribution	100%	5%	20%	24%	21%	16%	14%
Average Size	3.7	3.0	4.1	4.4	3.7	3.0	2.6
Family Income: Median	$5,956	$4,276	$5,902	$6,827	$7,040	$6,219	$3,204
Under $3,000	20%	31%	14%	12%	13%	19%	47%
$3,000–5,000	19	30	21	16	16	18	23
$5,000–7,000	22	25	31	24	20	21	12
$7,000–10,000	21	12	23	27	24	20	8
$10,000–15,000	13	2	9	16	19	15	6
$15,000 and over	5	0	2	5	8	7	4
Distribution all income	100%	3	19	27	25	17	9
Personal Debt:* Families having	50%	63%	67%	65%	50%	34%	18%
$500 or More	27	31	42	36	31	13	7
Type of Family:							
Husband-Wife	87%	90%	91%	89%	87%	86%	79%
Female Head	10	8	8	9	10	11	15
Other	3	2	1	2	3	3	6
Births: Per 1,000 families annually	105	517	251	79	14	2	0
Distribution all births	100%	28	51	18	3	0	0
Children: Families having:	59%	66%	87%	87%	58%	21%	4%
1	18	36	21	17	26	13	2
2	18	21	30	27	17	4	1
3	12	7	20	20	8	2	1
4+	11	2	16	23	7	2	0
Families with child under 6	33%	64%	75%	43%	12%	3%	1%
Distribution all children	100%	4	32	41	18	4	1
Wife Working:							
During Year	39%	55%	40%	40%	45%	37%	19%
27 Weeks or more	26	30	23	27	34	28	13
Earning $1,000 or more	24	30	25	25	29	23	10
Occupation							
Professional, technical	11	10	15	12	9	8	9
Managers, officials	13	5	10	14	15	15	15
Clerical	7	9	7	6	6	6	6
Sales	7	7	7	7	7	7	9
Craftsmen, foremen	22	20	22	24	23	22	15
Operatives	21	31	24	21	20	17	10
Service	5	4	4	5	5	8	11
Laborers	6	9	6	5	6	6	5
Farm	8	5	5	6	9	11	20
Education:							
16 years or more	9%	7%	14%	12%	9%	7%	4%
12 to 15 years	31	52	43	40	29	20	16
8 to 11 years	37	34	32	34	40	41	38
Less than 8 years	23	7	11	14	22	32	42
Mobility: Per cent moving annually	17%	61%	28%	15%	(9%	)	6%
Moving within same county	12	43	19	10	(7	)	4
Residence:							
In Urbanized Area	53%	51%	55%	55%	54%	53%	48%
Central City	31	33	31	30	31	33	32
Urban Fringe	22	18	24	25	23	20	16
Nonurbanized Area	47	49	45	45	46	47	52
Housing: Home owners (Households)	62%	21%	50%	66%	68%	68%	69%
1 or 2 rooms	6%	14%	6%	4%	5%	7%	9%
3 to 5 rooms	58	76	66	54	53	55	55
6 rooms or more	36	10	28	42	42	38	36
Ownership of Durables: Households having							
Washing Machine	74%	50%	77%	83%	78%	71%	63%
Clothes Dryer	17	8	23	26	18	12	6
Television	87	80	90	92	90	86	77
2 or More	10	3	8	15	13	9	5
Radio	91	87	91	93	93	91	89
2 or More	35	23	33	44	41	33	23
Air Conditioning	13	7	12	14	14	13	10
Food Freezer	18	5	16	24	23	18	13
Automobile	78	80	87	87	83	75	44
2 or More	22	12	20	28	29	21	10

Data on various characteristics are available for different years. All figures relate to 1960–1963.
* Excludes charge accounts or mortgage obligations. Data based on "Spending Units."

The changing age structure of our growing population influences many marketing decisions. Marketing strategists for consumer markets must recognize that shifts in preferences for various goods and services occur as families reach successive stages of the life cycle. Families are categorized by the age of the family head, and their spending patterns are reported.

18. CONSUMER MARKETS: FAMILIES BY AGE, II: EXPENDITURES*

Fabian Linden†

Never before in the nation's history—not even during the great immigration early in the century—has the age structure of our adult population gone through as sharp a change as in the present period. We are now experiencing the combined consequences of the sharp fall in births during the depression Thirties and the spectacular baby boom of the prosperous Fifties. All this means a shift in the goods and services that are in demand, and has a far-reaching effect on many aspects of merchandising strategy, from packaging to the phrasing of the promotion message.

This, the second of two articles on the characteristics of households at each stage in the life cycle, is concerned with spending patterns. The preceding story reviewed social and income traits. The observations that follow are based on the Bureau of Labor Statistics' recent study of spending habits of urban families and single consumers. The complete study covers the years 1960 and 1961; however, the only data released thus far are for the earlier year. This information was collected in 23 metropolitan areas and in 16 small cities. Since a similar survey was conducted in 1950, it is possible to examine the changes in consumer preferences over the past decade. In comparing past and present expenditure patterns, 1950 data have been converted to 1960 dollars.

HEAD UNDER 25

The typical consumer unit in this age bracket spent $4,500 for goods and services in 1960, or substantially less than the national average. In aggregate this group accounts for less than 5% of all buying.

---

* Reprinted from National Industrial Conference Board, "A Graphic Guide to Consumer Markets," *Monthly Supplement* (May, 1964).

† Consumer Economics Department, National Industrial Conference Board.

A large proportion of people in this bracket are single consumers, a fact reflected in the group's general expenditure profile. The percentage of income that goes for food, clothing, medical and personal care is below the all-country norm. Shelter is a significant item percentagewise at this age level, although actual dollar outlays for this purpose are below par. Expenditures for automobiles, on the other hand, are quite large, both in absolute and relative terms.

A much smaller proportion of the young household's budget now goes for food and clothing than did so 10 years ago. House furnishings and equipment, too, now make a smaller claim. Spending for housing on the other hand—shelter and particularly home operations—has grown more important than it was in 1950.

HEAD 25–34

Most of the spending units in this group are husband-wife families. Spending for consumption came to $5,600 in the survey year, which is fractionally above average. This group accounts for close to a fifth of total consumer buying.

Expenditures in this age bracket broadly follow the all-country pattern. The proportion of resources channeled into the home—shelter, household operations and home furnishings—is above par, while outlays for food and clothing are slightly below the national average, measured in relative terms, and about equal to the all-household figure in actual dollars. The automobile also takes a somewhat smaller share of total spending, although dollar outlays are higher than they are in the average American family.

The average household in this bracket spends about a quarter more on goods and services than does the typical under-25-year-old family. However, food, alcohol, tobacco and clothing expenditures are much more than 25% greater. (The consumer unit is bigger now—there are more persons to feed and clothe.) The rise in outlays for house furnishings, and particularly for autos, is less than for all spending.

As in the case of the youngest families, a substantially smaller share of this age group's spending now goes for food, clothing and home furnishings than did so a decade ago, while a much greater proportion is earmarked for shelter and household operations. Personal and medical care, too, have increased in importance in this bracket, and more is being spent on automobiles.

HEAD 35–44

Roughly a quarter of total consumer buying is represented by this age group. In the survey year the average household spent about $6,500, more than in any other bracket.

Although more money is now being spent on cars, home furnishings, and household operations than in the preceding age group, the increases for these items are less than the increment in all spending. The big rise in outlays is for food and clothing, which account for an above-average portion of this age group's budget. This is because, at this stage of the life cycle, the household has reached its peak size.

URBAN FAMILY EXPENDITURES

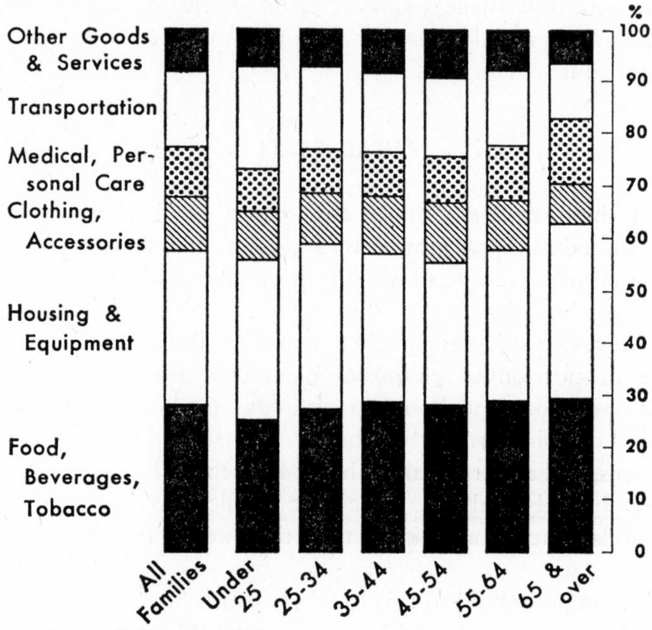

SOURCE: Department of Labor.

As observed in connection with the other age groups, food, clothing and home furnishings are less significant percentagewise than a decade ago, but shelter, particularly household operations, and the automobile are more important.

HEAD 45–54

Though the family is now at its peak earning level, expenditures for current consumption have declined moderately, to $6,200. Only about 90% of income after taxes finds its way to the market, as compared to 95% for the preceding age category. In large measure this development is explained by a decline in household size. Many of the offspring of these families have reached adulthood and left home. However, this age category is of most importance to marketers since it accounts for over a quarter of all consumer spending.

Summary of Expenditures, by Age of Family
All U.S. Urban Families and Single Consumers, 1960

	All Consumer Units	*Under 25*	*25–34*	*35–44*	*45–54*	*55–64*	*65 and over*
Consumer units							
Distribution	100.0%	6.2	18.1	19.2	21.9	15.9	18.7
Average size	3.1	2.6	3.7	4.0	3.2	2.4	1.8
Income							
Before taxes	$6587	$4870	$6425	$7791	$7972	$6746	$3983
After taxes	5822	4368	5767	6900	6959	5783	3637
Expenditures							
Per cent of income after taxes	92.2	101.3	96.6	95.0	89.6	85.0	89.1
Per cent of total demand	100.0%	5.2	19.0	23.8	25.8	14.8	11.4
Total expenditures (average)	$5365	$4425	$5571	$6555	$6238	$4916	$3241
Food, total	1311	950	1295	1621	1512	1241	867
Food prepared at home	1036	683	1005	1299	1196	967	719
Food away from home	274	267	290	321	316	274	148
Tobacco	96	81	112	117	110	87	44
Alcoholic beverages	94	65	97	113	126	84	43
Housing total	1587	1361	1754	1876	1713	1426	1077
Shelter	742	692	846	841	781	658	537
Rented dwelling	327	554	471	293	266	252	265
Owned dwelling	379	129	351	512	456	363	245
Other shelter	36	9	24	35	59	43	27
Utilities	239	130	218	285	272	247	195
Household operations	319	256	349	377	341	285	236
House furnishings	281	282	335	371	309	228	107
Clothing, materials, etc.	549	405	547	727	704	480	247
Personal care	153	120	154	185	183	139	92
Medical care	345	256	330	377	370	355	310
Recreation	214	195	245	287	260	164	81
Reading	50	38	52	58	55	48	37
Education	61	54	46	69	118	44	16
Transportation	790	848	859	978	928	708	344
Automobile	696	778	788	869	813	585	286
Other travel	93	70	71	109	115	123	58
Other expenditures	118	52	80	147	159	140	83
Total expenditures (per cent)	100.0%	100.0%	100.0%	100.0%	100.0%	100.0%	100.0%
Food, total	24.4	21.5	23.2	24.7	24.2	25.2	26.8
Tobacco and alcohol	3.6	3.3	3.7	3.5	3.8	3.5	2.7
Housing, total	29.6	30.8	31.5	28.6	27.5	29.0	33.2
Shelter	13.8	15.6	15.2	12.8	12.5	13.4	16.6
Utilities	4.5	2.9	3.9	4.3	4.4	5.0	6.0
Household operation	5.9	5.8	6.3	5.8	5.5	5.8	7.3
House furnishings	5.2	6.4	6.0	5.7	5.0	4.6	3.3
Clothing, materials, etc.	10.2	9.2	9.8	11.1	11.3	9.8	7.6
Personal care	2.9	2.7	2.8	2.8	2.9	2.8	2.8
Medical care	6.4	5.8	5.9	5.8	5.9	7.2	9.6
Recreation	4.0	4.4	4.4	4.4	4.2	3.3	2.5
Reading and education	2.0	2.1	1.7	2.0	2.8	1.9	1.6
Transportation	14.7	19.2	15.4	14.9	14.9	14.4	10.6
Other expenditures	2.2	1.2	1.4	2.2	2.5	2.8	2.6

Source: Department of Labor.

The decrease in family size is reflected in expenditure habits. Total outlays are roughly 5% below the next-youngest bracket but spending for food, shelter, and the home generally has declined by an even larger proportion. The decrease is also relatively big for automobiles. On the other hand, spending for some items is off by less than 5%. These include clothing and medical and personal care. Expenditure for alcohol increases.

Changes in this age group's spending habits over the past decade are typical. Food now claims a smaller share of the family's budget, housing and the car a somewhat larger share. The importance of clothing is unchanged.

HEAD 55–64

In this age bracket we find some significant changes in the composition of the family, its earnings and its spending habits. While the majority of household heads are at their peak earning capacity, many others are retired or semiretired. The average family now spends $5,000 for goods and services, or about 85% of post-tax income.

Total consumption of this group is a full fifth less than in the 45-to-54 bracket. Many items, however, are off by much more, notably house furnishings, clothing, recreation, alcohol and automobiles. On the other hand expenditures decline only moderately for medical care, shelter, and household operations. The decrease in food spending is also surprisingly small.

The share of the budget going for food has dropped from 29% to 25% in the last 10 years, while the portion devoted to housing has increased, largely because of the shelter and operation components. Autos and personal and medical care have become more important since 1950, but the weight assigned to clothing has remained the same.

65 AND OVER

The average household in this retired age bracket spent slightly over $3,200 in the survey year for all goods and services, representing about 90% of its post-tax income. About 19% of all consumer units are in this bracket, but they account for only a little better than 11% of total spending. The average household has declined to 1.8 persons.

With the sharp reduction in spending, essentials such as food and housing take a comparatively large share of the budget. Three fifths of total outlays go for these items. An additional 12% are for personal and medical care.

Consumption is more than a third less than in the 55-to-64 group. Many items, of course, have fallen by much more, notably tobacco and alcohol, clothing, house furnishings, transportation and recreation. Among items that have decreased by less than the drop in total spending are housing, food and medical care.

A decade ago, older families spent a larger share of their budget for food and clothing, but a smaller proportion for housing, than they do today. Outlays for medical and personal care are appreciably higher, having increased from roughly a tenth of the budget to about an eighth.

Segmentation analysis—the evaluation of all potentially useful ways of segmenting a market—may produce a more effective marketing strategy than does segmentation based solely on demographic characteristics. The strategic choice concept of segmentation broadens the scope of marketing planning to include the positioning of new as well as established products. Marketing must develop its own interpretive theory if it is to optimize the value of segmentation analysis.

19. NEW CRITERIA FOR MARKET SEGMENTATION*

Daniel Yankelovich†

The director of marketing in a large company is confronted by some of the most difficult problems in the history of U.S. industry. To assist him, the information revolution of the past decade puts at his disposal a vast array of techniques, facts, and figures. But without a way to master this information, he can easily be overwhelmed by the reports that flow in to him incessantly from marketing research, economic forecasts, cost analyses, and sales breakdowns. He must have more than mere access to mountains of data. He must himself bring to bear a method of analysis that cuts through the detail to focus sharply on new opportunities.

In this article, I shall propose such a method. It is called *segmentation analysis*. It is based on the proposition that once you discover the most useful ways of segmenting a market, you have produced the beginnings of a sound marketing strategy.

UNIQUE ADVANTAGES

Segmentation analysis has developed out of several key premises:

In today's economy, each brand appears to sell effectively to only certain segments of any market and not to the whole market.

* Reprinted from "New Criteria for Market Segmentation," *Harvard Business Review*, Vol. XLII, No. 2 (March–April, 1964), pp. 83–90.

† Daniel Yankelovich, Inc.

Sound marketing objectives depend on knowledge of how segments which produce the most customers for a company's brands differ in requirements and susceptibilities from the segments which produce the largest number of customers for competitive brands.

Traditional demographic methods of market segmentation do not usually provide this knowledge. Analyses of market segments by age, sex, geography, and income level are not likely to provide as much direction for marketing strategy as management requires.

Once the marketing director does discover the most pragmatically useful way of segmenting his market, it becomes a new standard for almost all his evaluations. He will use it to appraise competitive strengths and vulnerabilities, to plan his product line, to determine his advertising and selling strategy, and to set precise marketing objectives against which performance can later be measured. Specifically, segmentation analysis helps him to—

. . . direct the appropriate amounts of promotional attention and money to the most potentially profitable segments of his market;

. . . design a product line that truly parallels the demands of the market instead of one that bulks in some areas and ignores or scants other potentially quite profitable segments;

. . . catch the first sign of a major trend in a swiftly changing market and thus give him time to prepare to take advantage of it;

. . . determine the appeals that will be most effective in his company's advertising; and, where several different appeals are significantly effective, quantify the segments of the market responsive to each;

. . . choose advertising media more wisely and determine the proportion of budget that should be allocated to each medium in the light of anticipated impact;

. . . correct the timing of advertising and promotional efforts so that they are massed in the weeks, months, and seasons when selling resistance is least and responsiveness is likely to be at its maximum;

. . . understand otherwise seemingly meaningless demographic market information and apply it in scores of new and effective ways.

These advantages hold in the case of both packaged goods and hard goods, and for commercial and industrial products as well as consumer products.

Guides to Strategy

Segmentation analysis cuts through the data facing a marketing director when he tries to set targets based on markets as a whole, or when he relies primarily on demographic breakdowns. It is a systematic approach that permits the marketing planner to pick the strategically most important segmentations and then to design brands, products, packages, communications, and marketing strategies around them. It infinitely simplifies the setting of objectives.

In the following sections we shall consider nondemographic ways of segmenting markets. These ways dramatize the point that finding marketing opportunities by depending solely on demographic breakdowns is like trying to win a national election by relying only on the information in a census. A modern census contains useful data, but it identifies neither the crucial issues of an election, nor those groups whose voting habits are still fluid, nor the needs, values, and attitudes that influence how those groups will vote. This kind of information, rather than census-type data, is the kind that wins elections—and markets.

Consider, for example, companies like Procter & Gamble, General Motors, or American Tobacco, whose multiple brands sell against one another and must, every day, win new elections in the marketplace:

> These companies sell to the whole market, not by offering one brand that appeals to all people, but by covering the different segments with multiple brands. How can they prevent these brands from cannibalizing each other? How can they avoid surrendering opportunities to competitors by failing to provide brands that appeal to all important segments? In neither automobiles, soaps, nor cigarettes do demographic analyses reveal to the manufacturer what products to make or what products to sell to what segments of the market. Obviously, some modes of segmentation other than demographic are needed to explain why brands which differ so little nevertheless find their own niches in the market, each one appealing to a different segment.

The point at issue is not that demographic segmentation should be disregarded, but rather that it should be regarded as only one among many possible ways of analyzing markets. In fact, the key requirement of segmentation analysis is that the marketing director should never assume in advance that any one method of segmentation is the best. His first job should be to muster all probable segmentation and *then* choose the most meaningful ones to work with. This approach is analogous to that used in research in the physical sciences, where the hypothesis that best seems to explain the phenomena under investigation is the one chosen for working purposes. . . .

Conclusion

. . . let me stress three points:

1. *We should discard the old, unquestioned assumption that demography is always the best way of looking at markets.*

The demographic premise implies that differences in reasons for buying, in brand choice influences, in frequency of use, or in susceptibility will be reflected in differences in age, sex, income, and geographical location. But this is usually not true. Markets should be scrutinized for important differences in buyer attitudes, motivations, values, usage patterns, aesthetic preferences, or degree of susceptibility. These may have no demographic correlatives. Above all, we must never assume in advance that we know the best way of looking at a market. This is the cardinal rule of segmentation analysis. All ways of segmenting markets must be considered, and *then* we must select out of the various methods available the ones that have the most important implications for action. This process of choosing the strategically most useful mode of segmentation is the essence of the marketing approach espoused in this article.

In considering cases like those described, we must understand that we are not dealing with different types of people, but with differences in people's *values*. A woman who buys a refrigerator because it is the

EXHIBIT 1

Example of Segmentation in Different Industries

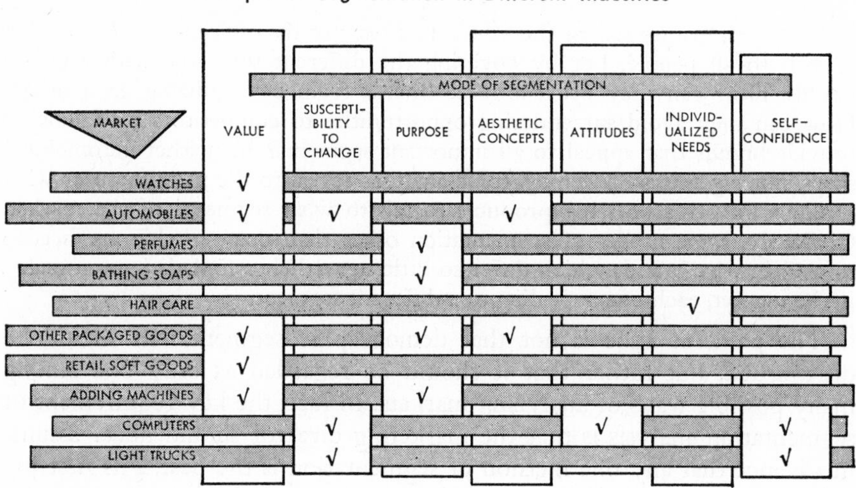

MODE OF SEGMENTATION
MARKET
VALUE
SUSCEPTIBILITY TO CHANGE
PURPOSE
AESTHETIC CONCEPTS
ATTITUDES
INDIVIDUALIZED NEEDS
SELF-CONFIDENCE
WATCHES
AUTOMOBILES
PERFUMES
BATHING SOAPS
HAIR CARE
OTHER PACKAGED GOODS
RETAIL SOFT GOODS
ADDING MACHINES
COMPUTERS
LIGHT TRUCKS

EDITOR'S NOTE: In Exhibit 1 the author shows schematically for ten markets the effect of seven different modes of nondemographic segmentation. The discussion of these examples is not included in this excerpt of the article. The seven modes are examples of how segmentation analysis can enlarge the scope of marketing thinking.

---

cheapest available may want to buy the most expensive towels. A man who pays extra for his beer may own a cheap watch. A Ford-owning Kellogg's Corn Flakes-eater may be closed off to Chevrolet but susceptible to Post Toasties; he is the same man, but he has had different experiences and holds different values toward each product he purchases. By segmenting markets on the basis of the values, purposes, needs, and attitudes relevant to the product being studied, as in Exhibit 1, we avoid misleading information derived from attempts to divide people into types.

2. *The strategic-choice concept of segmentation broadens the scope of marketing planning to include the positioning of new products as well as of established products.*

It also has implications for brand planning, not just for individual products but for the composition of a line of competing brands where any meaningful segment in the market can possibly support a brand. One explanation of the successful competing brand strategy of companies like Procter & Gamble is that they are based on sensitivity to the many different modes of market segmentation. The brands offered by P & G often appear very similar to the outsider, but small, marginal differences between them appeal to different market segments. It is this rather than intramural competition that supports P & G successes.

3. *Marketing must develop its own interpretive theory, and not borrow a ready-made one from the social sciences.*

Marketing research, as an applied science, is tempted to borrow its theoretical structures from the disciplines from which it derives. The social sciences offer an abundance of such structures, but they are not applicable to marketing in their pure academic form. While the temptation to apply them in that form is great, it should be resisted. From sociology, for example, marketing has frequently borrowed the concept of status. This is a far-reaching concept, but it is not necessarily the most important one in a marketing problem, nor even one of the important ones. Again, early psychoanalytic theory has contributed an understanding of the sexual factor. While this can sometimes be helpful in an analysis of buying behavior in a given situation, some motivation researchers have become oversensitive to the role of sex and, as a result, have made many mistakes. Much the same might be said of the concept of social character, that is, seeing the world as being "inner-directed," "other-directed," "tradition-directed," "autonomous," and so forth.

One of the values of segmentation analysis is that, while it has drawn on the insights of social scientists, it has developed an interpretive theory *within* marketing. It has been homegrown in business. This may explain its ability to impose patterns of meaning on the immense diversity of the market, and to provide the modern marketing director with a systematic method for evolving true marketing objectives.

Product differentiation efforts attempt to control demand through the promotion of product differences, while market segmentation efforts seek control by discovering and responding to different product preferences. Success in devising a product and services mix requires the use of both product differentiation and market segmentation as components of marketing strategy. The relationship of the two strategies in imperfectly competitive markets is discussed.

20. PRODUCT DIFFERENTIATION AND MARKET SEGMENTATION AS ALTERNATIVE MARKETING STRATEGIES*

Wendell R. Smith†

. . . Product differentiation and market segmentation are both consistent with the framework of imperfect competition.[1] In its simplest terms, *product differentiation* is concerned with the bending of demand to the will of supply. It is an attempt to shift or to change the slope of the demand curve for the market offering of an individual supplier. This strategy may also be employed by a group of suppliers such as a farm cooperative, the members of which have agreed to act together. It results from the desire to establish a kind of equilibrium in the market by bringing about adjustment of market demand to supply conditions favorable to the seller.

Segmentation is based upon developments on the demand side of the market and represents a rational and more precise adjustment of product and marketing effort to consumer or user requirements. In the language of the economist, segmentation is *disaggregative* in its effects and tends to

* Reprinted from "Product Differentiation and Market Segmentation As Alternative Marketing Strategies," *Journal of Marketing*, Vol. XXI, No. 1 (July, 1956), pp. 3–8.

† Marketing Science Institute.

[1] Imperfect competition assumes lack of uniformity in the size and influence of the firms or individuals that comprise the demand or supply sides of a market.

bring about recognition of several demand schedules where only one was recognized before.

Attention has been drawn to this area of analysis by the increasing number of cases in which business problems have become soluble by doing something about marketing programs and product policies that overgeneralize both markets and marketing effort. These are situations where intensive promotion designed to differentiate the company's products was not accomplishing its objective—cases where failure to recognize the reality of market segments was resulting in loss of market position.

While successful product differentiation will result in giving the marketer a horizontal share of a broad and generalized market, equally successful application of the strategy of market segmentation tends to produce depth of market position in the segments that are effectively defined and penetrated. The differentiator seeks to secure a layer of the market cake, whereas one who employs market segmentation strives to secure one or more wedge-shaped pieces.

Many examples of market segmentation can be cited; the cigarette and automobile industries are well-known illustrations. Similar developments exist in greater or lesser degree in almost all product areas. Recent introduction of a refrigerator with no storage compartment for frozen foods was in response to the distinguishable preferences of the segment of the refrigerator market made up of home freezer owners whose frozen food storage needs had already been met.

Strategies of segmentation and differentiation may be employed simultaneously, but more commonly they are applied in sequence in response to changing market conditions. In one sense, segmentation is a momentary or short-term phenomenon in that effective use of this strategy may lead to more formal recognition of the reality of market segments through redefinition of the segments as individual markets. Redefinition may result in a swing back to differentiation.

The literature of both economics and marketing abounds in formal definitions of product differentiation. *From a strategy viewpoint*, product differentiation is securing a measure of control over the demand for a product by advertising or promoting differences between a product and the products of competing sellers. It is basically the result of sellers' desires to establish firm market positions and/or to insulate their businesses against price competition. Differentiation tends to be characterized by heavy use of advertising and promotion and to result in prices that are somewhat above the equilibrium levels associated with perfectly competitive market conditions. It may be classified as a *promotional* strategy or approach to marketing.

Market segmentation, on the other hand, consists of viewing a heterogeneous market (one characterized by divergent demand) as a number of smaller homogeneous markets in response to differing product preferences among important market segments. It is attributable to the desires of consumers or users for more precise satisfaction of their varying wants. Like differentiation, segmentation often involves substantial use of advertising and promotion. This is to inform market segments of the availability of goods or services produced for or presented as meeting their needs with precision. Under these circumstances, prices tend to be somewhat closer to perfectly competitive equilibrium. Market segmentation is essentially a *merchandising* strategy, merchandising being used here in its technical sense as representing the adjustment of market offerings to consumer or user requirements.

THE EMERGENCE OF THE SEGMENTATION STRATEGY

To a certain extent, market segmentation may be regarded as a force in the market that will not be denied. It may result from trial and error in the sense that generalized programs of product differentiation may turn out to be effective in some segments of the market and ineffective in others. Recognition of, and intelligent response to, such a situation necessarily involves a shift in emphasis. On the other hand, it may develop that products involved in marketing programs designed for particular market segments may achieve a broader acceptance than originally planned, thus revealing a basis for convergence of demand and a more generalized marketing approach. The challenge to planning arises from the importance of determining, preferably in advance, the level or degree of segmentation that can be exploited with profit.

There appear to be many reasons why formal recognition of market segmentation as a strategy is beginning to emerge. One of the most important of these is decrease in the size of the minimum efficient producing or manufacturing unit required in some product areas. American industry has also established the technical base for product diversity by gaining release from some of the rigidities imposed by earlier approaches to mass production. Hence, there is less need today for generalization of markets in response to the necessity for long production runs of identical items.

Present emphasis upon the minimizing of marketing costs through self-service and similar developments tends to impose a requirement for better adjustment of products to consumer demand. The retailing structure, in its efforts to achieve improved efficiency, is providing less and less sales push at point of sale. This increases the premium placed by retailers upon products that are presold by their producers and are readily recognized by consumers as meeting their requirements as measured by satisfactory rates of stock turnover.

It has been suggested that the present level of discretionary buying power is productive of sharper shopping comparisons, particularly for items that are above the need level. General prosperity also creates increased willingness "to pay a little more" to get "just what I wanted."

Attention to market segmentation has also been enhanced by the recent ascendancy of product competition to a position of great economic importance. An expanded array of goods and services is competing for the consumer's dollar. More specifically, advancing technology is creating competition between new and traditional materials with reference to metals, construction materials, textile products, and in many other areas. While such competition is confusing and difficult to analyze in its early stages, it tends to achieve a kind of balance as various competing materials find their markets of maximum potential as a result of recognition of differences in the requirements of market segments.

Many companies are reaching the stage in their development where attention to market segmentation may be regarded as a condition or cost of growth. Their *core* markets have already been developed on a generalized basis to the point where additional advertising and selling expenditures are yielding diminishing returns. Attention to smaller or *fringe* market segments, which may have small potentials individually but are of crucial importance in the aggregate, may be indicated.

Finally, some business firms are beginning to regard an increasing share of their total costs of operation as being fixed in character. The higher costs of maintaining market position in the channels of distribution illustrate this change. Total reliance upon a strategy of product differentiation under such circumstances is undesirable, since market share available as a result of such a promotion-oriented approach tends to be variable over time. Much may hinge, for example, upon week-to-week audience ratings of the television shows of competitors who seek to outdifferentiate each other. Exploitation of market segments, which provides for greater maximization of consumer or user satisfactions, tends to build a more secure market position and to lead to greater over-all stability. While traditionally, high fixed costs (regarded primarily from the production viewpoint) have created pressures for expanded sale of standardized items through differentiation, the possible shifting of certain marketing costs into the fixed area of the total cost structure tends to minimize this pressure.

CONCLUSION

Success in planning marketing activities requires precise utilization of both product differentiation and market segmentation as components of marketing strategy. It is fortunate that available techniques of marketing research make unplanned market exploration largely unnecessary. It is the obligation of those responsible for sales and marketing administration to keep the strategy mix in adjustment with market structure at any point in time and to produce in marketing strategy at least as much dynamism as is present in the market. The ability of business to plan in this way is dependent upon the maintenance of a flow of market information that can be provided by marketing research as well as the full utilization of available techniques of cost accounting and cost analysis.

The Department of Defense is the largest single customer of American business. To be successful in the defense market, firms must recognize and adapt to the basic structure of the defense industry environment. Seven key factors in this environmental structure are discussed. A theory for organization of the defense marketing function is presented.

21. A THEORY ON PRINCIPLES AND PRACTICES IN DEFENSE MARKETING*

John J. Kennedy†

The defense industry has not been able to diversify successfully into commercial practice. A central reason is its reported lack of marketing; or conversely, its fixation on the technical aspects of the firm. The weaknesses of defense marketing practices are:

1. No marketing concept at all
2. Shotgun proposals
3. Speaking to yourself
4. Loss of customer pulse
5. The contract firehose
6. Horse trading and browbeating
7. No time

---

* Reprinted from "A Theory on Principles and Practices in Defense Marketing," *Proceedings of the Winter Conference of the American Marketing Association,* 1964, pp. 440–50. (See EDITORS' NOTE below.)

† University of Notre Dame.

EDITORS' NOTE: For a discussion of the structure, magnitude, and characteristics of the defense market, see Murray L. Weidenbaum, "The Nature of the Defense Market," *Business Topics,* Vol. II, No. 2 (Spring, 1963), pp. 61–67. This article contains a description of the magnitude and scope of the defense market. Discussed are the structure of demand, shifts in demand, and the effects of these shifts on suppliers. The treatment of the military market's major characteristics is of particular interest. For an evaluation of the marketing manager's role in focusing defense-oriented marketing efforts, see Sal F. Divita, "Selling R & D to the Government," *Harvard Business Review,* Vol. XLIII, No. 5 (September–October, 1965), pp. 62–75; and Philip L. Oster, "The Marketing Profile of the Defense Contractor," *Proceedings of the American Marketing Association* (June, 1965), pp. 538–53.

Only recently has systematic attention been given to the matter of marketing problems in the defense market. In various *Proceedings,* the American Marketing Association has published several papers that treat different aspects of military

The intent of this paper is to suggest alternatives that might partially remedy the weaknesses noted above. Structurally, the paper consists of three segments: (1) the significant environmental factors, (2) a theory on defense marketing organizational activities, and (3) concepts and principles for marketing practice.

The objectives of marketing are reasonably independent of the specific environment of a firm. They relate to maximizing long-run profit through the provision of value (goods and services) to the customer. However, specific activities relating to the achievement of marketing objectives are a function of basic environmental factors. Thus, prior to presenting the conceptual organization the significant environmental factors are evaluated. Within this context specific marketing activities are recommended. And finally, specific broad guidelines or principles for marketing practice are offered.

ENVIRONMENTAL FACTORS[1]

Scope

The defense industry is one of the largest industries in the world. Approximately 8–10% of the gross national product is allocated to the needs of the Department of Defense. About one-half of these dollars support the procurement of supplies and services. Total major military procurement actions fall in three areas: technical equipment items, services and non-equipment items. Technical equipment items consist of aircraft, missiles, ships, tanks, weapons, ammunitions, and electronics and communications equipment; and non-equipment items relate to subsistence, textiles, clothing and equipage, fuels and lubricants, miscellaneous hard goods, and construction. Of the categories, the technical equipment items account for over 70% of the allocated dollars. On the basis of corporate ownership, over 50% of defense contracts on a prime basis are

---

marketing. These papers, and two articles of interest, include: B. B. Gierer, "Marketing R&D For Military Products," *Harvard Business Review,* Vol. XL, No. 5 (September–October, 1962), pp. 111–20; William R. Boose, "Marketing to the Navy," *Journal* marketing. These papers, and two articles of interest, include: B. B. Bierer, "Market- *of Marketing;* Gerald A. Busch, "Marketing in the Defense Business," *Proceedings, American Marketing Association,* June, 1962, pp. 508–16; Joseph M. Hertzberg, "Measuring the Effectiveness of the Defense Marketing Operation," *Proceedings, American Marketing Association,* June, 1963, pp. 440–53; John J. Kennedy, "Strengths and Weaknesses of Defense Marketing Practices," *Proceedings, American Marketing Association,* June, 1964, pp. 869–79; Thomas L. Shubert, "The Defense Procurement Market," *Proceedings, American Marketing Association,* June, 1964, pp. 850–55; Earl W. Trantham, Jr., "Measuring and Selling the Defense Market," *Proceedings, American Marketing Association,* June, 1962, pp. 487–91; William C. Walter, "The National Space Program Market," *Proceedings, American Marketing Association,* June, 1964, pp. 856–68; Harry L. Williams, "An Economic Analysis of Future Defense Market Trends," *Proceedings, American Marketing Association,* June, 1962, pp. 517–20.

[1] John Joseph Kennedy, "Strengths and Weaknesses of Defense Marketing Practices," *The Marketing Concept in Action,* Robert M. Kaplan, Editor (Chicago: American Marketing Association, 1964), pp. 869–879.

allocated yearly to only four states—California, Texas, New York, and Massachusetts. This does not reflect the impact of sub-contracting which is substantial. Major defense companies often sub-contract between 40–50% of the contract dollar. However, in many instances the major sub-contracting segments are other major defense contractors. Although large defense weapon contractors predominate in the defense business, small business participation averages about 20%. Nevertheless, its participation in the defense contract industry is limited: 2.7% for aircraft, 1.2% for missiles, and about 10% for electronics.

The participation of small business is primarily in the non-technical category. In addition to military contracts, military installations in the United States account for a government, military, and civilian payroll of about $11 billion a year; and although this has been cut down recently by the actions of Defense Secretary McNamara, the payroll alone is still equal to one and one-half times the combined payrolls of iron and steel industry and all other basic metal producers, and is more than double the payroll of the automobile industry.

Zero Risk Conflict

What risk is the nation willing to take that Russia may establish military superiority. How many dollars must be spent to preclude this possibility? At present, this country commits about 8% of its GNP to the Department of Defense. What role does cost reduction play when viewed from this perspective?

Created Competition

The environment is artificial—created by the Department of Defense. The building blocks of this created competition environment include: (1) Classifications of Research and Development, (2) Program Definition, (3) Contractor Performance Evaluation, (4) Incentive Contracts, (5) New Management Control Systems such as PERT, and (6) Weighted Guideline Profit determination. The objective is to simulate an economic environment where competition will assure (1) a reasonable price, and (2) an incentive to provide quality on a timely basis.

The Real Product—Research and Development

The National Science Foundation reports that 58% of the Research and Development Expenditures of industry were financed by the federal government in 1964 and that 90 per cent of this was attributed to the Department of Defense and NASA. Hence, approximately 52% of total industry research and development is performed for defense space purposes.

Change and Obsolescence

Technical information is increasing at an increasing rate. It is not uncommon due to long lead times in development cycles that items finally readied for production are also ready for obsolescence. Defense firms must be able to adapt to rapid changes in demand.

Oligopolistic Supply

One-hundred companies and their subsidiaries account annually for 70 per cent or more of defense procurement dollars. The twenty largest companies alone receive over 50 per cent. Subcontracting is substantial, but a good part goes to other large firms numbered among the top 100. When the companies are grouped by product, only a handful of companies are seriously considered for any given contract award. This is particularly true for large systems.

Quasi-Legalistic Structure

About 80 to 90 per cent of defense dollars each year flow to industry through the mechanism of the negotiation process and the vehicle of the procurement contract. A unique and specific body of government contract law exists to which defense marketing must adapt. It is far more rigorous than the legal restrictions of commercial marketing practices. The contract entered into by both parties describes and defines specific performance for almost all aspects of the business. And the government is sovereign. The balance of power in the long run weighs heavily toward the Sovereign Power—the Federal Government.

Political Eyeball

The Department of Defense and the Defense Industry play their game in a stadium where the seats are filled with representatives of our political system. Each spectator has his favorite team. The Labor Surplus and Small Business "set asides clauses" compound the problem. The federal government influences our economic system principally by indirect means. The defense expenditures offer an excellent vehicle for direct input. This economic tool is of vital interest to the political body. It is an area that has not been evaluated objectively to date.

A THEORY ON DEFENSE MARKETING ORGANIZATIONAL ACTIVITIES

An organization reflects the needs of the situation. Although there often are many different approaches that could be effective for a given situation, a conceptual model or framework of reference is indispensable. It is important to have a way of thinking about marketing. From the conceptual model, adaptation can be made to varying circumstances.

An analysis of the defense environment suggests the following. (See Figure 1.)

FIGURE 1

Basic Marketing Functions

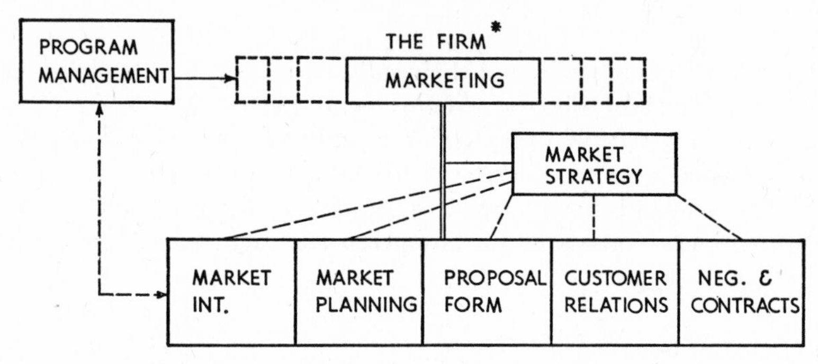

* Basic Functions include: Engineering, Material, Marketing, Operations, Quality, Customer Relations, and Controller.

The major marketing activities are:

1. *Market intelligence*—Information of a technical or general nature which contributes to improving a firm's competitive position.
2. *Market planning*—The analysis of market intelligence data, the evaluation of alternative courses of action, the establishment of target markets, and the development of marketing strategies related thereto.
3. *Proposal formulation*—The advertising media of defense marketing.
4. *Customer relations*—The personal sales activity.
5. *Negotiation*—The final phase of the selling process—the close. It is the determination by mutual agreement of the specific contractual terms and conditions under which the work is to be performed.

Market Intelligence

Contract award is highly correlated with (1) the firm that sells the idea initially to the government, and (2) the firm that finds out about the requirement before his competitors. Thus the importance of market intelligence is obvious. The need becomes particularly apparent when viewed in the context of the environment discussed earlier. The facets that are most dominant in shaping market intelligence needs are (1) orientation to research and development, (2) change and obsolescence, (3) the created competition, and (4) the political eyeball.

Market intelligence is derived from data from many sources: (1) customer requirements, (2) procurement awards, (3) Federal statistical data, (4) Congressional and Senatorial hearings, (5) political contracts, (6) military contracts, (7) competitive firms, (8) commercial publications, and (9) customer relations.

Market intelligence to be effective should be an integral unit of the marketing team. Indeed, it is the rock upon which success stands or falls. It must be a formal organization entity directed toward specific marketing goals. Marketing intelligence forms the basis for new goals and/or the revision of existing targets. Intelligence cannot be a haphazard non-goal oriented function and be effective. Where scope warrants, effective utilization can be made of the computer and quantitative analysis techniques. This provides a criterion for rapid impact analysis of new data and its potential implications.

Market Planning

The task of market planning is to define marketing goals and the means of their accomplishment. It relates to the development of marketing strategies and the variables to be considered in achieving the stated objectives. The Market Planning group should provide for the organization a list of targets ranked according to their significance to the organization and the probability of award. This will require an analysis of each specific procurement situation: Technical aspects, special facilities or know-how, competition, follow-on contracts, type of contract, time cycle, and so forth. These factors are then compared with a critical self-examination to establish a probability of award for each contract. The probability of award multiplied by the value to the organization provide the criteria for rank.[2] (See Figure 2.)

If an intuitive evaluation leads to a different criterion, an inconsistency exists in the assignment of probabilities of award, the values assigned, or both.

Proposal Formulation

Since the proposal is often the only source of knowledge that many government contractor personnel have of a particular firm, it is of vital interest. The proposal is the statement of how the firm plans to accomplish the specific goals established by the customer. As such, it must in a clear, concise, logical fashion define the reasons the firm believes it should be awarded the contract. The proposal is the communications link. It is the medium of the message to the customer.

Proposals reflect the efforts of the market intelligence and market planning groups. It is the implementation of the marketing planning function. Most contract awards go to companies whose proposal activity

[2] Expected value concept. Other techniques also applicable.

had started 24 to 36 months prior to formal requests for proposals. If a contractor waits until he is formally notified to develop and submit a proposal, his chances of award are extremely limited.

Proposals should be written to specific people and should be directed toward a particular target contract. The customer relations actively aids in orienting the proposal to the needs and wants of the decision channel. Too often proposals are written in a vacuum and the firm's orientation is itself;—i.e., talking to yourself.

FIGURE 2

	Profit	*Probability of Award*	*1 x 2*
Contract A	100	20	2000
Contract B	90	40	3600
Contract C	70	80	5600
Contract D	80	30	2400
Contract E	30	100	3000

Rank C, B, E, D, A.

The proposal formulation activity should be a formal, permanent organizational unit rather than an *ad hoc* committee that meets after receipts of requests for bid. It should participate in the market planning function through the market strategy committee. It works closely with customer relations to assure a rapport with the buyer. The guide for its activities is the overall market strategy plan.

The growth and importance of the proposal activity is directly related to defense marketing environmental factors. The predominant factors are (1) the emphasis of research and development, (2) created competition, (3) the quasi-legalistic orientation, and (4) the oligopolistic nature of the supply function.

Customer Relations

Customer relations personnel[3] develop the framework within which to develop the proposal. One of the basic tasks is to cultivate a compatible relationship with the decision channel. Thus it provides to the proposal group the orientation based on the needs, the personalities, the idiosyncrasies, and the receptiveness of the customer.

Customer relations must be cognizant of and participate in the overall market strategy plan. It is then oriented to specific tasks and plays the significant role in the execution, implementation, and feedback of the established strategy.

Too often customer relations personnel are "Charm Boys." Too often these "Charm Boys" are a loosely knit, non-directed group of geographically distributed representatives that operate in a vacuum apart from the

[3] Over 50% of these people usually have engineering backgrounds.

firm and distinct from the organizations of which presumably they are a part.

Negotiation[4]

Negotiation is the process by which mutual agreement is reached on conflicting positions. It is significant because since 1950 between 80 and 90 per cent of dollars have flowed to the defense industry through the process of negotiation. Negotiation, unfortunately, is often characterized by loss of customer pulse, the contract firehose, horse trading, and brow-beating.[5] The following is offered as an approach to the Negotiation Process in lieu of the above. (See Figure 3.)

FIGURE 3

The Negotiation Process*

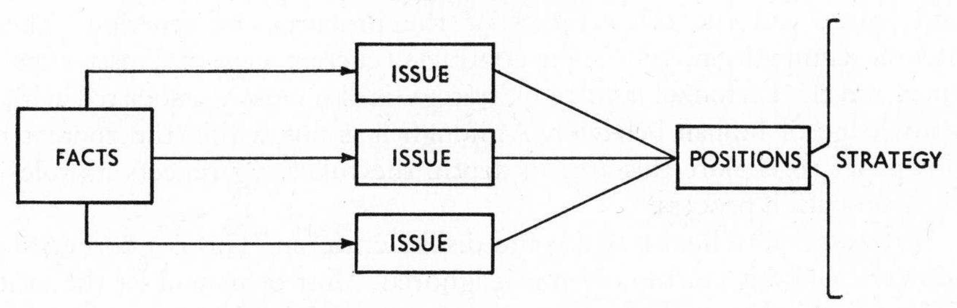

Facts:
1. Classify by issue and strategy
2. Catalog by degree and method of supportability

Issues:
1. Rank of importance
2. Use–non-use
3. Catalog for strategy use
4. Real–apparent

Positions:
1. Classified by importance
2. Facts cataloged by issue and related to positions
3. Maximum, minimum, and target positions

Strategy:
1. Analysis of procurement situation
2. Use of issues
3. Positions
4. Human behavior
5. Timing
6. Organization

* John J. Kennedy, "The Negotiation Process," unpublished paper, University of Notre Dame.

Negotiation, when viewed as a process, includes the variables of objectives, facts, issues, positions, strategy, and human behavior. These must be viewed in the context of the specific procurement situation. The manage-

[4] H. Kroecker of the Defense Management Center, Ohio State University, has performed much of the pioneering work in defense negotiation.

[5] Kennedy, *loc. cit.*

ment of the negotiation process relates to the planning, organizing, and controlling of these variables to maximize long-range corporate objectives.

The first step in a successful negotiation is to determine specific goals based on the factors prevalent for the given procurement. Facts are gathered and analyzed. Issues are identified through this analysis and the facts are then cataloged by issue. Issues are potential areas of disagreement that could preclude the accomplishment of the goals. The facts are classified by issue to facilitate the development of positions. Positions represent the companies' stand on the issues.

In the development of positions, the company must identify areas of possible agreement. Toward this end it is advisable that the range include maximum, minimum, and target positions. Facts, issues, and positions must then be woven into strategies.

The strategy is a function of the objectives, the positions based on facts and issues, and the other facets of the procurement situation. These include competition, follow-on contracts, current capacity, past experience, and the personnel involved. Strategy is also closely associated with a knowledge of human behavior. Although it is not within the context of this paper to explore this area in depth, the following reflects its role in the negotiation process.

We respond to honest praise and dislike criticism. This is a cornerstone of every sales kit but too often it is ignored. Most of us will let the other fellow lead—this can be important. It is often advisable to grasp the reins to guide the session. Leading often facilitates strategy implementation. You don't always change a person's mind with facts; human beings tend to interpret facts as necessary to preconceived ends. Once a pattern of decision making is established, it tends to persist. Therefore, start the negotiation session positively. Get off to a good start.

The marketing functions thus are parts of a whole—the fingers on a hand that work in rhythm and unison with a common goal. The following will assist the reader in the relationship of these functions to their environment. (See Figure 4.)

GUIDES TO MARKETING PRACTICES

Principles are statements of truth applicable under most conditions. The following represent a distillation of the ideas growing out of Parts I and II of this paper. They, of course, are not principles tested by thorough research; rather, they emerge as probable guides to action that must be adapted to specific circumstances.

1. Defense products must be sold.
2. Success in obtaining contracts, assuming previous good performance, is directly related to: (*a*) demand creation, (*b*) the level of proposal sophistication, (*c*) cultivation of the decision chain, (*d*) the expertise of

the customer relations function, and (*e*) the extent to which some market planning has been undertaken based on market intelligence.

3. A company cannot successfully ignore the government's role as sovereign. The government will win most arguments over the long run.

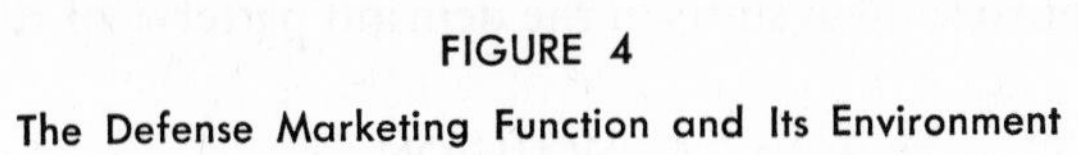

FIGURE 4

The Defense Marketing Function and Its Environment

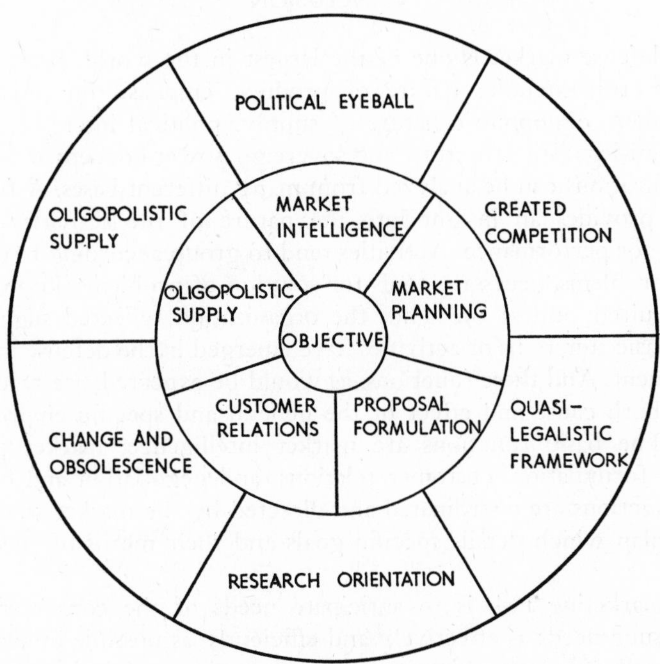

4. There is a definite correlation between the image of the company in the minds of those in the decision channel and the company's success in obtaining defense contracts.

5. The smaller the company and the more highly specialized its product, the greater the price flexibility.

6. An outstanding proposal will contribute to a capable company's chances for contract award. However, an outstanding proposal will not help a company whose image with a decision channel is highly negative.

7. Proposals have to be written for a specific purpose and oriented to specific individuals in the decision channel.

8. Prior knowledge of negotiation and its principles and theories and the ability to apply them is generally more important than specific product knowledge.

9. Satisfactory performance over a long period of time is not sufficient to warrant success in the defense market. The defense market can be as impersonal as you want it to be. Conversely, it can be as impersonal as you let it be.

10. A defense company's organization is directly affected by the organizational philosophy of the customer.

11. Proposals are advertising; they must be planned and budgeted.

12. A dominant factor that can cause marketing success or failure is the ability to adapt to sudden shifts in the demand patterns of the customer.

CONCLUSION

The defense market is one of the largest in the world. Basic environmental factors include: nature of product, emphasis on research and development, oligopolistic nature of supply, political interests and reactions, quasi-legalistic structure, and sovereign power concept.

Organizations can be analyzed from many different bases. A functional analysis provides an insight into the nature of the activities that are required for performance. Activities tend to group according to commonality of problems, necessary tools for solution of problems, knowledge or skills required, and so on. Thus the organization reflected suggests that certain basic functions or activities have emerged in the defense marketing environment. And these functions, as would be expected, are reactions to, and are both cause and effect of the general and specific environmental forces. The basic functions are market intelligence, market planning, proposal formulation, customer relations, and negotiation and contracts. These functions are coordinated and directed by the market strategy and general plan which details specific goals and their means of accomplishment.

The marketing task is to anticipate needs of the consumer and to provide such needs as effectively and efficiently as possible in accordance with overall corporate objectives. The marketing activities and practices related to the task vary with the environment; but nevertheless exist. Defense marketing needs *exist.* A framework of reference for the defense marketing sphere is the prerequisite.

Bibliography—Chapter III

BLISS, PERRY. *Marketing and the Behavioral Sciences,* 2nd ed. Boston: Allyn and Bacon, Inc., 1967.

BOYD, HARPER W., JR., AND LEVY, SIDNEY J. "New Dimension in Consumer Analysis," *Harvard Business Review,* Vol. XLI, No. 6 (November–December, 1963), pp. 129–40.

DICHTER, ERNEST. "Discovering the Inner Jones," *Harvard Business Review,* Vol. XLIII, No. 3 (May–June, 1965), pp. 6 ff.

FERBER, ROBERT, AND WALES, HUGH G. (eds). *Motivation and Market Behavior.* Homewood, Illinois: Richard D. Irwin, Inc., 1958.

FESTINGER, L. *A Theory of Cognitive Dissonance.* Stanford, Calif.: Stanford University Press, 1957.

GLOCK, CHARLES Y. AND NICOSIA, FRANCESCO M. "Uses of Sociology in Studying Consumption Behavior, *Journal of Marketing,* Vol. 28, No. 3 (July, 1964), pp. 51–54.

GOTTMAN, J. "Megalopolis: The Urbanized Northeastern Seaboard of the U.S.," *Twentieth Century Fund Report.* New York: Macmillan Co., 1961.

KATONA, GEORGE. *The Powerful Consumer.* New York: McGraw-Hill Book Co., Inc., 1960.

KRUGMAN, H. E., AND HARTLEY, E. L. "The Learning of Tastes," *Public Opinion Quarterly,* Vol. XXIV, No. 4 (Winter, 1960), pp. 621–31.

MCNEAL, JAMES U. *Dimension of Consumer Behavior.* New York: Appleton-Century-Crofts, 1965.

MARTINEAU, PIERRE. "Social Class and Spending Behavior," *Journal of Marketing,* Vol. 23, No. 2 (October, 1958), pp. 121–30.

NICOSIA, FRANCESCO M. *Consumer Decision Processes: Marketing and Advertising Implications.* Englewood Cliffs, New Jersey: Prentice-Hall, Inc., 1966.

SCHNORE, L. F. "The Socio-Economic Status of Cities and Suburbs," *American Sociological Review,* Vol. XXVIII, No. 1 (February, 1963), pp. 76–85.

VON ECKARDT, W. "The Challenge of Megalopolis," *Twentieth Century Fund Report.* New York: Macmillan Co., 1964.

IV. MARKETING DECISIONS: MODELS, TECHNIQUES, AND STRATEGIES

Marketing can be viewed as a function of business. It can also be studied and analyzed as a philosophy of business operation and as a prime focus for managerial decision making. In many business problems, the influence of marketing extends well beyond the commonly accepted functional limits of marketing in a business organization. Marketing decisions affect and are affected by decisions made in other functional areas of business, such as procurement, production, finance, credit, product development, and personnel. Some of the newer research techniques and strategies reflect this broader view of marketing and research in marketing.

A longtime goal of marketing researchers has been to make marketing practices and research more scientific. Some of the newer tools of analysis provide methods for making better marketing management decisions under uncertainty. The application of computer technology in business has been hailed as the second industrial revolution. Bayesian statistics is revamping conceptual approaches to problem solving. Marketing models are being developed to depict important marketing relationships; mathematical and statistical tools bring the quantitative methods of operations research to bear on marketing problems; electronic data processing provides valuable marketing information and the base for marketing intelligence.

The articles in this chapter are concerned with developing an integrated perspective for decision making. They indicate how decision tools can be utilized effectively to mobilize the total resources of the firm and capitalize on market opportunities. The research challenge to the marketing manager is to find a better way of performing the marketing function and helping the firm to achieve its goals in an environment in which marketing considerations are growing more important.

The concept of marketing models and their relevance to significant marketing problems are discussed. Marketing models are defined, and two approaches to model building are described. Generalizations are made about the role of models in marketing science.

22. THE ROLE OF MODELS IN MARKETING*

William Lazer†

Behavioral sciences and quantitative methods are both in the forefront in the current development and extension of marketing knowledge. It is no mere coincidence that both make frequent reference to two concepts: models and systems. Certainly models and systems have become powerful interpretive tools.[1]

Models and systems have relevance to such significant marketing problems as: (1) developing marketing concepts and enriching the marketing language by introducing terms that reflect an operational viewpoint and orientation; (2) providing new methods and perspectives for problem-solving; (3) conducting marketing research and designing experiments; (4) developing marketing theories; (5) measuring the effectiveness of marketing programs.

Although they may not be recognized as such, marketing models are fairly widely applied by both practitioners and academicians. The use of analogies, constructs, verbal descriptions of systems, "idealizations," and graphic representations are quite widespread in marketing. For example, pricing models, physical distribution models, models of marketing institutions, and advertising models are useful marketing tools.

DEFINITION OF MARKETING MODELS

A model is simply the perception or diagramming of a complex or a system. In marketing, it involves translating perceived marketing relation-

* Reprinted from "The Role of Models in Marketing," *Journal of Marketing*, Vol. 26, No. 2 (April, 1962), pp. 9–14. See also W. J. Baumol, *Marketing and the Computer* (Englewood Cliffs, N.J.: Prentice-Hall, Inc., 1963), pp. 202 ff.

† Michigan State University.

[1] Paul Meadows, "Models, Systems and Science," *American Sociological Review*, Vol. 22 (February, 1957), pp. 3–9, at p. 3.

ships into constructs, symbols, and perhaps mathematical terms. For example, an internally consistent set of statements concerning wholesaling, advertising, merchandising, or pricing comprises a model. It relates in a logical manner certain constructs or axioms that are envisaged.

Models are really the bases for marketing theories, since they are the axioms or assumptions on which marketing theories are founded. They furnish the underlying realities for theory construction. Where the perceived relationships are expressed in mathematical terms, we have a mathematical model. In this sense, any consistent set of mathematical statements about some aspect of marketing can be regarded as a model.

All marketing models are based on suppositions or assumptions. These assumptions do not correspond exactly with the real marketing world. Usually they are employed to simplify an existing marketing situation. Therefore, models cannot depict marketing activities exactly. Moreover, no matter how precise mathematical models may be, they do not correct themselves for false assumptions.

MODEL BUILDING

There are two approaches to the construction of marketing models: *abstraction* and *realization*.[2]

In abstraction, a real world situation is perceived and it is mapped into a model. If it is mapped into a mathematical system, a mathematical model results. This is illustrated by Figure 1.

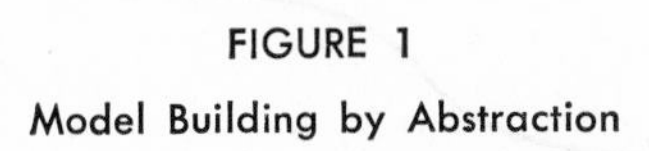

FIGURE 1

Model Building by Abstraction

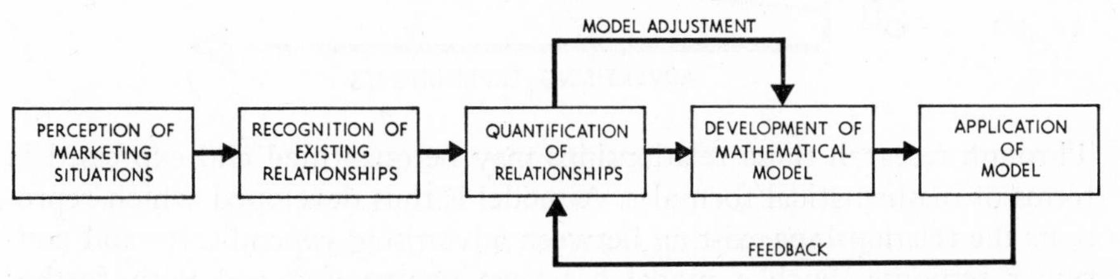

In abstraction, the model builder must perceive of a marketing situation in a way that permits him to recognize the relationships between a number of variables. For example, he may perceive of relationships between transportation costs, customer satisfaction, and the location of distribution centers; the number of sales calls and resulting sales and profits; the allocation of advertising expenditures and the achievement of favorable consumer response.

[2] See C. H. Coombs, H. Raiffa, and R. M. Thrall, "Some Views On Mathematical Models and Measurement Theory," in R. M. Thrall, C. H. Coombs, and R. L. Davis (editors), *Decision Processes* (New York: John Wiley and Sons, Inc., 1954), pp. 20–21.

Based on this, the model builder will become aware of logical conceptual relationships which he is able to state fairly succinctly and clearly. These relationships may then be quantified through the use of available records and data, experiments, or simulations. The basis for the establishment of a mathematical model is obtained.

Once the mathematical model is determined, it may be applied in "the real world." Feedback will result which will provide the basis for a further alteration of the quantification of the conceptual relationships perceived. It will lead to a refinement and improvement in the mathematical model.

As an example of model building by abstraction, consider the construction of a model representing consumer response to company advertising expenditures.[3] Through observation, analysis of relevant data, and experience, the model builder may recognize that with little or no advertising expenditures consumer purchases of a product are very small. Then it may appear that, as expenditures increase over a certain range, purchase responses increase quite sharply. While response increases even further with additional advertising expenditures, it is noted that eventually it tapers off and tends toward some limit.

The resulting model may be depicted graphically as in Figure 2.

FIGURE 2

Relationship of Consumer Response to Advertising Expenditures

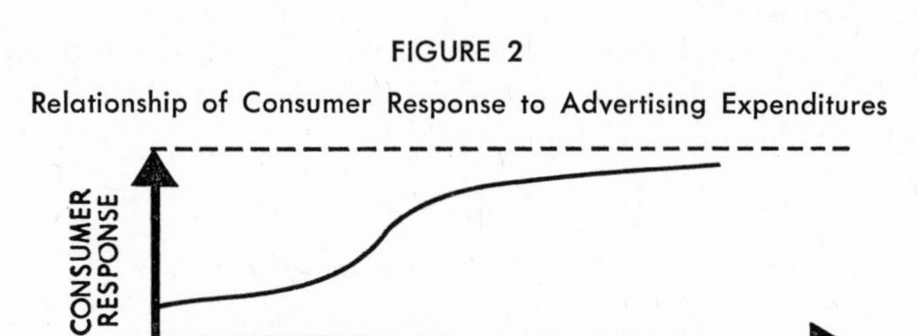

Through research these relationships may be quantified and expressed in terms of mathematical formulas. A model is thus developed which represents the relationships existing between advertising expenditures and consumer response. Such a model has been constructed and with further mathematical refinements was used to determine the optimum allocation of advertising expenditures.[4] The model also proved to be useful in developing advertising-response curves, analyzing the impact of time lags in advertising effect, evaluating the interaction of competing promotional effort and estimating the impact of varying promotional resources.

---

[3] A. P. Zentler and Dorothy Ryde, "An Optimal Geographical Distribution of Publicity Expenditure In A Private Organization," *Management Science*, Vol. 2 (July, 1956), pp. 337–52.

[4] *Ibid.*

Model Building by Realization

In realization, the process of model building is reversed. The model builder starts with a consideration of a logically consistent conceptual system. Then some aspect of the real world can be viewed as the model of the system. It is a process of going from the logical system to the real world.[5] This is portrayed in Figure 3.

FIGURE 3

Model Building by Realization

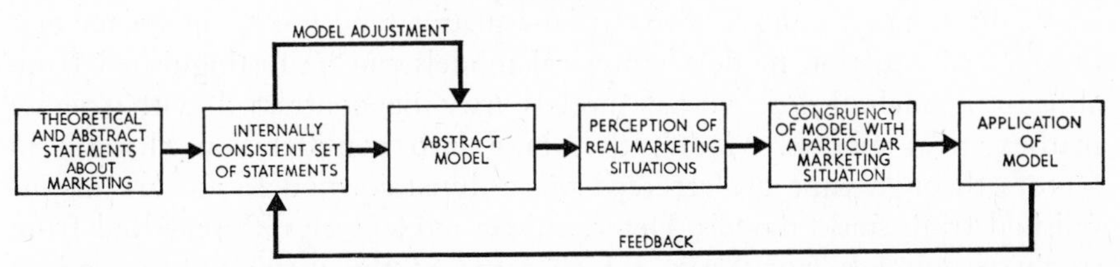

Model building by realization may be illustrated by considering the mathematical model known as a Markov process. This process is a model that is useful in the study of complex business systems. It studies the present state of a marketing system and what has happened through some transition time. For example, it can be of help in studying the users and nonusers of a product (the present state of the system), and what has happened as advertising is applied over a time period (the state transitions). It is a theoretical, logically consistent, and abstract model.

Starting with this model, the model builder may perceive that such marketing situations as the use of advertising to switch brand loyalties of consumers, or to change consumers from the state of nonusers to users, deal with the current state of a system and the transition of the system through time. Therefore, he may use the Markov process to study the effects of advertising impact. As experience from application of the model is developed, feedback will result and the model can be adjusted. In using this procedure, the model builder has gone from a logical mathematical system to the world of marketing.

Herniter and Magee and also Maffei have discussed the application of Markov process models.[6] Their research indicates that such models are extremely useful in determining the choice of promotional policy for maximizing profits in the long-run; in specifying the kinds of experimen-

---

[5] Coombs, Raiffa, and Thrall, *op. cit.*, p. 21.

[6] Jerome Herniter and John F. Magee, "Customer Behavior As A Markov Process," *Operations Research*, Vol. 9 (January–February, 1961), pp. 105–22. Richard B. Maffei, "Brand Preferences and Simple Markov Processes," *Operations Research*, Vol. 8 (March–April, 1960), pp. 210–18.

tation required to measure the impact of promotional effort, and in calculating cost and revenue changes resulting from the use of alternative marketing strategies over time.

KINDS OF MARKETING MODELS

It is difficult to classify marketing models since there are many dimensions and distinguishing characteristics that may be used as criteria for classification.

Mathematicians, for instance, might classify marketing models according to the type of equations used. They could distinguish among algebraic, difference-equation, differential-equation, and mixed-difference and differential equation models.[7] Physical models can be distinguished from abstract models. Loose verbal models may be contrasted with precise mathematical models. Models that take into consideration changes in factors through time are referred to as dynamic models and are distinguished from static models. Deterministic models are differentiated from stochastic models (models in which some of the variables are random factors and cannot be completely determined). Micro marketing and macro marketing models exist, as do linear and non-linear models. Perhaps one of the most meaningful distinctions from a marketing point of view is that of goal models and systems models.

Systems Models and Goal Models

A distinction has been made in the behavioral-science literature between *systems models* and *goal models*.[8]

In marketing, a goal model or end-means model starts with a marketing task to be achieved. For instance, it focuses on the marketing objectives and the uses of company resources to achieve them as efficiently as possible. It is the achievement of marketing goals, and not necessarily corporate goals, that become important.

The goal model does not lend itself readily to a representation of a multifunctional unit. The marketing department is not viewed as being comprised of a number of different departments with possible conflicting goals, but rather as one over-all unit with a major goal. The implication here is that if we increase the marketing means, we thereby increase our effectiveness in achieving marketing goals. In this model, moreover, the effectiveness of the marketing department is measured by the devotion to

[7] This breakdown is taken from an unpublished paper prepared by Dr. Paul Craig, at the Institute of Basic Mathematics for application to business, sponsored by the Ford Foundation at Harvard University during 1959–60. The actual classification of models was suggested by Dr. Samuel Goldberg.

[8] Amitai Etzioni, "Two Approaches to Organizational Analysis: A Critique and A Suggestion," *Administrative Science Quarterly*, Vol. 5 (September, 1960), pp. 257–78, at p. 258.

the achievement of marketing goals. Although the goal model is useful, it is Utopian and unrealistic.

In the systems model, the starting point is not a goal. The starting point is the model of a total functioning system, for example, the marketing department. It is the model of a marketing unit capable of achieving goals. The systems model recognizes that there can be many conflicting objectives within an organization and that concessions must be made. In this model, the multifunctional units involved in achieving marketing goals are recognized. This model also considers that some means must be allocated to non-goal directed effort, such as the resources necessary to maintain the marketing organization. Given certain marketing conditions and resources, the main consideration is—how can they be programmed to achieve the optimum position for the total business system?

The systems model is the superior model for marketing management. It is the model that the operations researcher uses when he perceives of a business as an over-all system of action as when he plans the optimal use of resources. The systems approach to the study of marketing is appearing in the literature and should result in a better understanding of the existing interrelationships among marketing elements, a clearer grasp of marketing behavior, and a more effective allocation of marketing resources.[9]

Models and Marketing Theory

The terms "models" and "theories" are often used interchangeably. An interesting and useful distinction for marketing can be drawn from an idea expressed by Coombs, Raiffa, and Thrall; "A model is not itself a theory; it is only an available or possible or potential theory until a segment of the real world has been mapped into it. Then the model becomes a theory about the real world."[10] As a theory, a marketing model can be accepted or rejected on the basis of how well it actually works. The actual model itself, however, is "right or wrong" (internally consistent) on logical grounds only.

One can distinguish between models and theories by considering marketing-research techniques. A stipulated technique for marketing measurement may be called a model. For example, the forecasting technique known as exponential smoothing, or forecasting by exponentially weighted moving averages, has proved to be a useful forecasting model.[11]

[9] See Wroe Alderson, *Marketing Decisions and Executive Action* (Homewood, Ill.: Richard D. Irwin, Inc., 1957); William Lazer and Eugene J. Kelley, "Interdisciplinary Contributions to Marketing Management" (Bureau of Business and Economic Research, Michigan State University, 1959); William Lazer, "Transportation Management: A Systems Approach," *Distribution Age*, Vol. 59 (September, 1960), pp. 33–35; and John F. Magee, "Operations Research in Making Marketing Decisions," *Journal of Marketing*, Vol. 25 (October, 1960), pp. 18–24.

[10] Coombs, Raiffa, and Thrall, *op. cit.*, pp. 25–26.

[11] Peter R. Winters, "Forecasting Sales by Exponentially Weighted Moving Averages," *Management Science*, Vol. 6 (April, 1960), pp. 324–42.

As a model it need only be internally consistent. It is a potential marketing theory.

When data are actually measured by the exponential smoothing technique and are mapped into the model, then the model becomes a theory about the marketing data. The resulting theory may be a good one or a poor one.

The relationship between marketing models, theories, and hypotheses now follows directly. Within a theoretical framework, we are able to test certain hypotheses. The assumptions of a marketing model itself, however, need not be subjected to tests, whereas hypotheses should be tested. It should be noted that assumptions in one model may be hypotheses in another.

USES OF MODELS IN MARKETING

Five major uses for models in marketing can be suggested.

1) *Marketing models provide a frame of reference for solving marketing problems.* They suggest fruitful lines of inquiry, and existing information gaps. Marketing models do this by playing a descriptive role. The descriptive model does not go beyond presenting a representation or picture of some aspect of marketing activity. However, it serves an extremely important function in the extention of marketing thought. The use of flow diagrams in depicting existing relationships or in developing a logical computer program is an example of the use of descriptive models.

2) *Marketing models may play an explicative role, and as such they are suggestive and flexible.* Such models are more than simple metaphors; they attempt to explain relationships and reactions. The marketing scientist not only is interested in describing marketing phenomena and examining them, but he desires to explain existing relationships and frames of references. For example, "switching models" often attempt to explain the relationships between advertising and brand loyalty.[12]

3) *Marketing models are useful aids in making predictions.* For instance, in answer to the question why models should be used, Bross explains that the real answer to this question is that the procedure has been followed in the development of the most successful predicting systems so far produced, the predicting systems used in science.[13] Marketing practitioners and scientists wish to predict and consequently employ various types of forecasting models and inventory models. These models become more than just an explanation and a representation of an existing situation. They become means of presenting future reality.

4) *Marketing models can be useful in theory construction.* Formulators of marketing models may hypothesize about various aspects of mar-

[12] See footnote 9.

[13] Irwin D. J. Bross, *Design for Decisions* (New York: The Macmillan Co., 1953), p. 169.

keting as they might exist. Thereby, we have "reality" as it is hypothesized. Simulation, for example, which really involves experimentation on models, can lead to valuable insights into marketing theory. In the same vein an ideal may be developed as a model. Although the ideal may not be achieved, it provides a useful vehicle for extending knowledge.

5) *Marketing models may stimulate the generation of hypotheses which can then be verified and tested.* Thereby, it furthers the application of the scientific method in marketing research and the extension of marketing knowledge.

Benefits of Mathematical Models

Why should marketing scientists and practitioners utilize mathematical models rather than other kinds of models?[14] Perhaps the most important reasons are four:

1) *The translation of a model from a verbal to a mathematical form makes for greater clarification of existing relationships and interactions.* It is a rigorous and demanding task; and conceptual clarity and operational definitions are often achieved. The models developed may also become more generally applicable.

2) *Mathematical models promote greater ease of communication.* Within business administration and related subject-matter areas, there is the difficulty of cross-communication because of the terminology used by specialized disciplines. Through the use of mathematical models, all of the disciplines may be reduced to a common mathematical language which may reveal interrelationships and pertinence of research findings not previously known.

3) *Mathematical models tend to be more objective, while verbal constructs lean heavily on intuition and rationalizations.* Scientific marketing can be advanced through the application of objective mathematical analysis.

4) *Analyses that are not feasible through verbal models may be advanced through mathematical models.* Mathematics provides powerful tools for marketing academicians and practitioners. Mathematical models lend themselves to analysis and manipulation. In the manipulation of verbal models, the inter-relationships and logic are easily lost.

CONCLUDING OBSERVATIONS

The usefulness of a marketing model is a function of the level of generalization the model achieves and the degree of reality it portrays. Symbolization is used in model building to achieve greater internal consistency and more correspondence with reality. The greater the level of symbolization, and the fewer the restrictions, the more adequate and more generally applicable is the model.

---

[14] See footnote 7.

For example, it is true that linear-programing models are more abstract, more general, and more valuable than are mere descriptive models representing a factory and warehousing complex. However, it may well be that the linear-programming model is by no means more widely used.

All marketing models are based on simplifications and abstractions. Only by making assumptions is a model molded to fit reality. Sometimes the reality beyond the boundaries of the model, however, is much greater than the reality within the boundaries. The model then becomes severely limited by the assumptions on which it is based.

To be effective, marketing models should be plausible, solvable, and based on realistic assumptions. The current level of model building in marketing is not yet a sophisticated one. It cannot compare favorably with the level of model building in the physical or biological sciences. As the discipline of marketing matures, however, it will use an increasing number of models and will develop more complex models that have broader application.

Logical flow models depict the sequence of events in a behavioral process. They are less cumbersome than prose models and do not require the degree of mathematical sophistication assumed in many mathematical models. The characteristics of prose, mathematical, and logical flow models are enumerated, and the development of a logical flow model is discussed.

23. LOGICAL FLOW MODELS FOR MARKETING ANALYSIS*

William F. Massy† and Jim D. Savvas†

The use of analytical models in marketing has become widely accepted. As direct aids to decision-makers, their use provides an increased understanding of the forces underlying marketing phenomena, and in some cases leads to improved forecasts of specific conditions like the level of sales or competitive prices.

Similarly, effective marketing research requires a systematic statement

* Reprinted from "Logical Flow Models for Marketing Analysis," *Journal of Marketing,* Vol. 28, No. 1 (January, 1964), pp. 30–37.

† Stanford University.

of hypotheses, logic, and conclusions. Such statements are the sum and substance of the analytical model.

What may not be widely enough recognized is that a high degree of mathematical knowledge is not necessary for the construction and analysis of many useful marketing models. The purpose of this article is to describe the *logical flow model*, to show where it fits into the spectrum of modeling activity, and to indicate how this kind of analysis can be conducted by even the mathematically unsophisticated.

TYPES OF MODELS

Models can be classified in a number of different ways:

Deterministic or probabilistic
Descriptive or normative
Empirical or theoretical
According to the language used in their construction.[1]

The models to be discussed in this article are: (1) deterministic—they do not explicitly consider uncertainty as to outcome;[2] (2) descriptive—they represent attempts to describe what *is* rather than what should be;[3] and (3) empirical—they are based on direct observation and testing rather than on abstract principles.[4]

The major question to be discussed is that of the language used in the construction of models. Models useful for marketing analysis are usually made up of English statements, mathematical equations, or logical flow sequences. Each of these languages will be considered in order to show the strong and weak points and the range of usefulness of each of them for marketing.

Prose Models

Everyone has constructed simple models of human or marketing behavior, using only "everyday English" as the language of representation. For example, a sales manager for a firm manufacturing consumer products might describe a competitor's reaction to his price cut by saying: "If I cut my price, my competitor will cut his an equal amount."

---

[1] For a generalized treatment of model building and simulation, see Ronald E. Frank, Alfred A. Kuehn, and William F. Massy, *Quantitative Techniques in Marketing Analysis* (Homewood, Illinois: Richard D. Irwin Co., Inc., 1962), especially pp. 106–124 and pp. 461–548.

[2] A treatment of uncertainty can be found in Robert D. Buzzell and Charles C. Slater, "Decision Theory and Marketing Management," *Journal of Marketing*, Vol. 26 (July, 1962), pp. 7–16.

[3] See Herbert A. Simon, "Theories of Decision-Making in Economics," *American Economic Review*, Vol. 49 (June, 1959), pp. 253–283.

[4] See William Lazer, "The Role of Models in Marketing," *Journal of Marketing*, Vol. 26 (April, 1962), pp. 9–14.

When the sales manager is pressed, he may give a more detailed description of his competitor's reaction: for example, the prose model in Part *A* of Figure 1.

While a one-sentence model is easy to grasp, more complicated formulations like the many-sentence model in the figure may be unduly cumbersome. It may be difficult to keep all of their important characteristics in mind when attempting to draw conclusions or make predictions about the behavior under study. Yet the many-sentence model meets the basic requirements for a model of behavior: It sets up initial conditions and inputs ("If I cut my price," "providing the price cut is likely to be permanent," etc.) and predicts responses ("my competitor will cut his [price] to meet mine," etc.).

Mathematical Models

Based on the sales manager's verbal statements, the mathematically inclined marketing analyst might build a model as described in the middle portion of Figure 1. Notice how the "everyday English" of the verbal model is still used in the definitions of the variables, but how relationships among them are described with equality signs, subscripts, and other mathematical relationships, in addition to English.

While the mathematical model in Figure 1 is quite brief, it can in principle be subjected to the gamut of mathematical techniques, ranging from optimization to sensitivity to comparative statics analysis.[5] It can easily be passed on to a technician or a computer for mathematical computations. However, it is backed up by a long string of definitions and restrictions which were used in its construction and which must be used again to translate the conclusions of the mathematical analysis back into "everyday English." In fact, these definitions must be kept constantly in mind during the mathematical analysis if absurd manipulations and conclusions are to be avoided.

Logical Flow Models

The third model of Figure 1 is also based on the sales manager's English statements. This model uses three types of language:

1. Everyday English—to describe questions asked and actions taken by the subject of the model.
2. Circles, diamonds, and squares—to enclose physically the sets of questions and actions described by the model.
3. Arrows—to indicate the flow of questions and actions: the sequence in which questions are asked and actions are taken.

[5] See Jay W. Forrester, *Industrial Dynamics* (Cambridge: M.I.T. Press and New York: John Wiley & Sons, Inc., 1961), as well as the comparative statics analysis of classical economic models as discussed in H. A. Simon, *Models of Man, Social and Rational* (New York: John Wiley & Sons, Inc., 1957), p. 103.

FIGURE 1

Three Models of a Competitor's Reaction to a Price Cut

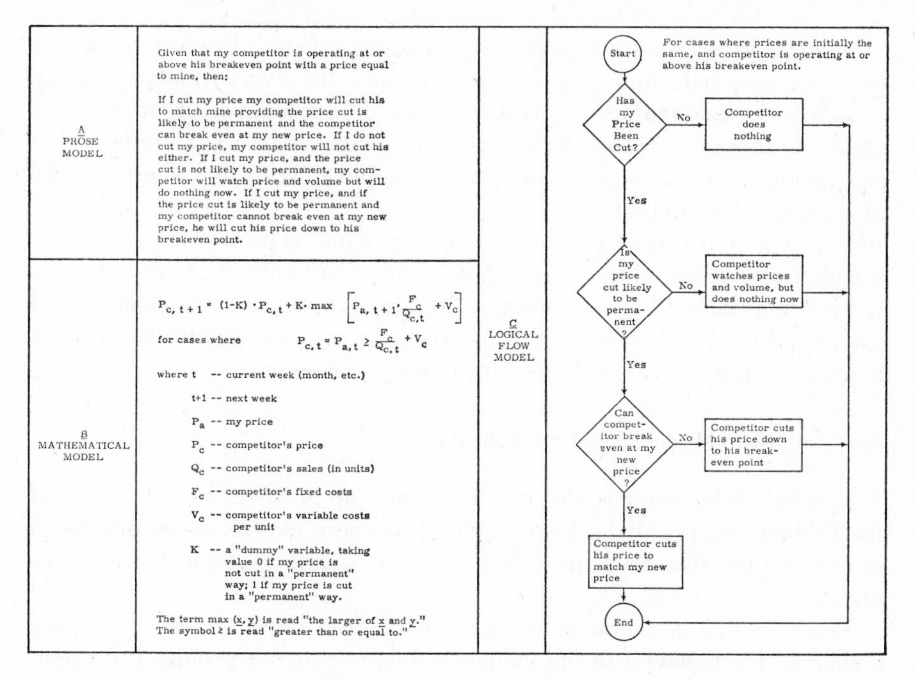

The logical flow model of *C* in Figure 1 is easily constructed from the prose model by simply describing the questions posed and actions taken. The statements of the latter are set down in the logical sequence in which they appear in the behavioral process. The simple devices of geometrical shapes and arrows help put together a picture one can "see." This picture is easily grasped or even memorized, and can be referenced readily. Conclusions obtained from the prose model can be reconstructed by following each possible path leading from "start" to "end."

COMPARISON OF MODELS

The important features of prose, mathematical, and logical flow models have been summarized in Figure 2 as an aid to comparing the three types of languages which are available to the marketing analyst. The following discussion is limited to the:

Expertise required of the researcher
Applicability to modeling various behaviors
Applicability of conducting various types of analyses
Understandability by businessmen

Expertise Required of the Researcher

The ability to reason logically in terms of everyday English (or whatever the national language) is a prerequisite for every model building endeavor. One advantage of prose and logical flow models is that this basic ability is sufficient to handle the technical aspects of their construction and manipulation, whereas mathematical sophistication is a must for the mathematical-model builder.

It is taken for granted that no matter what type of model the researcher is attempting to construct, he is able (and willing) to do intensive work along the well-known lines of literature research, the collection and analysis of field and/or secondary source data, and the important cycle of modeling—testing—remodeling—retesting—and so on.

Applicability to Modeling Various Behaviors

Logical flow models do not represent an answer to all kinds of model-building problems. Each of the three basic models under discussion is more applicable to some types of model-building situations than to others.

Prose models are best suited to the description of relatively simple aspects of the behavior of individuals and homogeneous groups. For example: "I will sell you a dozen apples in return for forty-nine cents," and "All scheduled airlines in the United States will begin collecting 5% federal excise tax, instead of 10%, on all taxable passenger tickets beginning in 1964."

Mathematical models are most applicable where the results of many independent decisions are "averaged out" to produce aggregate behavior patterns which are of interest. Continuous quantitative variables are usually handled best by mathematical means.

Also the behavior of heterogeneous groups of individuals, or behavior with respect to a broad class of decisions, is best modeled mathematically. Examples are the cost-volume-profit (break-even point) considerations of the examples in Figure 1, which represent in a continuous fashion the effect of many decisions; and the price-sales volume relationship which was deliberately left out of the models of Figure 1 but which would be essential in completing this model of competitive behavior.

By themselves, logical flow models are applicable for the description of both simple and fairly complicated aspects of the behavior of an individual, or a homogeneous group of individuals, with respect to particular decisions. An example will be given later. Simple mathematics may be combined with logical flow statements if the individual whose behavior is being modeled makes use of mathematical calculations in reaching a decision. These same calculations must then be incorporated, but the

FIGURE 2

Comparison of Features of Verbal, Mathematical, and Logical Flow Models

Feature of model	*Applicability of Feature to:**			
	(1) *Prose models*	*(2)* *Mathematical models*	*(3)* *Logical flow models*	*(4)* *Combination mathematical and logical flow models*
Expertise required of researcher				
Logic	+	+	+	+
Mathematics	−	+	−	+
Applicability to modeling				
Simple behavior of:				
individuals	+	−	+	+
homogeneous groups	+	−	+	+
heterogeneous groups	−	+	−	+
Complicated behavior of:				
individuals	−	−	+	+
homogeneous groups	−	−	+	+
heterogeneous groups	−	−	−	−
Applicability of conducting				
Computer simulation	−	+	+	+
Understandability by Businessman of:				
Models	+	−	+	+
Analysis of models	+	−	+	−
Recommendations based on models	+	−	+	+
Some examples of applicability				
To various subjects:				
A competitor's behavior	−	−	+	+
Market demand	−	+	−	−
Break-even points	−	+	−	−

* (+) is "yes" or "good," (−) is "no" or "poor."

general nature of the logical flow model (Figure 2, column 3) is not altered.

If the competitor calculates average costs per unit from his accounting data in order to determine whether he can break even at a given price, for example, the model builder must incorporate the same calculations, even though he is constructing a logical flow rather than a mathematical model. There is an important difference between including such calculations in a logical flow model and building a mathematical model of the cost-volume-profit structure for a firm. The former was concerned only with the way the competitor conducts his business—as good or bad as that may be. The latter would *abstract the essence* of the *true* cost-volume-profit relations for the competitor.

Logical flow models can be used jointly with mathematical models in a more meaningful sense than just considered (Figure 2, column 4). Consider the case where a series of logical flow models has been built to describe how buyers for department stores, discount houses, and chain stores set prices on, say, electric refrigerators. Assume a metropolitan area in which 90% of all electric refrigerators are sold by the stores already modeled, and the other 10% of sales can safely be ignored.

In such a situation, it might well be desirable to have a model of how consumers react to the prices set by the various stores. Instead of studying the millions of heterogeneous consumers in the metropolitan area and building a great many logical flow models to describe their reactions separately, it would be better to build and statistically test a summary mathematical model which first predicted the total yearly sales of electric refrigerators and then allocated the total sales to the various stores according to their prices. The two types of models could then be connected together to produce a replica of the overall retail market structure for refrigerators in the metropolitan area.

Applicability of Various Types of Analyses

Simulation has been defined as "the process of conducting experiments on a model instead of attempting the experiments on the real system."[6] In most business simulations, the model is translated from the language in which it was originally constructed into a language that can be interpreted by a digital computer (BALGOL, FORTRAN, MAD, IPL, LISP, or SIMSCRIPT, to mention but a few). A set of experimental conditions may then be fed into the machine, which after performing the operations indicated by the model produces the desired set of outcomes.

It is easy to see how mathematical equation models can be translated to a computer input language. After all, the computer was designed to perform arithmetic calculations—it can add, subtract, multiply, and divide, and with appropriate programing can take logarithms, perform exponentiation, and find determinants. The so-called "algebraic" programming languages like IBM's FORTRAN (FORmula TRANslation) are designed to speed the writing of mathematical programs.

What perhaps is not so well known is that computers enjoy an equal facility for non-arithmetic computation.[7] Computers can read, write, process, and compare a variety of kinds of symbols or patterns. These can be interpreted not only as numbers, but also as words, as sentences, or even as geometric diagrams.

Since computers can be programed to follow different courses of action (that is, branches), depending upon the relationships between patterns, it is possible to translate logical flow models like the one given in Part C of Figure 1 directly into a computer input language. Any of the

[6] Same reference as footnote 5, at p. 18.

[7] Geoffrey P. E. Clarkson and Herbert A. Simon, "Simulation of Individual and Group Behavior," *American Economic Review,* Vol. 50 (December, 1960), pp. 920–932.

"algebraic" languages can be used as nonnumerical symbol manipulators by concentrating upon their set of conditional branching instructions. In addition, certain languages (for example, IPL and LISP) have been constructed expressly for the purpose of translating logical flow models into terms that computers understand.[8]

Understandability by Businessmen

Marketing practitioners grasp even complicated-looking flow charts much more easily than mathematical or even prose models. This contrasts particularly with the kinds of initial barriers that are often "thrown up" against the use of mathematics.

A MODEL OF BUYER BEHAVIOR

Savvas has conducted research into the behavior of a department store organization, under the sponsorship of an important manufacturer of electrical appliances. Suggested by the pioneering efforts of Cyert, March, and Moore,[9] it has led to work on a logical flow model of the store's procedures for deciding what manufacturers' lines to carry in its major appliance department.

A portion of the model is presented in Figure 3. In addition to certain sectors that are not reported, some of the questions posed in the figure (such as, "Is it bad on service?") are determined through lower level flow sequences (how "bad" is determined).

The model includes two basic types of elements: lists, and questions or conditional branches. The product lines which the buyer carries, and others which he knows are potentially available, are arranged into lists—there are five lists represented in Figure 3. Particular lines are moved from one list to another according to the outcomes of the conditional branching operations. Sometimes the order of occurrence of lines in a list is important, as when the lines are rank-ordered by gross margin or some other attribute. The idea of *processing lists* is of key importance for the construction of computer programs from logical flow models. For example, the LISP programming language mentioned above stands for LIST Processing.

While the general nature of this part of the buyer's decision process is made apparent by inspection of Figure 3, a number of points are worth considering in detail.

1. Gross margin (last year's sales multiplied by markup) is used as the buyer's primary criterion for ranking lines. For lines not carried now, he

[8] See Allen Newell, editor, *Information Processing Language: V. Manual* (Englewood Cliffs, N.J.: Prentice-Hall, Inc., 1961).

[9] R. M. Cyert, J. G. March, and C. G. Moore, "A Model of Retail Ordering and Pricing by a Department Store," in Frank, Kuehn, and Massy, same reference as footnote 1, pp. 502–522.

FIGURE 3

How a Major Appliance Department Decides Which Supplier's Lines to Carry

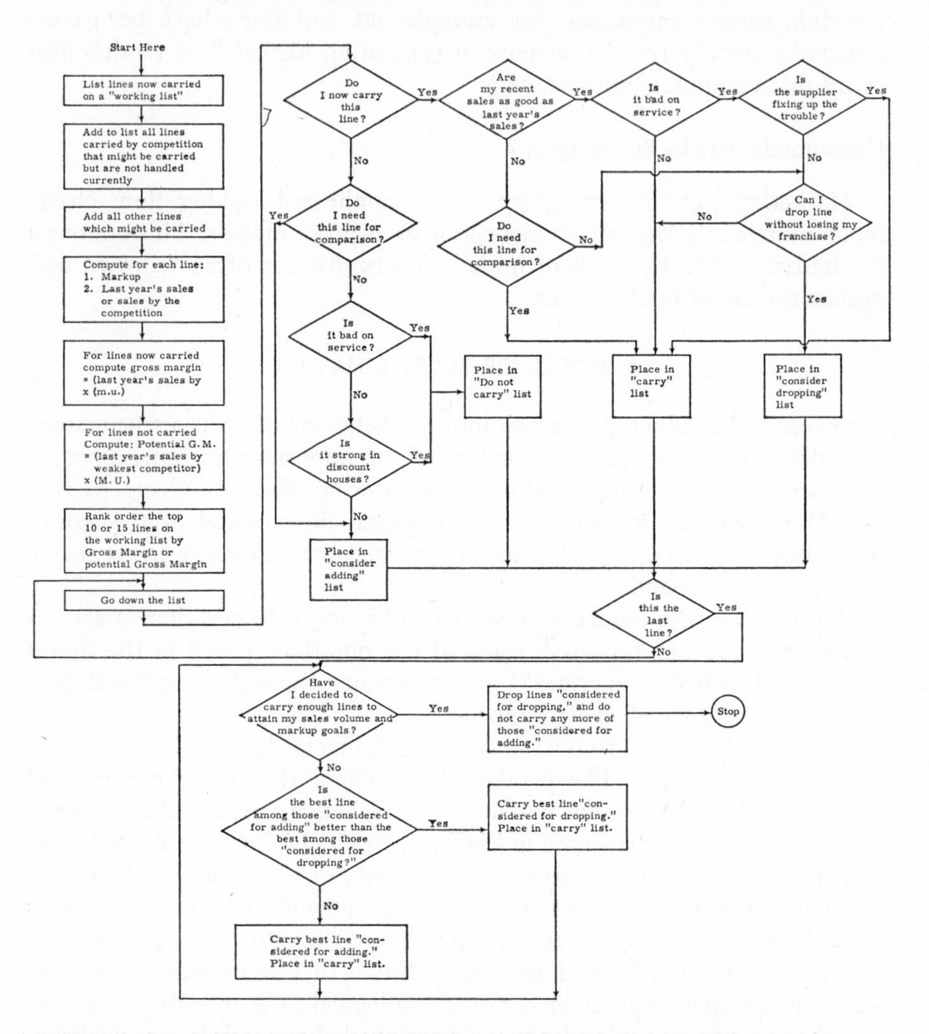

looks at his weakest major competitor's sales. Thus, his method for forecasting gross margin is biased in favor of products he now carries.

2. Lines now carried enjoy a second advantage. Provided that (a) they are among the top 10 or 15 lines on the working list (this cutoff is rarely effective for currently carried items), (b) their sales have not declined during the last year, and (c) service has been satisfactory, these products are automatically placed in the "carry" list regardless of other alternatives that might be available.

3. Satisfactory lines that are not currently carried are placed in the "consider-buying" list. They are considered further only if the buyer has not been able to meet his sales and markup goals exclusively from the "carry list." If additional lines are needed, the best potential new line is compared with

the best of the old lines on the "consider-to-drop" list; and the one with the highest gross margin is chosen.

4. Potential new lines must have satisfactory service and must not be strong in discount houses. The discount house question does not come up in evaluating currently carried products, although service considerations remain important. Exceptions are made when the lines are needed for comparison purposes (trading the customer up or down).

Figure 3 places significant limits on the decision processes which the buyer is expected to use. While no one would pretend that he always acts in the indicated way, the model will be useful if it replicates his behavior in a substantial number of cases. Unusual behavior can be discovered and analyzed against the backdrop of the average decision patterns as summed up by the model.

Finally, since this model was developed from observations upon the behavior of only two people—the buyer and his assistant—generalization of the present model without further research would be a serious mistake.

DEVELOPMENT OF A LOGICAL FLOW MODEL

The model from which Figure 3 was excerpted was constructed with the aid of three kinds of data: (1) interviews with the buyer, wherein he attempted to explain how he performed his job; (2) observations of current decisions as they were actually made; and (3) a careful analysis of the department's written records, which summarized the results of many past decisions.

Individuals can rarely describe all the details of their jobs with great accuracy—some things are easily forgotten and others are difficult to make precise or put into words at all. On the other hand, written records may be interpreted in many different ways, and the researcher cannot choose between them without help from the decision-maker himself.

Observation of current decisions is the most difficult kind of data to acquire—the researcher must obtain access to the decision-maker, and then be at the right place at the right time. Moreover, many decisions are made largely without benefit of oral or any other overt activity which can be noted by the observer. In such cases, it is sometimes possible to ask the respondent to "think aloud," although the biases possibly introduced by such a procedure are not well understood. Where such "live" observations can be obtained, however, they are well worth the effort since they can provide a basic understanding upon which other avenues of exploration can be based.

Testing the Model

Once a model has been developed, it should be tested against new data about the phenomena under study. The untested model represents a set of hypotheses, from which predictions about the real world may be obtained. Obviously the empirical verification of hypotheses is a crucial element in the development of a scientific discipline. It is no less important in the application of scientific methods to practical problems.

The formulation of research results in terms of a logical flow (or mathematical equation) model and the translation of the model into the input language of a digital computer provide an opportunity for testing. Once this has been done, the researcher can go back "into the field" and collect fresh data about a new set of decisions which have been made by the individual or group studied originally.

When the new data are fed into the computer and the program is allowed to run its course, the computer's decision can be compared with the one actually made by the subject of the simulation. If discrepancies between the two results are noted, the model can be improved and tested again with new data. If the test is successful, the success serves as evidence for the validity of the model. Thus, the logical flow model can be tested against actual behavior in the same way that theories in the physical sciences are tested against the results of new experiments.

The computer model of behavior allows more stringent tests than simple comparisons of predicted and actual decisions. Since the model is "couched" in terms of the decision process actually utilized by the individual in question, it is possible to compare the results of each of the intermediate tests that are performed on the way to determining the final solution (that is, the "questions" of Figure 3) with their real-world counterparts.

In theory, it is possible to compare the computer's determination of what is to be done; when, how, and where; and in what form the results are made available, with equivalent data derived from fresh observation and analysis of the real organization. If the model does well on these microscopic comparisons, the degree of confidence in its validity is increased immeasurably.

Strictly speaking, the computer is not necessary for any of these results. A man with a pencil and paper, and perhaps a slide rule or desk calculator, could follow the steps of the flow chart if the problem is not of too great magnitude. Since this method is often time-consuming and subject to clerical errors, however, the intermediate step of computer programming is usually desirable. Once a program is written and "debugged," the rules given in the flow chart can be applied to a variety of situations in a short time, without danger of mistakes or misinterpretations.

Use of the computer has another "payoff" as well. The computer is unable to fill in or gloss over situations where the researcher has failed to specify procedures clearly. Since the computer is essentially a blank slate to be filled in by the programmer, it is absolutely necessary that the flow chart be made complete, consistent, and unambiguous. The machine cannot determine whether the model is correct, in the sense of being a true replication of the real decision process; but it can and most certainly will find any gaps or inconsistencies in the model.

Since completeness and logical consistency are prerequisites for a valid model, the stringent requirements imposed by machine programming—and indeed by the modeling process itself—are entirely consistent with those for the advancement of knowledge of decision-making in marketing.

IMPORTANCE FOR MANAGEMENT

The logical flow model will take its place in the battery of techniques that promise to put marketing decision-making on a more scientific plane than has heretofore been possible.

Its use can lead to an increased understanding of the behavior of consumers, members of the channels of distribution, and even parts of firms' own marketing organizations. This kind of knowledge will allow better forecasts of marketing phenomena and hence improved management decisions. It is easier to make a good choice between alternatives if their respective outcomes are known or can be closely approximated.

An analysis of potential contributions of operations research to marketing science is presented. The methods of operations research are enumerated, its current status in marketing is discussed, and problems of communication between operations research and marketing are evaluated.

24. OPERATIONS RESEARCH AND MARKETING SCIENCE*

William Lazer†

THE OPERATIONS RESEARCH PERSPECTIVE

Many disciplines and fields of study are contributing to the development of marketing science. The interdisciplinary approach has been sug-

---

* Reprinted from "Operations Research and Marketing Science," *Science in Marketing*, ed. G. Schwartz (New York: John Wiley & Sons, Inc., 1965), pp. 430–45. For an illustration of how decision theory techniques can be applied to marketing problems, see Robert D. Buzzell and Charles C. Slater, "Decision Theory and Marketing Management," *Journal of Marketing*, Vol. 26, No. 3 (July, 1962), pp. 7–16.

† Michigan State University.

gested as a very fruitful avenue for the development of marketing knowledge and theory. The value of incorporating findings from the behavioral sciences and quantitative methods has been stressed.[1] Operations research which utilizes quantitative methods has a decided contribution to make to marketing science.

Operations research approaches vary from other marketing approaches in at least two respects. First of all, operations researchers use different tools for problem solving. They make frequent recourse to mathematical and statistical tools. Mathematical models are part of the normal problem-solving kit of the operations researcher. Marketing executives expect operations researchers to demonstrate a degree of skill in applying quantitative techniques not required of other management people. The application of mathematical models to marketing problems should advance the development of marketing science in the following ways:[2]

1. The models are useful in theory construction. When quantitative models are formulated and data from the real world are mapped into them, a theory about the data results.
2. Simulation, or experimentation, on the models can generate further theories and hypotheses about marketing and provide valuable insights for marketing science.
3. Models have provided the most successful predicting system so far produced, the predicting systems used in science.[3]
4. Quantitative models help portray marketing situations in simplified forms so they can be analyzed. They help explain relationships and reactions which are critical in developing marketing science.
5. Quantitative models tend to be objective rather than intuitive, and they can often pursue analyses not feasible through other techniques.

The second major difference in operations research approaches is one of perspective. Operations researchers adopt a systems perspective. In trying to solve marketing problems they view marketing not in terms of a group of functions that must be performed, or in terms of manufacturing, wholesaling, and retailing institutions, but as a total system of business action. The impact of systems thinking, advanced by the operations researcher, is being felt in marketing.

The most widely hailed marketing development in the postwar period is the acceptance of the marketing philosophy of business operation as was discussed by King in an earlier chapter. This viewpoint, however, is merely the outward manifestation of a more fundamental and significant development that has occurred. Marketing executives have adopted a new

---

[1] William Lazer and Eugene J. Kelley, "Interdisciplinary Contributions to Marketing Management," *Marketing and Transportation Paper No. 5*, Bureau of Business and Economic Research, Michigan State University.

[2] For a detailed discussion of models in marketing, see William Lazer, "The Role of Models in Marketing," *Journal of Marketing*, Vol. 26, No. 2 (April, 1962).

[3] Irwin D. J. Bross, *Design for Decisions*, Macmillan, New York, 1953, p. 169.

perspective of marketing operations. They are embracing the systems viewpoint of marketing action.[4] The systems approach is fundamental to the marketing concept, to the role of models in marketing, and to the application of computers.

Under the systems concept, marketing institutions and operations are viewed as complex, large-scale, dynamic action systems. A marketing system is comprised of a group of marketing elements and operations which are interrelated and connected and can be delineated conceptually or physically. The characteristic which differentiates a system from a jumble of parts and pieces is that they form a coherent group. Systems thinking, therefore, is based on the integration and coordination of marketing activity. A marketing organization is seen not merely as a number of separate departmental units, processes, and activities; it is a system of action.

The systems approach in marketing turns on the central theme that marketing reality occurs in systems. A business, or part of it, can be represented by some suitable system. The system may culminate in a simulation model, a flow diagram, a physical replica, or a chart. Marketing managers have the major responsibility of recognizing the relationships among the elements of the system, comprehending their potential combinations, and coordinating and integrating business factors so that goals are achieved effectively. This implies that the master model for marketing activity is the systems model.

The marketing management concept, which is a signal breakthrough in the management thinking, by its very nature implies a systems approach to the management of marketing effort. It requires a recognition of the interrelations and interconnections between marketing and other business elements. It involves the integration of all the components of the marketing program into a coordinated marketing mix. It demands the establishment of a communications network and linkages between the various functionaries and activities necessary for the accomplishment of marketing missions. It is concerned with the flows of information and resources through a firm to the marketplace. Even the implementation of the marketing concept requires the grouping of marketing activities and the designation of a top-level executive to integrate both authority and responsibility.

OPERATIONS RESEARCH APPROACHES

Operations research is suggested by such terms as waiting-line theory, simulation, linear programming, dynamic programming, game theory, Markov processes, and decision theory. This analytical technique empha-

[4] For a detailed discussion of the systems concept, see William Lazer and Eugene J. Kelley, *Managerial Marketing: Perspectives and Viewpoints*, revised ed., Richard D. Irwin, Homewood, Ill., 1962.

sizes the use of mathematical tools. Yet, operations research groups are not comprised solely of mathematicians. They include engineers, logicians, physicists, accountants, biologists, and statisticians as well as various types of business executives.

Operations research in one sense is broader in scope than any functional discipline. It cuts across functional lines and is applicable to all types of organizations, institutions, and activities, private and governmental, concerned with allocating scarce resources among alternative means to try to achieve objectives effectively. It stresses the similarities and analogies of quantitative approaches from widely diverse fields. It is not just a group of mathematical techniques. OR is eclectic in nature. It utilizes all branches of scientific endeavor to solve problems.

Operations research as applied to marketing science then is concerned with techniques and methodology for solving operating marketing problems. It is not merely concerned with knowledge for the sake of knowledge. It does not have an organized body of knowledge in the sense that cultural anthropology, social psychology, or political science does. The characteristic that links operations researchers in many fields is problem-solving techniques. Operations research then spans a wide and diverse subject matter, is concerned with a multitude of operational problems, and emphasizes problem solving rather than knowledge.

OR emphasizes individual and specialized applications of techniques. Analytical methods are developed for solving the marketing problems of individual organizations. The operations researcher is more concerned with attaining specific solutions to problems than he is in developing more generalized models. For although it is often possible to change a problem to fit some general solution method, in practice, when this is done, the actual solution may have very little meaning. It is the ability to generate solutions to real problems that is important rather than success in molding problems so that answers, however unrealistic, are obtained through available tools.

For the evolution of marketing science, it might be more useful to develop generalized models. The difficulties encountered, however, are enormous. Although there are similarities between marketing organizations, the problems confronting them are often exceedingly different. Marketing organizations differ in size, resources, objectives, complexity, scope, and limitations. This tends to preclude a high degree of generalization of models, and demands that operations researchers be adaptive, flexible, and creative so that specific techniques for specialized situations can be employed.

Operations researchers are concerned with investigating goal-directed or purposeful operating systems. OR studies systems of action rather than individuals. For example, researchers are interested in purposeful marketing systems in which specific objectives are pursued and in which choices from among alternative courses of action are present.

Operations researchers study patterns of marketing activities. However, they do not seem to study interactions of people. Operations researchers seem most interested in those properties of a marketing system that would not change if the people involved were replaced by others. This strips away many essential aspects of marketing operations and could lead to a concentration on some of the less significant factors.

One of the most important characteristics of operations research methods is its practical aim. It is not just a descriptive, theoretical activity. OR is concerned with the practical operation and management of an organization. It deals with practical decisions and programs of action. Costs, profits, losses, competitors' actions, and the impact of changing strategies, all are of concern to the operations researcher. While operations researchers use theory, and adapt abstract models and tools from various sciences, they must provide practical information and specific answers to problem situations. Their recommendations must face the demanding tests of the marketplace.

Operations researchers often work in teams. In dealing with new problems and technologies team effort has proven to be productive. The OR team is often composed of people who have diverse backgrounds, interests, and skills. The team brings together men from various disciplines, such as mathematics, statistics, logic, physics, engineering, biology, and philosophy, with a breadth of experience who focus attention on the same problem.

Although OR utilizes the synthesis of various disciplines in studying systems and operations, this does not mean that OR will take over other disciplines. For example, research findings from systems engineering, communications theory, and computer technology, are used by OR to solve marketing problems. The individual identities of each have and will continue to have an independent usefulness. At the same time, marketing science is benefiting from the higher order integration of sciences and technologies. Through such collaboration, broader approaches to marketing problems are being taken than would otherwise be the case.

Marketing problems, because of their complexity, often cannot be solved effectively by the tools, concepts, and findings of a specific discipline. "The aspects of the system which can be manipulated so as to improve its performance are likely to come from many different disciplines."[5] As the disciplines involved in the study of marketing increase their research power, the problem of selecting the most appropriate ones to improve organizational performance will become increasingly difficult to solve. It will require an integrated examination of marketing organizations as systems.

Operations research techniques have increased the effectiveness of the decision-making process in marketing. They hold great promise for

---

[5] Russell L. Ackoff, "The Meaning, Scope, and Methods of Operations Research," *Progress in Operations Research*, Vol. I, John Wiley & Sons, Inc., New York, 1962.

achieving more effective allocation of marketing resources and a better matching of resources and opportunities. Marketing is developing as a more scientific discipline. The factors in the marketing program and their impact are becoming measurable. Operations research methodology is assisting marketing in its progression as a scientific discipline. The sophisticated and rigorous tools of operations analysis are resulting in more adequate and pertinent data, the ability to multiply experimentation in marketing, and the development of measurements not previously available.

OPERATIONS RESEARCH AS A SCIENCE

Is operations research a science? Although many operations researchers may proclaim that it is, this may not be the case. For instance, Lathrop suggests that "Perhaps it is best described as the application of scientists from various disciplines to the solution of operating problems. The opportunity to be called a science and to do scientific research on top management problems must be earned and not demanded. The question facing the operations researcher is how to earn it."[6]

In the same vein, Stafford Beer in the *Operational Research Quarterly* (Vol. 9, 1958) states that OR as subject matter is not a science. Operations research emerges rather as a group of scientific methods appropriate to the analysis of activity. These methods *per se*, however, do not form a science. Rather, they refer to the attack of modern science on probability type problems which arise in the management, and the control of men, machines, materials, and money in their natural environment.

At present it appears that OR is not an applied discipline. Operations research might even be thought of as the application of scientists to new problems—problems which may be unrelated to the content of their original training and experience. OR may be considered as a stage in the development of an applied subject-matter field rather than the actual discipline itself. It reflects approaches or methods. Like most effective methods, OR is scientific. As such, it can extend the scientific approach to the study and management of marketing activity.

OPERATIONS RESEARCH DEFINED

There is no wide consensus on the definition of operations research. We may gain some perspective of its scope and boundaries, however, by considering a few of the definitions appearing in the literature. This will permit the delineation of some of OR's distinguishing major characteristics and methods of problem solving.

Among the many definitions offered of OR are (1) "a scientific

[6] John Lathrop, "A Letter to Ellis Johnson," *Operations Research* (July–August 1960), p. 576.

method of providing executives with the quantitative basis for making decisions with regard to operations under their control."[7] (2) "the application of scientific method of industrial problems leading to recommendations that in turn lead to action."[8] (3) "the convergence of a research region, concerned with the preparation of management decisions at various levels and in various contexts, and the application of a method of approach which is rigorously scientific a method which uses quite an arsenal of techniques and often employs speedy and powerful calculating tools. Therefore, operations research is above all dependent on an attitude of mind in regard to the problems put by management."[9] (4) "the exacting and critical application of the scientific method by scientists and subject specialists to the study of basic laws governing a given operation. Its purpose is to give administrators a basis for predicting quantitatively the most effective results of an operation under a given set of variable conditions and thereby narrow the area of choices of action in making final decisions."[10]

A careful scrutiny of the foregoing definitions, and others appearing in the literature, will reveal the following major characteristics of OR:

1. Scientists from a variety of fields and scientific methods are used to solve operating problems.
2. Quantitative techniques are emphasized.
3. Optimal solutions to problems, rather than mere description, are emphasized.
4. A systems or total perspective is adopted in problem solving.

Operations research then is research intended to help solve practical, immediate problems in the fields of marketing, and other business administration areas, as well as in governmental and military administration. As for its place in marketing, operations research serves as an adjunct to, not a substitute for, marketing research, distribution cost accounting, sales forecasting, and physical distribution. Operations research draws on information from these subjects, calls on the services of varied company specialists, and cuts across lines of functional authority in sublimating the objectives of subgroups to the over-all objective of the company. It is not designed to reduce the responsibilities of marketing management but rather to add new scope and dimensions to the marketing tasks and to help marketing managers deal more effectively with the crucial decisions they must make.

---

[7] W. G. Ireson and E. L. Grant (eds.), *Handbook of Industrial Engineering and Management*, Prentice-Hall, Inc., Englewood Cliffs, N.J., 1955, p. 1015.

[8] *Managements' Operations Research Digest*, Vol. 1, No. 11 (October 1955), back cover.

[9] Philip M. Morse and George E. Kimball, *Methods of Operations Research*, John Wiley & Sons, Inc., New York, 1951, p. 1.

[10] T. C. Schelling, *The Review of Economics and Statistics*, Vol. XL (August 1958), p. 221.

OR is oriented toward the similarities and analogies of quantitative problems from widely different fields. It is concerned with the application of models and theories to problem solving. Some of the OR approaches may even be suggested by the problems that marketing managers tackle, such as measuring advertising impact, determining the number of check-out counters to have in supermarkets, establishing inventory controls, and developing better sales forecasts.

Operations research as applied to marketing, therefore, should be viewed from two perspectives: (1) It is an attitude of mind toward the relation between a business and its marketing environment, and (2) it is a body of methods for the solution of marketing problems which arise in that relationship.[11] The former may result in increased understanding of the marketing environment and its resulting impact on company operations. This may be one of the most important contributions of OR methods to marketing science.

COMMENTS ON CURRENT STATUS OF *OR* IN MARKETING

The use of OR tools and techniques in marketing stems from three desires of marketing executives: (1) to obtain more pertinent, up-to-date, and adequate information for decision-making purposes, (2) to control marketing resources and operations more effectively, and (3) to develop more adequate and rational marketing objectives, policies, strategies, and programs. OR does not obsolete but tends to complement conventional marketing management. OR is directed toward "providing executive departments with the quantitative basis for decisions regarding the operations under their control."[12] By so doing, it should improve the effectiveness of marketing managers.

Despite these significant aims, the application of operations research methods in solving marketing problems, to date, has been quite limited. Marketing practitioners and academicians, nevertheless, are beginning to accept some of the newer approaches of OR. The development of skills in operations research and interest in applying the techniques has been slower in marketing than it has been in other areas, such as production, engineering, and the military sciences. Only recently have modern mathematical tools been applied to develop better marketing practice and theory.

A good proportion of the research that has been undertaken in marketing has been verbal rather than quantitative. Much of it reports evaluations made on a relative basis of good or poor marketing practice. Some of

[11] See "The Teaching of Operational Research," *Operational Research Quarterly*, Vol. IX, 1958, p. 267.

[12] Philip M. Morse and George E. Kimball, *Methods of Operations Research*, John Wiley & Sons, Inc., New York, 1951, p. 1.

it is definitional in nature, drawing functional distinctions among marketing institutions and activities. These research efforts have indeed made valuable contributions to science in marketing. They have led to improved marketing insights. However, they have also neglected the quantitative emphasis. In fact, marketing scholars themselves have often resisted analytical generalizations. They seem to do so by taking refuge in statements about the difficulties of analyzing marketing factors quantitatively.

It is true that to some extent the problems in the fields of marketing appear to be mathematically intractable. They tend to lie somewhere between problems in the applied areas of engineering on the one hand, which lend themselves to a quantitative approach, and those of the behavioral sciences, such as economics, sociology, social psychology, on the other hand, which often do not.

The problems faced in marketing are exceedingly complex, and many of the important factors surrounding marketing decisions are not quantifiable. Some factors, although quantifiable conceptually, elude actual measurement. Other factors are so inextricably intertwined that the operations researchers' models and analytical techniques are ineffective in sorting them out and evaluating their impact and significance. Marketing is a difficult discipline for operations research convergence. Despite such limitations, marketing managers should not adopt a defensive posture and ignore the benefits of operations research.

In trying to understand why OR has not caught on in marketing at a more rapid rate, one should remember the tastes and training of people in executive positions in marketing. Most are unskilled in mathematical and statistical methods. They are "people-oriented" rather than "technique and analytically oriented." They have intended to follow the lore of the trade, to use rules of thumb, and often to apply various generalizations. Moreover, many have been extremely successful.

Rationally, there ought not to be any distrust of mathematical tools and techniques on the part of marketing academicians and administrators. The fact remains, however, that business administrators are sometimes prone to look with a certain amount of disfavor, and even distrust, on anything that is not familiar and anything that is couched in abstract, mathematical, or statistical terms.

Only recently have people with quantitative training, aptitudes, and interests delved into the fruitful and significant areas of marketing. This trend has been encouraged by the establishment of formal marketing research departments, the availability of computers, and the use of external marketing research and management science services by companies.

Marketing presents a more difficult challenge to operations researchers than many other business areas do. Operations researchers face exceptional difficulties when they try to handle marketing factors and interpret market conditions. Part of the reason for this is that marketing operations introduce the human element, especially in terms of consumer attitudes, opinions, motives, and behavior, and the reactions of wholesalers, retailers, and manufacturers, and their employees as decision makers.

In developing marketing models, the operations researcher must deal with conditions of great uncertainty. Marketing factors that are not as concrete as those of certain production and inventory problems must be handled. Moreover, the specific facts necessary for generating solutions are often unknown. As a result, the operations researcher is forced to rely on complex mathematical techniques and manipulations, especially probability theory.

The fact that marketing executives do not understand OR and the associated mathematical techniques seems to result in two opposing executive reactions. On the other hand, there seems to be a tendency among marketing managers who are not trained in quantitative techniques, and who are immersed in operating problems, to treat operations researchers with a "halo effect." Individuals who can manipulate symbols, use computers, refer to the proper mystic and mathematical concepts, and arrive at solutions are accorded status. And yet, there is also a suspicion of, and negative reaction to, operations researchers and mathematical tools. This often leads to an outright rejection of the idea that marketing factors and activities can be quantified.

To improve marketing management and enhance marketing science, the role of computers, quantitative techniques, models, and operations researchers in the marketing decision process must be viewed in a positive light. All marketing organizations are confronted with a problem of making optimal use of scarce resources in a manner that maximizes profits and/or minimizes costs. The operations researcher can often approach such problems through mathematical programming by stating in algebraic terms the function to be minimized or maximized, the alternatives that may be used in achieving this objective function, the constraints which are imposed by various factors, and then achieve the best solution by manipulating the equations or inequalities. It is the realistic appraisal of the value of such methods to marketing that is one of the challenges now facing marketing academicians and practitioners.

OPERATIONS RESEARCH IN MARKETING: A CRITICAL ASSESSMENT

Operations researchers do not operate in an environmental vacuum. They function in a marketing setting. Although marketing parameters have the greatest impact on significant business decisions, they are often skirted and ignored. Operations researchers in their investigations tend to assume away marketing factors. They appear to place a heavy emphasis on problems outside the marketing area while neglecting more significant marketing considerations.

In reality, operations researchers have a great stake in the development of marketing thought and knowledge. They must concern themselves with the primacy of marketing factors in enterprise decisions. They must recognize the extended influence of marketing forces. They must realize that the development of a richer body of scientific knowledge pertaining to management is inextricably intertwined with a better understanding of marketing factors.

The virtues of operations research have been extolled in many articles readily available to the reader. It might be profitable to explore the limitations of operations research in marketing. A review of marketing-related articles appearing in operations research and management science journals suggest several criticisms of operations research approaches to marketing. The following material presents a critical assessment of operations research treatments of marketing problems.

Much of the progress made in the extension of management science has been attributed to the use of models. Models are truly useful tools of analysis. Some of the more sophisticated mathematical models have received widespread acclaim for their accomplishments. Yet, when evaluated against the spectrum of significant marketing problems, the accomplishments of models, and particularly mathematical models, have been sparse indeed. The value of mathematical models in solving marketing problems, perhaps with the exception of linear programming, is quite limited. In fact, it is the promise of *potential applications* in marketing, rather than *actual application*, to which operations researchers refer fondly.

Operations research models are not ends in themselves. They are the means to an end. In marketing they are the means to better marketing decisions. Yet, in model building, operations researchers seem to get lost in heroic mathematical abstractions. They appear to develop a preference for rigor over realism, for manipulative potentiality over practicality, and for mathematical sophistication over immediate problem-solving capability in marketing. Marketing models, like other kinds of models, seem to result in "the unlimited postulation of irrelevant truths,"[13] or what has been termed mathematicians' aphasia.[14]

Operations researchers tend to obliterate marketing factors. In their models, critical marketing factors are usually assumed away. For instance, demand is assumed; consumer behavior is taken as given; promotional effects are treated as knowns, competitive strategies and reactions are assumed; marketing share and sales potential are treated as known quantities. Given such assumptions, answers to important business problems are then found.

There exists at least one obvious flaw in this procedure. Despite the

[13] H. Theil, *Economic Forecasts and Policy*, Amsterdam, North Holland, 1958, p. 4.

[14] See Herbert A. Simon, *The New Science of Management Decision*, Harper & Row, Publishers, New York, 1960, p. 18.

intellectual and rigorous exercise pursued, the major aspects of the problem, the factors that usually impose the most serious management constraints, those factors that are most significant are whisked away. As a result, to a large extent, solutions reached are relatively impotent. The models developed often contain less reality within the model than actually exist outside the model.[15] What is often obtained by operations research procedures are neat mathematical formulations that need not pertain to marketing reality, that are ineffective as decision tools but that furnish impressive looking manuscripts for esoteric journals.

Operations research often provides fragmented solutions. In applying models and mathematical techniques, operations researchers often attack small segments of marketing problems. This approach seems to make good analytical sense. It can, however, result in rather poor operational results.

For instance, in dealing with transportation, warehousing, or inventory control problems, solutions are often obtained which reduce costs in one of these decision areas. Many of the solutions reached, however, place a burden on other business cost centers, such as personal selling and advertising, and can increase total costs.

Operations research studies neglect human factors. The very crux of marketing activities centers on humans and human behavior. Customers and consumers are focal points of marketing and, in essence, management action. Yet, the marketing models developed by management scientists do not portray this. They do not account for human behavior. They seem to consider human beings as "black boxes" with input-output characteristics. Most operations research models are developed, analyzed, and interpreted as though the interaction of people is of little consequence.

Operations researchers seem to tackle the least crucial problems. The types of marketing problems that have been handled reflect an unbalanced problem-solving emphasis. In marketing, quantitative techniques and models have been applied successfully to physical distribution and inventory-type problems. Although they are worthy problem areas, they are not the most crucial problems in marketing management today. Perhaps they are the easiest to handle mathematically. However, they may also be the easiest problems to handle by conventional and less exacting techniques.

There also seems to be a tendency for management scientists to ignore and sometimes even degrade other types of marketing problems that are more significant than those that have been handled. The problems surrounding personal selling and salesmanship, for instance, are often viewed with a jaundiced eye as to their academic respectability. Problems related

[15] A good example of this is the development of an advertising model which first appeared in a leading management journal and has since been reprinted in, and referred to in, marketing books. The model seems to be acclaimed by management scientists as the type of progress being made in the application of mathematical models to marketing. However, it is referred to by the company executives as being useless in solving their problems and as a waste of research funds.

to mass production, on the other hand, seem to be entirely respectable. Yet, the former are very significant to the welfare of individual firms and our economy. These problems cannot be skipped over lightly or ignored in the management of business systems.

Operations research models often fail to portray a proper perspective of marketing productivity. Marketing expenditures seem to be viewed as costs, expenses, and often as wastes. In reality, marketing activities are among the most productive management activities—they may even be more productive than the activities related to physical shaping, forming, and creating a product. Marketing tasks, including advertising, selling, sales promotion, and marketing research, should be perceived and treated as business investments. Surely they are as significant investments as expenditures on capital equipment, plant, warehouses, and furniture. Ownership of market position is as important to a company, and perhaps even more so, than ownership of productive capacity.

In reality, operations researchers do not understand our marketing system too well. They have failed to mark the pivotal role of marketing in management. In the future, operations researchers will recognize that they are challenged with understanding marketing not only to help our competitive economy function more effectively but also to help less mature economies achieve greater progress and to develop management science.

OR AND MARKETING SCIENCE: LACK OF COMMUNICATION

The field of operations research is a highly technical one. "Management opinion, or judgment about OR applications or techniques, can generally be accorded lay standing only. This does not mean, however, that management must assume a subordinate role to the practitioner in dealing with his problems."[16] It does mean that marketing managers should become acquainted with these newer techniques and apprised of OR achievements. Marketing executives must recognize the evolution that is occurring in the methodology for problem solving. Complex marketing problems do require the use, on a broad base, of more powerful decision tools than is currently the case. Marketing executives must strive to achieve better understanding of the newer techniques.

Communication between operations researchers and marketing academicians and executives, or for that matter with executives in other functional areas of management, is clearly lacking. Marketing personnel in general do not know what is happening in the operations research field that is, or should be, of interest to them. They are not familiar with the available tools that can be of assistance in solving marketing problems.

Most people in marketing cannot read the specialized journals and

---

[16] W. W. Cooper, "Operations Research and Economics," *The Review of Economics and Statistics*, Vol. XL (August 1958), p. 196.

volumes containing operations research material. This in turn tends to generate a defensive attitude and some skepticism of operations research. While operations researchers share common problems with top management, interestingly enough there has not yet been a common operating terminology developed and a satisfactory level of communication achieved.

Operations researchers, rather than striving for good communications, often help to create communication barriers. They adhere to the language and approaches which are useful for their purposes but are usually foreign and meaningless to others. In reality, they should avoid trying to overwhelm or impress management with the language developed for, and understood by, members of the OR fraternity only. Operations researchers should stress clearer communications with management.

Realistically, for adequate communications to take place between marketing personnel and operations researchers, each must understand some of the dimensions of the other's job. Only under these conditions can OR make its greatest contribution to marketing science. The operations researcher should be attuned to the fact that marketing problems requiring solutions first come to the attention of marketing management. If marketing management fails to perceive the problems, or fails to recognize the possibility that OR may be helpful in seeking a solution and is not willing to allocate the necessary budget, much of the effectiveness of OR is lost.

Lathrop adopts the view that the burden of communication is on the OR man, that the researcher must give "his answer to the impatient and fretting decision maker in the decision maker's own language in a form he can use at once." The burden and total responsibility, however, do not lie solely with OR personnel. Those in marketing must re-educate themselves to understand OR methods and techniques. Meaningful communication is one of the challenges confronting both the operations researcher in dealing with marketing and the marketing manager in dealing with effective problem solving.

Marketing scientists in the future will not have to become operations researchers or skilled mathematicians. They will not have to understand the many nuances and intricacies of the newer quantitative techniques. They will, however, have to attain a better grasp of what the new quantitative tools are, the types of problems for which operations researchers can furnish assistance, and the potentialities and limitations of operations research techniques.

An extensive body of operations research literature currently exists for the mathematically sophisticated person and for operations research technicians. Relatively little material is available to the professional manager who lacks a technical background. Yet, problem solving in marketing and marketing science cannot be advanced solely by operations researchers communicating among themselves. The institution of a two-way communication channel is necessary to ensure that operations researchers will have the required working laboratory and that the potential benefits from applying operations research to marketing will accrue.

It is essential that operations researchers communicate among themselves in a technical manner in order to advance the field of operations research. It is also necessary that they establish rapport with marketing scientists. They must understand marketing problems, see that operations research approaches and contributions to marketing are recognized. The veil of symbolism and mysticism that surrounds the application of mathematical models and techniques in marketing, and the semantic barriers raised by the technical nature of operations research materials, must be erased if operations research ideas and findings are to be presented to a broader marketing science audience.

There does not seem to be the free interchange of ideas in the area of operations research that exists in many other management areas where specialized staff personnel and consultants play an important role. One reason for this is that management executives do not feel competent or qualified to comprehend and assess operations research approaches and applications. A way must be found to communicate successful applications and potential application of OR to marketing, to erase some of the ignorance and suspicion of OR applications on the part of marketing personnel, and to open the way for greater professionalization of marketing and the development of marketing science.

The quantity of data available in marketing probably exceeds that available in any other functional area of business. Until the advent of the computer, data could not be assembled and analyzed rapidly enough to be operationally useful. The computer and its peripheral input–output devices have bridged the gap between data collection and operationally useful analysis. Marketing's use of EDP in inventory management is discussed.

25. COMPUTERS BEGIN TO SOLVE THE MARKETING PUZZLE*

. . . *Taking over.* The computer is flashing with dazzling speed across the panorama of marketing—which takes in the entire relationship between the designer of a product, the manufacturer, seller, buyer, and user.

---

* Reprinted from the April 17, 1965, issue of *Business Week* by special permission. Copyrighted © 1965 by McGraw-Hill, Inc. Developments in information technology have had a significant effect on marketing's decision-making processes. For an overview of information technology, its techniques, impact, and potential

Electronic data processing not only is managing inventory in nationwide chains of retail stores, it is telling large department stores which customers are the best prospects for certain merchandise, is "advising" a food company when to offer special "deals," is giving rifle-accuracy to the calls of an apparel manufacturer's salesmen, is forecasting crop yields for a canner, and is giving greater precision to the selection of media by advertising agencies.

There are still plenty of skeptics. A computer guided by programmers unfamiliar with the specific industry so thoroughly fouled up one heavy equipment maker's replacement parts production that it took two years to untangle. Most retailers, particularly supermarkets, are loathe to use computers as anything but bookkeepers.

Too late? Strictly marketing uses of EDP, going beyond inventory management, are still uncommon in U.S. business. But those who have sampled its magic are convinced the hour is late for the laggards. In a shockingly matter-of-fact way, a department store man in an Eastern metropolis says: "Our competition is finished; they can't compete with us any more. They started too late with their [EDP] systems and now we are getting so much of the business they'll never be able to afford the system to do the job."

His competition is about as old, as well-established, and as outwardly prosperous as his own store. But in the age of the computer, the hands on marketing's clock are at half-past eleven—30 minutes before the witching hour. The use of EDP is about to become routine in many marketing operations which until now have defied systemization.

Only a year ago, Richard F. Neuschel, a director of McKinsey & Co., wrote in Marketing and the Computer: "In none of the major functions of American business has the impact of the computer been so lightly felt as in marketing. Yet, in none of the major functions is its potential so great."

I. THE DATA COLLECTORS GO TO WORK

The potential of EDP in marketing is great simply because of a pervading belief that there are not enough good, hard numbers in marketing to make a fair-sized computer work up a mild sweat.

In the book, Decision Exercises in Marketing, Dr. Arnold Corbin, professor of marketing at New York University, Dr. George Blagowidow, and Dr. Claire Corbin, write: "To many people, marketing . . . is regarded as a business function in which most decisions are highly qualita-

---

contributions, see: Melvin Anshen, "Managerial Decision Making," in J. T. Dunlop, *Automation and Technological Change* (Englewood Cliffs, N.J.: Prentice-Hall, Inc., 1962); G. P. Schultz and T. L. Whisler, *Management and the Computer* (Glencoe, Ill.: Free Press, 1960); and Herbert A. Simon, *New Science of Management Decision* (New York: Harper & Row, Publishers, 1960).

tive in nature and strongly rooted in intangible factors. . . . Hence marketing decisions are often made on the basis of hunch, guess, or intuition, rather than on a rational analysis of the measurable relationships among the principal variables involved."

John F. Stolle, a Booz, Allen & Hamilton vice-president and specialist in operations research, comments that "marketing is the most difficult area to get quantification in."

You hear that strain throughout business: EDP, to do any good, needs hard data, tons of them, needs them fast—and there is a lack of data all through the marketing stream.

The automobile industry is about the only one that really knows who buys each of its products, where the customers live, and other useful bits of information about them. In contrast, another consumer goods manufacturer refuses to advertise in Indianapolis because his records show no sales there; actually, his Chicago distributor serves Indianapolis retailers, but the manufacturer's own positive information about sales stops at the distributor level.

Bridging the Gap. Yet, it simply isn't true that data do not exist in marketing; they exist in probably greater quantities than in any other business function. Until now there has never been a means to collect the information or to analyze it fast enough for it to be useful.

With the "peripheral" equipment associated with the computer—input-output devices such as the Data-Phone, tape, ticket and card readers, and high-speed printers, for feeding information to the computer and getting it out—the vast gap between collection of information and its analysis has been bridged.

Archibald J. McGill, an industry manager for the Data Processing Div. of International Business Machines Corp., figures that only 5% of the solution of what he calls the distribution problem is the computer, and 95% is the system. "Input-output devices are of more significance in distribution than the computer itself," he says.

There are computers whirring and blinking throughout U.S. business—for the accounting department. Now, with the input and output devices, the marketing department also is finding ways to get information for the computer to work on. . . .

Buyers' New Role. Management's daily report of stock condition is already changing one hallowed role in department stores: the preeminence of the buyer. Since retailing began, buyers have been the leading figures, responsible for keeping their stores stocked with salable merchandise. But because of the enormous increase in the number of items a store now carries, the buyer has become too busy with a physical count of stock to try to know what the customer wants and when.

At EDP-equipped stores, management knows before the buyer does what's moving and what isn't. Some buyers find this disconcerting indeed. In the words of Jack Jacobson, Goldblatt's director of electronic data processing, they "don't trust computers and are not analytically inclined."

But others use the freedom EDP has given them to get out on the floor once more to see what customers are like. Jack Hanson, senior vice-president of Macy's New York, says buyers now have a chance to "get back into the market where they were 30 years ago, to get better prices and better merchandise."

Penney's merchandise planning and control manager, Emerson Tolle, sees another advantage to the end of physical stock-taking (Penny's counts stock only every quarter): "Instead of being under the counter counting stock, the sales clerk can be standing up taking care of customers."

Precise Weapon. Putting accounts receivable—customer's charge account records—on the computer might seem to be only another accounting procedure. But it can be a merchandising weapon of profitable precision. Macy's has more than 1.3-million charge accounts on magnetic tape. Depending on what it is told to do, the computer will break up those accounts any way the store wants them—by alphabet, by house number, by size of average charge.

Not long ago Macy's had its computer print out a list of all charge customers of the Herald Square store who lived in four counties, and invited them to a special after-hours sale of furniture and furnishings.

The results can't be measured precisely because nothing like it had been done before; but compared with other special sales using radio and direct mail, the computer-based effort cost less and sold more.

Smaller Stock, but More Stores

In food retailing, the problems are different from those in a department store, and EDP has scarcely penetrated the retail end of food distribution.

For one thing, food retailing is about the most hidebound of all businesses dealing with the consumer. For another, a food store's after-tax profit is normally less than 2% on sales—so operators look at the cost of EDP and blanch. Yet, their low rate of return is in itself a reason to get involved with EDP; it offers opportunities for cutting costs and raising profits.

In food processing and warehousing, though, EDP has cut deep, mostly by use of an IBM-developed system known as Impact (Inventory Management Program and Control Technique). All major food manufacturers, as well as other companies that sell through supermarkets—Scott Paper Co. and Procter & Gamble Co., for example—have data links between sales offices, plants, distribution and shipping points, and are managing production, warehousing, and shipping by computer-programmed economics.

Latest Link. The newest trend is a data link between a manufacturer and a distributor for the automatic ordering of staple items.

This has barely started. Kellogg Co. warehouses are linked with warehouses of Safeway Stores, Inc., on the West Coast and of Wakefern Food Corp., a distributor for a group of New Jersey supermarkets. Pillsbury Co. has a similar hookup with Spartan Stores, Inc., a small chain in the Grand Rapids (Mich.) area—after having proved the procedure in experiments with Kroger Co. and Super Valu Stores, Inc.

Savings with this sort of system can be sensational; James Rude, Pillsbury director of information services and systems, quotes a Spartan official as saying the chain can save enough in lead time and storage to build another store.

There is no longer any question about the marketing power of a data link between supplier and customer. The clincher is what has happened in industrial selling. . . .

The Ultimate Question. . . . Carborundum Co. . . . has been using computers for about 10 years and, says Group Vice-President Robert W. Lear, is "still experimenting." Carborundum, with more than 1,000 programs on computers, is ready for the next plateau, which is defined best by a series of questions Lear asked in a recent speech:

"Which of our districts, salesmen, distributors, customers, markets, and products are the real profit producers? How much does it cost to make a sales call? What does it cost to process an order item? If it's four bucks, can we afford to continue accepting five-buck or even twenty-five-buck orders without some kind of a surcharge or premium?

"What was the return on investment from our last promotion? Did we even try to calculate it? Which is more profitable—a direct sale, or one through a distributor? Did our last price adjustment take into consideration the distribution cost for each item, or did we just study our factory gross margins and assume an arbitrary average for everything below the line?"

Those questions get to the heart of the reason for using computers in marketing, for you can't answer them without getting data. Then, for the first time in marketing, management can ask the question: "What if . . . ?"

II. MARKETING BY MATHEMATICS

Dr. Wendell R. Smith, president of the Marketing Science Institute, tells of a former business associate who constantly used computers to ask the question: "What if . . . ?" He explained to Smith: "I can ask the computer without starting a rumor. If I went to the controller and asked him what would happen to our profits if we dropped a certain product line, it would be all over the plant before lunch that we were getting ready to go out of that particular business."

Storage in a computer of mathematical models that simulate a market or that duplicate a marketing situation is perhaps the ultimate contribution EDP can make to marketing.

C. A. Swanson, manager of P&G's Data Processing Systems Department, lists four things his company expects from EDP: savings of money, accuracy, speed, and "doing things not otherwise possible."

There is wide agreement that model-building and simulation is perhaps the most significant of those things not otherwise possible without a computer. As of now, an electronic digital computer is the only device that can handle variable on top of variable and give management a choice of alternatives while there's still time to make a decision.

Changing Management. In a masterful little book, Mathematical Models and Marketing Management, published by the Harvard Business School last year, Prof. Robert D. Buzzell wrote: "The model-builder offers a general, systematic approach to the analysis of management problems. To the extent that this approach is accepted and implemented, fundamental changes may take place in the practice of marketing management."

The biggest change that model-building is bringing about in marketing management is almost defamatory to mention: It is forcing management to plan, and to define its goals. To John Stolle, of Booz, Allen & Hamilton, one of the things that has slowed down the use of EDP and model-building in marketing is simply the fact that "it exposes the non-planners."

As Buzzell brings out, few developments in marketing have churned up so much skepticism and downright suspicion among marketing executives as model-building and simulation. The man who rose through the ranks from salesman to vice-president for marketing usually has little sympathy for the "fellow who's never met a payroll"—and into that category fall most of the mathematicians who are skilled at model-building and simulation.

But already models are regulating some marketing programs. . . .

Bringing Marketing into Management

Advertising practitioners have always presumed that what they do is more art than science. So it may seem strange that all of the larger agencies now have people practicing operations research, which is presumed to be a science—the science of management. In reality it is not strange at all, for part of operations research deals with the weighing of alternatives—and the advertising man may have more numeric alternatives to deal with than anybody.

A media man with one ad and 30 media where he can spot it can be confronted with more than one billion combinations. The computer—that big adding machine—is the only way to run quickly through those combinations and weed out the obviously worthless.

What combinations remain are subject to management decision. The example used is in advertising, but it could just as well be in other marketing functions. Throughout marketing these days you are finding the computer used to weed out the obviously worthless things to do, leaving management with only a few alternatives to consider—sometimes, even, alternatives leading to a go or no-go decision:

What would be the returns now, compared to 60 days from now, on a cents-off promotion? Would it be more efficient to ship to Point A from Plant 1, or build a new distribution location to serve Point A and a potential future Point B? Would it be more economic to double our order for fast-moving baby food and receive shipments every other week rather than every week, even though it ties up more capital? Would it be more profitable to kill immediately Old Product, the life cycle of which is ending, and use the resources to push New Product harder?

Total. Decisions such as these involve determining the proper allocation of a company's total resources—in other words, operations research. Only now are the numbers so necessary for operations research being assembled for the marketing function, for only now is there a way to work with them: the computer. The more EDP sophistication pervades marketing, the closer a company moves toward a total management information system, toward true operations research. Says John Stolle, the OR man at Booz, Allen & Hamilton: "When we add marketing to our collection of trophies, we will be able to build models of total business systems."

It will still be some years before marketing's scalp hangs from the belt of the OR man, but the way marketing data already are being used indicates some changes the future may bring. . . .

Lots of Products and Plans for Retailers

In perhaps no area of marketing is EDP going to make as many changes as in retailing—which lags not only in use of EDP, but frequently in modern business thinking.

In a study of department store control systems, Douglas J. Dalrymple, assistant professor of business administration at the University of California at Los Angeles, found "that a small minority of the merchandising executives . . . believed that stock turnover was an important control factor, but to most executives it was only a vague concept of secondary importance." Yet, fast stock turnover was the weapon the discounters turned loose on department stores 15 years ago. The higher the turnover, the higher the profit on a constant amount of money used in the business.

But the computer is forcing retailers to become aware of the importance of stock turnover.

The EDP Way. Stock turnover is usually about four times a year for general merchandise and about twenty times for dry groceries. There's a traditional way to turn it faster: Simply sell more without carrying a higher inventory. But it's a rare merchant who can do that.

The EDP way to get a higher turnover is by keeping such fresh data on sales that you know what's moving fast and what isn't, and by having a data hookup that will give you automatic replenishment of the fast-moving or high-profit items. In food retailing, one estimate is that a 24-hour replenishment cycle will reduce inventory by 30%, without creating out-of-stock situations that hurt sales.

In general merchandising, Seymour Helfant, head of the Small Stores Div. of the National Retail Merchants Assn., says he has reports of stores using EDP that lower their inventory by 25% and increase profits by 25%. And a specialty store that formerly turned its stock six times a year has added one full turn.

Analysis of information handled by a store's EDP system can also guide store executives in when, what, and how to promote.

Big and Small. The benefits of EDP are not reserved for the big stores and chains. "Any retailer, regardless of size, will be able to be on-line to a big processing center," says James Hotchkiss, assistant director of product planning of National Cash Register Co., which probably has more experience than any other computer manufacturer with the problems of small retailers. NCR, of course, has data processing centers throughout the country as do GE, IBM, and other computer manufacturers. NRMA is sponsoring a cooperative processing center for small retailers.

An example of what a data processing center can do for small retailers is found at Santoro Management Consultants, Inc., in Houston. Santoro has 60 clients—whose volumes range from $50,000 to $500,000—for whom it provides a full package: budgets, advertising, merchandising, sales analysis and projection, inventory records. Says Mrs. Daisy Strother, of Fort Worth: "The service took the butterflies out of my stomach. We know which department is making money . . . our buying is controlled, dead merchandise eliminated and we have reorder money."

At present, most of the small stores mail or deliver tapes to the processing centers. But when Hotchkiss says small stores can be "on-line," he means a direct data link to some establishment using a computer. Once such a link is created, it will drive right through a barrier that (excepting, again, only the automobile business) still separates a manufacturer from sure knowledge of what's happening on the retail level.

A few months ago, B. S. Durant, president of RCA Sales Corp., did a little dreaming for a group of marketing executives. RCA, in common with other consumer electronics producers, is always in doubt as to how much of its product is in distributors' warehouses and how much is moving out of retailers' doors.

Durant began by conceding that a small retailer will probably never be able to afford a computer, "but he could afford a low-cost transactor of some type. . . . Before the dealer goes home at night, he would put the transactor device on standby. Somewhere along about a quarter after two, a central computer would interrogate the transactor and take from it the data covering the dealer's daily business transactions." Durant offered a new, and provocative thought: The independent distributor might have that central computer and be the retailer's data processing center.

If the distributor's computer could interrogate the retailer's transactor, then each night the manufacturer's computer could interrogate the distributor's computer. The next morning, the manufacturer's executives would have—for the first time in their experience—actual records of their product sales at retail the day before.

Gleaming Vistas. This opens vistas that gleam so brightly that any marketing man has to shield his eyes to avoid snow blindness. New product performance could be gauged day-by-day and promotion money deployed for maximum effectiveness. A product that isn't going to make it could be withdrawn from the market before it hurt either profits or reputation significantly. When you know precisely what is selling where, and when, you can identify your customers, plan future promotions intelligently, simulate all sorts of situations. . . .

Bayesian statistics, a formal structure of decision theory, is a valuable technique for the marketing manager. Until the the advent of Bayesian statistics, a gap existed between statistics and business judgment. Now, these two elements can be integrated in a single decision-making process. A sample application of Bayesian statistics to marketing is presented, and the technique's potential contributions are discussed.

26. BAYESIAN STATISTICS IN MARKETING*

Harry V. Roberts†

The application of statistics to marketing has grown substantially in recent decades. Yet statistics has remained more of a "sideshow" than an integral part of the process of decision-making. Too often, consumer

* Reprinted from "Bayesian Statistics in Marketing," *Journal of Marketing*, Vol. 27, No. 1 (January, 1963), pp. 1–4. See, also, Harry V. Roberts, "The New Business Statistics," *Journal of Business*, Vol. 33, No. 1 (January, 1960), pp. 21–30, for a summarization and appraisal of Robert Schlaifer, *Probability and Statistics for Business Decisions* (New York: McGraw-Hill Book Company, Inc., 1959). The Schlaifer book is fundamental to an understanding of decision theory and the use of statistical theory in making business decisions.

† University of Chicago.

surveys and sales analyses have been carried out with little thought about their contribution to management problems.

This is hardly surprising, because it is only recently that statistical theorists themselves have seen the potential contribution of statistics to decision-making and have begun to evolve a formal structure of *decision theory* that can actually be applied. Although the structure is still incomplete, its promise is bright. This structure is called *Bayesian statistics.*

The adjective "Bayesian" comes from Bayes's theorem, an elementary result of probability theory traceable to the Rev. Thomas Bayes, an English clergyman of the 18th century. His theorem typically, although not necessarily, plays an essential part in a Bayesian statistical analysis. Strangely enough, the really distinctive feature of Bayesian statistics is not Bayes's theorem but rather the personalistic interpretation of probability. That is, it is legitimate to quantify our feelings about uncertainty in terms of subjectively assessed numerical probabilities, even when confronted by a single unique decision and when there is no extensive past history on which to base the assessment of probabilities.

Assessments are made of probabilities of events that determine the profitability of alternative actions open to a decision-maker. Assessments are also made of profit (more generally, utility) for each possible combination of action and event. For each possible action, expected profit can then be computed, that is, a weighted mean of the possible profits, the weights being the probabilities mentioned above. The action is chosen for which expected profit is highest. The dominating principle of decision, then, is maximimization of expected profit (or utility).

AN EXAMPLE

Consider the following hypothetical, simplified, yet reasonably realistic marketing application.

A manufacturer of automobiles is testing a new direct mail approach B versus a standard approach A. An experiment is conducted in which each of the two approaches is tried out on random samples of size n (sample size $2n$ in total) from a large national mailing list. Suppose that $n = 100{,}000$, so that 200,000 is the total sample size of the experiment. During a three-month period, approach B has 761 sales and A has 753.

The problem is: should A or B be used on a national scale, or should a decision be deferred until more research has been done?

Suppose that additional evidence cannot be obtained and that a choice must be made between A and B. Many statisticians would suggest a test of significance. It turns out that the difference is not significant at any of the usual levels. What to conclude? One answer is that nothing can be decided from the experiment because A and B do not differ significantly. Another answer is that the standard method A should be continued because it is not significantly worse. Still another answer is that it does not matter whether *A* or *B* is used because they are not significantly different. The correct answer is that if all *other* considerations are evenly balanced, then the slight edge of *B* over *A* should be decisive.

While this common-sense answer can be given a justification of sorts by conventional statistical theory, it can be supported easily by a Bayesian analysis. Three assumptions about "all *other* considerations are evenly balanced" can be made explicit. First, it can be assumed that other evidence on the effectiveness of the two approaches is negligible by comparison with this statistical evidence. Second, it can be assumed that if the true effectiveness of each method were known, we would be willing to adopt the one with the higher effectiveness; that is, there are no differences in costs or side benefits: the "break-even" difference in true effectiveness is zero. Third, it can be assumed that the difference in effectiveness measured in sales rates per mailing is proportional to the difference in effectiveness measured in profit rates per mailing.

Under these assumptions a Bayesian analysis proceeds as follows. Compute a *posterior distribution* (posterior to the sample, that is) of the true difference of effectiveness between *B* and *A*. Under our present assumptions, Bayes's theorem shows that the posterior distribution of the true difference in sales rates per mailing can be approximated by a normal distribution with a mean of

$$\frac{761}{100{,}000} - \frac{753}{100{,}000} = \frac{8}{100{,}000} = .00008$$

and a standard deviation of

$$\sqrt{\frac{(.00761)\ (1 - .00761)}{100{,}000} + \frac{(.00753)\ (1 - .00753)}{100{,}000}}$$
$$= \sqrt{\frac{.00756}{100{,}000} + \frac{.00748}{100{,}000}}$$
$$= \sqrt{.0000001504}$$
$$= .00039,$$

where familiar classical formulas, $p_1 - p_2$ and

$\sqrt{\frac{p_1q_1}{n_1} + \frac{p_2q_2}{n_2}}$ are used in the calculation.

What does this mean? It means that we are attaching probabilities to the thing we are uncertain about, namely, the true difference in effectiveness between *B* and *A*, and that these probabilities are summarized approximately by a normal distribution with the stated mean and standard deviation. Once we attach probabilities to the things we are uncertain about, we can implement the rule of decision: Choose that action for which expected profit is highest.

In our present example, it can be shown that this rule tells us to compare the mean of the posterior distribution, .00008, with the break even point of true differential effectiveness, or 0. Since .00008 exceeds 0, we should choose appeal *B*.

Reasonably realistic numerical assumptions show that the expected superiority of *B* over *A* is $2,000,000. The assumptions are that the balance of the national mailing list has 50,000,000 names, and that the incremental profit per car sold is $500. Under these assumptions, 8 added cars per 100,000 names implies an expected differential profit of (.00008) (50,000,000) ($50) = $2,000,000. It is hardly a matter of indifference which approach is chosen.

The decision to choose *B* could, of course, be reached by unaided common sense. Even if the economic break-even point were different than zero, unaided common sense would still work. Suppose that it was judged that because of certain changeover costs, *B* would have to be at least .00020 units more effective than *A* to warrant its adoption. Then we would compare .00008 with .00020 and conclude that *A* should be retained, since .00008 is less than .00020.

THE ROLE OF JUDGMENT

Suppose, however, that other evidence is not negligible compared to the statistical evidence. For example, suppose that prior to the experiment management had felt that on balance *A* was better than *B*, but that the chances that they were wrong were enough to warrant the experiment.

More quantitatively, suppose that it had been judged that the odds were even that the true effectiveness of *B* over *A* did not exceed −.00010, but also that the odds were only even that the true effectiveness was within .000026 of −.00010. Note that .00010 is about 1.3% of the sales rate for *A*, and that .00026 is about 3.5% of it.

Moreover, management assumed that the normal distribution fitting these requirements, which will have a mean of −.00010 and a standard deviation of .00039, can be taken to be the *prior distribution* of the true difference in effectiveness. "Prior" simply means prior by comparison with the statistical evidence contemplated, which in this example was the experiment already described. Bayes's theorem again tells how this prior distribution should be revised in the face of sample evidence to arrive at a posterior distribution. It turns out to be approximately a normal distribution with mean

$$\frac{-.00010 + .00008}{2} = -.00001,$$

so that the decision would now go *against* approach *B*.

In order to make this calculation, the standard error of the sample difference, .00039, had to be used. It is an accident of this particular illustration that the reconciliation of judgment and sample evidence is achieved by a simple average; in general, the two would not be weighted equally. While the details of operation of Bayes's theorem will not be developed here, the important thing is that the theorem gives a formal reconciliation between managerial judgment, expressed quantitatively in the prior distribution, and the statistical evidence of the experiment. This reconciliation might be much harder to arrive at by common sense alone.

Incidentally, managerial judgment is not, as assumed at the outset, likely to be given negligible weight by comparison with the experiment evidence. There is likely to be good reason to believe that the differential sales effectiveness of *A* and *B* is rather small, as in this last illustration, because the direct mailing itself has a relatively small influence on total sales.

THE PROBLEM OF SAMPLE SIZE

Turn now to a more difficult question, that of deciding whether additional evidence should be sought, and if so, how much. This question is really the problem of sample size.

To give a concrete illustration of how it is solved, let us revert to the situation in which prior evidence was negligible compared to that of a sample, so that the posterior distribution is normal with mean .00008 and standard error .00039. This posterior distribution now can be regarded as a *prior* distribution with respect to additional experimental information that might be obtained.

In addition to this prior distribution, an assessment must be made of four key economic quantities: (1) the incremental profit to the company (assumed constant) of an added car sold; (2) the size of the national mailing list; (3) the fixed cost of an experiment; (4) the incremental cost per name (assumed constant) on an experimental mailing list.

For illustration, take $500, 50,000,000, $10,000, and $0.25 for these quantities. The result of a numerical calculation is that a further experiment involving about 500,000 names for each approach—1,000,000 in total—should be run, and then a final decision between *A* and *B* should be made based on the mean of the posterior distribution after that experiment. (The added or lost sales attributable to *B* during the experiment are not accounted for in this approximate calculation. The details of this calculation would be meaningless without a great deal more background than can be developed in a short exposition.[1])

---

[1] Robert Schlaifer, *Probability and Statistics in Business Decisions*, corrected impression (New York: McGraw-Hill Book Co., Inc., 1959), especially pp. 544–546.

POTENTIAL CONTRIBUTIONS

There are three potential contributions of Bayesian statistics illustrated by the example above:

1. How to choose between marketing alternatives on the basis of sample evidence when virtually no weight is to be given to managerial judgment.
2. How to choose between marketing alternatives on the basis of sample evidence when substantial weight is to be given to managerial judgment.
3. How to decide on how much research, if any, should be done before a final choice is made.

For completeness, there is a fourth potential contribution not indicated in the example above:

4. How to choose between marketing alternatives when no sample evidence is available: judgments would be expressed as a prior distribution, and the mean of this distribution would be compared with the break-even point.

IMPLICATIONS

Consider the importance of each of these contributions. The fourth, how to make a choice in the absence of sample evidence, is simply a way of formalizing what would otherwise be done informally and intuitively. It is like having a checklist to assure that nothing will be forgotten or given distorted importance.

The first, how to make a choice when the evidence is almost wholly statistical, can be made by common sense without Bayesian statistics. On the other hand, the Bayesian approach helps greatly to avoid errors that are common in practice, and especially those due to serious yet natural misunderstandings of traditional statistical methods.

The second, how to reconcile strong judgments with statistical evidence, is very difficult to do by common sense alone. The formal Bayesian apparatus is a great help.

The third, how to choose the best sample size, is not obvious at all to common sense. On no other problem are the recommendations of different statisticians likely to differ so much. The Bayesian calculation illustrated is the only defensible way to give an answer. Traditional statistical theory tells how to choose a sample size that will meet a specification for precision. It does not tell how much precision should be specified, except to give informal advice that the benefits of added precision must be balanced against the costs of attaining it. Such informal advice is not an adequate guide.

Not all marketing problems can be answered as easily as the one given in this example. However, a substantial fraction of marketing problems are of this type, although perhaps more complicated, as where a choice must be made between three approaches, *A*, *B*, and *C*, where *C* might be no direct mailing at all. The Bayesian apparatus has been worked out for these problems. Moreover, the apparatus has been extended to certain other kinds of problems.

There was not sufficient realism in this example to make it completely convincing. One defect is that an experiment of this kind would have to be carried out in selected markets rather than in a random sample of a national mailing list. There is uncertainty as to how the differential effectiveness of *A* and *B* in Denver, for example, might compare with differential effectiveness in the rest of the country. A formal Bayesian apparatus exists for dealing with such problems.

Of course, much needs to be done to work out Bayesian solutions for common marketing problems. But much has already been done, and important problems can be solved now.[2]

The real difficulty in applying statistics to marketing is that until recently no theoretical bridge existed between "statistics" and "business judgment." For the first time we now know how to fit both these elements into the process of decision-making. In particular, no statistical analysis is complete unless "business judgment" is incorporated into it. It *does* matter, for example, what management thinks about the comparative effectiveness of *A* and *B* before statistical evidence on the question can be intelligently sought or analyzed.

Marketing statisticians cannot pursue the illusory goal of trying to provide "definitive answers" in the sense that scientific research is sometimes supposed to do. "Definitive answers" might require exorbitant sample sizes, and even then the answers might not turn out to be really definitive.

Likewise, marketing executives cannot leave statistics solely to the statisticians. They must communicate the essence of their judgment about marketing problems before statisticians can make a fully satisfactory technical contribution; and they must understand the underlying rationale of decision theory.

[2] Schlaifer, same reference as footnote 1. Also, Robert Schlaifer and Howard Raiffa, *Applied Statistical Decision Theory* (Boston, Division of Research, Harvard Graduate School of Business Administration, 1961).

Marketing intelligence is information selected, evaluated, interpreted and expressed in a manner that facilitates its application to marketing problems. Marketing intelligence and the assessment of market opportunity are key factors in long-range planning. Long-range planning is more than a summation of short-range plans. Short-range plans cannot be expected to adequately assess long-range environmental trends.

27. MARKETING INFORMATION, INTELLIGENCE AND LONG-RANGE PLANNING*

Edward L. Brink†

At the very outset I should like to make clear my interest in the subject of this paper. It is marketing intelligence. During the past few years at the Wharton School we have been preparing a course in this subject as a part of the over-all remodeling of our curriculum. This academic year we presented it for the first time, with success I believe.

What is marketing intelligence? The following definition is the one which evolved from the first offering of the course.

> Marketing intelligence flows from marketing information, which is first gathered by utilizing such "tools" as marketing research, distribution cost analysis or even operations research, and then organized. Marketing intelligence is information which is selected, evaluated, interpreted and expressed in such a way that its application to a marketing problem, present or potential, is clear.

This concept predicates a flow from INFORMATION to INTELLIGENCE to use in DECISION MAKING AND LONG-RANGE PLANNING. It further stipulates a process through which the informa-

---

* Reprinted from "Marketing Information, Intelligence and Long-Range Planning," *Proceedings of the 47th National Conference of the American Marketing Association*, 1964, pp. 154–58.

† University of Pennsylvania.

tion must pass before becoming intelligence. This is the continuous cycle of SELECTION, EVALUATION AND INTERPRETATION.

The preceding stage of GATHERING and ORGANIZING information cannot be independent of the "intelligence cycle," there must be feedback for guidance in the gathering process. If this were not so one would gather every possible shred. I will mention this later as part of the economics of information gathering.

LONG-RANGE PLANNING

What does this have to do with long-range planning? To answer that I would like to restate the concluding remarks of Prof. Alderson's paper in this session.

"Thus, change comes because it is demand, because of the initiative of profit-seeking enterprises or because of inherent tendencies in human organization which are more sociological and political rather than falling within the scope of marketing economics."

Long-range planning cannot be the result of a series of short-range plans coupled with a pious hope that the sum or products, will be correlated with the long-run political and sociological changes. Having mentioned this I would like to make a comment that may give my answer to a question in your mind. The question is "What about marketing research?" I have been associated with it for quite a few years and personally I have found that the majority of its efforts are devoted to short-range fires with very little sense of continuity with the past.

Certainly there are exceptions to this and there are marketing research departments that would fulfill my concept of an intelligence department. These are far and few between. I am currently trying to question the 1,000 leading firms in our country on this subject and although the returns are only beginning to trickle in, there are many interesting comments—to wit, there is no need for a long-range intelligence effort. I think that a further questioning may lead to the real answer, that they can't afford long-range intelligence. This certainly can be true and leads me to a subject which I shall mention only briefly. How far you can afford to project your effort and how much you can gather as you go—that is how long and how much, is a matter for the economics of information. Prof. Paul Green has written extensively on this under the pen name of Dr. Bayes and I refer you in all seriousness, to his writings.

What are the typical long-range marketing problems that can be aided by an intelligence effort? We have considered them to be pricing, market share, product development, product mix and promotional mix.

Let us suppose as a case in point that we are looking at a drug firm where great interest is in technological research or product development.

The hypothetical example is based in a large part on a research proposal made by the management Science Center at the Wharton School.

TECHNOLOGICAL FORECASTING

Technological research (and development) is a scientific and financial gamble. It cannot be "rigged" in advance; one is dealing with things that are unknown until they are found. The most elusive and often inconsequential goals have to be pursued sometimes for years because one might possibly find a pleasant surprise awaiting when one gets there. Then, if one is willing and able to do all these things, perhaps once in a thousand times, success may be achieved. There is no doubt that the accumulated skill and experience of research administrators provides the fundamental basis for sound research judgment and direction. To provide management and research directors with the best combination of tools including schemes, models, programs, devices and data, to deal with this problem, and to enable management to profit fully from past experience in making future decisions, it appears that the basic element of the problem lies in the ability to predict or sense innovation. Note if you will, the similarity in the ability of the military to predict innovation in material and tactics, etc. If this is possible, then one will no longer have to wait for the once in a thousand success, or conversely, one can be ready to capitalize on the success as soon as it appears.

Technological forecasting can be viewed as being either a very profound systems problem or a simple statistical problem. The simple statistical problem simply seeks to match prediction with the events that do mature in breakthroughs. This is usually done by using some elementary unsophisticated correlation measures. In many instances this suffices.

Forecasting of technological breakthroughs normally goes out for five or ten years so that the statistical approach just mentioned is also impractical because of the elapsed time before the accumulation of data is complete. The other approach is retrospective, if you will, in which predictions of five years ago are measured against what has happened today. The method of phrasing the predictions (if any such predictions can be found) is so likely to be irrelevant to the present way of phrasing the predictions that retrospective validations are quite unconvincing. There have been studies, for example, in the medical research areas that show the fallacy of this method. Yet, retrospective follow-up may be the only way to get numbers within less than a year. One selects the events today and tries to guess the universe from which they arose randomly some time ago. The selection of this universe is so liable to fallacious sampling that the confidence in such statistics can be very shaky.

This leads to a conclusive viewpoint on technological forecasting: Validation lies in the persuasion that a valid method has been used and in the long-term success of the human enterprise which is based on the forecasts. Since personal opinions are suspect as methods of prediction, we look to structural relationships among factors, expressed explicitly, as the method of prediction. The communication of this structure from one scientific group to another is the vehicle for extending conviction in the validity of the method of the prediction. All of this is to say that, if you can show verbally or diagrammatically how all of the factors in your prediction relate to other factors, and if other persons agree with your integrated concept, then your method is more valid than the person's who merely gives an opinion. The validation then lies in the demonstration of the connectivity and relativity of the matrix of scientific factors determining the predicted scientific results. This would be my concept of an operating intelligence effort in such a firm.

In a less complex sense I would like to refer you to Prof. Ralph Cassidy's article in the Spring, 1964, California Management Review entitled "*The Intelligence Function and Business Competition.*" He summarizes in part as follows:

"One final point: While the role of intelligence in protecting markets is important in keeping up with new developments (as in the case of stainless steel blades) and price changes, it may be limited if only because one may have no idea from what direction innovations will be forthcoming and hence how to organize the intelligence effort. There is the additional problem of adjusting one's competitive effort to changes, because of absence of knowledge re the timing of the acceptance of the new development, as for example, pay television. This suggests that under certain circumstances there is little that existing vendors can do except to keep an eye on new developments (through trade papers and the company's sales force, for example) and remain on one's toes as it were in order to be able to adjust offerings to market changes if and when such adjustments are indicated. And this requires a certain degree of humility on the part of the decision-makers."

To date you have had my opinions and a reflection of some colleagues'. Now you may say well, what about the hard-headed businessman. I am trying to find this out in my survey, but I do know that one of our leading Management Consulting Firms has set up intelligence departments for two large clients.

Marion Harper, Jr., also wrote on this in an article entitled "A New Profession to Aid Management,"*Journal of Marketing*, Vol. 25, No. 3 (January, 1961), pp. 1–6. This article is best described by quoting the premises suggested by the writer: "To manage a business well is to manage its future and to manage its future is to manage information;" "Management decision making is becoming an increasingly complex process, with a multiplication of knowns and unknowns;" "We are entering upon an Information Revolution in which the supply of data increases by geometric progression;" "As information multiplies, management needs 'protection' from the specialist;" "Too many people take part in decisions—and too many decision-makers use the wrong tools." Each of these premises is explored in some detail with the conclusion that there is a need to develop a new profession "to provide an intelligence service for the shaping of strategy and policy." It would be headed by a Director of Intelligence Services "who would develop information for different possible recommendations and who would outline the probable consequences of moving in any direction." There are many other such articles appearing in other journals as well as trade publications.

CONCLUSION

I would like to say a few words in conclusion about organization. I don't propose to present any organization charts. As Mr. Harper stated the head of this effort must be much like a military intelligence officer. He and he alone must be responsible for the evaluation of the material itself, the evaluation of the source and the interpretation. Finally, he must be responsible for a presentation responsive to the problem at hand for the decision-maker.

I have tried to relate the nature of long-range planning to the nature of an intelligence effort as I see it.

Bibliography—Chapter IV

Ackoff, R. L. "The Meaning, Scope and Methods of Operations Research," *Progress in Operations Research* (ed. R. L. Ackoff), Vol. I, pp. 1–20. New York: John Wiley & Sons, Inc., 1961.

Alderson, W., and Shapiro, S. J. (eds.). *Marketing and the Computer.* Englewood Cliffs, N.J.: Prentice-Hall, Inc., 1963.

Banks, Seymour. *Experimentation in Marketing.* New York: McGraw-Hill Book Co., Inc., 1965.

Bass, F. M., et al. (eds.). *Mathematical Models and Methods in Marketing.* Homewood, Ill.: Richard D. Irwin, Inc., 1961.

Borko, Harold (ed.). *Computer Applications in the Behavioral Sciences.* Englewood Cliffs, N.J.: Prentice-Hall, Inc., 1962.

Buzzell, Robert D. *Mathematical Models and Marketing Management.* Cambridge, Mass.: Division of Research, Harvard Business School, 1964.

Crisp, Richard D. *Sales Planning and Control.* New York: McGraw-Hill Book Co., Inc., 1961.

Day, Ralph L. (ed.). *Marketing Models—Quantitative and Behavioral.* Scranton, Pa.: International Textbook Co., 1964.

Frank, R. E.; Kuehn, A. A.; and Massy, W. F. *Quantitative Techniques in Marketing Analysis.* Homewood, Ill.: Richard D. Irwin, Inc., 1963.

Howard, John. *Marketing Management.* Rev. ed. Homewood, Ill.: Richard D. Irwin, Inc., 1963.

Langhoff, Peter (ed.). *Models, Measurement and Marketing.* Englewood Cliffs, N.J.: Prentice-Hall, Inc., 1963.

Rigby, Paul H. *Conceptual Foundations of Business Research.* New York: John Wiley & Sons, Inc., 1965.

Schlaifer, Robert. *Probability and Statistics for Business Decisions.* New York: McGraw-Hill Book Co., Inc., 1959.

Simon, Herbert A. *The New Science of Management Decision.* New York: Harper & Bros., Inc., 1960.

V. MARKETING MANAGEMENT FUNCTIONS: THE SYSTEMS ORIENTATION

The achievement of predetermined marketing goals requires integration and coordination of all market-related elements of the firm. Marketing management's task is to combine these elements into an effective operating system and to manage the system in its interaction with a dynamic environment. Marketing management functions that must be performed to plan and manage a corporate marketing system are assessing marketing opportunity, planning and programming marketing activity, actuating marketing organization and leadership, and evaluating and adjusting marketing effort.

Assessment of marketing opportunity involves the identification of company goals and the analysis of established and new profit opportunities for the firm. The significance of this function is that market opportunities are continually changing, and marketing management must develop creative strategies to cultivate these market opportunities. A planned program of innovation is essential for marketing effectiveness. The firm must respond to the market and adopt a broad and dynamic view of marketing opportunity. Performance of the assessment function on a continuing basis assures the firm that it will be dynamic in its marketing and production operations, that identification of the set of challenges and problems facing the company is possible, and that changing marketing opportunities will be met effectively by the firm.

Planning is an integral component of the marketing management concept and is a vital element of the systems orientation. This func-

tion, when based on the assessment of market opportunity, is a key to successful marketing management and performance. Market planning is used to develop and define objectives and then derive programs that will enable the firm to achieve these objectives. The systems approach requires a concise statement of these goals and encourages a systematic analysis of the impact of the programs devised. Planning provides the basis for an integrated and coordinated marketing strategy. Coordination of the firm's marketing programs is a must if the planned objectives of the business are to be achieved. To make planning central to the marketing concept, both short- and long-range planning are involved.

The innovistic and dynamic nature of marketing activity places heavy demands on the marketing organization. The systems approach influences the firm's thinking about the marketing organization. Viewing the organization as a goal-directed system can stimulate fundamental thinking about the firm's marketing operations and problems. The interaction process between the organization and the environment is a central concern of the marketing discipline. Application of the newer organizational theories may have an impact on marketing operations. New product developments and the growing importance of international marketing are some of the marketing changes that have raised organizational problems for the firm. Implementation of the marketing management concept will be directly reflected in the organizational changes that occur.

Diverse changes are influencing the patterns and styles of leadership required for effective performance of marketing functions. Development of newer patterns of leadership are testing traditional views of management methods and practices. For example, one organizational problem is raised by the tendency toward centralization of responsibility for integration of the total marketing task. Balanced against this centralization tendency is the need for greater participation in management and decision making by people at subordinate levels. A solution requires analysis of management's philosophy, communication patterns, the scope of responsibility and authority, leadership abilities and staffing policies and practices, and the development of appropriate policies in the setting of the individual situation and firm.

In order to take advantage of profitable marketing opportunities, the marketing manager must continually evaluate and adjust the marketing effort. The firm must adjust to its ever-changing environment. To make an effective judgment, the marketing manager must have knowledge of the entire marketing system so that the components of the system can be evaluated, controlled, and adjusted to bring the system into line with marketing opportunity. Essentially, the major challenge confronting marketing management is that of creative adaptation to change. To meet this challenge, the firm should have a complete appraisal of its marketing operations through a marketing audit. The continuing problem for marketing management is to match marketing effort with market opportunity.

A. Marketing Opportunity Assessment

Management must recognize the necessity for planning, organizing, and controlling product and process innovation in the creation of market opportunity. Every marketing manager must develop a framework for analysis of the problems and opportunities involved in programmed innovation. Activities basic to innovation management are identified and related to two examples of the innovation process.

28. MANAGING INNOVATION IN MARKETING*

Eugene J. Kelley† and William Lazer‡

Despite all the speeches made about "marketing orientation" or "customer orientation," most businesses are still primarily product- or process-oriented rather than market-oriented.[1] Few firms today construct

---

* Reprinted from "Managing Innovation in Marketing," *Advanced Management-Office Executive* Vol. 1, No. 7 (July, 1962), pp. 10–13. For a discussion of managerial marketing functions, see Thomas A. Staudt, "The Managerial Functions of Marketing," in William Lazer and Eugene J. Kelley, *Managerial Marketing: Perspectives and Viewpoints* (rev. ed. Homewood, Ill.: Richard D. Irwin, Inc., 1962), pp. 385–92. Also see Thomas A. Staudt and Donald A. Taylor, *A Managerial Introduction to Marketing* (Englewood Cliffs, N.J.: Prentice-Hall, Inc., 1965), pp. 17–26.

† The Pennsylvania State University.

‡Michigan State University.

[1] Peter F. Drucker, quoted in Lazo, Hector and Corbin, Arnold, *Management in Marketing* (New York: McGraw-Hill Book Co., Inc., 1961), p. vii.

and execute corporate plans and strategy on the basis of careful study of market needs, forces, and opportunities. Competition will accelerate the change to a genuine marketing concept in more firms in the next five years, and stimulate more interest in the process of managing change through programmed innovation management. Programmed innovation will increasingly become the foundation of business strategy. The basic managerial response to accelerating change must be innovation.

In this article nine activities of innovation management are identified and are applied to the function and process of innovation. Experience in a number of firms indicates that while innovation may rest basically on the creative and managerial powers of a relatively limited number of individuals, innovation can be stimulated, produced, and managed by systematic attention to the task. The risks and costs of non-innovation are tending to overcome the fear of loss on unsuccessful innovations in more competitive situations in large and small firms.

Managers in all industries must produce and manage innovation on a scale sufficient to absorb unused and growing production capabilities and to achieve differential advantage in the market. To do this job, each manager must develop a framework for analysis of the problems and opportunities involved in innovation management. Increased understanding of the function and process of innovation is a basic requirement of executive and corporate growth.

To managers the fundamental notion underlying innovation is clear, i.e., the addition of something new and different to an existing situation. The managerial problem is administering the systematic injection of appropriate new insights, concepts, and techniques into existing business situations. Programmed attention to each of the following activities characterizes the innovation-directed firm. Their neglect is more typical in non-innovation-minded enterprises.

ACTIVITIES OF INNOVATION MANAGEMENT

1. Acceptance of the inevitability of change and innovation by management.
2. Programmed perception of new market needs and of dysfunctioning in the system.
3. Relating market opportunity to corporate resources.
4. Specifying innovistic opportunities of the firm.
5. Identifying practical alternative strategies.
6. Determining the expected profitability of each of the major strategies.
7. Making a decision on innovative action.
8. Promoting the innovation.
9. Assuring market acceptance of the innovation.

The relation of these nine activities is discussed below.

1. Acceptance of the inevitability of change and innovation by management.

This is primary and pervasive. Acceptance of the inevitability and necessity of change and innovation in a period of accelerating technology is a basic management and organizational responsibility. The point of view that change is accelerating, normal, and constructive must be held by the leadership of an enterprise. This is essentially a directorship responsibility which requires an awareness on the part of top management of the need for discerning unsatisfied market demands. Top management's tasks include provision of a motivated organization and a permissive environment for innovation. Innovation can not only be encouraged, but discouraged by top-management attitudes.

2. Programmed perception of new market opportunities and of dysfunctioning in the system.

The perception of new market needs, future market opportunity, and system dysfunctioning is a prerequisite for business dynamism. This perception grows out of an attitude of dissatisfaction with present performance. Market opportunity and dysfunctioning is recognized by comparing market response to products and services with market wants and needs. The discrepancy is one measure of innovistic and market opportunity. The discrepancy is measured through a combination of various techniques of consumer and market research and managerial judgment and vision.

The early stages of the innovation process require people able to perceive areas of human dissatisfaction as market opportunities. One of the major problems confronting corporate management committed to the generation of innovation is to identify, stimulate, and encourage the people in the system who are perceivers of dysfunctioning. Innovation and creativity do not flourish in overstructured situations. Perceivers can exist among customers and salesmen as well as executives and researchers. Management must plan to broaden the base of perceivers of dysfunctioning by stimulating and rewarding such people wherever they are found in the organization.

3. Relating market opportunity to corporate resources.

Perception of market needs does not mean an opportunity exists for any particular company. Available opportunities must be related to the particular company's resources including its personnel, financial, and physical resources. Profitable courses of action vary with individual corporate postures and goals. The overwhelming majority of innovative opportunities will be rejected. But it is necessary to screen the many to find the few that do relate to the resources and the mission of the company.

4. Specifying innovistic opportunities of the firm.

This function of innovation relates to specifying the company's innovistic opportunity by identifying the various practical alternatives which exist to remedy the discovered dysfunctioning. This is a job where the technician can assume a major responsibility. An analysis of total company operations and methods in light of market opportunities is helpful in sifting the opportunities to arrive at the few that are most relevant and profitable for the company's current situation.

5. Identifying practical alternative strategies.

Having specified the available opportunities the company is in a position of being able to outline alternative strategies for the profitable pursuit of innovistic opportunity. It can thereby indicate various courses of action that could be followed to overcome the market dysfunctioning or meet a new market need.

6. Determining the expected profitability of each of the major strategies.

One logical method of selection of the right strategy is to determine the expected dollar values in following each of the practical strategies. For example, market opportunity might indicate that five products could satisfy market wants at a particular point in time. Each product has inherent advantages and disadvantages, but each is capable of serving market demands. The question becomes one of determining the expected dollar values of each of the five strategies. The expected dollar value is determined by two items.

1. The anticipated dollar outcomes of following each of the five strategies.
2. The estimated profitability of success of each of the five strategies.[2]

Management usually does not know with certainty the likelihood of success of following any given strategy nor the exact payoff. However, it should attempt to determine specific values for them. A value of this approach is that management is forced to place an expected dollar value on the outcomes of each of the strategies. If the objective is to maximize profits, then the decision choice for the innovation becomes one of choosing that strategy which has the highest expected dollar value.

---

[2] For example, if it is estimated that the dollar value of following strategy "A" is a million dollars, this dollar value times the estimated probability of success of the strategy determines the expected dollar value. Therefore, if the probability of success is 0.5, the expected value of strategy "A" is $500,000.

7. Making a decision on innovative action.

Once the expected dollar values of alternative decision choices have been arrayed, a logical choice is facilitated. The expected returns, however, must meet corporate criteria before an innovation is adopted.

If the expected dollar return of the best alternative does not meet the rate of return or profit expectations of a company; or if the risk of the alternatives is too high, the innovistic opportunity may then be passed up by the company. The opportunity finally selected will determine the specific marketing program adopted.

8. Promoting the innovation.

This might be more broadly considered as marketing the innovation to the audience for which it has been designed. It is in this area, for instance, that advertising, salesmanship, and all the elements of the marketing mix must be coordinated to effectively cultivate the particular market. To promote an innovation to the market place, a firm must cultivate awareness on the part of consumers, build up its image, and overcome the natural resistance to innovation.

9. Assuring market acceptance of the innovation.

The last stage is the adoption of the innovation. The gradual overcoming of the resistance to change to any innovation becomes the focal point for management effort. Factors leading to possible refinement of the innovation are evaluated through appraisal of information fed back from the market. Such market feedback will enable management to measure market responses to innovation and help to indicate new market opportunities. Market acceptance of an innovation results not in a new equilibrium but in a new situation in which the seeds of further dysfunctioning exist.

THE PROCESS OF INNOVATION

The chart on page 281 illustrates one model of the innovative process and indicates the activities required at various managerial levels. It may suggest that different talents are needed at each stage of the process. The skills of the entrepreneur, the manager, the technician, the distribution expert, and the salesman are called for at various action stages of the innovative process.

The innovation time scale is collapsing. The period from the perception of dysfunctioning to the acceptance of the innovation has been consistently decreasing. This means more pressure will be placed on management to understand more fully the process of managing change through managing knowledge and the process of programmed innovation. Innovation approaches manageability when participation in the process becomes part of the continuing responsibility of all levels of management. Only then can a firm hope to deploy its resources profitably and be envisioned to meet the challenge of change.

INNOVATION ILLUSTRATIONS

Marketing innovation is influenced by technology and the physical sciences and by diverse social changes. Basic technological and social change combine to generate new areas of innovistic opportunity in marketing.

Marketing innovations occur in two main areas:

1. Product and service developments.
2. The facilitation of the processes of marketing.

An application of the innovative process in the introduction of a new product follows.

PRODUCT INNOVATION IN THE DRUG INDUSTRY

The drug industry offers many examples of product innovation. The competitive and social environment of the drug industry stimulates an acceptance of the inevitability of change and innovation. Individual drug companies typically recognize the nature of innovative opportunity and establish systematic programs for the perception of new market needs and the development of products to satisfy those needs. Research and development in drugs is based on the recognition that medical researchers, physicists and chemists must point towards the frontiers of knowledge in certain defined areas.

Basic research is usually encouraged. But, it is usually guided towards areas of strength of the company to relate new knowledge to corporate resources and marketing opportunities. For example, one drug company may have advanced research in steroids further than any competitor or any research group. Market opportunities in the development of steroids will present a particular innovistic opportunity for such a company. Top management in such a company tends to become more concerned with evaluating alternative strategies designed to achieve innovative opportunities in steroid drugs. For instance, four or five particular products with a steroid compound may be developed which seem likely to lead to successful treatment of particular diseases. With limited resources, the company must decide which is the most profitable and desirable opportunity to follow. Expected profit is usually the criterion in innovation-minded industries; it is only through profitable returns on innovation that further research and innovation are insured.

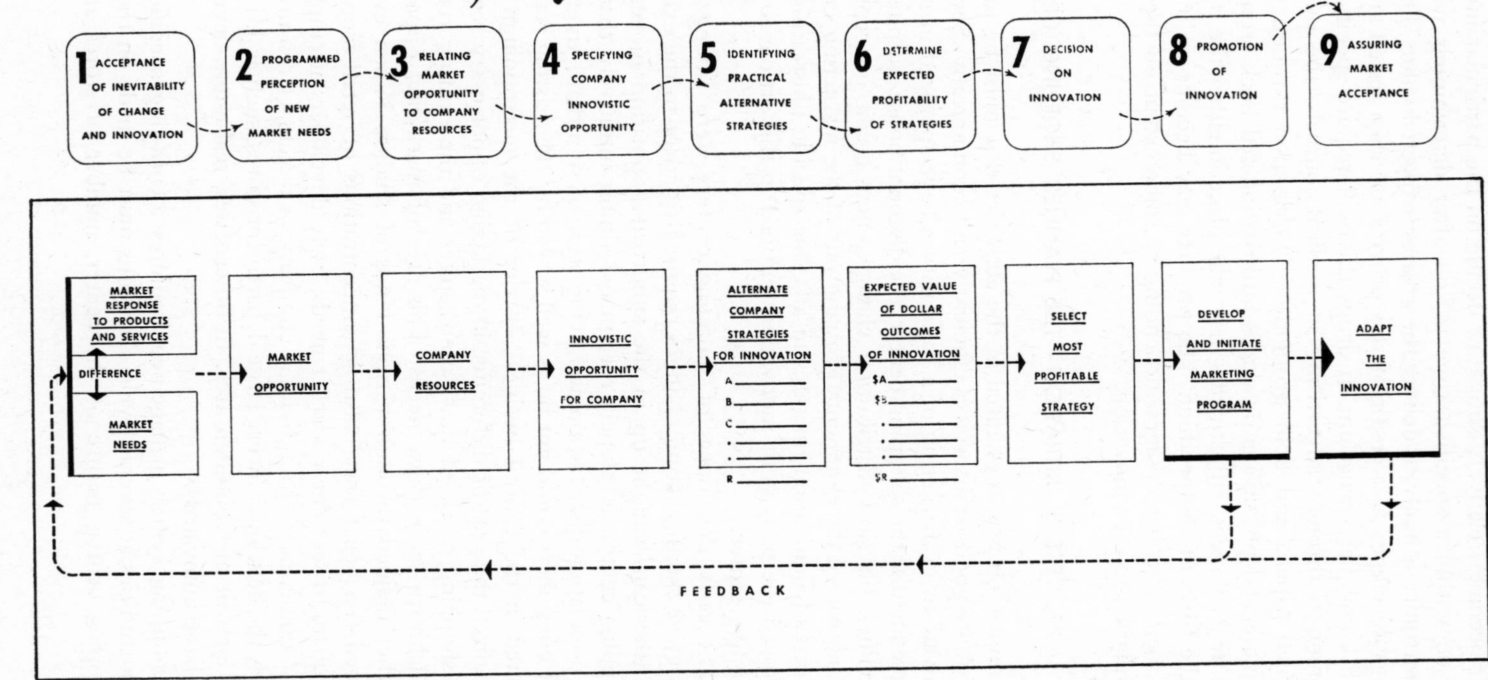
The Process of Innovation
1 ACCEPTANCE OF INEVITABILITY OF CHANGE AND INNOVATION
2 PROGRAMMED PERCEPTION OF NEW MARKET NEEDS
3 RELATING MARKET OPPORTUNITY TO COMPANY RESOURCES
4 SPECIFYING COMPANY INNOVISTIC OPPORTUNITY
5 IDENTIFYING PRACTICAL ALTERNATIVE STRATEGIES
6 DETERMINE EXPECTED PROFITABILITY OF STRATEGIES
7 DECISION ON INNOVATION
8 PROMOTION OF INNOVATION
9 ASSURING MARKET ACCEPTANCE
MARKET RESPONSE TO PRODUCTS AND SERVICES
DIFFERENCE
MARKET NEEDS
MARKET OPPORTUNITY
COMPANY RESOURCES
INNOVISTIC OPPORTUNITY FOR COMPANY
ALTERNATE COMPANY STRATEGIES FOR INNOVATION
A
B
C
R
EXPECTED VALUE OF DOLLAR OUTCOMES OF INNOVATION
$A
$B
$R
SELECT MOST PROFITABLE STRATEGY
DEVELOP AND INITIATE MARKETING PROGRAM
ADAPT THE INNOVATION
FEEDBACK

It becomes relatively simple to decide on the particular innovations to pursue within a specified time period after determining which steroid opportunity is likely to deliver the greatest expected value. The particular drugs developed as a result of this process are then tested and marketed with a complete program. In drugs this will require specific innovative promotion through advertising in medical journals, the publication of learned papers, and field promotion. Distribution through drug stores, hospitals and physicians produces information fed back from consumers and medical men. Adjustments may take place in either the product itself or the form of the product. The product may become an injection or a pill, or of varying dosages, depending to some extent on the reaction of the market to the innovation.

PROCESS ILLUSTRATION—THE PLANNED SHOPPING CENTER

Innovation is also essential in the activities that must be performed to distribute goods and services efficiently and economically. Several process innovations in marketing of a basic nature have appeared in recent years. These include the shopping center, the discount house, automatic vending machines, physical distribution changes, new credit concepts, and new organizational developments growing out of the marketing concept. The process of innovation operates in all. One specific illustration which has followed the pattern of innovation outlined in this article is the planned shopping center.

The early developers of shopping centers were among the first to recognize the marketing changes required to adapt to the evolving needs of Americans caught up in the suburban population movement. Early shopping center developers recognized almost intuitively that changes in the population distribution and living style of suburban Americans meant that consumers could not be as well served by the existing retail structure located in the central business district of the metropolitan area. They visualized the area of difference in marketing opportunity terms between the shopping needs of new suburbanites and the existing retail facilities available to serve those needs. This area of marketing opportunity was further defined through various kinds of studies. When evidence supported the belief that existing concentrations of retail stores were not adequate to serve new market needs, early developers attempted to relate those unmet needs to individual company or developer resources. In some cases, the developers were large department stores, such as J. L. Hudson in the Detroit metropolitan area. In other cases, real estate developers were the basic innovators.

Shopping center management requires identifying specific innovative opportunities at several levels. Decisions must be made on the size of the shopping center, nature of the center, number of stores and types of stores. The question of location and site selection is also one of analyzing specific innovative opportunities.

In site selection and locational innovation the problem becomes one of identifying various sites and attempting to determine the expected profitability of a location at each site. This involves trading area analysis, time-distance studies, and other efforts to get at the expected value of the dollar outcomes of locating shopping centers on a given site.

As with other process innovations, the decision once made must be promoted, not only to consumers, but to bankers, merchants, and others in the system. Finally, the innovation is modified through changes in the tenant mix or merchandise mix to fit more precisely the needs of the consumers served by the innovation.

Process innovation will be recognized as more important in marketing in the future. Fundamental concepts of marketing are changing and the entire field is being reoriented. The attitude of retailers, particularly, toward innovation is changing. The retailer must adapt to changes in the basic dynamic areas of consumer behavior, technology, changing competitive practices, and constantly altering business-governmental relationships.

CHANGE AND INNOVATION

All managers today must recognize product and process change as the constant in planning, organizing, and controlling marketing activity. Management's responsibility becomes that of anticipating, adapting, and innovating under accelerating change conditions. The emphasis, in many enterprises in the future, is not likely to be on operations. It will have to be on anticipating and adapting to change. Innovation is the essential element in such a strategy.

The programmed introduction of new or improved products and processes has become an essential part of the planning and strategy of many firms. It is a difficult task which requires a realistic evaluation of existing product lines, markets, trends, and competitive positions. This article defines and describes the various dimensions of the innovation process and their relations to the marketing functions.

29. THE CONCEPT AND PROCESS OF INNOVATION*

William Lazer† and William E. Bell‡

DIMENSIONS OF INNOVATION

Marketing and innovation are closely intertwined. Successful innovation is a necessary condition for effective marketing.[1] "Innovate or perish" is a trite statement, but one which has rich meaning for businesses operating in a consumeristic economy.

Marketing as an adaptive process seeks greater correspondence between the opportunities reflected in environments and a company's marketing mix. Since environments change continuously, and since technological developments are emerging at an increasing rate, greater attention is being directed at innovation. The result has been an acceptance of the concept of programmed innovation—the regular introduction of innovations to markets on a planned basis.

The significance of technological discovery to innovation has long been recognized. Now, in addition, the complementary and critical role of marketing in achieving successful innovation is underscored. The result is more market-directed research and development, the organization of marketing planning departments, and the extension of the activities and scope of marketing research departments.

---

* Not previously published.

† Michigan State University.

‡ Merrimack College.

[1] William Lazer, "Competition, Innovation, and Marketing Management," in Taylor W. Meloan and Charles M. Whitlo (eds.), *Competition In Marketing* (Department of Marketing and Business Logistics, University of Southern California, Los Angeles, 1964), p. 10.

This article explores innovation from a marketing point of view. It defines different categories of innovation, discusses the stages of the innovation process, and summarizes a few theories of new product and process acceptance.

THE INNOVATION PROCESS

Innovations are often distinguished from inventions. They are referred to as successful inventions. An innovation, essentially, is the act of developing a novel idea into a process or product. For an innovation to be successful, the process or product must be feasible and have commercial acceptability.[2]

Successful innovations go through three major phases: the idea, the implementation, and market acceptance. The idea is defined as the invention, and it is the result of creative work often done by researchers. Implementation refers to the development of the idea from its conceptual stage to an output—a developed product or service. This phase has received the greatest attention by business firms. Market acceptance, the third stage, is, by definition, crucial to any successful innovation.

The first two phases of the innovation process can be partially controlled by the firm. The acceptance decision, however, is largely exogenous to the firm. It depends upon consumers and their reactions. Although promotional and other marketing influences may be exerted, the decision per se is in the hands of potential consumers.

REASONS FOR INNOVATIONS

Innovations can be troublesome, risky, and may meet with great resistance. They require change on the part of manufacturers, distributors, and consumers. Yet innovation has become an integral part of modern marketing operations. Why do companies innovate?

Management innovates to solve problems—problems in the sense of untapped opportunities and not just immediate company difficulties. Innovations afford opportunities for:[3] (1) the use of excess plant capacity, (2) the use of available manpower, (3) better use of sales organization, (4) the utilization of by-products, (5) the employment of surplus capital, (6) the provision of a hedge against slack seasons, (7) the counteraction of declining market for a company's basic products.

Although risks may be great, the financial rewards for innovations can also be very large. Increasingly, a greater proportion of the earnings of

---

[2] William E. Bell, "Consumer Innovation: An Investigation of Selected Characteristics of Innovations" (unpublished D.B.A. dissertation, Michigan State University, 1962), p. 7.

[3] *Grey Matter*, Grey Advertising Agency, Inc., National Advertisers' Edition, Vol. XXXI (January, 1960), p. 2.

many companies come from new products and processes. Effective innovation assures corporations a niche in tomorrow's business setting. Similarly, inadequate innovation can render a company vulnerable to competitors' actions.

Company growth can be maintained through innovations. In fact, companies in industries classified as "growth industries" typically are oriented toward new product and process innovation. Examples of such industries are: chemicals, drugs, and electronics. For them, "It is about 'par' to have around 50 per cent of sales in products that are new since the war."[4]

Programmed innovation is also a defensive strategy. As old products decay and suffer loss of markets, new ones must be ready to accept the slack. The costs of not innovating can prove to be excessive. Given a competitive situation, a firm cannot hold its current market and profit position for long without innovating.

ADAPTIVE, FUNCTIONAL, AND FUNDAMENTAL INNOVATIONS

Innovations vary in both degree of complexity and application. The complexity of innovations may vary from minor adjustments to major technological breakthroughs. Minor product alternations, such as changes in packages or colors, constitute small changes in a product. They may, however, account for significant changes in the marketing task. At the other end of the continuum are completely novel products, such as missiles, laser beams, and computers. They may generate totally new industries and hitherto unrecognized markets.

Three main categories of innovation based on consumer reactions can be delineated: adaptive, functional, and fundamental. The least complex type of innovation is an adaptive innovation. It refers to the minor alteration of an existing product. Alterations in packages, color, design, trim, size, and style are examples. The adaptive innovation does not perform new functions for the user or the purchaser. It does not require any change in consumer behavior patterns or new consumer skills to use it. Adaptive innovations usually require the least investment in research expenditures, less ingenuity on the part of the firm, and little change on the part of consumer behavior. They constitute the most common type of innovation and also the easiest to emulate.

The second type of innovation is functional innovation. These are more complex for both consumers and producers than adaptive innovations. Functional innovations are those in which the product or service remains the same but the method of performing the function is new. For

[4] Ralph W. Jones, "Management of New Products," *The Journal of Industrial Engineering*, Vol. IX, No. 5 (September–October, 1948). Reprinted in William Lazer and E. J. Kelley (eds.), *Managerial Marketing: Perspectives and Viewpoints* (rev. ed.; Homewood, Ill.: Richard D. Irwin, Inc., 1962), p. 444.

example, electric and gas clothes dryers, or electric knives, perform the same functions for consumers as wringers and clothes lines, and ordinary knives, but do so in a different manner. Consumers, therefore, satisfy a previously fulfilled want in a new and better way.

Functional innovations can require considerable adjustments on the part of consumers. They may result in the purchase of tangible products to perform functions previously not requiring a physical product. For example, an electric or gas clothes dryer requires a different behavior pattern on the part of the consumer than did previous methods of drying clothes. Also a firm may need new processes or raw materials to effect such a change.

The third group of innovations are fundamental innovations. They are the most complex and rare of the three classes. Fundamental innovations incorporate original ideas or concepts which perform new functions for the consumer. They represent a complete break with the past on both the part of the consumer and the firm. They fulfill a need which was not previously recognized, or if recognized, was not previously fulfilled.

Fundamental innovations do not involve direct substitution, but focus on complete newness. Therefore, a firm may be faced with developing new raw materials and/or processes, as well as developing primary demand. The cultivation of markets and achievement of customer acceptance can be a difficult, expensive, and timely task for fundamental innovations.

An example of a fundamental innovation is the dehumidifier. The previously unsatisfied want or need is comfort in muggy or chilly weather, and freedom from the expense and nuisance of mildew. It had not been fulfilled previously. A new set of habits is required in the use and operation of this new product.

Any classification scheme of products or services suffers from the inability to establish categories that are mutually exclusive in all cases. There is some overlap in the categories established. It may even be more realistic to think in terms of an innovation spectrum ranging from various kinds of adaptive innovations at one extreme to several classes of fundamental innovations at the other. Yet, for purposes of understanding market reaction, the three categories suggested are useful.

Do products necessarily move from one category to another over time? For instance, does a fundamental innovation become an adaptive innovation? Part of the answer depends on how one defines a new product. If television, for example, is considered a completely new product, it is a fundamental innovation. But it may also be considered as an extension of radio with just the addition of sight to sound. Thus, the dilemma of what is new must be resolved before ascertaining whether or not a product started at the fundamental level.

A product or service does not necessarily have to move along the innovation continuum from category to category. All products need not

FIGURE I

Classification of Product Innovations

Type of Innovation

	FUNDAMENTAL	FUNCTIONAL	ADAPTIVE
CHARACTERISTICS	Requires: Absolute newness No substitutability Habit change New process New markets	Substitutability Improved product or process New or changed production	New in minor aspects: e.g., weight, color, design, package Much substitutability
	May Require: New skills New resources New consumption patterns New distribution systems	Change in consumption patterns New or changed distribution systems	Limited production change No changes in consumption pattern No change in distribution required Greater convenience
EXAMPLES	Missiles Dehumidifiers Airplanes Televisions Lasers Computers	Clothes dryers Electric knives Electric sharpeners Automatic dishwashers Jet planes	Flip-top box Filter and mentholated cigarettes New brands
MARKETING TASKS	Create primary demand Create new consumption habits New production facilities and/or processes Overcome resistance to change Gain acceptance	Create selective demand Change consumption habits New or changed production New service facilities Extend markets	Meet competition Extend markets Create selective demand Specialize product for market segments Differentiate product Create image of newness

emanate as fundamental innovations. On the other hand, it seems that the majority of them do at least move from functional to adaptive types of innovations. Few products do not have some kind of adaptation with regard to size, variety, number of parts, packaging, branding, and the like.

In Figure I, some of the salient considerations of fundamental, functional, and adaptive innovations are presented in tabular form. The characteristics of each innovation category, various examples of each, and a number of the marketing tasks are summarized.

ACCEPTANCE OF INNOVATION

Several theories have been advanced to explain the process of new product and process acceptance by consumers. In general, there has been no attempt to differentiate between types of innovations and their effects on consumer acceptance.

The "trickle down" theory is one of the most widely referred to explanations of the acceptance of innovations. The essence of this theory is that product or process acceptance starts at a top echelon of consumers, the upper income groups or social class, and trickles down until it reaches the lower echelons—the masses or lowest income groups. The acceptance of fashion is often explained in this way. While this theory has great appeal and may be useful in developing marketing strategy, it is an oversimplification and does not have applicability to all products.

A second theory might be called the theory of random selection. Proponents of this theory would assert there is a unique core market who will purchase an innovation regardless of socio-economic characteristics. The propensity to buy newness does not depend on the product but only on the fact that it is new and provides status, prestige, and recognition for the owners. A rational assessment of product characteristics is not involved in these purchases.

A third theory holds that there are opinion leaders and influentials within every peer group and these people are the tastemakers or pace setters within their own groups. They determine the acceptance of innovations for their respective groups.

The distinction between this theory and the "trickle down" theory is that each peer group will have its own pace setters, and product or process acceptors can be found within each. Further, the proponents of this theory argue that these opinion leaders are extremely influential in determining whether a product will achieve market acceptance. This approach has the benefit of matching kinds of innovations with different types of consumers.

THE ADOPTION PROCESS

An adoption process has been hypothesized by numerous researchers.[5] This process covers the steps that a consumer goes through in determining the feasibility of buying new products. The steps are described as

1. Awareness
2. Interest
3. Evaluation
4. Trial
5. Adoption

Awareness. At the awareness stage, a person first learns about a new idea, product, or practice. He has only general information about it. He knows little or nothing about any special qualities, its potential usefulness, or how it would likely work for him.

Interest. Here he develops an interest in the new things that he has learned about. He is not satisfied with mere knowledge of its existence. He wants more detailed information about what it is, how it will work, and what it will do. He is willing to listen, read, and learn more about it, and is inclined

[5] H. V. Lionberger, *Adoption of New Ideas and Practices* (Ames: The Iowa State University Press, 1960), pp. 22–23.

to actively seek the information desired. It makes little difference whether we call this the information or the interest stage. The personal need of the individual making the decision remains much the same.

Evaluation. At the evaluation stage a person weighs the information and evidence accumulated in the previous stages in order to decide whether the new idea, product, or practice is basically good, and whether it is good for him. In a sense, he reasons through the pros and cons mentally, and applies them to his own situation. Perhaps this stage could very well be referred to as the "mental trial stage." To be sure, evaluation is involved at all stages of the adoption process, but it is at this stage that it is most in evidence and perhaps most needed.

Trial. At this stage the individual is confronted with a distinctly different set of problems. He must actually put the change into practice. This means that he must learn how, when, where, how much, etc. Competent personal assistance may be required in putting the innovation to use. The usual pattern of acceptance is to try a little at first, and then to make large-scale use of it if the small-scale experiment proves successful.

Adoption. Here a person decides that the new idea, product, or practice is good enough for full-scale and continued use. A complete change is made with that end in view.

CHARACTERISTICS OF INNOVATORS

Do those who accept different kinds of innovations vary in their characteristics, or are the innovators the same regardless of the kind of

FIGURE II

Comparison of Profiles: Adaptive and Functional Innovators

VARIABLE	*ADAPTIVE INNOVATORS*	*FUNCTIONAL INNOVATORS*
Age		
Head	Very young	Young
Spouse	Very young	Young
Occupation		
Head	Dispersed between Professional-Managerial and Craftsmen-Foremen	Highly concentrated in Professional-Managerial
Spouse	No difference	No difference
Education		
Head	Above average education	Very highly educated
Spouse	Above average education	Very highly educated
Family Income	High income	Very high income
Ethnic Group	Negro, French, Italian	Jewish, British, German
Home Characteristics		
Ownership	Slightly higher than average	Very high
Structure	Highly concentrated in single units	More highly concentrated in single units
Home Value	High value	Extremely high value
Rent	High rent	Very high rent
Number in Family	Dispersed	Dispersed

innovation? Some research has shown that there are differences. Figure II presents several socio-economic characteristics of innovators for selected adaptive and functional innovations.[6]

Innovation is organized, goal-oriented, risk-taking change undertaken to optimize economic gain. Systematic planned innovation is essential to scientific, technological, and social progress as well as to the achievement of the firm's marketing objectives. Innovation strategy and the relationship of innovation to growth and corporate planning are discussed.

30. INNOVATION—A CENTRAL TASK OF MANAGEMENT*

For many reasons which touch virtually every aspect of our domestic and international problems, economic growth has become a paramount national concern. As this issue takes an unprecedented place in our economic and political spotlight, a new element is becoming more apparent in the growth process itself. It is one that is destined to have a powerful impact on the pace of economic growth in the future and, even more than that, on the structure of our society and the nature of our civilization.

That element, largely a post-war phenomenon, but with roots that go back to the first industrial revolution, is management's growing understanding of the importance of systematically planned innovation on a continuing basis. Economic growth is not a force of nature. It is the result of the action, the purposeful responsible risk-taking action, of men as entrepreneurs and managers. The immediate generator of economic growth is, of course, investment. Investment is set in motion partly by economic forces. But more basically, investment arises from new ideas, new knowledge, new developments in science and technology, from research. Innovations—new products, new processes, new resources, new services—are the real needs of long-term economic growth.

We have discovered that these innovations need not be the accidental, irregular things they have been in the past. By a new emphasis on

[6] William E. Bell, "Consumer Innovations: A Unique Market for Newness," *Proceedings of the Winter Conference of the American Marketing Association*, 1963, p. 92 with adaptation.

* Reprinted from "Innovation—A Central Task of Management," *Management Consultant*, No. 2, 1965 series.

research, by systematizing innovation—industry and government now make regular provision for the occurrence of new and unpredictable developments. This process is taking increasing hold in American business, though its use still varies widely from industry to industry. But already it is beginning to furnish the spur to growth that came in earlier periods from such individual developments as steam power, railroads, electricity, automobiles, and the concept of capital investment itself.

The discovery that innovation is at the heart of scientific, technological, and social advance in our rapidly changing and competitive economy is basic. But in itself, it does not guarantee adequate growth. That also depends on the underlying demand for goods and services, the over-all state of the economy, and on the balances within it, particularly on incentives for investment, innovation, and growth. If stability is present in the economy, economic growth will be determined in large part by our ability to master the process of innovation and by our skill in dealing with the economic and social problems which accompany change.

In view of its importance to companies and our free enterprise system, it is important to ask what the concept of innovation involves, and how managers can promote it?

WHAT INNOVATION INVOLVES

The central fact about economic activity is that it commits present resources to an unknowable and uncertain future. In effect, it is a commitment to future expectations rather than facts. To take risks is, therefore, the essence of economic activity, and risk-making and risk-taking constitute the basic function of enterprise. These are the facts that define the role of innovation. *Innovation is purposeful, organized, risk-taking change introduced for the purpose of maximizing economic opportunities.* It is the generation and introduction of some new element which will give the business a new economic dimension. Innovative ability is conceptual and creative rather than technical or scientific. It is the ability to look at the business as a system and to provide the missing element which will convert the already existing elements into a new and more productive whole. It involves the determination of what innovations will create and change the customer need-value-satisfaction relationship.

Innovation is the basic inner-law of business as we know it. It is non-specific; it applies to and discovers its particular shape and methodology from each specific area of activity. It occurs in two forms: (1) exploration and improvement within the various parameters of the business, and (2) the questioning, testing, and establishing of the parameters themselves. In relation to the other central tasks of managing, it cuts across all areas of a business. It is as important in the establishment of goals, objectives, organization, and the operating and procedural aspects of the business as it is in the technological areas of product and process. It may take the form of a change in design, in product, in packaging, in price, in service to the customer, or in over-all corporate or marketing strategy. Or it may involve the use of new materials or new automatic machinery, or the introduction of new knowledge, techniques, skills, organizational schemes or policies into the business. Thus there are two basic kinds of innovation in every business: innovation in product or service; and innovation in the various skills and activities needed to supply them. Since it extends across all functions, all activities of the business, every managerial unit should have clear responsibility and definite goals for innovation. Innovative performance should be built into the job and into the spirit of the organization, and be made an important criterion for personal progress in the company.

INNOVATION AND CORPORATE PLANNING

Every business must have some kind of informal or formal corporate strategy. To a large extent, the success of the company depends on how clearly defined, how well understood, and how smoothly it is geared to the company's environment. During the past decade, a host of activities has sprung up in a score of companies under such labels as long-range planning, corporate development, corporate planning, or corporate strategy. Corporate planning is deciding what the company ought to be and defining the major steps to reach and maintain that goal. A corporate strategy is an organized set of fundamental objectives, goals, and policies through which the purpose and missions of the corporation are realized. The effective strategic plan stresses what to do to preserve the long-term vitality of the business and to engineer its profitable growth.

A systematic approach to corporate planning implies two key elements: (1) the imposition of a planning discipline on the present operations of the business (that is, the establishment of a planning system for each division of the organization and the maintenance of this system); and (2) a reappraisal of the business and of the direction in which it should be heading. The essence of corporate planning is the application of the company's resources and talents to the most profitable uses. *Innovation* is at the core of such planning for change. It is the critical element in the total process of planning which enables management to accomplish its marketing goals and objectives.

INNOVATION STRATEGY

Overall innovation strategy involves the setting of objectives for technical and social innovation. Since technical innovation offers one of the best prospects for a company's growth and for achieving an expanding economy, top management should take an active, aggressive attitude toward it. Its most essential activities in this area should include (1) providing research with a clear understanding of company goals and strategies, and defining specific objectives for research within the context of these plans; (2) seeing that appropriate organizational arrangements are made (a) to assess carefully the major technological threats and opportunities the company faces, (b) to facilitate transfer of research technology into operations; and (3) developing a project evaluation procedure which results in a balanced package of projects to meet company objectives. From this point on, management must continuously evaluate its program of technical innovation to see that both research and operating units carry out their intended functions in developing and utilizing technology to support company goals.

The need for innovation in the social area is just as important as it is in the technical area. For the explosive development of technological progress and change will be largely unproductive unless it is accompanied by major innovations in the social area. The most important need for such innovation is in marketing and distribution. Also, urgently needed are real advances in methods, tools, and measurements for doing the managerial job, as well as improvements in the management and organization of knowledge workers and the structuring of their work. Obviously, objectives for social innovation should further and be closely correlated with those for technical innovation.

Social and technical innovation goals for the average business should include:

1. New products or services needed to attain marketing objectives.
2. Product improvements and new products or services needed to meet technological competition and offset technical and other forms of obsolescence.
3. New resources, new materials, new equipment, new processes needed to keep pace with technology.
4. Social innovations and improvements in all major areas of company activity.

CONCLUSION

While innovation does not lend itself to a magic formula, it should not be left to chance. If companies are to enjoy an increased rate of corporate growth, it is not enough to trust that random change, improvement, product development, invention, or research will do it. Management must itself take a hand in the process, giving full, vigorous, and continuous support to the work of technical and social innovation. Herein lies the key to an expanding economic system.

There is no such thing as a growth industry. Companies are organized and operated to create and capitalize on growth opportunities. Companies must respond to market requirements and must think of themselves as creators and satisfiers of customers rather than as producers of goods and services. The firm must adopt a broad and dynamic view of market opportunity.

31. MARKETING MYOPIA*

Theodore Levitt†

Every major industry was once a growth industry. But some that are now riding a wave of growth enthusiasm are very much in the shadow of decline. Others which are thought of as seasoned growth industries have actually stopped growing. In every case the reason growth is threatened, slowed, or stopped is *not* because the market is saturated. It is because there has been a failure of management.

FATEFUL PURPOSES

The failure is at the top. The executives responsible for it, in the last analysis, are those who deal with broad aims and policies. Thus:

The railroads did not stop growing because the need for passenger and freight transportation declined. That grew. The railroads are in trouble today not because the need was filled by others (cars, trucks, airplanes, even telephones), but because it was *not* filled by the railroads themselves. They let others take customers away from them because they assumed themselves to be in the railroad business rather than in the transportation business. The reason they defined their industry wrong was because they were railroad-oriented

* Reprinted by permission of the publishers from Edward C. Bursk and John F. Chapman (eds.). *Modern Marketing Strategy*, Cambridge, Mass.: Harvard University Press, copyright 1964, by the President and Fellows of Harvard College. This article also appeared in *Harvard Business Review*, Vol. XXXVIII, No. 4 (July–August, 1960), pp. 45–56. For a definition of the market opportunity concept that can be helpful in the management of innovation and change see Robert L. Clewett, "Market Opportunity and Corporate Management," *Proceedings of the Fall Conference of the American Marketing Association*, 1965, pp. 187–99.

† Harvard Business School.

instead of transportation-oriented; they were product-oriented instead of customer-oriented.

Hollywood barely escaped being totally ravished by television. Actually, all the established film companies went through drastic reorganizations. Some simply disappeared. All of them got into trouble not because of TV's inroads but because of their own myopia. As with the railroads, Hollywood defined its business incorrectly. It thought it was in the movie business when it was actually in the entertainment business. "Movies" implied a specific, limited product. This produced a fatuous contentment which from the beginning led producers to view TV as a threat. Hollywood scorned and rejected TV when it should have welcomed it as an opportunity—an opportunity to expand the entertainment business.

Today TV is a bigger business than the old narrowly defined movie business ever was. Had Hollywood been customer-oriented (providing entertainment), rather than product-oriented (making movies), would it have gone through the fiscal purgatory that it did? I doubt it. What ultimately saved Hollywood and accounted for its recent resurgence was the wave of new young writers, producers, and directors whose previous successes in television had decimated the old movie companies and toppled the big movie moguls.

There are other less obvious examples of industries that have been and are now endangering their futures by improperly defining their purposes. I shall discuss some in detail later and analyze the kind of policies that lead to trouble. Right now it may help to show what a thoroughly customer-oriented management *can* do to keep a growth industry growing, even after the obvious opportunities have been exhausted; and here there are two examples that have been around for a long time. They are nylon and glass—specifically, E. I. duPont de Nemours & Company and Corning Glass Works:

Both companies have great technical competence. Their product orientation is unquestioned. But this alone does not explain their success. After all, who was more pridefully product-oriented and product-conscious than the erstwhile New England textile companies that have been so thoroughly massacred? The DuPonts and the Cornings have succeeded not primarily because of their product or research orientation but because they have been thoroughly customer-oriented also. It is constant watchfulness for opportunities to apply their technical know-how to the creation of customer-satisfying uses which accounts for their prodigious output of successful new products. Without a very sophisticated eye on the customer, most of their new products might have been wrong, their sales methods useless.

Aluminum has also continued to be a growth industry, thanks to the efforts of two wartime-created companies which deliberately set about creating new customer-satisfying uses. Without Kaiser Aluminum & Chemical Corporation and Reynolds Metals Company, the total demand for aluminum today would be vastly less than it is.

Error of Analysis

Some may argue that it is foolish to set the railroads off against aluminum or the movies off against glass. Are not aluminum and glass naturally so versatile that the industries are bound to have more growth opportunities than the railroads and movies? This view commits precisely the error I have been talking about. It defines an industry, or a product, or a cluster of know-how so narrowly as to guarantee its premature senescence. When we mention "railroads," we should make sure we mean "transportation." As transporters, the railroads still have a good chance for very considerable growth. They are not limited to the railroad business as such (though in my opinion rail transportation is potentially a much stronger transportation medium than is generally believed).

What the railroads lack is not opportunity, but some of the same managerial imaginativeness and audacity that made them great. Even an amateur like Jacques Barzun can see what is lacking when he says:

> "I grieve to see the most advanced physical and social organization of the last century go down in shabby disgrace for lack of the same comprehensive imagination that built it up. [What is lacking is] the will of the companies to survive and to satisfy the public by inventiveness and skill."[1]

SHADOW OF OBSOLESCENCE

It is impossible to mention a single major industry that did not at one time qualify for the magic appellation of "growth industry." In each case its assumed strength lay in the apparently unchallenged superiority of its product. There appeared to be no effective substitute for it. It was itself a runaway substitute for the product it so triumphantly replaced. Yet one after another of these celebrated industries has come under a shadow. Let us look briefly at a few more of them, this time taking examples that have so far received a little less attention:

Dry cleaning—This was once a growth industry with lavish prospects. In an age of wool garments, imagine being finally able to get them safely and easily clean. The boom was on.

Yet here we are 30 years after the boom started and the industry is in trouble. Where has the competition come from? From a better way of cleaning? No. It has come from synthetic fibers and chemical additives that have cut the need for dry cleaning. But this is only the beginning. Lurking in the wings and ready to make chemical dry cleaning totally obsolescent is that powerful magician, ultrasonics.

Electric utilities—This is another one of those supposedly "no-substitute" products that has been enthroned on a pedestal of invincible growth. When the incandescent lamp came along, kerosene lights were finished. Later the

[1] Jacques Barzun, "Trains and the Mind of Man," *Holiday*, February 1960, p. 21.

water wheel and the steam engine were cut to ribbons by the flexibility, reliability, simplicity, and just plain easy availability of electric motors. The prosperity of electric utilities continues to wax extravagant as the home is converted into a museum of electric gadgetry. How can anybody miss by investing in utilities, with no competition, nothing but growth ahead?

But a second look is not quite so comforting. A score of nonutility companies are well advanced toward developing a powerful chemical fuel cell which could sit in some hidden closet of every home silently ticking off electric power. The electric lines that vulgarize so many neighborhoods will be eliminated. So will the endless demolition of streets and service interruptions during storms. Also on the horizon is solar energy, again pioneered by nonutility companies.

Who says that the utilities have no competition? They may be natural monopolies now, but tomorrow they may be natural deaths. To avoid this prospect, they too will have to develop fuel cells, solar energy, and other power sources. To survive, they themselves will have to plot the obsolescence of what now produces their livelihood.

Grocery stores—Many people find it hard to realize that there ever was a thriving establishment known as the "corner grocery store." The supermarket has taken over with a powerful effectiveness. Yet the big food chains of the 1930's narrowly escaped being completely wiped out by the aggressive expansion of independent supermarkets. The first genuine supermarket was opened in 1930, in Jamaica, Long Island. By 1933 supermarkets were thriving in California, Ohio, Pennsylvania, and elsewhere. Yet the established chains pompously ignored them. When they chose to notice them, it was with such derisive descriptions as "cheapy," "horse-and-buggy," "cracker-barrel storekeeping," and "unethical opportunists."

The executive of one big chain announced at the time that he found it "hard to believe that people will drive for miles to shop for foods and sacrifice the personal service chains have perfected and to which Mrs. Consumer is accustomed."[2] As late as 1936, the National Wholesale Grocers convention and the New Jersey Retail Grocers Association said there was nothing to fear. They said that the supers' narrow appeal to the price buyer limited the size of their market. They had to draw from miles around. When imitators came, there would be wholesale liquidations as volume fell. The current high sales of the supers was said to be partly due to their novelty. Basically people wanted convenient neighborhood grocers. If the neighborhood stores "cooperate with their suppliers, pay attention to their costs, and improve their service," they would be able to weather the competition until it blew over.[3]

It never blew over. The chains discovered that survival required going into the supermarket business. This meant the wholesale destruction of their huge investments in corner store sites and in established distribution and merchandising methods. The companies with "the courage of their convictions" resolutely stuck to the corner store philosophy. They kept their pride but lost their shirts.

[2] For more details see M. M. Zimmerman, *The Super Market: A Revolution in Distribution* (New York: McGraw-Hill Book Company, Inc., 1955), p. 48.

[3] *Ibid.*, pp. 45–47.

Self-Deceiving Cycle

But memories are short. For example, it is hard for people who today confidently hail the twin messiahs of electronics and chemicals to see how things could possibly go wrong with these galloping industries. They probably also cannot see how a reasonably sensible businessman could have been as myopic as the famous Boston millionaire who 50 years ago unintentionally sentenced his heirs to poverty by stipulating that his entire estate be forever invested exclusively in electric streetcar securities. His posthumous declaration, "There will always be a big demand for efficient urban transportation," is no consolation to his heirs who sustain life by pumping gasoline at automobile filling stations.

Yet, in a casual survey I recently took among a group of intelligent business executives, nearly half agreed that it would be hard to hurt their heirs by tying their estates forever to the electronics industry. When I then confronted them with the Boston streetcar example, they chorused unanimously, "That's different!" But is it? Is not the basic situation identical?

In truth, *there is no such thing* as a growth industry, I believe. There are only companies organized and operated to create and capitalize on growth opportunities. Industries that assume themselves to be riding some automatic growth escalator invariably descend into stagnation. The history of every dead and dying "growth" industry shows a self-deceiving cycle of bountiful expansion and undetected decay. There are four conditions which usually guarantee this cycle:

1. The belief that growth is assured by an expanding and more affluent population.
2. The belief that there is no competitive substitute for the industry's major product.
3. Too much faith in mass production and in the advantages of rapidly declining unit costs as output rises.
4. Preoccupation with a product that lends itself to carefully controlled scientific experimentation, improvement, and manufacturing cost reduction.

Beginning and End

The view that an industry is a customer-satisfying process, not a goods-producing process, is vital for all businessmen to understand. An industry begins with the customer and his needs, not with a patent, a raw material, or a selling skill. Given the customer's needs, the industry develops backwards, first concerning itself with the physical *delivery* of customer satisfactions. Then it moves back further to *creating* the things by which these satisfactions are in part achieved. How these materials are created is a matter of indifference to the customer, hence the particular form of manufacturing, processing, or what-have-you cannot be considered as a vital aspect of the industry. Finally, the industry moves back still further to *finding* the raw materials necessary for making its products.

The irony of some industries oriented toward technical research and development is that the scientists who occupy the high executive positions are totally unscientific when it comes to defining their companies' over-all needs and purposes. They violate the first two rules of the scientific method—being aware of and defining their companies' problems, and then developing testable hypotheses about solving them. They are scientific only about the convenient things, such as laboratory and product experiments. The reason that the customer (and the satisfaction of his deepest needs) is not considered as being "the problem" is not because there is any certain belief that so such problem exists, but because an organizational lifetime has conditioned management to look in the opposite direction. Marketing is a stepchild.

I do not mean that selling is ignored. Far from it. But selling, again, is not marketing. As already pointed out, selling concerns itself with the tricks and techniques of getting people to exchange their cash for your product. It is not concerned with the values that the exchange is all about. And it does not, as marketing invariably does, view the entire business process as consisting of a tightly integrated effort to discover, create, arouse, and satisfy customer needs. The customer is somebody "out there" who, with proper cunning, can be separated from his loose change.

Actually, not even selling gets much attention in some technologically minded firms. Because there is a virtually guaranteed market for the abundant flow of their new products, they do not actually know what a real market is. It is as if they lived in a planned economy, moving their products routinely from factory to retail outlet. Their successful concentration on products tends to convince them of the soundness of what they have been doing, and they fail to see the gathering clouds over the market.

CONCLUSION

Less than 75 years ago American railroads enjoyed a fierce loyalty among astute Wall Streeters. European monarchs invested in them heavily. Eternal wealth was thought to be the benediction for anybody who could scrape a few thousand dollars together to put into rail stocks. No other form of transportation could compete with the railroads in speed, flexibility, durability, economy, and growth potentials. As Jacques Barzun put it, "by the turn of the century it was an institution, an image of man, a tradition, a code of honor, a source of poetry, a nursery of boyhood desires, a sublimest of toys, and the most solemn machine—next to the funeral hearse—that marks the epochs in man's life."[4]

---

[4] Zimmerman, *op. cit.*, p. 20.

Even after the advent of automobiles, trucks, and airplanes, the railroad tycoons remained imperturbably self-confident. If you had told them 60 years ago that in 30 years they would be flat on their backs, broke, and pleading for government subsidies, they would have thought you totally demented. Such a future was simply not considered possible. It was not even a discussable subject, or an askable question, or a matter which any sane person would consider worth speculating about. The very thought was insane. Yet a lot of insane notions now have matter-of-fact acceptance—for example, the idea of 100-ton tubes of metal moving smoothly through the air 20,000 feet above the earth, loaded with 100 sane and solid citizens casually drinking martinis—and they have dealt cruel blows to the railroads.

What specifically must other companies do to avoid this fate? What does customer orientation involve? These questions have in part been answered by the preceding examples and analysis. It would take another article to show in detail what is required for specific industries. In any case, it should be obvious that building an effective customer-oriented company involves far more than good intentions or promotional tricks; it involves profound matters of human organization and leadership. For the present, let me merely suggest what appear to be some general requirements.

Visceral Feel of Greatness

Obviously the company has to do what survival demands. It has to adapt to the requirements of the market, and it has to do it sooner rather than later. But mere survival is a so-so aspiration. Anybody can survive in some way or other, even the skid-row bum. The trick is to survive gallantly, to feel the surging impulse of commercial mastery; not just to experience the sweet smell of success, but to have the visceral feel of entrepreneurial greatness.

No organization can achieve greatness without a vigorous leader who is driven onward by his own pulsating *will to succeed.* He has to have a vision of grandeur, a vision that can produce eager followers in vast numbers. In business, the followers are the customers. To produce these customers, the entire corporation must be viewed as a customer-creating and customer-satisfying organism. Management must think of itself not as producing products but as providing customer-creating value satisfactions. It must push this idea (and everything it means and requires) into every nook and cranny of the organization. It has to do this continuously and with the kind of flair that excites and stimulates the people in it. Otherwise, the company will be merely a series of pigeonholed parts, with no consolidating sense of purpose or direction.

In short, the organization must learn to think of itself not as producing goods or services but as *buying customers*, as doing the things that will make people *want* to do business with it. And the chief executive himself has the inescapable responsibility for creating this environment, this viewpoint, this attitude, this aspiration. He himself must set the company's style, its direction, and its goals. This means he has to know precisely where he himself wants to go, and to make sure the whole organization is enthusiastically aware of where that is. This is a first requisite of leadership, for *unless he knows where he is going, any road will take him there.*

If any road is okay, the chief executive might as well pack his attaché case and go fishing. If an organization does not know or care where it is going, it does not need to advertise that fact with a ceremonial figurehead. Everybody will notice it soon enough.

B. Planning and Programming Marketing Activity

Marketing planning, based on an assessment of market opportunity, is one of the key concepts in the marketing management approach. Sales forecasting furnishes "future information" for planning purposes. A comprehensive sales forecasting program is one of the essential ingredients in an integrated approach to marketing action.

32. SALES FORECASTING: KEY TO INTEGRATED MANAGEMENT*

William Lazer†

Business organizations are increasingly adopting the marketing management concept. This philosophy of business operation places greater emphasis on marketing planning and forces business executives to design marketing strategies and program marketing effort to achieve realistic and predetermined objectives.

Sales forecasting can aid management greatly in implementing the marketing management approach. It is a basis for developing co-ordinated and goal-directed systems of marketing action. The sales forecast is one of the vital tools of marketing planning since adequate planning and the effective deployment of marketing resources are based on sales forecasting data.

---

* Reprinted from "Sales Forecasting: Key to Integrated Management," *Business Horizons*, Vol. II, No. 3 (Fall, 1959), pp. 61–67.

† Michigan State University.

Sales forecasting promotes and facilitates the proper functioning of the many segments of a firm's total spectrum of business and marketing activities. It influences almost every other prediction of business operations. It is used in establishing budgets and marketing controls. Sales forecasts help determine various limiting conditions for management decisions and programs and are useful tools for coordinating the integral aspects of business operations. They provide bases for evaluating the functioning and productivity of various segments of business activity. They can guide marketing and other business action toward the achievement of implicit and explicit objectives.

This article investigates three aspects of sales forecasting as a key to integrated management action: (1) sales forecasting as a component of the marketing planning process, (2) sales forecasting as a focus for integrative planning, and (3) the basic components and procedures of a comprehensive sales forecasting program.

IN MARKETING PLANNING

Figure 1 illustrates the strategic role of sales forecasting in gathering information for marketing planning. Effective planning of marketing activities can be achieved only if adequate marketing-related information is available. Marketing planning is concerned with the application of analysis and judgment to available information and the prediction of likely occurrences and trends during some future period.

FIGURE 1

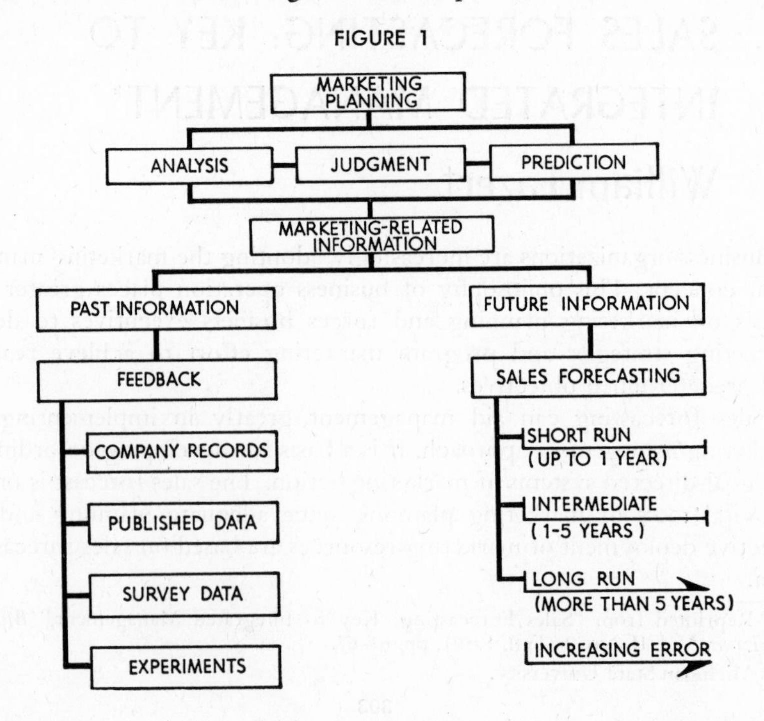

Marketing-related information can refer to either the past or the future. Information about past activities is often referred to as factual information. Information about the future is anything but factual, and might be characterized as assumptive. Past information is available to every business if it has an adequate record-keeping process. It is also available from other secondary data sources, such as information reported by governmental bureaus, university research bureaus, and trade associations. Past information may also be assembled through the use of various primary data-gathering research tools, such as surveys and experiments.

Future information requires the utilization of forecasting techniques and processes. Nevertheless, it is based on past data and is usually the result of the application of predictive tools to available past information.

Whenever a business gathers future data, varying degrees of error are bound to exist. Regardless of the forecasting techniques used and the degrees of sophistication achieved, future conditions will always deviate to some degree from the predictions of the forecasters. Thus, management must expect future information to contain some error.

For effective marketing planning, both types of information must be available for executive use. From a planning and decision-making point of view, future, or nonfactual, information may be more significant than information about the past. This becomes clear if one considers that plans and decisions made today are actually based on executive expectations of what will happen during some future period.

If we consider sales forecasting from the point of view of furnishing marketing-related information, we can state that management gathers information as a result of two complementary processes: feedback and sales forecasting. Feedback consists of relating information about past events and relationships back to management. Through the use of such factual data, management can adjust existing operations and plans and thereby improve the effectiveness of all business action.

Sales forecasting furnishes management with information about what market conditions will probably be like during a future period. Management can then use this information as a basis for planning broad company goals and the strategies to achieve them. Sales forecasting data are used in establishing various types of potential volume and profit targets that become the bases for guiding and controlling operations.

Past and future information, however, are constantly blending. A sales forecast, although it furnishes future information, eventually takes the form of feedback information. Once this happens, a comparison may be made between actual and forecast sales for a specific period. Through such an audit, deviations may be noted and explanations sought for them. This information can, in turn, help refine the assumptions about future sales forecasts and increase the total effectiveness of the forecasting procedure.

The various predictions made may take the form of short-run sales forecasts of less than a year, intermediate forecasts of from one to five years, and long-run forecasts for periods of more than five years. Generally, the longer range the predictions, the greater the forecasting error.

IN INTEGRATIVE PLANNING

Another facet of sales forecasting and its role in marketing planning is its position in the integrative planning process. A sales forecast is a useful tool for integrating the external business environment with the internal forces of the company. It reduces to workable management dimensions the external business environment over which management has relatively little control. It delimits those constraints that establish the boundaries

FIGURE 2

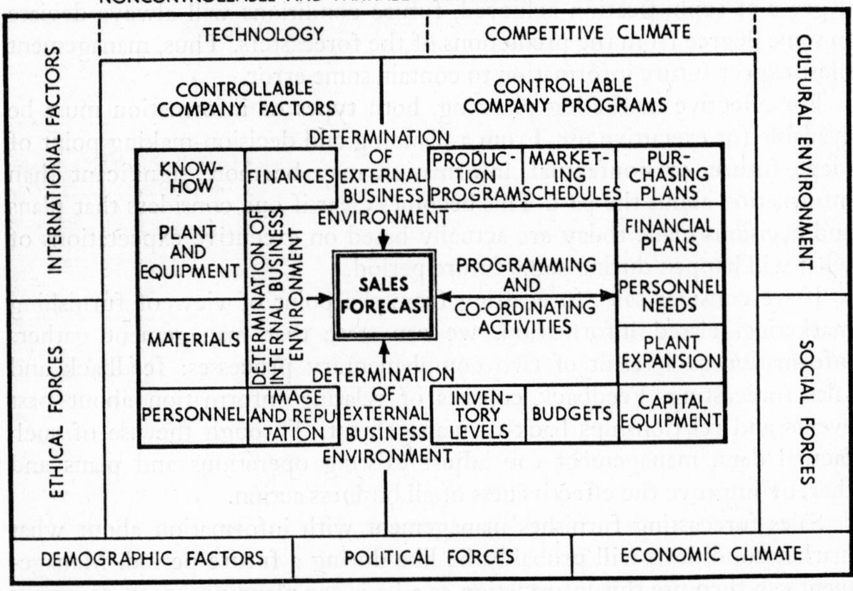

within which a company must make decisions and operate and translates them into company programs.

Figure 2 portrays sales forecasting as an aid to integrative planning. It indicates the controllable, partially controllable, and noncontrollable factors that management should integrate and take into account in making effective sales forecasts.

The noncontrollable forces determine the broad environmental limits within which the company will operate. These factors include cultural forces, the economic environment, demographic forces, political factors, ethical and social forces, and various international conditions. They cannot be influenced to any degree by company action; at best, they may be recognized and appraised in an intelligent manner.

On Figure 2, broken lines separate the competitive environment and technological factors from other noncontrollable factors. This is to indicate that management action may have some influence over at least these two external forces, which are considered partially controllable factors. However, even though company action can affect competition and technology, the forces *beyond* company control generally have a more significant impact.

As forecasts become longer run in nature, the necessity of recording the existing external climate becomes more imperative since, in the future, it will be these noncontrollable factors that set the over-all constraints and boundaries within which companies survive and grow or fail. Through an evaluation and projection of external forces, management attempts to make realistic assumptions about the future environment. These assumptions about noncontrollable and partially controllable factors are the foundations of sales forecasts, and intelligent sales predictions can be made only by implicitly or explicitly assuming relationships about these factors.

Management should not consider this initial step of determining the external company environment as merely a theoretical exercise that is of little use in practical sales forecasting. The external variables are factors that must be dealt with practically and realistically. Their influence cannot be ignored.

As an example of the importance of external forces, consider the development of a controlled shopping center. Several years may elapse from the initiation of the original idea and the first inquiry concerning site location until the actual opening of the center. Choices must be made from among alternative sites, and considerable negotiations may follow to obtain the property and construct and finance the center. Then there are a host of operating details to attend to, including the actual leasing of stores.

The profitability of the total investment and the sales realized by retail stores in the shopping center will be affected by external forces. Existing and potential competition, for example, can have great influence on future sales. Demographic and economic forces in the form of population shifts and income trends will shape the retail sales potential of the center. Existing and potential industrial development of the surrounding territory will influence employment and income and will be reflected in marketing opportunity.

Municipal, state, and federal regulations will have an impact on future pricing tactics, on the use of various promotional devices including trading stamps, on store hours, and even on the types of merchandise that may be sold in particular kinds of stores.

Other examples could be presented concerning such industries as wood products, chemicals, mining, petroleum, transportation, the power industry, and communications.

After determining the external business climate for a future period, the sales forecaster must estimate the impact that internal business factors will make on potential markets. This involves an evaluation of those factors over which the company has direct control. They can be adjusted over the longer run by the company itself.

For an effective forecast, the company's know-how, its financial position, the plant capacity, the material resources and personnel available, and the company's reputation, image, and position in the market place must all be evaluated. The market position that a company eventually earns and the sales that it achieves will depend on the impact made by the internal business factors as they are combined into planned management programs carried out within the external business system. A consideration of both climates, external and internal, will give management some guides by which to judge the potential sales opportunity for a company. Through the use of various analyses and by the application of sound judgment, management may map out a company's future sales position.

Thus, sales forecasting helps integrate the management-controllable and management-noncontrollable factors, or the given elements of a total business system within which the company operates and the internal factors of the business itself.

The sales forecast is also a device by means of which management may integrate its objectives, its operating programs, and its targets with potential market opportunity. This can be done by translating the sales forecast into specific profit and sales-volume goals to be realized in a given future period of time. The sales forecast thus becomes a basis for marketing programs, purchasing plans, financial budgets, personnel needs, production schedules, plant and equipment requirements, expansion programs, and perhaps most other aspects of management programming.

The right half of Figure 2 presents sales forecasting as a vehicle for translating the noncontrollable, partially controllable, and internal business environments into specific controllable management programs. The figure also emphasizes the interrelationships between sales forecasts and company programs.

FORECASTING PROGRAM

Figure 3 outlines the elements of a total sales forecasting program. Four major stages of forecasting, the specific procedures to be followed, and their sequence are presented. These stages are: assembling the forecasting information; evaluating and projecting the data; applying the sales forecast operationally; and auditing the forecast. These four steps are broken down further, and some of the techniques that may be utilized at each stage and the results achieved are described. Figure 3 starts with the noncontrollable business environment and internal business climate and works down through the various predictions about controllable business plans, programs, and objectives.

The first step in a comprehensive sales forecasting program is assem-

FIGURE 3

A Total Sales Forecasting Program

Stages of Process	*Techniques*	*Results*
Assembling Information		
Recognize noncontrollable and partially controllable business environment.	Observe and list significant external factors	Identification of pertinent cultural, social, economic, political, demographic, competitive, ethical, international technological forces
Gather information about noncontrollable and partially controllable forces	Investigate outside sources of information	Selection and gathering of data from government, industry, university research, Federal Reserve Board, company records
Gather information about controllable forces.	Investigate company records	Selection of relevant company forecasting information
Evaluating and Projecting Data		
Analyze data	Apply analytical tools: time series analysis, least squares, simple correlation, multiple correlation, input-output tables, breakeven charts	Determination of patterns and relationships: lead and lag indicators, cycles, seasonal indexes, trend lines, covariation
Forecast future sales	Employ extrapolation, constant percentage of increase, end-use analysis, executive opinion, historical analogy, panel of experts, grassroots techniques, surveys, models, experiments, samples, hunches, judgment, and crystal ball	Prediction and definition of future dollar sales, unit sales, maximum and minimum ranges
Operationally Applying Forecast		
Refine sales forecast	Break sales down by volume and profit control units: product lines, territories, customers, salesmen	Establishment of specific sales targets
Translate specific targets into operational programs	Establish and co-ordinate plans: marketing program, production schedules, purchasing plans, financial requirements, personnel needs, plant expansion, capital equipment budgets, inventory levels	Identification of controllable business environment
Auditing the Forecast		
Review forecast	Compare actual and forecast sales regularly and analyze discrepancies	Determination of reasons for deviations
Modify forecast and forecasting procedures	Re-evaluate projections and adjust forecasting techniques	More accurate sales forecasting

bling forecasting information. This involves the recognition of noncontrollable and partially controllable environments through observation and listing of significant external factors. The result is the identification of pertinent social, cultural, ethical, economic, political, demographic, international, technological, and competitive forces that will influence the projections.

Next, information can be assembled about these noncontrollable factors and an investigation made of such outside sources of information as governments, industries, and universities.

The third step in assembling forecasting information is that of gathering information about the controllable company environment, which involves research into company records. This should result in the selection of relevant company forecasting information.

After forecasting information has been assembled, the data must be evaluated and projected. This activity has two components: analyzing the data and making the actual forecast. To analyze the data, such analytical tools as time series analysis, least squares methods of fitting a straight line, fitting curves, simple and multiple correlation, the use of input-output tables, and breakeven charts may be used. This leads to the determination of patterns and relationships through lead and lag indicators, cycles, seasonal indexes, trend lines, and measures of covariation.

The actual sales projections may be made through extrapolation, a straight percentage increase in sales, executive opinion polls, end-use analysis, historical analogy, a panel of experts, the grass-roots approach, samples and surveys, models, experiments, hunches, judgments, and the oft-used crystal ball. After these projections have been made, the prediction and definition of future dollar and unit sales, and maximum and minimum sales ranges is possible.

Then the forecast must be applied operationally, which involves refining the sales forecast. This is done by breaking it down on the basis of volume and profit control units by product lines, salesmen, customers, territories, and other managerial units. Specific sales targets can thus be established, and sales forecasting data become the basis for programming marketing, production, purchasing, finance, plant expansion, capital equipment acquisition, personnel, and inventory needs. Controllable business programs have now been really determined.

The last step in a comprehensive sales forecasting program is that of auditing the forecast. This involves reviewing the forecast by comparing actual and forecast sales and analyzing any deviations or discrepancies. The purpose here is to determine the reasons for the deviations. Then future forecasts and even the forecasting techniques can be modified. The end result is more accurate sales forecasts.

The total sales forecasting process is one of refinement. It starts with the more general factors—the external noncontrollable environment and the internal business environment—quantifies them, and finally establishes specific operational goals and targets.

Marketing planning often suffers because management does not develop an effective sales forecasting program. One of the great inducements to ignore or neglect sales forecasting is the difficulty of making predictions. It is a trying task for anyone to try to determine future relationships and their implications for potential sales. It is much more comfortable to turn to the consideration of current operating problems, which are more concrete, are somewhat easier to grasp, and for which some corrective action may be initiated almost immediately.

However, professional marketing management cannot afford to neglect the sales forecasting process. It must become concerned with the development of well co-ordinated, planned, and forceful systems of business action. It must plan the use of company resources so that a firm can establish itself in the market place and grow.

The future marketing climate is likely to be one of keener competition, an exhilarating pace of market change, heavier fixed costs, and an increasing emphasis on innovation. Adequate marketing planning will become the foundation for integrated marketing action. Since one of the basic components of effective marketing planning is sales forecasting, it seems obvious that in the future an increasing amount of time and resources will be spent by companies in developing more adequate sales forecasts.

Long-range planning is "risk-taking decision making." Rational decisions require that long-range planning processes provide for the systematic organization and analysis of information. The need for and requirements of effective long-range planning are discussed. Long-range planning is viewed as a major opportunity for management science.

33. LONG-RANGE PLANNING*

Peter F. Drucker†

I

It is easier to define long-range planning by what it is not rather than by what it is. Three things in particular, which it is commonly believed to be, it emphatically is not.

1) *First it is not "forecasting."* It is not masterminding the future, in

* Reprinted from "Long-Range Planning," *Management Science*, Vol. V, No. 3, (April, 1959), pp. 238–249.

† New York University.

other words. Any attempt to do so is foolish; human beings can neither predict nor control the future.

If anyone still suffers from the delusion that the ability to forecast beyond the shortest time span is given to us, let him look at the headlines in yesterday's paper, and then ask himself which of them he could possibly have predicted ten years ago. . . .

This is the way the future always behaves. To try to mastermind it is therefore childish; we can only discredit what we are doing by attempting it. We must start out with the conclusion that forecasting is not respectable and not worthwhile beyond the shortest of periods. *Long-range planning is necessary precisely because we cannot forecast.*

But there is another, and even more compelling reason why forecasting is not long-range planning. Forecasting attempts to find the most probable course of events, or at best, a range of probabilities. But the enterpreneurial problem is the unique event that will change the possibilities, for the entrepreneurial universe in not a physical but a value-universe. Indeed the central entrepreneurial contribution and the one which alone is rewarded with a profit, is to bring about the unique event, the *innovation* that changes the probabilities. . . .

2) *The next thing to be said about what long-range planning is not, is that it does not deal with future decisions.* It deals with the *futurity of present decisions.*

Decisions exist only in the present. The question that faces the long-range planner is not what we should do tomorrow. It is what do we have to do today to be ready for an uncertain tomorrow. The question is not what will happen in the future. It is: what futurity do we have to factor into our present thinking and doing, what time spans do we have to consider, and how do we converge them to a simultaneous decision in the present?

Decision-making is essentially a time machine which synchronizes into one present a great number of divergent time spans. This is, I think, something which we are only learning now. Our approach today still tends toward the making of plans for something we will decide to do in the future. This may be a very entertaining exercise, but it is a futile one.

Again, long-range planning is necessary because we can make decisions only *in* the present; the rest are pious intentions. And yet we cannot make decisions *for* the present alone; the most expedient, most opportunist decision—let alone the decision not to decide—may commit us on a long-range basis, if not permanently and irrevocably.

3) *Finally, the most common misconception of all, long-range planning is not an attempt to eliminate risk.* It is not even an attempt to minimize risk. Indeed any such attempt can only lead to irrational and unlimited risk and to certain disaster.

The central fact about economic activity is that, by definition, it commits present resources to future and therefore highly uncertain expectations. To take risk is therefore the essence of economic activity. Indeed one of the most rigorous theorems of economics (Boehm-Bawerk's Law) proves that existing means of production will yield greater economic performance only through greater uncertainty, that is, through greater risk.

But while it is futile to try to eliminate risk, and questionable to try to minimize it, it is essential that the risks taken be the *right risks*. The end result of successful long-range planning must be a capacity to take a greater risk; for this is the only way to improve *entrepreneurial* performance. To do this, however, we must know and understand the risks we take. We must be able to rationally choose among risk-taking courses of action rather than plunge into uncertainty on the basis of hunch, hearsay or experience (no matter how meticulously quantified).

Now I think we can attempt to define what long-range planning is. It is the continuous process of making *present entrepreneurial* (*risk taking*) *decisions* systematically and with the best possible knowledge of their futurity, organizing systematically *the efforts* needed to carry out these decisions, and measuring the results of these decisions against the expectations through *organized, systematic feed-back*.

II

"This is all very well," many experienced businessmen might say (and do say). "But why make a production out of it? Isn't this what the entrepreneur has been doing all along, and doing quite successfully? Why then should it need all this elaborate mumbo-jumbo? Why should it be an organized, perhaps even a separate activity? Why in other words, should we even talk about 'long-range planning,' let alone do it?"

It is perfectly true that there is nothing very new to entrepreneurial decisions. They have been made as long as we have had entrepreneurs. There is nothing new in here regarding the essentials of economic activity. It has always been the commitment of present resources to future expectations; and for the last three hundred years this has been done in contemplation of change. (This was not true earlier. Earlier economic activity was based on the assumption that there would be no change, which assumption was institutionally guarded and defended. Altogether up to the seventeenth century it was the purpose of all human institutions to prevent change. The business enterprise is a significant and rather amazing novelty in that it is the first human institution having the purpose of bringing about change.)

But there are several things which are new; and they have created the need for the organized, systematic, and above all, specific process that we call "long-range planning."[1]

[1] "Long-range planning" is not a term I like or would have picked myself. It is a misnomer—as are so many of our terms in economics and management, such as

1) The time span of entrepreneurial and managerial decisions has been lengthening so fast and so much as to make necessary systematic exploration of the uncertainty and risk of decisions. . . .

Today practically every manager takes ten or twenty year risks without wincing. He takes them in product development, in research, in market development, in the development of a sales organization, and in almost anything. This lengthening of the time span of commitment is one of the most significant features of our age. It underlies our economic advances. But while quantitative in itself, it has changed the qualitative character of entrepreneurial decisions. It has, so to speak, converted time from being a dimension in which business decisions are being made into an essential element of the decisions themselves.

2) Another new feature is the speed and risk of innovation. To define what we mean by this term would go far beyond the scope of this paper.[2]

But we do not need to know more than that industrial research expenditures (that is, business expenditures aimed at innovating primarily peacetime products and processes) have increased in this country from less than $100 million in 1928 to $7 or 8 billion in 1958. Clearly, a technologically slow-moving, if not essentially stable economy has become one of violent technological flux, rapid obsolescence and great uncertainty.

3) Then there is the growing complexity both of the business enterprise internally, and of the economy and society in which it exists. There is the growing specialization of work which creates increasing need for common vision, common understanding, and common language, without which top management decisions, however right, will never become effective action.

4) Finally—a subtle, but perhaps the most important point—the typical businessman's concept of the basis of entrepreneurial decision is, after all, a misconception.

Most businessmen still believe that these decisions are made by "top management." Indeed practically all text books lay down the dictum that "basic policy decisions" are the "prerogative of top management." At most, top management "delegates" certain decisions.

But this reflects yesterday's rather than today's reality, let alone that of tomorrow. It is perfectly true that top management must have the final say, the final responsibility. But the business enterprise of today is no longer an organization in which there are a handful of "bosses" at the top who make all the decisions while the "workers" carry out orders. It is primarily an organization[3] of professionals of highly specialized knowl-

"capitalism," "automation," "operations research," "industrial engineering," or "depreciation." But it is too late to do anything about the term; it has become common usage.

[2] For a discussion see my new book, *The Landmarks of Tomorrow* (New York: Harper and Brothers, 1958).

[3] For a discussion of this "new organization" see again my *The Landmarks of Tomorrow* mentioned above.

edge exercising autonomous, responsible judgment. And every one of them—whether manager or individual expert contributor—constantly makes truly entrepreneurial decisions, that is, decisions which affect the economic characteristics and risks of the entire enterprise. He makes them not by "delegation from above" but inevitably in the performance of his own job and work.

For this organization to be functioning, two things are needed: knowledge by the entire organization of what the direction, the goals, the expectations are; and knowledge by top management of what the decisions, commitments, and efforts of the people in the organization are. The needed focus—one might call it a *model of the relevants in internal and external environment*—only a "long-range plan" can provide.

One way to summarize what is new and different in the process of entrepreneurial decision-making is in terms of information. The amount, diversity, and ambiguity of the information that is beating in on the decision-maker have all been increasing so much that the built-in experience reaction that a good manager has cannot handle it. He breaks down; and his breakdown will take either of the two forms known to any experimental psychologists. One is withdrawal from reality, i.e., "I know what I know and I only go by it; the rest is quite irrelevant and I won't even look at it." Or there is a feeling that the universe has become completely irrational so that one decision is as good as the other, resulting in paralysis. We see both in executives who have to make decisions today. Neither is likely to result in rational or in successful decisions. . . .

"Long-range planning" is more than organization and analysis of information; it is a decision-making process. But even the information job cannot be done except as part of an organized planning effort—otherwise there is no way of determining which information is relevant.

III

What then are the requirements of long-range planning? We cannot satisfy all of them as yet with any degree of competence; but we can specify them.

Indeed, we can—and should—give two sets of specifications: One in terms of the characteristics of the process itself; another in terms of its major and specific new-knowledge content.

1) Risk-taking entrepreneurial decisions, no matter whether made rationally or by tea-leaf reading, always embody the same eight elements:

a. *Objectives.* This is, admittedly, an elusive term, perhaps even a metaphysical one. It may be as difficult for Management Science to define "objectives" as it is for biology to define "life." Yet, we will be as unable to do without "objectives" as the biologists are unable to do without "life." Any entrepreneurial decision, let alone the integrated decision-system we call a "long-range plan," has objectives, consciously or not.

b. *Assumptions.* These are what is believed by the people who make and carry out decisions to be "real" in the internal and external universe of the business.

c. *Expectations.*—The future events or results considered likely or attainable. These three elements can be said to *define the decision.*

d. *Alternative courses of action.* There never is—indeed, in a true uncertainty situation there never can be—"one right decision." There cannot even be "one best decision." There are always "wrong decisions," that is, decisions inadequate to the objectives, incompatible with the assumptions, or grossly improbable in the light of the expectations. But once these have been eliminated, there will still be alternatives left—each a different configuration of objectives, assumptions and expectations, each with its own risks and its own ratio between risks and rewards, each with its own impact, its specific efforts and its own results. Every decision is thus a value-judgment—it is not the "facts that decide"; people have to choose between imperfect alternatives on the basis of uncertain knowledge and fragmentary understanding.

Two alternatives deserve special mention, if only because they have to be considered in almost every case. One is the alternative of no action (which is, of course, what postponing a decision often amounts to); the other is the very important choice between adaptive and innovating action—each having risks that differ greatly in character though not necessarily in magnitude.

e. The next element in the decision-making process is the *decision itself.*

f. But there is no such thing as one isolated decision; every decision is, of necessity, part of a *decision-structure.*

Every financial man knows, for instance, that the original capital appropriation on a new investment implies a commitment to future—and usually larger-capital appropriations which, however, are almost never as much as mentioned in the proposal submitted. Few of them seem to realize, however, that this implies not only a positive commitment but also, by mortgaging future capital resources, limits future freedom of action. The structuring impact of a decision is even greater in respect to allocations of scarce manpower, such as research people.

g. A decision is only pious intention unless it leads to action. Every decision, therefore, has an *impact stage.*

This impact always follows Newton's Second Law, so to speak; it consists of action and reaction. It requires effort. But it also dislocates. There is, therefore, always the question: what effort is required, by whom, and where? What must people know, what must they do and what must they achieve? But there is also the question—generally neglected—what does this decision do to other areas? Where does it shift the burden, the weaknesses, and the stress points; and what impact does it have on the outside; in the market, in the supply structure, in the community, and so on.

h. And, finally, there are *results*.

Each of these elements of the process deserves an entire book by itself. But I think I have said enough to show that both, the process itself and each element in it, are *rational*, no matter how irrational and arbitrary they may appear. Both the process and all its elements can therefore be defined, can be studied and can be analyzed. And both can be improved through systematic and organized work. In particular, as in all rational processes, the entire process is improved and strengthened as we define, clarify and analyze each of its constituent elements.

2) We can also, as said above, describe long-range planning in terms of its specific new-knowledge content.

Among the areas where such new knowledge is particularly cogent, might be mentioned:

a. *The time dimensions of planning*.

To say "long-range" or "short-range" planning implies that a given time span defines the planning; and this is actually how businesses look at it when they speak of a "five-year plan" or a "ten-year plan." But the essence of planning is to make present decisions with knowledge of their futurity. It is the futurity that determines the time span, and not vice versa.

Strictly speaking, "short range" and "long range" do not describe time spans but stages in every decision. "Short range" is the stage before the decision has become fully effective, the stage during which it is only "costs" and not yet "results." The "short range" of a decision to build a steel mill is the five years or so until the mill is in production. And the "long range" of any decision is the period of expected performance needed to make the decision a successful one—the twenty or more years above break-even point operations in the case of the steel mill, for instance.

There are limitations on futurity. In business decisions the most precise mathematical statement is often that of my eighth grade teacher that parallels are two lines which do not meet this side of the school yard. Certainly, in the expectations and anticipations of a business the old rule of statistics usually applies that anything beyond twenty years equals infinity; and since expectations more than twenty years hence have normally a present value of zero, they should receive normally only a minimal allocation of present efforts and resources. . . .

It is the nature of the business and the nature of the decision which determine the time spans of planning.

Yet the time spans are not static or "given." The time decision itself is the first and a highly important risk-taking decision in the planning process. It largely determines the allocation of resources and efforts. It largely determines the risks taken (and one cannot repeat too often that to postpone a decision is in itself a risk-taking and often irrevocable decision). Indeed, the time decision largely determines the character and nature of the business.

b. *Decision structure and configuration.*

The problem of the time dimension is closely tied in with that of decision structure.

Underlying the whole concept of long-range planning are two simple insights.

We need an integrated decision structure for the business as a whole. There are really no isolated decisions on a product, or on markets, or on people. Each major risk-taking decision has impact throughout the whole; and no decision is isolated in time. Every decision is a move in a chess game, except that the rules of enterprise are by no means as clearly defined. There is no finite "board" and the pieces are neither as neatly distinguished nor as few in number. Every move opens some future opportunities for decision, and foreclose others. Every move, therefore, commits positively and negatively. . . .

At the same time, entrepreneurial decisions must be fundamentally expedient decisions. It is not only impossible to know all the contingent effects of a decision, even for the shortest time period ahead. The very attempt to know them would lead to complete paralysis.

But the determination of what should be considered and what should be ignored, is in itself a difficult and consequential decision. We need knowledge to make it—I might say that we need a theory of entrepreneurial inference.

c. *The characteristics of risks.*

It is not only magnitude of risk that we need to be able to appraise in entrepreneurial decisions. It is above all the character of the risk. Is it, for instance, the kind of risk we can afford to take, or the kind of risk we cannot afford to take? Or is it that rare but singularly important risk, the risk we cannot afford not to take—sometimes regardless of the odds?

The best General Electric scientists, we are told, advised their management in 1945 that it would be at least forty years before nuclear energy could be used to produce electric power commercially. Yet General Electric—rightly—decided that it had to get into the atomic energy field. It could not afford not to take the risk as long as there was the remotest possibility that atomic energy would, after all, become a feasible source of electric power.

We know from experience that the risk we cannot afford not to take, is like a "high-low" poker game. A middle hand will inevitably lose out. But we do not know why this is so. And the other, and much more common kinds of risk we do not really understand at all.

d. *Finally, there is the area of measurements.*

I do not have to explain to readers of *Management Science* why measurements are needed in management, and especially for the organized entrepreneurial decisions we call "long-range planning."

But it should be said that in human institutions, such as a business enterprise, measurements, strictly speaking, do not and cannot exist. It is the definition of a measurement that it be impersonal and objective, that is, extraneous to the event measured. A child's growth is not dependent on the yardstick or influenced by being recorded. But any measurement in a business enterprise determines action—both on the part of the measurer and the measured—and thereby directs, limits and causes behavior and performance of the enterprise. Measurement in the enterprise is always motivation, that is, moral force, as much as it is *ratio cognoscendi.*

In addition, in long-range planning we do not deal with observable events. We deal with future events, that is with expectations. And expectations, being incapable of being observed, are never "facts" and cannot be measured.

Measurements, in long-range planning, thus present very real problems, especially conceptual ones. Yet precisely because what we measure and how we measure determines what will be considered relevant, and determines thereby not just what we see, but what we—and others—do, measurements are all-important in the planning process. Above all, unless we build expectations into the planning decision in such a way that we can very early realize whether they are actually fulfilled or not—including a fair understanding of what are significant deviations both in time and in scale—we cannot plan; and we have no feedback, no way of self-control in management.

We obviously also need for long-range planning *managerial* knowledge—the knowledge with respect to the operations of a business. We need such knowledge as that of the resources available, especially the human resources, their capacities and their limitations. We need to know how to "translate" from business needs, business results and business decisions into functional capacity and specialized effort. There is, after all, no functional decision, there is not even functional data, just as there is no functional profit, no functional loss, no functional investment, no functional risk, no functional customer, no functional product and no functional image of a company. There is only a unified company product, risk, investment and so on, hence only company performance and company results. Yet at the same time the work obviously has to be done by people each of whom has to be specialized. Hence for a decision to be possible, we must be able to integrate divergent individual knowledges and capacities into one organization potential; and for a decision to be effective, we must be able to translate it into a diversity of individual and expert, yet focused, efforts.

There are also big problems of knowledge in the entrepreneurial task that I have not mentioned—the problems of growth and change, for instance, or those of the moral values of a society and their meaning to business. But these are problems that exist for many areas and disciplines other than management.

And in this paper I have confined myself intentionally to knowledge that is specific to the process of long-range planning. Even so I have barely mentioned the main areas. But I think I have said enough to substantiate three conclusions:

a) Here are areas of genuine knowledge, not just areas in which we need data. What we need above all are basic theory and conceptual thinking.

b) The knowledge we need is new knowledge. It is not to be found in the traditional disciplines of business such as accounting or economics. It is also not available, by and large, in the physical or life sciences. From the existing disciplines we can get a great deal of help, of course, especially in tools and techniques. And we need all we can get. But the knowledge we need is distinct and specific. It pertains not to the physical, the biological or the pyschological universe, though it partakes of them all. It pertains to the specific institution, the enterprise, which is a social institution existing in contemplation of human values. What is "knowledge" in respect to this institution let alone what is "scientific" must therefore always be determined by reference to the nature, function and purposes of this specific (and very peculiar) institution.

c) It is not within the decision of the entrepreneur whether he wants to make risk-taking decisions with long futurity; he makes them by definition. All that is within his power is to decide whether he wants to make them responsibly or irresponsibly, with a rational chance of effectiveness and success, or as a blind gamble against all odds. And both, because the process is essentially a rational process, and because the effectiveness of the entrepreneurial decisions depends on the understanding and voluntary efforts of others, the process will be the more responsible and the more likely to be effective, the more it is a rational, organized process based on knowledge.

IV

Long-range planning is risk-taking decision making. As such it is the responsibility of the policy-maker, whether we call him entrepreneur or manager. To do the job rationally and systematically does not change this. Long-range planning does not "substitute facts for judgment," does not "substitute science for the manager." It does not even lessen the importance and role of managerial ability, courage, experience, intuition, or even hunch—just as scientific biology and systematic medicine have not lessened the importance of these qualities in the individual physician. On the contrary, the systematic organization of the planning job and the supply of knowledge to it, should make more effective individual managerial qualities of personality and vision.

But at the same time long-range planning offers major opportunity and major challenge to Management Science and to the Management Scientist.[4] We need systematic study of the process itself and of every one of its

[4] I would like to say here that I do not believe that the world is divided into "managers" and "management scientists." One man may well be both. Certainly, management scientists must understand the work and job of the manager, and vice versa. But conceptually and as a kind of work, the two are distinct.

elements. We need systematic work in a number of big areas of new knowledge—at least we need to know enough to organize our ignorance.

At the same time, long-range planning is the crucial area; it deals with the decisions which, in the last analysis, determine the character and the survival of the enterprise.

So far, it must be said, Management Science has not made much contribution to long-range planning. Sometimes one wonders whether those who call themselves "Management Scientists" are even aware of the risk-taking character of economic activity and of the resultant enterpreneurial job of long-range planning. Yet, in the long run, Management Science and Management Scientists may well, and justly, be judged by their ability to supply the knowledge and thinking needed to make long-range planning possible, simple, and effective.

A long-range plan is a formalized structure for coordinating the variables involved in establishing and achieving a set of corporate objectives. Strategy decisions based upon careful analysis of the firm's resources, competition, and market trends must precede the development of long-range plans. Long-range planning and goal determination are interdependent, and periodic re-evaluation of both is required if efficient operation is to be insured. Research and development timetables should be an integral part of long-range plans.

34. LONG-RANGE PLANNING AND RESEARCH AND DEVELOPMENT*

Wendell R. Smith†

INTRODUCTION

I think it is fair to say that an analysis of the subject matter areas being discussed at management seminars, trade conferences, and similar gatherings would indicate an increasing emphasis upon long-range planning and the associated problems of research and development programs. These are

* Not previously published.

† Marketing Science Institute.

critical business functions and hence worthy of the emphasis that they are receiving. Are these activities really new? If they are as important as the current emphasis would indicate, how have we been able to get along without them for so many years in the past?

With reference to long-range planning, a moment's reflection will lead to the conclusion that planning is now and always has been an *unavoidable* management function. What is happening is that we are beginning to make planning a conscious, explicit function and, in many cases, to recognize its existence by assigning the responsibility in a formal way on the organization chart. It seems quite obvious that the firm which does not develop a formal long-range plan, by virtue of its decision not to do so, has actually evolved a plan which says in effect, "In the future we will meet conditions as they arise and will not attempt to anticipate the opportunities and problems that will confront us as the years go by." Recognition of long-range planning, then, as a management function is very much like the decision to formulate policies. Looked at from a functional point of view, a policy is simply a prefabricated answer to a recurring question; the enforcement of which will produce continuity and consistency in the behavior of the firm and its employees. Similarly a long-range plan becomes a formal device for coordinating the activities of the firm toward a defined set of goals. It is important at this point for us to try to understand why it is that over the last few years so many firms have found it desirable to develop long-range plans, thus making explicit the important elements of the planning function.

Perhaps one of the most important reasons has been the increase in the size of the firm, associated with the tendency of companies to embrace activities that are less homogeneous than was true in the past. Growth and diversification create significant problems of coordination and control that are at least partially capable of solution by means of formalized plans.

A *second* reason is attributable to the fact that the "price of admission" to many of the growth areas of the economy is going up. The electronics industry is a case in point. Because of rapidly advancing technology, the opportunities that exist in the field are almost unlimited. However, the costs of exploring these opportunities and developing products and services that would result in their realization is of such magnitude that even the largest firms in the industry are incapable of pursuing them all. Therefore, there is a problem of selection and the associated problem of allocating an essentially limited research and development effort over the opportunities of greatest promise. Hence, long-range planning becomes mandatory as the inevitable result of the increasing cost of pursuing "new frontiers."

There are many who would argue that the increase of interest in long-range planning is, at least in part, the result of the availability of new management tools such as marketing research, operations research, model building, simulation techniques, and so forth. From my point of view such an argument tends to confuse cause and effect. History seems to indicate that new management functions which have a decent chance for survival are functions that have arisen in response to need rather than in response to the availability of new techniques. To some extent, this is the chicken and egg argument, but to me the identity of the creative element of the cycle seems reasonably clear.

Thus far I have referred to research and development as a rather general concept. It is important to note, however, that while most people think of the research laboratory as the focus of this activity, it is in reality a concept capable of much broader application. Developing new and better ways of doing things for the future should not be limited to the technical area of the business, but should also be recognized as important in connection with manufacturing, finance, personnel, and certainly in connection with marketing. Recognition of this latter point is evidenced by the fact that there is a current trend toward the rechristening of marketing research departments with the more appropriate title of *marketing research and development.* Admittedly, however, the main thrust of research and development is in the area of technology. As Dr. Rinfret of Lionel D. Edie and Company points out, "Technology is reshaping the industrial structure of the United States. In industry after industry it is becoming more and more apparent that research and development is creating chaos and opportunity." Chaos in industries and companies that do effective long-range planning is converted to opportunity as the result of recognizing that research and development has become one of the keys to the future and to growth.

LONG-RANGE PLANNING—OBJECTIVES AND A SUGGESTED APPROACH

I have already referred to some of the objectives that firms attempt to achieve through long-range planning. In a very real sense management is attempting, through long-range planning, to run the business rather than to be run by it. Further, long-range planning represents an attempt to coordinate the many and diverse activities of the firm toward a desired set of goals. It is a recognition of the increasingly long-term commitments that must be made in facilities, equipment, research and development, and in specialized personnel. Perhaps, the total benefits of long-range planning are best brought to light by consideration of a suggested approach to the development of plans and a review of the interrelationship between long-range plans and current operations.

Much has been said and written about the sequence in steps involved in the development of sound business plans. The first step is usually identified as the determination of goals or objectives to be accomplished by means of the business action that is being planned. This is true only to the extent that the firm has in its possession the results of a careful review of its present position as a foundation upon which to determine realistic goals and feasible objectives. The continuous or periodic availability of such a position is a prime responsibility of accounting, marketing research, and the other activities that are responsible for supplying the inputs of information and analysis that are essential to the planning process. Hence, determination of goals and objectives may turn out to be the second step in planning instead of the first.

Those experienced in the planning of business activities tend to approach the finalizing of goals and objectives cautiously, and often come to regard alternative sets of goals and objectives somewhat in the light of hypotheses to be tested, with the selection of the appropriate alternative as an important joint product of the planning operation itself. It seems clear that the feasibility of a goal can best be evaluated only by careful review of the action plan that would be necessary for its achievement. Therefore, viewed realistically, the initial stages of the long-range planning process may well tend to merge with the final steps in goal determination until the criteria of feasibility have been satisfied. It is at this early exploratory, perhaps experimental, stage in the planning process that considerations of business and marketing strategy become paramount as a true prelude to the development of the plans which will finally emerge, resplendent with timetables, budgets, campaigns, and schedules for the deployment and acquisition of personnel.

There are many ways in which the nature of business strategy can be described; but regardless of definition, business strategy is primarily concerned with the *creative* elements of a goal-directed, long-range plan. The strategy describes, in broad brush, the basic elements of the way in which the firm plans to get from where it is to where it wants to be. The strategy becomes the central theme that integrates and coordinates the many and diverse components of effort (tactics) to be stipulated in the plan itself.

While business strategies are inherently creative, this does not mean that the process of their generation depends upon the availability of an inspired genius. As a matter of fact, an orderly method of developing strategic concepts is one of the most basic aspects of the contemporary approach to planning. In general, business strategies evolve from study of the *firm* itself, from study and analysis of *competition* (both present and prospective future) and from analysis of the market and market trends.

As was pointed out earlier, the generation of business strategies essentially begins with a careful review of the present position of the firm in relation to competition and in relation to the markets that it serves. Such analysis rather quickly reveals whether the strategy should be essentially *defensive*, that is designed to compensate for and to correct weaknesses in the present operation, or *offensive* in the sense of leading to plans designed to fully capitalize upon the relative strengths and advantages that the firm enjoys. As contemporary economists have so eloquently pointed out, many business strategies are developed with primary reference to the present and prospective future behavior of competition. However, the most important and fundamental of business strategies are those that are related directly to the accomplishment of goals and objectives that are defined in terms of the market itself. Solid marketing research is the stuff out of which strategies can be built. Let us look at two examples of the ways in which market data may suggest an orderly method or approach to strategy generation.

In the first place, analysis of trends in demand for present and prospective future products or services becomes fundamental. An unfavorable trend in demand suggests a choice between strategies designed to reverse the trend or to accept and to adjust to the development. Similarly, a favorable trend in demand suggests a choice of strategies concerned with how the firm can profit most from this happy state of affairs without over-extending or producing imbalance in its situation.

Second, analysis of market structure or composition will reveal whether the market is characterized by *homogeneity*, a situation where the requirements of customers or users are very much the same; or *heterogeneity*, a situation where individual requirements vary and hence would be imperfectly satisfied by a limited offering to the market. In the first case, the situation of homogeneity, one would logically follow a business strategy designed to bring about the convergence of individual market demands upon a single or limited offering to the market. This is usually accomplished by the achievement of product differentiation through advertising and promotion. On the other hand, if the structure of the market is characterized by heterogeneity, the decision may be to the effect that it is better to accept divergent demand as a market characteristic and to adjust product line and market strategy accordingly. Such a strategy has been referred to as a strategy of *market segmentation* which consists essentially of approaching a heterogeneous market as if it were a group of smaller homogeneous markets (market segments) in response to differing product needs and preferences among important segments of the market. This strategy also often involves substantial use of advertising and promotion, but the objective becomes that of informing the market segments of the availability of goods or services produced for or presented as meeting their needs with greater precision. It has been my purpose thus far to suggest, first, that long-range business planning cannot proceed until the marketing goals to be achieved by means of the plan have been defined. Second, it seems clear that the "nuts and bolts" or the detailed activities concerned with the generation of the long-term plan must necessarily be preceded by one or more strategy decisions that will have been arrived at as a result of careful analysis of the position and capabilities of the firm, the position and capabilities of competition, and probable future market trends and changes in structure.

In its initial stages, planning draws heavily on industry and company records and other sources of internal data. Preliminary projections are often made, based for the moment on the assumption that future conditions and circumstances will represent little change from the current operating environment. These preliminary projections are then adjusted for expected changes in economic activity, product line, product design, or other company actions that will effect the operations of the firm. Normally the marketing segment of the long-range plan is the first to emerge, since it is necessary as the basis for plans relating to production, financial requirements, personnel and so forth. Not infrequently plans judged to be entirely feasible in terms of market opportunity and action must be revised because of production or financial limitations. The end product, of course, is a detailed blueprint of the actions to be taken during the period covered by the plan in all aspects of the business. It is truly a "flight plan" designed to meet in advance the thunderstorms and crosswinds that may be encountered along the way. One of its objectives is to minimize the crises and waste that are common where business activity is not planned and to save the panic button for real emergencies over which the firm may have no control.

The long-range plan will be incomplete if it fails to specify bench marks of expected performance against which actual performance can be checked at specified times. Just as the aircraft pilot periodically checks back with flight control, business progress must be checked against the plan or the "par" that has been established.

Deviation from planned performance may indicate that someone is falling down on the job, or it may turn out that predetermined plans are now unrealistic in terms of changed conditions. If the latter turns out to be the case, plans must of course be revised. One may very well ask, "What is the good of having long-range plans if they are constantly being revised?" It is a fact that "meeting developments" by revising plans results in a more successful and rational adjustment to changed conditions than is true of the business that has not planned ahead and thus is constantly "flying by the seat of its pants."

There is little argument among executives these days as to the general desirability of engaging in long-range planning and using the long-range plan as a method of controlling and evaluating the various activities of the firm. However, it is not generally recognized that it is just as dangerous to plan, control, and evaluate by intuition as it is not to plan at all. These three closely interrelated concepts imply the need for a rational approach if they are successful. A plan based upon hope and optimism alone is often worse than no plan at all because it produces a false sense of security about the hazards of the future that have not been taken into account.

The question is often raised as to what period of time should be covered by "long-range" plans. There is no uniform answer to this question. The answer must be found in each individual case, and the answer will depend upon many factors; among them, the period of time over which accurate forecasting is feasible, product life cycles, the time necessary to bring new or revised products to market, the relative importance of research and development activity, and all other factors that involve advance commitments, the payoff from which falls at sometime in the future. Arbitrary planning periods and resistance to revision of plans when warranted must be contained if the benefits obtainable through long-range planning are to be secured.

ORGANIZATIONAL ASPECTS OF LONG-RANGE PLANNING

The organizational placement of long-range planning responsibility is probably much less important than the degree to which the importance of long-range planning is recognized by the decision makers within the firm. Much time and money is wasted in firms where the development of plans consists primarily of determining what top management arbitrarily expects for the planning period and factoring back from there. This is one way of saying that there must be a substantial amount of high-level involvement in the planning process if it is to be successful. However, the evidence is piling up that it is not realistic to expect operating personnel to do an effective job of long-range planning unless they are effectively supported by the essential staff services. However, in my judgment, there is no one best answer as to where the planning responsibility should reside. In some companies it would make sense for it to become centered in the office of the controller. In other companies, where marketing capability represents a most important single element in success, marketing research personnel will be heavily involved. Suffice it to say that the reporting point of those having planning responsibility must be at a high level and, even if this is the case, they cannot operate effectively without active top-level support. It is a truism that the quality of long-range plans is a function of the degree to which they are used in guiding and controlling the operations of the business.

PLANNING FOR GROWTH

Thus far we have been concerned primarily with long-range planning as an operational device. Let us look now at the importance of the long-range plan as a means of achieving sound growth. Long-range planning is almost synonymous with planning for growth for the following reasons:

1. The long-range plan inevitably demonstrates the validity of the life cycle theory in products, thereby pointing up the necessity for new product development and product improvement if desired volume and growth are to be achieved. The long-range plan creates a sense of urgency about new business development that is difficult to achieve in any other way.
2. The long-range plan establishes the timetable for research and development because the anticipated results of R & D become a part of the plan.
3. The analysis that must precede the planning process frequently exposes

new areas of opportunity that can be pursued. This analysis compels the firm to match its capabilities against emerging market opportunities, and this is the basic process by means of which new business development occurs.

4. Analysis of competition, both direct and indirect, often reveals opportunities for growth by merger or acquisition; assuming, of course, that legal complexities do not intervene.

SIMULATIONS AND MODELS

We now stand on the threshold of a new era in both the development and use of long-range plans toward the goal of increasing the profitability of the firm. As a result of the simultaneous development of the mathematical model of the firm and its environment and the techniques of electronic data processing, it now becomes possible to "pretest" the results that would be achieved by plans based on alternative strategies or procedures. If the firm has accurately and effectively analyzed itself, its competition, and its market, relationships between these data can be expressed in the form of an equation or model. The model can then, in effect, be programmed into the computer. This makes it possible for the planner to experiment by varying certain elements of the plan and noting the impact upon the end result. For example, if such a program for the computer is available, one might determine in a matter of minutes the effect on sales and profits that would result from a 25% reduction in prices. These techniques are available. However, our ability to use them depends upon the generation of much more market information than most firms have readily available. Of more immediate utility is the use of the model and the computer for solving lesser problems of strategy that are subordinate to the overall strategy being followed in the long-range plan. The coming decade will see substantial progress in this area.

CONCLUSIONS

At this point it should be obvious that I am one of those who is convinced that planning, both short range and long range, is here to stay and will improve and increase in accuracy and utility as the result of experience and the evolution of new techniques. At first glance this would seem to imply an increase in the complexity of the management task. This may be true in the short run. In the long run, however, the reverse will be the case in that decision-making time may be reserved for consideration of major issues rather than dissipated by conjecture as to what the facts and interrelationships between them actually are.

According to the author, few current marketing planning processes follow sound planning principles. The function of marketing planning is the development of strategies that will lead to the attainment of corporate goals. Programs and controls must be devised to implement these strategies. The key elements in a marketing planning procedure are discussed.

35. ARE YOU REALLY PLANNING YOUR MARKETING?*

Leon Winer†

The biggest problem in marketing planning is the *planning*. Many companies have a marketing "plan," yet few of these plans represent any real planning. To demonstrate this point, five steps will describe practices encountered frequently. These practices were observed through intensive interviews with manufacturing firms and their advertising agencies, and have been reported by executives at meetings and seminars attended by the author.

Step 1: Set the market share objective of your brand by adding to its present market share, depending on how ambitious you are.

Step 2: Project total sales volume, for *all* brands of the product, in dollars, for the following year.

Step 3: Multiply the result of Step 1 by the result of Step 2. (Market share objective X projected total dollar market.) This gives the dollar sales objective for the brand.

Step 4: Subtract from the dollar sales objective: (a) total factory cost, (b) an allocated portion of the company's fixed marketing costs, and (c) desired profit. What is left, if anything, is "planned" marketing expenditure.

Step 5: Compose a "marketing mix" of advertising, marketing research, personal selling, price concessions, public relations, package design, point of sales materials, dealer aids, and so on, that will (a) just use up all the marketing funds and (b) yield exactly the forecasted sales volume.

---

* Reprinted from "Are You Really Planning Your Marketing?" *Journal of Marketing*, Vol. 29, No. 1 (January, 1965), p. 1–8.

† IBM Corporation.

These five steps represent the procedures of many companies, yet they are thoroughly unsound, for three reasons:

First, this procedure assumes that an increase in market share is profitable or, for that matter, possible. By definition, not *all* brands of a product can increase their market shares.

Second, this method of marketing planning reverses the cause-and-effect relationship between marketing effort and sales volume. Clearly, the sales volume forecast should depend on the amount of effort expended on marketing, not the other way around.

FIGURE 1.

Flow Model of a Marketing Planning Procedure

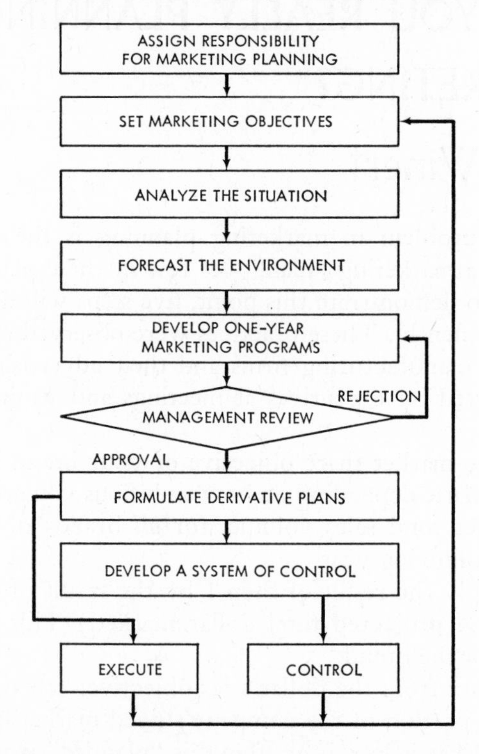

Third, this method requires the manager to select the "right" marketing mix from among the hundreds, or thousands, of possible marketing mixes. In other words, the manager is given a sales volume objective and a fixed amount of money for marketing, and he is expected to devise the combination of advertising, price reductions, personal selling, marketing research, public relations, point of sale materials, and so on, that will just use up the available money and will attain the sales objective. No human being has the knowledge or the calculating ability to do this, even if it were *theoretically* possible.

If the argument presented above is correct, and widely followed practice is inadequate, what alternatives are available?

To answer this question, a study was made of the marketing planning practices of companies recognized as leaders in this area, and of planning books and articles. The conclusion was that while a certain amount of adaptation is required in each case, a general procedure exists that is applicable to marketing planning. This procedure is presented as a flow model in Figure 1. The discussion of the steps in the model will follow the sequence shown, except that "assigning responsibility for planning" will be discussed last instead of first.

SETTING MARKETING OBJECTIVES

In setting marketing objectives, planners should keep in mind three properties of objectives: (1) multiplicity, the fact that organizations have many objectives; (2) time, objectives need to be set for varying lengths of time; and (3) level, the firm should have many levels of objectives, or a hierarchy of objectives.

Multiplicity

Generally speaking, marketers tend to focus on maximizing next year's profits as being the only proper objective for their efforts. Actually a company may be equally interested in stabilizing profits, or in seeking opportunities for investments for the longer term. Therefore, before doing any marketing planning, it is necessary to explore thoroughly with the company's management what *it* views the company's objectives to be and to derive marketing objectives from those of the company.

Objectives and Time

Given the company's objectives, it does not necessarily follow that these can be realized directly. A firm may not be able to capture a larger share of the market, economically, unless it has an improved product. Therefore, in order to attain a more distant objective of increasing its market share, it will set an intermediate objective of developing an improved product.

Since the firm possesses only limited management and financial resources, in setting the objectives described above, it will very probably have to forsake such alternative objectives as entering a foreign market or acquiring a potentially profitable competitor.

Therefore, in setting long-range objectives, and the intermediate objectives that will lead to their attainment, the firm must consider the alternatives it is forsaking, and select those most suitable to its circumstances.

Hierarchy of Objectives

Even though a firm sets long-term objectives and determines the appropriate intermediate objectives, that may not be enough. It does not do much good to tell the advertising department that the objective of the company is to increase its rate of return on investment unless this objec-

FIGURE 2.

Hierarchy of Objectives for the Interstate Telephone Company

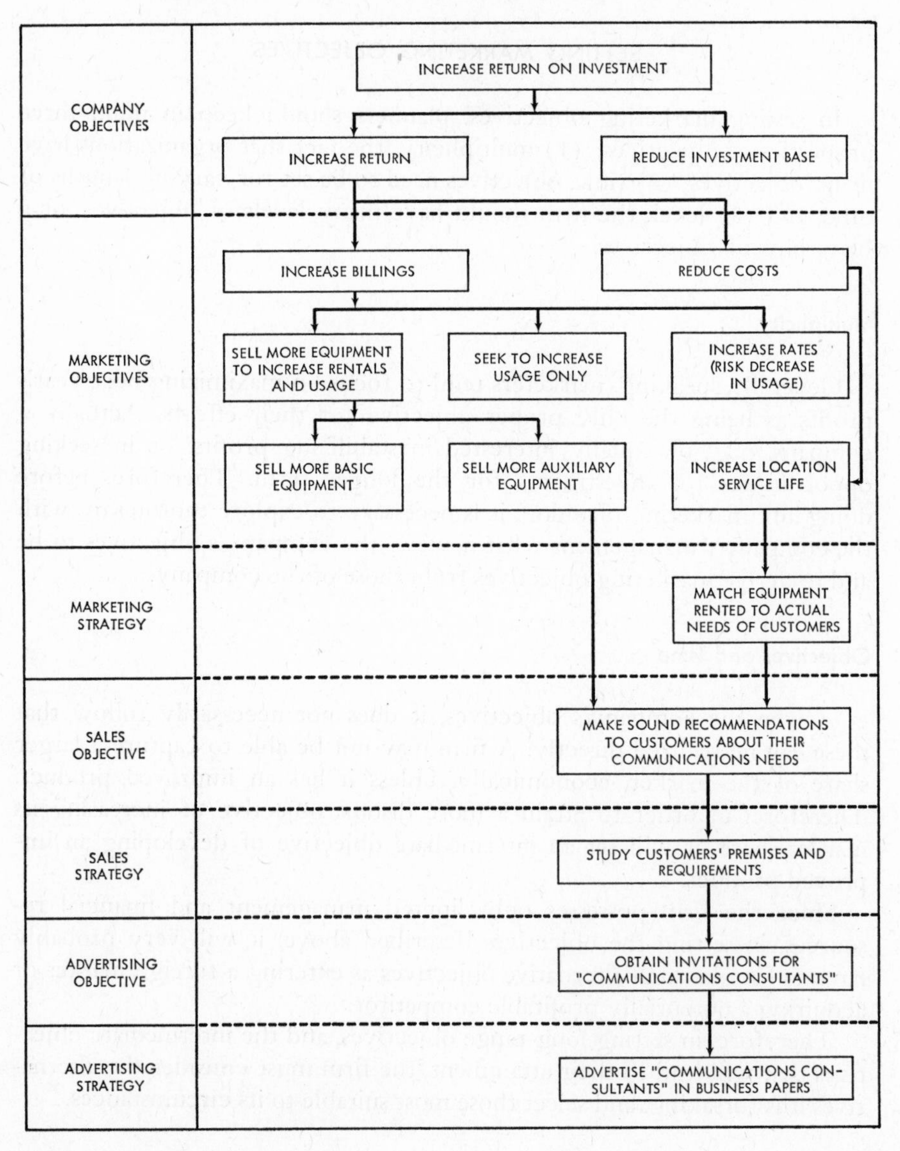

tive is translated into specific strategies. Therefore, it is necessary to develop a hierarchy of objectives.

Development of such a hierarchy of objectives is not a simple task. Careful study is required to make sure that sufficient alternatives are considered at each level and that suitable criteria are discovered for deciding which alternatives are to be selected, or emphasized.

An example, showing how a hierarchy of objectives may be derived through flow-modeling, is shown in Figure 2. This is the case of the business market (offices, factories, stores, hospitals, and so on) of the Interstate Telephone Company (a fictitious name for a real company). At the top of the chart is one of the Company's permanent objectives, that of increasing return on invested capital. A rate of return of 7½% is believed to be attainable. Two possible objectives were derived from this one: (1) increase return, or net profit, and (2) reduce the investment base on which return is computed. The second possibility was not believed to be attainable because of (1) population growth, (2) rapidly growing communication needs, and (3) trend toward mechanization and automation. Therefore, attention was focused on the first.

To increase profits, two objectives may be set, following the reasoning of the Interstate Company: (1) increase billings, or (2) reduce costs. Again, the second objective is unlikely to be attained because one of the important sources of the return on investment problem is the rising cost of labor and materials. (One exception should be noted, however. Costs may be reduced by reducing the rate of disconnections due to customer dissatisfaction, since the cost of installing complex equipment often exceeds installation charges.) This leaves the alternative of increasing billings.

To increase billings, the Interstate Company may (1) try to raise rates and risk reduction in usage, (2) persuade customers to increase usage of existing equipment, or (3) sell additional equipment and services in order to increase equipment rentals and, to some extent, usage. However, a public service commission will not grant a rate increase unless return on investment is *below* a certain minimum, say 5½%. Then a commission is not likely to grant a raise that will increase return by as much as two percentage points. The next alternative objective, persuading customers to increase usage, has been used as an objective for promotional efforts of the Company. The third objective, that of selling additional equipment and services, has been selected for particular emphasis. In particular, because of the saturation of the business market with respect to basic equipment, the marketing effort has focused on the sale of auxiliary services and equipment, such as "Call Directors," teletype units, modern switchboards, and interior dialing.

To achieve the objective of selling more auxiliary services and equipment, and reducing disconnections due to customer dissatisfaction, the Company needs to match equipment and services to the *needs* of the customers, by making recommendations based on careful study of these needs. To do this, it seeks to persuade customers, through advertising, to invite "Communications Consultants" to survey their communications problems. In this way, by deriving a hierarchy of objectives, Interstate identifies the specific marketing strategies that will lead to attainment of the Company's highest objectives.

ANALYZING THE SITUATION

Once the planner has a well-developed set of objectives, the next step is to begin discovering ways of attaining them. To do this, he has to form some ideas about what *actions* of the firm, under what *environmental conditions*, have brought about the *present* situation. He will then be able to identify courses of action that may be used in the future.

Logan[1] has suggested a four-step procedure for conducting the situation analysis:

Investigation—A wide range of data that may be relevant should be sought, with care being taken to distinguish between facts and opinions.

Classification—The planner sorts the data collected during the investigation.

Generalization—Classes of data are studied to discover relationships. Statistical techniques such as correlation analysis are used to determine whether dependable associations exist between types of events. For example, a distributor may find that leased outlets are more profitable than owned outlets to a degree that prevents attributing the differences to chance.

Estimate of the Situation—Causes are sought for the associations discovered in the previous step. The planner now has some ideas about what actions under past conditions have resulted in the present situation. In this way he has learned several courses of action that he may follow to achieve his objectives. In the example cited previously, the distributor may find, on searching further, that the higher profitability of leased outlets is caused by the superior location of the leased outlets. In other words, the fact that the outlet was leased was *not* the cause of the higher profitability. Rather *both* the leasing and the higher profitability were caused by a third factor—superior location. (Owners of well-located outlets were not willing to sell them and therefore the distributor had been forced to lease.) Consequently, the appropriate strategy for the future would not be to prefer leasing to owning, but to seek good locations and leasing, if necessary. Inadequate search for causes might have led to very poor results.

Ideally, the situation analysis should cover other firms in the industry,

---

[1] James P. Logan, "Economic Forecasts, Decision Processes, and Types of Plans" (unpublished doctoral dissertation, Columbia University, 1960), pp. 14–19, 76.

so that the company may benefit from their experiences, both successes and failures.

FORECASTING THE FUTURE ENVIRONMENT

The forecasting problem, from the viewpoint of the planner, is to determine *what* conditions he should forecast and *how* to do it. In this article we will limit ourselves to the first part of the problem because the literature of forecasting techniques is too vast to be reviewed adequately here.

Frey[2] has listed five factors that may affect purchases of a product:

1. Population changes.
2. Improvements in, and new-use discoveries for competing types of products.
3. Improvements in, and new-use discoveries for the company's own type of product.
4. Changed consumer attitudes and habits.
5. Changes in general business conditions.

Howard[3] suggests four criteria for identifying *key* factors:

1. Variability. If a factor is stable over time, there is no need to make a forecast of it.
2. Co-variation. There must be a relationship between changes in the factor and changes in demand.
3. Measurability.
4. Independence. The factor must not be closely related to another factor already considered.

Essentially, this means that the planner has to find out *which* uncontrollable factors, such as personal income, occupation of consumers, educational level, attitudes, affect sales of his brand, and then he has to forecast the future of these factors. Here, as in situation analysis, statistical methods must be used with care, to avoid erroneous conclusions.

DEVELOPING ONE-YEAR MARKETING PROGRAMS

Development of marketing programs requires three steps: (a) formulating alternative courses of action, (b) examining these alternatives, (c) comparing alternatives and selecting the ones to be recommended.

---

[2] Albert W. Frey, *The Effective Marketing Mix: Programming for Optimum Results* (Hanover, New Hampshire: The Amos Tuck School of Business Administration, 1956), p. 11.

[3] John Howard, *Marketing Management* (Homewood, Illinois: R. D. Irwin, Inc., 1957), Chapter VI.

Formulating Alternatives

The first step in conceiving alternative courses of action was described in an earlier section on situation analysis. We reviewed a four-step process for discovering factors that had brought about the present situation, and presumably could be manipulated to achieve future objectives.

However, in addition to the cause-and-effect relationships discovered in situation analysis, there is usually room for innovation, or the development of new courses of action.

The importance of the creative process cannot be under-estimated, because a plan can only be as good as the best of the alternatives considered. Therefore, it is highly rewarding to spend time evolving alternatives. Unfortunately, there is a strong human tendency to stop the search for alternatives as soon as an apparently acceptable course of action is discovered. This is a tendency that planners must guard against.

Examining Alternatives

This step consists of projecting all the outcomes of each alternative course of action evolved above. The outcomes considered should include (1) desirable and undesirable; (2) immediate and long range; (3) tangible and intangible; and (4) certain and only possible.[4]

Clearly, one of the outcomes that must be projected in every case is sales volume and/or profit. In making this projection, errors in both directions are possible. Eldridge[5] discusses the probable consequences of these errors and suggests a solution to the problem.

"If (the marketing manager) overestimates his sales volume and gross profit, and bases his marketing expenditures on that overestimate . . . he is likely to find . . . that profits are running well below the forecast. . . .

"If he underestimates his volume and gross profit, he runs the risk of spending less than the product needs—and thereby . . . makes certain that the results are less than hoped for.

"Nevertheless, it is probably preferable for the marketing manager, when weaving his way perilously between the devil and the deep sea, to err on the side of conservatism in budgeting sales, his marketing expenditures, and his profits. . . .

"For himself, his associates, the advertising agency, and the field sales department, it is wholly desirable that objectives should be set on the high side, in order that the attainment of those objectives shall require 'reaching . . .'."

---

[4] William H. Newman and Charles E. Summer, Jr., *The Process of Management* (Englewood Cliffs, New Jersey: Prentice-Hall, Inc., 1961), p. 302.

[5] Clarence E. Eldridge, "Marketing Plans," in E. R. French (editor), *The Copywriter's Guide* (New York: Harper & Bros., 1958), pp. 3–28, on pp. 24–25.

In other words, Eldridge suggests "keeping two sets of books." The implications of this suggestion will be discussed subsequently.

Comparing and Selecting Alternatives

In this step the planner compares the projected outcomes of the various alternative courses of action. The purpose is to rank the alternatives on the basis of the extent to which they achieve objectives and avoid undesirable results. Then the most desirable alternatives are recommended to management.

This point, after programs are prepared, and before they are reviewed by top management, is suitable for writing down the plans.

On the basis of the argument presented here, the written plan should discuss the following topics, if it is to enable management to evaluate it:

1. Specific objective(s) of the plan.
2. Relationship between the specific objective(s) and the objectives of the firm, or an explanation of the extent to which this plan will advance the higher-level and longer-term objectives of the firm. Quantitative measures should be included, if possible.
3. Other specific objectives considered, and the planner's opinion of the relative values of these specific objectives. This evaluation should also include quantitative measures, if possible.
4. Costs of executing the plan.
5. Forecasts of the firm's environment.
6. Course of action recommended: first, briefly, then in detail.
7. Alternative courses of action and reasons why they were considered inferior to the action recommended.
8. Projected results of the plan, if it is executed.
9. Listing of control standards and procedures to be used for controlling execution of the plan.

Before leaving this discussion of preparation of programs, an important point should be emphasized:

Marketing planning should not be done function by function, as has been the tradition for a long time and still is the practice in many firms. (By "functions" we mean the activities normally performed by a marketing department, such as advertising, personal selling, pricing, marketing research, and product and package development. *Within* these functions are many sub-functions. For example, within personal selling is recruitment, selection, and training of salesmen; assignment of territories; design of compensation systems; sales analysis, and so on. At least 50 functions and sub-functions could easily be listed.)

Marketing planning should be oriented to achieving objectives. Of course, if objectives may be fulfilled entirely within one function, the objective-directed plan will also be "functional." But the approach, even then, will still be from objectives to means rather than from means to objectives.

MANAGEMENT REVIEW

Criteria of reviewing executives may be grouped conveniently as follows: (1) economic, or financial; and (2) subjective.

Economic or financial criteria, such as return on investment, present discounted value of future income, alternative uses of funds, and cut-off rates, are sufficiently well known that they do not require comment here.

Subjective criteria, on the other hand, may require some discussion. Smith[6] has commented on the role of management as follows: "Management may simply accept the goals indicated. . . . More frequently . . . management's reaction will be one expressed by such comment as: 'Surely we can do better than that. . . .' "

In the case of the National Paper Company (a fictitious name for a real firm), during one year, management reduced the recommended marketing expenditures by 23%, *without* reducing the sales volume objective. Other, similar, reviewing actions could be cited. Therefore, it appears that management, in reviewing marketing plans, asks itself: "How much 'fat' does this plan contain?" and answers the question somehow, probably subjectively.

Are such reviewing actions justified? In other words, is it fair to the planner to suspect him of "padding" his plan? We have noted earlier the view that: ". . . when it comes to budgeting (setting sales, profit and marketing expenditure goals), the situation is different (from setting objectives for the advertising agency, the sales force, and the like). The forecasts for financial budgeting should be sufficiently conservative that . . . they are certain to be made. . . ."[7] This commentator appears to be suggesting that the planner should overstate consistently the expenditure needed to achieve the goals of the plan. This appears to recognize that a conflict may exist between the objectives of the planner and those of the firm.

The management literature has emphasized repeatedly that differences exist between the objectives of the employee and those of the employing organization. Therefore, it seems fair to conclude that the planner, in trying to achieve his personal goals of continued employment and approval of his superiors, may undermine organizational objectives such as maximum return on marketing expenditures. Following this, the problem of the reviewing manager would then appear to be not to decide *whether* there is "fat" in the plan, but rather to estimate the percentage.

---

[6] Wendell R. Smith, "A Rational Approach to Marketing Management," in Eugene J. Kelley and William Lazer (eds.), *Managerial Marketing: Perspectives and Viewpoints* (rev. ed.; Homewood, Illinois: Richard D. Irwin, Inc., 1958), p. 154.

[7] Eldridge, same reference as footnote 5.

FORMULATING DERIVATIVE PLANS

Ultimately, at the lowest level in the hierarchy, the result of planning has to be a list of actions, or a program, to be carried out.

For drawing up this program, Newman and Summer[8] suggest six steps:

1. Divide into steps the activities necessary to achieve the objective.
2. Note relations between each of the steps, especially necessary sequences.
3. Decide who is to be responsible for each step.
4. Determine the resources needed for each step.
5. Estimate the time required for each step.
6. Assign definite dates for each part.

In formulating its derivative plans, the Finchley (a fictitious name for a real company) Drug Company, uses the individual plans prepared for each of 50 products. The pertinent information is pulled out of each product plan and reassembled in three derivative plans: (a) detailing (personal selling) schedule, (b) advertising program, and (c) financial summary. These derivative plans are described below:

Detailing Schedule—The Detailing Schedule is structured very much like a calendar. For each month, three products are listed in the order in which they are to be presented to physicians. The schedule serves as a working document for the sales force. As the year passes, 500 copies of each page are made and distributed to Finchley's detail men to be carried out.

Advertising Program—The Advertising Program describes several thousand items of direct mail and journal advertising to be prepared during the course of the year. The items are arranged by month and by day of the month when they are to appear, or to be mailed. As the year progresses, this information is used by technicians and artists in the Advertising Department and the Company's agency to prepare advertisements, buy space and materials, and so on.

Financial Summary—The Financial Summary, unlike the other two documents, is not used by any functional department as a basis for action. Instead, it is essentially a communication and control device. Probably the best way to describe the contents of this document is to list the information presented for *each* actively promoted product:

1. Total market ($).
2. Company's share (%).
3. Company's sales ($).
4. Advertising expenditure ($).
5. Allocated detailing cost ($).

[8] Newman and Summer, same reference as footnote 4.

6. Total marketing cost ($).
7. Marketing cost as a % of sales.
8. Gross profit ($).
9. Gross profit as a % of sales.

This information is presented both for the current year and the following year.

As plans are executed, the Financial Summary is used for comparing actual results with plans, or controlling the execution of the plan. The point is that advertising, sales, and financial plans are derived from objective-directed product marketing plans and *not* prepared independently by the separate functions: Advertising, Sales, and Finance.

DEVELOPING A SYSTEM OF CONTROL

A system of control should (1) establish standards, (2) measure activities and results, (3) compare these measurements to standards, and (4) report variances between measurements and standards.

Control is relevant to planning because control standards have a greater effect in determining actual results than the objectives of the plan. Therefore, it is necessary that the standards which *are* set, reflect very closely the objectives of the plan.

In addition, a system of control informs the planner of the results obtained from execution of his plans. This is helpful because it becomes possible to change plans if they are found to be ineffective either because (1) the cause and effect premise on which they were based turns out to be faulty, or (2) the actual environment is sufficiently different from the forecast environment.

In the first instance, the objectives are still valid, but the method of attaining them needs to be changed. In the second instance, the objective may no longer be appropriate. Therefore, new objectives and strategies may be required, and with them, new courses of action.

ASSIGNING RESPONSIBILITY FOR MARKETING PLANNING

In practice, the management decision of assigning responsibility for marketing planning is the first step performed. In this paper, we have postponed discussion of this topic until the end, because organization of the planning function may depend on the kind of planning to be done. Therefore, it was necessary to describe first the steps in marketing planning.

Writers on the subject of marketing planning organization have described several alternatives:

1. Delegation of planning to functional executives, such as managers of the advertising, sales, pricing, sales promotion, marketing research divisions of the marketing department.

2. Planning done by a planning staff group.
3. Planning done by everyone who has a part to play in marketing the brand, including outside organizations.
4. Planning done by brand, or product managers.

However, criteria are lacking in the literature for selecting the appropriate planning organization.

Leading firms often rely on product, or brand managers for planning, although the practice is not universal, and where such managers are used, their responsibilities are not always the same.

To illustrate this point:

1. At the drug company discussed earlier, product managers plan advertising of two kinds, and personal selling.
2. At the household paper products company, brand managers plan consumer advertising and temporary reductions in price charged to retailers and consumers.
3. The telephone company, on the other hand, does not employ product managers. Instead, planning is assigned to sales and advertising executives, for their individual functions.

Possibly these differences in planning organization can be attributed to differences in the means used for communicating with the market. The telephone company needs to communicate with business market customers (that is, business firms, government agencies, and so on) on an individual basis. The reason is that no two customers (other than the very smallest) are likely to need exactly the same combination of products and services. Therefore, a centrally conceived, uniform approach, used alone, would not be suitable. The household paper products company and the drug company deal with mass markets where the potential profit made from individual customers is small. This rules out the possibility of tailoring a specialized approach to each customer. In addition, the needs and desires of large numbers of potential and actual customers are relatively similar. Therefore, grouping large numbers of customers into a market for a brand is an economical way of approaching the planning problem.

It follows that the "brand" manager is really a *market* manager, the market being the totality of actual and potential consumers of the brand. We may conclude, therefore, that a brand or product manager has a role to play whenever there is an opportunity to use standardized appeals in communicating with numerous customers.

Nevertheless, not all firms require brand managers, even though they may use mass communication media. For example, the Interstate Telephone Company permits all the advertising planning to be done in its advertising department, and delegates the major part of its sales planning to sales executives. The question arises then: what are the key differences that cause such marked differences in planning organization?

The answer that suggests itself is that there are important differences in the marketing objectives of these firms. Two illustrations can be given.

1. At the paper company, two of the important objectives are increase in market share, and product distribution in certain areas. Programming for these objectives requires crossing of functional lines. Therefore there appears to be a need for a special planning executive.

2. At the telephone company the important marketing objectives are: (1) to increase auxiliary equipment and service billings; and (2) to increase location service life of auxiliary equipment. These objectives are interpreted to require that "communications consultants" survey the operations and premises of business market customers. To achieve this, the company tries to persuade customers to avail themselves of the free services of these consultants. Thus, we have three levels of objectives: (a) persuade the customer to invite the communications consultant, in order to (b) have the communications consultant advise the customer, in order to (c) increase billings and service life.

Achieving objectives (a) and (b), the objectives that can be achieved by direct action—(c) obviously cannot—does not require any coordination among functions. Objective (b) is achieved by the Sales Department, and objective (a), by the Advertising Department.

The conclusion is that the planning organization should mirror the hierarchy of objectives: a planning manager is needed wherever there is an objective whose achievement requires coordination of, or selection from among, several functions. In practice, the existing organization may satisfy this requirement, in which case, no new responsibilities need be assigned. However, if existing planning responsibilities do not allow for this type of selection, or coordination, new ones need to be created.

IMPLICATIONS FOR MARKETING MANAGERS

When a new idea or concept is presented to the business world, its *form* often receives more attention than its *substance*. While attempts are made to adopt the new concept, old habits of thought, and procedures, are continued even though they may not be consistent with the new idea.

The central idea of marketing planning is to develop marketing objectives that will lead to attainment of the objectives of the firm, and then to devise programs and controls that will help to achieve these marketing objectives. In deciding to plan its marketing activities, a business firm has to stand ready to scrap its traditional budgeting and functional planning procedures and to re-think and reorganize its marketing. Only those methods and procedures should be retained that fit logically with the pattern of starting with the highest objectives of the firm and refining successive steps of instrumental objectives until courses of action are specified. Any other approach, or procedure, will give inferior results.

Admittedly, it is much easier to go through the five steps outlined in the first few paragraphs, and say that marketing is being planned, than to follow the procedure described in the body of this paper. However, in this instance, as in most, there are no easy short-cuts to the development of good, effective, and profitable plans. Also, there really is no escape from the need to plan conscientiously. Leading companies *are* planning in this way, with obvious financial success. Those who wish to attain similar success will have to apply themselves equally. Successful procedures will not be developed overnight, or even in one year. Most likely, it will take from three to five cycles of planning to establish an effective, smoothly working procedure. However, nothing will be accomplished if a sincere beginning is not made.

C. Marketing Organization and Leadership

The marketing concept must be translated into an organizational structure that provides an operating mechanism for systemic decision making and programmed marketing action. The objective of organizational design is the integration and coordination of people, facilities, and functions in a manner consistent with the marketing concept. Organization is often the weakest link in the marketing structure. Dynamic leadership is required to critically analyze the firm's needs and overcome the barriers of tradition in developing an integrated marketing subsystem.

36. ORGANIZATIONAL IMPLICATIONS OF THE MARKETING CONCEPT*

Anthony E. Cascino†

Modern marketing is both a philosophical and an organizational concept. As a philosophy, the modern marketing concept recognizes that the customer is king; that a business entity's only purpose for existence is to

---

* Reprinted from William Lazer and Eugene J. Kelley, *Managerial Marketing: Perspectives and Viewpoints* (rev. ed.; Homewood, Illinois: Richard D. Irwin, Inc., 1962), pp. 370–78. The decision to adopt the marketing concept requires top management to review corporate policies and practices in order to determine if an emphasis on departmental efficiency has been detrimental to the advancement of overall company interests. See Philip Kotler's "Diagnosing the Marketing Takeover," *Harvard Business Review*, Vol. XLIII, No. 6 (November–December, 1965), pp. 70–72.

† International Minerals and Chemical Corporation.

serve the customer; and that all commercial activity must begin with a determination of the customer's wants and desires and end with a fulfillment of them in a most expeditious and efficient manner.

Inherent in this philosophy is existence of a truly customer-conscious organization embracing all personnel from the lowest operating level to the president. Indelibly imprinted on each employee's mind must be the dictum: "We are forever beholden to the customer."

But a company cannot become customer conscious by edict. Since all organizations tend to emulate their leader, it is most important that the head of the business be thoroughly customer conscious. There can only be one marketing head in any business and that must be the president. He can develop a mood, an atmosphere, and an esprit de corps reflecting the pre-eminence of the customer that permeates every nook and corner of the company.

The best evidence of a truly customer-conscious company is that it is intimately acquainted with the customer's business. A market-oriented company acts and thinks in terms of the final end use of its product, raw materials, parts, or sub-assemblies. For example, the fertilizer business is not just concerned with selling fertilizers, it is involved in growing food. Therefore, it is necessary for fertilizer manufacturers to understand the farmer, in all of his requirements, to be in a better position to serve distributors who must ultimately appeal to farmers for the sale of fertilizer.

While this philosophical view is an essential prerequisite to successful marketing, it must be supplemented by a strong organizational approach. For in addition to being customer conscious and market oriented, a company must also organize and program marketing activities to provide the customer with adequate products and services. This is probably the weakest link in the marketing activities of most companies. Companies may have the will and the desire to serve the customer, but all too often, they are inadequately organized to do so.

Proper organization must result in a total integration and coordination of all of the factors that can influence the final sale. This is the very essence of the modern marketing concept. If advertising, direct selling, merchandising, transportation, publicity, and the other sales influences are treated as separate entities, and are autonomously executed, their respective contributions are fairly well vitiated. When they are integrated into a completely coordinated communications program, the total impact is greatly compounded.

For example, International Minerals & Chemicals (IMC) recently conducted a readership survey of an advertising campaign that had been directed to industrial customers. It was a good campaign and the readership score was expected to show up quite favorably. IMC was not prepared for the overwhelming results that this study disclosed. One hundred per cent of the respondents said they remembered the advertising, 80%

said they had actually read it, and the customers did an excellent job of playing back the message.

This is phenomenal and unheard of in the annals of advertising research. IMC does not get 80% readership of advertising, and would be foolish to expect such a high figure. What happened then? It is felt that the results stem from a sales effort that was effectively coordinated. The advertising message was the identical message being told by IMC salesmen. It was the same message being promoted through sales tools and merchandising. It was the exact message contained in advertising specialties (giveaways, direct mail, and displays). A whole host of influences were delivering the same message to the customer at the same time. Although the customer attributed his awareness of the message to advertising, it was the combination of many media working together in complete harmony that led to the surprising results.

Integration, to be effective, must be an inviolate practice in the execution of each major activity in the marketing program. As an example, about a year ago, IMC decided to acquaint customers (fertilizer manufacturers) with the transportation services offered. These services included custom tailored routes, economical combinations of various types of carriers, expeditious settlement of freight claims, advice and counsel in rate petitions before official bodies, and improved warehousing and materials handling activity. This activity is an important part of an overall marketing approach when products are low-cost, bulk commodities, and the cost of transportation often exceeds the cost of the product. The customer needs and appreciates assistance in reducing his landed cost. Any supplier who can fulfill this need, gains a strong competitive advantage.

Eight weeks were set aside for this campaign, and nine members of the Transportation Department were assigned to various sales territories. They travelled with individual salesmen and explained the full transportation service program to the customer. The Public Relations Department placed stories about this campaign in the trade press. Direct mail was sent to the customer in advance of the personal contact by the salesman and the transportation expert. Advertisements appeared in all trade books telling the same story of the wealth of transportation services which were available to the customer.

To help the salesmen and the transportation expert tell the story directly to the customer a colored sound-slide film was produced. The film was shown to the customer in his place of business through the use of a portable projector. At the conclusion of the visit, the customer was presented with a brochure which again repeated the transportation story.

The benefits of this completely integrated approach were manifold. Strong ties developed between the transportation department and the sales force. Also, the transportation people established a "first-name" relationship with the customer; they became as well known as the salesman who covered the territory. The communications cycle had been closed. On the one hand, the transportation people became intimately acquainted with the customers' transportation problems; on the other, the customers fully recognized, understood, and appreciated the IMC transportation service program. A favorable image was successfully established in a vital area.

While the concept of integration and coordination is not a profound one, in practice the integration of marketing activities is frequently lacking. One reason is that it is most difficult to put into practice and execute. Integration means a breakdown of the autonomous power of advertising managers, sales managers, and all others who communicate with the customer. Integration means a thorough and complete program of forward planning, regimentation, and discipline, and an ever aggressive follow-through.

While there are various methods for effecting integration, certain activities have universal application. They are:

1. Hold "planning sessions" to make a position audit, determine future objectives, and resolve marketing strategy. This requires that all participants in the total marketing effort be brought together, including agencies and other outside service and production sources. It demands that inhibitions and zealously held prerogatives be overcome by allowing each discipline to contribute to the formation of the marketing strategy covering all areas from training to top-level selling. In this way, each knows what the other is doing, each recognizes the place and importance of his respective responsibility, and each fully understands and appreciates the basic strategy and the objectives to be attained.

2. Establish a market calendar. The calendar facilitates putting everything on paper and in chronological order. It means spelling out each activity, when it will take place, and the procedure by which all elements will be synchronized to bear on the customer in a consistent and persistent manner. Control is paramount if integration is to be accomplished, and this calendar alerts everyone as to his obligations and deadlines.

3. Fully acquaint the field sales force. The sales force must become the hub around which all other corollary activities revolve. If such a meeting is expertly handled sufficiently in advance of the effective date of the marketing program, the salesman becomes a strong proponent and staunch supporter of that program. Such a meeting can give the sales team a complete perspective of the year's program—before its release to the trade. Being "in the know" is flattering, and the salesmen will assume a new marketing posture. No longer will they question the ability of the home office, doubt the value of the written message, and feel that they have been deserted. A field force's constant complaint is that it does not know what is going on at the home office. Nothing is more embarrassing to a salesman than being forced to display ignorance to the customer.

It is not enough that a sales meeting impart information; it must also provide inspiration and enthusiasm. Even the most revolutionary marketing approach will suffer if it lacks emotion and empathy. Salesmen need excitement and stimulation, and a sales meeting should provide the atmosphere through which these characteristics can be generated.

A successful marketing program must assume the profile of a human being so that it can command and capture the affection and loyalty of the sales force. For this reason, every good marketing program must have a name that has vitality and intrigue, an identity all of its own, and once the program has effectively invaded the heart and mind of the salesman it will become his exclusive property to support to the utmost. Despite the belief that a marketing program should produce a high degree of camaraderie and esprit de corps, a word of caution should be advanced. This emotional build-up must be superimposed upon a program of substance. Emotions will subside, and when they do, the salesman must recognize a plan that is credible and effective.

Experience is inadequate in the creation of a marketing program. Unfortunately, too many companies rely solely on the knowledge gained in a supplier-customer relation to guide them in their selling strategy. Management must not trust to intuition and hunch in determining the factors that will motivate customers to buy. The fact of the matter is that a supplier seldom really knows the deep-seated and hidden motives of his customers. Since conflicting interests exist between buyer and seller, honest, frank, and uninhibited conversations rarely occur. A marketing program that is based upon "what we have been told by our customer," runs the serious risk of being misdirected.

Since a buyer will never fully unburden himself to a seller it is often necessary to turn to a third party to probe the customer's mind. Independent research organizations tackle marketing problems skillfully, professionally, anonymously, and hopefully, without bias. Such information is the basis for good sales programs.

It is axiomatic that the best sales story is to little avail if it is diluted as it is transmitted from the home office, to the sales manager, to the regional manager, to the field salesman, and finally, to the customer. Therefore, not only is there a need to create an effective sales message, but also, to develop sales aids to assure effective delivery to the customer.

Two guides should be recognized in the development of sales tools. First of all, if they are to be effective, sales tools must be varied, kept fresh, provocative, and stimulating. After a salesman has used a given sales tool several dozen times, it becomes dull, boring and shopworn. Secondly, and equally important, sales tools should be of the type that help educate and train the salesman. In the act of delivering the sales message, the salesman should become more knowledgeable about the product and/or service, more adept at describing it in a convincing manner. Sales tools are image-building devices.

In addition to providing a completely integrated marketing blueprint that contains both substance and life, the marketing program must also build men. A well-rounded marketing program should include ways and means for the salesman to be exposed to the customer in a most favorable light. Opportunities should be created for the salesman to participate in industry conventions, or to conduct customer meetings. But the salesman must be thoroughly schooled and rehearsed in not only what to say but how to say it. He should be supported with charts, films, easels, anything that will make his presentation more professional, more dramatic. Once a salesman stands up before a customer group, and delivers an important message in a skillful and professional manner, he takes on the stature of an executive. Instead of being an order taker, he becomes a personal confidant to the customer on many phases of his business.

This is a large order: a marketing organization and program that embraces adequate research, factual findings, emotional appeals, dramatic sales meetings, complete integration and coordination of all marketing activities, professional and cultural upgrading of the salesman, and varied and stimulating sales tools. Yet more has to be done to achieve effective organization and use of marketing resources.

So far, this paper has concerned itself solely with the integration of those factors which are involved in the movement of ownership—including direct selling, advertising, and promotion, merchandising, and publicity. But marketing also embraces the activities involved in the movement of goods, consisting of inventory control, warehouse locations and operations, delivery, order processing, and material handling. These are marketing activities. They are an integral part of the overall marketing process.

At IMC, physical distribution is a part of the Marketing Division. That is where it will remain because it is a vital and pivotal activity in gaining the order and making the sale. In physical distribution, the need for integration is urgent in order to stem the tide of ever increasing costs of distribution.

Physical distribution is a major expense factor, representing the third largest cost of doing business, amounting to $100 billion a year. These expenditures are more than twice the net profits of all American corporations combined, and they are three times as much as will be spent in 1962 for modernizing and building plants and facilities.

Although physical distribution is a sizable and important part of the profit and loss statement this area has been seriously neglected. One expert says that "only 15% of the possible economies of physical distribution are now being realized."[1] Another calls it "the last frontier of industrial waste and inefficiency."[2] Unless the administration of physical distribution is pursued with the same coordinate approach now being directed toward the promotional aspects of marketing the already deplorable conditions will only further deteriorate under the pressure of ever-increasing transportation costs.

---

[1] "Distribution's New Trends: How Will They Change Markets?" *Salesweek* (May 2, 1960), p. 12.

[2] *Ibid.*, p. 13.

Transportation costs, in some instances, make up a third or more of the total costs of physical distribution. During the last decade, railroad costs have increased by 41%; trucking costs by 45%; and water transportation has gone up 33%.[3] We cannot expect the carriers to solve the shippers' problems. The financial plight confronting most railroads militates against any action that would tend to further reduce their revenues.

This is a rather sweeping indictment of all who have a responsibility in the physical movement of the product. It is recognized, however, that important contributions have been made within certain specific, but isolated, areas. Companies and industries have introduced product and packaging innovations which achieve efficiencies and economies of physical distribution. Linear programming models, computers, and electronic equipment for processing data have also been exploited to determine ideal locations for plants and warehouses, to select the most economical routes to the customer, and to expedite the handling of materials and documents. Even the carriers, despite their fiscal problems, have designed new equipment and improved old equipment to increase capacity, reduce handling, and inject flexibility in combining various forms and types of products.

Nevertheless, despite these advancements by both shippers and carriers, the criticism that the field of physical distribution is "the last frontier of industrial waste and inefficiencies" is still valid and proper.[4] While all of the accomplishments are most commendable, they are based upon a foundation of sand, and much of their potential economies and efficiencies are dissipated through improper organization and control.

The real and comprehensive solution to efficiency and the elimination of waste lies in a progressive and intelligent administration and manage-

---

[3] For rail increases, Interstate Commerce Commission General Freight Rate Increases Proceedings, *Ex Parte* 175, *Ex Parte* 196, *Ex Parte* 206-A, *Ex Parte* 212.

For truck increases, Central States Motor Freight Bureau, Rate Increases, Tariff 220-C:

Date	*Increase*
12–12–51	General—10%
5– 6–52	Surcharge—$1.50
4– 7–54	General—10%
4–15–55	Surcharge—$1.50 cancelled
5– 1–56	General—7%
6–20–57	General—6%—Interim
3–21–57	General—7%
9–30–58	Commodity—5%
6– 1–60	Surcharge—(10¢ LTL) (2¢ TL)

For water transportation increases, American Waterways Operators Association, Interstate Commerce Commission Freight Rate Increases Proceedings, *Ex Parte* 175, *Ex Parte* 196.

Wesley Rogers' Increase Tariffs, *Ex Parte* 1, *Ex Parte* 1A.

[4] *Salesweek, op. cit.*, p. 13.

ment of the several interrelated functions. Physical distribution will never reach the level of proficiency, achieved by other areas of the business, until every function is regimented into a system that is integrated and coordinated. The activities of inventory control, transportation and traffic, warehouse operations, order processing, customer service, materials handling, and special packing are inseparable and interrelated. When they are administered as separate and distinct functions, the economies effected in one area tend to be lost as they become a part of a disjointed system with nebulous and perhaps even conflicting objectives.

Yet, in most companies, the functions of physical distribution are divided in an illogical, non-workable manner between manufacturing and sales. Frequently, this arrangement is not conducive to coordination. Fragments of the total effort are usually assigned to executives of equal status who use their respective portions to foster their own vested and primary interests. Thereby they vitiate the opportunity to establish a smooth running, harmonious, and integrated system of physical distribution. Even worse, some of the important functions are as one observer states, "left to fall between the chairs," creating gray areas that are devoid of purpose and organization.[5] Unless the various functions of physical distribution are forced into a regimented and disciplined whole the ultimate in economy and efficiency will never be accomplished.

Marketing managers must recognize that physical distribution is a single, integrated, and coordinated whole; that it is a major activity within the corporate framework; and finally, that all of the activities must be subjected to the unified authority of one person, the director of distribution. The corollary benefits to this approach are manifold. First, these activities are entrusted to professional hands on a full-time basis. Second, the responsibility for decision and action are concentrated in one identifiable person eliminating the need for mass meetings dominated by divergent and discordant views. Third, it relieves sales and manufacturing personnel of extracurricular activities so that they can devote full energies to their primary obligations. Fourth, it provides an objective and neutral intermediary between the sales department's demands for unrestrained customer service on one hand, and the manufacturing department's overly concern for the cost of service on the other. Fifth, for companies with autonomous divisions, line control may remain with the division while functional direction is under the corporate distribution director. Through this structure coordination is realized, not only between manufacturing and sales of a given division, but also, and most importantly, there is sound integration among the several divisions.

---

[5] American Management Association Report No. 49, *Management of the Physical-Distribution Function*, 1960, "Organizing for Effective Physical-Distribution Management—How to Eliminate the 'Gray Areas' between Manufacturing and Sales" by Philip E. Cannon, vice president, Barrington Associates, Inc., New York, N.Y., p. 15.

The mere thought of creating a centralized distribution group will bring a cold sweat in certain quarters. The old allegations promiscuously hurled about during the integration of the promotional functions of marketing will be restated with even greater apprehension. Again, marketing managers will be accused as "empire builders" and "self-seekers." However, the dissenters should recognize that the successful, progressive, forward-thinking companies have already embarked upon this intelligent course. Through sound organization they enjoy the fruits of efficiency, service, and economy. Anyone who has any responsibility for developing and implementing marketing programs should do all in his power to provide the forceful and courageous leadership necessary to break down the barriers of tradition and to develop well designed, integrated and coordinated programs of marketing action.

Exchange is a process of interactions. The central concern of marketing is the interaction process between the organization and its environment. The term "ecosystem" is used to describe an organization functionally linked to its environment through a pattern of dynamic interactions. A model of a transacting ecosystem is presented to aid in the development of a total marketing system.

37. MARKETING ORGANIZATION: AN ECOLOGICAL VIEW*

Hans Thorelli†

Every biological organism, human being and organization is dependent on its *environment* for survival. No one is self-sufficient. To obtain necessary sustenance from the environment we all must have something to offer it in exchange. Neither nature nor human civilization is in the end an eleemosynary institution. Conceptually, universal dependence on exchange means that every person, plant or organization (be it a boy scout troop, a government agency or a private firm) is really engaged in marketing.

Exchange is often thought of as a simple swap of "tit for tat," just as

* Not previously published.

† University of Indiana.

many people tend to think of decision-making simply as the flick of a switch in the mind of an executive.[1] To the student of marketing, however, it must be clear that exchange in this narrow sense is the result of a *process of interaction* between the organization and its environment. Indeed, this process of interaction and its determinants is the central concern of our discipline.

The interdependence of organism and environment stems from the incessant drive towards specialization, or division of labor, or nichemanship, as the prime means of survival in a world characterized by an all prevailing relative scarcity of resources. In the plant and animal world, this specialization is brought about by the glacial interplay of forces resulting in the survival of the fittest. In industrialized societies humanity achieves division of labor primarily through organizations. Organizations whose output is economic utilities are called firms. It is important to emphasize that firms represent a species of organization. Progress in understanding the firm and its behavior is linked intimately with progress in the general area of organization theory.

ECOLOGY CUTS ACROSS THE DISCIPLINES

An emerging vital strain of thought is aimed directly at linking organization theory and theories of markets and marketing. This development—heralded by some of the writings of John R. Commons, Kurt Lewin, Wroe Alderson and others—involves the application of the concepts and viewpoint of ecology. The term ecology originates with that branch of biology which deals with the mutual relations among organisms (or populations of plants or animals) and, especially, between organisms (or populations) and their environment. While the prime attention in biology[2] as well as in the more recent field of "human ecology"[3] generally has been on spatial, demographic and physical aspects of the environment, there is an unmistakable tendency to broaden the concept to apply to the interrelations of an organism with its *total* setting. It is in this latter sense the notion will be used here.

Traditionally, the focal points of inquiry in biological ecology have been succession and evolution and the laws of survival and extinction. Adaptation tends to be viewed mainly as a one-way proposition: the organism which can adapt to a changing environment will survive. Adap-

[1] We may observe in passing that both of these notions are part and parcel of the classical economic theory of the firm.

[2] Sample references: W. B. McDougall, *Plant Ecology* (Philadelphia: Lea & Febiga, 1931); W. C. Allee, A. E. Emerson, O. and T. Park, K. Schmidt, *Principles of Animal Ecology* (Philadelphia: Saunders, 1949).

[3] Sample references: A. H. Hawley, *Human Ecology; A Theory of Community Structure* (New York: Ronald, 1950); O. D. Duncan, "Human Ecology and Population Studies," in P. M. Hauser and O. D. Duncan, eds., *The Study of Population: An Inventory and Appraisal* (Chicago: University of Chicago Press, 1959), pp. 678–716.

tation also tends to be viewed as an objective, largely non-conscious process.

While research on human organization may derive considerable inspiration from plant and animal ecology there are important distinctions to be made. Humans have long-term objectives, and they have a certain amount of foresight (as well as hindsight). They can plan for and administer change. Man and the organizations he creates are to a certain extent the masters of their own destiny. To some degree we may shape our own environment, and are not merely shaped by it. This is most clearly evident in the case of such powerful entities as national governments or large corporations, but it is actually characteristic of all human organizations.

The fact that in the environment of human organization constraints are less immediate, the range of discretion is greater, and the alternative means to reach given ends are more numerous is of tremendous significance. It provides the explanation for two vital phenomena, largely neglected in economic and sociological theory. The first is the emergence of a multiple goal structure in every organization once its immediate survival seems assured. The second is the viable coexistence of different organization structures and strategies of interaction in the same general environment.

THE UBIQUITOUS ENVIRONMENT

A constellation of an organization, or several organizations, functionally linked to its (their) environment through a pattern of dynamic interaction may be labeled an ecosystem. At least if the organization is a business firm the principal manifestation of this interaction is found in the *transactions* taking place. Fig. 1 represents a model of a transacting ecosystem at what is admittedly a very high level of abstraction.

To simplify the representation of interaction between the organization and its environment they are depicted as being entirely distinct. Actually, the organization is totally immersed in the environment, and it is frequently difficult to distinguish the borderlines between them. This is why any "black box" concept of organization is so artificial.

FIGURE 1

Model of Transacting Ecosystem

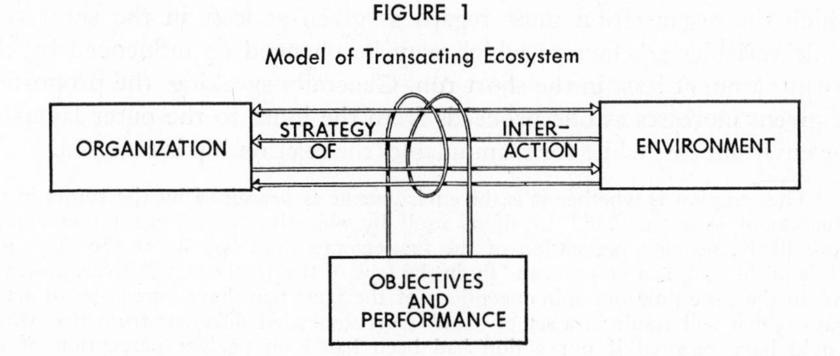

Since little would be gained by studying the entire universe in order to understand the operations of any given organization (for example, a corner drugstore), it is clear that we are also faced with the problem of defining the *relevant* environment. For the time being it may be sufficient to say that the sum of all the factors and phenomena which may affect an organization, or which may be affected by the organization, constitutes the relevant environment.[4]

An action system based on four interdependent sets of variables is envisaged. A sample of variables in each category might include:

Organization	*Interaction Strategy*	*Environment*	*Objectives and Resultant Performance Criteria*
Size	Product	Size	Survival
Centralization	Promotion	Geographical dispersion	Growth
Integration	Place	Competition	Profitability
Structuring by area, product, function, clients	Price	Diversity of customers	Sales volume
		Stage in growth cycle	Customer satisfaction
			Productivity

It is frequently useful to speak of three different environmental layers. The first might be labeled intra-organizational. It is relevant whenever a semi-autonomous part of a broader organization is studied. A highly relevant sector of the total environment surrounding the Chevrolet Division, for example, is all the other divisions of GM as well as the corporate headquarters of the concern. The second layer is represented by what we might call the *task environment*, i.e., generally the market in which the principal offering (cars of a certain price, performance, quality, prestige, etc.) of the organization is exchanged for the customer dollars on which the survival of the organization directly depends. The third layer includes such factors as the general social, economic, political and technological climate in which the organization finds itself operating.

From the viewpoint of interaction between the organization and its habitat it is pertinent to observe that the factors encountered at each layer of the environment may be divided into parameters and variables. While there is no hard and fast borderline, parameters may be viewed as factors which the organization must regard as given at least in the short run, while variables are factors which may be changed or influenced by the organization, at least in the short run. Generally speaking, the proportion of givens increases as one proceeds from the inner to the outer layers of the environment, while for manipulables the relationship is reversed.

[4] The question is whether it is the environment as *perceived* by the actors in the situation or as it "actually" manifests itself by objective measurement that counts. Most likely, people's perception of the facts counts most heavily in the short run, while in the long run no one can "fly in the face of the (real) facts." Note, however, that in the meantime our misconceptions of the facts may have caused us to act in ways which will result in a set of "real" facts somewhat different from that which would have resulted if our action had been based on perfect perception of the environment and our own situation in it.

The set of factors labeled Objectives and Performance have been placed in an intermediary, inductive-deductive position between the organization and the environment. This stems from the hypothesis that the objectives of an organization must be meshed with those of relevant groups in its environment. Organization leaders may think their objectives are new and unique. Nevertheless, if they are not in tune with the environment they will either have to be modified or the organization is doomed. Objectives yield performance criteria. If performance is not up to par objectives are again likely to be revised, as is suggested by psycho-sociological theories about aspiration levels and their revision.

EFFECTS IN SEARCH OF CAUSES

Managerial decision-making as well as scientific inquiry presupposes the existence of at least one independent variable, the action of which affects at least one dependent variable. Even the schematic model of an ecosystem presented earlier is quite powerful as a generator of hypotheses. For example, relating environment to organization we might postulate that increased geographical dispersion is associated with decreased centralization, and that the later stages of the market growth curve tend to be associated with a high degree of integration. Or, relating environment to strategy, we might assume that the greater the diversity of customers, the greater the degree of product differentiation.

To complicate matters, we must assume mutual interaction between all four sets of variables with a cacophony of causal arrows bringing to mind Moussorgski's *A Night on Bald Mountain*. The problem of intervening variables is, however, far from new, and improved techniques of handling this difficulty are being developed in the areas of statistics and experimental design. The direction of causal arrows, whenever they happen to be one-way, can frequently be traced by analysis over time.

A further complication stems from interaction *within* each set of variables. Within organizations, for example, it is often held that size and centralization are inversely related. Among objectives, profitability and sales volume often evidence high collinearity. Looking at the strategy variables, marketing men are apt to emphasize the gestalt effect: any marketing strategy worth its salt is something more than a marketing mix; that is, it represents a whole that is greater than an odd conglomerate of so many parts of product, price, and promotion. To some extent the problem may be alleviated by factor analysis, but in the long run it will be handled more effectively once we are able to classify strategies more meaningfully than at present. Until then, there is nothing wrong with studying the effects of individual variables, such as price or advertising, and combinations thereof. Plant ecologists frequently study the effects of climate and soil conditions, taken separately, on plant populations, even though it is clear that there is considerable interaction among climate and soil variables themselves.

MERITS OF ECOLOGICS

The simplified model displayed in Fig. 1 may be extended (or contracted) in various ways. It is not difficult, for instance, to nominate twice as many variables signifying dimensions of organization, interaction strategies, and environments, although there is little reason to believe that a great many more are needed for adequate explanation. (On the other hand, no claim is made that the sample of variables given here includes all the most important ones). The model may also be focused on what Alderson used to call market behavior systems, comprising the entire chain of inter-linked organizations from primary producer to consumer, and the relations between parallel systems. Biologists have made observations concerning food chains and dominant species in plant and animal communities, insights which may prove quite helpful in applying ecological approaches to manufacturer-distributor interaction in channel systems.

A major advantage of eco-models is that they generally lend themselves fairly well to operationalization, that is, to empirical testing. It is true that there are no self-evident or universally accepted measures for almost any of the variables which we have listed by way of example. But for most of them, operational substitutes have been used in many studies which were not ecological in character. Organization theory has several useful measures of "size" and "centralization," economics, "price" (listed, quoted, actual, with and without discount, etc.) and "productivity." Geographers and location theorists have widely used measures of spatial dispersion.

The relative ease with which eco-models lend themselves to operationalization sets them apart from some otherwise intriguing models about the behavior of firms and markets, such as the attempts to explain such behavior as a manifestation of the interplay of interest groups[5] or in terms of Galbraith's countervailing powers. The prime advantage of eco-models in relation to Operations Research type models is that the former are less ephemeral, less focused on the short term and less casuistic than the latter. In relation to classical economic theories of the firm and competition, eco-models would seem to offer quite a set of major advantages:

1) recognition of the idea of multiple goals, and the related notion of the niche, i.e., the "market within a market";
2) recognition of the entire arsenal of marketing strategy variables;
3) recognition of relevant aspects of the environment generally neglected by these economic theories (spatial aspects, differential customer characteristics, market life cycle notions, and so on);
4) recognition of the fact that competition and cooperation are really two different dimensions rather than simply opposite poles on a continuum of interaction;

---

[5] H. B. Thorelli, "The Political Economy of the Firm: Basis for a New Theory of Competition?" 101 *Schweizerische Zeitschrift für Volkswirtschaft und Statistik* (1965:3), pp. 248–62. Also published in Graduate School of Business, Indiana University, *Reprint Series,* No. 15.

5) recognition of the vital role of structural and functional variables *inside* the organization in conditioning (and being conditioned by) objectives, interactive strategies and the environment itself.

Ecological approaches have already proved to be useful in marketing as well as organization theory.[6] There is every reason to believe that these pioneering efforts will be followed by a tidal wave of intellectual endeavor in the near future, to the benefit of theory and practice alike.

The relationship between a marketing orientation and emerging patterns of organization and administration in industry are discussed. The characteristics of two models of organization—production-oriented and market-oriented—are described and evaluated.

38. MARKETING ORIENTATION AND EMERGING PATTERNS OF MANAGEMENT AND ORGANIZATION*

David G. Moore†

I. INTRODUCTION

The analysis of the Sears, Roebuck organization was based primarily on a conceptual frame of reference provided by social anthropology. It might, therefore, be useful to review briefly certain social anthropological concepts, since these will enter into our discussion later on. The point of view of the social anthropologist is drawn from his studies of primitive,

[6] Cf., e.g., W. R. Dill, "Environment as an Influence on Managerial Autonomy," Administrative Science Quarterly (1957–58), pp. 409–43; and J. F. Kane, *Marketing Strategy and the Environment—An Ecological Study of the Adaptive Behavior of Marketing Agencies in a Small Retail Service Station Market,* D.B.A. thesis, Microfilm HF17, Washington University, 1964. The present author has made use of eco-models in field research on the General Electric industrial sales organization and on Sears, Roebuck operations in Latin America, studies to be accounted for elsewhere.

* Reprinted from William Lazer and Eugene J. Kelley, *Managerial Marketing: Perspectives and Viewpoints* (rev. ed. Homewood, Ill.: Richard D. Irwin, Inc., 1962), pp. 351–56.

† Cornell University.

relatively self-contained societies. It is not surprising, therefore, to find him viewing social organization as an interdependent, functionally interrelated system. In traditional homogeneous societies, there is a manifest organic unity which cannot be denied. The technology merges into the social organization, which in turn is sanctioned by the religious and philosophic system. Each element of the society is bound together with every other element in intimate relationship. No single element can be understood separate from the others. Thus, the social anthropologist tends to concentrate his attention on functional interdependency and to view society as a kind of living system which maintains a certain equilibrium or balance among its many and diverse segments.

Now, while this rather organismic view of society is not as appropriate to the discordant, complex, dynamic confusion which we call modern civilization, as it is to small, homogeneous, primitive social systems, it is extremely useful in analyzing industrial organizations. Here we find functional interdependency more or less imposed by management in its quest for coordination, efficiency, and control. There is an underlying logic to industrial organization growing out of management's conscious efforts to gear the various functions to the overall strategic aims of the enterprise. Thus, we find organizations evolving in systematic ways as management attempts to relate one function to another and cope with new problems as they arise. We find the typical industrial organization held together by an intricate syllogistic pattern in which there are certain major premises or strategic ideas from which a whole series of minor premises are deducted in an orderly and predictable fashion.

The social anthropologist also views society as having a structure consisting of various positions. In primitive, traditional societies, each position requires of the individuals in it particular ways of behaving which can be readily identified.

Again we find this way of looking at social systems useful in analyzing industrial organizations. From the standpoint of structure, a company can be viewed as a collection of occupations representing various technologies and points of view. However, there is more to it than this. An occupation is more than a job; it is to the individual in it a way of life with which he identifies. It provides more than a particular set of skills; it also provides a set of interests, a sense of purpose, a philosophy, a reason for being. Why this is so we won't take time to develop here except to state that our society provides few other possibilities for personal identification. Ours is a work-oriented society and the job that we perform is not only the way we are known to others but the way we know ourselves.

Within the industrial organization, particularly at the level of management but at other levels as well, the various occupational values and points of view are in constant contention. Indeed, the politics of business are intimately bound up with occupational values. Each functional group strives to realize its own interests and thereby comes into collision with other interests. These conflicts are resolved in various ways usually by the dominance of particular functional groups so that the values and points of view of these groups become the major propositions to which the values of contending groups must be reconciled and subordinated. Thus, the personnel director subordinates his basic humanistic interests to the tangible, concrete cost and efficiency interests of the manufacturing executive.

The dynamics of organization emerge primarily out of the flux and flow of internal politics and power struggles. But external influences have much to do with who gains power and why. Economic conditions, cultural values, and social trends all play their part but the more personal factors of politics are important too.

II. EMERGING ORGANIZATIONAL PATTERNS

During the past ten years, we have witnessed important shifts in the basic patterns of organization and administration in American industry. These shifts have been related primarily to a trend toward managerial decentralization. Various arguments have been offered for this trend. Industry has grown large; it is impossible to administer large, sprawling, geographically dispersed organizations. Decentralization is the latest administrative fad which management has picked up from style leaders like General Motors, General Electric, and General Wood. Decentralization is an effort to introduce democratic principles into industry, or it is a result of the "insidious" influence of the purveyors of group dynamics, ego-involvement, and participative techniques.

Describing these shifts in organization patterns in terms of managerial decentralization, however, is in my opinion too simple an explanation. There is considerably more to it than that. In order to illustrate my point, I shall describe two models of organization. The first represents what, for the moment, I shall designate the old model. The essential characteristics of this model are as follows:

1. *Concern with System and Internal Process.* This is the major premise on which the old model is built. There is a constant and abiding concern with internal system and process. In a sense this concern appears to be a reflection of the Protestant Ethic which holds, among other things, that, if the internalized character of a man is in balance, then the external world and his adjustment to it will take care of itself. Thus, we find in the "old" model an interest in developing neat, logical, efficient work systems and procedures. The ideal is the machine, an interacting system in which all of the parts work together in the intricate choreography of a well-oiled, well-designed mechanism.

2. *Inexorable Logic of the System.* It is assumed that there is one, and only one, best way to get a job done. This "one best way" is to be sought principally at the tangible level of time-motion economy, although other elements may enter in. Building an organization represents a gradual, but

consistent unfolding of the fundamental and inexorable logic of the "one best system."

3. *Primacy of the System.* Since the system is held to represent the one best way of getting the job done, then it is imperative that it be followed exactly and that no deviations be permitted. Cooperation and coordination of human effort is built into the system so that, if each individual performs his part of the total task as it is supposed to be performed, then the total effort will be harmonious, efficient, and unified. The system as a means of insuring coordination and cooperation is thus imposed on the work force. Indeed, one of the principal tools of management becomes that of policing the work force at the various levels to insure that the system is being followed.

4. *Centralization of Authority.* The primacy of the system tends to centralize authority. The system cannot be changed indiscriminately but must be adjusted carefully and in accordance with so-called principles of logic and science. Control and design of the system become management's main tasks. There can be only one system and this must be guaranteed through the highest authority of management.

5. *Multiple Layers of Supervision.* With the need for close control, there is also the need for many layers of supervision, each level breathing down the necks of the next lower level. There is also a demand for detailed reports and information about each step in the work process. Constant control is exercised. Problems of coordination are typically solved by the addition of more supervision and/or a more intricate system of work. In other words, the answer to the problem of coordination is either more supervision and control or more system.

6. *Specialization.* The so-called "old" pattern of organization places a heavy emphasis on specialization. Employees at all levels are pegged in either square or round holes and cannot be shifted about. The emphasis is on functional skill rather than the whole man.

7. *The Subordination of Human Values to the Machine.* The system is a machine involving human and mechanical production units which merge together and are hardly distinguishable. Expressions of purely human sentiments and needs are regarded almost as sinful. Basically the machine is more moral than the human being. Employees and customers alike are subordinated to the great machine. The customer is supposed to take what the machine turns out. His sentimental, aesthetic, and purely social needs are regarded as capricious, willy-nilly, and irrational. If the sales force can't sell what the machine turns out, then there's something wrong with the sales force, not with the product.

8. *Concern with the Job Within the System Rather than Over-All Results.* Following the system oftentimes becomes more important than overall results to management and employees alike. There is a tendency to become lost in the system and to forget what the system was set

up to accomplish. The system becomes an end in itself rather than a means to an end.

There are a number of other characteristics of this older pattern of management and organization which can be described. For example, the heavy emphasis on standardization, the notion of narrow span of control, the utilization of human relations findings primarily in a manipulative sense, the primacy of the line organization and vertical authority, and so on. However, most of these additional characteristics can be deduced from the elements already described.

Another mode of management and organization has been emerging, as we have indicated, over the past decade. This pattern by no means completely supplants the older model but has somewhat different emphases. It is perhaps best represented by such organizations as Sears and the Kroger Company. The characteristics of this newer pattern are as follows:

1. *Concern with External Ends.* If the older model is concerned with internal processes, the newer model concentrates far more on the problems of external adjustment. The business is viewed basically as a problem of relationship among various claimant groups with varying interests which must be integrated and reintegrated in a dynamic, changing world. Attention is concentrated on this external reality.

2. *Subordination of System to Overall Results.* The system of work is regarded simply as a means to an end and is not deified as it is in the older pattern. There is rather an experimental attitude toward administrative and organizational practices. There is a willingness to accept diverse and often discordant modes of operation so long as results are achieved. The organization is viewed as an *ad hoc* arrangement which can always be adjusted and changed if need be. There is nothing sacred about it; it is fluid and dynamic.

3. *Decentralization.* The newer mode of management tends to be more decentralized with broader spans of control and fewer layers of supervision since a police force does not have to be maintained to insure that the system is being followed. More than this, there is the acceptance of the idea of decentralized decision-making. The conviction develops that those closest to the scene of action can make certain kinds of decisions which are more appropriate and valid than higher levels of authority.

4. *Overlapping Job Duties and Responsibilities.* The newer model of organization is sloppy by older standards. There is frequently a considerable overlapping of job responsibilities and less of a tendency for employees, particularly at executive levels, to stay put in the organization. There is a willingness and acceptance of the idea of stepping across job lines to get the overall task accomplished.

5. *Reliance on Men Rather than Systems.* As General Wood has said,

"While systems are important, we must place our main reliance in men." The emphasis is on the whole man, his motivation, character, personality, general knowledge, and intelligence rather than on his special skills and technical know-how. It is assumed that most of the technical knowledge required in a business organization can be readily learned by men of the "right" type. The notion of interchangeable executives thus becomes a dominant precept.

Again, a number of additional characteristics can be deduced from the foregoing, but the major elements are clear and sufficient for our purposes.

III. MARKET-ORIENTED MANAGEMENT

It seems fairly obvious that what we have been describing here is not simply the difference between centralized and decentralized management. It is, rather, a difference between a production-oriented and market-oriented management. The dominant values in industry have shifted from those of the manufacturing executive to those of the marketing executive. It is the manufacturing executive or the engineer, who is concerned with system, who models his organization after the machine, who gets excited about input, output, and feedback, who strives to eliminate human sentiments and values from the work and market place, who strives to develop the one and only system, and who places a premium on standardization. It is the marketing manager who looks out into the external world and views the changing, shifting needs of the market, the relativity of business objectives, the need for flexibility, the importance of constant adjustment, etc. These shifts in organization patterns would appear to represent a shift in occupational dominance and a reintegration of industry in terms of marketing values.

Obviously, the new marketing externally-oriented emphasis is not applied uniformly throughout industry. It is not by chance that the purest examples of the newer model are both merchandising organizations. However, bits and pieces of the externally-directed theme are found everywhere—for example, the emphasis on general executive skills, the decentralization fad, the tremendous proliferation of staff functions and horizontal authority, the increasing emphasis on style, and the shift from the engineer to the industrial designer. An external orientation, while it frees business from internal compulsions, places also a heavy burden of responsibility on management. A business will survive and grow in the long run only if it achieves the end of developing the character of the people it serves. This means that management itself must have character. As we move from inner direction to external direction, we must acquire a better understanding of mental health, personal growth, intellectual, aesthetic, and spiritual needs and, in the final analysis, how to take mass consumption and change it to mass development.

The relationship between McGregor's Theory Y, concerned with human resources management, and the marketing concept are explored, and some implications of the relationships are examined. The underlying theme of both the marketing and Theory Y concepts is dependence upon participation and cooperation by subordinate units. Both theories need to be extended before widespread endorsement occurs.

39. A COMPARISON OF MANAGEMENT THEORY Y WITH THE MARKETING CONCEPT*

John Douglas†

One of the most important problems faced by men in all professions is that of "keeping up." For the executive, this means reading in a multitude of areas. Wendell Willkie's One World concept has descended upon business. As interrelationships and interdependencies appear, the scope of the businessman's "specialty" broadens. To keep up in his reading, the executive must not only read but also develop the criteria for sifting through the volume of materials.

The acquisition of an up-to-date posture is difficult at best. So time-consuming can this be that the most important questions rarely are formed. How does this report relate to the one read last week? What implications do the new empirical research findings pose for the future? How valid are the assumptions underlying the newer theories?

This article represents an attempt to gain this broader vision. In an effort to approach current business topics in such a manner, this writer focuses upon two recent major developments in business—the newer management and marketing theories. The following paragraphs contain a discussion of these theories organized around four basic questions. What are the management and marketing theories that are receiving attention in

* Reprinted from "A Comparison of Management Theory Y With the Marketing Concept," *Quarterly Review of Economics and Business*, Vol. IV, No. 3 (October, 1964), pp. 21–32.

† University of Kentucky.

current literature? What are the similarities of these theories that suggest a more basic trend or characteristic? How is this basic trend identified? What are the implications of this trend for marketing and management operations and therefore for society? Starting with the first question, then, the following discussion will attempt to relate these theories and to present possible implications.

THE CONTEMPORARY THEORIES

The New Management Theory

In 1960, Douglas McGregor of the Massachusetts Institute of Technology presented in book form some ideas that represented the more advanced management thought of the time.[1] In particular, Professor McGregor emphasized the management thought that related to the managing of the human resources of the firm—a topic appearing in more and more academic and professional journals[2] and one which gains international attention daily. In McGregor's words,

> This volume is an attempt to substantiate the thesis that the human side of enterprise is "all of a piece"—that the theoretical assumptions management holds about controlling its human resources determine the whole character of the enterprise. They determine also the quality of its successive generations of management.[3]

In his book McGregor stated that every managerial act rests on theory and that theory and practice are inseparable; thus, he suggested that the assumptions about human nature and human behavior (and so also the statements underlying managerial decisions and thus theory) should be clearly delineated and expressed. In short, McGregor contended that the traditional management practice (Theory X) should give way to a more contemporary Theory Y.[4] He built his case by analyzing the basic assumptions of both the traditional and the "called for." A brief summary of the major points will provide a common reference point.

THEORY X ASSUMPTIONS

The assumptions about human behavior are

(1) The average human being has an inherent dislike of work and will avoid it if he can.

---

[1] Douglas McGregor, *The Human Side of Enterprise* (New York: McGraw-Hill, 1960).

[2] See, for example, David W. Belcher, "Toward a Behavioral Science Theory of Wages," *Journal of the Academy of Management*, Vol. 5, No. 5 (August, 1962), pp. 102–17; Perry Bliss, *Marketing and the Behavioral Sciences* (Boston: Allyn and Bacon, Inc., 1963); Rensis Likert, *New Patterns of Management* (New York: McGraw-Hill, 1961).

[3] McGregor, *op. cit.*, pp. vi–vii.

[4] When McGregor uses the term "theory" he means certain managerial assumptions about the behavior of subordinates.

(2) Because of this human characteristic of dislike of work, most people must be coerced, controlled, directed, threatened with punishment to get them to put forth adequate effort toward the achievement of organizational objectives.

(3) The average human being prefers to be directed, wishes to avoid responsibility, has relatively little ambition, wants security above all.[5]

With these assumptions as a base, McGregor held that traditional methods actually stress direction and control of subordinates since the direction and control of operations includes people as well as things. Although this pattern seems to have expressed the management practice of past years, McGregor contended that these practices should change because the basic assumptions of Theory X are in error and also are lacking in validity.

This is a brief summary of some of the characteristics of the traditional theory of management; a review of what McGregor hoped would replace it will follow.

Theory Y Assumptions and Practice

The more appropriate assumptions about man should be

(1) The expenditure of physical and mental effort in work is as natural as play or rest.

(2) External control and the threat of punishment are not the only means for bringing about effort toward organizational objectives. Man will exercise self-direction and self-control in the service of objectives to which he is committed.

(3) Commitment to objectives is a function of the rewards associated with their achievement.

(4) The average human being learns, under proper conditions, not only to accept but to seek responsibility.

(5) The capacity to exercise a relatively high degree of imagination, ingenuity, and creativity in the solution of organizational problems is widely, not narrowly, distributed in the population.

(6) Under the conditions of modern industrial life, the intellectual potentialities of the average human being are only partially utilized.[6]

The central principle which derives from these assumptions is that conditions should be created to encourage subordinates to achieve their own goals best by working for the success of the enterprise.

In summary, McGregor believed that the traditional management practice is based upon assumptions about human nature which are the *consequences* of a management practice using organizational concepts derived from early military and church organizations—authority through direction and control. If management were to change its practices, the propo-

---

[5] McGregor, *op. cit.*, pp. 33–34.

[6] *Ibid.*, pp. 47–48.

nents of Theory Y say, the truer nature of man would be revealed. This position, of course, gains support from psychology and sociology research. The manager under Theory Y would create positive conditions or a climate wherein the subordinate would see that fulfilling the needs of the organization would in turn enable him to fulfill his own personal needs. The subordinate, therefore, would become much more involved in the matters that affect his work behavior. He would plan, organize, direct, and maintain self-control over work that was his responsibility.

This review presents only the highlights of the newer management theory presented by Douglas McGregor—a theory finding widespread acclaim, acceptance, and expression in other articles, in executive development courses, and in graduate and undergraduate curricula.

Now, let us turn to the development of another new theory—one representing changing thought in the marketing field. At the moment, there should be no attempt by the reader to compare the new marketing concept with Theory Y; this discussion will occur later in the article.

The New Marketing Concept

This new theory sounds almost naive in its simplicity; that is, all marketing activity should start with the consumer. While the consumer has always been important, he has not always been the key figure in the design and manufacture of the product. In past years, the problems of reducing cost and increasing efficiency have required the major efforts of the corporation; however, a new focal point is being discussed. No longer can the engineer demand the most attention. The important man on the emerging scene is now the consumer.

In some instances, men have expressed the newer concept as part of an evolutionary process.[7]

> The function of marketing is still growing within the corporate organization, and it will continue to grow for some time to come. Business has come a long way since the day when most corporations were production-oriented manufacturing companies. The swing to the customer-minded philosophy has brought the marketing-oriented manufacturing company into full bloom today.[8]

But not all the experts hold the newer marketing theory to be a natural evolutionary outgrowth. Much more urgency and change is expressed by such persons as Robert J. Keith. In his article, "The Marketing Revolu-

---

[7] The evolutionary character of the concept found expression in a recent article "AMA Beats the Drum for Innovation," *Business Week*, No. 1764 (June 22, 1963), pp. 88–91. The retiring president of the American Marketing Association, Donald R. Longman, said, "It's not a revolution, but a rapid evolution."

[8] "Transition To A Marketing Company," *Sales Management*, Vol. 87, No. 2 (July 21, 1961), pp. 36–38 and 102.

tion,"[9] Mr. Keith likens the relationship between the new marketing concept and the traditional one to the revolution in science created by Nicolaus Copernicus. "The market is the center of the economic universe as the sun is the center of our universe." A similar picture is expressed by Fred J. Borch, new president of the General Electric Company. "Under marketing, the customer becomes the fulcrum, the pivot point about which the business moves in operating for the balanced best interests of all concerned."[10]

The operating idea in the last statement quoted is supported by those persons who look at the marketing concept in terms of the decision process of the corporation. Peter Drucker, long associated with dealing with the managerial problems of firms, suggests that even (perhaps he meant to say especially) the corporate officers should view marketing as the starting place for policy, for criteria in decision-making, and for the testing of corporate effectiveness.[11] Professors Lazo and Corbin go so far as to say that the new marketing concept means that all business decisions (whether made by marketing personnel, engineers, research and development workers, or financiers) should be made with the market in mind; the decision should be viewed in terms of the impact upon the market.[12] And finally, A. P. Felton has stated that the marketing concept is

> A corporate state of mind that insists on the integration and coordination of all the marketing functions which, in turn, are melded with all other corporate functions, for the basic objectives of producing maximum long-range corporate profits.[13]

Thus, the marketing concept has been viewed from a number of different bases: an evolutionary concept, a revolutionary concept, an integrating concept, and others. Common to all views is this important thought: while the movement toward the new theory or concept will be a function of the type of industry, the character and vision of top manage-

---

[9] Robert J. Keith, "The Marketing Revolution," reprinted from the *Journal of Marketing*, Vol. 24, No. 3 (January, 1960), pp. 35–38, in Parker M. Holmes, Ralph E. Brownlee, and Robert Bartels (eds.), *Readings in Marketing* (Columbus: Merrill, 1963), pp. 65–70.

[10] Fred J. Borch, "The Marketing Philosophy as a Way of Business Life," in *The Marketing Concept: Its Meaning to Management*, Marketing Series, No. 99 (New York: American Management Association, 1957), p. 4.

[11] Peter Drucker, *The Practice of Management* (New York: Harper, 1954), pp. 37–41.

[12] Hector Lazo and Arnold Corbin, *Management in Marketing* (New York: McGraw-Hill, 1961). These authors also mention that some persons believed it was not the early efforts of educators like Paul Converse, J. F. Pyle, and R. S. Vaile nor the efforts by Ralph Cordiner at General Electric to act on marketing matters that ushered in the marketing concept. Rather, it may have been "the graduated taxes, high wages, and inflation which followed in the wake of World War II which finally made management focus its attention on the importance of marketing" (p. 9).

[13] Arthur P. Felton, "Making the Marketing Concept Work," *Harvard Business Review*, Vol. 37, No. 4 (July–August, 1959), p. 55.

ment, the nature of the product, and other factors, the movement is inevitable. Marketing in its many ramifications must start with the customer.

The preceding paragraphs have served the purpose of answering the first question: What are the contemporary management and marketing theories that represent newer trends of thought? With this material as a framework, we are now ready to ask, What are the similarities of these theories that suggest a more basic trend or movement?

SIMILARITIES OF THE NEW THEORIES

Timing

Perhaps it was not unusual that the new management theory and the new marketing concept came on the scene about the same time. The fields of management and marketing almost by definition tend to overlap each other in both day-to-day operations and longer-range policy matters. Because the marketing activity of a firm must be managed, the management concepts relate to all processes of marketing. Similarly, the higher levels of management (divisional level and up) must be concerned with marketing matters—products, prices, markets, competition, and so on. This relationship probably explains the emergence of the two new ideas at approximately the same time—the early fifties.

Heralds of New Truth

Both theories have received so much attention and acclaim that the outsider might feel that major breakthroughs had been accomplished and that the search for truth had ended. Theory X represented the traditional management thought and although no analogy has been made to the coin, there is the feeling that the other side of Theory X is Theory Y. Theory Y is presented as *the* theory for the management of human resources.

Often the new marketing concept, too, is presented as an absolute or ultimate law: ". . . once the importance of marketing has been accepted *as a matter of survival*, the company creed itself will undergo vital changes. . . ."[14] A business executive of General Electric has said that the reason many older business firms had been successful was that "their businesses were customer-oriented because they knew that this was the only way to run a business!"[15] As a final example of the critical nature of the concept, J. W. Keener believes that "the marketing-oriented organizations will be the winners in the exciting, risk-filled, and opportunity-filled decade ahead."[16]

---

[14] Lazo and Corbin, *op. cit.*, p. 30.

[15] Borch, *loc. cit.*

[16] J. W. Keener, "Marketing's Job for the 1960s," reprinted from the *Journal of Marketing*, Vol. 24, No. 3 (January, 1960), pp. 1–6, in Holmes *et al.*, *op. cit.*, p. 174.

Both these concepts, therefore, represent advanced stages in the respective fields. Both also are described as major changes in emphasis and direction incorporating the latest information from the allied fields of economics, psychology, and sociology.

Shift in Emphasis

Figure 1 shows the pre-concept relationship of both the marketing area in its relationship to the market and the management area in its relationship through supervision.

From Figure 1, we see that communications and decisions have flowed

FIGURE 1

Relationships under Theory X and Production Orientation

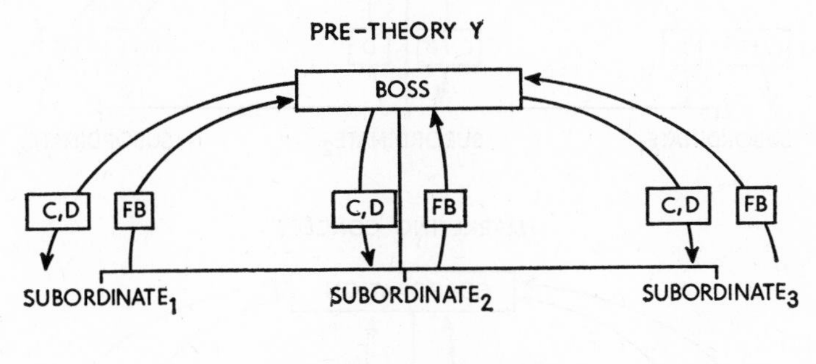

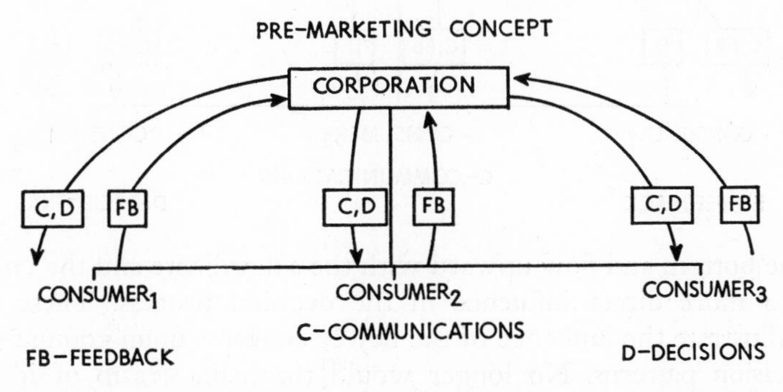

downward through the organization, the subordinate and the consumer responding with feedback. In management circles, the subordinate feedback has been in the form of productivity; in the marketing context, the consumer has responded with his feedback in terms of the purchasing dollar.

Theory Y and the new marketing concept seem to suggest that the orientation needs revision; the new emphasis should be on customer or market orientation. In management, the new emphasis should be on employee orientation to the management process. In both these concepts the call is for greater involvement by the lower-level units (i.e., the subordinate or the consumer).

If the new relationships were to be diagrammed, they would appear as in Figure 2.

Communications are now (or would be) originating in two areas: the boss and the corporation; the subordinate and the market or consumer. Each is to be a more equal partner in the relationship. Feedback also stems from both as information concerning needs and wants as well as reactions to decisions are continually transmitted to both parties. Decisions emanate

FIGURE 2

Relationships under Theory Y and Consumer Orientation

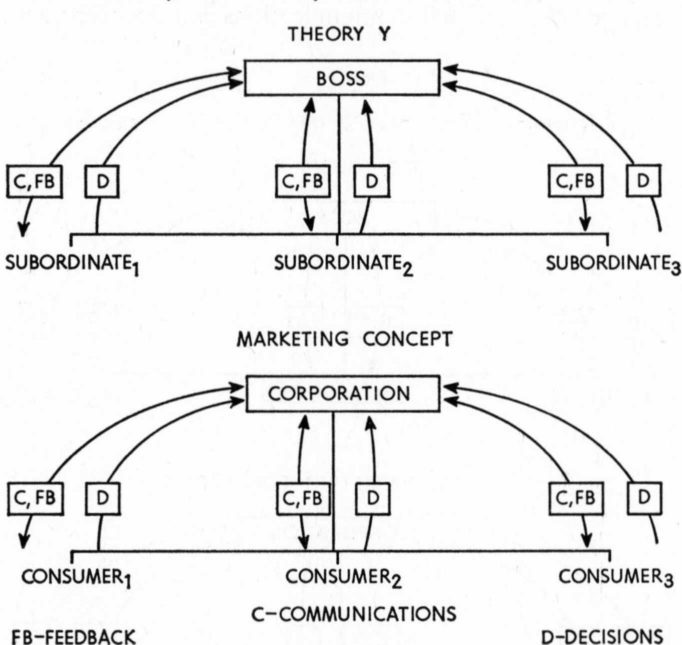

from the bottom and flow upward with the subordinate and the consumer having a more direct influence in the decision process. These figures should illustrate the influence of the newer concepts upon communication and decision patterns. No longer would the main stream of ideas and communication be downward. Under the new plans, the pattern would be modified in favor of a bottom-to-top direction.

The preceding paragraphs have served to suggest that many similarities exist between the new marketing and management theories. These newer theories began to be discussed about the same time. The supporters of both the management and the marketing theories claim the presence of new or ultimate truth in these ideas. And both theories represent a shift of emphasis in decision and communication patterns.

The presence of many common elements, then, points to the possibility of a more basic relationship or factor common to both movements. Thus far, such a relationship has merely been suggested but the following section will directly support a case for the common element. This time the question is, How is this basic characteristic identified?

THE COMMON CHARACTERISTIC

To me the underlying theme permeating both the marketing concept and the management concept is the dependence upon participation. The new concepts call for the subordinate and the consumer to participate in activities once reserved for those persons in higher management levels and positions.

Participation in Management

The rationale in management thought follows logically in this way. Who should perform the management process? Who should do the planning, organizing, directing, and controlling of activities? In earlier days the answer might have been a resounding "the boss," but today many would say "the subordinate." Many consultants know that solutions to company problems exist within the ranks of the company personnel and that the consultant's job is to clarify the problem, locate the persons with the solutions to these problems, and then convince top management of the value of the solutions. This very characteristic is basic to the participation concept. Theoretically, the subordinate manager, who has to work on the project, is best able to plan the project and set the objectives he believes are attainable. If the subordinate manager is best able to plan the operation that he will perform, it follows that he will be the one who can best organize and direct it. In the process of performing these management functions, the subordinate applies control, which has become self-control. Under this kind of system of subordinate participation in the management process, the primary role of the executive manager or boss is in the *coaching* of the subordinates as they participate and in the *coordination* of the activities of the subordinates.

Participation in Marketing

The American economic system has always had an element of consumer participation in it. As put forth in the basic economic texts or even in the contemporary language of Robert Heilbroner's *The Making of Economic Society*,[17] America chose the market system (as opposed to tradition and command) for finding an economic answer to such questions as what is to be produced, how it is to be produced, and to whom it should be distributed. In the market system, the consumer is supposed to have the

[17] Robert Heilbroner, *The Making of Economic Society* (Englewood Cliffs, N.J.: Prentice-Hall, 1962).

greatest voice by actually deciding whether to purchase or not. The dollar is the consumer vote. This point is relevant to the marketing concept.

The role of the consumer is theoretically elevated through the implementation of the new marketing concept. This is not a drastic step, as the consumer role is already on a high plane. In 1944, Ludwig von Mises wrote:

> Within the market society the working of the price mechanism makes the consumers supreme. They determine through the prices they pay and through the amount of their purchases both the quantity and quality of production. They determine directly the prices of consumers' goods, and thereby indirectly the prices of all material factors of production and the wages of all hands employed.
>
> . . . in that endless rotating mechanism the entrepreneurs and capitalists are the servants of the consumers. The consumers are the masters, to whose whims the entrepreneurs and capitalists must adjust their investments and methods of production.[18]

If the American economic system has already given the consumer such an elevated role, how does the newer theory stress greater participation by the consumer?

It appears that the major difference between the consumer roles under the traditional market system and under the new marketing concept is that the consumer in the past has participated in response to corporate activity (through buying or not buying the products) whereas the new marketing concept describes consumer participation in the *planning phases* of production as well as in the setting of the criteria for decision-making throughout the total enterprise.

This participation in the new marketing concept is manifested in two ways.[19] The consumer now assumes a much greater role and voice in the decision-making processes of the firm *and* those persons involved with the marketing activity assume a much more important place among the executive elite. Most writers, when describing the implementation of the marketing concept in the firm, speak in terms of the change that must take place within the organization. The "proper state of mind" or the "changed attitude" refers to that of the corporate officials, who must be willing to see the significance of operating *from* the market rather than *to* the market. Thus this type of participation (the other was consumer participation) is an internal type where the person in charge of marketing activities becomes more involved.

Considerable effort has been devoted to illustrating where this new,

---

[18] Ludwig von Mises, *Omnipotent Government* (New Haven: Yale University Press, 1944), pp. 49–50.

[19] In the Foreword to Lazo and Corbin, *op. cit.*, p. v, Peter Drucker uses the terms "marketing view" and the "management of marketing" to convey a similar idea.

greater stress upon participation occurs in the new marketing and management theories. This is not to say that these newer theories contain no other factors or ideas in common; however, basic to them both and crucial to their implementation is consumer or subordinate participation. It is this dominant characteristic which permeates both trends.

The identification of this common denominator is important for two reasons. First, it enables us to see more easily the relationship of these newer theories to others outside the business area. Certainly, participation or ego involvement is an important term in many fields. The newer art expression rests upon it; education and training insist upon it; and psychology thrives upon it. To this extent, then, Theory Y and the new marketing concept are part of a broader social trend. This insight helps to understand better the "why" of the newer theories.

The second reason for identifying the common characteristic is more directly relevant to the final topic of the implications of the newer theories. If the theories are perceived as being related to other movements also stressing participation, a possible danger presents itself. Because of the inertia created by similar movements, the newer theories may be acclaimed and accepted before their merits have been investigated extensively. Participation is neither good nor bad. It must be weighed with a specific set of conditions in mind. There are many questions of limitations and extent. Therefore, the next question is, What are the implications of this increased participation for marketing and management and indirectly for the whole of society?

The following discussion is intended to locate probable problems if the greater-participation trend is supported. This is not to say that the raising of questions necessarily denies the point. In other words, the succeeding paragraphs are not included to condemn participation but to provide an awareness of the more far-reaching consequences of participation by greater numbers of people in decisive areas of management and marketing. It is hoped that such an examination of problem areas may aid the reader in evaluating the newer theories from a broader and wiser base.

IMPLICATIONS OF PARTICIPATION

Benefits

Many claims have been made by the proponents of the participation movement as to its advantages. These proponents, coming primarily from the university ranks as social scientists, believe participation provides significant benefits for both the individual participating and the corporation. Included in these advantages are such items as productivity increases, improvements in morale and motivation, a greater sense of well-being for the participating subordinate, and enhancement of the individual's identification with the corporation goals.[20] The picture that emerges is of an individual growing and developing through participation in the decision process of the enterprise. This individual is a cooperative person and is thus able to find much more meaning in his work and the work of others around him.

These benefits to the individual are not at the expense of the corporation, however, since it too benefits from this participation. The productivity increases of the individual will also improve the cost picture of the corporation; efficiencies from the cooperation of the subordinates should be more attainable; the corporate image becomes more easily accepted by all parties, who, because of their participation, become salesmen for the enterprise.

Problems and Criticisms

Not everyone agrees that the benefits just described are the natural extension of participation. The first charge thrown at the participation proponents is that of manipulation.[21] The social scientists, particularly the newer group of behavioral scientists who have worked in industry, have been labeled by Loren Baritz as the "servants of power."[22] The behavioral servants respond to the wishes of their masters, the corporation executives, who have hired them at salaries far above their meager university earnings to conduct "research studies" that will "uncover the truth." Baritz maintains that most of these "findings" are really *post facto* findings: a company needs data to support some point and data are found. The Harwood studies, for example, which are purported to exemplify the benefits to be derived from participation, are seen by Baritz as ingenious methods for having the employees "participate" in a management-planned situation so that the goals of the corporation would be better achieved.[23]

Baritz' criticism has been used here to exemplify some thinking and uneasiness about the use of social findings. Actually, one of two possible assumptions must be made before carrying the discussion further. One assumes that subordinate units can help set objectives in the best interests

---

[20] See, for example, Victor H. Vroom, *Some Personality Determinants of the Effects of Participation* (Englewood Cliffs, N.J.: Prentice-Hall, 1960).

[21] Douglas McGregor was well aware of the criticisms of participation. In his Chapter 9, "Participation in Perspective," he criticizes those proponents of participation who believe that the magic formula has been found for the elimination of conflict and disagreement; he also attacks the critics who believe participation is merely manipulation. In his words, ". . . participation is not a panacea, a manipulative device, a gimmick, or a threat. Used wisely, and with understanding, it is a natural concomitant of management by integration and self-control." See McGregor, *op. cit.*, p. 131.

[22] Loren Baritz, *The Servants of Power* (Middletown, Conn.: Wesleyan University Press, 1960).

[23] Others have raised their voices in protest. See the writings of Arthur Kornhauser, C. Wright Mills, and Wilbert E. Moore.

of the firm or one assumes that they cannot. If the latter position is held, then efforts to guide behavior in the direction of predetermined patterns must be vulnerable to the charge of manipulation. The control of individual behavior is beset with many problems of ethics. The reader can surely extend his thinking along these lines to see how involved this charge of manipulation can become.

But the other assumption may also hold. Perhaps the majority of the proponents of the newer management and marketing theories sincerely believe that goals and methods advocated by subordinate units will in fact work for the greatest good of the organization. What then?

If subordinate units in fact were encouraged to make corporate plans and decisions, the mind would immediately turn to difficulties emerging in many directions. How could responsible leadership be encouraged?[24] How could such units handle complex commodities such as defense mechanisms or drugs? Does the consumer know what he wants?[25] These are only some of the pertinent questions. Even though such reflections conjure up a multitude of problems, the discussion here will center about a broader area. Perhaps the most serious and far-reaching implication of the participation movement is the subtle impact it would have upon the standards of society.

The Social System

It has been suggested that the pursuit and questioning of implications is important because so many forces in society (management and marketing, in this case) are striving toward the goal of participation. True, not all factions of the business society may completely achieve this end but because of the striving, the question of direction is critical.

If a corporation actually becomes consumer oriented, it takes on the values of the consumers. This transformation does not come overnight but in the day-to-day attempts to have "the customer's wants become the very criteria for corporate decision-making." What will happen to society when participation encourages the acceptance of mass values? Can society's goals be achieved when mass values may delay the process of innovation and individual creativity? And as Irving Kristol suggests,[26] if segments of our nation resist taking on the values of the masses, the government may become the protector or guardian of these segments—resulting in increased bureaucratic organization.

The point is that the very process of placing participation as *the* goal may erode the forces within this nation that have been balanced basically

[24] John Douglas, "Our Lopsided Concept of Accomplishment," *Business Quarterly*, Vol. 28, No. 1 (Spring, 1963), pp. 10–18 and 77.

[25] "Tiffany's Off On a Spree," *Business Week*, No. 1727 (October 6, 1962), p. 56.

[26] Irving Kristol, "Is the Welfare State Obsolete?" *Harper's Magazine*, Vol. 226, No. 1357 (June, 1963), pp. 39–43.

by our Constitution (the doctrine of checks and balances). The individual's values can be lost to those of the mass. Can minority or individual rights continue to be respected with this greater emphasis upon mass values?

In the same way that followership should be viewed as the countervailing[27] force to leadership, participation should be viewed as the countervailing force to autocratic decision-making, and cooperation the countervailing force to conflict. In more specific terms, the two new theories being discussed contain an emphasis upon participation by subordinate units. In effect, this movement would invest new power in these groups. If the pendulum swings radically to one side, then it would be possible for the new power groups to overbalance the power of the executive organization. To provide an effective and constructive change, then, the new theories must include more specific corollaries relating to limitations, extent, and scope.

SUMMARY

Two concepts, one in marketing and one in management, were reviewed with special attention given to the relationship of each to a more fundamental movement of the times. Stress upon participation by subordinate units in management and marketing and the resulting aim of cooperation among the forces appeared as primary goals. The implications of such goals suggested that the newer theories in marketing and management—indeed, in all areas—need to be extended to their broader ramifications before widespread endorsement occurs.

---

[27] See John Kenneth Galbraith, *American Capitalism* (Cambridge, Mass.: Riverside Press, 1962) for the development of the countervailing power concept.

D. Evaluation and Adjustment of Marketing Effort

Marketing must be treated as a total interacting system of business management, and the components of this system must be carefully evaluated and controlled. While a complete marketing audit may not be a feasible goal, much misplaced and misdirected marketing effort can be uncovered and corrected by a comprehensive analysis of sales volume and marketing costs.

40. EVALUATING MARKETING EFFORT*

William J. Stanton†

The concept of an audit is not new to business management. Traditionally it has carried the connotation of a review and evaluation of some business activity. It has long been used in accounting and financial operations. Management is also accustomed to manpower or personnel audits.

* Reprinted from William Lazer and Eugene J. Kelley, *Managerial Marketing: Perspectives and Viewpoints* (rev. ed. Homewood, Ill.: Richard D. Irwin, Inc., 1962), pp. 393–97. This article is based on part of a longer paper, "Planning and Controlling Selling Efforts," delivered by the author and reprinted in *Marketing Adjustment to the Environment*, 1961 University of Illinois Marketing Symposium, Bureau of Business Management Bulletin (Urbana: University of Illinois, 1962).

† University of Colorado.

Editors' note: Other marketing control articles of interest include: F. M. Bass, "Marketing Research Expenditures: A Decision Model," *Journal of Business*, Vol. XXXVI, No. 1 (January, 1963), pp. 77–90; A. A. Brown, F. T. Hulswit, and John D. Kettelle, "A Study of Sales Operations," *Operations Research*, Vol. IV, No. 3 (June, 1956), pp. 296–308; J. Dearden, "Management Information Systems and the Computer," in R. N. Vancil, J. Dearden, and R. N. Anthony, *Management Control Systems* (Homewood, Ill.: Richard D. Irwin, Inc., 1965); Cyril Freeman, "How to Eval-

A complete marketing audit is something of an ideal or goal for management to work toward. Rarely does a firm conduct an audit of the total components of its marketing mix and the interactions among these elements. The reason is that such an audit is too expensive and time consuming. Also, a total marketing-mix audit would be based to some extent upon data whose validity would be doubted by management.

Consequently it may be more reasonable first to conduct a complete analysis and investigation of the separate components of the marketing mix and to maximize the productivity and effectiveness of each of these elements before evaluating the interaction among them. With respect to field selling efforts, for example, such an approach to evaluation would involve an appraisal of the sales volume results, the related marketing expenses, and the performance of individual salesmen.

Often in individual firms there is a considerable amount of misdirected or misplaced marketing effort. Marketing efforts and cost follow the *number* of territories, customers, products, or other selling units, rather than the *actual or potential sales volume or profit* in these units. In a retail sale which is to be charged and delivered, approximately the same order-filling and delivery expenses are involved whether the sale is a mink coat or a necktie. Manufacturers will assign one salesman or one branch office to each territory, yet there may be substantial differences in the volume and profit return from each of these districts. This lack of balanced marketing effort has been characterized as the 80–20 principle.

There are several reasons for the occurrence of misdirected marketing effort. First, many businessmen are simply unaware of the situation. They do not know what percentage of total sales and profits comes from a given product line or customer group. Ordinarily these executives have done little or nothing toward analyzing and appraising their marketing operation. Executives frequently lack sufficiently detailed information with which to uncover their misdirection of effort. The lack of detailed information has been likened to an iceberg and serves as the basis of the so-called principle.

A second reason for misplaced marketing effort is that, in the past, management has relied upon sales volume as the sole criterion for measuring the success of a marketing program. The increasing acceptance of the marketing concept should blunt this eagerness for volume alone. The emphasis on sales volume, however, remains among manufacturers who set volume quotas for their salesmen, among wholesalers who pay their

---

uate Advertising's Contribution," *Harvard Business Review*, Vol. XL, No. 4 (July–August, 1962), pp. 137–45; E. A. Pessemier, "Models Using Experimental Data to Appraise Marketing Strategy," *Experimental Methods of Analyzing Demand for Branded Consumer Goods with Application to Problems in Marketing Strategy* (Pullman: Washington State University Press, 1963), chap. 6, pp. 74–125; and C. H. Sevin, "Measuring the Productivity of Marketing Expenditures," in W. Alderson and S. J. Shapiro (eds.), *Marketing and the Computer* (Englewood Cliffs, N.J.: Prentice-Hall, Inc., 1963), pp. 164–76.

salesmen a commission on net sales, and among retailers whose goal is to beat last year sales volume figures.

A third and more fundamental reason for misplaced marketing effort is that marketing executives must make decisions even though two decision elements often are very inadequate: (1) their knowledge of the exact nature of marketing costs, and (2) their managerial tools for controlling these expenses. In other words, marketing management has lacked knowledge of the disproportionate spread of marketing effort, and reliable standards for determining what should have been spent on marketing, and what results should have been obtained from these expenditures.

As an illustration, a marketing executive really does not know how much to spend on sales selection, marketing research, or sales training. Even more troublesome is the fact that after the money is spent there is no satisfactory yardstick to determine whether the results are satisfactory. If a firm adds two new sales branches, marketing management cannot state precisely what the resulting increase in volume or profit should be. Furthermore, management cannot equate the value of two marketing expenditures. For example, if a company spends $250,000 more on advertising this year than last year, management cannot state with certainty what change in sales volume or profit these expenditures will bring as compared with putting an equivalent sum into an improved salesmen selection program, management training institutes for middlemen, or some other phase of the marketing program.

In the markets of the 1960's this misdirection of marketing effort will not be tolerated by management to the same extent as it has been in the past two decades. Rising costs, higher break-even points, and shrinking profit margins are forcing management to focus increasing attention on the task of cutting marketing expenses and generally improving the efficiency of marketing operations. Probably nowhere in the marketing program will this trend of interest be more evident than in the control of costs related to the field selling efforts. Each phase of field selling will have to justify its existence and the expenditures related to it. In management's eagerness to reduce and control this marketing cost, there is some danger that a short-sighted, meat-axe approach will be used. So often when operating costs must be reduced, the first place management looks is to the activities supporting the field selling effort. There is the risk that management will curtail activities which in the short run may cut costs, but which in the long run will reduce profits.

One significant step a firm can take to remedy its misdirected marketing efforts is to conduct a careful, detailed, and complete sales volume and marketing cost analysis. The evaluative process is essentially a three-stage procedure. First, the facts must be gathered and analyzed. This includes a comparison of the actual results with the budgeted figures to determine the extent of the variation. Next, the executives must determine what specific factors in the market or in the marketing program are responsible for these results. Finally, management should develop plans, policies, and procedures with the intent of improving unsatisfactory conditions, while at the same time capitalizing on the favorable ones. To summarize, the administrator's job is to find out *what happened*, *why it happened*, and then decide *what to do* about it.

None of these three steps is an easy one. Determining *what* has happened means management must provide for an information flow which will adequately report the data to be used in the sales and cost analyses. Whether management is analyzing its sales volume, marketing costs, or salesmen's productivity, the success of the evaluation depends largely upon the extent to which quantitative performance standards can be established. These performance standards may be set for sales volume, gross margin, or net profit. Each of these criteria may be computed for territories, product lines, or customer groups. Quantitative standards also may be set for such evaluative factors as the call rate, the number of orders per call, the size of orders, the salesmen's expense ratio, etc.

In a marketing cost study which is made to determine what has happened, the executives face the problem of cost allocation. Costs appearing in ledger accounts have to be allocated to functional groupings, and then these functional costs must be apportioned among the selling units (products, territories, etc.) being studied. Also management must decide whether it will seek to determine the net profit in each selling unit or whether it will be satisfied with the contribution-margin approach.

After management knows what has happened, it may take considerable further study and insight to determine what accounts for the results realized. For example, when the sales volume in a given territory or product line falls short of the predetermined norm, the administration must determine whether the results stem from weaknesses in the company's operations or from strengths in the competition. Within the firm's marketing operation, there are almost limitless possibilities accounting for substandard results. Something may be wrong with the product itself—its styling, design, or color. Possibly some aspect of the price structure and price policies are the problem. Or the weakness may lie in some phase of the advertising such as the choice of media or the ads themselves. Finally, there is the entire area of sales force management for the administrator to examine in his search for an explanation for the inadequate performance. On the other hand, it may be that the firm's operations are as good as they ever were, but the competitors have shown marked improvement. There may be more competitors, or some of these firms may have made significant improvements in some phase of their own marketing programs.

The third step in the evaluative procedure is the one in which an executive has full opportunity to display his marketing acumen and his administrative ability. At this point presumably he knows what has happened and why it happened. His responsibility now is to make effective use of this information in the course of managing his sales force. These findings can be helpful particularly in such activities as training, stimulating, directing, and supervising the salesmen and planning the selling effort. For example, a sales volume analysis and a marketing cost analysis are sources of information which may be used in developing a job description, preparatory to recruiting sales applicants. Sub-par performance in certain territories, products, or customer groups should influence the salesmen's training program and their supervision. Additional training and supervision may be necessary, for instance, to increase the sales of high-margin products or to improve handling of key accounts. Sometimes sub-par performance in territorial coverage or in dealings with certain groups of accounts results in management's decision to reroute the salesman. In another case the quota system or compensation plan may be altered when the results of a volume and cost analysis show unbalanced coverage of territories, products, or customer groups. A sales contest may be set up to stimulate the salesmen toward better performance of some activity. Based on the findings of these studies, management may decide to revise some territorial boundaries, possibly increasing the size of some, decreasing others, adding new districts or eliminating territories.

The key point here is that management is really in the dark with respect to the strengths and weaknesses in the field selling program until a sales volume and marketing cost analysis is made, preferably along with an evaluation of the salesman's performance. Only then is an executive reasonably in a position to take administrative action to correct, or capitalize on the situation.

The everchanging environmental factors facing marketing management are increasing the importance of evaluating and controlling the marketing effort. These factors manifest themselves in such forms as higher break-even points, fixed costs accounting for a larger share of total cost, fiercer competition, and increased innovation in products, distribution structures, and promotional programs. In the face of these conditions, it is imperative that marketing be treated as a total interacting system of business management and that the components of this system be carefully evaluated and controlled. This, in turn, should result in a more effective marketing program bent toward generating profitable volume within the framework of the marketing concept.

A marketing audit is a programmed appraisal of the total marketing operation that focuses on an evaluation of the objectives, policies, and assumptions that underlie the operation. Its objective is prognosis as well as diagnosis—a search for opportunities and the means for exploiting them as well as for weaknesses and the means for eliminating them.

41. THE MARKETING AUDIT: ITS NATURE, PURPOSES, AND PROBLEMS*

Abe Shuchman†

The notion of an audit—a periodic review and appraisal of a business activity—is familiar to all executives. In most companies, financial audits to establish the adequacy and accuracy of accounting and financial operations are accepted practice. Periodic inventories for the evaluation of physical assets are also commonplace. In addition, many firms today make periodic reviews of the records and achievements of all employees, and there is evidence that such "personnel audits" are fast becoming standard practice.

In recent years there has been increasing awareness that the future growth—indeed, the very survival—of most companies depends primarily upon the success of their marketing operations. There has been widespread recognition of the central and critical role of marketing activities in the shaping of a firm's destiny. It has not, however, been generally recognized that, because marketing operations are of such crucial importance, it is necessary to apply to these operations a type of stock-taking analogous to that currently applied to financial and personnel activities. Very few firms have yet come to realize that a *marketing audit* is as essential as an audit of the company's books, physical assets, or employees.

---

* Reprinted from "The Marketing Audit: Its Nature, Purposes, and Problems," *American Management Association Report No. 32,* 1959.

† Columbia University.

NATURE OF THE MARKETING AUDIT

Most marketing executives would probably deny indignantly that they do not recognize the need for auditing the operations which are their responsibility. They would insist, in fact, that they are *constantly* evaluating these operations—and they would probably be right. Within every modern marketing organization, evaluations of many different kinds *are* constantly being made. It is important to recognize, however, that not every marketing evaluation is a marketing audit. Neither, except very rarely, does the sum of all the evaluations currently being made equal a marketing audit.

Some Distinguishing Characteristics

There are a number of reasons for asserting that current appraisals do not, either singly or as a group, constitute a marketing audit. The principal reason, however, is that they are far too limited in scope. Executives review and appraise the effectiveness of the field sales force, the advertising program, the company's product mix, and the like, but they evaluate each of these elements at different times, and in no planned or coherent pattern. They do not, within a specified interval, examine each and every facet of the *total* operation. There is no integrated, coordinated, comprehensive appraisal encompassing all marketing activities and executed systematically in accord with a planned program and schedule. Yet the principal characteristic of the marketing audit is that it *is* such a systematic and comprehensive survey and evaluation of the total marketing operation—a programmed appraisal of *all* of the activities included within the marketing function.

Current appraisals are much more limited than the marketing audit in another respect. They are, in general, confined to the review and evaluation of performance, methods and procedures, and personnel, concentrating on the manpower and tactics used and the results achieved within a given framework of objectives and policies. Rarely is the framework itself subjected to systematic and critical analysis and appraisal.

Now a marketing audit is, to be sure, an appraisal of performance and tactics—of methods, procedures, personnel, and organization. Beyond this, however, it is a great deal more. In fact, its principal focus is on those elements of the marketing function which are almost never subjected to careful, regular, and orderly scrutiny but which are of fundamental importance because they comprise the base from which methods, procedures, and organization are derived. In short, the marketing audit is primarily a re-examination and evaluation of marketing objectives and policies—an appraisal not only of a company's marketing program but also of the framework which has given the program its direction, structure, and shape.

The preoccupation of the marketing audit with objectives and policies is one of its most salient and distinguishing characteristics, for it implies that, unlike other appraisals, the audit is a searching inquiry into the character and validity of the fundamental premises underlying a company's marketing operations. It is a review and evaluation of the assumptions, conceptions, and expectations that guide executives in their planning and operating decisions. It is a planned effort to test and assess executive beliefs and opinions about the character of the market, the company's position in the market, the company's objectives and capabilities, and the effectiveness of the various policies, methods, personnel, and organizational structures which are or might be employed.

As Wroe Alderson of Alderson Associates, Inc. has observed:

> The marketing executive may be visualized as operating on the basis of a sort of map. There are boundaries or limits marking off the class of customers he is trying to reach or the trade channels through which he is willing to sell. There are routes over which he can move in attaining his objectives which experience or investigation has indicated are better than other routes. This map may have to be brought up to date by a validation or a revision of operating assumptions . . .[1]

In this context, the marketing audit becomes essentially an effort to step back and take a penetrating look at the basic ideas which are the ultimate source of a company's marketing programs. It is an attempt to explicitly define and verify these ideas about the company, the market, and methods of reaching the market by testing them against current and accurate information.

The Basic Purposes

The marketing audit may thus be defined as a *systematic, critical, and impartial review and appraisal of the total marketing operation: of the basic objectives and policies of the operation and the assumptions which underlie them as well as of the methods, procedures, personnel, and organization employed to implement the policies and achieve the objectives.* This definition, however, is not complete. It conveys no sense of the purpose of the audit, as it should, for it is important to understand that the audit is a prognostic as well as a diagnostic tool—a search for opportunity as well as for malfunction.

Too many executives take a static view of appraisals. In examining the marketing operation or one of its component activities, they are concerned almost exclusively with the here and now. They are intent on identifying *existing* problems or weaknesses and discovering their causes,

[1] Wroe Alderson, *Marketing Behavior and Executive Action* (Homewood, Ill.: Richard D. Irwin, Inc., 1957), p. 419.

so that appropriate remedies can be applied. A marketing audit, too, aims at locating existing weaknesses, at pinpointing current problems and their sources. Like other types of evaluations, therefore, the audit too is a diagnostic tool. But diagnosis is not the only, or even the most important, purpose of the marketing audit. It is concerned as much with the future as with the present. It is a search not only for weaknesses that clearly exist but also for those that may arise. It is aimed at identifying current problems and determining their causes, but at the same time it probes for incipient problems—those just beginning or likely to emerge. This is what we mean when we say that the marketing audit is a prognostic as well as a diagnostic tool.

Executives tend also to conceive of audits almost exclusively as means for locating and defining problems. The identification of problems and possible remedies is, however, only one of the purposes of the marketing audit. The audit is, in addition, concerned with identifying the particular strengths of the marketing operation. It is a search for opportunities, existing and potential, to apply the factors which create strength in one marketing activity to others. And it is a search for opportunities in the market which had previously been overlooked or which have only recently emerged.

Thus, the marketing audit has several purposes. It is intended to reveal potential as well as existing strengths and weaknesses in a company's marketing operation, and it is intended also to bring into sharp focus possibilities for capitalizing on the strengths and eliminating the weaknesses. In consequence, the marketing audit is a tool that can be of tremendous value not only to the less successful, crisis-ridden company but also to the highly successful and profitable industry leader. No marketing operation is ever so good that it cannot be improved. Even the best can be made better. In fact, even the best *must* be made better, for few if any marketing operations can remain successful over the years by maintaining the status quo. Continued success requires continual adaptation to a constantly changing environment. It requires, therefore, continual scrutiny of the environment and of the firm's relationship to the environment, with the aim of spotting the cues which indicate both a need for modifying the firm's marketing program and the direction such modification should take. It requires an unremitting search for emerging opportunities that can and must be exploited if the marketing operation is to remain highly successful. The marketing audit, therefore, is not only a prescription for the sick firm but also preventive medicine for the currently healthy and successful firm.

A Total View

To summarize, then, the most prominent characteristics and most important purposes of the marketing audit are these:

It is a carefully programmed appraisal of the total marketing operation.

It is centered on an evaluation of objectives and policies and of the assumptions which underlie them.

Its aim is prognosis as well as diagnosis.

It is a search for opportunities and means for exploiting them as well as for weaknesses and means for their elimination.

It is the practice of preventive as well as curative marketing medicine.

WHY AUDIT—AND WHEN?

Every marketing executive recognizes that he operates in a highly fluid environment. He is fully aware that unceasing change is the most salient characteristic of his company's marketing situation. He knows that there is constant and continuous—sometimes even abrupt and dramatic—change in the size, composition, and geographic distribution of the population; in the size and distribution of incomes; in tastes, preferences, and habits; and in technology. He has, in short, absorbed the truth that has so often escaped other executives: The modern market is highly dynamic.

Keeping Abreast of the Times

Unfortunately, recognition of the dynamic quality of the market has not led marketing executives to recognition of all its implications. Many executives have not yet fully realized that continual flux in the market signifies continual alteration of the relationship of a company to its market and of the competitive relationships between companies, and that such constant and widespread change in the environment makes some facet of almost every existing marketing operation obsolete. As Arthur Felton has described the situation in the *Harvard Business Review:*

> There is probably no marketing plan in industry today that is not out of date. . . . The reason is that there are so many constantly changing factors in any company's marketing situation that it is practically impossible to keep revising a plan so rapidly and so accurately that there is no lag in it. The factors that keep a plan dated are not only those of the "changing American market" which *Fortune* and other publications have discussed—suburbia, the new middle class, the Negro market, etc. The dating factors have also to do with changing selling problems growing out of the major upheavals—shifts in consumer psychology that necessitate different kinds of advertising and packaging, trends in distribution that affect the company's relations with wholesalers and jobbers, changes in the "customer mix" that affect the efficiency of the sale organization, and so on.[2]

The significance of market dynamism, then, is that a firm's marketing operation tends continually to fall out of phase with current conditions and incipient trends. Elements of every marketing program are always losing their effectiveness. Methods, procedures, and organizational struc-

[2] Arthur P. Felton, "Conditions of Marketing Leadership," *Harvard Business Review,* March–April, 1956, p. 119.

tures rapidly become outmoded, and objectives and policies become inappropriate as the validity of the assumptions on which they are based is destroyed. The continual change in a company's marketing situation means, in fact, that no marketing program is ever completely and precisely adapted to the environment in which it is executed; indeed, it means that every program becomes ever more poorly adapted with the passage of time. This is evidenced by the fact that, almost from the moment a marketing program takes effect, a drift away from the program commences which accelerates as time goes by. This drift arises from the efforts of managers and their subordinates to cope with the many specific problems engendered by the lack of adjustment between the marketing program and the changing marketing environment. It is symptomatic of the inability to be always in perfect tune with the times. It is also dangerous if not arrested, for the drift implies that the planned marketing operation is degenerating into a patchwork of opportunistic and expedient actions. It implies that confusion and even chaos increasingly supplant the originally integrated and coherent plan for the application of marketing effort. In time, therefore, unless the marketing operation is revamped—unless objectives, policies, methods, procedures, personnel, and organization are once again combined in a carefully articulated plan which is better adapted to the company's current marketing situation—the drift and its accompanying confusion will almost certainly precipitate a company crisis.

Thus, the dynamic quality of the market implies a need for constant vigilance on the part of marketing executives. It compels recognition of the need for awareness of the nature of the changes taking place within and without the firm, and of the directions in which the marketing organization and program can be and must be modified in order to adapt to these changes. It emphasizes the need for improvement-consciousness, and thus for a continual search for new cost reduction possibilities and new sales opportunities. In other words, the rapid pace of change in our modes of living and the continually accelerating technological revolution in industry make it imperative that the marketing executive appraise and reappraise every element of his operations and organization. Moreover, if the executive wants the best results from these appraisals he must *plan* them, for only a systematic, careful, and orderly program of appraisal can assure that no activity or element of the marketing operation is neglected or subjected to only the most cursory examination. It follows, therefore, that the marketing audit is a necessary and important tool which can provide a marketing manager with the knowledge required to keep his operations abreast of the times and thus in a strong competitive position.

Auditing under Crisis Conditions

Many executives who recognize the effectiveness of a marketing audit seem to believe that it is needed primarily by companies which are problem-ridden and which face a deteriorating market and profit position. They regard the audit as an effective remedy for a marketing operation which is in critical condition. Such a conception of the audit is entirely erroneous, however, for, as we have already noted, the audit is preventive as well as curative marketing medicine. Nevertheless, this conception of the audit is so widespread that it may be worthwhile to give some reasons for believing that it is wrong.

Executives who conceive of the marketing audit as being unnecessary for a smoothly functioning, highly successful marketing operation have really failed to understand fully its nature and purposes. They fail to see, therefore, that appraisals made in an atmosphere of crisis are unlikely to have the character of a marketing audit. This is true for two reasons:

1. In a crisis situation there exists a compulsion to do something quickly which will resuscitate the marketing operation before it reaches a point of no return. Under crisis conditions, therefore, the aim of an appraisal must be to find an appropriate stimulant rather than a basic therapy. As a result, such an appraisal inevitably assumes the nature of a rapid scanning rather than a penetrating look at the marketing operation; and even this scanning is limited to those facets of the operation which experience and intuition indicate are most likely both to require attention and to respond quickly to treatment.
2. Since a crisis in a company's marketing operation often means that the company is experiencing financial difficulty, any appraisal undertaken at such a time will almost surely be allotted far less money than is required to do the job properly.

Thus, both for financial reasons and because of the need for haste, an appraisal under crisis conditions is likely to be far more superficial, far more limited in both scope and depth, than a true marketing audit.

Auditing the Successful Operation

The smoothly running and successful marketing operation can, therefore, be more effectively audited than a sick operation. More important, however, is the fact that it *needs* to be audited. Success tends to foster complacency, laxity, and carelessness. It permits tradition and habit to become the dominant shapers of marketing programs. It allows dry rot and excessive costs to develop and spread. It leads some marketing executives to become so deeply involved with existing policies and methods that they never bother to examine the possibility of performing the marketing task in other ways—ways which, although once inappropriate, may now be more closely attuned to the company's needs. Yet none of these well-known concomitants of success may be immediately apparent. A successful operation can move along well, for a time at least, propelled by the momentum which has been generated in the past. The growing waste of marketing effort and the increasing frequency of failures to pioneer innovations are not reflected at once in shrinking profits and market share.

Their effect is delayed, for marketing wastes and failures erode rather than shatter the company's market position. Sooner or later, however, the erosion of market position must find expression in reduced volume and profits—and, when it does, the "healthy" marketing operation appears suddenly to have contracted a very severe illness.

The dangers of success clearly suggest that in marketing as in home maintenance the time to fix the roof is when the sun is shining. They point clearly to the need for continual, systematic, critical, and objective appraisal of even the most successful marketing operation *while it is successful.* The negligence and waste, the complacency and blind obedience to tradition and habit which breed so easily in the culture of success can become extremely noxious viruses if permitted to develop unchecked. They can appear anywhere in a marketing organization, and they can in time sap the strength of the most vigorous marketing operation. The maintenance of health and vigor in the operation requires, therefore, that such factors be identified and eliminated just as soon as they appear. The marketing audit serves this end. It is, consequently, of considerable importance to the successful marketing organization, for it constitutes a kind of insurance against subversion by success.

SOME PROBLEMS OF AUDITING

The dynamism of the market and the awareness that continued success may have undesirable by-products point to a general need for marketing audits. They strongly suggest that every marketing operation can be improved through a systematic and comprehensive program of evaluation. Such a program of evaluation is not likely, however, to be executed without difficulty. It may be helpful, therefore, to indicate the nature of some of the more important difficulties that are likely to be encountered.

Some of the problems that will arise as an executive seeks to inaugurate and execute a marketing audit are of such moment that they have been treated more fully than is possible here by other contributors to this volume. The problem of defining appropriate standards or criteria for each marketing activity and each element of each activity which are valid and operational measures of effectiveness is an example. Other problems, such as that of obtaining the funds needed to pay for a full-scale audit, are so obvious that they require little more than mention. In addition to these problems, however, there are three others which merit attention. These involve (1) the selection of auditors; (2) the scheduling of the audit; and (3) the impact of the audit on marketing personnel.

Selecting the Auditors

No audit can be better than the people who make it. Consequently, no audit will yield the benefits that it is possible to obtain unless it is made by the right kind of people. As is implied by the definition of the audit, such people must be not only critical and impartial but also knowledgeable and creative. They must not be so involved with or "married" to existing policies and procedures that they cannot really be critical and objective in their assessments. In addition, they must possess the experience, know-how, and creative imagination needed to recognize problems and opportunities that are just beginning to appear on the horizon of the company's marketing situation and to define feasible courses of action for solving the problems and exploiting the opportunities. Finding enough such people to staff the audit can be a tall order. Few companies have an abundance of men with these characteristics. The quality of the audit is, nevertheless, determined largely by the extent to which the auditors possess these characteristics, and successful solution of the staffing problem is therefore of singular importance.

Scheduling the Audit

Since the marketing audit is an evaluation of the total marketing operation, it cannot be properly executed in a matter of days or weeks; it must be a relatively long-term project. And, as in any long-term project, there is always the danger that distractions may intervene to delay execution or that interest in the audit may be dissipated, with the result that the audit drags on and on. If the audit is permitted to drag on, however, conditions within and without the firm may change to such a degree that the findings when reported describe the marketing situation as it *was* rather than as it *is*. Any modification of the marketing operation on the basis of such findings could, of course, impair rather than improve the operation. Clearly then, the audit, if it is to yield accurate information about the company's current marketing situation, must be executed in accord with an established timetable. Preventing the many deviations from the timetable which can easily be rationalized is a central problem of any marketing audit.

Impact upon Marketing Personnel

The success of a marketing audit requires the full cooperation of all marketing personnel, from the chief executive and department heads to the salesmen in the field. The evaluation of an activity for which one is responsible, however, is often regarded by those carrying on the activity as a personal evaluation. These people often perceive in the audit a threat to their status and aspirations, and they therefore tend to resist it. They do not necessarily refuse to cooperate, but they may attempt to sabotage the audit wherever they feel it is possible to do so with impunity. Their resistance may make it extremely difficult—if not, in fact, impossible—to obtain accurate information. Moreover, the feeling that they are being threatened may impair their morale and reduce their effectiveness on the job.

It is extremely important to be aware of these possible side-effects of the audit so that pains are taken to obviate them through precautionary measures. Every effort must be made to create a genuine appreciation of the fact that the audit is not a fault-finding expedition but a search for ideas and tools that will enable everyone to do a better job. Marketing personnel must be educated to the fact that the audit is a management tool used to "help us help you" and not a device for "getting" anybody. They must be convinced that the audit is a full-scale effort to provide everyone in the marketing organization with important information that could not possibly be obtained through normal channels and routines. Before inaugurating a marketing audit, therefore, the possibilities of resistance and lowered morale must be dealt with through an educational campaign within the marketing organization.

* * *

Change is a dominant fact of life. It is also a dominant consideration in planning and executing marketing strategies and programs. In fact, appropriate and timely adaptation to change is the key to marketing success. Such adaptation requires appraisal and reappraisal of the total marketing operation to insure that inefficiencies are detected quickly and opportunities recognized as they appear. The marketing audit, if executed properly and in the proper atmosphere, can insure management against the inertia and astigmatism which retard growth and may even bring destruction. No marketing executive can escape the need, therefore, for giving serious consideration to the inauguration of a program of periodic marketing audits.

Networks of feedback loops link the company and its market. The dynamic nature of this interacting network should be investigated through the factors that comprise these linkages or connections. Simulation of significant behavioral relationships can determine causes of stagnation, growth and other disturbances. A successful interaction between company and market can be achieved only through knowledge of the entire marketing system.

42. MODELING OF MARKET AND COMPANY INTERACTIONS*

Jay W. Forrester†

All of you in marketing recognize that many linkages connect a company to its market. Some of these linkages are tangible like the flow of orders toward the company and the counterflow of product to the customer. Other linkages are obvious like the sales effort and advertising expended to communicate with the market. But many linkages are subtle and tenuous like those that carry customer attitudes and needs back to the decision-making points in the company.

But recognizing these linkages between company and market does not mean that one can see clearly the time-varying responses caused by interactions between them. It is in the interplay of forces caused by these interacting linkages that we find the causes of company and product growth and conversely find the influences which can cause stagnation and decline.

These company–market linkages form networks of feedback loops. In these loops an action by the company causes a response in the market which in turn produces the information on which decisions are based to control future company actions. The dynamic behavior of these feedback loops is poorly understood and contains many surprises.

The complexity of these interactions is far too great for analytical solution using conventional mathematical approaches. With trivial excep-

---

* Reprinted from "Modeling of Market and Company Interaction," *Proceedings of the Fall Conference of the American Marketing Association*, 1965, pp. 353–64.

† Massachusetts Institute of Technology.

tions, mathematics deals only with linear systems. Yet some of the most important behavior mechanisms in marketing depend for their very existence on nonlinear relationships. The only effective tool for understanding nonlinear, multiple-loop, feedback systems is the construction of a model that permits simulation of the behavior relationships which we perceive within the company and market.

The construction of models to represent market dynamics is now possible. The problem is not, as often supposed, the need for more empirical data. The pace of progress will be set entirely by the availability of investigators who understand the kinds of factors that are important in feedback system behavior and who can conceptually structure the presently available information and data.

Some of the linkages between a company and market appear in Figure 1. The company uses incoming information from the market as the basis for generating the outputs from company to market. These outputs generated by the company include price and the quality of products and services. Another output from the company is delivery delay which reflects the relationship between incoming order rate and production capability. Product suitability reflects the adequacy of new product development and the degree of perception by the company of market needs. Sales effort is a result of the company's resource allocation policies.

In the opposite direction from market to company, there is, of course, a flow of orders and payments. But there are also other important information streams. These might be defined in a variety of ways. One useful structuring of information from the market to the company is in terms of reflections of those linkages which the company projects to the market. The company should be interested in the market reactions toward price, quality, delivery delay, and product suitability.

Starting from Figure 1, to construct a dynamic simulation model requires that we define the responses that we believe exist in the two separate sectors—the company and the market. In each sector the task is to take the incoming inputs as a basis for generating the outputs. Within the company the time delays and policy interactions must be represented which convert market information into the outputs of price, quality, delivery delay, product suitability, sales effort, and product flow. Within the market the characteristics must be conceptualized and defined which we believe react to the inputs from the company and generate a stream of orders as well as the sources of information flowing to the company. This means that the model represents our operational knowledge about the management processes in the company and the customer processes in the market.

Figure 1 implies the futility of attempting to teach marketing as an isolated corporate function. In the corporation, marketing shares with the area of management information systems the characteristic that it depends on an unusually high number of linkages to other parts of the business system. It is not self-sufficient. By contrast, production is a more self-contained corporate function. I feel that this high degree of interconnectedness in marketing explains many of the difficulties encountered in attempting to teach the subject. Marketing can not be successfully isolated from its dynamic interactions with other company functions.

In Figure 1 we see implied many of the simpler feedback loops in the system. Company activities to generate quality lead to an actual product quality that produces a market reaction to quality and an information return to the company about the reaction to quality which is one of the inputs to the future management of quality. Likewise, a loop connects company price policy through prices to the market and back through the reaction of the market to price. But the system is not a collection of

FIGURE 1

Company–Market Linkages

COMPANY
PRICE
QUALITY
DELIVERY DELAY
PRODUCT SUITABILITY
SALES EFFORT
PRODUCT
PAYMENT
ORDERS
REACTION TO PRICE
REACTION TO QUALITY
REACTION TO DELIVERY DELAY
REACTION TO PRODUCT SUITABILITY
MARKET

separate and isolated loops controlling the separate company outputs. There are many important cross couplings. For example, a policy which reduces price can reduce the payment stream and thereby company profits so that pressure is brought on the activities controlling quality which then may lower the quality output from the company and in time cause a decrease in market orders. The feedback loops connecting company and market have many devious interconnections. The dynamic interactions within these loops can defeat our attempts at intuitive judgment about system behavior.

Some of the feedback loops between company and market are so-called "negative feedback loops" which attempt to adjust system operation toward some reference goal. Other loops are "positive feedback" in character and these latter account for the processes of growth and decline.

Figure 2 shows an example of a positive feedback loop involved in the growth of a new product. The sales effort operating at some sales effectiveness produces a sales rate. The sales effectiveness is a reflection of the desirability of the product and is a measure of the ease with which it can be sold. The sales rate generates revenue. A part of the revenue becomes available in the sales budget to support future sales effort. If the sales effectiveness is high enough and the fraction of revenue going to the sales budget is large enough, then a given sales effort will produce a sales rate and budget higher than necessary to sustain the initial sales effort. Under these favorable circumstances, sales effort leads to a growing sales budget which then supports an increasing sales effort. The regenerative growth process continues until something within the loop, perhaps the sales effectiveness, changes in an unfavorable direction. The rapidity of growth depends on the coefficients in the system such as the sales effectiveness and

FIGURE 2

Positive Feedback in Sales Growth

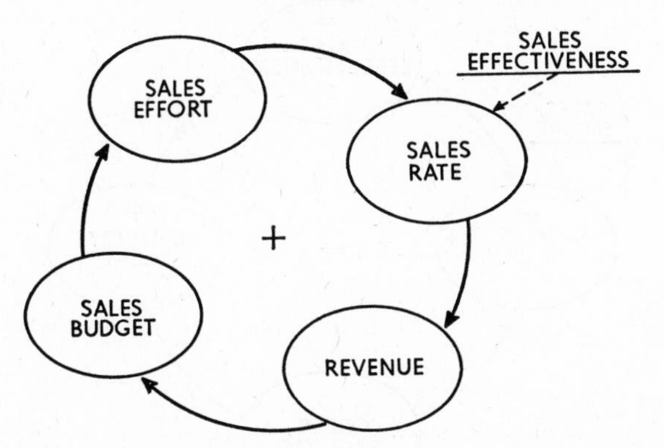

the fraction of revenue going to the support of sales effort. The rapidity of growth is also directly influenced by the delays around the loop. Because of the market delays, the sales rate lags behind the corresponding sales effort; because of manufacturing and invoice collection delays, the revenue lags behind the sales rate; because of the corporate budgeting procedures, the sales budget lags behind the incoming revenue; and because of the time to locate and train salesmen, the sales effort lags behind the budget. Other conditions being equal, the rate of sales growth will be doubled if the delays around this positive feedback loop can be reduced to half.

Conversely, a positive feedback loop can show degenerative decline. In the example of Figure 2, if the sales effectiveness is low, the sales effort may not support its own sales budget leading to a future reduction in sales effort that further reduces sales. Positive feedback loops can exhibit either growth or decay. By contrast, negative feedback loops tend to adjust activity toward a reference goal, but in the attempt they often produce fluctuation.

Figure 3 shows a negative feedback loop coupling sales rate, order backlog, delivery delay, and sales effectiveness. In this diagram it is assumed that sales effort remains constant. The relationship between order backlog and sales rate depends on the production capacity characteristics of the company. For illustration, assume that the production capacity is constant and the sales effort is more than adequate to create the corresponding sales rate if delivery delay is short. Under these circumstances, sales rate will exceed production capacity and the order backlog will increase. The increase in the order backlog will continue until the resulting increase in delivery delay becomes sufficient that some customers become unwilling to wait for delivery. As the delivery delay becomes longer, the product becomes less attractive and the product becomes less

FIGURE 3

Negative Feedback Limiting Sales

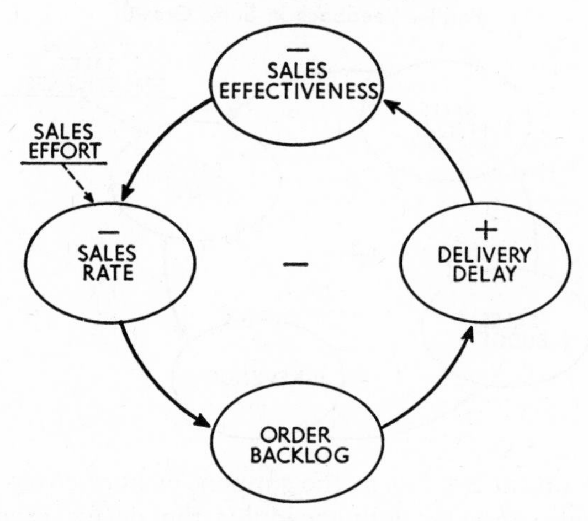

easy to sell. This means that, as delivery delay increases, the sales effectiveness declines until sales rate falls to the production capability. This negative feedback loop is at work in any market situation where delivery delays are long enough to be of concern to the customer. A negative feedback loop as shown in Figure 3 can exhibit instability. There are delays at each point in the loop. The sales rate does not respond immediately to changes in delivery delay because many of the orders under negotiation are already committed and cannot be redirected. Order backlog is an accumulation over time of discrepancies between the sales rate and the production capacity and backlog lags behind a change in sales rate. Delivery delay here represents the delay recognized by the market, and this lags behind the true delay as indicated by the order backlog. These delays, coupled with the other characteristics of the loop, can lead to overcorrection. A sales rate which is too high goes unrecognized until the backlog builds up and until the delivery delay is recognized. By this time delivery delay is excessive and leads to a reduction in sales rate below the production capacity. Then, order backlog declines unduly before the low delivery delay is recognized and sales again rise.

An important part of the negative feedback loop of Figure 3 is the nonlinear relationship between delivery delay and sales effectiveness as shown in Figure 4. Sales effectiveness is a maximum when delivery is zero. For very small delivery delays (measured in seconds for a drugstore item and up to months for a digital computer) there is no reduction of sales as delivery delay increases. However, with longer delivery delays, a region of steep slope is encountered where the delay is sufficient to discourage a progressively larger fraction of customers. For still longer delays, the curve levels out as it approaches zero sales effectiveness, representing the fact that a few customers find the product particularly suitable and are willing to plan ahead and wait unusually long.

FIGURE 4

Nonlinear Relationship

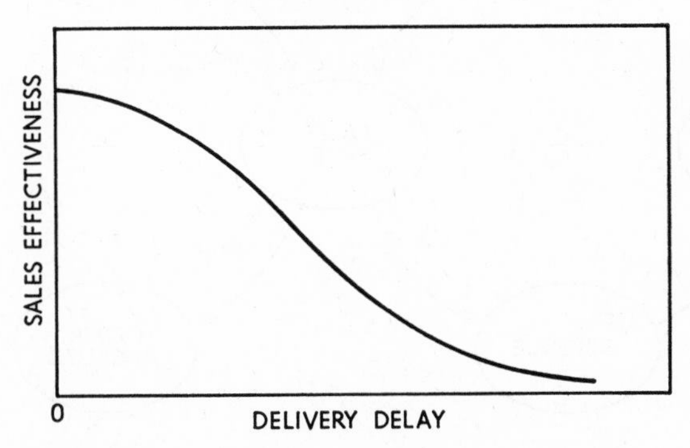

Now what would happen in a coupled company and market system involving the two control loops of Figures 2 and 3? These are shown interconnected in Figure 5. Here, if we assume that only a limited production capacity is available, the positive feedback loop will regenerate a rising rate of sales until the production capacity limit is reached. When the production rate no longer increases with sales, the negative loop would show an increasing delivery delay, and this would produce a declining sales effectiveness to limit further growth. This process of growth limitation is commonly encountered in many subtle ways in new product situations. A new product may enjoy adequate production as long as it does not encroach seriously on established products. As the new product grows, it may find increasing difficulty in competing for available capacity. Capacity limitation is often not recognized because its effect can occur even before the plant facilities are operating at maximum output. As the plant begins to reach its full capacity, flexibility is lost and orders for special variations in the product cause congestion and confusion. Average delivery delay increases even though it appears that the manufacturing capacity is still not fully occupied. Any situation where order backlogs are long enough to be viewed unfavorably by customers implies that this negative feedback loop is active in partially suppressing sales. Figure 5 can be recognized as an extremely simplified subset of the possible interactions contained in Figure 1. Even in this severely simplified form of Figure 5, the implied system behavior cannot be intuitively estimated as one contemplates changing the many factors within the two coupled loops.

The growth behavior of the double-loop system under one set of system conditions is shown in Figure 6. The figure is taken from a

FIGURE 5

Coupled Negative and Positive Feedback Loops

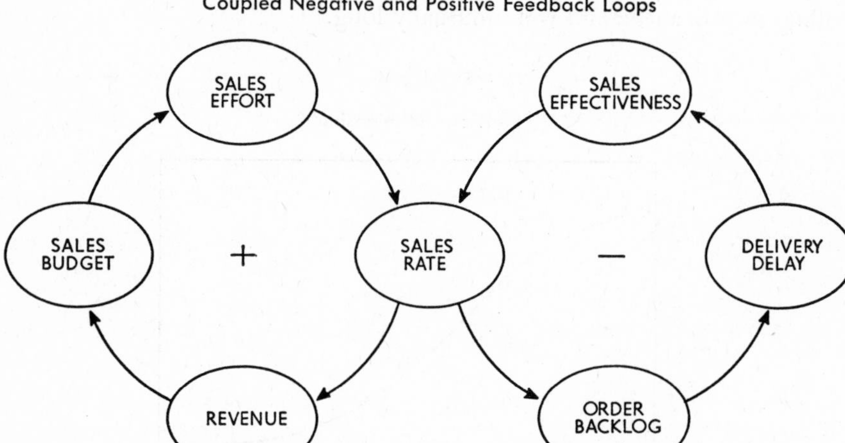

simulation run using "industrial dynamics" methods[1] and the DYNAMO compiler[2] for simulating the model. Growth in sales rate occurs during the first 60 months. Thereafter sales tend to fluctuate because the production capacity limit has been reached. During the early period of growth, sales effectiveness remains constant and high while at the same time the delivery delay remains constant and low. As the sales rate begins to approach the production capacity, the delivery delay increases and the sales effectiveness falls. After month 60, the system fluctuates because of the characteristics of the negative feedback loop in which readjustments within the loop are delayed and instability occurs on either side of the equilibrium position.

The major characteristics of Figure 6—the rapidity of early growth and the fluctuation during the stagnation period—depend on the parameters and the time delays in the two loops. The positive feedback loop of

---

[1] J. W. Forrester, *Industrial Dynamics* (Cambridge, Mass.: M.I.T. Press, 1961).

[2] A. L. Pugh, III, *DYNAMO User's Manual,* (2d ed.; Cambridge, Mass.: M.I.T. Press, 1963).

Figure 2 is the primary determinant of the growth phase shown in Figure 6; and the negative feedback loop in Figure 3 is the primary determinant of the behavior after sales growth has been arrested by reaching the production capacity. In Figure 6 we see a transition from positive feedback loop behavior to negative loop behavior which is triggered by the nonlinear characteristics represented in the production capacity and the sales effectiveness.

In Figures 5 and 6, the cessation of sales growth could not be forestalled by improved or expanded marketing activities. A larger fraction of revenue devoted to sales effort would only cause the delivery delay to

FIGURE 6

Growth and Stagnation in Sales

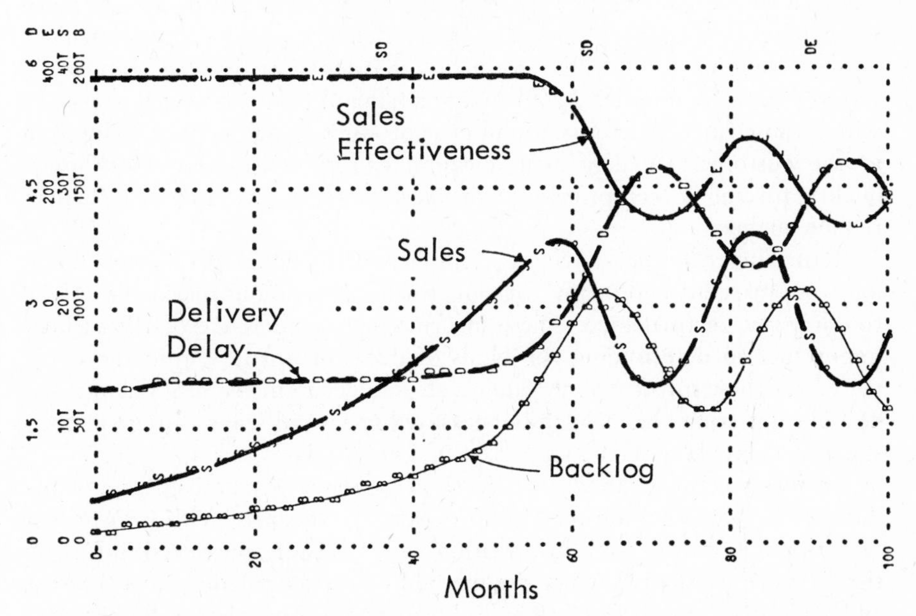

increase further and drive down the sales effectiveness to still lower values. Similar interactions, within the multiple channels of the far greater complexity of real-life situations, can invalidate marketing decisions by the inner workings of the market-company system.

It is sufficient to say that any marketing decision considered by itself is apt to become a victim of other interacting factors.

When one examines a model of the interactions between company and market, he discovers many mechanisms which can cause limitation in sales and stagnation in growth. In fact, one should reverse the common query, "How can I increase sales?" A better question is "How should one limit sales?" It is clear that one must limit sales. If the product has the highest quality, immediate delivery, the most suitable design, the widest distribution, the best salesmen, and the lowest price, sales will exceed the physical or financial capability of the company.

The oversimplified economic view suggests that price is the mechanism which balances supply and demand. But as a practical matter this is not true. There is no way to determine a price which will cause exact balance between supply and demand. Price is established on the basis of manufacturing cost, past traditions, competitors' prices, or in response to financial pressures on the company. If the price is set lower than the economic equilibrium value, then other influences must share the burden of limiting orders. The first effect will usually be a rise in delivery delay to make the product less attractive. After a period of long deliveries, the company may grow careless and allow quality to decline so that the lower quality contributes to limiting sales. The company profitability is, however, very sensitive to the balance of factors at work in the limitation of sales. As more of the burden is shifted to long delivery delay, lower quality, obsolete design, and unskilled salesmen, the price must be correspondingly lowered to maintain sales. Profit margins fall and create financial pressures which cause further deterioration in the product characteristics of interest to the customer. A degenerative spiral can then develop with lower quality forcing lower prices which exert financial pressure and further reduce quality.

Returning to Figure 1 we see a number of information channels flowing from market to company carrying information about market reactions to company performance. These information channels are of the utmost importance in determining the kinds of decisions made within the company. Yet these information channels are subject to many ills. The quality of an information channel can be measured in several ways—by its persuasiveness, delay, bias, distortion, error, and cross-talk.

An information channel usually shows greater persuasiveness and influence on the decision-making processes as it deals with short-term factors and as it deals with information which is easily measured. Information is more persuasive when the method of measurement is well known and widely accepted. For example, inventory information is highly persuasive since it appears monthly on the balance sheet measured to five decimal places (even though it may not be truly meaningful even in the first decimal place). By contrast, information indicating what the customers think of the company's product quality lacks persuasiveness because it is difficult to measure and hard to define. Oftentimes the most important information is the least persuasive.

Delay represents the time it takes information to travel along a channel. Information delays can be very long. For example, there can easily be a five-year delay between the quality actually produced in a product and the reputation for quality which is prevalent in the market. The time taken to judge quality is partly controlled by the natural life of the product. A meaningful measure of quality in an electric refrigerator can only be made if one waits through the normal life of the refrigerator. Even after quality is observed directly by a user, further delays are encountered before this reputation is transmitted to potential customers who have not been users.

Bias is the offset in an information channel where the perceived information deviates consistently from the true conditions. One often sees bias in a company's belief about the degree to which customers are satisfied. The company wants to believe it is doing well. Favorable reports bolster the self image and are remembered and circulated. Unfavorable reports are dismissed as exceptions or as unfortunate accidents.

Distortion is a deviation between the input and output of an information channel which is a function of the nature of the information itself. Distortion is sometimes intentional as in an averaging process. Averaging of sales data suppresses short-term fluctuation while allowing longer term deviations to be transmitted. The fidelity of the process therefore depends on the periodicity of the information being transmitted.

Error refers to random deviations and mistakes in an information channel. More effort is expended in reducing error than in reducing any of the other types of information deficiencies. Yet of the six types of information degradation, error is probably least important in affecting the feedback systems that couple a company to its market.

Cross-talk is a term borrowed from telephone usage and represents the tendency of information to be transposed from one channel to another. Transposition of the meaning of information is conspicuously evident in the channels flowing from market to company. There is a tendency for all customer dissatisfaction to take the form of indicating that the price is too high. This can happen at many points in the information channels. Price is too high for the low quality, or price is too high for the poor delivery, or price is too high for the discourteous salesmen. But the qualification is lost and only the reference to price is transmitted. Suppose that the customer is dissatisfied with the performance of his last purchase. He has decided not to buy again. When the salesman appears, the socially acceptable and most expeditious reason for not buying is to say that the price is too high. That is a value judgment which the salesman can not effectively counter. Were the customer to complain of quality, the salesman might offer to send a service engineer or he might explain how quality control at the factory has been improved. Or he might offer to take back the equipment for repair. But, if the customer wants none of these and wants not to be bothered, he says the price is too high. Suppose, however, that the customer does complain about the low quality and the obsolete design. Will the salesman risk the wrath of the development department and the factory by carrying these complaints back to the home plant? Probably not. He will simply report that the price is too high. But suppose that the salesman has courage to press complaints of an obsolete product. What will the management do to restore falling sales? It may well reduce price because it knows how to accomplish that, whereas a redesign is uncertain and far in the future.

From simulation of the information channels and decision-making policies that create the company-market system one can learn much about the behavior which in real life is so baffling. Interactions are complex. The human mind is not well adapted to intuitively estimating the behavior of complex feedback linkages. Marketing is a function which can not exist by itself. It is intimately coupled to production, capital investment policies, product design, and the company's educational programs. As one makes changes in a particular set of market linkages he may simply create greater difficulties in another area. It is only through knowledge of the entire system that successful coupling between company and market can be achieved.

Modern advertising requires a highly complex, thoroughly integrated communications system, extending from the initiating firm to the consumer. A model that simulates a communications network in a generalized advertising situation is presented in this brief excerpt from a longer article.

43. ADVERTISING OBJECTIVES, CONTROL, AND THE MEASUREMENT CONTROVERSY*

Charles E. Lee† and Jarvis Wolverton Mason‡

. . . Advertising is generally regarded as a form of communication the purpose of which is to convey concepts about companies, goods, and services by means of words, pictures, diagrams, sounds, music, color, shapes, and symbols on two levels of significance—the rational and the emotional. Rarely, however, is this definition followed through in the

* Reprinted from "Advertising Objectives, Control, and the Measurement Controversy," *Business Topics*, Vol. XII, No. 4 (Autumn, 1964), pp. 37–42.

† University of Connecticut.

‡ Consultant.

application of available measurement techniques or in the search for new ones. Apparently a desire for results in terms of sales and sales only all too frequently intervenes and, of course, the most effective communication may be negatively correlated with sales or profits.[1]

THE COMMUNICATIONS SYSTEM

Modern advertising requires the services of a highly complex and thoroughly integrated communications system stretching from the initiating firm to the consumer or other intended receptor of the message. The functions performed, however, fit a very simple pattern: the source or

DIAGRAM I

The Process of Communication

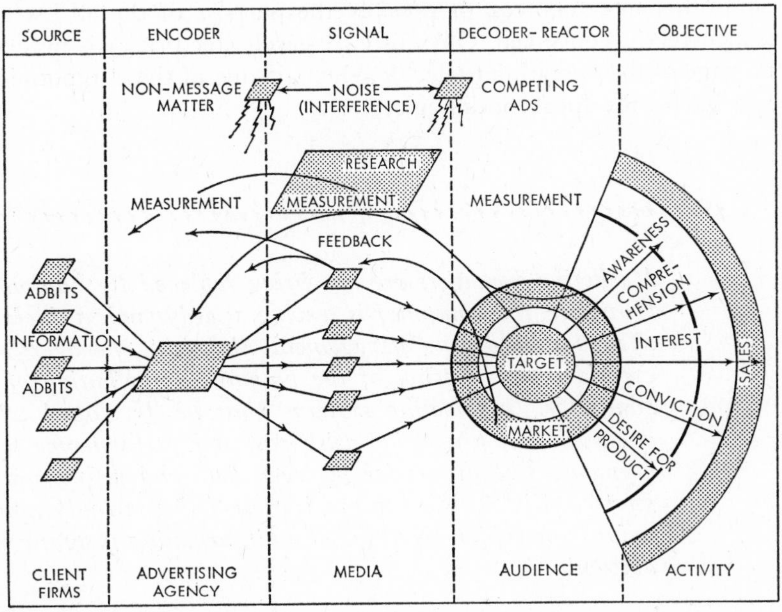

instigating firm, the encoder—the advertising agency that puts the ideas into symbols of some kind, the connector (media) required to convey the information (the signal), the decoder (reader of the ad) and the reactor (usually the same reader) who carries out the *objective* or purpose of the communication. Each stage, of course, is a potential source of measurement data. The accompanying model (Diagram 1) portrays the essential features of this process as a generalized advertising situation.

While this model simulates the network through which information[2]

[1] C. K. Raymond, "Profitable Advertising is Everybody's Business," speech to the Marketing Association of Canada, May 14, 1963.

[2] See Francis Bello, "The Information Theory," *Fortune,* December 1953.

flows, it is incomplete without a consideration of its purpose. This undoubtedly includes the exchange of intelligence between at least two minds, one of which is informed and motivated to communicate, the other capable of understanding, and willing to receive, the message. The connection must, of course, be adequate and complete; the message should be suited to the situation; it must have a definite purpose and the desired sales response should be readily and rapidly realized.

In advertising, many who receive the communication (signal) fail to enter the market. This may be because the message does not adequately relate, stimulate, or persuade; it may be improperly encoded or decoded; the connection may be faulty or associated with the wrong receptor, the timing may be bad, the environment unfavorable, and the response delayed or impossible to carry out. And, of course, it may be that the message has been confused with non-message matter, offset by competing ads and other interferences, or possibly the purpose of the ad itself has been incorrectly conceived. Obviously, research (feedback) is needed at every stage of the operation to decide which, if any, of these hypotheses is responsible for the apparent difficulty. . . .

Marketing managers are not being replaced by computers. However, the computer is serving as a dynamic vehicle for change in marketing management. Marketing managers must expand their estimates of the potential contribution of the computer. Information systems must be developed which combine data processing with cost and performance measurement. The difference between data and information is stressed. The decision process is presented as the only vantage point from which the value of an information system can be determined.

44. COMPUTER TECHNOLOGY AND THE CONTROL PROCESS*

Wayne Nelson†

For the past several years trade magazines, national news media, and professional journals have carried articles which allege that there is a

* Not previously published.

† Burroughs Corporation.

revolution taking place in management because of computers. Recently a leading national magazine carried a cover banner which indicated that "marketing" was the latest conquest of a computer. Both "revolution" and "conquest" have the connotation that something is replaced or made subservient. Marketing is not being replaced, automated, or made subservient to a computer. On the other hand, change is taking place in the marketing management process. The change is not dictated by a computer. The computer is the vehicle for change. The change is motivated by and stimulated by the pressures of a dynamic competitive business economy.

The most serious problem for American Business is and will continue to be the selection of executives who can make wise and effective decisions. The business organization also, however, has the responsibility to assure that its executives are provided with the tools and techniques which will maximize their effectiveness.

For more than 50 years we who have participated on the "management side" of business have charged our associates in production with the responsibility of keeping up with the latest technology in our manufacturing process in order that we can maintain a competitive position. In many if not most instances this has meant that the manufacturing professional has had to re-educate himself in terms of basic technology of production two if not three times during this span of operation. It wasn't that we couldn't continue to hand assemble a product or continue to custom design something, it was that technology offered an opportunity to increase productivity thus gaining competitiveness. Alternatively, because others in an industry group changed, we had to change to maintain competitiveness.

Today marketing managers stand challenged in the same way. The new information technologies offer significant potential. Competitive pressures force us to adopt that which is practical and feasible in order that we may maintain our position in an industry. The problem in most areas is not the need for a new theory or a new technique. The problem is to understand the process and thus define the problem so that an evaluation can be made of the practical and feasible ways of capitalizing on an existing body of knowledge. This is the opportunity that is available.

COMPUTER APPLICATIONS

Four major classes of application have emerged to date for electronic data processing systems. Each class has provided sufficient return on the investment to justify the acquisition of a computing system by the using organization. The first was the need for powerful computational instruments to support scientific and engineering research. This application accounts for an important segment of the total demand for computers and has stimulated the development of powerful and sophisticated computing equipment. Research in the social sciences, including Management Science, is part of this class. The second is the automatic control of physical processes. This would include control of production machine operations in commercial manufacturing as one example, and fire control of advanced weapons in defense operations as another. The computers that are used in these applications vary in many respects and would include both analog and digital types. However, they are generally lumped into one major class called "Scientific Computers."

A RESOURCE CALLED MARKETING MANAGEMENT

What is Marketing Management?

Several decades ago we demonstrated our attitude toward "management" when we presented a profit analysis for a new item which we might be interested in adding to our product line. The format of such a profit analysis ran roughly as shown in Figure 1. We computed the manufacturing and marketing costs, fixed and variable. We drew a subtotal. Then we added an element called *burden*. We added this burden to the project cost. Essentially the term "burden" was synonymous with "management." This is where we put the cost of management. The form pretty clearly illustrated our attitude to its contribution to the profitability of a product. Say "management" to the people in a production shop and you often get a definition like this—"It's them guys upstairs" or—"them guys back East." There usually was the general connotation of "non-productive."

FIGURE 1

Profit Analysis			
Investment: Project X			
Cost			
Manufacturing			
	Fixed	____	
	Variable	____	____
Marketing			
	Fixed	____	
	Variable	____	____
Subtotal			____
BURDEN			____
Total Cost			____

Our understanding of and our attitude toward management has changed significantly in the last several decades. We understand that marketing management is an essential resource to be consumed in an industrial process just as production capacity, transportation capability, money, time, or inventory are consumed. As a resource it has several unique characteristics. We can count inventory, money, and time. We have measures for the value of production and transportation. But we do not understand enough about management, as yet, to have a convenient unit of measure for it. There is no "erg" of management yet defined. We can change its value. We can increase its value. We can decrease its value. For a given value it is a substitute for other resources. Within limits, for example, we can substitute management for inventory, management for production capacity, management for transportation capability, or management for inventory and, needless to say, vice versa. We can "over capitalize" this resource in the same way and with the same detrimental effect that results from over capitalizing production capacity or inventory.

Although the immediate objective in this new class of application is to use the computer to increase the value of the management resource, it is important to understand that this alone will only increase the cost of operations. It is only when this added value is used as a substitute for alternative resources which are of higher cost that the real objective of the program is realized. For example, if the value of the management resource can be increased by one unit for $1.00 and if this additional unit of management resource will substitute for two units of production capacity which costs $1.00 per unit, obviously the process as a whole will produce a greater output for the same level of investment or the same level of output for the smaller investment. The basic question is the determination of the best mix of resources in a given industrial process. This is really the "name of the game." It is a complex process requiring not only an understanding of the interchangeability of the various resources consumed in a given industrial process.

Marketing capability, which is the term we generally use to describe marketing worth, is the product of a very complex interaction that takes place between three major components, as shown below.

The policy structure, embodying the goals of the organization, defining what it is the organization is attempting to do.

The tools and techniques, defining the precision which can be brought to bear in the attainment of the goal.

The organizational structure, a social structure which is the mechanism through which we communicate and administer.

Let me discuss each of these areas and their significance in more depth. The policy structure is the embodiment and reflection of the goal of the organization. The definition and understanding of the goal of the organization is of crucial importance in designing a management system. Let me emphasize its importance in this way. Given a goal, we will proceed to establish an elaborate and complex process called "marketing" whose primary purpose is the accomplishment of the organization's marketing goal. If we misunderstand or incorrectly define that goal, it is possible to create an operation which will "move" the organization in a direction that is not desired.

A business organization, even the corner grocery store, is a system living in systems. It is a system which lives in an economic system, a political system, a social system, a governmental system. It acknowledges allegiance toward or is constrained by these embedding systems. The interface between the business and these various external systems influences the goal of an organization. In practice, the goal of an organization is complex. In most instances we find the profit motive tempered with the desire to stay in business. The willingness to give up some increment of "today's" profit to be in business "tomorrow" (a "going concern" concept). The goal must be defined but this does not mean that it is static. The world is dynamic, therefore, the goals of an organization must be dynamic. The problem of defining, interpreting, and assuring an understanding of the goal is one of the more difficult problems of executive management.

Once we have defined the goal, the next step is to assure that the policy structure of the organization appropriately reflects that goal. This is not always so. In most business organizations of any size and complexity we find volumes of company publications in the book shelf which contain the official statement of corporate policy. All too often these policies are so embedded in procedural language as to be unidentifiable. And often they are completely out of touch with the goal.

Once we have an understanding of the goal and an assurance that the goal is interpreted into appropriate major policy statements, the next requirement is to assure that these policies are appropriately reflected in the decision process. This is not merely a requirement for literal representation. It adds a tremendous dimension of complexity to this process. Traditionally we have structured our American businesses along vertical resource lines. We find resource managers even at the executive management level. Typical are Vice President of Manufacturing, Vice President of Marketing, Vice President of Research and Development, Vice President of Distribution. In keeping with the resource orientation, most efforts to improve "management capability" have been localized and limited to these resource areas. As problem solvers became members of the management team, they obviously began their activity within the resource areas. They worked toward an optimal solution for each manager. We can visualize the answer one would get to the question: What is best for each resource manager? To the salesman the best answer is a large inventory—immediately available to his commitment—and well priced. The result is that he never loses a deal. The optimal solution to the man in charge of distribution generally tended to the desire to "pack everything in square boxes." He can have efficient material handling procedures and get efficient utilization of warehouse space. His common complaint is "stop adding items to the line and taking items out of the line." Why? Because this migration caused rewarehousing, and he got stuck with the salvage problem as well. For the manufacturing manager, the best answer was a large order backlog. It facilitated efficient lot sizes and assured a smooth work flow. Put all of these solutions together and you have something that is far from being the best system for the organization. One of the key elements in translating policy structure into the decision process is to *create balance*. This, of course, is where we implement the "best mix" decisions. Maximizing efficiency in each resource area is not a valid objective. In some circumstances some degree of relative inefficiency in manufacturing is desirable in order to absorb the variability and uncertainty of demand in manufacturing rather than in inventory safety stock. The resultant savings in investment in inventory may be greater than the cost of flexibility in manufacturing. Production capacity is generally a common resource to several items.

This concept of balance and interrelation is known as "the system concept." While it has been misunderstood, maligned and grossly misapplied, there is a real and important substance foundation for the concept. It must be understood.

There is yet a further complicating aspect to this process. We must establish the mechanism for the proper function of the relationship between the "time horizons" of marketing management. What I call the "time horizons" of marketing management are related to what other professionals would term the functions of management. The longest time horizon which management deals with is that associated with the planning process. Here management's responsibility is to acquire every shred of relevant information from which they can create an image of the "world" at some future point in time. Given this image, the question they address themselves to is what mix of resources can they acquire, create or otherwise bring into being, within their debt capacity, which will maximize the goals that they have established for the organization at that future period?

A dichotomy exists in planning. It became clear that in the "today" time horizon management's responsibilities and indeed its objectives are different from the longer range time horizon found in the planning function. The objective in the planning function was to determine the "best mix" of resources to meet a stated objective within some defined condition of the environment. But when that cloudy uncertain tomorrow becomes the stark reality of today any complex industrial process finds itself out of balance. That is, it finds itself with too much of something and too little of something else. In this "today" world, management's objective is to maximize the utilization of resources in being, regardless of the planning rationale for their creation. This apparent dichotomy is of significance in management system development.

Systems emphasize the value and the need for an adaptive capability in the management process. We are aware that in most instances the adaptive mechanism is indeed the logistical backbone of the management resource. One aspect of this adaptive mechanism is the monitoring and sensing system which tells us what we have and where, what we need and where, and the relative importance of the needs. It also requires procedural mechanisms for re-allocating resources and changing standards of performance throughout the system, so that we can adjust in the near term to assure the most effective utilization of the resources in being.

Having established a balanced operational structure, both in terms of resource and time horizon actions, marketing management must assure that its performance measuring systems do not violate the integrity of the structure. In most situations there is a management review process "overlayed" on the operation. It acts as an intelligence system by which management exercises control. This review process can take one of a host of administrative forms, for example, a periodic management review process involving direct transaction between executive management and operating level officials, or a more impersonal management reporting system. Often the specific items upon which organizational units are measured are not consistent with the structure of operation envisioned in the policy/decision system.

Supporting the information processing function we find performance and cost measuring and related data collection systems, data communication systems, data processing, data storage, and data display systems.

There is a distinction between information and data, as information is the *right* data, at the *right* time, in the *right* place, in the *right* form, to be consumed by the *right* man in making a decision. That definition is a play on words, but it embodies an important distinction which unfortunately has not been well understood in many application programs. Only in the decision process can one determine the relevance and the value of information. Here information value is stated in terms of form and content, accuracy, precision, and responsiveness. The information value is a function of the decision technique and the efficacy of the decision relative to other decisions.

Many organizations came into the "fascinating world of computers" at the time when the practical goal was economy in data processing. They attained their objective and then as we humans are prone to do, said to themselves, "we are good," "what can we do now?" The answer was to "strive to be of service to management." If they continued to maintain their same perspective of the world—essentially the data processing operation—they were in danger of becoming enamoured with the number of ways that you can aggregate, manipulate, graph and display the same basic set of data. They created a "report factory." Management was inundated with paper. We learned a lesson. When the information circuits to a decision point become overloaded, management, rather than using more information to support its decision process, puts on "a heavier filter" and begins to rely less and less on quantitative data and more and more on intuition, judgment and experience as the basis for its decisions.

As avenues of investigation and validation are completed, a new and complex phase called "implementation" begins.

Bibliography—Chapter V

ALDERSON, WROE. "Marketing Innovations and the Problem Solver," *American Marketing Association Proceedings,* June, 1965.

ALDERSON, WROE, AND GREEN, PAUL E. *Planning and Problem Solving in Marketing.* Homewood, Ill.: Richard D. Irwin, Inc., 1964.

ALEXANDER, RALPH S., AND BERG, THOMAS L. *Dynamic Management in Marketing.* Homewood, Ill.: Richard D. Irwin, Inc., 1965.

AMERICAN MANAGEMENT ASSOCIATION, MARKETING DIVISION. "Analyzing and Improving Marketing Performance," *Management Report No. 32,* 1959.

ANSOFF, IGOR. "Planning as a Practical Management Tool," *Financial Executive,* Vol. XXXII, No. 6 (June, 1964), pp. 34–37.

DAVIS, KENNETH R. *Marketing Management.* 2d ed. New York: The Ronald Press Co., 1966.

DRUCKER, PETER F. *Managing for Results.* New York: Harper & Row, Publishers, 1964.

HESKETT, J. L.; IVIE, ROBERT M.; AND GLASKOWSKY, NICHOLAS A., JR. *Business Logistics: Management of Physical Supply and Distribution.* New York: The Ronald Press Co., 1964.

LANGHOFF, P. (ed.). *Models, Measurement and Marketing.* Englewood Cliffs, N.J.: Prentice-Hall, Inc., 1965.

LEVITT, THEODORE. *Innovation in Marketing.* New York: McGraw-Hill Book Co., Inc., 1962.

LUCK, DAVID J., AND NOWAK, THEODORE. "Product Management—Vision Unfulfilled," *Harvard Business Review,* Vol. XLIII, No. 3 (May–June, 1965), pp. 143 ff.

OXENFELDT, ALFRED R. *Executive Action in Marketing.* Belmont, Calif.: Wadsworth Publishing Co., Inc., 1966.

OXENFELDT, ALFRED R. *Pricing for Marketing Executives.* Belmont, Calif.: Wadsworth Publishing Company, Inc., 1961.

SCHIFF, M., AND MELLMAN, M. *Financial Management of the Marketing Function,* New York: Financial Executives Research Foundation, Inc., 1962.

VI. MANAGING THE MARKETING MIX

The marketing mix consists of the inputs and resources utilized in marketing programs to achieve business objectives. An optimal marketing mix evolves from a creative blending of ingredients, or elements, so that the product or service is offered to the market under the conditions most favorable to the attainment of marketing objectives. The marketing mix is an example of the systems approach to marketing discussed in Chapters I and V. An efficient business adjusts to its changing environment by developing a coordinated marketing mix that meets the needs and wants of particular markets at different periods of time. Each firm's relative efficiency in the marketplace is determined by its own operational performance and by its success in meeting actions of competitive firms which are attempting to profitably satisfy demand in the same markets.

The marketing mix is composed of three submixes: the product and service mix, the distribution mix, and the communications mix. The product and service mix is concerned with all the ingredients that comprise the bundle of utilities consumers purchase. This includes such items as the product per se, the package, branding, labeling, warranties, and services accompanying the product. The distribution mix has two major components: (1) channels of distribution, including all the middlemen and facilitating agencies involved in getting products and the title to products to consumers; and (2) physical distribution, which is concerned with transporting, warehousing, storing, and handling products. The communications mix is concerned with all the persuasive and informational ingredients employed in communicating with the marketplace. Included are personal selling, advertising, sales promotion, merchandising, and special sales aids.

Marketing managers are continuously challenged to select the mix of ingredients that best conforms to market demands, returns optimal profits, and is consistent with attainment of other objectives. The selections presented in this section emphasize major problems and policy issues in designing each of the three mixes as well as the overall marketing mix.

A. Product and Service Mix

Corporate health depends on a continuing flow of new products and improvements in existing ones. While many firms have written statements of new-product objectives, few of these broadly written policies are of real value in product development effort. The formulation of logical objectives is the key to achieving effective, efficient new-product planning, research, and development.

45. NEW PRODUCTS AND CORPORATE STRATEGY*

Taylor W. Meloan†

IMPORTANCE OF NEW PRODUCTS

No phase of marketing management has received greater attention in industry during recent years than has new product planning, research, and development. The reasons for this stress are obvious. In most industries, competitive pressures require a constant flow of technologically new goods or improvements in existing ones if corporate sales and profits are to be sustained or enhanced. In chemicals, metal working machinery, industrial installations, and transportation equipment, as examples, new products have accounted for 40 to 80 percent of sales increases during the past five years. The same is true in many consumer goods markets. The drug, cosmetic, photographic, toy, and household goods fields have been especially prolific in new product introductions in the immediate past. Some

* Not previously published.

† University of Southern California.

relatively small firms have blossomed overnight on the basis of a single new development that has caught on.

Current inflationary pressures in our economy are not likely to result in less emphasis on new products. Indeed, they will probably lead to an increase in overall research and development and more new technology as firms continue to scramble for the consumer and/or the industrial dollar. There is every reason to believe that the Johnson administration will continue to expand its support for "basic" and military research from which commercially feasible developments may emerge. Thus, it seems logical to assume that overall R&D budgets, which include allocations for new product research in most firms, will spurt ahead of the estimated current $21 billion annual total.[1]

NEW PRODUCT BATTING AVERAGES

For years, we have read that four out of five new products fail. This cliché stems from an early postwar study of 200 leading packaged goods manufacturers. Since respondents were asked about their success with products actually introduced, it is contended that the failure rate would have been even greater if those which never reached the commercialization stage, on which management spent considerable time and talent in laboratory, field, and office, had also been included in the calculations.[2] Also, since the sample was restricted to large firms, it is often argued that the success ratio would have been much less had smaller, and presumably less sophisticated firms, been included in the survey. However, these are unproven hypotheses that are at least partially refuted by later data. In a 1960 study of 922 new products introduced by 65 prominent concerns, 49 percent were considered to be successful, 34 percent were in the doubtful category, and only 17 percent were outright failures.[3] But most of the doubtful ones eventually became failures unless they were revamped to remedy marketing and/or production deficiencies. This analysis showed surprisingly little difference in the success–failure ratio between industries, but there were startling variations within industries. A limited number of firms have outstanding new product "batting averages." Of the 22 products which S. C. Johnson & Son have launched in the past decade, for example, 20 are still on the market.[4]

---

[1] See Edgar A. Pessemier, "Directing R&D for Profitable New Product Development," *Marketing and Economic Development* (Chicago: American Marketing Association, 1965), pp. 279–87 for an overview of the diverse nature of research activities which fall within the purview of corporate and governmental research and development.

[2] *A Survey of 200 Leading Package Goods Manufacturers on Experiences and Problems Prevalent in the Introduction of a New Product* (New York: Ross Federal Research Corporation, 1945), p. 1.

[3] *Management of New Products* (New York: Booz, Allen & Hamilton, Inc., 1960), pp. 14–15.

[4] "The New Product Boom," *Sales Management* (August 3, 1962), p. 46.

Success Criteria . . . In part, these differing ratios stem from lack of common norms for defining product succsss. While sales volume and profits are traditional ones, ancillary success criteria cited by marketing managers include the following: tapping new markets, making other orders possible, absorbing excess capacity, providing potential for expansion, reinforcing a firm's reputation as a leader, and reducing returns or complaints about performance. A high score on one or more of the foregoing criteria could result in a new product with a mediocre sales record being considered a satisfactory addition to a line.

Failure Rates in Consumer versus Industrial Fields . . . There is reason to believe that consumer goods producers often experience a higher new product failure rate than do those making industrial goods. Generally, there are more distribution variables to consider in successfully launching new consumer items than is the case with industrial products. Furthermore, the extensive promotional budgets required for many nationally distributed consumer goods in highly competitive lines create difficult-to-achieve breakeven points which are not common in job-order industrial fields where limited markets and small volume do not necessarily spell failure. Admittedly, however, large research investments in technologically new industrial products can lengthen pay-out periods unduly, thereby creating situations comparable to those faced by new consumer goods in intensely competitive markets.

NEW PRODUCT POLICY GUIDES

Although many firms now have written statements covering their new product emphasis or objectives, there is considerable evidence indicating that these policy guides are frequently so broad that they are of limited value in channeling effort. Product scope, desirable mix, and profitability criteria are too often inadequately covered. The marketing managers of other concerns indicate that written product policy statements are unnecessary because of the close rapport among members of the top management team; but, when they give differing replies to questions about new product plans, there is obvious reason to question their agreement.

Clear Cut Goals Needed . . . The first and most elementary step in achieving new product planning, research, and development maturity is to formulate logical accomplishment goals. This implies a complete audit of company strengths and weaknesses. An objective analysis of production capacity, availability of materials, adequacy of labor, management talent, and distribution facilities provides the basis for future planning. What one firm may reasonably expect to accomplish may be a pie-in-the-sky dream for another.

Production and Marketing Fit . . . In many successful companies, the key factor influencing the selection of new products for development and commercialization is the degree to which they fit or mesh with the present line. A high degree of production accord exists when present plant, labor, equipment, and manufacturing processes can be used in making new products. Acceptable adjustment requires minimum additions or alterations in one or more of these production categories. Such firms also consider it desirable when a contemplated addition to the line can be manufactured with materials and components identical or similar to those used in current production. This is the rationale of the Ekco Products Company, a subsidiary of the American Home Products Company. Ekco is probably best known to most of us for its housewares and cutlery. Because of this firm's know-how with metals and plastics, its primary areas of product interest are other houseware items and builders' hardware.[5]

From a marketing standpoint, new product harmony exists when established distribution outlets and sales organizations can be used to move a new good or line through the pipelines. The Bristol-Myers Products Company, for example, is interested chiefly in new items that may be sold through drug, grocery, discount, and department stores—its traditional channels.[6] The possibility of using the same service or repair facilities and personnel enhances the fit between current products and new ones as does blanket brand identification. The Hoover Company's half-century image as a leading producer of vacuum cleaners has facilitated its introduction of other products for home maintenance purposes.

Decisions Depend Upon Objectives . . . Lack of a high degree of production or marketing adjacency between established products and contemplated new ones does not necessarily mean that new product ideas should be discarded. This decision depends upon a firm's objectives. As the Cheshire Cat commented to Alice (in Wonderland), where one goes depends a great deal on where he wants to get to. Textron successfully overcame low profits in the textile industry by expanding into more lucrative fields. Its key diversification objective was to earn 20 percent after taxes on net worth.[7] Smoothing out seasonal fluctuations in sales is reported to have been a prime consideration behind recent diversification moves by Bell and Howell. Virtually all West Coast aerospace companies have established commercial divisions largely because of short-run insecurity over hot–cold war temperature changes, and also the longer-run phasing out of military air frame construction.[8] In short, there are many

---

[5] Interview with John J. Kane, Vice President-Marketing, Ekco Products Company, Chicago, Illinois, September 14, 1966.

[6] Interview with Arthur Pearson, Director of Market Planning, Bristol-Myers Products Company, New York, May 19, 1966.

[7] Royal Little, "The Pitfalls of Corporate Diversification," *Transcript of the Third Annual New Product Seminar* (Irvington-on-Hudson, New York: The New Products Institute, Inc., 1956), p. 8.

[8] See John S. Gilmore and Dean C. Coddington, "Diversification Guides for Defense Firms," *Harvard Business Review* (May–June, 1966), pp. 144–155. This study of the product mix and diversification criteria of 13 firms revealed that all of them

pertinent and often interrelated reasons why firms move into new lines or industries.

Propagation and Acceptance of Criteria . . . In most companies, including those previously cited, product scope and mix are usually determined on the basis of multiple criteria. Regardless of what they are, such considerations should be *recorded*, *disseminated*, *understood*, *promoted*, and *accepted* by all appropriate personnel through the intermediate management levels of the enterprise. The establishment of product line parameters should not stifle management imagination but rather guide it in directions designed to maximize the achievement of company objectives. Consideration of ideas which clearly fall outside of the boundaries that have been set up should require exceptional justification.

Annual review of product policy statements is desirable to make sure that they continue to reflect corporate objectives. If they have been carefully drafted initially, only minor changes should be needed from time to time in the absence of an abrupt shift in management thinking.

NEW PRODUCT IDEA SOURCES

Study of a large number of new product case histories fails to show any single source of ideas as the most fruitful one. Generally, however, internal sources are cited more often than external ones as creative seedbeds. Some companies seem to have a dearth of suggestions while others are deluged with them. The key factor stimulating the internal flow of ideas appears to be an innovational philosophy which pervades the entire organization. A highly motivated management team in a permissive organization that is known to be willing to accept the risks of new product evolution is almost sure to be more productive of ideas than equally competent men in an authoritarian, or "fat and tired" firm that is primarily interested in maintaining the status quo.

In part, however, the number of product ideas available for consideration is a function of a firm's definition of "newness."[9] Concerns that limit product change to minor variations in operation, design, color, or packaging are likely to have more ideas to consider than those that seek true technological newness. Companies with well structured R&D facilities and engineering laboratories typically get more worthwhile ideas internally than do smaller companies that perforce often turn to external sources such as customers, raw material suppliers, competitors, firms in allied fields, government agencies, consulting organizations, research institutes, or free lance product analysts.

---

consider a 50–50 split between defense and non-defense business to be ideal. But our deepening involvement in Vietnam has lessened the pressure to achieve such a balance in most defense-space companies.

[9] Chester R. Wasson, "What is 'New' About a New Product?" *Journal of Marketing* (July, 1960), pp. 52–56.

Legal Hazards . . . A confidential relationship may be thrust unwillingly upon a company for alleged or actual use of an unsolicited idea. Cautious firms that decline to consider unpatented suggestions from outsiders often return such letters with covering notes stating that mail clerks stopped reading when the nature of the correspondence became apparent. Other companies return suggestions with release forms for the signature of those submitting ideas. Generally, these waivers disclaim liability if the company examines the proposal. They specify further that payment shall be at the firm's sole discretion and shall not exceed a stipulated amount. The obvious purpose of these steps is to preclude a confidential relationship developing unless and until agreement is reached regarding compensation, if any, for the idea.

Rather than enter into royalty arrangements with outsiders, many companies prefer to buy outright ideas or information which interests them, or they may escrow the proposition with a third party who is technically qualified to evaluate its merits. In any event, most attorneys consider it highly unwise to submit unsolicited ideas to a panel or a committee of technical or management personnel for evaluation prior to limiting corporate obligations to the outsider.[10]

In recent years, the doctrine of "strict liability" has added a new hazard with which manufacturers of new products must be prepared to cope. For more than a century, the concept of "privity" meant that the buyer could only sue the seller for damages caused by product malfunction. No longer is that the case. A manufacturer may now be held responsible for injuries resulting from the use of his products even though he used all reasonable care in making them. In a major bench mark case involving a defective automobile which caused personal injury, the court held that by placing the car in the stream of commerce and promoting the brand aggressively to the public a warranty was implied that it was safe for the use intended.[11] The long standing legal need to prove negligence in manufacture was set aside. As a result of this and other similar decisions, personal injury lawsuits are becoming much more common.[12] This trend points up the need to develop and to test more adequately than ever new products before they are released.

New Products by Merger . . . Firms can expand their product lines via internal development or they may buy an existing business or product. Of course, some companies pursue both policies simultaneously. Those who favor mergers generally rely on brokers, consultants, bankers, business friends, and aggressive "scouting" for leads. One well-known, highly diversified company is reported to have developed a list of approximately

---

[10] John W. Bohlen, "Legal Considerations in Product Development and Introduction," in *Establishing a New Product Program* (New York: American Management Association, 1958), pp. 30–36.

[11] *Henningsen* v. *Bloomfield Motors, Inc.*, 32 N.J. 358, 161 A.2nd 69 (1960).

[12] Arthur F. Southwick, Jr., "The Disenchanted Consumer—Liability for Harmful Products," *Michigan Business Review* (January, 1966), pp. 5–11.

1,500 influential businessmen and community leaders who are reminded regularly of the firm's interest in other enterprises.

Securing acquisition leads is no less difficult than generating ideas for internal development. However, well-financed, respected companies that are considered to be merger conscious apparently do not lack for candidates from whom to choose. The Glidden Company and Hunt Foods are reported to be contacted regularly by firms that wish to affiliate with them. While it may be assumed that there are many "cats and dogs" among the list, well-managed, desirable firms are also available for consideration.[13] Sometimes they favor merger with a larger and stronger company in order to secure new capital for continued growth. In many other instances, the management of a closely held corporation may want to sell out in order to realize a capital gain, or to make possible an exchange of stock that has inheritance tax advantages.

ORGANIZATION FOR ACTION

Regardless of whether a firm expands its line by development of products within the firm, through purchase of existing business or products, or by pursuing an ambidextrous policy, organization for action is necessary. Without *motivation*, *direction*, and *coordination* of staff specifically charged with new product responsibility, it is unlikely that anything will happen. In many firms, initial discussions about the desirability of new products have not led to the creation of appropriate plans and procedures for internal development because executives were too absorbed in day-to-day operations.

New Product Departments . . . In recognition of the importance of new product evolution as a full-time activity, more and more firms are setting up new product planning departments. As yet, they rarely exceed four or five managerial members. In fact, many of them initially consist of only a director. The key purposes of these managers and departments are to mesh the gears of the new product creation process and to insure continuity of effort. Liaison between technical and marketing research and development must be maintained, as well as multidirectional communication between staff and line production, finance, and sales personnel. Frequently, too, the work of independent design, marketing, or management consultants must be coordinated with that of the company. Usually product planning managers report directly to top management; common alternatives provide for reporting to the president or executive vice president, to the vice president of research and development, or to the vice president of marketing or sales.[14]

---

[13] See James B. Boulden, "Counter-Intelligence in Corporate Mergers," *Business Horizons* (Winter, 1965), pp. 47–52; and L. A. Casler, "Pitfalls of Acquisitions," *Dun's Review and Modern Industry* (June, 1966), pp. 34–35.

[14] Jay W. Lorsch and Paul R. Lawrence, "Organization for Product Innovation," *Harvard Business Review* (January–February, 1965), pp. 109–119.

Use of Committees . . . Because of the inter-functional nature of successful new product evolution many companies use one or more kinds of committees to facilitate action in addition to or in lieu of product planning personnel. In some firms, product idea teams plus product screening or evaluation committees have been set up. Creative, divergent thinkers are sought for the former groups, while the latter committees are usually composed of those with analytical, convergent minds who review critically the output of the idea teams. In other firms, these functions are performed by one committee. It generates ideas of its own, passes judgment on those submitted by others within the firm, and reviews suggestions from outsiders that have been cleared by the legal department. If the company has a product planning department, one or more members are usually assigned to each committee. Often the product planning manager is either chairman or secretary of idea and/or screening committees. He seeks to establish a creative climate and a sense of momentum in their deliberations. This is important because committee members usually have day-to-day responsibilities that often seem more pressing. Another common responsibility of product planning department members who are assigned to committees is the maintenance of records about group decisions. Such committees may also be chaired by a member of general management, marketing management, or by an R&D officer. In any event, all of the foregoing areas plus marketing research, finance, production, and sales are likely to be represented.[15]

While the use of new product departments and/or committees are common ways of expediting new product evolution, this responsibility is borne in some companies solely by the research and development department, by the sales department, or by a member of top management, even the president.

Initial Appraisal . . . Preliminary screening is an obvious initial step in winnowing new product wheat from chaff. Regardless of whether it is done by a committee, a department, or an individual, experience and judgment are used at this stage far more than formal research. If a firm has established its overall objectives and scope of product interest, the delineation of preliminary screening criteria should not be too difficult. Ideas are considered in the light of these factors. Reference tools largely consist of the telephone, knowledgeable people in the firm, and the reference library. In many companies, from one hour to two days is a common range per idea. Of course, obviously inappropriate ones are rejected immediately.

Feasibility Analyses . . . Ideas that survive preliminary screening are generally subjected next to more detailed technical and marketing analyses. To facilitate research and inter-departmental communications, product proposals are usually prepared at this stage describing the idea

[15] Ferdinand F. Mauser, "Which System Works Best," in *New Products Marketing, Printers' Ink* (May 29, 1964), pp. 88–90.

and its purposes in concrete terms. Some companies have forms for this purpose that are quite detailed. That of Beckman Instruments is eight pages long. Like many others, it provides space to record the results of research and the estimates of functional specialists about project feasibility. A majority of companies use checklists of some sort for this purpose. Those that conduct analyses-in-depth commonly include sections covering the project cost and time schedule, the target date for completion, estimated average return on investment, patent possibilities and restrictions, projected sales in dollars and units for X years, pricing, product life, the effect, if any, on the current line, the competitive situation, manufacturing fit, channels of distribution, promotional investment, and a project P&L statement or break-even chart.

Evaluation Formulas . . . A few companies have experimented with numerical formulas or equations to secure a quantitative indication of an idea's worth. They include the Quaker Oats Company, Monsanto Chemical Company, Olin Industries, Inc., and American Alcolac. In most of these schemes, the rater assigns a point score from a specified range to each of a series of product criteria. In some of them, plus and minus values are used. Others require simple mathematical calculations, but they all provide a total point score or an index number.[16] Their purpose is to establish priorities for developmental consideration. A few firms using new product rating systems have scored past projects, successful and unsuccessful, as bench marks for comparison. These schemes have been controversial. Opponents argue that they are arbitrary and lack flexibility. Supporters rebut with the contention that they force consideration on an organized basis of all of the key variables influencing product success. They point out also that the ratings can be supported or refuted by other data.

The foregoing implies that all companies conduct a detailed study of projects that have survived preliminary screening. This is not always the case. Some firms seek only a broad spectrum of executive opinion about ideas under consideration. They reserve more detailed analysis until the project has been authorized. In other companies, the depth of analysis depends largely upon the investment in the contemplated product.

Coordination of the Analysis Phase . . . Like preliminary screening, the analysis phase of new product investigation is coordinated in most firms either by the new products department, by a committee, or cooperatively by both. In companies favoring committees, the preliminary screening group may also coordinate the feasibility investigation. In other firms, these activities are kept separated. In large concerns with many projects under consideration, several teams or sponsor groups may be coordinating feasibility studies simultaneously. Team membership depends upon the research requirements. If the firm has a new products

[16] Barry M. Richmond, "A Rating Scale for Product Innovation," *Business Horizons* (Summer 1962), pp. 37–44.

department, it is usually represented on each group, and part of the data gathering is done by that department. Naturally other areas and functional specialists must be called upon for help. In firms that do not rely upon new products departments and/or committees to coordinate idea analyses, this phase of product evolution will likely be directed by a designated member of general management, marketing management, sales, or R&D.

When the feasibility investigation is complete, the data must be summarized with a recommendation—usually by the executive in charge of the research. Often segmental approvals by area heads are secured. Then, proposals are examined *in toto* by the executive committee of the firm and/or by the officials in charge of new products. They may approve the project, table it, or reject it; or they may authorize additional research before a final decision is made.

Acquisition Screening . . . Organization for action is equally necessary if a company embarks upon an acquisition program. However, the screening arrangements for mergers are usually less complex than those required for internal evolution of products. The former is often done under the direction of the president, chairman, or a designated member of top management. Of course, functional specialists are called upon as needed in the evaluation process. Consultants are often used too, especially to conduct management audits.

Many merger-minded firms use evaluation checklists to make sure that they do not overlook key factors which should be considered.[17] The Brown Engineering Company, which has acquired three firms within the past two years, screens potential acquisitions with a point scored "merger matrix" with 17 factors which must be reviewed. They include suitability, non-defense orientation, past earnings on investment, tax loss carry forward, marketing orientation, financial rating, price–earnings ratio, size of cash outlay required, position on ogee (growth) curve, status of competition, product outlook and protection, industry outlook, strength of top management, and resource interchange. Study teams independently score firms under consideration and reconcile rating differences.[18]

SUMMING UP

Most concerns are still experimenting with organizational procedures and techniques for new product evolution. There is no one best way that will fit every firm. The foregoing approaches must be adapted creatively to meet specific company needs and situations. Intelligent planning, an

[17] See George D. McCarthy, *Acquisitions and Mergers* (New York: Ronald Press Company, 1963). Appendix A consists of a checklist for proposed acquisitions, pp. 269–286.

[18] Robert B. Anderson, "How to Evaluate a Potential Acquisition," *Business Management* (August, 1966), pp. 26–36.

intense pioneering spirit, and continuity of effort are the key attributes in achieving success.

Successful new product strategy should be viewed as a planned totality that looks ahead over some years—a plan for a timed sequence of conditional moves. At each stage in a product's life cycle, management decisions must consider the competitive requirements for the next stage. Four stages in the product life cycle are introduced. Focusing on these stages will aid management in determining the feasibility of product change, the introduction of new products, and profit optimization.

46. EXPLOIT THE PRODUCT LIFE CYCLE*

Theodore Levitt†

Most alert and thoughtful senior marketing executives are by now familiar with the concept of the product life cycle. Even a handful of uniquely cosmopolitan and up-to-date corporate presidents have familiarized themselves with this tantalizing concept. Yet a recent survey I took of such executives found none who used the concept in any strategic way whatever, and pitifully few who used it in any kind of tactical way. It has remained—as have so many fascinating theories in economics, physics, and sex—a remarkably durable but almost totally unemployed and seemingly unemployable piece of professional baggage whose presence in the rhetoric of professional discussions adds a much coveted but apparently unattainable legitimacy to the idea that marketing management is somehow a profession. There is, furthermore, a persistent feeling that the life cycle concept adds luster and believability to the insistent claim in certain circles that marketing is close to being some sort of science.[1]

* Reprinted from "Exploit the Product Life Cycle," *Harvard Business Review*, Vol. XLIII, No. 6 (November–December, 1965), pp. 81–94.

† Harvard University.

AUTHOR'S NOTE: This article will appear in a forthcoming book, *Marketing Vision*, edited by Lee Adler.

[1] For discussions of the scientific claims or potentials of marketing, see George Schwartz, *Development of Marketing Theory* (Cincinnati, Ohio: South-Western Publishing Co., 1963); and Reavis Cox, Wroe Alderson, and Stanley J. Shapiro, editors, *Theory in Marketing* (Homewood, Illinois: Richard D. Irwin, Inc., Second Series, 1964).

The concept of the product life cycle is today at about the stage that the Copernican view of the universe was 300 years ago: a lot of people knew about it, but hardly anybody seemed to use it in any effective or productive way.

Now that so many people know and in some fashion understand the product life cycle, it seems time to put it to work. The object of this article is to suggest some ways of using the concept effectively and of turning the knowledge of its existence into a managerial instrument of competitive power.

Since the concept has been presented somewhat differently by different authors and for different audiences, it is useful to review it briefly here so that every reader has the same background for the discussion which follows later in this article.

HISTORICAL PATTERN

The life story of most successful products is a history of their passing through certain recognizable stages. These are shown in Exhibit I and occur in the following order:

Stage 1. Market Development—This is when a new product is first brought to market, before there is a proved demand for it, and often before it has been fully proved out technically in all respects. Sales are low and creep along slowly.

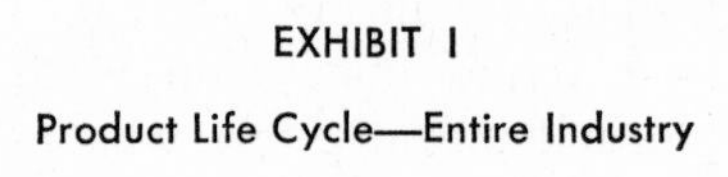

EXHIBIT I

Product Life Cycle—Entire Industry

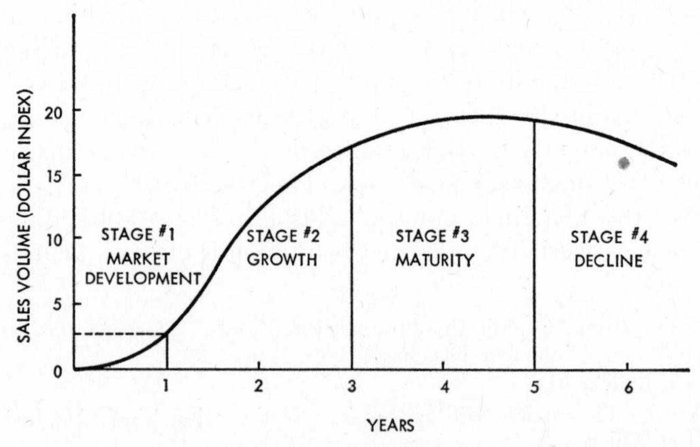

Stage 2. Market Growth—Demand begins to accelerate and the size of the total market expands rapidly. It might also be called the "Takeoff Stage."

Stage 3. Market Maturity—Demand levels off and grows, for the most part, only at the replacement and new family-formation rate.

Stage 4. Market Decline—The product begins to lose consumer appeal and sales drift downward, such as when buggy whips lost out with the advent of automobiles and when silk lost out to nylon.

Three operating questions will quickly occur to the alert executive:

Given a proposed new product or service, how and to what extent can the shape and duration of each stage be predicted?

Given an existing product, how can one determine what stage it is in?

Given all this knowledge, how can it be effectively used?

A brief further elaboration of each stage will be useful before dealing with these questions in detail.

Development Stage

Bringing a new product to market is fraught with unknowns, uncertainties, and frequently unknowable risks. Generally, demand has to be "created" during the product's initial *market development stage*. How long this takes depends on the product's complexity, its degree of newness, its fit into consumer needs, and the presence of competitive substitutes of one form or another. A proved cancer cure would require virtually no market development; it would get immediate massive support. An alleged superior substitute for the lost-wax process of sculpture casting would take lots longer.

While it has been demonstrated time after time that properly customer-oriented new product development is one of the primary conditions of sales and profit growth, what have been demonstrated even more conclusively are the ravaging costs and frequent fatalities associated with launching new products. Nothing seems to take more time, cost more money, involve more pitfalls, cause more anguish, or break more careers than do sincere and well-conceived new product programs. The fact is, most new products don't have any sort of classical life cycle curve at all. They have instead from the very outset an infinitely descending curve. The product not only doesn't get off the ground; it goes quickly under ground—six feet under.

It is little wonder, therefore, that some disillusioned and badly burned companies have recently adopted a more conservative policy—what I call the "used apple policy." Instead of aspiring to be the first company to see and seize an opportunity, they systematically avoid being first. They let others take the first bite of the supposedly juicy apple that tantalizes them. They let others do the pioneering. If the idea works, they quickly follow suit. They say, in effect, "The trouble with being a pioneer is that the pioneers get killed by the Indians." Hence, they say (thoroughly mixing their metaphors), "We don't have to get the first bite of the apple. The second one is good enough." They are willing to eat off a used apple, but they try to be alert enough to make sure it is only slightly used—that they at least get the second big bite, not the tenth skimpy one.

Growth Stage

The usual characteristic of a successful new product is a gradual rise in its sales curve during the market development stage. At some point in this rise a marked increase in consumer demand occurs and sales take off. The boom is on. This is the beginning of Stage 2—the *market growth stage*. At this point potential competitors who have been watching developments during Stage 1 jump into the fray. The first ones to get in are generally those with an exceptionally effective "used apple policy." Some enter the market with carbon-copies of the originator's product. Others make functional and design improvements. And at this point product and brand differentiation begin to develop.

The ensuing fight for the consumer's patronage poses to the originating producer an entirely new set of problems. Instead of seeking ways of getting consumers to *try the product*, the originator now faces the more compelling problem of getting them to *prefer his brand*. This generally requires important changes in marketing strategies and methods. But the policies and tactics now adopted will be neither freely the sole choice of the originating producer, nor as experimental as they might have been during Stage 1. The presence of competitors both dictates and limits what can easily be tried—such as, for example, testing what is the best price level or the best channel of distribution.

As the rate of consumer acceptance accelerates, it generally becomes increasingly easy to open new distribution channels and retail outlets. The consequent filling of distribution pipelines generally causes the entire industry's factory sales to rise more rapidly than store sales. This creates an exaggerated impression of profit opportunity which, in turn, attracts more competitors. Some of these will begin to charge lower prices because of later advances in technology, production shortcuts, the need to take lower margins in order to get distribution, and the like. All this in time inescapably moves the industry to the threshold of a new stage of competition.

Maturity Stage

This new stage is the *market maturity stage*. The first sign of its advent is evidence of market saturation. This means that most consumer companies or households that are sales prospects will be owning or using the product. Sales now grow about on a par with population. No more distribution pipelines need be filled. Price competition now becomes intense. Competitive attempts to achieve and hold brand preference now involve making finer and finer differentiations in the product, in customer services, and in the promotional practices and claims made for the product.

Typically, the market maturity stage forces the producer to concentrate on holding his distribution outlets, retaining his shelf space, and, in the end, trying to secure even more intensive distribution. Whereas during the market development stage the originator depended heavily on the positive efforts of his retailers and distributors to help sell his product, retailers and distributors will now frequently have been reduced largely to being merchandise-displayers and order-takers. In the case of branded products in particular, the originator must now, more than ever, communicate directly with the consumer.

The market maturity stage typically calls for a new kind of emphasis on competing more effectively. The originator is increasingly forced to appeal to the consumer on the basis of price, marginal product differences, or both. Depending on the product, services and deals offered in connection with it are often the clearest and most effective forms of differentiation. Beyond these, there will be attempts to create and promote fine product distinctions through packaging and advertising, and to appeal to special market segments. The market maturity stage can be passed through rapidly, as in the case of most women's fashion fads, or it can persist for generations with per capita consumption neither rising nor falling, as in the case of such staples as men's shoes and industrial fasteners. Or maturity can persist, but in a state of gradual but steady per capita decline, as in the case of beer and steel.

Decline Stage

When market maturity tapers off and consequently comes to an end, the product enters Stage 4—*market decline.* In all cases of maturity and decline the industry is transformed. Few companies are able to weather the competitive storm. As demand declines, the overcapacity that was already apparent during the period of maturity now becomes endemic. Some producers see the handwriting implacably on the wall but feel that with proper management and cunning they will be one of the survivors after the industry-wide deluge they so clearly foresee. To hasten their competitors' eclipse directly, or to frighten them into early voluntary withdrawal from the industry, they initiate a variety of aggressively depressive tactics, propose mergers or buy-outs, and generally engage in activities that make life thanklessly burdensome for all firms, and make death the inevitable consequence for most of them. A few companies do indeed weather the storm, sustaining life through the constant descent that now clearly characterizes the industry. Production gets concentrated into fewer hands. Prices and margins get depressed. Consumers get bored.

The only cases where there is any relief from this boredom and gradual euthanasia are where styling and fashion play some constantly revivifying role.

PREPLANNING IMPORTANCE

Knowing that the lives of successful products and services are generally characterized by something like the pattern illustrated in Exhibit I can become the basis for important life-giving policies and practices. One of the greatest values of the life cycle concept is for managers about to launch a new product. The first step for them is to try to foresee the profile of the proposed product's cycle.

As with so many things in business, and perhaps uniquely in marketing, it is almost impossible to make universally useful suggestions regarding how to manage one's affairs. It is certainly particularly difficult to provide widely useful advice on how to foresee or predict the slope and duration of a product's life. Indeed, it is precisely because so little specific day-to-day guidance is possible in anything, and because no checklist has ever by itself been very useful to anybody for very long, that business management will probably never be a science—always an art—and will pay exceptional rewards to managers with rare talent, enormous energy, iron nerve, great capacity for assuming responsibility and bearing accountability.

But this does not mean that useful efforts cannot or should not be made to try to foresee the slope and duration of a new product's life. Time spent in attempting this kind of foresight not only helps assure that a more rational approach is brought to product planning and merchandising; also, as will be shown later, it can help create valuable lead time for important strategic and tactical moves after the product is brought to market. Specifically, it can be a great help in developing an orderly series of competitive moves, in expanding or stretching out the life of a product, in maintaining a clean product line, and in purposely phasing out dying and costly old products.[2]

Failure Possibilities . . .

As pointed out above, the length and slope of the market development stage depend on the product's complexity, its degree of newness, its fit into customer needs, and the presence of competitive substitutes.

The more unique or distinctive the newness of the product, the longer it generally takes to get it sucessfully off the ground. The world does not

---

[2] See Philip Kotler, "Phasing Out Weak Products," *Harvard Business Review* (March–April, 1965), p. 107.

automatically beat a path to the man with the better mousetrap.[3] The world has to be told, coddled, enticed, romanced, and even bribed (as with, for example, coupons, samples, free application aids, and the like). When the product's newness is distinctive and the job it is designed to do is unique, the public will generally be less quick to perceive it as something it clearly needs or wants.

This makes life particularly difficult for the innovator. He will have more than the usual difficulties of identifying those characteristics of his product and those supporting communications themes or devices which imply value to the consumer. As a consequence, the more distinctive the newness, the greater the risk of failure resulting either from insufficient working capital to sustain a long and frustrating period of creating enough solvent customers to make the proposition pay, or from the inability to convince investors and bankers that they should put up more money.

In any particular situation the more people who will be involved in making a single purchasing decision for a new product, the more drawn out Stage 1 will be. Thus in the highly fragmented construction materials industry, for example, success takes an exceptionally long time to catch hold; and having once caught hold, it tends to hold tenaciously for a long time—often too long. On the other hand, fashion items clearly catch on fastest and last shortest. But because fashion is so powerful, recently some companies in what often seem the least fashion-influenced of industries (machine tools, for example) have shortened the market development stage by introducing elements of design and packaging fashion to their products.

What factors tend to prolong the market development stage and therefore raise the risk of failure? The more complex the product, the more distinctive its newness, the less influenced by fashion, the greater the number of persons influencing a single buying decision, the more costly, and the greater the required shift in the customer's usual way of doing things—these are the conditions most likely to slow things up and create problems.

. . . versus Success Chances

But problems also create opportunities to control the forces arrayed against new product success. For example, the newer the product, the more important it becomes for the customers to have a favorable first experience with it. Newness creates a certain special visibility for the

[3] For perhaps the ultimate example of how the world does *not* beat such a path, see the example of the man who actually, and to his painful regret, made a "better" mousetrap, in John B. Matthews, Jr., R. D. Buzzell, Theodore Levitt, and Ronald E. Frank, *Marketing: An Introductory Analysis* (New York: McGraw-Hill Book Company, Inc., 1964), p. 4.

product, with a certain number of people standing on the sidelines to see how the first customers get on with it. If their first experience is unfavorable in some crucial way, this may have repercussions far out of proportion to the actual extent of the underfulfillment of the customers' expectations. But a favorable first experience or application will, for the same reason, get a lot of disproportionately favorable publicity.

The possibility of exaggerated disillusionment with a poor first experience can raise vital questions regarding the appropriate channels of distribution for a new product. On the one hand, getting the product successfully launched may require having—as in the case of, say, the early days of home washing machines—many retailers who can give consumers considerable help in the product's correct utilization and thus help assure a favorable first experience for those buyers. On the other hand, channels that provide this kind of help (such as small neighborhood appliance stores in the case of washing machines) during the market development stage may not be the ones best able to merchandise the product most successfully later when help in creating and personally reassuring customers is less important than wide product distribution. To the extent that channel decisions during this first stage sacrifice some of the requirements of the market development stage to some of the requirements of later stages, the rate of the product's acceptance by consumers at the outset may be delayed.

In entering the market development stage, pricing decisions are often particularly hard for the producer to make. Should he set an initially high price to recoup his investment quickly—i.e., "skim the cream"—or should he set a low price to discourage potential competition—i.e., "exclusion"? The answer depends on the innovator's estimate of the probable length of the product's life cycle, the degree of patent protection the product is likely to enjoy, the amount of capital needed to get the product off the ground, the elasticity of demand during the early life of the product, and many other factors. The decision that is finally made may affect not just the rate at which the product catches on at the beginning, but even the duration of its total life. Thus some products that are priced too low at the outset (particularly fashion goods, such as the chemise, or sack, a few years ago) may catch on so quickly that they become short-lived fads. A slower rate of consumer acceptance might often extend their life cycles and raise the total profits they yield.

The actual slope, or rate of the growth stage, depends on some of the same things as does success or failure in Stage 1. But the extent to which patent exclusiveness can play a critical role is sometimes inexplicably forgotten. More frequently than one might offhand expect, holders of strong patent positions fail to recognize either the market-development virtue of making their patents available to competitors or the market-destroying possibilities of failing to control more effectively their competitors' use of such products.

Generally speaking, the more producers there are of a new product, the more effort goes into developing a market for it. The net result is very likely to be more rapid and steeper growth of the total market. The originator's market share may fall, but his total sales and profits may rise more rapidly. Certainly this has been the case in recent years of color television; RCA's eagerness to make its tubes available to competitors reflects its recognition of the power of numbers over the power of monopoly.

On the other hand, the failure to set and enforce appropriate quality standards in the early days of polystyrene and polyethylene drinking glasses and cups produced such sloppy, inferior goods that it took years to recover the consumer's confidence and revive the growth pattern.

But to try to see in advance what a product's growth pattern might be is not very useful if one fails to distinguish between the industry pattern and the pattern of the single firm—for its particular brand. The industry's cycle will almost certainly be different from the cycle of individual firms. Moreover, the life cycle of a given product may be different for different companies in the same industry at the same point in time, and it certainly affects different companies in the same industry differently.

ORIGINATOR'S BURDENS

The company with most at stake is the original producer—the company that launches an entirely new product. This company generally bears most of the costs, the tribulations, and certainly the risks of developing both the product and the market.

Competitive Pressure

Once the innovator demonstrates during the market development stage that a solid demand exists, armies of imitators rush in to capitalize on and help create the boom that becomes the market growth, or takeoff, stage. As a result, while exceedingly rapid growth will now characterize the product's total demand, for the originating company its growth stage paradoxically now becomes truncated. It has to share the boom with new competitors. Hence the potential rate of acceleration of its own takeoff is diminished and, indeed, may actually fail to last as long as the industry's. This occurs not only because there are so many competitors, but, as we noted earlier, also because competitors often come in with product improvements and lower prices. While these developments generally help keep the market expanding, they greatly restrict the originating company's rate of growth and the length of its takeoff stage.

All this can be illustrated by comparing the curve in Exhibit II with that in Exhibit I, which shows the life cycle for a product. During Stage 1 in Exhibit I there is generally only one company—the originator—even though the whole exhibit represents the entire industry. In Stage I the originator is the entire industry. But by Stage 2 he shares the industry with many competitors. Hence, while Exhibit I is an industry curve, its Stage 1 represents only a single company's sales.

Exhibit II shows the life cycle of the originator's brand—his own sales curve, not that of the industry. It can be seen that between Year 1 and Year 2 his sales are rising about as rapidly as the industry's. But after Year

EXHIBIT II

Product Life Cycle—Originating Company

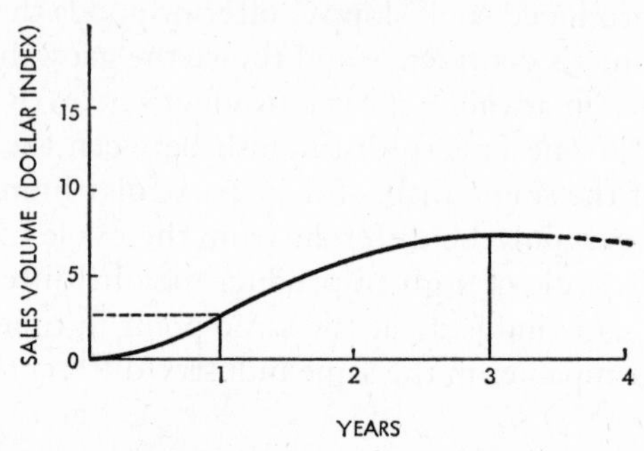

2, while industry sales in Exhibit I are still in vigorous expansion, the originator's sales curve in Exhibit II has begun to slow its ascent. He is now sharing the boom with a great many competitors, some of whom are much better positioned now than he is.

Profit Squeeze

In the process the originator may begin to encounter a serious squeeze on his profit margins. Exhibit III, which traces the profits per unit of the originator's sales, illustrates this point. During the market development stage his per-unit profits are negative. Sales volume is too low at existing prices. However, during the market growth stage unit profits boom as output rises and unit production costs fall. Total profits rise enormously. It is the presence of such lush profits that both attracts and ultimately destroys competitors.

Consequently, while (1) industry sales may still be rising nicely (as at the Year 3 point in Exhibit I), and (2) while the originating company's sales may at the same point of time have begun to slow down noticeably (as in Exhibit II), and (3) while at this point the originator's total profits may still be rising because his volume of sales is huge and on a slight upward trend, his profits per unit will often have taken a drastic downward course. Indeed, they will often have done so long before the sales curve flattened. They will have topped out and begun to decline perhaps around the Year 2 point (as in Exhibit III). By the time the originator's sales begin to flatten out (as at the Year 3 point in Exhibit II), unit profits may actually be approaching zero (as in Exhibit III).

At this point more competitors are in the industry, the rate of industry demand growth has slowed somewhat, and competitors are cutting prices. Some of them do this in order to get business, and others do it because their costs are lower owing to the fact that their equipment is more modern and productive.

EXHIBIT III

Unit Profit Contribution Life Cycle—Originating Company

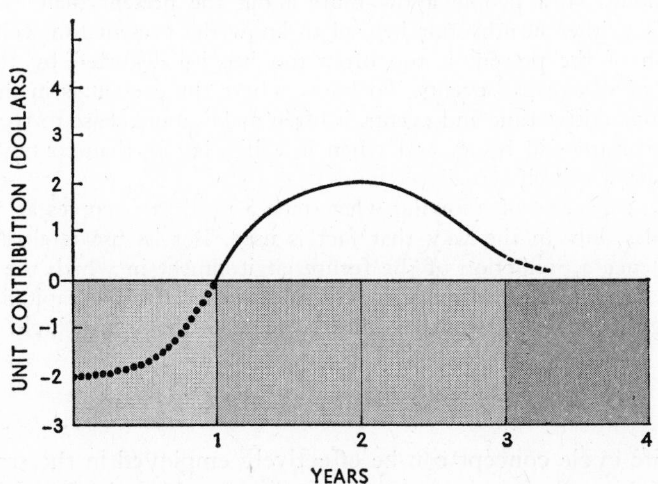

The industry's Stage 3—maturity—generally lasts as long as there are no important competitive substitutes (such as, for example, aluminum for steel in "tin" cans), no drastic shifts in influential value systems (such as the end of female modesty in the 1920's and the consequent destruction of the market for veils), no major changes in dominant fashions (such as the hour-glass female form and the end of waist cinchers), no changes in the demand for primary products which use the product in question (such as the effect of the decline of new railroad expansion on the demand for railroad ties), and no changes either in the rate of obsolescence of the product or in the character or introductory rate of product modifications.

Maturity can last for a long time, or it can actually never be attained. Fashion goods and fad items sometimes surge to sudden heights, hesitate momentarily at an uneasy peak, and then quickly drop off into total obscurity.

Stage Recognition

The various characteristics of the stages described above will help one to recognize the stage a particular product occupies at any given time. But hindsight will always be more accurate than current sight. Perhaps the best way of seeing one's current stage is to try to foresee the next stage and work backwards. This approach has several virtues:

It forces one to look ahead, constantly to try to reforesee his future and competitive environment. This will have its own rewards. As Charles F. Kettering, perhaps the last of Detroit's primitive inventors and probably the greatest of all its inventors, was fond of saying, "We should all be concerned about the future because that's where we'll have to spend the rest of our lives." By looking at the future one can better assess the state of the present.

Looking ahead gives more perspective to the present than looking at the present alone. Most people know more about the present than is good for them. It is neither healthy nor helpful to know the present too well, for our perception of the present is too often too heavily distorted by the urgent pressures of day-to-day events. To know where the present is in the continuum of competitive time and events, it often makes more sense to try to know what the future will bring, and when it will bring it, than to try to know what the present itself actually contains.

Finally, the value of knowing what stage a product occupies at any given time resides only in the way that fact is used. But its use is always in the future. Hence a prediction of the future environment in which the information will be used is often more functional for the effective capitalization on knowledge about the present than knowledge about the present itself.

SEQUENTIAL ACTIONS

The life cycle concept can be effectively employed in the strategy of both existing and new products. For purposes of continuity and clarity, the remainder of this article will describe some of the uses of the concept from the early stages of new product planning through the later stages of keeping the product profitably alive. The chief discussion will focus on what I call a policy of "life extension" or "market stretching."[4]

To the extent that Exhibits II and III outline the classical patterns of successful new products, one of the constant aims of the originating producer should be to avoid the severe discipline imposed by an early profit squeeze in the market growth stage, and to avoid the wear and waste so typical of the market maturity stage. Hence the following proposition would seem reasonable: when a company develops a new product or service, it should try to plan at the very outset a series of actions to be employed at various subsequent stages in the product's existence so that its sales and profit curves are constantly sustained rather than following their usual declining slope.

In other words, advance planning should be directed at extending, or stretching out, the life of the product. It is this idea of *planning in*

[4] For related ideas on discerning opportunities for product revivification, see Lee Adler, "A New Orientation for Plotting a Marketing Strategy," *Business Horizons*, Winter 1964, p. 37.

advance of the actual launching of a new product to take specific actions later in its life cycle—actions designed to sustain its growth and profitability—which appears to have great potential as an instrument of long-term product strategy.

Nylon's Life

How this might work for a product can be illustrated by looking at the history of nylon. The way in which nylon's booming sales life has been repeatedly and systematically extended and stretched can serve as a model for other products. What has happened in nylon may not have been purposely planned that way at the outset, but the results are quite as if they had been planned.

The first nylon end-uses were primarily military—parachutes, thread, rope. This was followed by nylon's entry into the circular knit market and its consequent domination of the women's hosiery business. Here it developed the kind of steadily rising growth and profit curves that every executive dreams about. After some years these curves began to flatten out. But before they flattened very noticeably, Du Pont had already developed measures designed to revitalize sales and profits. It did several things, each of which is demonstrated graphically in Exhibit IV. This exhibit and the explanation which follows take some liberties with the actual facts of the nylon situation in order to highlight the points I wish to make. But they take no liberties with the essential requisites of product strategy.

Point A of Exhibit IV shows the hypothetical point at which the nylon curve (dominated at this point by hosiery) flattened out. If nothing further had been done, the sales curve would have continued along the flattened pace indicated by the dotted line at Point A. This is also the hypothetical point at which the first systematic effort was made to extend the product's life. Du Pont, in effect, took certain "actions" which pushed hosiery sales upward rather than continuing the path implied by the dotted line extension of the curve at Point A. At Point A action #1 pushed an otherwise flat curve upward.

At points B, C, and D still other new sales and profit expansion "actions" (#2, #3, #4, and so forth) were taken. What were these actions? Or, more usefully, what was their strategic content? What did they try to do? They involved strategies that tried to expand sales via four different routes:

1. Promoting more frequent usage of the product among current users.
2. Developing more varied usage of the product among current users.
3. Creating new users for the product by expanding the market.
4. Finding new uses for the basic material.

Frequent Usage. Du Pont studies had shown an increasing trend toward "bareleggedness" among women. This was coincident with the trend toward more casual living and a declining perception among teenagers of what might be called the "social necessity" of wearing stockings. In the light of those findings, one approach to propping up the flattening sales curves might have been to reiterate the social necessity of wearing stockings at all times. That would have been a sales-building action, though obviously difficult and exceedingly costly. But it could clearly have fulfilled the strategy of promoting more frequent usage among current users as a means of extending the product's life.

Varied Usage. For Du Pont, this strategy took the form of an attempt to promote the "fashion smartness" of tinted hose and later of patterned

EXHIBIT IV

Hypothetical Life Cycle—Nylon

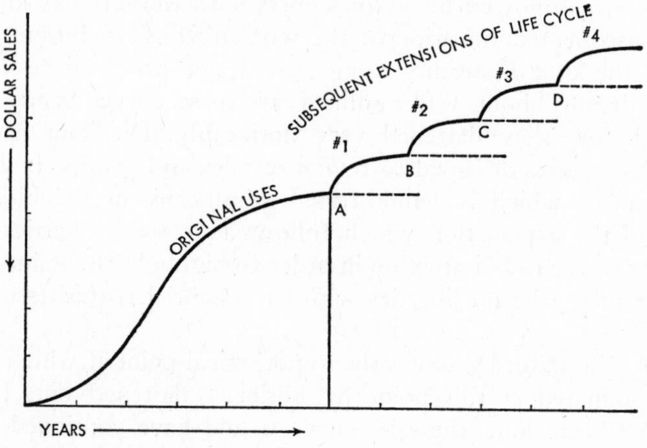

and highly textured hosiery. The idea was to raise each woman's inventory of hosiery by obsolescing the perception of hosiery as a fashion staple that came only in a narrow range of browns and pinks. Hosiery was to be converted from a "neutral" accessory to a central ingredient of fashion, with a "suitable" tint and pattern for each outer garment in the lady's wardrobe.

This not only would raise sales by expanding women's hosiery wardrobes and stores' inventories, but would open the door for annual tint and pattern obsolescence much the same as there is an annual color obsolescence in outer garments. Beyond that, the use of color and pattern to focus attention on the leg would help arrest the decline of the leg as an element of sex appeal—a trend which some researchers had discerned and which, they claimed, damaged hosiery sales.

New Users. Creating new users for nylon hosiery might conceivably have taken the form of attempting to legitimize the necessity of wearing hosiery among early teenagers and subteenagers. Advertising, public relations, and merchandising of youthful social and style leaders would have been called for.

New Uses. For nylon, this tactic has had many triumphs—from varied types of hosiery, such as stretch stockings and stretch socks, to new uses, such as rugs, tires, bearings, and so forth. Indeed, if there had been no further product innovations designed to create new uses for nylon after the original military, miscellaneous, and circular knit uses, nylon consumption in 1962 would have reached a saturation level at approximately 50 million pounds annually.

Instead, in 1962 consumption exceeded 500 million pounds. Exhibit V

EXHIBIT V

Innovation of New Products Postpones the Time of Total Maturity—Nylon Industry

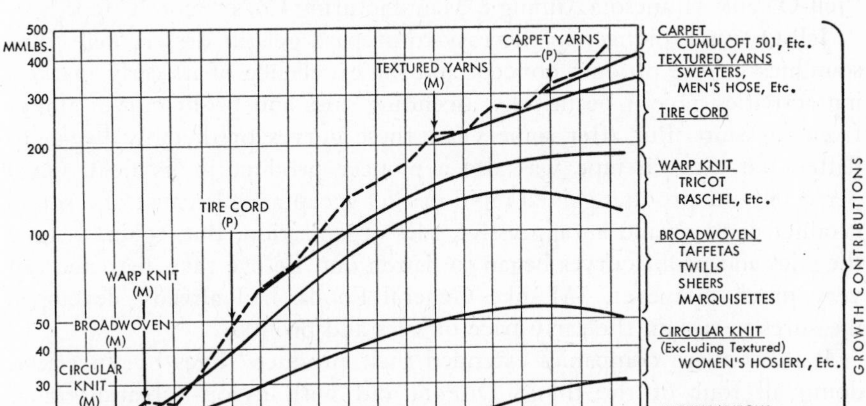

SOURCE: *Modern Textiles Magazine*, February, 1964, p. 33. © 1962 by Jordan P. Yale.

demonstrates how the continuous development of new uses for the basic material constantly produced new waves of sales. The exhibit shows that in spite of the growth of the women's stocking market, the cumulative result of the military, circular knit, and miscellaneous grouping would have been a flattened sales curve by 1958. (Nylon's entry into the broadwoven market in 1944 substantially raised sales above what they would have been. Even so, the sales of broadwoven, circular knit, and military and miscellaneous groupings peaked in 1957.)

Had it not been for the addition of new uses for the same basic material—such as warp knits in 1945, tire cord in 1948, textured yarns in

1955, carpet yarns in 1959, and so forth—nylon would not have had the spectacularly rising consumption curve it has so clearly had. At various stages it would have exhausted its existing markets or been forced into decline by competing materials. The systematic search for new uses for the basic (and improved) material extended and stretched the product's life.

Other Examples

Few companies seem to employ in any systematic or planned way the four product life-stretching steps described above. Yet the successful application of this kind of stretching strategy has characterized the history of such well-known products as General Foods Corporation's "Jell-O" and Minnesota Mining & Manufacturing Co.'s "Scotch" tape.[5]

Jell-O was a pioneer in the easy-to-prepare gelatin dessert field. The soundness of the product concept and the excellence of its early marketing activities gave it beautifully ascending sales and profit curves almost from the start. But after some years these curves predictably began to flatten out. Scotch tape was also a pioneer product in its field. Once perfected, the product gained rapid market acceptance because of a sound product concept and an aggressive sales organization. But, again, in time the sales and profit curves began to flatten out. Before they flattened out very much, however, 3M, like General Foods, had already developed measures to sustain the early pace of sales and profits.

Both of these companies extended their products' lives by, in effect, doing all four of the things DuPont did with nylon—creating more frequent usage among current users, more varied usage among current users, new users, and new uses for the basic "materials":

(1) The General Foods approach to increasing the frequency of serving Jell-O among current users was, essentially, to increase the number of flavors. From Don Wilson's famous "six delicious flavors," Jell-O moved up to over a dozen. On the other hand, 3M helped raise sales among its current users by developing a variety of handy Scotch tape dispensers which made the product easier to use.

(2) Creation of more varied usage of Jell-O among current dessert users involved its promotion as a base for salads and the facilitation of this usage by the development of a variety of vegetable flavored Jell-O's. Similarly, 3M developed a line of colored, patterned, waterproof, invisible, and write-on Scotch tapes which have enjoyed considerable success as sealing and decorating items for holiday and gift wrapping.

(3) Jell-O sought to create new users by pinpointing people who could not accept Jell-O as a popular dessert or salad product. Hence during the Metrecal boom Jell-O employed an advertising theme that successfully affixed

[5] I am indebted to my colleague, Dr. Derek A. Newton, for these examples and other helpful suggestions.

to the product a fashion-oriented weight control appeal. Similarly, 3M introduced "Rocket" tape, a product much like Scotch tape but lower in price, and also developed a line of commercial cellophane tapes of various widths, lengths, and strengths. These actions broadened product use in commercial and industrial markets.

(4) Both Jell-O and 3M have sought out new uses for the basic material. It is known, for example, that women consumers use powdered gelatin dissolved in liquids as a means of strengthening their fingernails. Both men and women use it in the same way as a bone-building agent. Hence Jell-O introduced a "completely flavorless" Jell-O for just these purposes. 3M has also developed new uses for the basic material—from "double-coated" tape (adhesive on both sides) which competes with ordinary liquid adhesives, to the reflecting tape which festoons countless automobile bumpers, to marker strips which compete with paint.

EXTENSION STRATEGIES

The existence of the kinds of product life cycles illustrated in Exhibits I and II and the unit profit cycle in Exhibit III suggests that there may be considerable value for people involved in new product work to begin planning for the extension of the lives of their products even before these products are formally launched. To plan for new life-extending infusions of effort (as in Exhibit IV) at this pre-introduction stage can be extremely useful in three profoundly important ways.

1. *It generates an active rather than a reactive product policy.*

It systematically structures a company's long-term marketing and product development efforts in advance, rather than each effort or activity being merely a stop-gap response to the urgent pressures of repeated competitive thrusts and declining profits. The life-extension view of product policy enforces thinking and planning ahead—thinking in some systematic way about the moves likely to be made by potential competitors, about possible changes in consumer reactions to the product, and the required selling activities which best take advantage of these conditional events.

2. *It lays out a long-term plan designed to infuse new life into the product at the right time, with the right degree of care, and with the right amount of effort.*

Many activities designed to raise the sales and profits of existing products or materials are often undertaken without regard to their relationship to each other or to timing—the optimum point of consumer readiness for such activities or the point of optimum competitive effectiveness. Careful advance planning, long before the need for such activity arises, can help assure that the timing, the care, and the efforts are appropriate to the situation.

For example, it appears extremely doubtful that the boom in women's hair coloring and hair tinting products would have been as spectacular if vigorous efforts to sell these products had preceded the boom in hair sprays and chemical hair fixers. The latter helped create a powerful consumer consciousness of hair fashions because they made it relatively easy to create and wear fashionable hair styles. Once it became easy for women to have fashionable hair styles, the resulting fashion consciousness helped open the door for hair colors and tints. It could not have happened the other way around, with colors and tints first creating fashion consciousness and thus raising the sales of sprays and fixers. Because understanding the reason for this precise order of events is essential for appreciating the importance of early pre-introduction life-extension planning, it is useful to go into a bit of detail. Consider:

For women, setting their hair has been a perennial problem for centuries. First, the length and treatment of their hair is one of the most obvious ways in which they distinguish themselves from men. Hence to be attractive in that distinction becomes a crucial. Second, hair frames and highlights the face, much like an attractive wooden border frames and highlights a beautiful painting. Thus hair styling is an important element in accentuating the appearance of a woman's facial features. Third, since the hair is long and soft, it is hard to hold in an attractive arrangement. It gets mussed in sleep, wind, damp weather, sporting activities, and so forth.

Therefore, the effective *arrangement* of a woman's hair is understandably her first priority in hair care. An unkempt brunette would gain nothing from making herself into a blond. Indeed, in a country where blonds are in the minority, the switch from being an unkempt brunette to being an unkempt blond would simply draw attention to her sloppiness. But once the problem of arrangement became easily "solved" by sprays and fixers, colors and tints could become big business, especially among women whose hair was beginning to turn gray.

The same order of priorities applies in industrial products. For example, it seems quite inconceivable that many manufacturing plants would easily have accepted the replacement of the old single-spindle, constantly mantended screw machine by a computerized tape-tended, multiple-spindle machine. The mechanical tending of the multiple-spindle machine was a necessary intermediate step, if for no other reason than that it required a lesser work-flow change, and certainly a lesser conceptual leap for the companies and the machine-tending workers involved.

For Jell-O, it is unlikely that vegetable flavors would have been very successful before the idea of gelatin as a salad base had been pretty well accepted. Similarly, the promotion of colored and patterned Scotch tape as a gift and decorative seal might not have been as successful if department stores had not, as the result of their drive to compete more effectively with mass merchandisers by offering more customer services, previously demonstrated to the consumer what could be done to wrap and decorate gifts.

3. *Perhaps the most important benefit of engaging in advance, pre-*

introduction planning for sales-extending, market-stretching activities later in the product's life is that this practice forces a company to adopt a wider view of the nature of the product it is dealing with.

Indeed, it may even force the adoption of a wider view of the company's business. Take the case of Jell-O. What is its product? Over the years Jell-O has become the brand umbrella for a wide range of dessert products, including cornstarch-base puddings, pie fillings, and the new "Whip'n Chill," a light dessert product similar to a Bavarian Creme or French Mousse. On the basis of these products, it might be said that the Jell-O Division of General Foods is in the "dessert technology" business.

In the case of tape, perhaps 3M has gone even further in this technological approach to its business. It has a particular expertise (technology) on which it has built a constantly expanding business. This expertise can be said to be that of bonding things (adhesives in the case of Scotch tape) to other things, particularly to thin materials. Hence we see 3M developing scores of profitable items, including electronic recording tape (bonding electron-sensitive materials to tape), and "Thermo-Fax" duplicating equipment and supplies (bonding heat reactive materials to paper).

CONCLUSION

For companies interested in continued growth and profits, successful new product strategy should be viewed as a planned totality that looks ahead over some years. For its own good, new product strategy should try to predict in some measure the likelihood, character, and timing of competitive and market events. While prediction is always hazardous and seldom very accurate, it is undoubtedly far better than not trying to predict at all. In fact, every product strategy and every business decision inescapably involves making a prediction about the future, about the market, and about competitors. To be more systematically aware of the predictions one is making so that one acts on them in an offensive rather than a defensive or reactive fashion—this is the real virtue of preplanning for market stretching and product life extension. The result will be a product strategy that includes some sort of *plan for a timed sequence of conditional moves.*

Even before entering the market development stage, the originator should make a judgment regarding the probable length of the product's normal life, taking into account the possibilities of expanding its uses and users. This judgment will also help determine many things—for example, whether to price the product on a skimming or a penetration basis, or what kind of relationship the company should develop with its resellers.

These considerations are important because at each stage in a product's life cycle each management decision must consider the competitive requirements of the next stage. Thus a decision to establish a strong branding policy during the market growth stage might help to insulate the brand against strong price competition later; a decision to establish a policy of "protected" dealers in the market development stage might facilitate point-of-sale promotions during the market growth state, and so on. In short, having a clear idea of future product development possibilities and market development opportunities should reduce the likelihood of becoming locked into forms of merchandising that might possibly prove undesirable.

This kind of advance thinking about new product strategy helps management avoid other pitfalls. For instance, advertising campaigns that look successful from a short-term view may hurt in the next stage of the life cycle. Thus at the outset Metrecal advertising used a strong medical theme. Sales boomed until imitative competitors successfully emphasized fashionable slimness. Metrecal had projected itself as the dietary for the overweight consumer, an image that proved far less appealing than that of being the dietary for people who were fashion-smart. But Metrecal's original appeal had been so strong and so well made that it was a formidable task later on to change people's impressions about the product. Obviously, with more careful long-range planning at the outset, a product's image can be more carefully positioned and advertising can have more clearly defined objectives.

Recognizing the importance of an orderly series of steps in the introduction of sales-building "actions" for new products should be a central ingredient of long-term product planning. A carefully preplanned program for market expansion, even before a new product is introduced, can have powerful virtues. The establishment of a rational plan for the future can also help to guide the direction and pace of the on-going technical research in support of the product. Although departures from such a plan will surely have to be made to accommodate unexpected events and revised judgments, the plan puts the company in a better position to *make* things happen rather than constantly having to react to things that *are* happening.

It is important that the originator does *not* delay this long-term planning until after the product's introduction. How the product should be introduced and the many uses for which it might be promoted at the outset should be a function of a careful consideration of the optimum sequence of suggested product appeals and product uses. Consideration must focus not just on optimum things to do, but as importantly on their optimum *sequence*—for instance, what the order of use of various appeals should be and what the order of suggested product uses should be. If Jell-O's first suggested use had been as a diet food, its chances of later making a big and easy impact in the gelatin dessert market undoubtedly would have been greatly diminished. Similarly, if nylon hosiery had been promoted at the outset as a functional daytime-wear hosiery, its ability to replace silk as the acceptable high-fashion hosiery would have been greatly diminished.

To illustrate the virtue of pre-introduction planning for a product's later life, suppose a company has developed a nonpatentable new product—say, an ordinary kitchen salt shaker. Suppose that nobody now has any kind of shaker. One might say, before launching it, that (1) it has a potential market of "x" million household, institutional, and commercial consumers, (2) in two years market maturity will set in, and (3) in one year profit margins will fall because of the entry of competition. Hence one might lay out the following plan:

I. *End of first year: expand market among current users*
Ideas—new designs, such as sterling shaker for formal use, "masculine" shaker for barbecue use, antique shaker for "Early American" households, miniature shaker for each table place setting, moisture-proof design for beach picnics.

II. *End of second year: expand market to new users*
Ideas—designs for children, quaffer design for beer drinkers in bars, design for sadists to rub salt into open wounds.

III. *End of third year: find new uses*
Ideas—make identical product for use as a pepper shaker, as decorative garlic salt shaker, shaker for household scouring powder, shaker to sprinkle silicon dust on parts being machined in machine shops, and so forth.

This effort to prethink methods of reactivating a flattening sales curve far in advance of its becoming flat enables product planners to assign priorities to each task, and to plan future production expansion and capital and marketing requirements in a systematic fashion. It prevents one's trying to do too many things at once, results in priorities being determined rationally instead of as accidental consequences of the timing of new ideas, and disciplines both the product development effort that is launched in support of a product's growth and the marketing effort that is required for its continued success.

Traditionally economists have attempted to explain marketing strategy in terms of price theory and market structures. The research reported here indicates the limitations of this approach and stresses the importance of nonprice competition. The key determinants of nonprice market strategy were found to be the firm's product and market rather than industry structure or firm size.

47. HOW IMPORTANT IS PRICING IN COMPETITIVE STRATEGY?*

Jon G. Udell†

In an effort to ascertain the key elements of business success in the market place, the author conducted a study among 200 producers of industrial and consumer goods. A sample of fairly well-known and successful manufacturing companies was selected from *Martindell's Manual of Excellent Management*. Listed are companies which are supposedly well managed, evaluated according to the criteria developed by the American Institute of Management. The use of the manual seemed appropriate in that the two most heavily weighted criteria are sales vigor and management efficiency.

The present study attempted to answer the question: "What are the key policies and procedures common to successful marketing managements in various manufacturing industries?"

Management's interest in the study was reflected by a 75% response to a 4-page mail questionnaire. The first section of the questionnaire listed 12 general policy areas of marketing management—among them, sales research and sales planning, pricing, management of sales personnel, and product service. The respondent, usually the vice president in charge of marketing, was asked to select the five areas which he regarded as most vital in his company's marketing success.

Importance of Product Development

The results indicate that product research and development, selected by almost 80% of the respondents is most important in modern-day

* Reprinted from "How Important Is Pricing in Competitive Strategy?" *Journal of Marketing*, Vol. XXVIII, No. 1 (January, 1964), pp. 44–48.

† University of Wisconsin.

competitive strategy. Four other policy areas, relating to either product or sales effort, were selected by more than half of the respondents. Table 1 presents a percentage analysis of the responses.

It appears that business management did not agree with the economic views of the importance of pricing—one-half of the respondents did *not* select pricing as *one of the five* most important policy areas in their firm's marketing success.

Also, the two major facets of nonprice competition (product and sales effort) were subdivided into a number of policy areas; for example, sales effort was subdivided into sales research and sales planning, management of sales personnel, and advertising and sales promotion. In short, *the competitive activities relating to the product and to sales effort were selected as most important in the success of these firms.*

Pricing

The emphasis on product and sales effort does not imply that price is unimportant. Three factors probably account for the relatively low ranking of pricing:

1. In today's competitive economy, *supply*—or production capacity—*generally exceeds demand;* and, therefore, nearly all sellers are forced to be either completely competitive or almost collusive in their pricing. Because there may be little or no freedom for a company to deviate from the market price, heavy reliance must be placed on product differentiation and sales effort.
2. *The relatively well-to-do consumers of today are interested in more than just price.* They are interested in product quality, distinctiveness, style, and many other factors which lead to both physical and psychological satisfaction. Consumers not only can afford but want product differentiation and sales promotion. From them the consumer receives a great deal of psychological satisfaction and utility. It is only logical that consumer-oriented managements would choose to emphasize products and sales efforts in an attempt to satisfy consumer desires.
3. *It is through successful product differentiation that a manufacturer may obtain some pricing freedom.* Products known to be identical must be priced identically in the market place. A departure from identical prices would result in all patronage going to the seller or sellers with the lowest price.

MARKETING STRATEGIES ACCORDING TO PRODUCTS AND CUSTOMERS

Economists have proposed several theories that give recognition to the nonprice factors of competitive strategy.[1] However, they have not cred-

[1] Lawrence Abbott, *Quality and Competition* (New York: Columbia University Press, 1951); Hans Brems, "The Interdependence of Quality Variations, Selling Effort and Price," *Quarterly Journal of Economics,* Vol. 62 (May, 1948), pp. 418–440; C. A. Stocking, "Advertising and Economic Theory," *American Economic Review,* Vol. 21 (March, 1931), pp. 43–55.

ited the nature of the product and the characteristics of the buyers as the dominant factors in explaining how companies organize to market their products. Instead, the dominant factor is usually assumed to be the market structure of the industry (competitive, oligopolistic, or monopolistic).

A producer of machine tools would not be expected to compete in the same manner as a producer of perfume; and a comparison of the structures of the machine-tool and perfume industries would not explain the differences in their marketing strategies. *Common business sense would lead one to believe that a company's use of nonprice competitive strategy should vary according to the nature of a firm's product and the characteristics of the buyers for that product.*

TABLE 1

HOW MANAGEMENT RANKS THE FACTORS OF MARKETING SUCCESS

Rank	*Policy areas*	*% of firms selecting the policy area**
1	Product research and development	79
2	Sales research and sales planning	73
3	Management of sales personnel	59
4	Advertising and sales promotion	56
5	Product service	52
6	Pricing	50
7	Organizational structure	44
8	Distribution channels and their control	41
9	Marketing cost budgeting and control	17
10	Financing and credit	14
11	Transportation and storage	7
12	Public relations	7

* Based on a tabulation of 135 usable questionnaires. Percentages here are rounded.

Accordingly, the data were classified according to the respondents' type of industry: industrial goods, consumer durable goods, and consumer nondurable goods.

Producers of Industrial Goods

The producers of industrial goods stressed the product facet of competitive strategy.

Two of the policy areas listed in the marketing management study pertain directly to the product—product research and development, and product service. (Product service refers to those activities performed by a manufacturer in the attempt to guarantee that a product gives satisfactory performance to its users.)

As shown in Table 2, both of these policy areas were selected by about 80% of the industrial users.

The policy areas relating to sales effort were relegated to a lesser role by the successful manufacturers of industrial goods. The average selection for the policy areas pertaining to sales effort was 50%, as compared with the average product selection of 80%.

The industrial-goods producers' primary emphasis on the product facet of marketing strategy was also emphasized in letters received from various respondents. A Pratt & Whitney Aircraft executive said: "Our two most

TABLE 2

POLICY AREAS SELECTED BY INDUSTRIAL GOODS PRODUCERS

Policy areas	*% of firms selecting the policy area**
Product:	
Product research and development	.79
Product service	.79
Average product selection ratio	.79
Sales efforts:	
Sales research and sales planning	.63
Management of sales personnel	.49
Advertising and sales promotion	.37
Average sales efforts selection ratio	.50
Pricing	.47
Other areas:	
Organizational structure	.50
Distribution channels and their control	.34
Financing and credit	.18
Marketing cost budgeting and control	.12
Transportation and storage	9
Public relations	7

* Based on the questionnaires of 68 industrial goods producers. Percentages here are rounded.

valuable assets sales-wise are the technical excellence of our products, and our policy of rendering the best possible product service to our customers both before and after the sale."

Producers of Consumer Goods

The manufacturers of consumer goods placed a much greater emphasis on the sales effort facet of competitive strategy. This emphasis was especially great in the case of the firms producing nondurable goods.

As shown in Table 3, the nondurable goods producers had an average sales effort selection of 85%, as compared with an average product selection of 45%. Durable goods producers had an average sales efforts selection of 79%, as compared with the product selection of 60%.

The differences were accounted for by the low selection ratios for product service, in that most consumer goods manufacturers selected product research and development.

It is understandable that consumer-goods producers selected product research and development with such a high degree of frequency in light of their emphasis on sales efforts. It is less difficult to promote a differentiated product than it is to promote an undifferentiated product.

Product research and development are important, but sales efforts are *most* important to manufacturers of consumer goods.

Product research and development was not broken down into research

TABLE 3

POLICY AREAS SELECTED BY CONSUMER GOODS MANUFACTURERS

Policy areas	Manufacturers of nondurable goods	Manufacturers of durable goods*
Sales efforts:		
Advertising and sales promotion	.89	73
Management of sales personnel	.64	91
Sales research and sales planning	.82	73
Average sales efforts selection ratio	.85	79
Product:		
Product research and development	.83	75
Product service	.14	36
Average product selection ratio	.45	60
Pricing	.50	46
Other areas:		
Distribution channels and their control	.54	46
Organizational structure	.39	27
Marketing cost budgeting and control	.29	9
Financing and credit	.11	9
Transportation and storage	4	9
Public relations	7	..

* Based on the questionnaires of 28 nondurable goods producers and 11 durable goods producers. Figures here are rounded.

related to physical (real) product improvement and research related to psychological (fancied) product improvement. It would be immaterial to the consumer-goods manufacturer if a product change were *real* or *fancied*, so long as the change was regarded as an improvement by his customers.

The second section of the questionnaire subdivided the general areas of policies and procedures into more specific categories of business activities. When product research and development was subdivided into three categories of activities, the following selections were obtained:

	Manufacturers of		
	Industrial goods	*Consumer nondurables*	*Consumer durables*
Technical research and development	.75	54	56
Marketing research related to new products	.30	62	56
Product evaluation	.16	19	22

As might be expected, the technical development of products was most emphasized by the industrial-goods producers, whereas marketing research related to new products was most emphasized by the consumer-goods producers.

This analysis indicates that all three groups of manufacturers—industrial, consumer durable, and consumer nondurable—stressed the non-price facets of competitive strategy, and that *the relative emphasis on product and sales efforts varied according to the nature of the products and the characteristics of the buyers.*

To further test this proposition, the questionnaires were grouped according to specific industries. If the proposition were valid, there should have been a high degree of similarity in the marketing strategies of respondents of a specific industry. That is, the respondents of a given industry, producing similar products for like customers, should select similar policy areas as most important in their marketing success.

Here are three examples that demonstrate the validity of this proposition.

Case No. 1—Capital Goods Industry

The most homogeneous grouping of companies with similar products and similar customers consisted of 12 producers of major installations—capital goods. As Table 4 illustrates, *all 12 producers selected product research and development and product service.*

TABLE 4

Selection of Major Policy Areas by Twelve Producers of Major Installations

Rank	*Policy areas*	*Selection ratio—%*
1	Product research and development	100
2	Product service	100
3	Distribution channels and their control	67
4	Organizational structure	42
5	Management of sales personnel	42
6	Sales research and sales planning	42
7	Advertising and sales promotion	33
8	Pricing	25
9	Financing and credit	17
10	Public relations	17
11	Marketing cost budgeting and control	8
12	Transportation and storage	8

Distribution channels and their control was selected by 8 of the 12 producers. This may be because sales servicing before and after is often performed by the distributors of capital goods.

The 100% selection for product research and development and for product service were high. Statistically one would expect such an occurrence only twice in 100,000 trials due to random sampling error.

Assuming that each policy area is actually of equal importance, there is a .00002 probability of getting a policy area with a 100% selection ratio due to random sampling error (binomial theorem used). The fact that *both* of the policy areas pertaining to product were selected by all 12 respondents provides further statistical proof that the selection ratios are *not* due to chance.

Case No. 2—Metals Industry

Another grouping of companies was comprised of producers of steel, zinc, aluminum, and other processed metals. The companies have similar markets and similar products, in that their products are the raw materials for the manufacture of other goods.

TABLE 5

SELECTION OF MAJOR POLICY AREAS BY EIGHT PRODUCERS OF METALS

Rank	*Policy areas*	*Selection ratio—%*
1	Product service	100
2	Product research and development	75
3	Sales research and sales planning	63
4	Pricing	63
5	Distribution channels and their control	50
6	Management of sales personnel	38
7	Organizational structure	25
8	Transportation and storage	25
9	Financing and credit	25
10	Public relations	13
11	Advertising and sales promotion	13
12	Marketing cost budgeting and control	—

It would be anticipated that the product facet of competition would have prevailed in the competitive strategies of these companies; and Table 5 shows that this was true.

Case No. 3—Chemical Industry

A third grouping of companies highlights the importance of customers in determining marketing strategy. Of the six chemical manufacturers participating in the study, three produced for the consumer market and three for the industrial market.

All six firms responded by selecting product research and development, but at this point the similarities ceased.

As shown in Table 6, the average product selection ratio of the industrial chemical manufacturers was much higher than that of the consumer chemical manufacturers. The average sales effort selection ratio of the consumer products manufacturers was higher than that of the industrial producers.

HOW IMPORTANT IS SIZE?

To ascertain the influence of company size on management's selection of the facets of marketing strategy, the responses were classified according to the sales volume of each company: less than $50 million, $50 to $100 million, $100 to $500 million, and over $500 million.

TABLE 6

SELECTION OF MAJOR POLICY AREAS BY CHEMICAL AND DRUG PRODUCERS

Policy areas	*Selection ratio of industrial chemical producers* (3)		*Selection ratio of consumer chemical producers* (3)	
Product research and development	100		100	
Product service	67			
Average product selection ratio		83		50
Advertising and sales promotions			100	
Sales research and sales planning	100		67	
Management of sales personnel	33		67	
Average sales efforts selection ratio		44		78

The differences among the selection ratios of the various size classifications were so small that none was found to be statistically significant. Apparently size had little influence on the relative importance that a company attached to the various facets of its marketing mix.

IN CONCLUSION

The ranking method provided only a rough measure of the importance of price, product, and sales efforts; *but it was a measurement.*

As for another possible limitation—lack of differentiation between responses related to "what is" and what the respondents felt "should be"—one might ask, "Who is better qualified to select the most important areas of a successful firm's marketing program than the firm's marketing management?"

The study reported illustrates two major points:

1. In today's market, the nonprice facets of competition occupy a prominent role.
2. The explanation of the roles of nonprice competitive facets does *not* lie solely in the structure of the industry (or the size of the firm), but instead primarily in the nature of the product and its market.

The importance of the nonprice aspects of the marketing mix and the variations among industries can be explained by the nature of today's economy. To compete successfully in a setting characterized by oligopolistic firms offering rival products to a customer-dominated market, the firm must be customer-oriented. In appealing to the customer, management finds success in utilizing the nonprice facets of competitive activity, adjusting its strategy to the needs and desires of the buyer.

The major objectives of new product price determination are: gaining product acceptance, maintaining market position in the face of growing competition, and producing profits. New product pricing strategy involves the choice between skimming pricing and penetration pricing. Five pricing factors—demand, costs, marketing targets, promotion, and distribution channels—are discussed.

48. PRICING A NEW PRODUCT*

Joel Dean†

New product pricing is important in two ways: it affects the amount of the product that will be sold; and it determines the amount of revenue that will be received for a given quantity of sales. If you set your price too high you will be likely to make too few sales to permit you to cover your overhead. If you set your price too low you may not be able to cover out-of-pocket costs and may face bankruptcy.

WHAT IS DIFFERENT ABOUT NEW PRODUCTS?

New products that are novel require a different pricing treatment than old products because they are distinctive; no one else sells quite the same thing. This distinctiveness is usually only temporary, however. As your product catches on, your competitors will try to take away your market by bringing out imitative substitutes. The speed with which your product loses its uniqueness will depend on a number of factors. Among these factors are the total sales potential, the investment required for rivals to manufacture and distribute the product, the strength of patent protection, and the alertness and power of competitors.

Although this process of competitive imitation is almost inevitable, the

* Reprinted from "Pricing a New Product," *The Controller*, Vol. XXIII, No. 4, (April, 1955), pp. 163–165.

† Columbia University.

company that introduces the new product can use price as a means of slowing the speed of competitive imitation. Finding the "right" price is not easy, however. New products are hard to price correctly. This is true both because past experience is no sure guide as to how the market will react to any given price, and because competing products are usually significantly different in nature or quality.

In setting a price on a new product you will want to have three objectives in mind:

Getting the product accepted.
Maintaining your market in the face of growing competition.
Producing profits.

Your pricing policy cannot be said to be successful unless you can achieve all three of these objectives.

WHAT ARE YOUR CHOICES AS TO POLICY?

Broadly speaking, the strategy in pricing a new product comes down to a choice between (1) "skimming" pricing, and (2) "penetration" pricing. There are a number of intermediate positions, but the issues are made clearer when the two extremes are compared.

Skimming Pricing

For products that represent a drastic departure from accepted ways of preforming a service or filling a demand, a strategy of high prices coupled with large promotional expenditures in the early stages of market development (and lower prices at later stages) has frequently proven successful. This is known as a skimming price policy.

There are four main reasons why this kind of skimming price policy is attractive for new and distinctive products:

First, the quantity of the product that you can sell is likely to be less affected by price in the early stages than it will be when the product is full-grown and imitation has had time to take effect. This is the period when pure salesmanship can have the greatest effect on sales.

Second, a skimming price policy takes the cream of the market at a high price before attempting to penetrate the more price-sensitive sections of the market. This means that you can get more money from those who don't care how much they pay, while building up experience to hit the big mass market with tempting prices.

Third, this can be a way to feel out the demand. It is frequently easier to start out with a high "refusal" price and reduce it later on when the facts of product demand make themselves known than it is to set a low price initially and then boost the price to cover unforeseen costs or exploit a popular product.

Fourth, high prices will frequently produce a greater dollar volume of sales in the early stages of market development than a policy of low initial prices.

If this is the case, skimming pricing will provide you with funds for financing expansion into the big-volume sectors of your market.

A skimming-price policy is not always the answer to your problem, however. High initial prices may safeguard profits during the early stages of product introduction, but they may also prevent quick sales to the many buyers upon whom you must rely to give you a mass market. The alternative is to use low prices as an entering wedge to get into mass markets early. This is known as penetration pricing.

Penetration Pricing

This approach is likely to be desirable under the following conditions:

First, when the quantity of product sold is highly sensitive to price, even in the early stages of introduction.

Second, when you can achieve substantial economies in unit cost and effectiveness of manufacturing and distributing the product by operating at large volumes.

Third, when your product is faced by threats of strong potential competition, very soon after introduction.

Fourth, when there is no "elite" market—that is, a body of buyers who are willing to pay a much higher price in order to obtain the latest and best.

The decision to price so as to penetrate a broad market can be made at any stage in the product's life cycle, but you should be sure to examine this pricing strategy before your new product is marketed at all. This possibility certainly should be explored as soon as your product has established an elite market. Sometimes a product can be rescued from a premature death by adoption of a penetration price policy after the cream of the market has been skimmed.

The ease and speed with which competitors can bring out substitute products is probably the most important single consideration in your choice between skimming and penetration pricing at the time you introduce your new product. For products whose market potential looks big, a policy of low initial prices ("stay-out pricing") makes sense, because the big multiple-product manufacturers are attracted by mass markets. If you set your price low enough to begin with, your large competitor may not feel it worth his while to make a big production and distribution investment for slim profit margins. In any event, you should appraise the competitive situation very carefully for each new product before you decide on your pricing strategy.

WHAT SHOULD YOU LOOK AT IN SETTING A PRICE?

When you have decided on your basic pricing strategy you can turn to the task of putting a dollars-and-cents price tag on your new product. In order to do this you should study at least five important factors:

Potential and probable demand for your product.
Cost of making and selling the product.
Market targets.
Promotional strategy.
Suitable channels of distribution.

DEMAND

The first step in estimating market demand is to find out whether or not the product will sell at all—assuming that the price is set within the competitive range. That is, you should find out whether or not this product fulfills a real need, and whether enough potential customers are dissatisfied with their present means of filling that need. To do this, you should make some estimate of the total potential market for the new product and all its competing substitutes and then estimate the portion of this potential that your product is likely to get.

Next, you should determine the competitive range of price. This will be easier when substitutes are relatively close or when customers are familiar with the cost and quality of substitutes and act rationally on the basis of performance.

The next step is to try to guess the probable sales volume at two or three possible prices within the price range. The best way to do this is by controlled experiments; next best is by a close estimation of buyers' alternatives in the light of market preference.

Finally, you should consider the possibility of retaliation by manufacturers of displaced substitutes. If your new product hits any one of your competitors hard enough, you may be faced with price retaliation. The limit to this price cutting is set by the out-of-pocket cost of the price-cutting competitors. Therefore, some knowledge of the out-of-pocket cost of making competing products will be helpful in estimating the probable effects of a particular price.

COSTS

Before going ahead with your new product, you should estimate its effect on your investment, your costs, and your profits. First you should estimate the added investment necessary to manufacture and distribute the new product. This investment estimate should include estimates of increased working capital that will be required at various sales volumes. Then you should estimate the added costs of manufacturing and selling the product at various possible sales volumes. The way to estimate costs is to calculate what your total costs would be with and without the new product; the difference should be assigned to the new product. Allocations of overheads that you are already incurring should not be assigned to the new product because they will be the same whether or not you go ahead with the addition to your product line.

In building up your two sets of cost and investment figures—one showing the situation *without* the new product, and the other showing the contrasting situation *with* the new product added to your line—be sure to take into account *all* pertinent items. It often happens that companies which lose money on new products have run into trouble because of unanticipated costs or investment requirements which have absorbed most of or all the profits realizable from the new idea.

New product costs may be segregated into half a dozen main categories:

Direct labor.
Materials and supplies for production.
Components purchased outside.
Special equipment (such as jigs, dies, fixtures and other tools).
Plant overhead.
Sales expenses.

Direct Labor

Methods of estimating direct labor may be built up in one of three ways: (1) You can compare each operation on each component with accumulated historical data, from your files, on similar operations for similar components, (2) you can develop a mockup of the proposed work-place layout and actually time an operator who performs a series of manufacturing operations, simulated as accurately as possible, (3) you can apply one of several systems of predetermined, basic-motion times which are currently available from private sources.

Make certain, however, that you include any added time used for setup work, or needed to take the item from its transportation container, perform the operations, and return the item again to its transportation container. When the total direct labor time is determined multiply it by the appropriate labor rates.

Materials and Supplies for Production

In developing reliable cost figures for materials and supplies make a methodical list of all requirements. Having listed everything in an organized fashion, you can enter the specifications and costs on a manufactured-component estimate form. Remember to include any extra costs which may be incurred as a result of requirements for particular length, widths, qualities, or degrees of finish. Allowances for scrap should also be made as accurately as possible and corrected by applying a salvage factor if the scrap can be sold or reused.

Components Purchased Outside

Place your specification for parts purchased from other concerns with more than one reliable supplier and get competitive bids for the work. But in addition to price considerations be sure to give proper weight to the reputation and qualification of each potential producer. Moreover, if you use a substantial volume of purchased parts you may want to use a "plus" factor above the cost of the components themselves to cover your expenses involved in receiving, storing, and handling the items.

Special Equipment

Take careful precautions against making a faulty analysis of your expense and investment in special jigs, dies, fixtures, and other tools which you will need to produce the new product. To avoid trouble in this area make a table showing all cases where special equipment will be needed. The actual estimating of the costs of such equipment is best done by a qualified tool shop—your own if you have one or an outside organization. Here again, competitive bidding is an excellent protection on price. Do not include costs of routine inspection, service, and repair; these are properly charged to plant overhead.

Plant Overhead

The overhead item may be estimated as a given percentage of direct labor, machine utilization, or some other factor determined by your accountants to be the most sensible basis. In this way you can allocate satisfactorily charges for administration and supervision, for occupancy, and for indirect service related to producing the new product. Overhead allocations may be set up for a department, a production center, or even, in some cases, for a particular machine. In calculating plant overhead make certain that in setting up your cost controls, your accountants have not overlooked any proper indirect special charges which will have to be incurred because of the new product.

Sales Expenses

Your estimates of sales revenue at various potential volumes can now be compared with your estimates of added costs at those volumes. The difference will be the added profits of introducing the new product. Although the costs themselves probably should not be used as a basis for setting price, you should not go into any venture that will not produce for you a rate-of-return on the added investment required that is adequate to compensate for the added risk and still be at least as high as the return you could get by investing your money elsewhere. If no price that you set will provide enough revenue to produce an adequate profit over your added costs, then you should either drop the venture, try to cut costs, or wait for a more favorable time to introduce the product.

MARKETING TARGETS

Assuming that the estimates of market demand and of cost and investment have been made and that the profit picture looks sufficiently rosy, you are now in a position to set up some basic goals and programs. A decision must first be made about market targets—that is, what market share or sales volume should be aimed at? Among other factors, you should probably consider what effect it will have upon investment requirements, whether or not your existing organization can handle the new product, how it fits in with the rest of your present product line, and so forth. These decisions should be made after a cold-blooded survey of the nature of your new product and of your company's organization and manufacturing and distributive facilities.

PROMOTION

Closely related to the question of market targets is the design of promotional strategy. As an innovator, you must not only sell your product, but frequently you must also make people recognize their need for this kind of product. Your problem here is to determine the best way of "creating a market." You must determine the nature of the market and the type of appeal that will sell the product and secure prompt acceptance by potential buyers. And you should also estimate how much it will cost you to achieve this goal.

CHANNELS OF DISTRIBUTION

Frequently, there is some latitude in your choice of channels of distribution. This choice should be consistent with your strategy for initial pricing and for promotional outlays. Penetration pricing and explosive promotion calls for distribution channels that promptly make the product broadly available. Otherwise you waste advertising or stymie mass-market pricing. Distribution policy also concerns the role you wish the dealer to play in pushing your product, the margins you must pay him to introduce this action and the amount of protection of territory and of inventory required to do so.

YOUR DECISION

These are the factors you should look at in setting a price. Estimating these factors shrewdly and objectively requires specialized training and experience. Good estimates will make your pricing more realistic and successful. But pricing cannot be established by formula. Combining these factors into a pricing policy requires judgment. In the last analysis you must pull all the estimates of the experts together and arrive at your own decision. You will want to make sure that the pricing analysis is guided by sound principles and that the activities of your specialists are all geared toward the same end—devising a sound, effective marketing and promotional program in conjunction with a price that will meet your objectives of market acceptance, competitive strength, and profits.

Pricing is one of the important policy decisions facing marketing management. A sequential, multi-stage, long-range view of pricing and price action is presented. A market approach, rather than a cost approach, is followed. This facilitates the construction of a pricing decision framework and permits a decision to be made in stages rather than requiring a simultaneous solution of an entire price problem.

49. MULTI-STAGE APPROACH TO PRICING*

Alfred R. Oxenfeldt†

Of all the areas of executive decision, pricing is perhaps the most fuzzy. Although unanimity in marketing decisions is a custom more remarkable in its occurrence than in its absence, agreement in pricing decisions is even more rare.

This article accordingly presents a long-run, policy-oriented approach to pricing which should reduce the range of prices considered in specific situations and consequently improve the decisions which result. This approach, which to the best of my knowledge is new, calls for the price decision to be made in six successive steps, each one narrowing the alternatives to be considered at the next step.

Is this method just another mechanical pricing formula? Hardly, for it is my conviction that the quest for mechanical pricing methods is unduly optimistic, if not downright naive. Nevertheless, many businessmen consistently employ almost mechanical formulas for pricing.

Yet, even if mechanical pricing formulas are the hope of the optimistic, it would be excessively pessimistic to resign ourselves to a *formless* consideration of all the relevant factors and to a random exercise of judgment.

* Reprinted from "Multi-Stage Approach to Pricing," *Harvard Business Review*, Vol. XXXVIII, No. 4 (July–August, 1960), pp. 125–33.

† Columbia University.

SEQUENTIAL STAGES

In order to organize the various pieces of information and considerations that bear on price decisions, a multi-stage approach to pricing can be a very helpful tool. This method sorts the major elements in a pricing decision into six successive stages:

1. Selecting market targets.
2. Choosing a brand "image."
3. Composing a marketing mix.
4. Selecting a pricing policy.
5. Determining a pricing strategy.
6. Arriving at a specific price.

The sequence of the stages is an essential part of the method, for each step is calculated to simplify the succeeding stage and to reduce the likelihood of error. One might say that this method divides the price decision into manageable parts, each one logically antecedent to the next. In this way, the decision at each stage facilitates all subsequent decisions. This approach might also be regarded as a process of selective search, where the number of alternatives deserving close consideration is reduced drastically by making the decision in successive stages. Of course, one could arrive at the same result by simultaneously considering all the factors mentioned—but it might require a computer to do so.

While it appears that this approach is applicable over a broad range of industry and trade, the great diversity of business situations precludes the possibility of its being a universally applicable method. It must be adapted to prevailing circumstances; consequently, information, experience, and the application of rigorous logic are required for its optimum utilization.

1. Market Targets

A going concern is "committed," confined, and tied down by several important circumstances which can be altered only over a considerable period of time. It must live with many conditions, even while it may attempt to alter them. Also, an operating business possesses specified resources on which it will strive to capitalize in achieving its objectives. For example, a firm will have:

A fixed production location, given physical facilities, and a particular production and sales labor force.

A set of distribution arrangements through which the firm generally sells, including particular distributors with whom it has established relationships.

Contracts with suppliers, customers, laborers, and lenders of funds.

A portfolio of customers who have a definite opinion of the firm's reliability, and the quality of its offerings and service.

These commitments and resources of a firm contain pricing implications. Mainly, they determine the type of product that it can make, the type of service it can render, and its probable costs of operation. What is more, these circumstances form the basis for the most fundamental pricing decision that management should make—namely, the types of customers, or market segments, it will attempt to cultivate.

By virtue of its fixed commitments, then, a firm is limited to the several market segments it can reasonably hope to capture. It has customer connections on which it can capitalize, and it has a variety of strengths and weaknesses that limit its choice among potential submarkets for intensive cultivation. *One important criterion in the selection of market targets is customer awareness of and sensitivity to price.*

II. Brand "Image"

Once management has defined the submarkets it wishes to cultivate most actively, it must select the methods it will use to achieve its goal.

Success in the market place for more and more products seems to depend on creating a favorable general image (often vague and formless) of the product or company among prospective customers. The selection and development of this image become of prime importance and have a direct bearing on price, as will be explained subsequently. A favorable image is especially important when one sells consumers' goods, but only rarely is it completely unimportant even in the sales of producers' goods. Buyers' very perceptions are affected by their prior attitudes, the actions and opinions of others, first impressions and early associations. It is a rare firm that can ignore the total impression its potential customers have of it and of what it is selling.

The firm's selection of its company and brand image should be dictated by the types of customers it is trying to attract. Submarkets may be likened to targets at which the seller is firing, and "images" are powerful weapons that can be used to hit the targets.

Almost every going concern has invested—often very heavily—in the creation of a favorable image. Most businesses know what image they wish to achieve and are concerned lest they or their products fail to have a favorable "meaning" to potential customers. At the very minimum, almost every management knows there are certain images that customers might have of it and its product that would prove disastrous.

The type of image a firm can create of itself and its wares depends to a considerable degree, again, on its fixed commitments and resources. With its physical and personnel resources, there is a limit to what it can do to alter the prevailing opinions—for they reflect all that the company was and did in the past. In that sense, the basic commitments limit the type of image a firm can establish, how much time it will require to establish it, and the cost. Even as brand image is frequently an effective weapon in cultivating particular submarkets, price helps to create the brand image. It is for this reason that the selection of a brand image which is consistent with the firm's market targets implies particular forms of price behavior.

III. Marketing Mix

The third stage in multi-stage pricing calls for the selection of a combination of sales promotion devices that will create and re-enforce the desired company and product brand image and achieve maximum sales for the planned level of dollar outlays. In this stage, a role must be assigned to price. The role in which price is cast should be selected only after assessment is made as to the relative effectiveness and appropriateness of each sales promotion device that might be employed. The short-term gains of certain sales promotion devices may entail injury to the image objectives of the firm. Conflicts of such a nature must be resolved at this stage.

Then, too, a firm might achieve precisely the *desired* image and still find customers very hard to get. It is not enough to establish the desired image; it must be an *effective* image. Furthermore, even though a firm may establish highly favorable impressions of itself and its wares, the company and its products must live up to the image they foster. Not only must its product be "within reach" in price, but it must be accessible by being offered through convenient channels of distribution, and must be sold in outlets where customers like to buy.

The third stage builds directly upon the second. The need to conform to the prior decision about company and brand image greatly limits the number of price alternatives that a price setter can reasonably consider.

The marketing-mix decision at this stage need not be translated into specific dollars and cents amounts to be devoted to each sales promotion device; however, it does at least call for crude answers to the following questions:

How heavily to advertise?
How much for salesmen?
How much for product improvement?
How much of an assortment to carry?
How large an inventory to hold?
How best to provide speedy delivery?
How much emphasis on price appeal?

The composition of a marketing mix (arrived at by answering the type of questions just listed) is admittedly very difficult and highly subjective. But the job is facilitated greatly when answers are subjected to the test of conforming to the desired company and brand image and to the firm's fixed commitments.

Few firms can afford to switch "images," usually because they have invested heavily in them in prior years and should, therefore, not abandon them lightly. Moreover, past images persist and blur any future attempts at image building. Although it cannot easily scrap its brand image, a firm can vary its marketing mix within moderate limits and remain consistent with the image it seeks to create. Thus, the selection of an image sets limits and gives direction to the decision about the elements to be included in the marketing mix. In that way, it facilitates the decision and also increases the likelihood that it will be correct. However, it does not isolate a single marketing mix as the only correct one.

IV. Determining Policy

The fourth stage in multi-stage pricing calls for the selection of a pricing policy. But before a pricing policy can be determined, answers to the following questions must be obtained:

How should our price compare with "average" prices in the industry? Specifically, should we be 2% above or 4% below the average? And, when we speak of the average, which firms' prices are we going to include in the computation?

How fast will we meet price reductions or increases by rivals?

How frequently will it be advisable to vary price? To what extent is stability of price advantageous?

Should the firm make use of "fair trade" price maintenance?

How frequently should the firm run price promotions?

These are simply illustrative of the aspects of a pricing policy which management can and should spell out—in proper sequence. By virtue of having made the evaluations and decisions called for in the first three stages, management will find itself limited in the number of choices on these points.

In addition, each company must take account of the valuations placed on its product-service "package" as well as the valuations of rival products by the market segments it is most anxious to cultivate. On the basis of such considerations, plus its target market segments and marketing mix, it will decide whether it can afford to charge much more or less than its rivals.

"Bracketing" the Price. Before proceeding further, let us summarize. Surely, a price setter would be some distance from a specific price decision even after completing the fourth step. We must ask ourselves whether he would not also have covered considerable distance toward a price decision. By taking account of the firm's basic commitments and resources, the images it desires to establish, its decision about marketing mix, and the selection of a detailed pricing policy, has not the price setter reached the point where he is very strongly circumscribed in the price decision he will ultimately make?

V. Pricing Strategy

It is difficult to draw a sharp line between policy and strategy, but it is possible and useful to make some sort of distinction between them. Policy is formulated to deal with anticipated and foreseeable situations of a recurrent type. However, markets frequently are beset and dominated by *special* situations that basic policy was not designed to meet. For example:

A Congressional committee might threaten to investigate the company's or the industry's pricing arrangements.

A sizable firm may have fallen into a desperate financial situation so that it was forced to raise cash through a liquidation of its inventories.

A large new firm may have entered the market.

Business may have fallen off precipitately for the entire industry or economy.

The company may have introduced a model that is either a "dud" or a "sure winner."

Special situations like these ordinarily require an adjustment in price—and the formulation of a strategy to guide management in setting price *during the time that the special situation endures.*

There generally are several strategies which would be compatible with the firm's basic commitments and resources, its market targets, its image objectives, its convictions about the relative emphasis to attach to various elements in the marketing mix, and its specific pricing policies. Others would be incompatible with earlier decisions and therefore might endanger precious values. A threat to one's very survival might justify a scrapping of these, but impetuousness, shortsightedness, or avarice would not. Explicit recognition of these earlier stages of the pricing decision should prevent hasty short-run actions that are painful, but quite common.

VI. Specific Price

Here is the final step—the selection of a specific price. At this point, the price setter will usually find himself sharply circumscribed in the specific sums he can charge. Nevertheless, he usually will have some range of price possibilities that are consistent with the decisions made in the preceding five stages of the price decision. How may he best select among the alternatives?

To the extent that he is able, he should be guided by the arithmetic of pricing—that is, by a comparison of the costs and revenues of the alternative prices within the zone delimited by the prior stages of his pricing decision. Once he has taken into account his market targets, brand image, marketing mix, pricing policy, and strategy, he can afford to ignore everything but the calculations of costs and revenues. *The first five stages of decision are designed to take account of the business considerations which may be ignored if one selects price solely on the basis of prevailing cost and revenue conditions.*

It often is impossible to obtain reliable information about sales at different prices; this difficulty is present whatever method of pricing one employs. But the multi-stage policy approach facilitates research and experimentation into demand conditions by limiting the number of alternatives to be considered.

The price that would be established under this multi-stage policy approach would rarely be the same as that set by balancing marginal cost and marginal revenue. The former probably would exclude, as incompatible with the firm's basic commitments and resources, desired brand image, and so on, the prices that would be most profitable in the very short term.

THE ADVANTAGES

First, this approach breaks up the pricing decision into six relatively manageable pieces. In that way, it introduces order into the weighing of the many considerations bearing on price. This approach, therefore, should increase the likelihood that all major factors will be taken into account and that their large number will not overwhelm the price setter.

Second, this method of pricing reduces the risk that the price setter will destroy the firm's valuable investments in corporate and brand images. Also, it requires the price setter to determine and take into account the limitation on the firm's freedom of decision. In that way, it would discourage the pricing executive from undertaking what he is powerless to accomplish. Similarly, the multi-stage policy approach should militate against a short-run policy of opportunism that would sacrifice long-term values.

Third, the multi-stage policy approach to pricing should be valuable to those executives who are compelled to delegate pricing responsibilities. In the first place, high-level executives are virtually required by the method to make the decisions for several stages, which thus limits their dependence on their subordinates. In the second place, as explained, it simplifies the making of a price decision so that greater success can be expected. Then, too, its use should make it easier for subordinates to raise questions and obtain advice from their superiors, should they be unable to reach a decision.

Fourth, this approach to pricing puts considerable emphasis on the intangibles that are involved in pricing—particularly on the total impression that customers have of the vendor and of the things he sells. Price is far more than a rationing device that determines which potential customers will be able to afford to make a purchase. Generally it is one of the most important actions in creating an impression of the firm among potential customers. Especially as tangible differences among rival products shrink, these intangibles will grow in significance for marketing success.

THE LIMITATIONS

This approach does not indicate all the considerations that should be taken into account at each stage in the pricing decision. In other words, the price setter is compelled to isolate the significant factors operating at each stage and weigh them for himself.

Second, this approach does not indicate what price to charge in any specific situation. The most that can be claimed for it is that it narrows down the zone of possible prices to the point where it may not matter a great deal which particular price is selected. As stated at the outset, one must beware of any pricing method that does lead to a single price, for such a method could not possibly take into account all of the special circumstances which are relevant to a price decision and which vary so greatly from market to market and from time to time.

Third, this method does not guide price setters in recognizing the factors that dominate the market at any time and in knowing when to switch basic strategies. Also, there may well be more than one dominant condition which must be considered in selecting a basic strategy.

On balance, then, the multi-stage approach to pricing at best only takes an executive fairly close to his ultimate destination. Although the multi-stage policy approach does not do the whole job of pricing, the part of the job that is left is relatively easy to finish in many cases. Where this is not so, one can only assume that the task would be almost hopeless without the assistance of a method that reduces the pricing decision to a series of relatively manageable steps in a prescribed sequence.

CONCLUSION

The multi-stage policy approach outlined here differs from usual approaches to pricing in two major respects. First, it demands a long-range view of price by emphasizing the enduring effects of most price actions on company and brand image. One might say this approach constructs a policy framework for the price decision. And, second, it allows the price decision to be made in stages, rather than requiring a simultaneous solution of the entire price problem.

Credit is a service that must be marketed. Sellers perform a credit service by creating an identifiable value—possession utility. When viewed from a marketing perspective, credit is the financing of markets rather than merely the financing of assets. It is a means of increasing market potential and implementing selective distribution. Seven marketing objectives that can be at least partially achieved through credit service are presented.

50. CREDIT MANAGEMENT AS A MARKETING FUNCTION*

Robert Bartels†

Although the concept of functional integration has been widely adopted in both general management and marketing management, the employment of *credit* for the accomplishment of marketing objectives has not progressed as far as it might. There are several reasons for this, all of which stem from a limited concept of the role of credit in business.

CREDIT AND CREDIT SERVICE

For one thing, the essential nature of credit continues to be misunderstood. The idea persists that sellers "give credit." More accurately it should be said that they *perform a credit service*.

In selling on credit, sellers provide a service which must be regarded like any other service they perform. It is offered for the satisfaction of the market; for the differentiation of their market offering; and for additional income, either indirectly through the increased sale of products or directly through a charge made for the credit service.

Credit service must be marketed like any other service or product. The character of market demand for it must be ascertained. Operating costs are incurred in the performance, and these must be taken into consideration in setting price or in estimating profit.

The market for credit service arises from the utility which buyers

* Reprinted from "Credit Management as a Marketing Function," *Journal of Marketing*, Vol. XXVIII, No. 3 (July, 1964), pp. 59–61.

† Ohio State University.

attribute to it. Both sellers and buyers, however, have erred in their interpretation of credit, and this view has obscured the role of credit both in business and in the economy.

Sellers sometimes believe that in meeting credit competition they are forced to provide a "free" service. Thus, they may fail to allocate to this function all costs involved and neglect to program their credit service as part of their total product-service offering.

Buyers at times believe that they "get nothing" for the credit service charge or that they are charged more *for the goods bought* because of credit. As a result, they form attitudes antagonistic to those who provide credit service, tending to regard creditors as extortioners and themselves as defenseless customers.

Many legislators and public critics of credit also overlook the service inherent in credit operations, and tend to equate all credit business with the simple lending of money.

CREDIT AND POSSESSION UTILITY

Many of these misconceptions are traceable to conditions which antedated the present prominence of credit in business.

Prior to about 1920, in the effort to give theoretical justification to marketing activity, use was made of the economists' concept of "utilities." In marketing literature at that time it was claimed that marketing activity created time, place, and possession utilities. By the latter was meant a value supposedly created in the transaction itself. Embracing a number of factors, possession utility never really received explicit definition but appeared to result from such activities as selling and merchandising. It was not related specifically to credit business.

So long as markets were essentially cash markets, that explanation sufficed; but with growth of the credit economy a new explanation of credit was needed. This is offered in the following interpretation of credit service as creating possession utility.

When a cash transaction is contemplated, buyers estimate the value or utility of a product to them *at that time*, and sellers calculate the cost and price of providing it then. If buyers must defer purchasing until cash is accumulated at a future time, immediate evaluation of the product's usefulness *now* may in the mind of the buyer exceed his appraisal of it if no delay in use were imminent. Thus, if through credit service he may acquire the product at once, the sum of utilities gained may include both that of the *product* and that of *using* the product prior to the time when it could otherwise be obtained through cash purchase.

Credit service, therefore, creates an identifiable value which might be called "possession utility." Such utility is not limited to the field of consumer buying, but is also involved in mercantile transactions and in lending.

LITTLE INTEREST IN CREDIT WORK

The notions that "sellers give credit," that credit service is not distinct from the commodities to which it is applied, that credit service has no value, and that the offering of credit service is primarily a finance function—these are fallacies which have hindered the development of credit theory and practice.

For many years credit was regarded as an unproductive business activity, and the position of credit manager was at a much lower level than other marketing roles. Generally credit management has been assigned to the finance and bookkeeping departments and has been concerned mainly with allocation and utilization of working capital, turnover of receivables, sources of long-term and short-term funds for carrying receivables, credit loss ratios, cash discount tactics, economic indicators of the quality of receivables, and the like.

Although business use of credit was one of the functional fields of business first studied, the conceptual framework of credit management has remained essentially the same since the 1920s. A study of the location of the credit function in general organization structure was made by the National Association of Credit Management following World War II; but little progress has been made either among credit practitioners or among marketing theoreticians in developing a unified theory of the relation of credit to marketing. Only in recent years has credit management been regarded somewhat as a sales function, or more recently as a marketing function.

As a consequence of this narrow view, credit courses in business schools have specifically borne the adverse criticism made of specialization in the business curriculum. Furthermore, although employment in credit work is today at an all-time high, and although the importance of marketing has increased, relatively little interest in credit management is shown by college men preparing for business careers.

MARKETING PERSPECTIVE OF CREDIT

In proper perspective, credit has very broad marketing significance. A credit operation is not merely the financing of an asset. It is the *financing of markets*—both ultimate and intermediate markets. It is the financing not merely of an *asset held* by the seller but of an *inventory sold* and in possession of buyers. It is the financing of the distributive channel, and of the processes involved in moving goods through channels. It is the providing of an auxiliary service essential to the marketing of goods and one which may also be income-bearing. It is a means whereby mere buying desires may be converted into effectual demands.

Credit service is a means of reaching new segments of a heterogeneous market. Credit terms increase market potentials by creating a new form of purchasing power. Credit classifications of customers serve as a basis for selective distribution policies.

Moreover, through the offering of credit service the following marketing objectives also may be achieved:

Creation of a service "image" for the organization
Addition of a marketable line of service
Increase of revenue directly through the sale of credit service or indirectly through the increased credit sale of the commodities
Profitable employment of available working capital
Meeting of competition through terms of sale
Extension of markets so as to utilize production capacity
Counteraction of seasonal and cyclical trends through manipulation of credit sale terms

ORGANIZATION FOR CREDIT MANAGEMENT

From the decisions implicit in the marketing objectives toward which credit policy may be directed, it is evident that credit management is not solely the function of the position traditionally designated as "credit manager." Rather, the credit function is involved in *marketing management;* and as a means for accomplishing broad corporate objectives credit management is a function for which *top management* should be responsible.

Recognition of this marketing character of credit operation has not always been evident in credit organization structure or in job specifications. As a rule, credit organizations have taken form in line, staff, and functional relationships. Usually line relationships have been established within the credit department itself, or among credit personnel, for the allocating of responsibility and duties. Within the broader organization structure of the firm, however, the credit group usually have occupied staff and functional positions. In staff capacity they have served to advise general management; and in functional roles they have worked collaterally with the sales organization, which has always performed as a line function.

This concept of credit organization has been altered somewhat in recent years, as the direct marketing contribution of credit work has been acknowledged. This has been evident even in the terminology by which credit management has been designated: at first, Credit Manager; and later, as Credit Sales Department and Manager of Credit Sales.

Not semantics but a new concept of credit is involved. Insofar as credit management initiates marketing policies and plans, participates in the formulation of overall corporate objectives and programs involving credit service, and works directly with customers (particularly in providing income-bearing credit service)—to this extent the credit organization presents the characteristics long regarded as line organization. Authority and responsibility commensurate with this concept are implied.

The division of credit responsibility among credit management, sales management, and top management is *not* a question of usurpation of rights or of subordination of operational activity. Rather, it is a division of responsibility for achievement of objectives for which different levels of management are responsible with respect to the offering of credit service.

SHIFTS IN THE CREDIT FUNCTION

As a means to the achievement of corporate, marketing, and credit operational objectives, the credit operation should be regarded only as a *means*.

Thus, the performance of this function must be appraised economically like any other function. In the absence of adequate data on the cost of performing credit service, such appraisal has not always been made. Consequently, credit policy often has been determined on the basis of custom, belief, and personal preference; but today credit performance increasingly is regarded as the offering of a service—a marketable service.

This means that business management has to consider and decide how *in their particular circumstances* they can best perform the three basic functions inherent in credit operation; investment of capital in receivables, bearing of credit risk, and performance of the routine of the credit operation.

In other areas of marketing, such considerations have at times resulted in shifting functions to specialists for the most effective, most efficient performance. Advertising agencies, manufacturers' and selling agents, brokers, warehouses, and common carriers are a few examples of functional specialists engaged by business. In credit operations, functions have not been so commonly shifted, although the opportunities to do so are increasing.

The use of factors by manufacturers' and selling agents is one example of the shifting of all of the credit functions; and economy and efficiency are presumed to result. Similarly, credit insurance companies and financing organizations accept part of the credit functions when circumstances warrant using them.

Also in the field of consumer credit such shifting of functions to specialists is occurring, with the rise of credit-card companies and of charge-account banks and companies.

Thus, as a marketing function the credit operation may be managed as a marketable service creating valuable utility in the market. It is a function for which several echelons of management are responsible. And it is a function which may be performed either by the business firm itself or shifted elsewhere, depending on business conditions.

The Bayesian approach to decision making provides a framework for evaluating the economic costs of alternative courses of action. The initial judgment of the decision maker as well as information obtained during the decision process are key determinants in the Bayesian decision framework. An application of the Bayesian approach in a pricing decision is presented.

51. BAYESIAN DECISION THEORY IN PRICING STRATEGY*

Paul E. Green†

Since the publication of Robert Schlaifer's pioneering work, *Probability and Statistics for Business Decisions,*[1] the Bayesian approach to decision making under uncertainty has received much comment, pro and con, by theoretical and applied statisticians alike.

However, in contrast to the large number of theoretical contributions being made to decision theory in general and Bayesian statistics in particular, reported applications of these procedures to real-world problem situations have been rather meager. Applications appear especially lacking in the marketing field.

In highly oversimplified terms, the Bayesian approach to decision making under uncertainty provides a framework for explicitly working with the economic costs of alternative courses of action, the prior knowledge or judgments of the decision maker, and formal modification of these judgments as additional data are introduced into the problem.

In the Du Pont Company, the decision theory approach, often augmented by computer simulation, has been used experimentally over the past few years in a variety of market planning applications, ranging from capacity expansion problems to questions concerning the introduction of

* Reprinted from "Bayesian Decision Theory in Pricing Strategy," *Journal of Marketing,* Vol. XXVII, No. 1 (January, 1963), pp. 5–14.

† University of Pennsylvania.

[1] Robert Schlaifer, *Probability and Statistics for Business Decisions* (New York; McGraw-Hill Book Co., Inc., 1959). In addition, two excellent general articles dealing with the Bayesian approach are: Harry V. Roberts, "The New Business Statistics," *Journal of Business,* Vol. 33 (January, 1960) pp. 21–30, and Jack Hirshleifer, "The Bayesian Approach to Statistical Decision—An Exposition," *Journal of Business,* Vol. 34 (October, 1961) pp. 471–489.

new products and long-range price and promotional strategy. The application to follow concerns the use of Bayesian decision theory in the selection of a "best" pricing policy for a firm in an oligopolistic industry where such factors as demand elasticity, competitive retaliation, threat of future price weakness, and potential entry of new competitors influence the effectiveness of the firm's courses of action. Although the content of this case is aprocryphal, its structure has been compounded from actual situations.

No attempt will be made to describe even superficially all of the many facets of the Bayesian approach to decision making under uncertainty. The content of this article is focused on only two main considerations.

First, in dealing with actual marketing situations, for example, pricing problems, the opportunity to obtain field information may be nonexistent. Second, in dealing with actual marketing problems, the complexity of the situation may force the analyst to develop a problem structure in much greater detail than has been described in the literature.

AN ILLUSTRATIVE APPLICATION

Since early 1955, the Everclear Plastics Company had been producing a resin called Kromel, basically designed for certain industrial markets. In addition to Everclear, three other firms were producing Kromel resin. Prices among all four suppliers (called here the Kromel industry) were identical; and product quality and service among producers were comparable. Everclear's current share of Kromel industry sales amounted to 40%.

Four industrial end uses comprised the principal marketing area for the Kromel industry. These market segments will be labeled A, B, C, and D. Three of the four segments (B, C, and D) were functionally dependent on segment A in the sense that Kromel's *ultimate* market position and rate of approach to this level in each of these three segments was predicated on the resin's making substantial inroads in segment A.

The Kromel industry's only competition in these four segments consisted of another resin called Verlon, which was produced by six other firms. Shares of the total Verlon-Kromel market (weighted sums over all four segments) currently stood at 70% Verlon industry, and 30% Kromel industry. Since its introduction in 1955, the superior functional characteristics per dollar cost of Kromel had enabled this newer product to displace fairly large poundages of Verlon in market segments B, C, and D.

On the other hand, the functional superiority per dollar cost of Kromel had not been sufficiently high to interest segment A consumers. While past price decreases in Kromel had been made, the cumulative effect of these reductions had still been insufficient to accomplish Kromel sales penetration in segment A. (Sales penetration is defined as a market share exceeding zero.)

In the early fall of 1960, it appeared to Everclear's management that future weakness in Kromel price might be in the offing. The anticipated capacity increases on the part of the firm's Kromel competitors suggested that in the next year or two potential industry supply of this resin might significantly exceed demand, if no substantial market participation for the Kromel industry were established in segment A. In addition, it appeared likely that potential Kromel competitors might enter the business, thus adding to the threat of oversupply in later years.

Segment A, of course, constituted the key factor. If substantial inroads could be made in this segment, it appeared likely that Kromel industry sales growth in the other segments not only could be speeded up, but that ultimate market share levels for this resin could be markedly increased from those anticipated in the absence of segment A penetration. To Everclear's sales management, a price reduction in Kromel still appeared to represent a feasible means to achieve this objective, and (even assuming similar price reductions on the part of Kromel competitors) perhaps could still be profitable to Everclear.

However, a large degree of uncertainty surrounded both the overall attractiveness of this alternative, and under this alternative the amount of the price reduction which would enable Kromel to penetrate market segment A.

PROBLEM STRUCTURING AND DEVELOPMENT OF THE MODEL

Formulation of the problem required a certain amount of artistry and compromise toward achieving a reasonably adequate description of the problem. But it was also necessary to keep the structure simple enough so that the nature of each input would be comprehensible to the personnel responsible for supplying data for the study.

Problem components had to be formulated, such as: (a) length of planning period; (b) number and nature of courses of action; (c) payoff functions; and (d) states of nature covering future growth of the total Verlon-Kromel market, interindustry (Kromel vs. Verlon) and intra-Kromel industry effects of a Kromel price change, implications on Everclear's share of the total Kromel industry, and Everclear's production costs.

Initial discussions with sales management indicated that a planning period of five years should be considered in the study. While the selection of five years was somewhat arbitrary, sales personnel believed that some repercussions of a current price reduction might well extend over several years into the future.

A search for possible courses of action indicated that four pricing alternatives covered the range of actions under consideration:

1. Maintenance of status quo on Kromel price, which was $1.00/lb.
2. A price reduction to $.93/lb. within the next three months.

3. A price reduction to $.85/lb. within the next three months.
4. A price reduction to $.80/lb. within the next three months.

Inasmuch as each price action would be expected to produce a different time pattern in the flow of revenues and costs, and since no added investment in production facilities was contemplated, it was agreed that cumulative, compounded net profits over the 5-year planning period would constitute a relevant payoff function. In the absence of any unanimity as to the "correct" opportunity cost of capital, it was decided to use two interest rates of 6 and 10% annually in order to test the sensitivity of outcomes to the cost of capital variable.

Another consideration came to light during initial problem discussions. Total market growth (for the Kromel or Verlon industry) over the next five years in each market segment constituted a "state of nature" which could impinge on the Everclear's profit position. Accordingly, it was agreed to consider three separate forecasts of total market growth, a "most probable, optimistic, and pessimistic" forecast.

From these assumptions a base case was then formulated. This main case would first consider the pricing problem under the most probable forecast of total Verlon-Kromel year-by-year sales potential in each segment, using an opportunity cost of capital of 6% annually. The two other total market forecasts and the other cost of capital were then to be treated as sub-cases, in order to test the sensitivity of the base case outcomes to variations in these particular states of nature.

However, inter- and intra-industry alternative states of nature literally abounded in the Kromel resin problem. Sales management at Everclear had to consider such factors as:

1. The possibility that Kromel resin could effect penetration of market segment A if no price decrease were made.
2. If a price decrease were made, the extent of Verlon retaliation to be anticipated.
3. Given a particular type of Verlon price retaliation, its possible impact on Kromel's penetration of segment A.
4. If segment A were penetrated, the possible market share which the Kromel industry could gain in segment A.
5. If segment A were penetrated, the possible side effects of this event on speeding up Kromel's participation in market segments B, C, and D.
6. If segment A were not penetrated, the impact which the price reduction could still have on speeding up Kromel's participation in segments B, C, and D.
7. If segment A were not penetrated, the possibility that existing Kromel competitors would initiate price reductions a year hence.
8. The possible impact of a current Kromel price reduction on the decisions of existing or potential Kromel producers to increase capacity or enter the industry.

While courses of action, length of planning period, and the payoff measure (cumulative, compounded net profits) for the base case had been fairly quickly agreed upon, the large number of inter- and intra-Kromel industry states of nature deemed relevant to the problem would require rather lengthy discussion with Everclear's sales personnel.

Accordingly, introductory sessions were held with Everclear's sales management, in order to develop a set of states of nature large enough to represent an adequate description of the real problem, yet small enough to be comprehended by the participating sales personnel. Next, separate interview sessions were held with two groups of Everclear's sales personnel; subjective probabilities regarding the occurrence of alternative states of nature under each course of action were developed in these sessions. A final session was held with all contributing personnel in attendance; each projection and/or subjective probability was gone over in detail, and a final set of ground rules for the study was agreed upon. A description of these ground rules appears in Table 1.

TABLE 1

SUBJECTIVE PROBABILITIES AND DATA ESTIMATES ASSOCIATED WITH EVERCLEAR'S PRICING PROBLEM

1. If Kromel price remained at $1.00/pound and market segment A were not penetrated, what market share pattern for Kromel industry sales pounds would obtain in segments B, C, and D?

Base Assumption—Kromel Industry Share

	Segment B	*Segment C*	*Segment D*
1961	57.0%	40.0%	42.0%
1962	65.0	50.0	44.0
1963	75.0	80.0	46.0
1964	76.0	84.0	48.0
1965	76.0	84.0	50.0

2. If Kromel price remained at $1.00/pound, what is the probability that Kromel would still penetrate market segment A?

Probability of Penetration—Segment A

1961	.05
1962	.10
1963	.20
1964	.25
1965	.40

3. Under price strategies $.93/pound, $.85/pound, and $.80/pound, what is the probability of Verlon industry price retaliation; and given the particular retaliation (shown below), what is the probability that Kromel would still penetrate market segment A?

Pricing Case (entries are probabilities)

Verlon Industry Retaliation	*$.93 Case*	*$.85 Case*	*$.80 Case*
Full match of Kromel price reduction	.05	.15	.38
Half match of Kromel price reduction	.60	.75	.60
Stand pat on price	.35	.10	.02

Given a Particular Verlon Retaliatory Action, the Probability that Kromel Would Still Penetrate Segment A

	$.93 Case			*$.85 Case*			*$.80 Case*		
	Full Match	*Half Match*	*Stand Pat*	*Full Match*	*Half Match*	*Stand Pat*	*Full Match*	*Half Match*	*Stand Pat*
1961	.15	.20	.35	.20	.40	.80	.75	.80	.90
1962	.25	.30	.60	.30	.60	.90	.80	.85	.95
1963	.35	.40	.65	.40	.65	.95	.85	.90	1.00
1964	.60	.65	.75	.70	.75	.98	.90	.95	1.00
1965	.65	.70	.80	.75	.80	.98	.95	.98	1.00

4. If penetration in market segment A were effected, what is the probability that Kromel would obtain the specific share of this segment (a) during the first year of penetration, and (b) during the second year of participation?

Share	*First year*	*Second year*
25%	.15	.00
50	.35	.00
75	.40	.00
100	.10	1.00

5. If Kromel penetration of market segment A were effected, what impact would this event have on speeding up Kromel industry participation in segments B, C, and D?
   Segment B—Would speed up market participation one year from base assumption shown under point 1 of this Table.
   Segment C—Would speed up market participation one year from base assumption shown under point 1 of this Table.
   Segment D—Kromel would move up to 85% of the market in the following year, and would obtain 100% of the market in the second year following penetration of segment A.

6. Under the price reduction strategies, if Kromel penetration of market segment A were *not* accomplished, what is the probability that Kromel industry participation in segments B, C, and D (considered as a group) would still be speeded up one year from the base assumption shown under point 1 of this Table?

	Probability of Speedup
$.93 Case	.45
$.85 Case	.60
$.80 Case	.80

7. If Kromel price at the end of any given year were $1.00/pound, $.93/pound, $.85/pound, or $.80/pound respectively, *and* if market segment A were not penetrated, what is the probability that present competitive Kromel producers would take the specific price action shown below?

If Kromel price	*Action*	*Probability*
@ $1.00/pound	$1.00/pound	.15
	.93	.80
	.85	.05
	.80	.00
@ $ .93/pound	.93	.80
	.85	.20
	.80	.00
@ $ .85/pound	.85	1.00
	.80	.00
@ $ .80/pound	.80	1.00

8. Under each of the four price strategies, what is the probability that competitive (present or potential) Kromel producers would add to or initiate capacity (as related to the price prevailing in mid-1961) in the years 1963 and 1964? (No capacity changes were assumed in 1965.)

Competitor	*$1.00/pound*	*$.93/pound*	*$.85/pound*	*$.80/pound*
R	.50	.20	.05	.00
S	.90	.75	.50	.20
T	.40	.10	.05	.00
U	.70	.50	.25	.00
V	.70	.50	.25	.00

Timing and amount available beginning of year

Competitor	*1963*	*1964*
R	10 million pounds	20 million pounds
S	12	20
T	12	20
U	6	12
V	6	6

USE OF TREE DIAGRAMS

The large number of alternative states of nature which were associated with inter- and intra-industry factors necessitated the construction of "tree diagrams" for each pricing alternative. These diagrams enabled sales management to trace the implications of their assumptions. Figure 1 shows a portion of one such tree diagram.

A word of explanation concerning interpretation of the probability tree is in order. The two principal branches underneath the *$1.00 case* refer to the event of whether or not Kromel penetrates segment A in the first year of the planning period. Sales personnel felt that a 5% chance existed for penetration, hence the figure .05000 under A.

However, if A were penetrated, four market participations were deemed possible: 25, 50, 75 and 100% carrying the conditional probabilities of .15, .35, .40 and .10 respectively.

Multiplication of each conditional probability, in turn, by the .05 marginal probability leads to the four joint probabilities noted in the upper left portion of the chart.

Next, if Kromel did not penetrate segment A during the first year, a probability of .80 was attached to the event that competitive Kromel producers would reduce price to $.93/lb. Multiplying the conditional probability of .80 by .95 results in the .76000 probability assigned to the joint event, "did not penetrate segment A and Kromel price was reduced to $.93/lb."

However, if Kromel price were reduced to $.93/lb., Verlon retaliation had to be considered, leading to the joint probabilities assigned to the next set of tree branches. In this way probabilities were built up for each of the over-400 possible outcomes of the study by appropriate application of the ground rules noted in Table 1.

A mathematical model was next constructed for determining the expected value of Everclear's cumulative, compounded net profits under each price strategy. See Table 2.

FIGURE 1

Portion of a "Tree Diagram"; Kromel Price Simulation

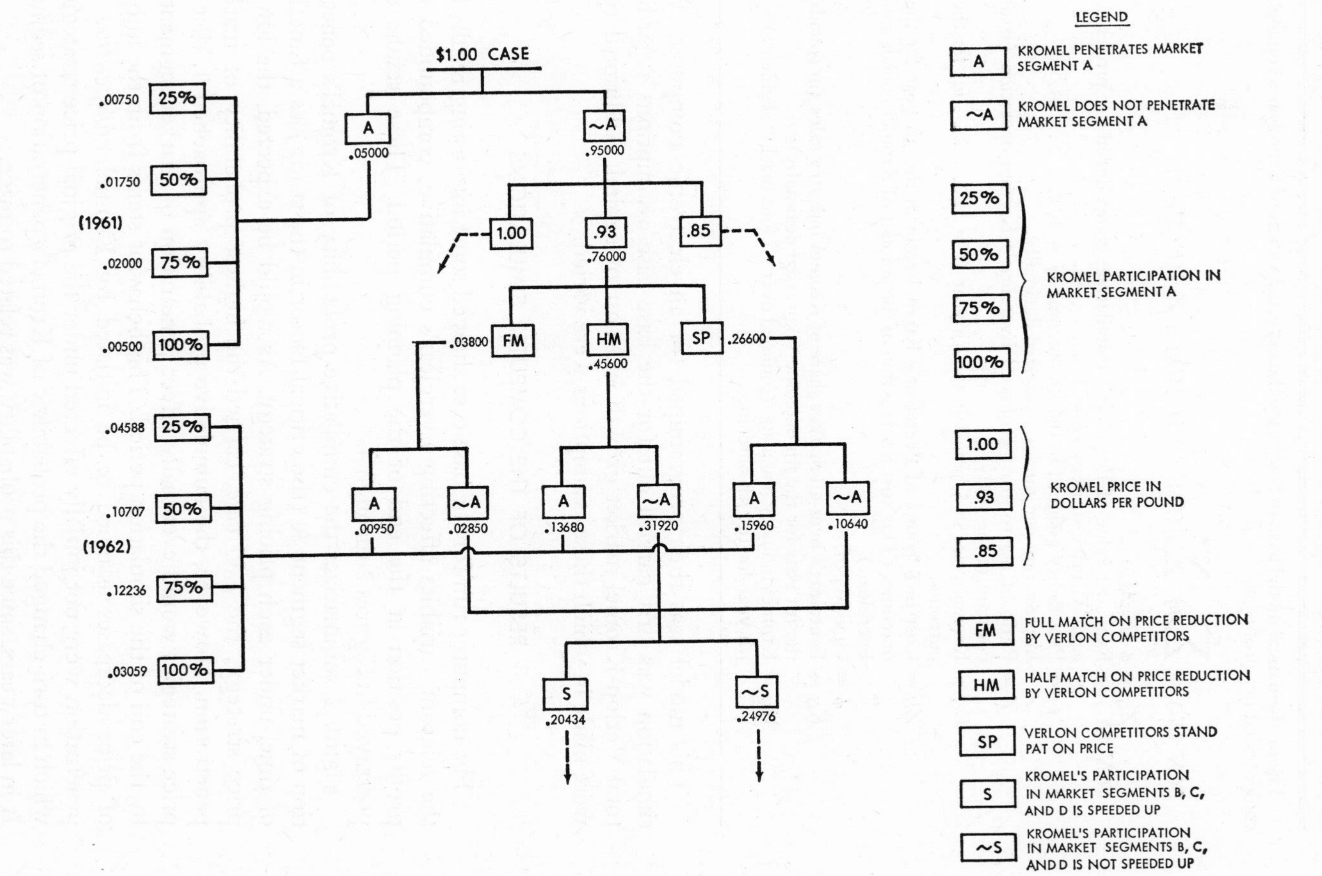

$1.00 CASE
A
.05000
~A
.95000
1.00
.93
.76000
.85
FM
.03800
HM
.45600
SP
.26600
A
.00950
~A
.02850
A
.13680
~A
.31920
A
.15960
~A
.10640
S
.20434
~S
.24976
(1961)
.00750 25%
.01750 50%
.02000 75%
.00500 100%
(1962)
.04588 25%
.10707 50%
.12236 75%
.03059 100%
LEGEND
A KROMEL PENETRATES MARKET SEGMENT A
~A KROMEL DOES NOT PENETRATE MARKET SEGMENT A
25% 50% 75% 100% KROMEL PARTICIPATION IN MARKET SEGMENT A
1.00 .93 .85 KROMEL PRICE IN DOLLARS PER POUND
FM FULL MATCH ON PRICE REDUCTION BY VERLON COMPETITORS
HM HALF MATCH ON PRICE REDUCTION BY VERLON COMPETITORS
SP VERLON COMPETITORS STAND PAT ON PRICE
S KROMEL'S PARTICIPATION IN MARKET SEGMENTS B, C, AND D IS SPEEDED UP
~S KROMEL'S PARTICIPATION IN MARKET SEGMENTS B, C, AND D IS NOT SPEEDED UP

TABLE 2

KROMEL MODEL—EXPECTED VALUE OF CUMULATIVE, COMPOUNDED NET PROFITS

The mathematical model used to determine the expected values of Everclear's cumulative, compounded net profits was as follows:

$$CCN\ (X_k) = \sum_{j=1}^{n} p_j \cdot \sum_{i=1}^{m} [(1 + r)^{m-i} T\ \{(D_{ij} - Z_{ij})(K_{ij}M_{ij})\}]$$

$Z_{ij} = \phi\ (K_{ij}M_{ij})$

$CCN\ (X_k)$ = Expected value of Everclear's cumulative, compounded net profits under each X_k price strategy ($k = 1, \ldots, 4$).

p_j = Probability assigned to the jth outcome ($j = 1, 2, \ldots, n$).

r = Interest rate per annum, expressed decimally.

T = Ratio of net to gross profits of Everclear's Kromel operation (assumed constant in the study).

D_{ij} = Kromel price in \$/pound in the ith year ($i = 1, 2, \ldots, m$) for the jth outcome.

Z_{ij} = Cost in \$/pound of Everclear's Kromel resin in the ith year for the jth outcome. (This cost is a function of the amount of Kromel pounds sold by Everclear.)

ϕ = Function of.

K_{ij} = Everclear's over-all market share of Kromel Industry sales (in pounds) in the ith year for the jth outcome (expressed decimally).

M_{ij} = Kromel Industry poundage (summed over all four market segments) in the ith year for the jth outcome.

This model was then programmed for an electronic computer. The simulation was first carried out for the base case assumptions regarding total Verlon-Kromel market growth and cost of capital. Additional runs were made in which these assumptions were varied.

RESULTS OF THE COMPUTER SIMULATIONS

The computer run for the base case showed some interesting results for the relevant variables affecting Everclear's cumulative, compounded net profits position at the end of the planning period. These results are portrayed in Figures 2 through 4.

Figure 2 summarizes the cumulative probability of Kromel's penetration of market segment A (the critical factor in the study) as a function of time, under each pricing strategy. As would be expected, the lowest price strategy, the *\$.80 case*, carried the highest probability of market penetration. However, the cumulative probability approached 1, that *all* price strategies would eventually effect penetration of market segment A by the end of the simulation period. This behavior stems from the impact of price decreases assumed to be initiated by Kromel *competitors* (if penetration were not initially effected under the original price strategies) which in turn changed the probability of Kromel's penetration of segment A in later years, since this probability was related to price.

Figure 3 shows the expected incremental sales dollars (obtained by subtracting the expected outcomes of the *\$1.00 case*, used as a reference base, from the expected outcomes of each of the other three cases respectively) generated for Everclear under each price strategy. While some tapering off in average sales dollars generated from the price reduction cases compared to the *$1.00 case* can be noted near the end of the simulation period, this tapering off is less pronounced than that which would be experienced by the total Kromel industry.

The reason for this different pattern is that the price reduction strategies (by reducing the probability of future capacity expansion on the part

FIGURE 2

Cumulative Probability of Kromel's Penetration of Market Segment A (as a Function of Time and Initial Price)

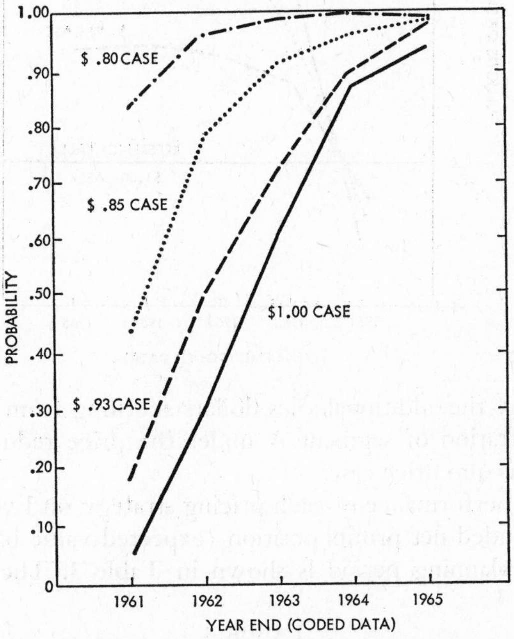

of existing and potential Kromel competitors) led to gains in Everclear's market share, relative to market share under the *$1.00 case.* These increases in Everclear's market share, under the price reduction strategies, partially offset the decline in incremental sales dollar gains (experienced by the Kromel industry near the end of the period) and thus explain the difference in sales patterns that would be observed between Everclear and the Kromel industry.

Figure 4 summarizes the behavior of Everclear's average, year-by-year (compounded) net profits performance again on an incremental basis compared to the *$1.00 case.* As would be expected, time lags in the penetration of segment A, under the price reduction strategies, result in an early profit penalty compared to the *$1.00 case.* This penalty is later

FIGURE 3
Kromel Sales Volume—Everclear Plastics Co.
(Incremental Sales Dollars Generated over
$1.00 case)

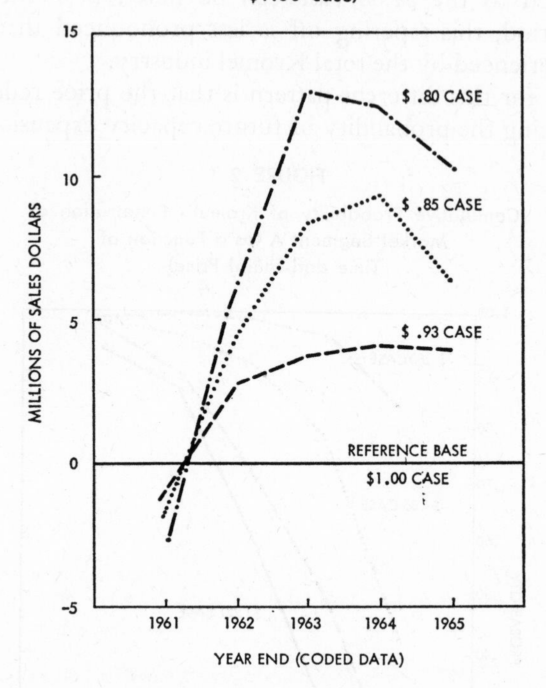

overbalanced by the additional sales dollars accruing from earlier (on the average) penetration of segment A under the price reduction strategies versus the status quo price case.

The overall performance of each pricing strategy on Everclear's cumulative, compounded net profits position (expected value basis) at the *end* of the 5-year planning period is shown in Table 3. These values were

TABLE 3
CUMULATIVE, COMPOUNDED NET PROFITS—EVERCLEAR PLASTICS CO.
(1961–65)

Price strategy	*End of period profit position*
$1.00 case	$26.5 million
.93 case	30.3 million
.85 case	33.9 million
.80 case	34.9 million

obtained by application of the formula shown in Table 2.

Table 3 shows that all of the price reduction strategies yield expected payoffs which exceed the *$1.00 case*. These additional profits stem from two principal sources: (a) the higher profits generated in the middle portion of the planning period, as a function of the increased probability of effecting penetration of market segment A, and its associated effect on Kromel industry sales in market segments B, C, and D; and (b) the higher market share for Everclear, resulting from the influence of the price reduction strategies on lowering the probability of capacity expansion and/or entry by Kromel competitors (existing or potential). These combined factors overbalance the lower profit margins per pound associated with the price reduction strategies compared to the *$1.00 case.*

However, a relevant question arose concerning the influence of the

FIGURE 4

Compounded Year-by-Year Net Profits of Everclear Plastics Co. (Compound Rate Equals 6% Annually)

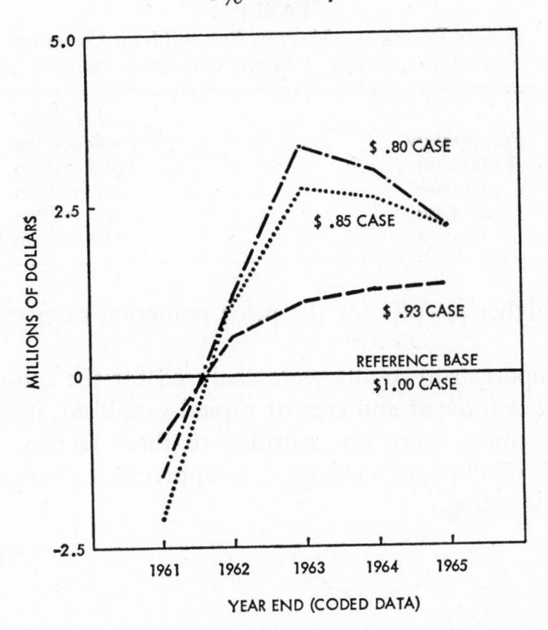

more favorable market share factor (under the price reduction cases) on the outcomes of these strategies vs. the *$1.00 case.* Suppose that no favorable difference in market share were obtained under the price reduction strategies compared to the no-price reduction case. That is, suppose the probability that lower Kromel price would discourage future competitive expansion of Kromel industry capacity in the 1963–64 period were zero. How would this affect Everclear's profit position?

In order to test the impact of this variable on Everclear's cumulative, compounded net profits, the market share factor was held constant at the trend level estimated under the no-price reduction, or *$1.00 case,* over the simulation period. This analysis resulted in the information given in Table 4.

It is clear from Table 4 that the market share factor is important in producing Everclear's higher profit position as associated with the price reduction alternatives noted in Table 3. If increased share for Everclear were *not* obtained in the 1963–65 period (relative to the share expected under the *$1.00 case*), all strategies would yield close to equal payoffs. That is, over the planning period, the increased sales volume resulting from earlier (on the average) penetration of segment A under the price reduction strategies just about balances the less favorable profit margins associated with these strategies.

However, beyond the planning period, all strategies have for all practical purposes accomplished penetration of segment A. The impact of *higher market share* for Everclear thus assumes an important role toward maintaining higher payoffs for the price reduction cases versus the *$1.00 case.*

TABLE 4
PROFIT POSITION—MARKET SHARE HELD CONSTANT
(EVERCLEAR'S CUMULATIVE, COMPOUNDED NET PROFITS; 1961–65)

Price strategy	*End of period profit position*
$1.00 case	$26.5 million
.93 case	26.9 million
.85 case	27.4 million
.80 case	25.2 million

When computer run results were analyzed for the sub-cases (varying the total market forecast and cost of capital variables), it was found that the study outcomes were not sensitive to these factors. Although the absolute levels of all payoffs changed, no appreciable change was noted in their relative standing.

In Summary

This illustration has shown two principal findings regarding the expected payoffs associated with the alternative courses of action formulated by Everclear: (a) all price reduction strategies result in higher expected payoffs than that associated with the status quo pricing case and of these, the *$.80 case* leads to the largest expected value; (b) the higher payoffs associated with the price reduction strategies are quite sensitive to the assumption that Everclear's future market share would be favorably influenced by reductions in Kromel price.

Everclear's management is now at least in a position to appraise the *financial implications* of its marketing assumptions in order to arrive at a reasoned selection among alternative choices.

IMPLICATIONS

The preceding illustration indicates the extent of problem detail which can be (and frequently must be) introduced to reflect adequately the characteristics of real market situations. Nevertheless, this illustration omits some important features of Bayesian decision theory.

First, payoffs were expressed in monetary terms (cumulative, compounded net profits) rather than utility in the von Neumann-Morgenstern sense, as discussed by Schlaifer.[2] One assumes implicitly, then, that utility is linear with money. As tempting as this assumption may be, some small-scale studies at Du Pont in which attempts were made to construct empirical utility functions raise some questions regarding the assumption of linearity. However, this feature of the Bayesian approach may well take many years of further education and development before it may find regular application on the industrial scene.

Second, while a plethora of Bayesian prior probabilities were used in this problem, no mention was made of analyzing sample data and calculating *posterior* probabilities. How does one investigate states of nature in problems of this type? Certainly the problems of conducting meaningful experiments are hardly trivial in pricing problems, or the general area of market planning.

Third, just how detailed a structure can be warranted, particularly when the inputs to the problem are largely subjective in character? One may obviously over-structure as well as under-structure a problem. This *caveat*, however, applies to all model building. While sensitivity analysis may be used to shed light on which variables "make a difference," the fact remains that the model-building process is still based largely on the builder's intuitive grasp of problem essentials and the interplay between analyst and decision maker. The structure of the problem discussed in this article turned out to be complex precisely because the variables included *were* deemed important by the decision maker(s). And part of the analyst's job is thus to examine the impact of supposedly important variables on the relevant payoff junction and then feed back his findings to the decision maker.

Finally, in conducting this study, realistic problems have a way of generating quite a lot of arithmetic detail, for example, a multi-stage set of alternative states of nature and payoffs. Implementation of the Bayesian approach must, therefore, frequently be aided by recourse to a high-speed computing device. Moreover, a computer model also facilitates the task of running sensitivity analyses concerning either changes in probabilities originally assigned to states of nature or changes in the payoff values

[2] Same reference as footnote 1, Chapter 2.

related to any particular combination of state of nature and course of action.

Our experience has indicated that the Bayesian approach, even coupled with the ancillary techniques of computer simulation and sensitivity analysis, does not offer any foolproof procedure for "solving" market planning problems. Still, it would seem that this method *does* offer definite advantage over the more traditional techniques usually associated with market planning. Traditional techniques rarely consider *alternative* states of nature, let alone assigning prior probabilities to their occurrence. Moreover, traditional market planning techniques seldom provide for testing the sensitivity of the study's outcomes to departures in the basic assumptions.

At the very least, the Bayesian model forces a more rigorous approach to market planning problems and offers a useful device for quickly finding the financial implications of assumptions about the occurrence of alternative states of nature. In time, this procedure coupled with a more sophisticated approach to the design, collection, and interpretation of field data appears capable of providing an up-to-date and flexible means to meet the more stringent demands of dynamic decision situations, so typical in the problems faced by the marketing manager.

B. Distribution Mix

Retailing systems are influenced by both internal and external factors. Adoption of a systems perspective permits the effective analysis of the impact of markets, stores, social factors, and competition and their interactions. Each retailing unit within a specified shopping district must be viewed as part of the total convenience offering that differentiates the district from area competitors. The adaptation of shopping districts to changing consumer demands should be based on an evaluation of the social and demographic characteristics of consumers.

52. COMPETING RETAIL SYSTEMS: THE SHOPPING CENTER AND THE CENTRAL BUSINESS DISTRICT*

Paul E. Smith† and Eugene J. Kelley‡

One breakthrough in retailing thought may develop from increased understanding of how the success of one store depends on its relationship with the group of stores of which it is a part. Within the group are flows of markets, merchandise, information, money, manpower, and equipment

* Reprinted from "Competing Retail Systems: The Shopping Center and the Central Business District," *Journal of Retailing*, Vol. XXXVI, No. 1 (Spring, 1960), pp. 11–18.

† Michigan State University.

‡ Pennsylvania State University.

which make up a retailing system. An analysis of how these elements interact is the key to determining how well the system works.

Retail systems have the characteristics of any large input-output systems. Retail systems are large because of the many degrees of freedom or dimensions of variability in the system. They are input-output systems because the inputs assembled and combined by managements, supplemented by external inputs, determine the outputs in the form of sales and profits. Sound retailing management requires that as many input factors as possible be recognized and manipulated to influence the results achieved.

The systems notion of feedback is a useful one in appraising operating results. The return flow of information in the form of customer responses can be used to redesign and improve the efficiency of the system as a whole.

In retail systems analysis, the interaction between several factors must be considered, including the location of the store or stores, their general character, source of customers, parking, traffic, and merchandise as well as advertising, promotion, and personnel. The interaction of these components to a large extent determines whether sales and profit objectives are realized and ultimately whether this system survives and grows. Systems analysis can contribute to an understanding of how retail selling efforts are influenced by other forces than those within the formal company organization and can focus attention on the external factors which influence the operation of the system.

The two retail business systems examined in this article are each competing marketing institutions. The planned or controlled shopping center has developed over the past ten years; the central business district has evolved institutionally over thousands of years of trial and error. Yet, systems analysis can be applied to both.

THE SHOPPING CENTER AS A TOTAL BUSINESS SYSTEM CONTRASTED WITH THE CENTRAL BUSINESS DISTRICT

The shopping-center planner has an opportunity to plan the center scientifically in terms of its total environment and review the plan as the environment changes. The market is analyzed and the center planned in terms of the market within the appropriate driving-time zone. The data obtained from the analysis are used to project the size of the center, the merchant-tenant mix, and merchandise assortments at the beginning and over a period of time. These same data are used by the stores in the center to plan store size, merchandise assortments, and price lines. Such market studies require continuous revision. Frequently a city or suburb will change over the years from a high- to middle-income area, or a good trading area may deteriorate and become a blighted section of the city.

Shopping-center growth will be determined not only by the projected population growth in the area but by the ability to attract patronage from existing competition. This attraction is determined in part by such factors as customer satisfaction and loyalty to individual stores. Systems analysis indicates that discounts have to be made for competition as well as population and different time-distance zones to reflect such factors.

A shopping center does not always meet the needs of shoppers nearby because of lack of understanding of the nature of the market served by the total system. One example is a regional shopping center located near a medium-sized city with average family incomes of $16,000. This center leased space to stores that cater to the $7,000 family income. As a result, its natural customer group has been forced to shop in the central business district of a neighboring city. The shopping center, in turn, derives the greatest share of its customers from a section of the city which is not its natural trading area.

Balanced Tenancy

Another important systems concept in shopping center development is the theory of balanced tenancy or planned competition. In *Shopping Center Planning Management*[1] attention was called to the fact that retail shopping districts tend to develop over the years on the basis of trial and error. If any large retail business district lacks any part of the total one-stop shopping environment, customer demands will force additional retail stores to fill the vacuum. A shopping center that lacks important units of total planned competition will encourage the establishment of competing shopping centers or flagship stores in the area.

The systems approach to retail competition also involves determining the optimal mix of various kinds of stores. Every retail district needs prestige or magnet stores. Central business districts need outstanding stores, especially those which will pull customers from great distances. These stores are the traffic-generating stores of the system. Regional shopping centers have the same problem since they must also be able to pull customers from some distance from the center.

One of the complicating factors in establishing planned competition is the change in merchandise assortments carried by retail stores. Drug stores stock variety store merchandise, supermarkets are selling drugs, and variety stores are becoming junior department stores. All of this complicates the competitive situation in any given area and is a reason why the systems mix must be reviewed regularly.

Location and Layout

A retail business system is primarily a merchandising operation. Real-estate factors are secondary in planning shopping centers and the locating

[1] Paul E. Smith, *Shopping Center Planning Management* (New York: National Retail Merchants Association, 1956), p. 17. See also Eugene J. Kelley, *Locating Controlled Regional Shopping Centers* (Westport, Connecticut: Eno Foundation, 1956), pp. 162–78.

of the kinds of stores within the center itself. The location of a store in any shopping district must consider its location systematically in relation to complementary and compatible stores, traffic patterns, dominant stores, and available parking facilities. In one new shopping center, a nut shop was located off the main traffic lane. It is not prospering since it depends on impulse purchases of people going past that location. There are other examples where stores have been located in string streets off main traffic arteries either in shopping centers or in downtown business districts that were not located in the proper way from the standpoint of pedestrian traffic.

Frequently shopping centers are planned in such a way that stores are spread over a large area without considering the effect on shopping and internal shopping center traffic. This encourages customers to move their cars from one section of the center to another, creating internal traffic problems and hazards to pedestrians.

Complementary Store Concept

Complementary stores are frequently located some distance apart. Nelson in *The Selection of Retail Locations*,[2] states a rule of retail compatibility:

> Two compatible businesses located in close proximity will show an increase in business volume directly proportionate to the incidence of total customer interchange between them, inversely proportionate to the ratio of the business volume of the larger store to that of the smaller store, and directly proportionate to the sum of the ratios of purposeful* purchasing to the total purchasing in each of the two stores.

He goes on to say:

> These relationships may be expressed in the equation:
>
> $$V = I\,(V1 + Vs) \times \frac{Vs}{V1} \times \left(\frac{P1}{V1} + \frac{Ps}{Vs}\right)$$
>
> in which:
>
> V1 equals volume of larger store (total purchasing)
> P1 equals purposeful purchasing in larger store
> Vs equals volume of smaller store (total purchasing)
> Ps equals purposeful purchasing in smaller store
> V equals increase in total volume of two stores
> I equals degree of interchange

---

[2] Richard Nelson, *The Selection of Retail Locations* (New York: F. W. Dodge Corporation, 1958), pp. 66–67.

* A purposeful purchase is one made by a shopper who, when interviewed, states that a visit to the store was a major purpose of the shopping trip. Total purchases, of course, include incidental and impulse purchases as well.

If there are two retail stores side by side and one customer in 100 makes a purchase in both, the rule indicates that together they will do one per cent more business than if separated by such a distance as to make this interchange impossible or unlikely. If one customer in 10 makes purchases in both stores, their total increase in business will be about 10 per cent. Theoretically, if every customer bought in both stores, their total business volume would double, if both businesses did about the same dollar volume.

This theory may explain why two competing stores tend to do better if they are located near each other, assuming sufficient market to support the stores. This is particularly true of traffic-generating shopping goods stores.

Layout

The location of parking in relation to the stores in the center must be considered. Supermarkets should be located near each other in order to invite comparison shopping and prevent the movement of cars from one place in the center to another. The layout of other stores should be in terms of the complementary stores concept. A department store should be surrounded by stores that sell the same kind of merchandise that it sells. This is so, both from the standpoint of the department store and its satellite stores. Variety stores and similar stores that live off traffic generated by other stores should be located on a main pedestrian artery either downtown or in shopping centers. Some shopping centers and downtown business districts tend to have complementary stores near each other in relation to the price of the merchandise. Fifth Avenue in New York City and Michigan Avenue in Chicago are dominated by expensive shops while some of the department stores cluster on other nearby streets. In some shopping centers the tendency is to place the better-quality-type stores near each other and group the stores catering to the medium-price merchandise in other locations within the center. Thus there is considerable similarity in the spatial arrangement of the shopping center and the downtown business district. The chief difference is the shopping-center advantage of beginning with a plan and, of course, in the smaller number of stores in the center.

Traffic and Parking

Frequently merchants in a central business district attempt to act jointly on traffic problems. But there is evidence to indicate that merchants tend to take a highly individualistic view of traffic and parking surrounding their stores. In several cities merchants have been most firm in their reluctance to change the parking situation. Investigations sometimes indicate that the merchant himself is the one who parks in front of his own store and thereby occupies the most valuable parking area.

Research in regional centers indicates that most customers do not like to walk much more than 600 feet from parked cars. Therefore, a retail business district, either downtown or in the shopping center, must include sufficient parking within 600 feet or customers will tend to move their cars from one location to another. This creates hazards and eventually results in customer reluctance to shop in the area.

Central business districts have made some efforts to enhance shopping environment. Toledo, Ohio, on a 45-day trial basis and Kalamazoo, Michigan, on a permanent basis have attempted to create a park-like atmosphere downtown by taking traffic off the main street. These are attempts to create the same kind of shopping environment one finds in a well-designed and architecturally sound planned shopping center. It will be interesting to see what the effect of this will be over an extended period of time. At this point, the initial results appear to be favorable. Such innovations in downtown layout are frequently tied in with many bargain promotions which are not indicative of the real ability of the downtown business district to draw people. Retailers seem to feel consistently that people are only interested in price. This attitude is reflected in newspaper advertising and other promotional efforts. Before the actual effect of these parklike atmospheres in the city can be evaluated, something other than price promotions should be attempted. These promotions attract bargain hunters and people residing near the downtown area, but do not consistently attract suburban customers.

Promotion of the Total Retail Business System

The planned shopping center has one great competitive advantage over other business districts: shopping centers offer opportunities for stores to cooperate in promotions, services, and other joint efforts. In contrast, the downtown business district historically has been viewed as comprising a group of merchants pursuing their own individual store operations unrelated to other district stores. What would happen if a central business district put together a complete promotion package extending over a period of time and publicized the offerings to be found in the downtown business district as contrasted to competing shopping centers? There is not a single shopping center in the country that could compare with the merchandise assortment and combined market magnetism of the central business district of its metropolitan area.

Perhaps the most important element needed is the leadership of intelligent, interested businessmen concerned with the welfare of an area. The total system concept can be used by merchants, bankers, and public officials to develop a trading and social environment which complements the type projected in individual stores and institutions. If merchants can transpose their thinking from exclusive concentration on their own stores to thinking of the total retail system, more sales for their individual stores and the whole downtown business complex would probably result.

It may be too much to hope that system-wide promotion will ever be shared by merchants in central business districts. However, in the case of the shopping center where the land and stores are owned by one landlord, it is a comparatively easy thing to do. The landlord has a very important stake in the sales of the stores in the center. For this reason, landlords should share in the cost of promotion. There is indeed a growing interest in total shopping-center promotion by many shopping centers throughout the country. Northgate Shopping Center in Seattle was one of the first to realize this potential. This center continuously secures the total efforts of all the merchants in center-wide promotional efforts. The Eastland and Northland shopping centers in Detroit have also given center-wide support to many successful promotional programs.

Most downtown business districts as well as planned shopping centers consider only seasonal promotional efforts such as Christmas and Easter as total system-wide promotions. These promotions are usually successful. However, such promotions are often limited to cut-price and bargain appeals to attract people to the downtown business district or shopping center. There are few consistent quality and value promotions in central business districts comparable to those conducted by some regional centers.

Retail Systems and the Community

The success of a retail system is determined by many factors in addition to stores. New York retailers get a substantial amount of business because of the attractions of theaters and civic affairs. Northland Center and other shopping centers have established a number of auditoriums and clubrooms which attract people to the center for social reasons. These people develop the habit of considering the center and the central business district as community gathering places. Since shopping habits tend to follow other habits, consumers not only tend to buy when attending civic affairs in shopping centers, but to carry with them a feeling of friendship and respect for the center itself. This potential is almost completely neglected by central business districts and neighborhood shopping districts. Very seldom does a string-street business district or a small-town business district support community activities to attract people to the area.

One of the characteristics of the shopping-center movement has been a substantial effort by the more successful developers to integrate their new shopping centers into the communities served. As mentioned, various devices such as auditoriums, clubrooms, restaurants, recreational facilities, and community services seem to be part of the integrated planning of center operators. What these people may have recognized instinctively is that shopping has both economic and social dimensions. Because the shopping center is developed as an entity it can consider all of these elements before it is built. This does not preclude the retailers in any established district from making efforts to attract people downtown. If the downtown merchants do not think of the customer as an economic and social being, the further decline of the downtown business district is likely. The decline of motion picture theaters as a downtown attraction may have increased the reluctance of people to go downtown for shopping. Merchants must make an organized effort through the Chamber of Commerce or merchants association to promote activities in addition to their stores and merchandise.

The Merchants Association

The merchants association in a shopping center or in an unplanned business district should think of itself as a service organization serving the total merchant mix in the system. The merchants association should combine the efforts of all the merchants to analyze and act on the total system situation. When a store submerges part of its identity to become known as a component of the total system, it will gain benefits. When its merchants identify their store as a part of the system, the total impact of this act on the community is likely to be greater than would be obtained by the individual promotional efforts of each merchant acting independently.

A merchants association should be concerned with answering some of the following questions: Has there been a change in the customers coming into the system in terms of numbers, sources, income levels, and other pertinent data? Has there been a relative change in the ability of the business district to attract people from a distance? Has there been a movement of the stores in the district toward other geographical locations, and what has been this effect on the ability to attract the kind of people needed in the downtown business district? Is the business system effectively serving the customer in terms of assortments and services? Is transient traffic an important source of customers, and is this transient traffic changing, increasing, or decreasing? The new federal expressway program may increase the relative pull of the city.

A PROGRAM FOR SYSTEMS ANALYSIS

Merchants wishing to study and change the business system of which they are a part might well consider a program such as the following:

1. *Markets.* An extensive economic and marketing analysis should be made of the trading area served by the system. This study should be revised every three or five years depending on the rate of change. Included in the analysis would be a study of customers shopping in the business district, classification of personal data for these customers such as residence, income level, husband's occupation, wage earners in the family,

the stores visited when they enter the business district and in what order, the length of time they spend in each store, their reasons for coming to the business district, the merchandise purchased while they are shopping, merchandise not usually bought there, the number and kinds of people in cars, and the movement of the cars within the system.

2. *Stores.* The retail stores in the system should be surveyed and analyzed in relation to the customer. Included would be an analysis of the merchant mix in the business district, the number of businesses that have changed their location, and the reasons for mortalities. Data should be gathered about traffic and parking, the changing income levels in the area as related to the merchandise assortments in the center, and changes in the financial or leasing or tax structure in the downtown business district as related to the profits derived from store sales. Such studies can be useful in updating the tax structure.

3. *Social factors.* Elements of other social and economic factors involved in the system should be studied to determine their effect on the shopping habits of consumers in the city. For example, there may be changes in the political, cultural, and social activities in the various areas.

4. *Competitive co-operation.* Stores in the system should be studied and analyzed in relation to such things as co-operative sales efforts, advertising, maintenance, merchants associations, and employee relations. In older districts or in new planned districts where an organization structure exists, these should be analyzed in terms of the functions of the merchants association and interrelationships existing between stores in the district.

A retail system is effective when it offers values in merchandise, services, and convenience to its customers greater than the sum of the attractions of the individual stores. The value difference accounts for the profit rewards of shopping center promoters and is available to other groups of merchants willing to act in systems terms. Profits can be earned from the differential value added to a planned, integrated shopping center over an unplanned, nonintegrated business district. The sources of the greater difference lie in the greater customer attraction based on the combined promotional and service effort, merchandise assortments, location differentiation, and parking.

Differential value can be added by retailers operating in unplanned business districts if a system-wide view of the district is taken. The suggestions for co-operative action on customer analysis, planned competition, location and layout, traffic and parking, promotion, community development, and cooperative merchants' activity which are made in the article should be explored and acted upon.

Members of retail systems are likely to gain a competitive advantage over other retailers who persist in outmoded ways of thought about the nature of retail competition. The real competition of a merchant is not necessarily found in the next store. It is equally likely to be a competing, better-organized business system.

Retail managers are faced with the challenge of planning and developing an effective retailing mix to adjust profitably to changing market conditions. Sound planning is the basis for developing coordinated and goal-directed retailing strategy. The retailing mix, like the marketing mix, is comprised of three submixes: a product and services mix, a communications mix, and a distribution mix. Consumer satisfaction is achieved through optimal submix blending.

53. THE RETAILING MIX: PLANNING AND MANAGEMENT*

William Lazer† and Eugene J. Kelley‡

Some retail managers have been observing the rapid growth of the marketing management concept in manufacturing firms with considerable interest. This concept of marketing is resulting in the acceptance of a new perspective for business activities in which marketing is viewed as the basis of an integrated system of business action. Adaptation of the marketing management approach has significance for retail managers concerned with designing a total retail capability to achieve realistic and attainable objectives.

The marketing management concept in retailing is characterized by:

1. *Planning.* An emphasis on planning to achieve clearly defined retailing targets is the key concept. It stresses that retailing objectives can be identified and that an integrated program of action be designed to achieve these objectives through orderly retail planning.

2. *Customer Orientation.* The customer orientation is adopted as the focus for retail decision making. A philosophy of customer orientation is more important than any body of retailing techniques, personnel policies, or organizational arrangements. It ensures that retail decisions are viewed through the consumer's eyes.

3. *Systems Approach.* The systems perspective of retailing action is used. In this approach, a retail organization is viewed as a total system of retail

* Reprinted from "The Retailing Mix: Planning and Management," *Journal of Retailing,* Vol. XXXVII, No. 1 (Spring, 1961), pp. 34–41.

† Michigan State University.

‡ Pennsylvania State University.

action. The interaction between the components of the retailing system is stressed as is the functioning and structure of the whole organization. This approach focuses on the integrated use of all retail resources to satisfy current market needs and future opportunities.

4. *Change*. Change is recognized as the "constant" in planning, organizing, and controlling retailing activity. The prime managerial responsibility is seen as that of adapting retailing organizations creatively to conditions of accelerating change. Retailing leadership's charge becomes that of planning for a managing change.

5. *Innovation*. There is a new emphasis on research and innovation. Innovation is seen as the basis for retailing action. The important fact is that innovation is becoming programmed and a basic part of the retail management process. In short, research, a system of commercial intelligence, and innovation are becoming standard factors in modern retail action. This is resulting in the application of findings from the behavioral and quantitative sciences to retailing. The effect is new techniques of retail control, better management of inventories, improved communications, and a greater awareness of the usefulness of theory in understanding and solving retailing problems.

The crucial factor for retail management to recognize is that socio-economic developments are operating so as to stimulate the emergence of more accurate and intelligent planning on the part of retail executives. Retailing executives are operating in an economy which is characterized by rapid change and explosive cultural and economic developments. The increasing degree of competition from both downtown and suburban areas, the impact of population shifts, trends in income and expenditures, the degree of innovation in both areas of products and services, the availability and utilization of more information about customers and markets, are examples of forces which require retail management to accept change as a normal way of life and to assign high priorities to developing creative adaptations to change. It is in such a climate that the marketing management movement, with prime emphasis on planning, has made its greatest headway.

To manage retailing effort effectively in such an environment requires planning. Yet retail planning is more than just a tool of growth. It is a rational means of achieving continuing profitable adjustment of the retail system to current and future marketing conditions.

Retailing planning, in its broadest terms, may be thought of as the utilization of analysis and foresight to increase the effectiveness of retail action. Planning retailing effort, therefore, is necessarily concerned with the objectives and goals that the retailing organization seeks to attain, the development of retailing systems, the operating system, through which retail management is attempting to achieve these goals, the availability of capacity and resources within the firm and existing facilitating agencies to exert the quantity and quality of effort necessary for their achievement. The planning process in retail management is portrayed in Chart I. Although this chart is necessarily a simplification, it does indicate the requisite arrangements of various factors in retail planning.

Retail plans must be conceived as functioning within an external framework determined by various forces beyond the control of the management of a given retail enterprise. This is one reason why it is becoming increasingly important in retail planning to consider environmental business factors as well as to identify the many retailing inputs, their interactions, and expected outputs.

The retail planning process involves at the first level three actions on the part of executives: analysis, evaluation, and prediction. The analysis of

CHART I

The Planning Process in Retail Management

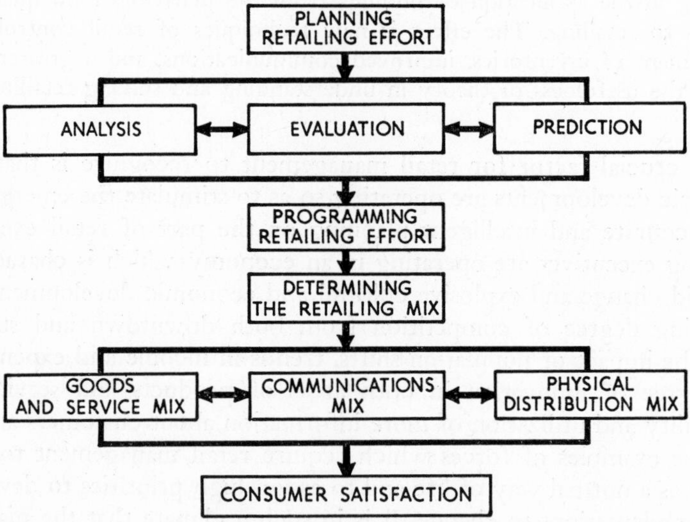

PLANNING RETAILING EFFORT

ANALYSIS
EVALUATION
PREDICTION

PROGRAMMING RETAILING EFFORT

DETERMINING THE RETAILING MIX

GOODS AND SERVICE MIX
COMMUNICATIONS MIX
PHYSICAL DISTRIBUTION MIX

CONSUMER SATISFACTION

available information, and an evaluation of trends and relationships will give retail management the frame of reference from which to perceive current and future problems. It will afford executives a perspective of the future. Past data is useful to management mainly as it helps predict the future.

Retailing Mix

The analysis and evaluation of data and the predictions made place executives in a position of being able to program total retailing effort. Retail programming is achieved through the determination of a retail store's retailing mix. Such a mix becomes the total package of goods and services that a store offers for sale to the public. The retailing mix, then, is the composite of all effort which was programmed by management and which embodies the adjustment of the retail store to its market environment.

The retailing mix, as such, is comprised of three submixes: a goods and service mix, a communications mix, and a distribution mix. Consumer satisfaction is achieved through optimal submix blending. It is through the achievement of a high customer satisfaction that a store prospers and grows. Some of the components of each of these submixes are depicted in Chart II.

In Chart II the consumer is presented as the focus for all market planning and programming. The retail program is designed specifically to bring the offerings of a retail organization into line with the wants and

CHART II

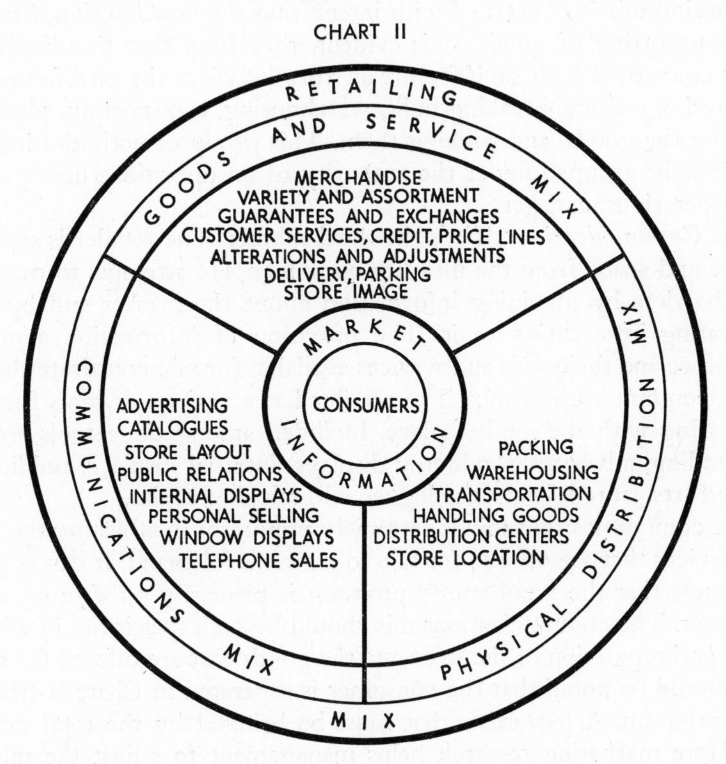

needs of its customers and the natural market areas. The established program, therefore, sets the tone for all retailing activity.

The submix that is most apparent in retailing is the *Goods and Service Mix*. Retailers are often well aware of the impact of the variety and assortment of goods offered for sale and the customer services that are extended. Other components of the goods and service mix are various credit plans that are offered, the price lines that a store will adhere to, the guarantees that are made and exchanges, alterations and adjustments, the image of the store and the goods it offers for sale, delivery, sales service, and parking facilities. The total goods and service mix should be so integrated that it will tie in with the store's own marketing goals. For example, if the image of the store is one of high quality then the customer lines offered, the price lines offered, and the types of service offered should be such that they will blend with this concept, rather than clash with it.

The *Physical Distribution Mix* essentially has two components: a channels of distribution component and a physical distribution component. The channels of distribution component is concerned with the number and type of retail outlets that comprise the total retailing complex. For example, the number and type of branch stores that are part of the retail enterprise, and the types of suburban stores that are members of the organization, are part of the mix. The physical distribution part of the distribution mix is concerned with integrating the warehousing, handling, and transporting of goods. It is evident, therefore, that the distribution mix is concerned with such factors as store location, the establishment of distribution centers, breaking bulk, warehousing, transporting, physically handling the goods, and packing them. This group of activities has been traditionally grouped under the authority of an operations manager or a store operations manager.

The *Communications Mix* is the third submix. The retailer is separated in time and space from the ultimate consumer. He attempts to overcome these barriers by obtaining information about the market and by communicating information to it. The provision of information about the retail store and the goods and services available for sale constitute the crux of the communications mix. The retailer has a variety of tools for communicating with the market place. Included among these tools are personal selling, advertising, window displays, internal displays, public relations efforts, store layouts, catalogues, and telephone sales.

The communications mix is extremely important in adjusting the goods and services that are offered for sale to consumer demand. It can convince consumers that the retail store's program is primarily satisfactory to the consumer. The communications mix should be such that it ties in with the image and reputation of the store and the goods that are offered for sale.

It should be noted that the consumer is separated in Chart II from the retail program. A gap exists that must be bridged by the total retailing mix. Here marketing research helps management to adjust the mix and become aware of future trends in order to plan and make rational decisions. As retail organizations grow larger, develop more branches, and become more decentralized, the existing gap between top retail management and consumers becomes wider. Therefore, more pertinent and readily available marketing information becomes a requisite for proper programming and control of retailing effort.

The Retail Management System

Planning an optimal retailing mix involves viewing a retailing operation as an integrated action system affected by both internal and external forces. The success of a retail system depends not only on proper selection of each element and submix but on the interaction between them.

The retail management system can be perceived as an input-output system. All of the ingredients of the retailing mix may be viewed as the inputs which flow through the retail organization and attain the outputs realized by the retailing organization. Hopefully, the outputs achieved match the accepted objectives of the organization. The response of consumers in the market place ultimately determines whether or not the store actually achieves its objectives, or the outputs planned by the programmer. In this sense, consumers hold veto power over the entire retail system.

The retail management system, as an organization, has been studied in various books and research studies. It is composed of various levels of "departmental" managers. In Chart III, five levels are depicted from the

CHART III

The Retail Management System

RETAIL MANAGEMENT ORGANIZATION
RETAIL PLANNING
CONSUMER BEHAVIOR
RETAILING OBJECTIVES
MARKET INFORMATION
"DEPARTMENT" MANAGER
"GROUP" MANAGER
"DIVISION" MANAGER
"MERCHANDISE" MANAGER
"TOP" MANAGER
SELLING TACTICS MARKET/SEGMENT MANAGEMENT
COORDINATED DEPARTMENTAL MARKETING EFFORT
COORDINATED STORE MARKETING EFFORT
INTEGRATED CORPORATE POLICY AND ACTION
MARKET IMPACT
PROFITS
SHARE OF MARKET
VOLUME
INDUSTRY LEADERSHIP
COMMUNITY STATUS
STORE IMAGE
CHANNEL CONTROL
MARKET INFORMATION

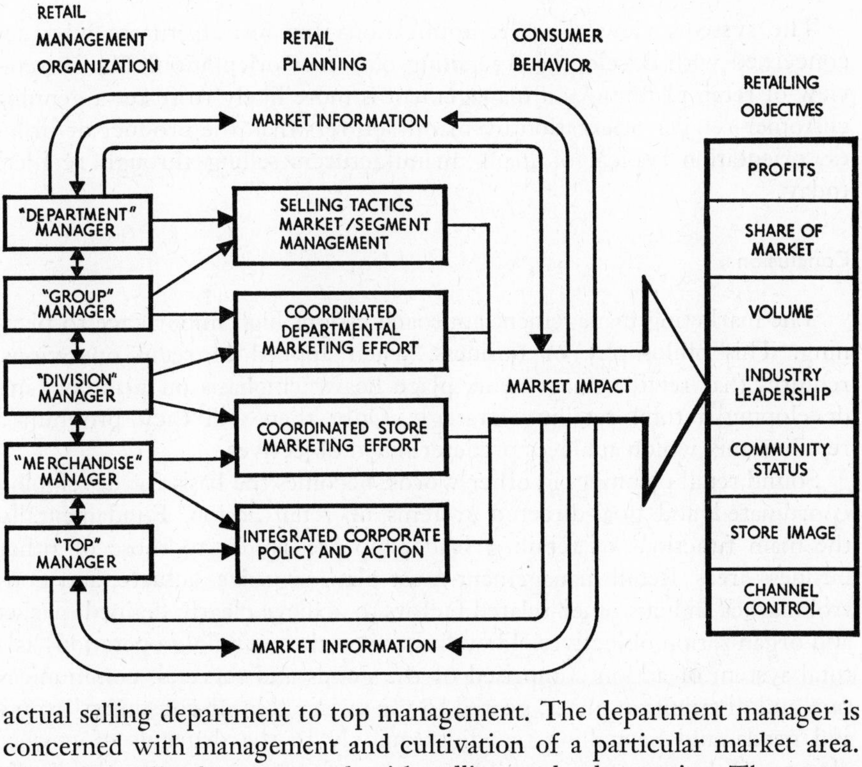

actual selling department to top management. The department manager is concerned with management and cultivation of a particular market area. He is immediately concerned with selling and sales tactics. The group manager coordinates the departmental marketing effort of several departments. Therefore, his is an integrative function to alleviate dysfunctioning between the departments. The division manager has a higher-level integrative point of view and is concerned with coordinating the stores marketing effort with the marketing effort of a number of departments. The merchandise manager is more concerned with integrated corporate policy and action as it relates to the total marketing effort within the store. Top management, of course, is concerned with the broader corporate issues including store adjustment to non-controllable environmental forces.

The consumer reactions to the retailing mix determine the profits that are achieved by the organization, its volume, its share of markets, its image as an industry leader, its status in the community, and the degree of channel control that retail management earns. If the proper planning has taken place, the outputs that are achieved through consumer behavior will be in line with the retailing objectives originally, planned by management. If this alignment does not occur, then retail management has three alternatives:

1. Alter the objectives of the retail organization
2. Adjust the retailing mix
3. Combine the two

The systems view also has implications for manufacturers who are concerned with developing a retailing-customer orientation. The systems view of retail planning and management is more likely to foster a genuine customer-retailer orientation by manufacturers than the product or process orientation typical of many manufacturers selling through retailers today.

Conclusion

The marketing management approach assigns high importance to planning. This philosophy of business, when applied to retail operations, requires that retail managements place heavy emphasis on planning and developing a total retailing strategy. Only then will they program a retailing mix which achieves predetermined objectives.

Sound retail planning, in other words, becomes the basis for developing coordinated and goal-directed systems of retail action. Fundamentally the main functions of retailing leadership are similar to those of other business areas. Retail management must plan, organize, actuate, and control market and customer-related factors to achieve clearly defined market and organization objectives. They must view their retailing operations as a total system of action comprised of the goods and services, communication and distribution mixes, geared to the satisfaction of consumers' wants and needs, and be willing to adjust quickly to the demands of market change. Only through such enlargement of perspective can the profit thrust of a retail organization be maximized.

Retail management is faced with major shifts in American living and spending patterns in an era of rapid technological change. Retailing concepts and techniques must adjust to meet and satisfy new purchasing patterns and shopping motivations. Some current and probable future trends in retailing are noted.

54. SOCIOECONOMIC CHANGE AND RETAIL MANAGEMENT: PRESENT AND FUTURE*

Robert D. Entenberg†

The intensity of consumer demand is one of the most important factors determining total business activity. In any general economic analysis, major attention must be devoted to the way the consumer divides his expenditures between durable goods (homes, cars, furniture), non-durable goods (groceries, apparel, accessories), and services.

The consumer, without knowing it, is the agent of change in marketing processes and techniques. That consumer, often acting in the grip of social and economic changes, has caused retailers, wholesalers, and manufacturers to drastically change their products, their methods of selling as well as the sales environment itself.

Great shifts in the American living patterns underlie these changes . . . new social desires, new purchasing patterns, and new shopping motivations. The consumer today is better educated, better read, afforded more leisure, more apt to own his home (maybe even two), either very much older or younger than his predecessor of a quarter century ago, and has focused his interest in new products, new merchandising techniques, and new services. And, he has left in his wake an amazing debris of outdated sales methods and marketing philosophies.

More specifically, since 1940 there has been an approximate eightfold increase in the discretionary spending power of individuals. There are today eight and one-half times more spending units (families and individ-

* Not previously published.

† University of Denver.

uals) in this country with incomes in excess of $3,000 than there were in 1941. . . . The inflation factor does not apply here since incomes generally have been rising at a faster rate than the consumer price index.

During the past 15 years, subsistence-level families have been disappearing rapidly from the American scene. As a result, consumer spending in the aggregate is becoming more typical of the spending patterns of the higher-income families of the past. The "real income" of consumers can be expected to continue to increase.

Rapidly changing technology and more efficient mass production techniques have and are still changing all economic philosophies. Our primary problem today is the creation of demand. . . . Consumption demand is and has been far below the capacity of our consumer goods manufacturers to produce. For example, since 1948, ultimate consumers have been absorbing *less* than two-thirds of the total output of goods and services produced in the United States. Fully a third of the productive capacity of our consumer goods manufacturers has gone unused in the last 17 years.

Obviously, then, an understanding of what consumers want, where they are willing to go to buy and what they are willing to accept in the way of goods and services is of major importance to the entire economy. Manufacturers have understood the changes in the production-consumption functions all too well. Unfortunately, understanding among most retail management has been limited. . . . One result has been the rapid disappearance of the smaller grocery stores.

The major interest in consumer expenditures centers around the more specific breakdowns of income allocations to certain merchandise lines. . . . For example, the tremendous increase in consumer expenditures for services. While total consumer expenditures are a function of income, the various ways money is spent are far from stable. Shifts in consumer spending can and do occur quite rapidly, and not necessarily with any advance notice. For example, the expansion of sales of non-foods in supermarkets.

New operating practices of a "non-price" as well as of a "price" competition among discount houses are now taking place. Some discount stores are now offering full-service selling in some departments in addition to self-service and simplified-selling procedures. Nevertheless, discounters are still managing—not always—to give the consumer more for his money. Their greatest appeal, however, is that they allow the consumer to feel thrifty and clever, whether he really is or not.

This combination of appeals, price plus service, has led to an ever-increasing dollar volume by discounters: in 1965, the writer estimates, approximately $10.2 billion in sales was generated by some 11,500 retail establishments of all kinds generally identified as discount houses. It is further estimated that an additional $32 billion of the nation's $285 billion in sales in 1965 was made on a discount basis by so-called "conventional" retailers and wholesalers. These "discount" sales do not refer to clearance items, but to new merchandise sales only.

The growth and prosperity of the discount house and other new types of competition have forced department stores, supermarkets, specialty stores, chains and other conventional retailers to reevaluate their store policies, services, pricing and overall methods of doing business. . . .

In this new environmental setting, there has been a wide geographic dispersion of "controlled shopping centers" (preplanned and limited to certain types of stores in which to shop). The result is that the American consumer has so many stores in which to shop and so many kinds of merchandise from which to choose that buying has become even more of an emotional than a rational process.

CONCURRENT TRENDS

Because of an evident reluctance to change and because of organizational inflexibility, a dwindling percentage of family income is being spent in retail stores. The competitive struggles now taking place in the market place have, in some cases, grown to almost panic proportions. . . .

Yet, many stores have completely changed their methods of doing business. Many others, still "ignoring" the discounter as a temporary innovation, have reemphasized their previously developed store image and institutional appeal as *The Place to Shop*. Some "conventional" retailers have become discount houses themselves. Still others have dropped merchandise lines wherein chaotic pricing conditions developed. Some stores are meeting the challenge of competitive prices in key merchandise areas; others have cut services and changed their selling procedures in attempts to lower expenses and reduce prices.

Emerging from the chaos of the discount house struggle has been a significant fact: no form of retailing can completely dominate the field. Retailing always has been and will continue to be essentially small scale and personal in character. Fortunately, during the current period of economic stress, the principal beneficiary of all the evolutionary tumult has been the intelligent consumer.

THE FUTURE

1. Decline in institutional loyalties to particular stores.
2. Changes in general and supermarket pricing practices; supermarkets are evolving into general merchandise stores.
3. Development of department store brands into separate "twig" units of a specialty variety; i.e., tire stores, children's stores, etc.
4. The slowup of center city decay, the acceleration of planned urban renewals, and the initiation of a new system of parking and intra-city public transportation.

5. Junior department stores are becoming full-line department stores; the discount houses will become "all things to all people"—department stores, specialty stores, drug stores, durable goods stores, food stores, etc.

6. Continued growth of credit acceptance and use of alternative credit plans.

7. The store of the future will benefit in added volume from the increased acceptance of in-home, catalogue and telephone order selling.

8. Separate prices of services attached to commodity offer as costs increase.

9. Stronger attempts to shift sales promotion and inventory functions to manufacturer.

10. Cyclical movements in the acceptance of trading stamps and appearance of alternative "discount" plans.

11. Further growth of "scrambled" merchandising: i.e., drugstores are evolving into variety and junior department and appliance stores.

12. Increase in "consignment" selling, particularly in non-foods sales to supermarkets.

13. More brand offerings by more manufacturers on all product categories.

14. Growth in uneconomic standardization of supermarket policies and price strategies in spite of geographic differences . . . further acceleration of non-food sales in supermarkets.

15. Continuing shifts in peak shopping hours both downtown and in suburban areas.

16. Innovators will introduce new concepts in "service departments" just as we have had continuing innovations in merchandise departments. The future retail environment will see more combinations of service-convenience stores and clusters.

17. There will be more manufacturer- and wholesaler-sponsored retail operations vertically integrated (through all phases of production, handling and sales) so that they can be assured of control of ultimate markets at the consumer level. This trend is evident in men's clothing and shoes. Horizontal integration will continue its present pace.

18. Food, gasoline, garden supplies, hardware and children's apparel will continue to be bought primarily at stores located immediately adjacent to zones of residence in suburban areas. Specialty and shopping goods such as fashion apparel, accessories and home furnishings, as well as men's clothing and shoes, will continue to be bought primarily downtown where selections are more complete.

19. Greatest growth areas in department and specialty stores will be those specifically geared to the "senior" and "under 25" mass markets. The department stores will strive to reverse their dwindling popularity among the "young marrieds" and the youth market. The growing competition for the senior citizens' market will result in their becoming more fashion conscious and selective in their purchasing.

20. There will be a decline in one-stop shopping centers of the regional variety, chiefly because of their difficult parking and walkathon situations. "Freestanding stores" conveniently located adjacent to major traffic arteries will become more important in suburban areas. This trend will be a reaction to the growing size and inconvenient locations of the shopping centers.

21. The problem of the "walkathons" now involved in any regional, diversified shopping areas may be solved through use of moving sidewalks, moving sidewalks with chairs, or continuous customer shuttle services.

22. Competition among an increasing number of shopping centers being built in marginal and "over-store" areas will result in a disheartening array of empty stores and shopping center failures.

These are only a few of the probable changes in the future. . . . The implications for ourselves as educators, businessmen and consumers are clear. We must develop an understanding of change and its underlying causes. Only through this understanding can we develop the necessary flexibility to deal with whatever new marketing techniques will be required.

The characteristics of goods and consumers are key factors in the formulation of retail expansion policies. A strategy for growth based on consumer orientation, profit through innovation as well as merchandising, and long-range planning is presented in this excerpt from a longer paper.

55. RETAIL EXPANSION: A STRATEGY FOR GROWTH*

Eugene J. Kelley†

FORMS OF RETAIL EXPANSION POLICY

1. Expansion of Present Business Through Adding Stores and Increasing Store Size

Most growth retailers are now actively adding new and larger stores. They have found that new stores have been a major influence on sales and earning gains in the past few years. Macy's alone added one million square feet of floor space in a recent 18-month period. This square footage, like most added by growth-minded managements, is in areas of high suburban

* Adapted from Eugene J. Kelley, "Retail Concentration and Expansion: Scope, Problems and Opportunities," presented at *Thirty-fifth Annual Boston Conference on Distribution*, October 14–15, 1963, pp. 101–10.

† Pennsylvania State University.

growth potential and in the more vital and promising central business districts.

The pace of new store openings for some retailers may be slower in the next year or two than it has been in the last two or three. One reason for the slowdown is that some managements are struggling to get out from under some of the financial and operational problems produced by the strong expansion programs of the last few years. In some cities a point of oversaturation may be being reached in certain lines such as food. But in spite of such problems, the new 1963–1964 stores, added to the growing volume of other new stores, are likely to extend the volume leadership of the current leaders.

2. Entry into New Retail Businesses

Many large retailers are redefining the scope of their business and modifying the character of their present operations by broadening the definition of corporate mission. For instance, Kroger has established discount food stores and has opened an experimental discount store handling food, drugs and general merchandise in Orange, Texas. They are continuing to construct drug units adjacent to Kroger stores and at separate locations. Kroger added 48 drug stores in 1962, bringing its total drug store operation to 66.

The entire supermarket industry is becoming more aggressive in non-foods. Jewel Tea Company is developing its "Main Street" drug variety stores in medium sized cities, Jewel-Osco Neighborhood Centers as neighborhood facilities in the Chicago area and its Turnstyle Family Centers of 100,000 or more square feet in size in other areas. The Family Centers feature a complete Jewel supermarket and a line of drugs and general merchandise. This merchandising flexibility is a recognition of the broad nature of the retail market and of the range of competition. J. C. Penney Company is moving into hard goods, credit, larger stores, and a national catalog organization with such vigor that the character of this soft goods merchandiser will change substantially over the next few years.

3. Entry into New Markets

Many retailers are breaking into new regions domestically and internationally. The day of the multinational retailer is coming fast. Woolworth's, for example, has 2,130 stores in the United States and Puerto Rico, and has 1,477 or 40 per cent of its stores in Canada, West Germany, West Berlin, England, Ireland and Mexico. Sears, Roebuck has demonstrated a pattern of operation in Latin America which offers both a guide to profits and to retailer contributions in economic development.

4. Addition of New Services and Departments

The services area offers a challenge to many retailers. Sears has branched into travel services, motor clubs and insurance. This services growth, added to their extensive foreign operations, mail order business and new fashion mindedness, suggests a pattern of distribution more retailing companies are likely to follow.

There will be more opportunities to organize new merchandise and service assortment packages for consumers as the rising level of real consumer income translates to greater spending power. Manufacturers are making more varied product mixes available, and consumers have the time and mobility to buy and to use what they buy.[1]

Perhaps the greatest services potential exists for department stores. These stores have the traditions and affinity for service retailing, yet by and large have not begun to tap the potential. As Entenberg said, assuming that present trends continue, "More money will be spent for consumer services than for nondurable goods within the next five years."[2] Department stores and other retailers can find attractive growth opportunities in rentals and leasing, personal services, travel, drugs, investments and other sectors not now developed. Smaller retailers must expand the personal services component in order to retain their present position against the giant retailers.

5. Extension of the Concept of the Store

Retailers are moving away from "four wall" thinking towards a realization that even the largest store is part of a total retail system. The success of shopping centers is due partly to the fact that consumers are offered a total shopping experience greater than the sum of the attractions of individual stores. The same increase in pulling power is being noted by merchants participating in urban renewal projects. One reason Macy's opened a 300,000 square foot branch store in New Haven was because they were attracted by the new vitality of the renewed central business district of New Haven.

Retailers are now large enough to shape the character of an entire shopping center or area. A new retail pattern is emerging in the McCrory Villages, Jewel Family Centers, Grant Villages and Korvette Cities. The

[1] Growth areas for expansion-minded merchants to consider are travel, leisure equipment of all types, products used at home, such as swimming pools, hi-fidelity equipment of all sorts, convenience products of all types and personal services. These lines offer a natural field for giant retailers. But, they also can be served by smaller operators.

[2] Robert D. Entenberg, "Customer Services: A New Look at an Old Technique," *Department Store Economist*, August, 1963.

shopping center super tenant has burst his walls and is integrating horizontally. The McCrory Corporation is an interesting example of a business which now includes a women's and children's wear chain (Lerner Shops), variety stores (McCrory-McLellan-Green and Cassels), a men's and boys' clothing chain (National Shirt Shops) and a house and auto supply chain (Otasco-Economy Auto Stores). This is in the pattern suggested of a retailer becoming a system of distribution rather than a store operator.

A STRATEGY FOR GROWTH

Basic to the achievements of growth retailers are a management philosophy and a customer service orientation which can be utilized profitably by more retailers. The elements include:

1. A Genuine Customer Orientation

Customer consideration and needs, not history, must be given priority in the definition of the business. Just as manufacturing-oriented firms can become preoccupied with products at the expense of customers, retailers can become overly enamoured of institutions and merchandise classifications. Mr. Baker indicated the Sears, Roebuck view at this conference in 1961 when he said, "Sears must conceive of itself as a distributor rather than as a retailer—and the company must think of the future in terms of the customer rather than products." Thinking of a store as a customer-oriented distribution system is the key to profitable expansion or to a defensive strategy towards expanding competitors.

2. Profits through Innovation as Well as Merchandising

Profit goals of retailers are not likely to be fulfilled in the future simply through repeating past merchandising triumphs. New consumption experiences must be delivered to precisely defined market segments. Retailers must constantly seek ways to reduce costs and improve present operations. The long-run profit payoff will go to customer-oriented merchants able to create and deliver new customer satisfaction while their routine operations are being steadily improved. These are the two parts of the profit concept in retailing. Profits, not profitless volume, will be most certainly achieved through programmed product and process innovation.

Competitive pressures arising from concentration places a premium on management's ability to anticipate and adapt creatively to change. Manufacturers and retailers must adjust product, price, promotion, and distribution policies and programs to meet the new competition and the complex market problems and opportunities generated by concentration in retailing.

One starting point for retailers is to study and participate in new product developments continuing as a result of technological progress. The buying committees of large retailers have a stake in participating in and shaping the consumer goods fallout. New products will not necessarily fall within established retail classifications or buying patterns. Products such as fiberglass boats, household dehumidifiers, low-calorie foods, and transistor radios added to changing consumption and life style patterns, make the struggle for retail position in the new lines increasingly complex. Mr. George Struthers, Vice President in Charge of Merchandising of Sears, recently suggested some other products which will be retailed in the next several years. These could include nonwoven disposable functional clothing, thermoformed furniture, fuel cells powering portable tools and the voice-operated typewriter.[3]

Such new products may constitute a significant share of retail volume by 1970. How will these products and others on the drawing board be retailed? Some merchants will find answers and grow through creating new retailing concepts and plans to parallel the new products.

The burden of promoting individual brands is on the owner of the brand—the manufacturer or the private brander. But, the task of generating new consumption experiences is shared by manufacturer and retailer. Both manufacturer and retailer are part of the market technology and both must adopt a systems view to improve it.

Product innovation must be accompanied by process innovation in retailing. A generous amount of process innovation in retailing has already altered the balance of competitive power. Process innovations have included the shopping center, discount merchandising, automatic vending, new physical distribution and credit concepts, information management systems and new organizational arrangements growing out of the marketing concept. Continued research and development by retailers is likely to produce more such innovations. Larger retailers willing to establish Research and Development departments with a broad charter will stimulate innovation in the goods and services as well as the processes of retailing. These retailers are likely to share in the benefits of innovation to a greater extent than those who wait to follow the leader. Each retailer has to pinpoint his place on the cycle of innovation in distribution to develop appropriate strategies.

Today's department store profit and share of market figures may reflect the propensity of some managements to move ponderously to the challenge of providing new consumption experiences. A foot dragging resistance to change style can, in the long run, result in lost profit opportunities as already experienced by some retailers.

---

[3] George Struthers, "The Long-Range Outlook for Consumer Goods," National Industrial Conference Board Panel Presentation, September 21, 1961, 4 pages, mimeographed.

3. Long-Range Planning

The planning horizon in retailing is lengthening. The industry is lagging behind industrial firms in the commitment made to long-range planning, but this time lag is being overcome by a few leading retailers.

In the final analysis, profits and satisfactions will be maximized for retailers, large and small, who possess the true merchant's commitment to serve consumers and the management capability to create and deliver consumption experiences to precisely defined retail market segments. The wheel of retailing is still spinning and offering ample opportunity for smaller merchants and the greatest opportunity in American business history for large retailers willing to adjust concepts and strategies to meet the challenges and opportunities of retailing growth.

Wholesalers have responded to secular change by vertical integration, both forward and backward, and by increased specialization in terms of goods and specific markets. Trends indicating increased efficiency and improved wholesaling services are discussed.

56. TRENDS IN WHOLESALING*

Edwin H. Lewis†

The period since World War II has demonstrated that wholesaling is still a very vital marketing activity and that the independent wholesaler is a necessary part of the channel of distribution. A comparison of the Census of Business for 1948 and 1963 indicates this very clearly.

During this 15 year interval the sales of retail establishments increased approximately 80 per cent whereas sales of merchant wholesalers increased 98 per cent. The independent wholesaler is also holding his own against manufacturers' wholesale branches with stocks. Sales of the latter have increased 88 per cent since World War II.

The strength of the independent wholesaler is particularly noticeable in the major consumer goods areas where wholesalers historically have been

---

* Not previously published.

† University of Minnesota.

important but where it was believed they had been losing out. Wholesalers of grocery products, hardware, furniture, drugs, appliances, confectionery, footwear, and jewelry have had greater increases in sales than retailers in these same lines. These increases in sales occurred in the face of a decline in the number of retail stores in the grocery, hardware, electrical appliance, and confectionery fields. The number of grocery and confectionery stores declined by nearly one-half. Stores in the hardware and appliances category were reduced by about one-seventh.

In the grocery field an increasingly large share of the wholesale business is handled by voluntary-group cooperatives and retailer cooperatives. In 1948, voluntary-group cooperatives accounted for 27½ per cent of the general line wholesale grocery business, and retailer cooperatives had 10 per cent. In 1963, the voluntary groups had 45 per cent and the retailer cooperatives 25 per cent, or 70 per cent of the grocery business taken together.

This trend in the growth of cooperatives undoubtedly will continue. In some cities nonaffiliated grocery wholesalers no longer exist. Frequently, cooperative groups have proved more than a match for the centrally owned grocery chains and have become the strongest grocery establishments in their area. Between 1948 and 1963 the operating-expense-to-sales ratio of voluntary groups declined from 8.3 per cent to 6.2 per cent. The ratio of retail cooperatives held constant at about 4.5 per cent while expenses of other general line wholesale grocers increased from 8.7 per cent to 9.2 per cent.

In order to consolidate their position and to secure control over good retail store locations, cooperatives especially of the voluntary type have given increasing help to retailers in securing leases and in financing the new business. In some cases the cooperatives either have established the stores themselves and run them until a good prospect appears or they have engaged in partial ownership of the stores. This type of financial assistance as well as some equity arrangements will undoubtedly be continued.

Voluntary-group activities also have assumed major importance in hardware and automotive supplies; and there has been further development of retailer cooperatives in the drug field.

The greatest sales increases by independent merchant wholesalers, however, have come not so much in the lines mentioned above as in industrial products and consumer durables. The following ranking shows the fields of greatest percentage increase in wholesale sales between 1948 and 1963.

One significant development of the post World War II period has been the growth of highly specialized merchant wholesalers, some of which are new types. This has occurred in consumer goods, as in drugs and furniture, but particularly in industrial goods. For example, electronics parts and equipment wholesalers were listed for the first time in the Census of

1954 when there were about 1,900. In the 1963 Census, there were nearly 3,900. In 1948, there were less than 200 wholesalers of aircraft, aeronautical equipment and parts. In 1963 there were over 900.

The extent of wholesale specialization may be illustrated by the electrical supplies field where some distributors sell to utilities and to industrial organizations while others specialize in sales to hotels, theaters, shipyards, electric-sign manufacturers and other specialized markets. In metropolitan areas, some electrical distributors may handle lighting fixtures and supplies only. Some of the smaller distributors obtain virtually all of their business from residential contractors who buy in relatively small quantities. Others do not cultivate the residential business but sell primarily to contractors engaged in industrial and commercial work.

Merchant Wholesalers	*Percentage Change in Sales 1948–63*
Stationery and Office Supplies	482
Professional Equipment and Supplies	263
Amusement, Sporting Goods	260
Transportation Equipment	242
Construction, Mining Equipment	232
Automobile Tires	200
Industrial Chemicals	193
Electrical Appliances	180
Furniture	180
Meats	168
Construction Materials	167
Drugs	165

Since highly specialized wholesalers are available in a number of fields, manufacturers can select those wholesalers who cater to the particular markets they want to reach. Therefore, they can serve well-defined market segments effectively and at comparatively low cost.

At times, over the years, manufacturers have been unhappy with the kind of coverage and service they have received from the older general line type of wholesaler who attempted to blanket a particular geographical area. The newer, more-efficiently operated specialty wholesalers have a high competence in a limited market and give manufacturers the kind of service they require.

Although the merchant wholesaler is holding his own overall against manufacturers' sales branches which carry stocks, the latter have outpaced wholesalers in several fields as shown in the tabulation on page 519. In the listed categories the dollar sales of manufacturers' branches in commercial and industrial machinery and paint exceed the sales of merchant wholesalers. The sales of footwear by the two groups is about the same. Dollar sales by manufacturers' branches, relative to merchant wholesalers, are increasing for drugs and amusement, sporting goods. For the other commodity fields wholesaler sales are much higher than sales of branches.

In the other major merchandise categories not listed, the sales growth of independent wholesalers has exceeded that of manufacturers' stock-carrying branches. In some categories: meat; confectionery; dry goods; plumbing, heating and air-conditioning; and service-establishment equipment, the dollar sales of manufacturers' branches actually declined substantially over the period indicated.

Not all manufacturers' branches displace independent wholesalers. Some of them are actually regional warehouses which carry back-up stocks on which wholesalers as well as other customers draw.

Wholesaling is still concentrated in the largest cities. At one time, it was believed that wholesaling was becoming more decentralized, but this is not entirely borne out by the census data. Some wholesale establishments have appeared in smaller communities, but the great bulk of wholesale business is still done in large cities. In 1954, 68 per cent of the sales of merchant wholesalers were in cities over 100,000 population. In 1963, the

Commodity Field	*Increase in Sales 1948–63*	
	Manufacturers' Sales Branches	*Merchant Wholesalers*
Construction, Mining Machinery	525	232
Lumber, Millwork	520	103
Printing and Writing Paper (except stationery), Wrapping Paper and Other Coarse Paper	500	119
Amusement, Sporting Goods	366	260
Commercial and Industrial Machinery and Equipment	343	65
Drugs	322	165
Electrical Appliances	316	180
Footwear	278	94
Hardware	150	26
Paint	66	58

percentage had risen to 83 per cent. This increasing centralization of wholesaling has occurred even in such commodity fields as groceries and tobacco which typically have had the smallest wholesale trading areas.

Among the agent middlemen, the greatest growth has occurred in the sales of manufacturers' agents. Sales of these agents over the 1948–63 period expanded one and a half times, and there was also a net increase of some 2,100 agent establishments. This growth reflects the entrance into the market of many small firms who wish to sell through agents rather than their own organizations. It also reflects the very great importance of agents in the industrial field, an area which has depended heavily on highly specialized agents who know their market and can secure efficient coverage of it. Even fairly large manufacturers in the industrial field continue to use agents whenever they have been able to secure and retain high caliber people. Often, these companies will retain some agents after they have made a decision to sell directly to their customers.

Wholesalers engaged in the assembly of farm products decreased substantially in numbers in the postwar period (about 25 per cent), and their sales declined 10 per cent between 1948 and 1963. These changes reflect a general trend toward shortening the marketing channels for farm products as processors and large-scale retailers increase their direct buying from farmers.

Several changes have occurred which result in shorter channels for agricultural products. The increased specialization of poultry producers has led to more direct selling to processors, and these processors tend to be located closer to their source of supply. With the growth of milk shipments by bulk tank trucks, there has been a decline in country milk plants and cream stations. Meat slaughtering plants also have been located closer to livestock producers, and this likewise has increased direct buying. Cotton assemblers have become less important with the increase in direct-mill buying of cotton and increased sales of cotton cooperatives.

In view of the major interest in steadily rising food prices, it is not likely that these trends will be reversed. Rather, it may be expected that continuing steps will be taken to reduce the costs of marketing farm products. Also, it is probable that some new types of integration will occur in this field. One large milling company, for example, has recently entered the poultry business.

Wholesalers have become more cost conscious and more control conscious. Many of the larger wholesalers and voluntary groups have installed computer systems which have facilitated office routines and have helped to control inventories. In addition, some wholesalers have been able to use their computers to furnish additional information to retail customers to help in their own operations.

One significant innovation with major long-run implications has been the use of automatic shipments from manufacturer to wholesaler and, to some degree, from wholesaler to retailer. This procedure has been used both in the introduction of new products and in the reordering of staples. This is another use of the computer which has major long-run possibilities.

Wholesalers have been aided in their efforts to improve costs through the efforts of their trade associations, some of which have developed uniform accounting procedures for their members. This has occurred in electrical goods and in groceries.

In some commodity fields, which have experienced a substantial increase in wholesaler sales since the war, operating-expenses-to-sales have decreased. This is true of specialty drug wholesalers and wholesalers handling construction materials (other than lumber), and professional equipment and supplies.

Wholesalers have improved their selling activities through the use of better trained salesmen and better use of sales aids. Some wholesalers, in drugs for example, have built up their telephone sales activities through the use of trained batteries of telephone order salesmen.

Manufacturer–distributor relations and distributor–retailer relations have been generally improved and strengthened. The marketing concept, which has been widely accepted by manufacturers, now has been adopted by leading wholesalers as well. To an increasing degree, wholesalers are helping retailers with various facets of their business. This includes help in locating and modernizing stores, aid in financing, training courses for store owners and store personnel and store management counseling.

One large drug wholesaler instituted group selling to retailers for seasonal promotions. This has involved a dinner followed by the presentation.

The postwar period has seen the greater use of policies of selective distribution on the part of manufacturers. This has been coupled in some cases with a wholesaler policy of stocking a limited number of competing lines. These policies contribute to stronger manufacturer–distributor ties especially when the manufacturer has a stated policy of selling exclusively through wholesalers. One manufacturer of heating units, for example, established some lines as "wholesaler designated." These lines are not sold directly to installers. The manufacturer helps to create a demand for the line through contacts with architects and engineers. Wholesalers who carry this line have a complete line under favorable terms, and the manufacturer trains the wholesaler's salesmen.

Some large wholesalers are integrating back into manufacturing, for example in the food and drug fields. There may be some rather limited opportunities for this type of integration, but few wholesalers are large enough to undertake it. However, in the grocery field some exploratory work has been done which might lead to joint manufacturing activities on the part of several voluntary chains.

Whether or not wholesalers integrate into manufacturing, they are likely to put greater emphasis on their own brands. This has already been a major factor in voluntary-chain operations and may be expected to grow as voluntary-chain activities expand and as large wholesalers, especially those of the chain type, take a larger share of their markets.

The complex structure of our wholesaling system presents buyers and sellers with many channel options. Until recently, executive judgment has been the main performance standard used in measuring the contribution of wholesaling systems. The author proposes measurement of performance by the "value added" concept—the evaluation of an enterprise's or institution's contribution in terms of the gross economic values created by it. The advantages of this method of measurement are discussed.

57. SUMMARY STATEMENT FROM "CHANGES IN WHOLESALING STRUCTURE AND PERFORMANCE"*

Theodore N. Beckman†

SUMMARY ON NATURE OF THE WHOLESALING STRUCTURE AND CHANGES THEREIN

. . . The wholesaling structure in the United States is extremely comlex. It consists of 59 major kinds of business groupings and a total of 140 individual kinds of business classifications. It consists further of six major segments by type of operations and many of the kinds of businesses are shown separately for each of two or more of the segments, making a total of 303 kinds of individual business classifications. Again, five of the six major segments are further divided into more functional classifications, making a total of about 30 types of operation classifications. Although the major groupings and segments remain essentially the same, there is great variety by kind of business and by type of operation, and the composition is constantly changing in each of the two classification categories in obedience to changes in technology, mode of living, and economic enterprise.

---

* This summary statement is reprinted from "Changes in Wholesaling Structure and Performance," *Proceedings of the Fall Conference of the American Marketing Association*, 1965, pp. 603–18.

† The Ohio State University.

Such a structural variety offers buyers and sellers many channel choices, as dictated by such considerations as size, market segmentation, financial strength, and chosen method of operation. It also makes possible a high degree of functional shiftability, whereby all wholesaling functions or a small part thereof may be shifted from one type of functionary to another and from one kind of business to another. Furthermore, the adaptive character of the structure facilitates adjustments to changing markets.

It is believed that a careful study of the structure in the United States with its complexity, variety, and changing character should be of help in understanding the structures existing in different countries at given stages of economic growth, as modified by relevant cultural differences, and in affording some predictive value with changes in the economy from one stage to another.

THE TEST OF PERFORMANCE

In the final analysis the existence and perseverance of a given structure or any of its components, in a freely competitive economy, depends upon need for it, opportunity provided by the environment, and its performance—results of its functioning. Structure, in its literal meaning, is anatomical in nature and as such merely provides the skeleton. It is the physiology or functioning of the structure that gives it life, meaning, and makes for possible growth. It is the effectiveness and efficiency of the functioning that is determinant in the long run, and that is why it is important that adequate measurements be provided for the purpose.

QUALITATIVE EVALUATION OF PERFORMANCE

The only measurement of performance of the wholesaling structure or any part of it until this year has been of the judgmental value type. This is based on the hypothesis that in a free economy an institution will not come into being unless there is a need for it and an opportunity for its development and that it cannot continue to exist unless it does an essential job better, more economically, and more efficiently than it can be done by possible alternatives under the same conditions. This, then, resolves itself into an analysis of exactly what the institution does, for whom, and what the consequences would be in its absence. In the case of the wholesaler it is a matter of analyzing point by point what he does for his customers on the one hand and for his suppliers on the other and the effects of all that upon society. Its strength lies in the fact that it is a logical approach to judge an institution by its functioning, it provides the basic rationality for any other explanation, and it may be illustrated with many specific examples.

This method is, however, largely or entirely qualitative and hence the results cannot really be measured. Whatever factual data can be used are on a case basis or in other limited terms. Most important, it does not permit comparison with any other institution or segment of the economy.

MEASUREMENT OF PERFORMANCE BY VALUE ADDED

For some twelve years the author of this paper has felt that an analysis of wholesaling (as well as other marketing) institutions in terms of services rendered or functions performed is not enough. Such analysis must be supplemented by one in terms of *value added,* to be derived in the same manner as has been done for value added by manufactures for a number of years. It amounts to a deduction from gross margin of the cost of containers, other supplies and materials, fuel, electric energy, water, and contract work. The result is a figure of the contribution made by an enterprise or an institution in terms of gross economic values created by it similar to those that are used in computing our Gross National Product. Some of the advantages of this kind of measurement are:

1. It is the best available *absolute* measure of value created.
2. It is the best *relative* measure for comparison with manufacturing, etc.
3. It helps to view costs in their proper perspective, shifting emphasis from costs to values created—a more positive approach.
4. It leads to improved public relations about wholesaling and marketing generally.

Following a number of papers, speeches, and special publications on the subject,[1] many parts of the American business community have enthusiastically accepted the concept, and attempts have been made to implement it through the collection of data that would help measure the values added. After several years of consistent effort along this line, including the persistent support of the National Association of Wholesalers, the Bureau of the Census of the U.S. Department of Commerce has conducted a sample study to determine whether the necessary information for the measurement of value added by wholesalers could be obtained. The results of this empirical approach were in the affirmative. In consequence, and after considerable deliberation, the Bureau decided to collect such data for the year 1963, the preliminary results of which were published in January of this year.

Thus, at long last the values added by wholesalers, who account for

[1] Theodore N. Beckman, "The Value Added Concept as Applied to Marketing and Its Implications," in Stewart A. Rewoldt (ed.), *Frontiers in Marketing Thought* (Bloomington: Bureau of Business Research, Indiana University, 1955), pp. 83–99; "Value Added as a Measurement of Output," *Advanced Management,* April, 1957; "Le concept de la "valeur ajoutee comme measure de la production," *Organization Scientifique,* Bruxelles, Belgium, Octobre 1957. See also "Value Added by Distribution," sponsored and published by The Chamber of Commerce of the United States, Washington, D.C., Fall, 1956.

over two-fifths of total wholesale trade, have been determined. This is the first of its kind and was based on a sample of about 10,000 firms. The preliminary published data show that for all of them in the aggregate the gross margin was 18.0% of total operating receipts. The *value added*, computed in the same manner as for manufacturing, was 17.2% of total operating receipts. The remaining 0.8 percentage points included in the gross margin consisted of *values contributed* by others, mostly in the form of contract work.

One must not assume from the above that gross margins could be used as approximations of values added. While such may be true of the aggregate for all wholesalers and for some other large group, it is far from true for any given kind of business or type of operation. For the dry goods and apparel wholesalers, for example, the difference between the gross margin and value added was 2.2 percentage points (18.4% gross margin and 16.2% value added) and for individual firms the difference may be quite gross and varied from the aggregate even of its own group.

As such data become available in greater detail, are carefully analyzed and properly interpreted, more emphasis will no doubt be placed on the positive contributions of wholesaling to our economy and its growth and less on items that have led to the misconceptions surrounding the subject. This is indeed a breakthrough long overdue and one that is hoped to spread into retail trade, other parts of the wholesaling structure, and into other areas of economic endeavor for effective scientific comparison and analysis. It is further hoped that similar approaches will be made in a number of other countries, so that the comparison and analysis can be enriched through insights into possible effects of differences in culture and in economic background.

The advent of management science and management's acceptance of the marketing concept have fostered increased awareness of the significance of physical distribution. Physical distribution and its two major subsystems—transportation and warehousing—are integrated with the systems concept of marketing management.

58. THE DISTRIBUTION MIX–A SYSTEMS APPROACH*

William Lazer†

INTRODUCTION

The past 15 years have witnessed dramatic changes in the management of business enterprise. Some of these changes are reflected in new organizational patterns such as the breaking out of new line and staff activities, or the development of new centers of authority, i.e. physical distribution. Others are embodied in the applications of mathematical techniques and computer technology to solve business problems. In distribution for example, linear programming, waiting-line theory, and simulation techniques have been employed successfully to improve business policies and to arrive at optimal solutions to problems.

A dramatic management shift has occurred in the marketing domain. It stems from management's recognition of the increasingly important and pervasive role of marketing in the business system. It culminates in the acceptance by management of the marketing concept of business operations. This change fosters a new perspective for distribution activities and an increased understanding of the significant role of distribution in company operations.

Corporate management today functions in an economy of abundance. In such a business environment, marketing problems in general, and distri-

---

* Not previously published. For a discussion of the importance of coordination and administration in manufacturer–dealer systems, see Valentine F. Ridgeway, "Administration of Manufacturer–Dealer Systems," *Administrative Science Quarterly*, Vol. 1, No. 4 (March, 1957), pp. 464–83.

† Michigan State University.

bution problems in particular, receive increasing emphasis. The task of matching the technical excellence of mass production with parallel progress in mass distribution becomes as crucial as any confronting management. Customers and consumers cannot enjoy the benefits of mass production without efficient distribution systems. This is as true in Russia as it is in the United States. An automated economy produces only filled warehouses and clogged supply pipelines unless great progress is made in distribution.

Our economic climate places heavy burdens on marketing activities. Continuous production is accompanied with increasing marketing responsibilities. Yet, marketing is constantly criticized for high costs, wastes, and inefficiencies. The significant progress that has been made in increasing marketing effectiveness is often unrecognized. Distribution is one area of marketing that has evidenced considerable progress in increasing efficiency and in reducing costs. It is the purpose of this article to discuss the relationship between distribution and the marketing mix. . . .

DISTRIBUTION AND MARKETING STRATEGY

The distribution mix essentially is comprised of two sub-mixes. One centers on the selection of distribution channels and the determination of channel strategy. The other is concerned with physical distribution. The latter will receive the major focus in our discussion. However, the physical distribution task can only be perceived properly in terms of its relationship to the various mixes and to overall marketing strategy.

Chart I illustrates the key role of physical distribution in marketing strategy. It also relates the distribution mix to the other elements in marketing programs which are directed at achieving such corporate goals as profit, volume, market share, image and reputation.

DISTRIBUTION STRATEGIES

Distribution strategies are concerned with overcoming forces of space, costs, time and competition. Distribution adds value to goods by meeting such barriers. In so doing it creates time, place, possession and information utilities. As a result of distribution activities consumers and customers are able to obtain goods and services at the time and place they desire them, possession is greatly facilitated, and more pertinent information is made available.

Distribution has been termed the dark continent of our economy.[1] Increasing attention must be paid to distribution problems in the future. To achieve the proper perspective and fully understand distribution problems they must be perceived in a marketing setting. Distribution strategies

[1] See Peter F. Drucker, "The Economy's Dark Continent," *Fortune*, April, 1962, pp. 103 and 270.

are part of the overall marketing strategy. They have a great impact on marketing operations and vice versa. They establish certain parameters within which marketing policies are determined and marketing decisions are implemented. Yet, in reality, it is market forces which govern distribution operations.

In essence, marketing distinguishes business organization from other forms of organization. Marketing is the vital part of any business enterprise. Marketing factors are the fundamental considerations in establishing

CHART I

Distribution and Marketing Strategy

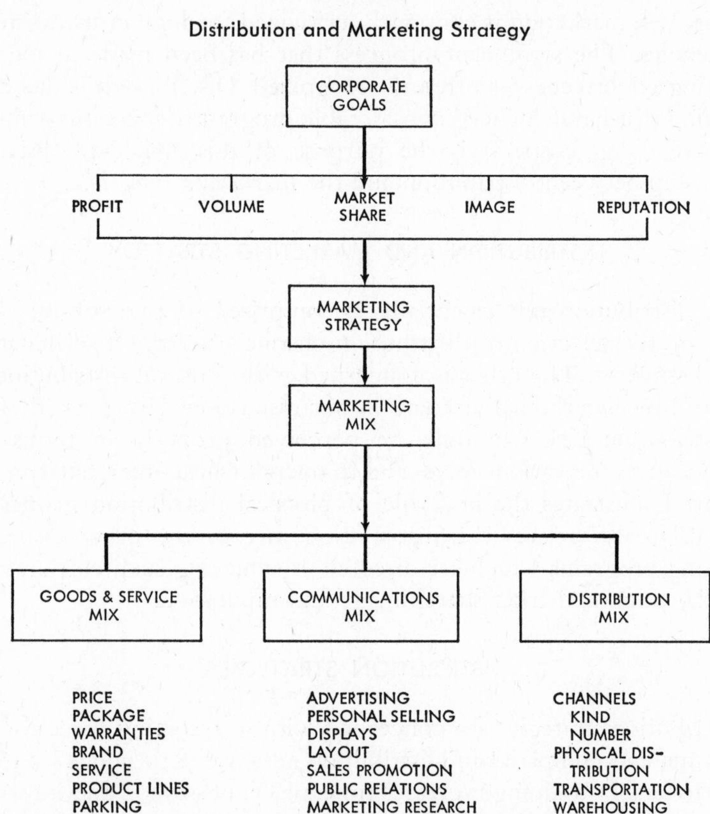

corporate policies and strategies and programming effective systems of action. In a very real sense questions of distribution policy and strategy (like those of other business areas) cannot be separated from dominant marketing influences.

Distribution strategies are more likely to be successful when two essential elements are combined. First there must be management understanding of the concept of marketing as a philosophy of business action. This involves the recognition of the significance of environmental forces which shape market opportunity. It emphasizes an understanding which must be reflected in distribution policies. It establishes the fact that distribution decisions must be brought into line with market wants, needs and opportunities. The consumer then becomes the ultimate force in distribution activities.

The second ingredient of effective distribution strategies is that of translating marketing perspectives into an operational distribution program. This results in the choice of effective distribution channels and the efficient distribution of products.

The relationship of distribution strategy to marketing strategy is portrayed in the bottom half of Chart I. It indicates that distribution managers are increasingly concerned with the planning and strategy aspects of their jobs. To a large extent, planning and the development of effective distribution strategies depend upon the utilization of market information to design an effective total marketing mix.

THE PHYSICAL DISTRIBUTION SYSTEM

The physical distribution system is comprised of two major subsystems. The first is a transportation system. The second is a warehousing system. These are illustrated in Charts II and III. The transportation system in turn is comprised of two major components: transportation carriers and transportation agencies. The carriers consist of rail, air, truck, pipeline and water. The agencies consist of such institutions as freight forwarders, railway express, parcel post, air express, and shippers' associations. In constructing a transportation system, transportation carriers and agencies are linked and integrated to form economic units that are more

CHART II

Transportation System

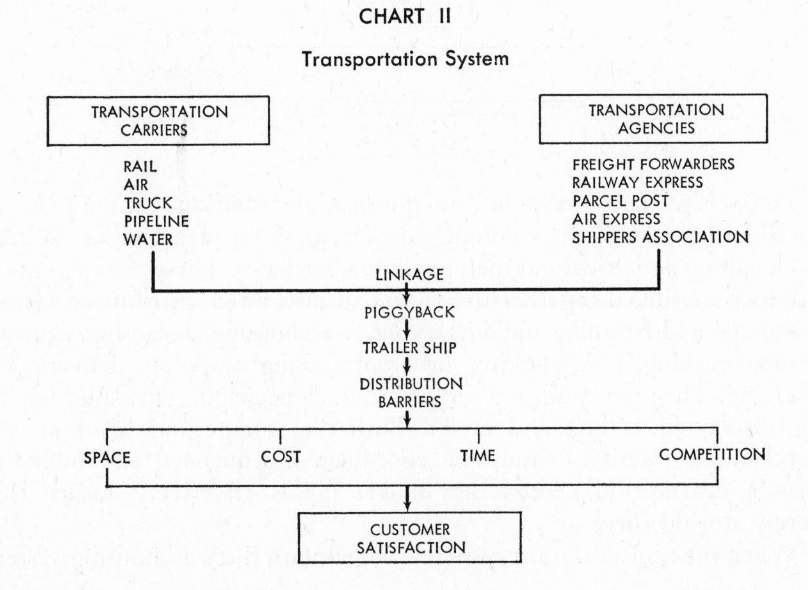

efficient from the user's point of view. As a result, an integrated and coordinated transportation system is developed which leads to the establishment of new types of carriers, services, and methods of movement and handling, such as piggyback and trailer ship.

The transportation system is designed to overcome the barriers separating a company from its customers and consumers. These barriers include time, place, cost and competitive elements. The integration of separate transportation institutions and activities into a transportation system is resulting in new economies of movement and more adequate servicing of market wants, needs, and opportunities.

CHART III

Warehousing System

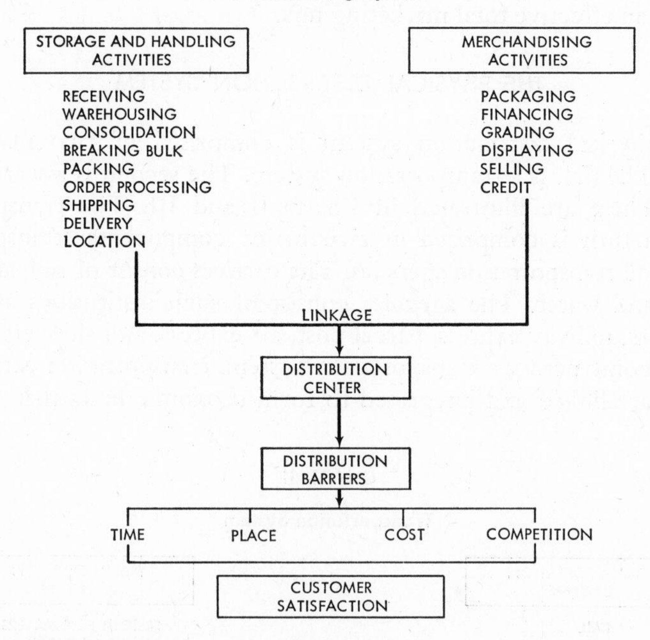

The second subsystem in the physical distribution complex is the warehousing system. It is comprised of two types of activities: storage and handling activities, and merchandising activities. These two groups of activities are linked together to achieve an integrated distribution center.

Storage and handling include layout, warehousing, receiving, consolidation, breaking bulk, packing, order processing, shipping, delivery and receiving. The merchandising services include packaging, grading, financing, displaying, selling and credit. Both the storage and handling and merchandising activities must be coordinated, sequenced and linked to form a distribution center that moves goods effectively rather than merely storing them.

When the transportation system is linked with the warehousing system, we achieve an integrated physical distribution system. This system is able to overcome barriers that separate the company from the market place thereby rendering services to customers and consumers and achieving better market posture for the firm. The physical distribution system is portrayed in Chart IV.

The physical distribution system operates within a larger marketing setting. It is one part of the marketing mix. It pertains directly to the distribution mix and must be designed to support and coordinate the activities that occur in distribution channels. Moreover, it must be in line

CHART IV

Physical Distribution System

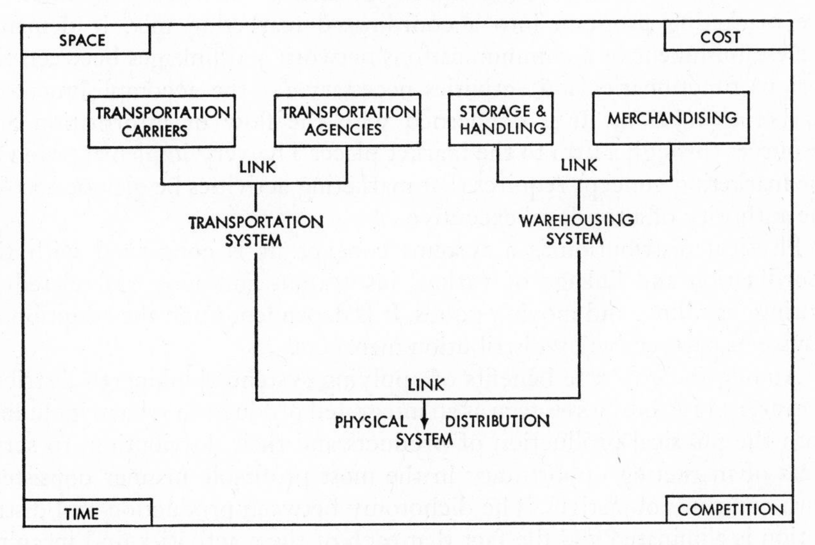

with both the goods and service mix and the communications mix. As a result, physical distribution activities and policies can only be properly perceived in their marketing framework. Marketing activities, problems, policies and decisions must be linked to physical distribution factors.

SYSTEMS THINKING

Such widely hailed marketing developments as the physical distribution concept, the marketing philosophy, and the marketing mix, which we have been describing, are merely manifestations of a more fundamental and significant management development that has occurred. In essence management has adopted a new perspective of distribution operations. They are embracing the systems viewpoint of distribution.

The characteristic which differentiates a system from a jumble of parts and pieces is that the elements form a coherent group. Systems thinking, therefore, is based on the integration and coordination of business activity.

Under the systems concept distribution agencies and operations are viewed as complex, large-scale, dynamic action systems.

Distribution managers have the major responsibility of recognizing the relationships existing among the elements of the distribution system, comprehending their potential combinations, and coordinating and integrating business factors so that goals are achieved effectively. This implies that the master model for distribution activity is the systems model.

The marketing management concept, which is a signal breakthrough in the management thinking, by its very nature, implies a systems approach to the management of marketing effort. It requires a recognition of the interrelationships and interconnections between marketing and other business elements. It involves the integration of all the components of the marketing program into a coordinated marketing mix. It demands the establishment of a communications network and linkages between the various functionaries and activities necessary for the accomplishment of marketing missions. It is concerned with the flow of information and resources through a firm to the market place. The very implementation of the marketing concept requires that marketing activities be grouped under the authority of a top-level executive.

Physical distribution is a systems concept. It is concerned with the coordination and linkage of various institutions and activities related to storing, handling, and moving goods. It is dependent upon the adoption of a systems perspective by distribution managers.

Among the concrete benefits of applying systems thinking to distribution are: (1) A business is seen as an integrated production system including both the physical production of products and their distribution, to serve areas of marketing opportunity in the most profitable manner consistent with company objectives. The dichotomy between production and distribution is eliminated and the fact that each of these activities find meaning in the other is stressed. This approach gives distribution forces the increased stature they deserve as an integral part of the business decision making framework. (2) A more realistic viewpoint is gained of the role of distribution in the management of an enterprise. Distribution activities are grouped under the direction of a top-level executive. Changes in organizational structures have resulted to adapt business enterprise more effectively to changing market needs. (3) Systems thinking fosters the coordination of related distribution activities to develop a total system of distribution action. It does not splinter distribution management into a number of distinct specialized operations such as storing, handling and transportation. (4) The application of the systems concept to distribution has resulted in savings in cost, time, and spoilage, and has increased distribution effectiveness. The entire distribution process from start to finish is viewed and engineered as a total system and savings are gained in the total costs of physically handling and distributing goods rather than in any one cost center.

Business logistics is concerned with the creation of time and place utility. Changes in business logistics management and some important probable future trends in the field are identified. The implications of these probable trends include greater involvement in both the physical and promotional capabilities of distribution systems, and more concern with logistical variables external to the firm's formal organization.

59. SOME THOUGHTS REGARDING TRENDS IN BUSINESS LOGISTICS*

J. L. Heskett†

Because there are as many definitions of business logistics as there are definers, it is first of all important to know what is meant by any individual attempting to assess past and future developments in the field. For the purposes of this discussion, the term business logistics will refer to the management of all activities which facilitate movement and the coordination of supply and demand in the creation of time and place utility in goods. Activities logically related to the field include transportation, warehousing, materials handling, order processing, supply scheduling, and inventory control.

SIGNIFICANT POSTWAR CHANGES IN BUSINESS LOGISTICS

Conceptual and organizational changes have taken place in the management of business logistics activities since World War II. These changes are the product of the combined causes suggested below.

Changes

Conceptually, objectives in the management of logistics activities have shifted from those concerned with the minimization of costs concerned with one type of activity such as transportation, warehousing, or inventory management to the minimization of costs resulting from the combi-

---

* Not previously published.

† Harvard University.

nation of these activities. "Trading-off" increased transportation costs against even greater savings in warehousing and inventory costs, for example, has become not only possible, but popular in recent years through the analytic philosophy of total cost analysis—a look at the way changes in method concurrently affect all costs of logistics.

It is not necessary to restructure the corporate organization to achieve the benefits of total cost analysis. However, to facilitate analyses and actions of broader scope, many companies have reorganized to assign responsibility and authority for all or many logistics activities to one individual with some stature in the organization.

Causes

Many reasons, mostly exogenous to logistics activity management, can be advanced for the marked increase in the development of interest and thought in logistics at this particular point in time. Among them are:

1. A growing interest in profit maximization rather than cost minimization as an underlying objective of management activity. This has been fostered most in distribution by the so-called marketing concept.
2. The ability of marketing to stimulate consumer preferences for various types of mass-produced goods, thereby allowing increased emphasis to be placed on controlled selling to more profitable customers, differentiated from all possible customers by, among other things, geographic location, size of individual shipments, and regularity of patronage.
3. A growing awareness, mainly through the educational programs of retail and wholesale trade associations, of the costs and relative undesirability of maintaining excessive inventories in a distribution channel. This has forced an increased consideration of the problems of doing business in low-inventory channels of distribution.
4. The tremendous post-war proliferation of products. Three products together selling at the rate of one previously can be expected to double inventory needs in relation to sales as a rough rule of thumb. Whether to meet the growing diversity of consumer desires or as a non-price competitive device, product proliferation has produced increasingly important logistical strains on distribution systems.
5. The development and recent growth of several forms of transportation has increased the number of alternative components to be considered in designing a logistics system. Perhaps the two most important developments of this type have been the increased availability of lower-cost air freight services and coordinated forms of transportation such as piggyback (trailer-on-flat-car). Although relatively insignificant in terms of volume and revenue among methods of transportation, the availability of air freight service has, because of its impact on costs of transportation, warehousing, and inventory maintenance, contributed to the growth of total cost analysis as an analytic philosophy.
6. The encouragement of carrier experimentation in pricing on the part of the regulatory agencies of the Government. A milestone in this process was

the Transportation Act of 1958 which allowed the Interstate Commerce Commission to place greater emphasis on rational (cost) measures in ruling on the desirability of carrier rate proposals.

7. The development of quantitative techniques particularly effective in the analysis of logistics problems. Foremost among these is linear programming. But the list also includes waiting line theory, graph theory, and heuristic programming employed to varying degrees in the construction of inventory and location models.

8. The development and popularization of the computer.

PROBABLE FUTURE TRENDS AND DEVELOPMENTS IN THE FIELD

It is not difficult to predict the direction of future efforts in the field of business logistics. Among the more important of future efforts will be:

1. Increased emphasis on total profit as opposed to total cost analysis. Basically, this involves an assessment of the effect of various logistics systems on sales as well as costs, resulting in profit-oriented analyses.

2. The extension of logistics systems analysis to include activities carried out by suppliers and customers as well as a firm in question. The goal of such efforts should be to an increasing extent the maximization of the long-run profit performance of a channel of distribution composed of more than one firm or profit center.

3. The increased systematic capture of data on an interfirm basis. Typical of efforts in this regard is the recent establishment of a Standard Transportation Commodity Code for identifying various commodities transported in the United States. Additional codes to provide the framework for collecting data about shipments methods, origins, destinations, transit times, commodity components, and weights will be designed for Governmental and inter-firm computer storage. The authorization of the first Census of Transportation carried out in 1963 provided the impetus for much of this effort.

4. Increased emphasis on approximating as opposed to optimizing techniques in logistics systems analysis. As the scope of systems analysis is expanded to (a) allow the design of dynamic rather than static models and (b) provide for additional logistics activities simulation techniques for arriving at good rather than the so-called best answers will be used to an increasing extent.

5. The computerization (or programmed control by whatever method) of routine tasks such as carrier rate and route determination, freight bill auditing, and inventory control will continue. While industrial shippers will be developing logistics systems alternatives to a growing extent by computer, governmental regulatory agencies should be able to develop the basis for more effectively assessing policy alternatives by the same method.

IMPLICATIONS FOR MARKETING STUDENTS AND EXECUTIVES

In view of the trends which might be expected to take place in business logistics, one might expect marketing management to become increasingly involved and interested in physical as well as promotional capabilities of distribution systems. This should lead to a greater concern for the measurement and control of customer responses to various levels of physical service. In terms of research efforts, it should produce more interest in measuring the behavior of customers other than ultimate consumers, for logistical considerations often outweigh those of a promotional nature in the distribution effort conducted at the wholesale and retail levels of consumer product channels and in industrial marketing.

Traditional management theory dealing with organization has imposed an unrealistic view of organization relationships on marketing and logistics management. Business relationships external to a firm's formal organization are perhaps more important to the firm's success than those of an internal nature. For reasons of economy in both promotional and logistical effort, attempts will be made to an increasing degree on the part of "channel captain" firms to extend managerial control to include certain aspects of the operations of suppliers and customers. A current example of this is the plan by which retailers' inventory control programs can be linked to their suppliers in a system featuring automatic inventory monitoring, ordering, order-filling, and billing by the supplier.

The increased role of logistics management in distribution should have a leavening effect on decisions formerly controlled by promotional or manufacturing executives or negotiated by both. The result should be the type of logistics program which can meet the needs of customer and supplier alike at a lower cost to the former and a higher profit to the latter.

Because of the variety of organizational arrangements by which logistics activities will be managed, it will be incumbent upon logistics and promotional managers to coordinate efforts and communicate ideas and programs. The isolation and identification of responsibility for logistics activities and costs should make this task somewhat easier in the future.

C. Communications Mix

A systems view of the marketing concept enables each member of the sales organization to better understand his job in terms of the firm's total market objectives. This broadened perspective facilitates adjustments in the sales mix and results in more effective intra- and interfirm organization.

60. BASIC DUTIES OF THE MODERN SALES DEPARTMENT*

Eugene J. Kelley† and William Lazer‡

How *should* the marketing concept affect sales management and the field sales force? What *should* the modern sales department contribute to its company's success?

Sales department responsibilities increase under the marketing concept. Sales personnel, at both the managerial and field levels, are asked to broaden their area of interest and "raise their sights."

Under the marketing concept, salesmen are urged to look beyond quotas and calls per customer, and assist the other levels of the company in achieving clearly defined objectives. The marketing concept emphasizes this interaction and interrelationship of selling and other marketing-related activities.

The sales manager *and field sales force* must now perform important management functions. An increasing number of companies are insisting

* Reprinted from "Basic Duties of the Modern Sales Department," *Industrial Marketing*, Vol. XLV, No. 4 (April, 1960), pp. 68–83. Note: Charts I and II did not appear in the original article.

† Pennsylvania State University.

‡ Michigan State University.

that their sales managers demonstrate an ability to plan and execute creative field sales strategy and to integrate sales activities with the other elements of the marketing mix.

In short, the marketing concept is resulting in a re-evaluation of the nature and scope of the sales department.

SALES MANAGER'S DUTIES

Under the marketing concept, the sales manager is concerned with management of the total sales effort. His job consists of more than recruiting, selecting and training salesmen. His major responsibility is one of creating a growth atmosphere and planning and coordinating sales force strategy in order to achieve company objectives.

Sales management operating under the marketing concept recognizes innovation and experimentation as the essential ingredients of sales and marketing progress. Under this concept, sales management realizes that change not only produces problems, but also presents marketing opportunities.

The duties of sales managers operating under the marketing concept fall into two broad areas: (1) sales administration, and (2) sales force management. These are portrayed in Chart I.

Sales administration includes the planning and organizing functions,

CHART I

The Sales Management System

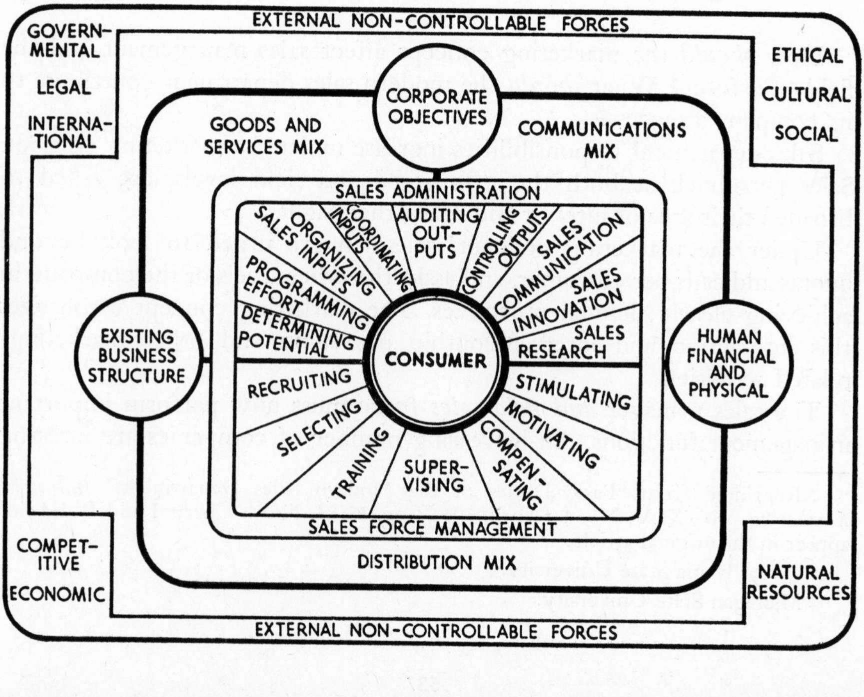

such as determining sales potentials, programming sales effort, coordinating sales inputs, and controlling sales outputs. In addition, the increasingly important functions of sales innovation, sales communication and sales research are sales administration responsibilities.

Sales force management includes the important functions of recruiting, selecting, training, supervising, compensating and motivating the field sales force.

Both sales administration and sales force management are of crucial importance. To date many sales managers have done a better job of recruiting, selecting, and training salesmen than they have of executing their sales administration responsibilities. In the future various pressures of competition, innovation, automation, high fixed costs and changing markets will force increased emphasis on sales administration.

SALES STRATEGY EMPHASIS

The modern sales manager is concerned with the strategy inherent in a total approach to overall sales. He still has the bread-and-butter tasks of achieving quotas and directing salesmen in the accomplishment of predetermined objectives; but he also is charged with helping to create market acceptance, establish brand or corporate images, provide research information, develop marketing manpower and establish harmonious dealer relationships.

The vital role of the sales manager in achieving corporate goals is emphasized in the marketing concept approach to sales strategy.

TWO DIMENSIONS

Marketing has two dimensions. First, marketing is an increasingly significant element in the total complex of business operation. Management makes a marketing decision after consideration of its effect on the whole business system and the overall objectives.

Second, marketing is an integrated subsystem. The marketing program is comprised of a mix of communications, distribution elements and goods and services "inputs." The essence of an integrated marketing program is that managerial attention is given to coordinating the interacting elements of the marketing mix to achieve predetermined goals.

It is not possible for a sales manager to understand the true dimensions of marketing change if he thinks only in terms of traditional sales management functions. Thinking of marketing as a cooperative effort—as a "system"—enables him to understand the place of sales in the total marketing effort.

TOTAL SALES PERSPECTIVE

Actually, sales operates within a framework determined by various forces beyond the control of management. These include competitive, social and political forces. Sales managers will have to be more sensitive to the influence on sales strategy of these forces. Nonbusiness disciplines such as psychology and sociology can be useful in supplying information on the external business environment.

A sales manager with a total sales perspective is less likely to see a particular problem as an isolated entity. For example, the problem of sales compensation is appraised in its relation to other components of sales, such as manpower development, selection, training, motivation, supervision and control.

Sales managers able to think in terms of how the field sales force is affected by the flows of information, money, and manpower are needed. These men will be in a better position to execute the policies of marketing-minded corporate managements. Since sales management will be working under this "systems concept" approach, understanding it will be a prerequisite for advancement.

SALESMEN'S DUTIES

The systems concept should be important to salesmen as well as sales managers. This is particularly true if the salesman's job is seen as that of managing a market area as it is in Chart II. If, on the other hand, the salesman is looked upon as an order taker, the concept is not as applicable.

An increasing number of companies are realizing that the job of the salesman has strategic and innovative dimensions, just as does sales force management. Many salesmen are faced in their own territories with problems of goal determination, planning and long-run market development. Acting in these capacities, the field man is a manager of a market area.

The distinction between a salesman and a manager of a market area is important; it is the difference between viewing salesmen as employees or as members of management. More important, it affects the way the salesman sees his own job. Under the market area management concept, the creative, strategic, and innovative powers of the field sales force are more likely to be tapped and utilized. In short, the market area management concept of field selling can bring about a fundamental change in the character of the salesman's job.

This new conceptual outlook of the sales job is not easy for some managers, or some salesmen, to accept. Viewing salesmen as managers at first blush seems to de-emphasize the importance of present managers. Actually it does not. It raises the sights of managers to higher strategic and planning levels. It may be the means of greater understanding and growth for present managers as well as one way of releasing the inherent creative energy of a force of salesmen.

A man's ability to maintain this subtle but fundamental perspective in

CHART II

The Sales Management System

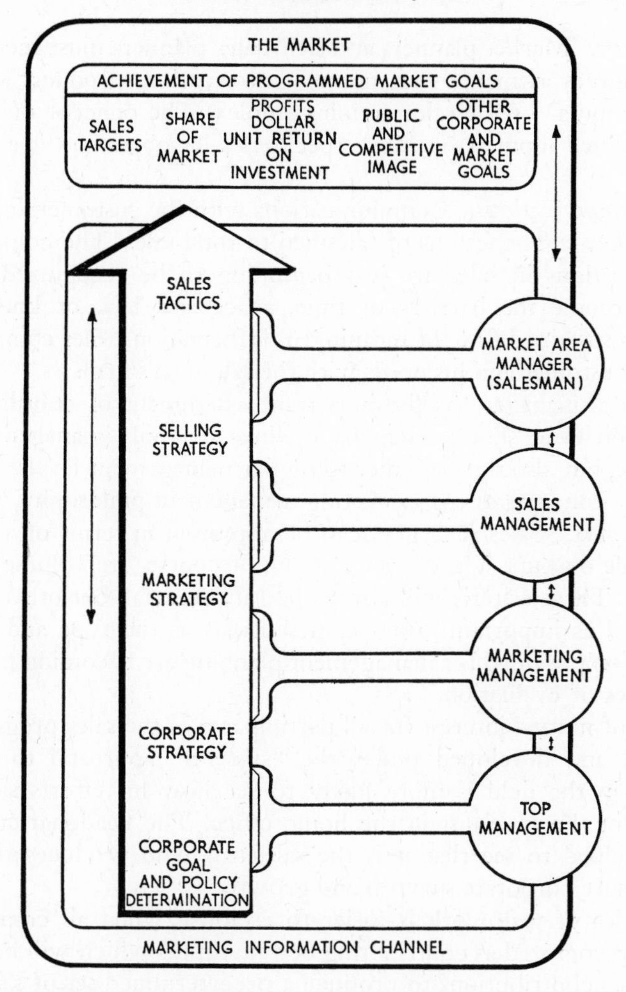

the management of his territory or his sales force is a basic criterion of his development potential for higher positions of managerial and administrative responsibility.

ELEMENTS OF TOTAL SALES

It is important for corporate success that sales personnel view the interaction of marketing elements as a single system. Many successful and sophsiticated sales managers have been aware that change in one component of sales action has an impact on the rest of the system. But organized, systematic, and intensive attention to such interaction is relatively new in marketing and selling.

The three components of the overall marketing effort which are particularly relevant to sales management are: input, communications and output.

1. *Inputs.* Market planners and field sales planners must recognize that such resources as manpower, money, information, products and service are the "inputs" of the sales action complex. The concept of assembling predetermined inputs to achieve specified sales objectives is a useful notion.

2. *Communications.* Communications with the customer and the company are key contributions of salesmen to total sales. The complexities of communications in sales are just beginning to be recognized. Salesmen must overcome the barriers of time, space and lack of knowledge to produce a sustained flow of meaningful information. Sales communication links the customer and his needs with the salesmen's firm.

The sales manager has the important assignment of coordinating this information flow. The sales manager links not only management to the sales force, but also the customer to higher management levels. This is one of the key concepts of the marketing management philosophy.

3. *Outputs.* Sales managers can be appraised in terms of a variety of measurable outputs. The most common, of course, are volume and profit standards. These criteria will always be fundamental, but others are being recognized as important. Such contributions as the type and quality of information provided for management planning are becoming more significant bases of evaluation.

Areas of mutual interest for all participants in the sales program can be identified and developed under the "systems" approach to sales. The salesman in the field is more likely to see how his efforts support and supplement the specialist in the home office. The headquarters specialist can be helped to see that it is the salesman who produces the markets which insure corporate survival and growth.

The idea of teamwork is easier to establish when all components of sales are recognized as contributing certain inputs which will be combined with other contributions to produce a predetermined set of sales outputs.

SCOPE OF CONCEPT

This concept of the sales action complex is also a way of looking at new areas of market opportunity.

In an era when technology is developing new products and new product applications at an accelerating rate, it behooves marketing and sales management to investigate the possibilities of "systems concept" selling.

In fact, many firms can view markets not only in terms of single companies but as complex business "systems." It is possible that a number of new products can be introduced simultaneously on a "systems" basis. The Air Force, for example, finds it necessary not only to buy individual products, but to purchase complete weapons systems including supporting service facilities.

And the same cooperative attitude should also carry through into manufacturer-dealer relations.

Many manufacturers do not recognize the mutual dependency aspects of their relations with suppliers and dealers. Frequently, distributors and manufacturers fail to recognize the community of interest involved in serving customers. How many manufacturers see their dealers as part of an extended sales system? Many say they do, but often unnecessary conflict exists where cooperation should prevail.

CONCLUSIONS

The specific benefits of the adoption of the systems approach to sales management are:

1. Coordination of corporate, marketing and sales efforts.
2. Integration of volume and profit targets established by the company with the operating activities of sales management.
3. Establishment of a circular and continuous relationship between corporate objectives and customer wants, needs and desires.
4. Combination of all sales inputs into an integrated marketing thrust. Through coordinated impact on the market place, effective and efficient sales action will result.
5. The systems concept approach requires sales management to achieve a perspective of marketing and corporate activities extending beyond the normal activities on such functions as production, purchasing and personnel.
6. The approach promotes teamwork. Decision makers at various corporate levels recognize the ramifications of their decisions at all levels. The salesman executing tactics in particular sales situations recognizes the contribution to the field sales team made by the men who devise sales strategy.

Changes occurring in personal selling and sales management have important implications for marketing. This article places in perspective factors that have influenced marketing generally, changes that are taking place in the sales force, and the significance of these factors to corporate-level marketing management.

61. DEVELOPMENTS IN SALES MANAGEMENT AND SALES*

W. J. E. Crissy†

If we are to place in perspective the changes which have occurred in sales management and sales in the recent past, we must first note some factors that have influenced marketing generally.

1. The evolution and acceptance of the marketing concept itself

A marketing-oriented firm places selling in perspective as the personal force in marketing. Because of the flexibility and personal nature of selling as a demand-cultivation force it becomes a major part of the total strategy and tactics of the firm that is oriented to its markets and the individuals therein who make purchasing decisions.

2. More precise delineation and definition of markets

A critical implication of this is that a given salesman often cannot be all things to all men. This in turn has caused specialization by customer groups within the sales force; in some instances, specialization by product groups; and in some wide-line companies both of these. Another organizational impact in some instances has been the creation of "special knower" posts as the staff part of the field sales organization.

3. Acceleration in the rate of change in technology and the "state of the art"

This has foreshortened the life expectancy of both products and markets. In turn it has influenced the sales effort by changing talent require-

* Not previously published.

† Michigan State University.

ments, the extent and scope of sales training, and the need for more frequent review of the sales organization structure lest it become obsolescent in terms of market needs and products and services offered.

4. Increased direct and indirect competition in many sectors of the economy

This has underscored the need for more systematic marketing intelligence information and in turn has imposed on the sales force a greater need to be the company's "eyes and ears" in the market place.

5. Systems thinking

The impact of this has been pervasive in terms of optimizing the product-service mix and, antecedent to that, gaining greater insight in depth of customers' needs. The key impact of this on the selling effort has been to accentuate the importance of the *values added* provided by the salesman in terms of ideas of worth and feasible solutions to problems. There has been a two-way application of this *values added*, primarily to the customers but also to the salesman's own firm.

6. Increased service demands associated with product lines

This has both lessened and narrowed product margins and caused much closer coordination between the field sales force and the field service group. In fact in many sectors of the economy these two have been combined organizationally to insure optimum service relative to profit potentials of accounts.

7. Increased discretionary spending

This has had its impact on marketing generally by increased focus on "trade up" as a key strategy. In turn, of course, product lines have been expanded toward the high end in terms of prices.

8. The knowledge explosion

All companies are dealing increasingly with sophisticated buyers. This in turn has had its impact on marketing generally and the sales force in particular by causing a necessary upgrading in the sophistication of sales personnel. In turn, this affects recruitment, selection, and training.

9. Increased tempo of business

This has had its impact on marketing generally by forcing greater decentralization for "on the spot" decision making. Inasmuch as the salesman is uniquely the transactional force in the marketing scheme of things he has to be vested with greater authority to act. Otherwise sales are lost through time delays.

10. Profit-centered accountancy

This is a change which has had pervasive influence on the total mission of the firm but it finds its greatest impact on the marketing group. More and more firms are viewing accounts, market segments, territories, products, and product groups as profit centers with planned return on investment objectives. This in turn has influenced the sales organization by imposing the need for greater fiscal sophistication on the part of salesmen and sales managers. It has also shifted thinking in many sectors of the economy on compensation plans. The company cannot preach profit and pay salesmen a straight linear commission on revenue. Rather, more and more firms associate compensation with profit contribution.

11. Alternatives to purchase

This is a widespread change in the industrial sector on big ticket items and is invading the consumer sector on such items. Leasing and rental are facts of life. Where such alternatives exist there is a direct influence on the sales force. These alternatives must be considered in optimizing the product/service mix and ultimately in what the salesman seeks to offer to a given account.

12. The rise of credit

As one executive put it, "Even in the industrial market place it is increasingly unfashionable to pay for anything." From the marketing standpoint credit can be viewed both as a demand cultivating force as well as a major ingredient in profitable operation. The sales organization must necessarily be privy to credit policies and practices and administer them consistently.

13. The computer

Potentially, the computer has larger use in the marketing part of the firm than in the fiscal or production end. With it the firm is able to handle the multi-variate problems involved in optimizing the customer/prospect mix, the product/service mix, the distribution mix, and the promotional mix. The computer hastens the flow of information to and from the field. Yet the computer is no better than the basic inputs. Hence, the sales organization must be more and more sophisticated on the place of the computer in the scheme of things and knowledgeable on the interpretations of the data generated by this new and amazing tool. Further, the computer is enabling management to make more and more precise cost/revenue analyses for planning and control purposes.

14. Evolution of new channels of distribution

There have been innumerable kinds of business entities developing since World War II. In the consumer sector, illustratively, the discount house and the shopping center. In the industrial sector, illustratively, firms involved exclusively in the renting and leasing of equipment with and without operators. The impact of this on the sales organization is manifold. The salesman must be alert to new categories of customers and prospects that may grow up in his territory. More importantly, once discovered, their unique needs must be explored if profitable business is to be developed.

15. Increased and more pervasive governmental influences

The marketing arm of a firm must be knowledgeable on tax and regulatory legislation and administrative entities and indeed must try to anticipate the changes in stance in the latter. Because the sales force performs the transactional role sales personnel must in turn be knowledgeable on what can and cannot be committed.

16. Government as a market

In reality, of course, there are government markets! For many companies this is a significant slice of their total business. The impact of this on the sales force is that both line salesmen and "special knowers" must be informed on the peculiarities of this market place. It is quite a different problem to sell equipment on a bid basis to a municipality as contrasted with selling the same equipment to firms within the municipality.

OTHER CHANGES IN THE SALES FORCE SINCE WORLD WAR II

Some of the points listed below have been alluded to above. It may be worthwhile to summarize these changes under five major headings.

1. Organization

a. Closer tie between sales and both pre- and post-transactional services.
b. Increased number and variety of "back up" specialists.
c. Closer coordinational relationship between selling and other demand cultivating groups within the market organization.
d. Creation of profit centers within the sales force.

2. The salesman's role

a. Marketing tactician.
b. Marketing intelligence along with staff-generated marketing research.
c. Idea man and problem solver for customer and for company.
d. Greater concern with posttransactional distribution of goods.

These imply that the salesman's "knower areas" will include people, money, products and services, and market place.

3. Sales manager's role

a. Manager rather than "lead salesman."
b. Collator and disseminator of marketing intelligence information.
c. Greater participation in market delineation and forecasting.
d. Increased concern with posttransactional distribution.

4. Compensation and incentives associated with profit rather than with revenue

5. Training

Greater need for systematic continuing training at all levels within the sales organization. Wider use of sales training managers and outside resources.

WHAT LIES AHEAD

Generally speaking the trends as noted in this memorandum all appear to be occurring at an increasing rate. In addition, I predict the following:

1. Sharper analysis of cost of selling leading to optimum mix of mass demand-cultivating forces *vis à vis* the personal selling effort.
2. More and more firms will find that the only major avenue for differential competitive advantage is in the knowledge and service areas. The salesman will be a key factor in providing the *values added* through his knowledge and sophistication as well as his authority to commit the firm's technical resources in solving customers' problems.
3. Increased professionalization of marketing generally and of the sales role in particular. Organizations as well as individual companies will commit resources to a positive program to break down the unfavorable stereotype of the salesman.
4. More and more companies will complement intrafirm training with professional training from outside sources such as universities.
5. More and more firms will differentiate levels of career salesmen and associate with these levels of competence additional compensation, incentives, and status.

SIGNIFICANCE FOR MARKETING

In summary, I see these seven points of increasing concern to corporate-level marketing management:

1. Increased attention on selling as the personal force in the total marketing effort.
2. More research on concepts, principles, methods, and techniques of personal salesmanship.
3. Positive strategy to offset "Willie Loman" stereotype.
4. Organizational changes designed to speed information flow from and to action points in the market place.
5. The evolution of new and improved observational and inquiry methods which salesmen can use for gauging business potential.
6. The translation of marketing knowledge into application terms for use by the sales force.
7. More precise cost-revenue analysis applied to markets, products, channels, and promotion.

Advertising focuses on the pretransactional phase as a market cultivating force. However advertising may also be used effectively during the posttransactional time period of a marketing program. Personal selling's major importance lies in the transactional phase. Differences and similarities between these two basic marketing activities are presented, and specific suggestions for the effective use of advertising are discussed.

62. COMPARISON OF ADVERTISING AND SELLING*

Harold C. Cash† and W. J. E. Crissy‡

Advertising, like selling, plays a major role in the total marketing effort of the firm. The degree to which each is important depends upon the nature of the goods and the market being cultivated. In the industrial

* Reprinted from "Comparison of Advertising and Selling," *The Salesman's Role in Marketing, The Psychology of Selling*, Vol. 12 (1965), pp. 56–75.

† Personnel Development Associates.

‡ Michigan State University.

product field, personal selling is generally the major force. Here the nature of the goods often requires specific application information that is best presented in person by the salesman. The dollar value of the order generally makes it economically feasible to finance this more effective and expensive method of presentation. Comparable effort to sell a box of soap powder to the housewife would be a ridiculous extravagance. On the other hand, it is likely that personal selling will be used to get this consumer product into the channels of distribution—through the wholesaler or chain store buying organization.

The person-to-person two-way communication of personal selling makes it a superior means of selling every time. Advertising by contrast is only a one-way communication system and is necessarily generalized to fit the needs of many people. Where the unit value of the sale is small, however, advertising is more economical. For example, a full page advertisement in an issue of *Life* magazine, which costs upward of $30,000 will deliver the message at a rate of less than ½ cent per copy. And since, on an average, about 4 persons read each copy, message exposure per reader is in the neighborhood of ⅛ cent per copy-reader. A full-color page advertisement provides exposure for about ⅙ cent per copy-reader. Of course, not every reader is likely to see a particular advertisement but even if only 25% of the exposures capture attention, the cost is minute. Comparable costs of message delivery apply to radio, T.V. and other mass media. Recent figures indicate a total of $31.31 as the cost of a typical sales call when all expenses are considered.

The worth of the sales call and an advertising impression is not likely to be equal. If the prospect is serious and has sincere interest in the proposal, the sales call is definitely worthwhile. If, on the other hand, the prospect is not nearly ready to place an order, a reminder of the existence of the product or services in the form of an advertisement would have been more economical.

Generally speaking, advertising needs additional support, either through personal selling or through promotional activities, to effect the sale. In most cases, its basic function is in the demand-cultivation area. Hence it is more significant in the pretransactional phase of marketing. There are, of course, instances where advertising alone makes the sale, as in the case of mail-order selling. This channel, however, represents only a very small volume of total sales in any year. To a lesser extent, advertising can help in the posttransactional area of demand-fulfillment by providing a rationalization to the purchaser after the buying decision has been made.

Advertising can be thought of in many ways. Perhaps, however, the most useful perspective to take is in terms of primary objectives. Most advertising is aimed at inducing purchase of a particular brand of product. Sometimes this is referred to as preselling since the aim is to lead the person to the transactional stage, even though the transaction itself is not accomplished. This type of advertising is essentially competitive.

There are many things that can be accomplished through advertising. Perhaps the most obvious is to create an awareness of, an interest in, or demand for a product. When fluoride was added to toothpaste, large-scale advertising was conducted to let customers know that the product was available. Concurrently, the sales organization obtained distribution in retail outlets so that customers could acquire the product. It is doubtful that many sales could be accomplished without the advertising program. The alternative to advertising would be to have retail store personnel personally sell the toothpaste to customers. This is not feasible because the unit sale is too low to support the salary and expense of a sales person. In this sense, advertising paves the way for the salesman because, without the promise of a huge advertising and promotion campaign, retailers would not cooperate in finding display space. It has been said "Salesmen put products on shelves and advertising takes them off."

Less frequently, advertising is used to introduce an entirely new idea. The educational effort may be underwritten by a single company or, where there are a number of producers in the field, it may be the cooperative effort of the industry. Here the advertising is designed to win for the industry a share of the consumer's dollar. Again it is a preselling activity. Such advertising is often called "pioneering" as contrasted with "competitive" advertising.

Many advertisements are aimed at reinforcing the product name or brand in the minds of the buying public. This may be considered as reminder advertising. It is normally used when a product has a dominant share of the market and cannot expect to attain any marked increase in volume within the economic limits of the extra promotional cost.

Some advertisements are primarily designed to convey a favorable image of the company as a good firm with which to do business. This institutional or public relations advertising is used by public utilities and major corporations which have an important stake in gaining a favorable public acceptance.

It is not unusual for a single advertisement to attempt to achieve a combination of these objectives.

As was noted before, generally speaking, advertising plays a more significant role in the marketing of consumer goods than it does in the case of industrial products. This is particularly true with respect to contact with the end users. However, even consumer goods depend to a significant extent on personal selling to move them through the channels.

When the item represents a substantial outlay and when there are complexities to be explained to the prospect, obviously, personal contact is both practical and necessary. Advertising for such goods, however, is often used in specialized media for the purpose of generating leads for the field sales force.

When goods flow through indirect channels, advertising grows in complexity. It may be used to cultivate demand on the part of the ultimate users through nationally distributed media. It may also be used in selected specialized media to encourage the various intermediaries to stock the merchandise.

When advertising is used with industrial products, it has different functions. As mentioned above, one function is to generate leads for salesmen. It is common for the advertisement to carry a coupon. When the coupon is received at the home office, it is relayed to the salesman covering that territory who then makes a sales call.

A second function of the advertising of industrial products is to keep the name of the company and product before the customers between sales calls. Good advertising also reassures a customer that he is buying from a good supplier. The advertising adds prestige to the product, the company, and the salesman, especially when it equals or excels that of competitors.

When a company has a substantial advertising program, salesmen can use tear sheets of the advertisements to good advantage. These can appropriately be shown to both prospects and customers. With prospects, consideration should be given to leaving copies of the advertisements as they create a feeling of stability and solidity with regard to the supplier. When prospects see advertisements, normally in the trade press, this paves the way for salesmen.

In a well organized and disciplined industrial sales force, there will be a similarity between the content of the advertisement and the sales presentation. Thus the advertisement and the sales call reinforce each other.

Many products must be used in a certain way to produce the desired results. Complaints arise when the product does not fulfill the salesman's claims. Advertising can carry instructions on using the product. This will help to insure satisfactory performance. If the product has already been used inappropriately, the advertising may cause the customer to understand the poor performance and give it another chance. In this way, it holds customers that might otherwise be lost.

SIMILARITIES AND DIFFERENCES BETWEEN ADVERTISING AND SELLING

From the viewpoint of communications, advertising and selling have much in common. Both must meet four criteria. They need to be *understandable*, *interesting*, *believable*, and *persuasive* if they are to achieve their purpose. There are, however, some noteworthy differences. Communication through advertising is one-way. In contrast, selling is uniquely two-way. There is an inherent weakness in advertising—"*noise*." This is likely to be present in greater amounts in advertising than in the case of the sales interview where misunderstandings can be cleared up on the spot. Whatever the medium being used, advertising must compete with other messages. For example, in a magazine the ad competes with surrounding editorial copy. The message conveyed by the salesman does not compete with other messages, at least at the time of the presentation.

Advertising may be used to generate either primary or selective demand; for example, an industry group may collaborate on its advertising with a view to enlarging the total market. In contrast, selling is aimed invariably at selective demand, that is, preference for the products and services being sold by the particular company over those available from competitors.

From the standpoint of persuasion, a sales message is far more flexible, personal, and powerful than an advertisement. An advertisement is normally prepared by persons having minimal personal contact with customers. The message is designed to appeal to a large number of persons. By contrast, the message in a good sales presentation is not determined in advance. The salesman has a tremendous store of knowledge about his product or service and selects appropriate items as the interview progresses. Thus the salesman can adapt his message to the thinking and needs of the customer or prospect *at the time of the sales call.* Furthermore, as objections arise and are voiced by the buyer, the salesman can treat the objections in an appropriate manner. This is not possible in advertising.

Company control over the advertising message is more complete than over a sales presentation. When an advertisement is prepared, it is submitted for the approval of all interested executives before it is released to the media. Thus there is little likelihood of any discrepancy between company policy and the content of the advertisement. In theory, salesmen receive training so that they understand the product or service and company policy. With the best possible training program, there are two possible sources of error or bases for deviation from company doctrine. One is loss of memory. Salesmen just cannot remember everything they are told. Also, they may meet situations that are unforeseen, and their reaction may not be identical with what the company management would specify if the problem were referred to them.

There is little a prospect can do to avoid a well planned advertising campaign. With the number of media available, he is almost certain to be exposed to one or more advertising messages. Buyers can refuse to see salesmen. When the salesman arrives at the premises of the buyer's company, he is subject to the will of the buyer as to whether he enjoys an interview. Thus, over a period of time, advertising will bring the product to the attention of persons who would be missed by salesmen.

Perceptual Similarities and Differences

In terms of perceptual process, there are also similarities. Both must penetrate the sensory mechanisms of the customer or prospect if they are to be effective. With both, careful selection of the stimuli to be presented is important. However, significant differences do exist from the standpoint of perception.

In selling, it may be possible to enlist not only the senses of vision and audition, but taste, smell, and the tactual senses as well. Time and space restraints on advertising limit the number and array of stimuli that can be presented. In selling, it is possible to vary the stimuli and to apply them as the salesman deems appropriate. Actual time duration of an ad generally limits the opportunity to summate and reinforce the message. In contrast, during the sales interview, frequent repetition and reinforcement are possible. In most instances, advertising commands less full attention than does selling. This limits the number of concepts that can be conveyed and places a high premium on careful construction of the ad copy and selection of the illustrations. In the case of the "commercial" on radio or television, few opportunities for reinforcement are possible within the ad itself. The salesman, too, must have a well planned presentation. However, it can be varied and adjusted as the sales interview progresses. Further, the salesman on the spot is able to re-arrest attention when he detects it is waning. This is not possible with an advertisement.

Cognitive Similarities and Differences

In terms of cognitive process, both advertising and selling are designed to induce favorable thoughts toward the company, its products and services, and its people. Both are aimed at conveying an image of *different* and *better vis-à-vis* competition. Advertising is far more limited than selling in influencing thought process. A relatively small number of ideas can be conveyed by an ad. There is no way to check on understanding. In the sales interview, the ideas and concepts can be tailored to the understanding of the prospect or customer. Because advertising employs mass media, the message must often be geared to the less sophisticated segment of the readership or audience. In contrast, the salesman who is effective gears his message to the sophistication of the person with whom he is conversing. Only to a limited extent can advertising carry the person exposed to the message through a reasoning process about the product or service. Instead, suggestion must be utilized.

In contrast, the salesman is able to employ suggestion or reasoning as the sales interview progresses, depending upon the perception of his message on the part of the customer or prospect. In the case of relatively complex products and services, the most that can be hoped for from advertising is a whetting of the prospect's appetite for more information. Questions can be raised but relatively few answers can be provided. In the case of those same goods and services, the salesman is able to cope with problems and questions at first hand. In fact, in some instances he plays an important role as a problem-solver for the prospective customer.

Feeling State Similarites and Differences

Advertising and selling both try to induce favorable feelings. In the case of selling the salesman himself becomes an important determiner of the customer's feeling state by the manner in which he conducts himself while he is with him. In advertising, too, it is important to induce a favorable feeling state or mood in order to provide more favorable receptivity to the message itself. This may be attempted directly within the ad by means of pleasant illustrations, anticipatory enjoyment attending the use of the product, emotional words, phrases, analogies and comparisons. This is accomplished less directly, where the medium permits it, by the entertainment bonus preceding and following the ad, as in the case of a television show or a radio program. In the case of printed media, the surrounding editorial copy may be employed to set the mood. Even with these direct and indirect efforts, it is unlikely that any advertisement meets the objective of emotional reinforcement with all those who are exposed to the message. In fact, what may please one person may annoy another. Paradoxically, there is some research evidence from the radio field that if an ad doesn't please the person it is next best to have it annoy him rather than to leave him in a neutral feeling state.

Selling, in contrast, has a tremendous advantage in the domain of feelings. The salesman in the first few seconds of face-to-face contact gauges the mood of the other person and adjusts his own behavior accordingly. Further, if he detects an unfavorable feeling state he may provide the other individual the opportunity to vent his feelings, or he may, in an extreme case, decide to withdraw and call on a more favorable occasion. This option is not open to the advertiser.

Advertising permits the firm far less control over the ultimate buying decision than does selling. The person exposed to the ad may turn the page or spin the dial, or walk out of the room. In contrast, once a salesman has gained entry, if he is effective, he is likely to be able to make a reasonably full presentation of the sales message.

Transactional Similarities and Differences

If the market is viewed as having the three phases . . . , *pretransactional*, *transactional*, and *posttransactional*, it is evident that advertising fits mainly in the pretransactional phase as a market cultivating force. It may also enter into the posttransactional phase by providing a rationalization to the purchaser. Only in rare instances does it accomplish the transaction itself. In contrast, selling is of importance in all three phases. (Figure 1.)

Advertising may be viewed as readying the market for the salesman's personal efforts. Even with carefully selected media and well-conceived

FIGURE 1

Relative Importance of Advertising and Selling

Market Phase

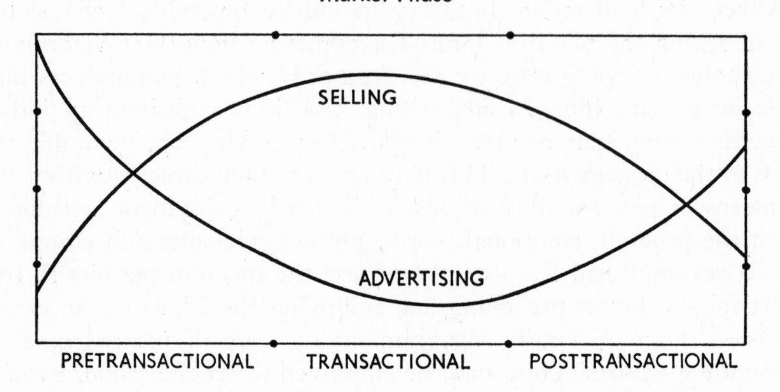

advertising, the strategy employed must be relatively general. In the case of selling, not only can strategy be formulated for each account and each decision maker in the account, but tactical adjustments can be made on the spot in order to influence those accounts.

SALESMAN'S USE OF ADVERTISING

Even though the salesman may not be directly involved in planning and formulating the advertising campaign of his firm, he certainly must be aware of the company's advertising plans, the media in which the advertisements are appearing, and the objectives that are being sought. If this information is not being furnished to him, it is legitimate for the salesman to request it. It can be very embarrassing to have a customer or prospect refer to an ad of which the salesman is unaware. The astute salesman is not only aware of his own company's ads, but he is also observant of the advertising done by competitors. The latter is often an important input for his own selling strategy. . . .

Certainly if the demand cultivation of the compay is to be coordinated, there must be a congruency between the content of the advertising and the salesman's presentations to customers and prospects. If this is accomplished, the summation principle discussed in Volume 2 can be effectively utilized. Temporally, the exposure to the advertisements plus the periodic sales calls combine to reinforce the message. From a spatial summation standpoint the ads plus the sales messages bring to bear a varied array of stimuli on the customer and prospect.

Many companies accomplish this mutual reinforcement of advertising and selling by furnishing the sales force with selling aids, reprints and tear sheets of advertisements from printed media. If this is done, the salesman has a direct means of reinforcing his oral presentation with advertising copy. Further, he is able to leave copies of ads as reminders to the persons called on.

When such ads are taken from prestige media they contribute to the building of a favorable image of the salesman's company. Sometimes local spot advertisements on radio and television make specific references such as "advertised in *Life* (or *Time*, or some other medium)" as an attempt to build up the prestige of the product and the company. The salesman accomplishes the same result with effective use of reprints and tear sheets.

The salesman is in a prime position to gauge the effectiveness of advertising. He is able to determine by inquiry how many of his customers and prospects have actually seen or heard the ad. By judicious questioning he also can learn of their reactions to the ads. This provides management useful feedback. He also may be able to suggest changes that will render the advertising more effective.

If suggestions are to be meaningful to management and the personnel who work on the advertising program, they must be in sufficient detail so that they can understand the reasoning of the salesman who submits them. They should include the following kinds of information:

1. Specific reasons why the campaign was not maximally successful. This should be supported by comments or behavior of customers and other interested parties, not merely an opinion of the salesman.
2. Sales figures which are directly related to the advertising campaign. If advertising mats are supplied, a comparison of the relative use of mats with those of other campaigns may be appropriate.
3. Comparisons can be made with competitive advertisers in the local area. In this case, samples of the competitive advertising should be submitted along with comments.

The foregoing observations should relate primarily to large scale print or broadcast media. In the case of dealer aids and point-of-purchase materials, the salesman is in an even stronger position to offer sound criticism. He can give first-hand reports of the ease with which display stands could be erected. He can report dealers' reactions to the materials and, even better, tally the actual use of the materials. When the materials have not been well received, he can inquire into the reasons for the poor reception and pass the information through the proper channels. It is perfectly proper for a salesman to state his opinion as well as the data he has collected, but to preserve his intellectual honesty and make his ideas more useful to management and advertising personnel, he should indicate which ideas are his own and which are opinions or behavior of dealers and customers.

Salesmen who wish to have their ideas considered should find out when advertising campaigns are in a formative stage and submit their ideas so that they can be considered before the final ideas have been selected for development.

Lead Generators

Advertising containing a coupon or a request to write to a box number or to phone may be a useful lead generating device for the salesmen. An important caution: Such leads must be carefully screened before an appreciable investment of time and effort is made. A recent study of leads generated through reader service cards in a trade magazine indicated that only ten to twelve per cent were bona fide prospects for the goods offered. The remainder were curiosity seekers, literature collectors, and high school students.

In some sales situations, an added value expected by the reseller is assistance from the salesman with his own advertising. In such instances, the salesman must be knowledgeable on the actual principles, methods and techniques of advertising. Usually, however, if this is a job duty, his firm furnishes instructional materials and specimen ads for use directly or with some modification. To the extent that the salesman can convince the customer of the worthwhileness of advertising, he is likely to generate increased profitable business for himself. Some firms encourage their intermediaries to advertise by sharing the costs. When this is the policy, it becomes even more imperative for the salesman to be astute in his recommendations. He is investing his company's money in the suggestions he makes. Ideas expected of him may range from choice of media, size of advertisement, frequency of insert, optimum time, to co-ordination of the advertising with other promotional efforts.

Where indirect channels are employed, the salesman may be able to use his firm's national advertising program as a potent force in his sales presentation. He can demonstrate as a *value-added* that his company is applying a powerful, demand generating force on the ultimate user which will develop increased business for all intermediaries. This is the "push-pull" effect. In this connection, if the salesman has information concerning an impending campaign, this can become a means of creating increased business in anticipation of likely demand. Inadequate inventory or "stock-out" can be translated into a loss of profit for the reseller as well as an attendant loss of good-will by not having the merchandise available when the customer wants it.

SALESMEN'S ATTITUDES TOWARD ADVERTISING

A company's emphasis on advertising will vary depending on the nature of the product, the price, and the distribution of its customers. Salesmen's attitudes will vary with the relative importance of selling and advertising in the promotional mix. One common finding, however, is that salesmen tend to become critical of their own company's advertising.

In some instances, salesmen, especially those handling industrial goods, feel too much money is spent on advertising. There is no point in discussing this problem, except in a specific instance. It can be pointed out that a salesman in his territory seldom has all the facts necessary to decide on the proper ratio of advertising and selling. It may be that he is entitled to more facts but that is an internal management decision, not one for outsiders. The best assumption for a salesman to make is that his company has established sound marketing objectives and has selected the right tools to achieve them. If the salesman feels differently, he should offer constructive criticism or, in the extreme case, consider seeking other employment. (Few salesmen have any idea of the cost of advertising per prospect. While the figures cited earlier in this chapter apply to consumer mass media, the cost per reader of industrial media is not too much greater.)

The content of advertising messages is often criticized by salesmen. As salesmen are face to face with customers and prospects every day, they are in a good position to gauge the impact of the firm's advertising. This does not mean they should compose the advertising because, as in the case of the amount of advertising, the company may have some objectives not known to the salesmen. It may wish to use part of the budget to promote what the salesmen feel is a minor rather than a major product in the line. This could very well happen if the salesmen are not informed on the profitability of each item in the line. In any event, each salesman should back up the company advertising because, however little immediate value he sees in it, he is in a stronger position supporting the advertising than opposing it.

Another area of possible disagreement between salesmen and management may be the media used. When the number of available advertising and promotional media is considered (T.V., radio, magazines [general and trade], newspapers, direct mail, transportation [car cards], outdoor, point of purchase, and sampling), it is not surprising that there may be disagreement. Indeed, there have probably been prolonged and exhaustive discussions within the management group before the media decision was reached. There are specialists in advertising agencies to help in selecting appropriate media. The likelihood of salesmen making constructive suggestions in this area of advertising is minimal except for some local conditions which may not have come to the attention of those making the final decision.

SUMMARY

Advertising and selling play major roles in the total marketing effort of the firm. Advertising, however, focuses mainly on market cultivation, though it sometimes plays a part in the actual transaction, and with some frequency, in the posttransactional aspect of the marketing program. The most useful way for the salesman to view advertising is in terms of its three key objectives—to induce an intention to purchase, to keep the product or brand in conscious awareness in the market place, and to project a favorable image of the firm. Similarities and differences between advertising and selling are discussed in terms of communication, perception, thought-process, feelings, and degree of control. Specific suggestions are made for effective use of advertising by the salesman, as well as ways and means the salesman can employ for apprising his management of the impact of the company's advertising efforts and for suggesting ways of improving them.

Advertising effectiveness is a function of several marketing variables. This article discusses several of these variables, and evaluates the potential contribution of mathematical models to their understanding and manipulation. The model presented depicts the advertising implications of lagged advertising effects and habitual brand choice behavior by consumers of a seasonal product.

63. HOW ADVERTISING PERFORMANCE DEPENDS ON OTHER MARKETING FACTORS*

Alfred A. Kuehn†

The budgeting of advertising is frequently discussed as though the appropriation were independent of competitive behavior, product characteristics, price, retail distribution, and the habits of potential customers. An advertising budget is commonly set as a percentage of past or expected future sales, in relation to the advertising-to-sales ratio prevalent in the industry, or more recently, by estimating the expenditures required to achieve some desired sales or promotion objective.

Can we be more precise in our budgeting of advertising? Can mathematical models sharpen our thinking about the effects of advertising and guide advertising practice? How do consumer product preferences, price,

* Reprinted from "How Advertising Performance Depends on Other Marketing Factors," *Journal of Advertising Research,* Vol. 2, No. 1 (March, 1962), pp. 2–10.

† Carnegie Institute of Technology.

retail availability, and costs of production influence the payoff of advertising for competing brands of a product? How should advertising appropriations be allocated throughout the year for seasonal product classes? This paper will discuss these questions in some detail. It will outline results of research which appear to provide sound guides to advertising and merchandising policy for low priced, frequently purchased products distributed through retail grocery and drug outlets.

MATHEMATICAL MODELS

Mathematical model building has achieved prominence in recent years as a means of studying a wide range of complex problems: the effectiveness of military weapons systems, the design of nuclear reactors, production and inventory control in industrial operations, prediction of voting behavior, and the routing of vehicular traffic. In most of these applications, the value of model building has been demonstrated beyond doubt. In marketing and advertising the use of mathematical models has generally met with less success, perhaps because of the difficulty model builders encounter in understanding the total merchandising system. Moreover, some aspects of marketing appear to be more complicated than the problems solved by model builders in other areas of business. This may be misleading, however, since any problem understood and solved then appears simple.

I am personally convinced that working with models will help us understand the mechanisms underlying the marketing process and enable us to make better advertising and merchandising decisions. A sound foundation of research on the behavior of consumers and the interaction between merchandising variables is needed, however, to reach this goal. Care must be taken to weed out the unstated assumptions from the hypotheses and factual evidence. Results which at first appear reasonable are easy to achieve in model building; a more difficult task is to maintain internal consistency and to test the assumptions, implications, and predictions of the model. The latter requires concurrent empirical research. We are not likely to solve many advertising problems by theorizing alone. Nor, in my opinion, are we likely to solve the broader aspects of these problems until we take into account the interaction of a firm's advertising with other marketing factors.

To show how a model can help determine advertising policy, let us examine the budgeting implications of lagged (carry-over) effects of advertising and habitual brand-choice behavior by consumers for the purchase of a seasonal product.

TIMING OF ADVERTISING

Many products have a seasonal demand. Given this condition, how should a firm allocate its advertising appropriation throughout the year?

This problem has been studied for low-cost grocery products. Two aspects of the problem appear most significant.

1. *Advertising carry-over.* An advertising impulse is generally thought to have both immediate and delayed effects. Such evidence as is available suggests that the advertising impulse carries over to the future but decays with the passing of time. The rate of decay appears to vary with the type of advertising, sale-price advertising decaying rapidly, and institutional advertising declining more slowly (see Figure 1).

2. *Habitual behavior in customer choice of brands.* To what extent do consumers change their brand mix of purchases over time? There appears

FIGURE 1

Carry-Over Effects of Two Types of Advertising

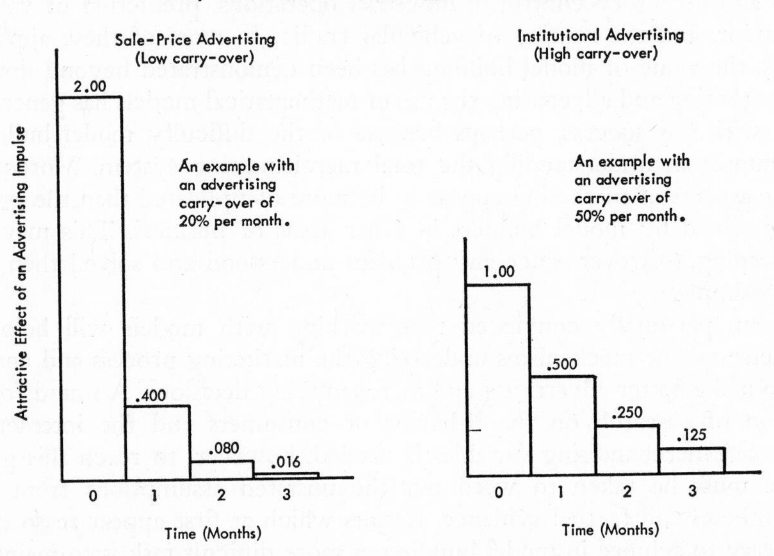

to be a high probability of a consumer's maintaining a relatively stable mix of brand purchases of grocery products from one month to the next. A study of frozen orange juice purchases indicated a decay rate in a consumer's brand purchase probability of approximately seven per cent per month, or a holdover due to habit, inertia or "brand loyalty" of about 93 per cent per month. This phenomenon is illustrated in Figure 2. Factors influencing the rate of decay include the extent to which consumers even consider buying brands which they do not currently purchase and the extent to which their evaluation of such products on trial purchases is influenced unfavorably by a predisposition to favor the well-known previously used brand.

Products with Habitual Brand Choice

Figure 3 shows a hypothetical seasonal sales curve together with three curves illustrating how firms should advertise in a competitive environment for various levels of advertising carry-over. The first curve shows the "optimal" advertising rate for the case assuming no advertising carry-over, the second assumes a 50 per cent carry-over from month to month, and the third curve assumes a 75 per cent carry-over. In each case it is also assumed that there is a high level of habitual purchasing in the choice of brand from month to month, namely, a 90 per cent holdover due to habit. Note that each of the advertising curves leads the sales curve: the greater the advertising carry-over the more the advertising cycle should lead the sales cycle. Note also that the amplitudes of the advertising cycles are very small relative to the sales cycle. Whereas the sales cycle at its peak is three times the level of the trough, the peak-to-trough ratio for the "optimal" advertising response by a firm

FIGURE 2

Effect of Habitual Buying Behavior upon a Consumer's Choice of Brands

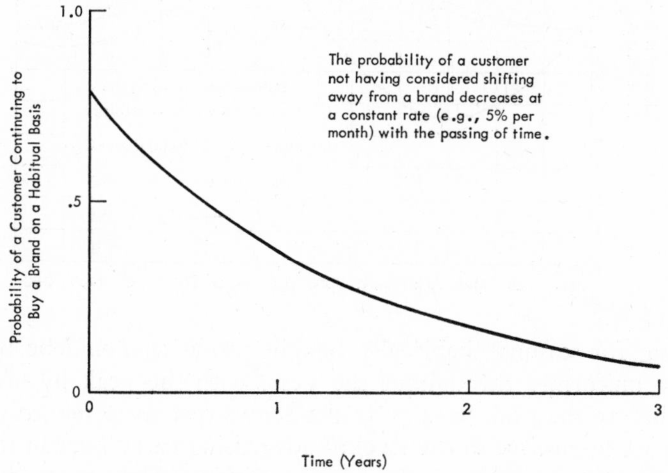

ranges from 1.25 (when there is no advertising carry-over) to 1.50 (when there is 75 per cent advertising carry-over). The ratio with 50 per cent advertising carry-over is 1.28, very close to that observed for no carry-over.

How can these "optimal" advertising curves help a merchandiser of grocery products budget his advertising? First we should recognize the meaning of the phrase "at competitive equilibrium" used in the title of Figure 3. This phrase reflects the assumption that each competitor in the market is independently budgeting his advertising expenditures at that level which will maximize his profits. This may not be true—perhaps some competitors are trying to maximize share of market, subject to certain profit constraints. If a firm's competitors were not to follow a policy consistent with maximizing profits, we could use the underlying advertising model to compute for the firm an "optimum" reaction to the advertising budgeting behavior established by competitors and, in general, obtain some relative advantage as a result. Only by outlining stated objectives for all competitors as we have done here with the assumption of competitive equilibrium, however, can we abstract generalized rules for advertising budgeting strategy from the model.

The "optimal" budgeting strategy illustrated in Figure 3 suggests that

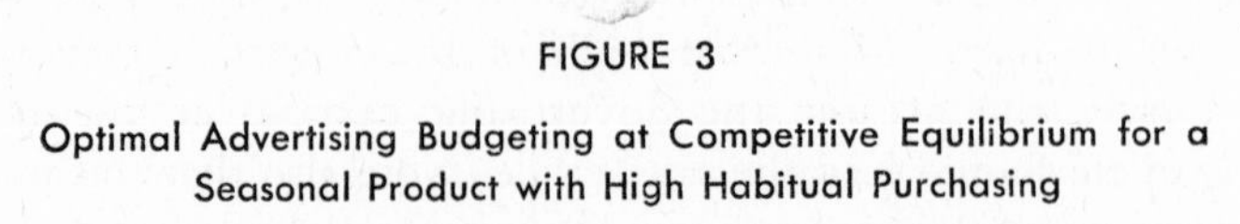

FIGURE 3

Optimal Advertising Budgeting at Competitive Equilibrium for a Seasonal Product with High Habitual Purchasing

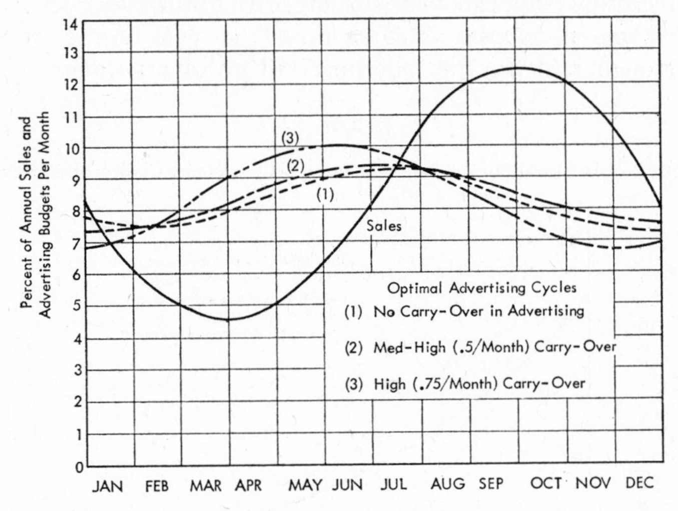

advertising for seasonal, habitually bought products *should* be budgeted relatively uniformly throughout the year, with the peak in advertising coming before the peak in sales. It also shows that these monthly appropriations are insensitive to the level of advertising carry-over in the range of 0 to 50 per cent per month, a range within which most advertising seems to lie.

Six additional assumptions underlie the above and subsequent analyses.

1. *Relationship of consumer planning-to-buy and purchase periods.* In the case of low-priced grocery and drug products there is apparently no substantial lag between a consumer's planning-to-buy and the actual purchase. Thus there is no need to determine the planning period during which time the consumer might decide upon the brand to be purchased, as distinct from the industry's sales period. This would probably not be true for major household appliances. If the planning period differs from the consumer purchase period, the sales curve should be replaced by a curve reflecting the brand *choice decisions* made in each time period.

2. *Price level throughout the sales cycle.* Gross margin from sales before advertising is assumed to be constant throughout the year. If it is not, the industry sales cycle should be replaced in the analysis by the

cycle of total gross margin potential for the firm, that is, industry sales multiplied by the firm's gross margin apart from advertising.

3. *Effect of advertising.* The sales cycle used in these analyses is assumed to be consistent with the advertising cycles computed for the industry. If the level of industry advertising influences total industry sales this assumption would be invalid. (However, if we were to know or assume some relationship as to the effect of industry advertising upon industry sales, a solution consistent with such a relationship could easily be computed.) For many established products, at least in the short run, it would appear that advertising has a greater effect in shifting consumers among brands than in influencing the level of total industry sales.

4. *The influence of other merchandising variables.* It is assumed that product characteristics, retail availability, and price of competing brands maintain a constant relative appeal to consumers throughout the sales cycle. In addition, the effectiveness of each firm's advertising is assumed to be constant throughout the year.

5. *Influence of advertising upon the retail trade.* These analyses consider the influence of advertising only on the consumer. Advertising also has a short term effect upon the availability of retail space for special displays. Since advertising intended to influence retailers (including consumer advertising) should be budgeted proportional to current sales, consideration of this aspect of the problem would result in a revised optimal advertising cycle, a weighted combination of the sales cycle and the advertising cycles computed here.

6. *Growth of the industry.* A stable industry is assumed in these analyses. Growth effects can be added, however, merely by increasing the plotted percentage budget of each month after the initial month by the rate of growth and renormalizing so that the sum of the percentages will again equal 100 per cent.

Products with Nonhabitual Brand Choice

In Figure 4 we see the same sales curve outlined in Figure 3, with three "optimal" advertising curves reflecting no advertising carry-over, 50 per cent carry-over, and 75 per cent carry-over from month to month. The difference between advertising curves in Figures 3 and 4 results from the assumption in Figure 4 that consumer brand choice is *not* influenced by habit. In the earlier analysis, it was assumed that 90 per cent of each brand's monthly sales reflect a continuation of habitual purchases from the previous month.

For what types or products is habitual brand choice low? Likely candidates are infrequently purchased items with a low level of brand identification, and products which the consumer can to some degree evaluate first-hand. Some industrial goods might also meet these qualifications.

In summary, the optimal advertising cycle under competitive equilibrium is identical to the sales cycle if there is no advertising carry-over and no habitual purchasing of brands. Both advertising carry-over and habitual behavior by customers results in the advertising cycle leading the sales cycle.

Increasing the level of habitual purchasing by brand within a product

FIGURE 4

Optimal Advertising Budgeting at Competitive Equilibrium for a Seasonal Product with No Habitual Purchasing

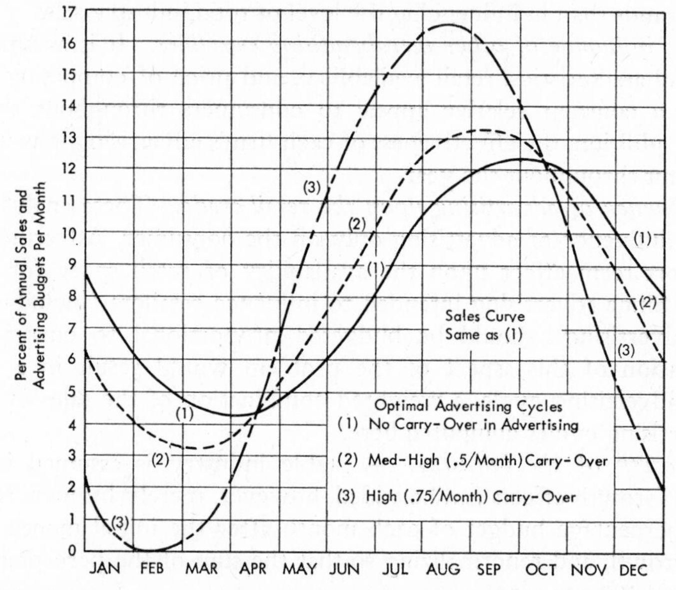

NOTE: The advertising curve assuming no advertising carry-over and no habit is identical to the sales curve. The curve for 25 per cent advertising carry-over, not shown here, deviates very little from this sales curve. Note also that the 50 per cent and 75 per cent curves increase progressively in amplitude and, to a lesser extent, with respect to the lead time of the advertising cycle relative to sales. The advertising cycle observed for a 25 percent per month level of habitual behavior deviate only slightly from those presented above, having somewhat smaller amplitudes and increased lead times of about a week with respect to sales.

class serves to *decrease* the amplitude of the "optimal" advertising cycles. In contrast, an *increase* in advertising carry-over results in an *increase* in the seasonal amplitude of advertising.

COSTS, PRICES, QUALITY, AND DISTRIBUTION

Many variables influence the profitability of advertising, and thereby the "optimal" level of a firm's advertising appropriation. Some are: manufacturing and shipping costs, price and product characteristics relative to competition, the distribution and advertising expenditures of competitors, the relative effectiveness of each brand's advertising message and choice of media, price and advertising elasticities, and the growth rate of the industry coupled with the rate of return required on investments. Since so many variables influence the value of a firm's advertising, we are frequently on shaky ground when making broad generalizations for the budgeting of advertising. These same considerations also limit the value of certain techniques of market testing advertising.

Since the various elements of marketing activity and consumer behavior are closely entwined, it would seem to be risky to study advertising without incorporating all of these factors into our analysis. This can *be* done by first building a model of consumer purchasing behavior and the influence of merchandising variables. Such a model might then be evaluated empirically, with respect to both its assumptions and its predictions. In addition, the theoretical implications of the model can be examined. I have attempted to construct such a model, much of which is contained in an earlier paper, "A Model for Budgeting Advertising" (Kuehn, 1961). More recently, the complete model has been incorporated in the Carnegie Management Game and in the C.I.T. Marketing Game for use as an educational tool and in research. The results outlined earlier for seasonality in advertising are included in this model. Similarly, the comments which follow are consistent with it and represent my current understanding of the interaction of advertising with other market variables.

Price and Retail Availability

Most advertising models ignore price and retail availability. Such models in effect assume price and retail availability to be equal for all brands. They also generally assume that no consumers would be attracted to an unadvertised brand. But we all know of the success of unadvertised brands whose appeal to potential customers is based primarily upon their price and retail availability. Given such assumptions within a model, price and availability would not be likely to appear as variables in the resulting advertising decision rules derived therefrom.

In practice, competing brands do differ in retail availability. These differences are accentuated when we recognize that shelf space, location and special displays affect brand availability as much as does its mere presence in the retail outlet. There may also be differences in price. How do these factors influence the profitability of advertising?

Sales gain resulting from increased advertising expenditures is generally correlated with the availability of the brand. On the other hand, advertising can be an effective vehicle for obtaining increased distribution, shelf space and special displays. Consequently, we get some insight with respect to the classic problem of where to allocate additional funds for a brand: to areas where it is doing poorly? or to areas in which it is selling well?

Briefly, increased advertising where the brand is relatively strong generally appears to be more profitable in the short run, unless the brand is already near its maximum potential penetration of the consumer market.

Expenditures in areas where the brand is weak must generally be looked upon as investment spending directed at obtaining distribution and shelf position. And these activities will succeed only if the balance of the sales program is closely coordinated with them. How frequently has a firm wasted its advertising or promotional budgets by failing to utilize its sales force concurrently to sell the retailer?

In allocating advertising dollars to regional or metropolitan markets, planners frequently must decide whether to allocate extra funds to some areas at the expense of others. Generally, however, they find it difficult to temporarily withdraw funds from areas in which a brand is doing poorly since they see the problem as one of survival. Under such circumstances, *pulsation* in advertising or promotion coordinated with sales force efforts, offers better prospects of profits and gains in distribution than a continuous dribble of advertising. In many such cases, it would also appear desirable to withdraw funds from some territories to concentrate on others, a result contrary to that suggested by most advertising models. By concentrating on a few markets, a brand frequently has a better chance of forcing distribution and increasing its over-all short term profitability, thereby obtaining the means for subsequent investment expenditures in other territories. It can be expensive to hold one's own in every market simply as a matter of principle, especially if this prevents the brand becoming firmly established and profitable in any one region.

A brand with greater retail availability than its competitors will tend to have a favorable differential in consumer response to its advertising. Such an advantage can generally be translated into a somewhat greater profit differential, all other factors being equal. For example, if one brand in a two-brand market were to have twice the availability of its competitor (i.e., a situation in which the first brand would outsell the second by a 2:1 ratio if price and sales promotion levels were equal), its profitability at competitive equilibrium would be 2½ times that of its comparable rival given an inter-brand price elasticity of four. The relative increase in profits for the first firm under conditions of competitive equilibrium would be a result of increased advertising expenditures by the firm due to its stronger retail distribution.

A decrease in price also improves consumer response to the brand's advertising. However, a reduced unit profit due to the lower price accompanies the increased response to advertising. Thus, only if a firm has lower costs than its competitors should it price below competition at equilibrium. If a brand has both lower costs and certain advantages in terms of basic product attributes, however, it should in most cases apply its added gross margin to increased advertising and sales promotion rather than to price cutting. In general, a brand with *product* advantages as well as *lower* costs would charge a premium *price* under conditions of competitive equilibrium.

Competitive Advertising

The effect of competitive advertising on a brand's optimal advertising budget depends on the relative strength of the brand's appeal to consumers in terms of its product attributes, price, and retail availability *as well as* on the effectiveness of its advertising story and its choice of media. If all competitors are about equal in these variables, we can easily compute the equilibrium price and advertising-promotion budgets in terms of the number of competitors (N), the industry price and advertising elasticities (η_p and η_a, respectively), the share-of-market price elasticity for brands (ϵ), the cost of manufacturing and distributing the product, and the probability (b_{pda}) of the consumer's brand choice being influenced in part by advertising or promotion:

$$\text{Price/unit} = \text{cost/unit} \cdot \frac{\eta_p + \epsilon(N-1)}{\eta_p + \epsilon(N-1) - N}$$

and

$$\begin{array}{c}\text{Sales}\\ \text{promotional}\\ \text{expense/unit}\end{array} = \text{cost/unit} \cdot \frac{\eta_a + b_{pda}(N-1)}{\eta_p + \epsilon(N-1) - N}$$

The industry price and advertising elasticities in the above expressions are consistent with the use of these concepts by economists. That is, all other factors being held constant, we have

$$D(p,a) = D(p_o,a_o)\left[\frac{p}{p_o}\right]^{-\eta_p}\left[\frac{a}{a_o}\right]^{\eta_a}$$

where $D(p,a)$ = industry demand at price p and advertising-promotion level a, where the industry price is the weighted average price of all brands in the market, each brand's contribution being weighted with respect to its share of market, and $D(p_o,a_o)$ = industry demand at some base price level p_o and base advertising-promotion level a_o.

Thus an increase in industry price or a decrease in industry advertising expenditures will decrease industry demand. The larger the absolute values of the price and advertising elasticities, η_p and η_a, the greater is the sensitivity of industry demand to changes in industry price and sales promotional expenditures.

The term b_{pda}, which represents the probability of a consumer's choice of a brand being influenced by advertising, has no direct counterpart in economic theory. In effect, at any given time the market can be treated as being divided into two segments; the first contains $(1 - b_{pda}) \cdot 100\%$ of the market and is influenced only by the effects of price, product characteristics and retail availability; the second contains $b_{pda} \cdot 100\%$ of the market and is influenced by advertising *in interaction with* price, product characteristics and availability. Thus if b_{pda} is near 0, advertising will affect only a small portion of the market. But if b_{pda} is near 1, competitive advertising will influence virtually all consumers. Product classes in which the customer either cannot or will not evaluate the brands in terms of their intrinsic merits have high values of b_{pda}. This reflects the ability of advertising to project status, confidence, or other desirable attributes to the product.

The share of market price elasticity (ϵ) for brands also deviates from the economists' treatment of cross-product elasticity except in certain limiting cases. As noted in the above discussion of advertising, price has influence in both market segments. In each segment, the relative attraction of each brand in terms of the combined effects of product characteristics, retail availability and, in the b_{pda} segment, advertising appeals, is modified (multiplied) by its relative price appeal computed as $\frac{p_i - \epsilon}{\Sigma p_i - \epsilon}$. This might be thought of as "share of price appeal," the numerator being the brand's price taken to the negative power of the share of market elasticity, the denominator being the same term summed over all brands. Note that an increase in the price of a brand, all other brands holding price constant, will reduce its share of market. The greater the elasticity ϵ, the higher the brand shifting sensitivity of the market to the relative prices of competing brands.

The share of market price elasticity generally ranges between three and six, while the industry price elasticity is on the order of two or less. It follows that the equilibrium relationships indicated above suggest two things. First, the industry equilibrium level for pricing and promotional expenditures is much more sensitve to ϵ than to η_p. Second, the industry price elasticity plays a minor role in determining prevailing prices when several firms are competing in the market. Similarly, the effect of advertising on brand shifting, represented by b_{pda} ranging from 0 to 1, generally tends to influence prevailing industry advertising levels for mature products more than does the industry advertising elasticity η_a, whose value is frequently on the order of 1/10.

In practice, individual competitors might be expected to deviate from these competitive equilibrium values, either because of goals other than profit maximization, the lack of price competition, or because of the absence of sound guides for implementing an appropriate budgeting policy. To evaluate the implications of such deviations from profit maximizing behavior by competitors, let us consider two promotional counter-strategies suggested by the decision rules derived from the merchandising model:

1. *Suboptimal advertising expenditures by competitors.* If all members of an industry are about equal with respect to operating costs, product appeal, retail distribution and promotional effectiveness, and if one's competitors *underspend* on advertising and other forms of sales

promotion, then the firm could increase its profit by also spending less than the equilibrium rate. The optimal size of its reduction would be *less*, however, than that of the firm or firms initiating the underspending.

2. *Excessive advertising expenditures by competitors.* If a firm's brand is equal in costs, product quality, distribution, and advertising effectiveness to its competitors, and the latter *overspend* on advertising, the firm could increase its profit by reducing its expenditures below equilibrium. To do so, however, would also increase the competitors' profits and, on balance, competition would gain a relative advantage. Consequently it may be desirable here to compete with overspending by also overspending, reducing the profitability of the industry at least temporarily, but hopefully bringing one's competitors to their senses.

Note that a firm operating at a competitive disadvantage in terms of costs or product appeal cannot easily counter competitive overspending with an increased advertising budget. The weaker firm tends to be at the mercy of its stronger competitor. Insofar as the stronger firm is willing to absorb some reduction in profit, it can keep a weaker competitor "on the ropes" by overspending, or by engaging in more advertising research to improve its promotional effectiveness. If the weaker firm counters by overspending, it helps dig its own grave. Interestingly enough, the share of market held by a firm does not necessarily indicate its competitive strength. Under many conditions the model suggests that the stronger firm, to maximize its profits, should permit its weaker rivals to maintain a significant share of the market. The underdog position of the rivals is, however, fully apparent when profits are compared.

SUMMARY AND CONCLUSIONS

The above model decision rules do not make decision-making easy or contradict our thinking about optimal strategy. Instead, they quantify relationships generally discussed only in qualitative terms. By making explicit our assumptions about market behavior and examining their consequences, we can test and thereby understand advertising phenomena. The use of such models does not eliminate the need for managerial judgment, but rather assists it by providing a new set of reference points.

The model from which these results were derived is relatively complex when viewed in its entirety. This research was begun some seven years ago with a very simple model—a model which has been modified and extended repeatedly in the light of additional evidence. As a result of these experiences, I now feel reasonably confident that a very simple model cannot hope to portray the intricacies of marketing processes. This is not to say that we cannot gain insight from simple models, but rather that we must be very careful that the factors these models ignore do not have a large effect upon the specific problem being studied. Only rarely do we get sound decisions from a model whose assumptions are not in tune with reality.

Because of the complexities of consumer behavior and the merchandising process, it is difficult to state widely applicable marketing decision rules for the guidance of management. The simplicity of the above solution for the seasonality of advertising budgets, for example, holds only when there is stability in the relative distribution, product attractiveness, and price of competing brands. And the effectiveness of each brand's advertising message and choice of media must be constant throughout the year. When these conditions are not met, we can still determine a firm's optimal budget in terms of the expected changes in these variables, but the results cannot be easily generalized. To date we have not been able to derive simple equilibrium decision rules for market situations in which there are more than two types of firms, that is, n_1 brands having one set of product, cost and distribution characteristics, and n_2 brands each having another common set of characteristics. The generalized rules available to us today are of limited value in practice. They serve to outline the broad aspects of the problem but, to solve any specific marketing problem, we must revert to the underlying detailed model.

What about the limitations of the model? First, there are difficulties in estimating some of the parameters and variables of the model. For example, it is not clear that we will ever be able to estimate very adequately the industry advertising and price elasticities. This being the case, we cannot make much practical use of the model in what appears to most marketing executives to be the simplest type of market—the situation in which a single brand virtually controls an entire product class. Our inability to estimate these parameters precisely is not a problem, however, in studying markets with multiple-brand entries. Here the industry elasticities have only a very minor influence upon optimal merchandising decisions.

We must reckon with other inadequacies in the model. For example, we know little of the effect of advertising and sales force activity, along with the brand's share of market, in obtaining retail distribution and shelf space for a brand. The problem is accentuated by the fact that we do not yet have a good measure of the effects of display space and location upon retail sales. I have attempted to make plausible assumptions, where necessary, to incorporate these aspects of the marketing process into the C.I.T. Marketing Game. Future research, both empirical field studies and analyses within the framework of this game, should enable us to evaluate these relationships and incorporate improvements into the model. Such untested portions of the model require us to exercise extreme care in its application.

The model cannot be used mechanically. Analyses of the sensitivity of decisions to the untested assumptions are generally required. In some instances, these gaps in the model can be filled by management's judgmental estimates. This is often feasible because management is required to estimate only competitive ratios (e.g., the effectiveness of our advertising copy relative to that of competition) rather than absolute levels.

An interesting sidelight of this research is its implications for the field testing of advertising campaigns. It suggests that controlled market by market testing contains a variety of pitfalls. For example, it is *not sufficient* that we "control" market conditions throughout the period of the test, assuming that such control is in fact possible. We must also know the *level* at which each of the variables is being controlled. This suggests, as a minimum, that we would have to match territories.

A more promising approach is to build a model of the marketing process, obtain the needed market measures through continuous monitoring, and evaluate these market activity data regularly by estimating the parameters required to determine the effectiveness of competitive strategy. Is this far in the future? I don't think so. Will the costs of monitoring the market be too high? Not once we know how to use these data in developing improved marketing decisions.

Models will grow in importance as guides to marketing management. They will not, however, take over management's role, or preclude creative approaches to merchandising. All they can do is help direct management toward better use of the firm's resources. The ultimate success of a brand will still depend upon how well its total marketing program meets the physical and psychological needs of the consumer.

REFERENCE

KUEHN, ALFRED A. "A Model for Budgeting Advertising," in Frank M. Bass *et al.*, eds., *Mathematical Models and Methods in Marketing*. Homewood, Ill.: Richard D. Irwin, Inc., 1961.

Bibliography—Chapter VI

BACKMAN, JULES (ed.). *Price Practices and Price Policies.* New York: Ronald Press Co., 1953.

BARGER, HAROLD. *Distribution's Place in the American Economy Since 1896.* Princeton, N.J.: Princeton University Press, 1955.

BARTELS, ROBERT. *Credit Management.* New York: The Ronald Press Company, 1967.

BECKMAN, THEODORE N. *Credits and Collections: Management and Theory.* 7th ed. New York: McGraw-Hill Book Co., Inc., 1962.

BERG, THOMAS L. AND SHUCHMAN, ABE. *Product Strategy and Management.* New York: Holt, Rinehart & Winston, Inc., 1963.

BERLO, DAVID K. *The Process of Communication.* New York: Holt, Rinehart & Winston, Inc., 1960.

BOYD, HARPER W. JR., AND LEVY, SIDNEY J. *Promotion.* Englewood Cliffs, N.J.: Prentice-Hall, Inc., 1967.

BRINK, E. L., AND KELLEY, W. T. *The Management of Promotion.* Englewood Cliffs, N.J.: Prentice-Hall, Inc., 1963.

CLEWETT, RICHARD M. (ed.). *Marketing Channels.* Homewood, Ill.: Richard D. Irwin, Inc., 1954.

COX, REAVIS; GOODMAN, CHARLES S.; AND FICHANDLER, THOMAS C. *Distribution in a High-Level Economy.* Englewood Cliffs, N.J.: Prentice-Hall, Inc., 1965.

CRANE, EDGAR. *Marketing Communications: A Behavioral Approach to Men, Messages, and Media.* New York: John Wiley & Sons, Inc., 1965.

DUNCAN, DELBERT J., AND PHILLIPS, CHARLES F. *Retailing: Principles and Methods.* Homewood, Ill.: Richard D. Irwin, Inc., 1963.

EPPERT, RAY R. "Passport for World Markets," *Business Topics,* Vol. XIII, No. 4 (Autumn, 1965), pp. 7–17.

FRAM, EUGENE J. "Applications of the Marketing Concept to Retailing," *Journal of Retailing,* Vol. XLI, No. 2 (Summer, 1965), pp. 19–26.

HALL, EDWARD T. *The Silent Language.* Greenwich, Conn.: Fawcett Publications, Inc., 1959.

KATZ, ELIHU, AND LAZARSFELD, PAUL F. *Personal Influence: The Part Played By People in the Flow of Mass Communications.* Glencoe, Ill.: Free Press, Inc., 1957.

KLINE, CHARLES H. "The Strategy of Product Policy," *Harvard Business Review*, Vol. XXXIII, No. 4 (July–August, 1955), pp. 91–100.

LUCAS, DARRELL BLAINE, AND BRITT, STEUART H. *Measuring Advertising Effectiveness.* New York: McGraw-Hill Book Co., Inc., 1963.

REVZAN, DAVID A. *Wholesaling in Marketing Organizations.* New York: John Wiley & Sons, Inc., 1961.

ROBINSON, PATRICK J., AND LUCK, DAVID J. *Promotional Decision Making Practice and Theory.* New York: Marketing Science Institute, McGraw-Hill Book Co., Inc., 1964.

SMYKAY, EDWARD W.; BOWERSOX, DONALD J.; AND MOSSMAN, FRANK H. *Physical Distribution Management.* New York: The MacMillan Co., 1961.

TILLES, SEYMOUR. "How to Evaluate Corporate Strategy," *Harvard Business Review*, Vol. XLI, No. 4 (July–August, 1963), pp. 111–21.

WASSON, CHESTER R. "What is New About a New Product?" *Journal of Marketing*, Vol. XXV, No. 1 (July, 1960), pp. 52–56.

WEIGAND, ROBERT A. "The Management of Physical Distribution: A Dilemma," *Business Topics*, Vol. X, No. 3 (Summer, 1962), pp. 67–72.

VII. INTERNATIONAL MARKETING

Many dynamic forces are contributing to the new importance of international marketing. These include the emergence of trading blocs, the worldwide population explosion, changes in the distribution of the world's wealth and resources, technological change, urbanization, mobility, industrialization of the developing nations, and what has been termed the revolution of rising expectations. These forces are causing more firms to enter global markets in the search for profitable market opportunities.

In one sense, international marketing does not differ from domestic marketing; international marketing involves the same basic marketing tools, concepts, techniques, and know-how. Differences arise in terms of the applications of these fundamental domestic marketing practices to international markets, which are characterized by complex environmental differences and conditions.

Fundamental differences exist in the economic, cultural, and political systems encountered in different international markets. Each market has unique characteristics which influence marketing management decisions and policies. Marketing management must develop empathy with the outlook, needs, and desires of consumers in different international markets and must adapt its basic marketing concepts to the environment of these individual markets.

The purpose of this section is to identify and discuss a number of issues involved in the coordinating, planning, and controlling of international marketing activities. Methods are suggested for creating a more satisfactory international operation, including development of local national executives, better communication, sharing financial returns with the countries, and building markets. The growth of world markets makes it vital for marketing management to develop specific forward-looking plans to improve worldwide competitive effectiveness.

A. Management of International Marketing

Comparative marketing involves study of marketing systems, operations, and practices in various parts of the world. Geographic factors, economic elements, and human factors—the significant inputs of a national marketing system—are examined. Comparative marketing is embryonic in nature, and the tools and concepts of affiliated disciplines must be used to achieve understanding of global similarities and differences.

64. COMPARATIVE MARKETING*

David Carson†

Comparative marketing is one of a number of contemporary developments in the practice and study of marketing which has broadened its scope far beyond the basic processes of buying, selling, pricing, sales promotion, channel selections, and facilitating services. In addition to economics and the quantitative disciplines—long recognized as marketing's major foundations—useful insights into marketing structure and operations have also been gained in recent years from geography, and from politics, philosophy, sociology, anthropology, social psychology, history, and other social sciences. Comparative marketing involves the study of marketing systems, operations, and practices in various parts of the world, and it is therefore natural that it should avail itself of all needed skills, tools, and concepts to analyze and to relate common factors and

* Not previously published.

† Boston University.

differences. Without the aid of the affiliated disciplines, comparative marketing is likely to remain more descriptive than analytical, since marketing in various regions must be related in terms of such basic factors as social, economic, and political systems if one is to understand the reasons for the likenesses and differences.

Because of the embryonic nature of comparative marketing, any generalizations must necessarily be tentative, especially since they are frequently based upon data from economics, the quantitative disciplines, and the social sciences which themselves have a high degree of uncertainty. While this magnifies the tenuous nature of these generalizations, it should stimulate comparative marketing to keep in close touch with these basic disciplines so that comparative marketing will develop along with these affiliated fields, and its tentative generalizations acquire a surer footing.

A CONCEPT OF A NATIONAL MARKETING SYSTEM

Just as the major inputs of an individual firm may be considered as a trinity of physical assets, financial assets, and people, so the most significant inputs of a national marketing system may be conceived of as geographic factors, economic elements, and human factors. The human factors are the sum total of the nation's characteristics with reference to vital statistics, education, cultural patterns, social structure and relationships, ethnic configurations, psychological viewpoints, religious precepts, political beliefs and governmental systems, etc. Naturally there is a large degree of mutual interaction among the geographic, economic, and human factors. This analysis of inputs into the national marketing system will, nevertheless, focus on these three categories since they are fairly well defined entities.

GEOGRAPHIC FACTORS

Geographic features which exert a major influence on an area's marketing system include land topography, the availability and location of water surfaces, soil fertility, climate, and mineral resources. Nations with large undeveloped areas of land tend to have highly concentrated marketing centers, such as Iran. The growth of long-range transportation and communications enables a country's marketing system to become more highly integrated, as currently observed in the Soviet Union and in Australia. The United States, with its complex network for transferring goods and information, has largely overcome the physical barriers posed by vast mountain ranges and deserts. Great Britain, on the other hand, has had a rather closely integrated marketing system for several centuries, due to its small size, its high population density relatively well dispersed throughout the nation, and an absence of formidable geographic barriers.

Agricultural industrialization, often going hand in hand with a breakdown of traditional social patterns in rural areas, frequently drives multitudes of people from the hinterlands to the urban centers, sometimes swelling the population of the cities to enormous proportions within relatively short periods. While industrial development has enabled metropolitan areas to absorb many newcomers in an adequate manner at certain periods, more frequently these recent arrivals have been crowded into deteriorating neighborhoods or into newly constructed slums, greatly affecting the geographic patterns of marketing activities. Cities with a basic Latin culture have tended to reinforce the nuclear characteristics of their city centers, often because of the strategic locations of cathedrals and other major churches, of principal governmental buildings, and of residences of the elite. Newer industries and the mass of immigrants are likely to be dispersed to the cities' peripheries.

The dominant form of expansion for cities with basically Anglo-Saxon cultures, on the other hand, has been the movement of the upper classes to new communities on the cities' outskirts or in the suburbs, with the depressed elements within the city and recent immigrants replacing the upper classes in the downtown residential neighborhoods. The building of better retail facilities in the newer neighborhoods tends to be accompanied by the downgrading and even deterioration of the older city centers. This movement depends to some extent upon the availability of open land in the countryside, since shopping centers tend to be more prevalent in nations with low densities of population, such as Canada, Australia, and the United States. Yet such new retail centers may also be found in relatively smaller numbers in West Germany, Great Britain, and Switzerland. In still other areas, urban districts tend to be defined more along ethnic lines, and while minor shifts may take place within these "quarters," the boundaries of the districts themselves may not change appreciably for decades. Bangalore, India, is such a city.

The location of large factories is usually more dependent upon geographic relationships to supply and distribution points than to specific urban neighborhoods, assuming the availability of employees, power, and transportation facilities within the metroplitan area. In many industries smaller plants are concentrated in specific neighborhoods, with many of their suppliers clustered about them. Smaller manufacturers and wholesalers in turn often locate close to the major retail centers of cities, further extending the symbiotic market relationships.

In addition to population growth, mobility of people among and within nations sets up pressures to which marketing systems must respond. For decades the dispersion of Canada's population was considered a deterrent to large-scale methods of distribution, but recent developments along the Southern tier have altered this situation, and Canada's marketing system is responding accordingly. Powerful centripetal economic and cultural forces are focusing many marketing operations (and even more of the major decisions) on large business and political capitals, within individual nations as well as on a world-wide scale. Spread effects serve as a countervailing pressure reminding marketers of the necessity of catering to unique characteristics of each region, or even neighborhood. On balance, though, areal differences in merchandise preferences within nations appear to be leveling off, even as they are among nations.

ECONOMIC FACTORS

Foreign trade and other aspects of international business are major forces shaping nations' marketing systems, sometimes directly by causing product standardization and more efficient means of assembly and/or distribution, and at other times more indirectly by the introduction of new ideas and methods. Since international business as a rule is concentrated in the hands of a more limited number of enterprises than domestic trade, each individual enterprise tends to wield considerable influence on the import and export of marketing ideas by means of foreign trade, and also through finance (including banking), and through direct foreign investments in manufacturing, in the distributive trades, and in service companies such as advertising agencies.

Shortages of goods, of skilled services, and of funds tend to restrict competition, and thus to dampen experimentation and innovation of marketing institutions and operations. The increased availability of merchandise experienced by a number of Western European countries since the end of the Second World War has spurred the large-scale introduction of new marketing methods and institutions which, judging from earlier records, might have been repressed. National economic planning, increasingly evident throughout the world, has also strongly shaped domestic marketing systems and operations.

The sparse settlement of many areas, their low levels of economic demand, and the scarcity of transportation caused the introduction of market rings centuries ago in many parts of the world, and they are still functioning in many less highly industrialized regions of Africa, Asia, and Latin America. The increased availability of goods, and consumers' ability to purchase them, resulted in the establishment of permanent sales outlets, initially as stalls and workshops in market places and in bazaars and, at a later period, in stores, display rooms, auction houses, and other facilities. Occasionally older forms of market organization have been adapted to more recent requirements, a most notable example being the development of the contemporary shopping center essentially based upon the traditional market place and the bazaar.

Few elements of the economic infrastructure affect marketing as directly as transportation, with the effects ranging from the shipment of agricultural products to points of processing and of consumption, to the transfer of goods from places of production to those of use, to the movement of sales personnel and of potential customers in order to expedite the sales transaction. Less highly industrialized regions frequently suffer from lack of a modern transportation system to support their marketing efforts, while many of the most highly industrialized regions—especially metropolitan areas—experience inadequacies because their transportation systems are unbalanced in terms of rolling stock, permanent facilities (e.g., roads, airports, railroad trackage, distribution points), and time of use. The clogged industrial and commercial cores of some of the major cities of the world are prime examples. Another element of the economic infrastructure of import to marketing is communication, which runs the gamut from sporadic messenger services in some remote corners of the earth, to the teletype systems tied into electronic data-processing systems in the most highly industrialized nations.

Of all the economic factors basic to marketing, none is so potent as production, whether of raw materials, of finished products, or of other goods. Unquestionably marketing under certain circumstances has stimulated production, as was true after the entrance of Sears, Roebuck & Company into Mexico following the Second World War. But by and large marketing systems appear to take their major cues from a nation's production, and adjust to it accordingly. Small-scale agricultural units producing minute quantities of perishables at sporadic intervals must sell their output at high costs. Even when national productivity in agriculture, manufacturing, and other industrial segments increases appreciably, it may be difficult to adjust marketing practices to the new conditions.

Poorer nations, with a high ratio of individuals existing partially or wholly in a subsistence economy and otherwise not involved with a monetary economy (e.g., India), have little need for a highly developed, hyperactive marketing system. A nation's pattern of income distribution is the primary indicator of its market segmentation, especially in the triangular design exhibited in most low-income nations; that is, a tiny elite group at the top, and myraids of very poor at the base. Even so, social, ethnic, psychological, and other cultural variations also play a role in these countries, although it is in the most affluent nations with a square-type pattern of income distribution that nonincome factors are much more significant as determinants of market segmentation.

HUMAN FACTORS

A wide array of explanations has been offered for the origins of trade, ranging from the ceremonial exchange of prestige goods (often of religious significance) to payment for services rendered. In a number of civilizations widely separated geographically and in time, trade in prestige merchandise and over long distances and in large quantities has been considered a high-status occupation, whereas person-to-person dealings on a small scale have been viewed as demeaning, perhaps because of a lack of understanding of the expenses needed to perform marketing functions and the fact that "huckstering" in the market place does require the seller to forego some personal dignity.

Trade has historically been a major vehicle for cultural transmissions from one area to another, but in recent decades the prevalence and the dispersion of this process have been greater than ever. Frequently specific ethnic groups have played major roles in spreading trade concepts and practices to other regions, with notable contemporary examples including the Chinese in Southeast Asia, Levantines in West Africa and parts of Latin America, and East Indians in South Africa and East Africa. Although traders have often arrived in the wake of military conquest, in recent times merchants were more likely to be migrants in search of opportunities to earn a better living. The pace with which larger manufacturers and retailers in the more highly industrialized nations, anxious to expand their potential markets, have been tempted to cross borders into other countries has been stepped up considerably since the end of World War II. And major retailers, no longer content merely to expose their customers to sporadic assortments of imported merchandise, have conducted major promotions on the wares of a single country or region, with many of these events exposing the clientele to more than the produce of foreign nations. Not all countries have welcomed foreign entries of people, produce, or ideas and some have actively opposed them.

Closed societies, best illustrated by the vanishing caste system of India, have long regulated distribution in accordance with traditional status levels in many lands, but essentially Western concepts of the open society are now making themselves felt throughout the world. As a result merchandise and services once limited to particular classes have become available on a broader social basis, and social restrictions and taboos are being lifted. The predisposition of people to accept change apparently is not necessarily related to their socio-political framework, however, since marked evidences of tradition-directed choices have been observed in the freest nations of the West (e.g., France, Great Britain, and Italy) while Iran, until recently steeped in feudalism, has for centuries been noted for its willingness to accept new modes.

Religion has been intertwined with trade since the dawn of history, and has frequently been the dominant factor in the regulation of marketing transactions. Although it is rare for religion to function so prominently today, it still forms an important ethical base to guide buyer–seller relations, and it is at the root of many market customs. Colors associated with religious occasions may be used in various societies to spur sales or, on the other hand, their employment may be taboo. Other societal customs pertinent to marketing may once have had religious foundations, but their derivations have been lost. Nevertheless an acquaintance with them is often vital for the modern marketer.

An individual's age is an important factor not only as an influence on his purchases, but also on the readiness with which a marketing entrepreneur or executive accepts and applies new ideas. A nation's educational system molds future customers by helping develop their value judgments, their interests, and their general cultural and technological knowledge. In addition, the educational system is largely responsible for supplying personnel to the marketing system. Illiteracy poses many obstacles in the way of marketers, sometimes causing them to substitute nonliterary means for more common forms of advertising and sales promotion. As distribution of many products becomes more international, pressures are created for advertising to serve many nations. Despite difficulties in the efforts to internationalize advertising, considerable progress has already been made.

A society's achievement syndrome affects both the will of consumers to work to acquire possessions and the wish of marketers to build and maintain successful enterprises. Value judgments concerning income taxes, social status, and social security may discourage individual enterprise, as may less rational factors—e.g., the Cargo Cultists of New Guinea. A group's ethical viewpoints may assist marketing practices, as was the case with the Chinese in Indonesia; or they may hinder them, as was true in the United States in the late 1950's and early 1960's following the revelation of several scandals implicating certain marketing organizations.

Except in societies where women by tradition are sheltered in the home, they frequently form a considerable part of the work force in marketing, especially at the retail level. As a rule, however, as the marketing system becomes more complex, men assume more important roles, especially in raw materials and manufacturing, and particularly as entrepreneurs and at higher organizational echelons. Countering this move in the more highly developed economies is the growing power of women as purchase decision-makers within the family.

The pressures which political governments bring to bear on marketing systems and practices vary from tacit approval or disapproval, to outright support or rejection. Today most of the more highly industrialized, democratically oriented Capitalist nations attempt to balance individual property rights and the public welfare, while at the same time seeking to increase the overall standard of living. Government direction of and assistance to marketing concentrates on legislation involving taxation, both personal and business; foreign trade; antitrust; pricing; advertising and sales promotion; and business hours. In addition, governments may offer a wide array of services to marketing, ranging from the standardization of goods and services, to the sponsorship of trade fairs both at home and abroad.

Although overt political colonialism fostered by Western powers has waned considerably since the end of the Second World War, close economic ties are still widely maintained between the former ruling powers and their erstwhile colonies, France and its former colonies in West Africa being an instance. Moreover, a new kind of relationship with some semblance to colonialism has sprung up between the Communist nations. The socialization of economic activities—including marketing—has also become more pronounced during this period, not only in the Communist states but also in many "new" socialist-type states in Asia and Africa. Consumer cooperatives have often been encouraged as a means (and sometimes as a guise) of expediting the socialization of marketing in the Communist and new socialist-type nations. The formation of common economic markets in several regions of the world has progressed at diverse rates, with political differences frequently forming the major barriers to closer integration. The continued growth of common markets would speed the transfer of concepts of marketing institutions and practices, and act as a strong propellant for the further internationalization of marketing.

Marketing managers must recognize the necessity of developing new ideas and methods to serve their international markets. Three billion world consumers want to buy, but their ability to do so is greatly limited or nonexistent. Marketing managers must help to build markets as well as sell to them. Extensive demographic and marketing information is presented.

65. THE INTERNATIONAL CONSUMER*

Virgil D. Reed†

HOW MANY INTERNATIONAL CONSUMERS?

After many millions of years the number of international consumers on the earth reached *one billion* by about 1820. Then, 110 years later (1930), there were *two billion* of them. But, only 35 years later (1965), there were three billion. Only 11 years from now (1977) they will exceed *four billion.* In 1990 there will be over *five billion.* This century will close with the unbelievably vast population of *six billion* international consumers, with all the accompanying dangers, problems, tragedies—and opportunities, too. Mankind's ability to find the way to make the benefits of the civilization we have so laboriously developed over millions of years

* Not previously published. For a discussion of attitudes and motivations of peoples of various countries as they influence consumption patterns, see Ernest Dichter, "The World Customer," *Harvard Business Review,* Vol. XL, No. 4 (July–August, 1962), pp. 113–22.

† American University.

available to these hordes will be the measure of these opportunities—and tragedies.

These projections are based on the *medium* population series of the United Nations.[1] High and low projections were also made by the U.N. using certain differing assumptions. The implications of these facts should be as challenging and as shocking to business leaders as to the U.N. and national leaders. They are the basis for the world's greatest problem—assuring peace and assuaging hunger and hopelessness. The revolution of expectations and the dreams of simple, easy solutions are outrunning the possibilities of satisfying them. The high birth rate bestowed on humanity to assure its survival has now become its greatest problem.

At mid-year 1963 the population of the world was estimated to be approximately 3,160,000,000 and is projected to the year 2000 as approximately 6,000,000,000. The distribution by continents or regions of these populations are shown below.

COMPARATIVE POPULATIONS 1963 AND 2000[2] BY CONTINENTS OR REGIONS
(In millions)

Continent or Region	*Population 1963*	*Percent of Total*	*Population 2000*	*Percent of Total*
World Population	3,160	100	6,267	100
Africa	294	9.3	421	6.7
North America (excluding Mexico)	208	6.6	312	5.0
Latin America	231	7.3	592	9.4
Asia	1,748	55.3	3,966	63.3
Europe (including U.S.S.R)	662	20.9	947	15.1
Oceania (including Australia, New Zealand, Melanesia, Polynesia and Micronesia)	16.8	0.5	29	0.5

In most cases the United Nations includes the U.S.S.R. in Europe but for comparative purposes the 1963 (mid year) estimate of Russian population was 225,000,000 and for U.S. population 189,375,000. At the time of writing this chapter U.S. population was approximately 195,000,000.

Approximately 450,000,000, or about 14% of present world population, live in 20 countries with a relatively high standard of living. There are at present 120 countries. The U.S., with by far the highest standard of living, accounts for about 6.0% of world population and 7.0% of world land area. However, it accounts for roughly 11.0% of world imports and 15.0% of world exports; over 25.0% of steel production; about 55.0% of motor vehicles in use; a gross national product almost twice that of the

[1] Provisional Report on World Population Prospects as Assessed in 1963. Department of Economic and Social Affairs, United Nations.

[2] Based on data from Statistical Yearbook 1964, United Nations and Provisional Report on World Population Prospects as Assessed in 1963. Department of Economic and Social Affairs, United Nations.

European Common Market (Belgium, France, West Germany, Italy, Luxembourg and the Netherlands) and more than twice the per capita gross national product of the Common Market; and total consumer expenditures two and a half times those of the Common Market. Our per capita annual steel consumption is 1,190 pounds and is in sharp contrast to India (35lbs.); Indonesia (5 lbs.); Communist China (35 lbs.); Pakistan (17 lbs.); Brazil (97 lbs.); Philippines (44 lbs.); South Vietnam (10 lbs.); U.S.S.R. (758 lbs.); Mexico (123 lbs.); and United Kingdom (811 lbs.)[3]

Of the present 120 countries those having populations of approximately 100 million or more are, according to the most recent estimates available (in millions):

China	700
India	480
U.S.S.R. (Russia)	229
United States	195
Indonesia	105
Pakistan	103
Japan	98
Total for all countries	1,910

Of these countries, which account for almost two-thirds of the world's population, China, India, Indonesia and Pakistan are technologically simple peasant societies with largely illiterate agrarian populations living mostly in scattered rural villages. Approximately 80% of the population is rural and agricultural practices are so primitive that all these countries have chronic food deficiencies often reaching the famine stage in large areas. The Far East has slightly more than half the world's population but produces little more than a fourth of the world's food. Maldistribution of available food is as chronic as the shortage. The 20% urban population of these countries is largely concentrated in a few very large cities.

Japan and the United States are highly developed, industrial nations. The U.S. has large agricultural surpluses and adequate sources of most raw materials. Russia (in Europe particularly) is developing her industrial economy rapidly, but erratically, and her agricultural problems have not yet been solved. At great social costs and through ruthless methods her steel output has been increased to the point where her tonnage output has actually exceeded ours for short periods of time. Consumer goods are still inadequate in quantity, quality, variety, and distribution.

The only large areas of food surpluses left in the world are the United States, Canada and Australia. Even Latin America, with about 7% of world population, produces only about 6.5% of the world's food, and coffee, largely exported, is about the only item in surplus.

The greatest need for the future is painfully and threateningly evident—a "production explosion" in agriculture and industry greatly ex-

[3] All figures used in this paragraph are for 1963, the latest year for which comparable data are available.

ceeding the scale of the "population explosion." If this and drastic population controls do not come soon, the Malthusian remedies—war, pestilence and famine—will operate on a vast scale to reduce the number of international consumers before they become even potential customers for anyone.

MISERY AND MARKETS

Markets are people with at least some disposable income. Good markets are people with both disposable and discretionary purchasing power—and the desire to use them. Most of the world's consumers have very little disposable purchasing power. With the exception of some 20 countries with relatively high standards of living there is precious little discretionary purchasing power. What there is in most other countries is restricted to a top layer or "class market." What we think of usually as the middle-classes, on which we place so much stress in our marketing, are very small in numbers and in proportion to the population. The mass-market, as we use that term, is nonexistent except for the most inexpensive and indispensable items. The American with his frame of reference and experience restricted to the economy of plenty of North America must learn an entire new scale of values in judging the international consumer and the markets of the world outside of Western Europe, where his own standards partly apply.

About half the world's people already suffer from hunger and malnutrition and only about one sixth are well fed according to a study by the Food and Agriculture Organization (F.A.O.) of the United Nations. In most of the world, population growth continues to exceed production growth in both agriculture and industry. This is true of nearly all the underdeveloped countries, where, unfortunately, population is increasing at the highest rates and in the largest numbers.

Approximately 25% of our North American diet is made up of animal products but only 17% in Europe and 3% in Asia. Our urban consumer eats about 5 pounds of food per day. The Indian consumer eats 1.23 pounds per day and about 85% of it is rice, deficient in proteins, fats and vitamins. The effects of diet are well illustrated in Japan—with a very high standard of living as compared to the rest of Asia. Changes in diet since World War II are said to have increased the height of Japanese sons by almost two inches over that of their fathers.

Hungry and malnourished people do not make good markets. They cannot work well, learn readily, resist disease or think of much beyond finding the next inadequate meal and the fuel, grass, sticks or cow dung, with which to cook it. And, all radical ideologies use hunger, hopelessness and want as their most effective weapons.

No country attains a dynamic and rapidly growing economy until approximately half its labor force has moved from agriculture to industry and business, thus providing a reasonable minimum of construction, communication, transportation and goods other than agricultural. Most countries have far to go before reaching even this limited stage of development necessary to provide the basic necessities beyond a subsistence level of existence. The industrial equivalent of present day China with its 700 million people, for instance, is probably that of little Belgium or little Holland.

A few indications of comparative purchasing power and living standards should be of interest to the marketing man and convince him of the need for the best marketing research that can be done, usually under very trying circumstances.

From India with its 480 million consumers, the following is quoted from a report of The Perspective Planning Division of the Planning Commission:

"Poverty is not confined to groups of unfortunates or to backward areas. It engulfs almost the entire population. The average per capita product is barely $80.00 per year. The consumption of the poorest 10% is as low as five cents a day and, notwithstanding the conspicuous consumption and the riches of the tiny minority at the top, the consumption of the richest 5% aggregates to no more than fifty cents a day."

There are only 10 to 12 million in India who constitute a market for American products, except those selling for a few cents.

India is threatened with widespread famine at the time this is written. To prevent this, or at least give substantial relief, the United States has scheduled shipment for 1966 of the following: 10 million tons of wheat; 200 thousand tons of corn; 150 million pounds of vegetable oils; 125 million pounds of powdered milk; and up to 700 thousand bales of cotton. These are being sent under our P.L. 480 surplus disposal program. Canada is providing another million tons of wheat. France is the only other wheat surplus country. Undoubtedly another two million tons of wheat will be needed to give adequate relief. The 1966 wheat crop of India is expected to be 12 million tons short of last year's crop.

In South Africa (the country) the *urban* "African" (Negro) buying power is relatively high. About 10% of these "Africans" are classed as skilled and their earnings range roughly from $125 and $225 per month. The 25% who are classed as semi-skilled earn approximately $60 to $120 per month. The other 65%, classed as laborers and domestics usually earn less than $60 per month. With a family subsistence level estimate at about $75 per month there is considerable discretionary spending power for the upper 35%, particularly if more than one member of the family works.

In Yugoslavia in 1947 the per capita income was only $180 and about 80% of the population were peasants. Now industry accounts for a little over half the national income compared to 9% in 1939. The national income is about four times that of 1947. Yugoslavia has already become a semi-industrialized economy with 19,500,000 consumers, is still developing rapidly, and is now attracting a surprising number of tourists.

Canada with a population approaching 20 million has a per capita income exceeding $2,200 (in constant 1957 Canadian dollars). Its farm population has shrunk to 11% and is still decreasing rapidly. Its major industrial development has taken place since 1939. As an indication of the standard of living it has already attained—and in a surprisingly short time after it reached the "take-off point"—the percentage of households equipped with the following items is quite revealing:[4]

Refrigerators	96%
Television	93
Telephones	89
Washing Machines	86
Central Heat	75
Cars	75

Africa accounts for 20% of the world's land area; about 11% of world population; about 4% of the world's trade; and less than 2% of the Gross "National" Product of the world.

These three countries and an entire continent give a good idea of the range of potentialities afforded by international consumers in various parts of the world. Any comparison with our American market, excepting Canada, is disappointing.

China, India and Indonesia possess astoundingly great wealth in both human and natural resources but their populations are still poverty stricken, having no or tiny disposable purchasing power and no discretionary income. Brazil is an extremely wealthy nation in natural resources but little of them are being turned into a standard of living. Only the Atlantic rim of the southern part of the country has shown much industrial development and coffee is still the major source of foreign exchange.

In all these countries not even the human resources have yet been developed. Management, technical skills, education, attitude favoring organization, competitive spirit and capital are all sadly lacking. It is easier for such countries to envy the economic blessings of North America and Western Europe—attained largely as a result of different basic attitudes of people—than to change the status quo and organize to turn their human and natural resources into a better way of life. They too can prosper if they organize to do so.

The North American Indians had more natural resources than Canada and the United States now have, because we have used or destroyed part of them. But the Indian did not use his resources to turn them into a high standard of living. The major differences lie in the attitudes, desires and organizational abilities of the two peoples.

The great majority of the international consumers of the world are figuratively beggars starving while sitting on huge bags of gold—and not knowing what to do with the gold. This is all the more tragic because the industrial and agricultural techniques and machines aggressively developed

[4] Dominion Bureau of Statistics, Canada

over the last century and a half in Europe and the United States are available to them *now*. Capital from those and other industrialized countries is available to them *now* if only there were trained managements to make effective use of it and narrow nationalism were not so rampant. Know-how, developed in our businesses and our universities, is available to them *now* and tomorrow, not a decade or a century in the future. An unbelievable wealth of potential electric power *now* runs wasted and unused into the oceans bordering these undeveloped and poverty stricken countries while millions yearn for the light, factories and goods which this water power could bring them if utilized. Each American workman has more than 10 horsepower at his elbow to multiply his output of goods.

Even adequate capital cannot quickly eliminate the handicaps of status quo and unstable government, traditional social attitudes, maldistribution of income, physical and regional isolation, cultural deprivation, lack of education, communal and religious tensions, class and caste differences and language and ethnic variations.

The world-wide craving for a better and more abundant way of life, more and better food, better health, more education, has for the first time in history become a major and dominant force in international affairs, in relations between nations and in the United Nations, in vast intergovernmental aid and relief programs, in newspapers, magazines, television and public discussion. The difficulty is: can we solve the problem before the world-wide craving and envy grow into aggressive impatience, then deteriorate into widespread violence?

In the meantime the world is the marketing man's oyster bed and the countries his oysters, but the number of oysters containing big pearls are few. Even the small pearls are not plentiful and it takes good research to find any of them.

EXPORTING ISN'T ENOUGH

When you merely export goods to international consumers you are only taking advantage of the markets others have built. That is not enough today with a world grown small for its teeming consumers and dangerously impatient for better living. Businessmen must help build markets as well as sell in them.

When Sears, Roebuck and Company established its store in Mexico City, a revolution in distribution and small industries resulted. The antiquated and moribund French department stores suffered shock convulsions over Sears' aggressive methods—then found out they could do the same with better profits. Sears encouraged and assisted in the establishment of several relatively small manufacturers to supply Sears and others with goods. This was intended to cut imports to a minimum, increase employment and raise more consumers into the middle class.

Many of the people trained in Sears have established their own stores, and that was expected, and they are much better stores. This kind of operation doesn't call down the all too common malediction of "Yankee Imperialism." It's simply built on the very obvious, but usually overlooked, principle that what is best for the most people is best for business—yours and mine.

In 1956 J. Walter Thompson Company (international advertising agency) opened an office in Tokyo. As a Vice President of the company your author was present at the opening. Our largest Japanese competitor, as its president told me a year later, did not believe we could be successful in Japan with our methods of operation. About a year later our competitor's management was both convinced and surprised and asked if I would spend some time with them explaining in detail how we operated. With my company's approval I spent an entire week in the offices of our competitor, lecturing on, discussing and explaining our methods, and concealed nothing except confidential client information. Our competitor doubted that my company would permit this but was most appreciative and grateful for our frank assistance. Why did we do this? Because, it is obvious that *good* competition raises the standards of the entire profession of advertising and marketing. It is an undeviating policy of this American company "to be a good neighbor" in any country in which it operates and its objective wherever it operates is to help raise the standard of living of international consumers.

During the next few decades American management will not be doing an adequate job unless it *develops international markets.* In most of the world they have to be developed and made dynamic before much can be sold to them. Why stop at an imaginary line called a national border in marketing outlook?

A good marketing man must learn to live with the slogan "When you're through changing, you're through,"—and most changes emanate from the consumer.

In addition to exporting, other methods of reaching the international consumer—and developing markets into better ones—are: (1) establishing wholly owned branches abroad; (2) establishing jointly owned or "partnership" branches; (3) licensing foreign manufacturers to produce the product under your patent or other proprietary rights on a royalty paying basis. All three of these methods avoid tariff barriers which are sometimes insurmountably high. The last two methods have the additional advantage of avoiding such common criticisms as "Yankee Imperialism" and draining off excessive profits from the country. The second method, joint ventures or "partnership" arrangements, has the very great advantage of local participation in capital and management and freedom from government objections and discrimination. It also gives the feeling of participation and encourages a much better understanding of the problems and social as well as economic rewards of our private enterprise system.

Mr. Edgar F. Kaiser, whose companies operate in several countries.

including producing automobiles in Argentina and aluminum and Jeeps in India, recently said, "Only by the experience of business association and partnership can there be a real understanding of our system and its great benefits to the masses of people. . . . The constructive roles of capital and management and the inadequate indigenous supply of both are beginning to be recognized. . . . Indians are getting a better look at how our capitalistic system operates, the opportunities it creates, . . . and the resulting increase in the standard of living for all."[5] It is quite obvious that everything businessmen say or do abroad has a favorable or unfavorable influence on employees, business associates and competitors, government officials and politicians, opinion leaders and rabble rousers, and all the rest of international consumers. Many times the reaction is neither the expected nor the rational one. Anti-foreignism or xenophobia—nationalism turned bitter—is widespread and unreasoned in most of the underdeveloped countries, and a grave handicap to cooperation in development. It is a form of militant traditionalism which resists change. As always the leading nation draws most of the criticism. Being the "good neighbor" in every country where American businesses operate is the best way to slay the bogeyman of "Capitalist Imperialism."

SOME MARKETS ARE OUT OF BOUNDS

At present China, Cuba, North Viet Nam and North Korea are under embargo so far as U.S. trade is concerned. Public attitude and certain limitations very greatly restrict trade with the U.S.S.R. also. These countries account for approximately a billion international consumers. Russia is approaching a decent standard of living, at least in her European area, but market potentialities are very limited for the others and will long remain small.

DIFFERENCES CAN BE DEVASTATING

On is the biggest small word in Japan and its meaning is all pervasive. Until you understand the complex meaning of *on* you will not know what makes the Japanese "tick." It is a system of ethics which is the foundation for the entire code of obligations of a Japanese toward everybody from the lowest employee to his Emperor, and "one never returns one ten-thousandth of an *on*." The power of the *on* "always overrides one's own personal preferences." You will even embarrass a Japanese by offering him a cigarette or by admiring something in his home unless you know him well and he understands Western customs. Either of these courtesies makes him *wear* another *on* or obligation. You too will be embarrassed when your host insists on giving you the thing you admired and is doubly embarrassed if you refuse the gift because he believes you do not consider it a worthy gift. There is no adequate English translation for the meaning

[5] Article in special section on India, *New York Times*, March 20, 1966.

of *on* because the whole concept is alien to us. Not knowing about *on* can get you into trouble socially or in your business affairs.

It is often said that people are alike all over the world. They are—*except for the differences*—but those differences can be devastating to the marketing executive. True, normal people have the same "chassis," "engine," "equipment," and "accessories," but even these vary considerably. Try wearing a Japanese necktie or look at an American necktie on a Japanese! In the first case the tie is far too short, in the second far too long. The Japanese is quite self-conscious of the fact that his legs are much shorter than ours from knee to ankle. The Chinese and Japanese call Europeans "big noses." Color, hair, size, eyes, lips and length of arms or legs vary widely throughout the world.

It is true that all people are motivated by the same basic instincts, senses, affections, passions and aspirations, but the different manner of expressing these motivations and aspirations can wreck marketing plans and advertising campaigns, as can customs and many other differences. Naturally, we share many common characteristics with the consumers of Canada, Western Europe, Australia and New Zealand, but having disposed of these countries the differences become more marked and more important in marketing.

One American marketing man, after spending a few years in Brazil expressed the power of differences there by saying, "It is only after considerable time that the practitioner begins to realize he must reexamine every idea he ever had about marketing." Two years experience there convinces me how true this is, even though Brazil's population is largely of European origin.

Symbolism varies widely. The cow is a sacred religious symbol among Hindus and must not be associated with commercial products. There too, a fountain pen (worn always on the left side of the chest) is such an important symbol that if you can't afford the pen you get the cap at least. Many a home in Holland has a TV antenna but no TV. In Brazil you do not wear deer designs in sweaters and in Venezuela duck designs are out. They denote homosexuals. In Sub-Sahara Africa "power" is the great symbol among the Negroes and for them encompasses a wide range of ideas—health, strength, influence, virility and vitality. In spite of all, a "white image or association" for a product is very important there. The lion, leopard and elephant have very favorable symbolic meaning. In Japan, the camera is so universal that one feels convinced every Japanese must be born with a camera attached.

HETEROGENEITY IS A HEX

Indonesia is 3,000 islands with about half its 105 million people living on one—Java. It is a very complex society in three layers:

1. Europeans, with their own social and economic organizations.

2. Foreign Orientals—mostly Chinese, Indians and Arabs—each group retaining its own customs and social organization.
3. Javanese, mostly farmers, small traders and cottage industry workers with a very thin layer of the elite.

The Europeans formerly dominated heavy industries and plantations, but recently they have been divested of much of their property and power. The foreign Orientals dominate small industry, wholesaling and larger scale retailing.

Only about 8% of the country's gross domestic income is from manufacturing.

The Philippines are a country of 7,000 islands with only 4,000 of them named and about 400 permanently inhabited by about 40 million consumers. About 19% of this country's gross domestic income is from manufacturing.

Yugoslavia, with a population of 19.5 million, is made up of six republics, five nationalities with three different languages written in two different scripts. It has three major religions, several national minorities and a wide range of regional cultures, customs and levels of economic development.

India, with its 480 million consumers, has 16 states, 14 basic languages, 102 distinct dialects and, until abolished or "ruthlessly integrated" in 1950, there were 500 "princely states." Its rural population lives in approximately 550 thousand farm villages. It is a land of minorities with the following given official recognition:

Muslims	(150,000,000)
Christians	(11,000,000)
Sikhs	(8,000,000)
Parsees	(250,000)
Anglo-Indians	(50,000)

Within the Hindu majority there also are the Scheduled Castes and the Scheduled Tribes.

Only 19% of the country's gross domestic product comes from manufacturing and construction combined.

In the United States there are far more similarities than differences among our states from a marketing standpoint. In most other countries there are many more regional differences than similarities.

COMMUNICATION PROBLEMS

The Minister of Commerce of India once chided me in the following terms: "Your people do not know even how to communicate with mine. Those astounding chrome trimmed kitchens and appliances you show us in your exhibits at our international fairs are so far beyond the average

Indian's comprehension and scale of values that they lack all credibility. He doesn't believe they are even used in your homes but are only propaganda. He thinks he is being spoofed and misled. He can't even dream of owning or using such things. They are so incredible they do not impress but annoy him. The Communists really impress him though with the promise of a pair of shoes a year and a quarter of an acre of land. He thoroughly understands those promises. They are entirely credible." That Minister was a top executive from one of India's greatest industrial complexes and he was thoroughly at home in solving marketing problems. Knowing how to communicate and convince is a necessity in marketing.

In countries with low educational levels and high illiteracy it is even difficult to get brand recognition, let alone brand preference or insistence. It requires unbelievable repetition of very simple impressions and messages. In India, for instance, movie documentaries should run 1,500 to 1,800 feet of film instead of our 1,000 to 1,200 feet. Village radios with loud speakers attached are common, but there are practically no radios in rural homes and there are probably not more than 2,000 TV sets in India.

Interestingly enough, the moving picture houses are about the only place you can get the castes together as an advertising audience.

The media available in different countries vary widely in number, coverage, availability and cost. Sound trucks, village radios, motion picture trucks, sampling, promotional teams, show-boats and even singing troubadours all belong in the media list of the rural and small town areas of many countries. Most of the highly developed countries have fairly adequate media of the same types as used in the United States and Canada. However, in several of these countries radio and TV advertising is not permitted.

Language has its problems, even when there is only one or two in a country. Copy should be written and programs prepared only by those who know thoroughly the idioms, customs, and language nuances of the country. It must have been very embarrassing for the management of one of our largest soft drink manufacturers, for instance, when it found that advertising prepared for Brazil using a slogan which has been very effective in the U.S. could not be used. Translated literally in Brazil it is the common slang term for the menstrual period.

Even within the same language, regional differences are great and often produce pitfalls for advertising and selling. A cigarro is a cigarette in Chile but a cigar in other Latin American countries. Pico means a pick or beak in most of Spanish America but you don't use it in polite circles in Chile. Mantequilla is butter, except in Argentina. Manteca is butter in Argentina but means grease or lard in other Spanish American countries. A comment that is polite and gracious in Venzuela may be off color in Peru or Argentina. Communication in other countries with diverse languages, customs and religions is even more of a problem.

BUYING HABITS DIFFER TOO

In Indonesia most people who come to the markets to buy are either villagers or townspeople of the lower or middle class. Influential townspeople usually have their poor relatives, servants or dependent neighbors do their shopping, except for such things as clothing.

In South Africa, in spite of apartheid, there is no color bar in shops and stores but there is in ownership of the stores, and in company cafeterias and locker rooms. In the "African" (Negro) townships children do most of the shopping. In all of Sub-Sahara Africa, Negro women are chattels and your advertising must influence the men who approve all purchases.

The men of Holland are gradually delegating more of their grocery shopping to their wives, excepting meat. Meat buying is a man's job and will probably remain so indefinitely. The butcher is the historical meat outlet but super markets are increasingly common. In introducing meat departments in these markets the sales promotion is directed at men. The meat department is called "man's world" and the meat counters are called "men's shelves."

Reciprocity in buying is carried to unusual extremes in Holland, particularly in the towns and smaller cities. Inter-dependence of people is much more pervasive in Holland than is common to us. A Dutch housewife may buy half a loaf of bread from each of four bakers in a day "to maintain good relations." A little hardware store may buy something from every distributor in its area. Most merchandise is still delivered to the homes. It is not uncommon for three milk men, three vegetable retailers, two poultry and two fish retailers to make deliveries to one home.

These examples of differing buying habits could be multiplied by hundreds—and such differences greatly influence marketing plans and strategies. Fixed prices, for instance, as we know them, prevail in only a small portion of the world. Higgling and haggling is far more universal.

FINDING POTENTIAL CUSTOMERS

A former business associate from Egypt was asked, "Why don't we see any market surveys from Egypt?" His answer was direct and frank, and applies to a great majority of the world's consumers. "It took Allah only six days to make the world but even Allah couldn't make a good market survey in Egypt in a year. Nobody knows anything about marketing research. Interviewing in homes is impossible. If you try to send out male interviewers they cannot get into homes and may be shot or stabbed for trying. If you send women interviewers they are admitted to homes but the women of the house are so gossip hungry the interviewer can neither complete her interview nor get away for hours. The 'facts' she gets are undependable—and besides the women of the house seldom do the buying nor do they know much about what is bought."

Aside from North America, most Western European countries, Australia, South Africa and Japan there is little bench-mark or basic data, let alone current detailed facts useful in determining the size and characteristics of the market. It is usually either difficult or impossible to find enough recent data to construct good samples. Even the numbers of married men and married women were far apart in the 1960 Brazilian census published almost five years late. Ecuador took its first population census in 1950. It too was incomplete, late and of questionable accuracy.

Telephone and mail surveys are impossible in most countries because: (1) There are few telephones and the service is poor; (2) Telephone directories are often useless for sampling or listing because in many countries you lose your telephone if the listing is changed—so they aren't changed; (3) Post-office efficiency is usually very low and if the employees strike, the accumulated mail may be sold to paper dealers or burned; (4) Literacy is so low that most people cannot fill out a questionnaire; (5) Returns even from educated people are extremely low; (6) There is usually a basic suspicion that the information is being sought by government for "checking purposes"; (7) The questionnaires returned are usually incomplete; (8) You can't depend on the answers, even if you get them, because they will often try to give you the answer they think you want.

Some rough relative measures can be made from the restricted and "ancient" census facts usually available in most areas of the world but they must be discounted for their shortcomings—inaccuracy, spottiness, incompleteness, poor tabulation and analysis, questionable quality of the interviewers, attitudes of respondents and poor publication.

It is evident that original research in most markets is difficult and costly. However, even "spot-checking" and careful research among leaders who *can* be reached and interviewed pays big dividends.

Noncompetitive businessmen, who do know the market in a general way at least, are usually helpful. The educated classes can be interviewed in practically all countries, if you can win their confidence. School teachers can usually get into homes in their own community and if carefully trained and supervised can gather a generous amount of information.

In spite of the handicaps limiting marketing research in most lands, anyone considering entering a new market must exhaust all reasonable possibilities to get what facts are available and collect as many more as is feasible under local conditions.

Don't substitute romance for facts insofar as they are available. The world has over three billion consumers and will have twice as many at the end of the century. All are yearning to buy, but the ability to do so is lacking or greatly limited for most at present. Finding those who can buy, and helping to raise standards of living to the point where increasing numbers can do so, are the major objectives of every intelligent marketing-oriented business executive. There are already several pearls of varying sizes in the oyster bed. It's up to American businessmen to help plant the grains of sand that will develop into many more.

Problems in developing policies for international operations confront many marketing managers. International competition is rigorous; it must be met while the firm stays abreast of the changing political and social developments in its areas of marketing interest. Meeting the threats of nationalism and competition by sharing financial returns with residents of host countries, developing local executives, and internationalizing management are suggested methods of achieving satisfactory international operations.

66. LRP FOR INTERNATIONAL OPERATIONS*

John Fayerweather†

"What will be the key policy questions for international managements in the next five to ten years?" . . .

At the risk of oversimplification, I will single out three areas which I believe present the critical problems which must be resolved in every company which hopes to have an effective international operation five to ten years hence. A few companies have already gone a long way in the direction of solving these problems, but for most international managements these will be major preoccupations for the next few years. The three are:

1. Establishment of operations which are viable in highly nationalistic environments with particular attention to the ownership question and joint ventures.
2. Development of local national executives for senior posts in overseas managements.
3. Welding and molding world-wide operations into an integrated unit.

---

* Reprinted from the *California Management Review*, Vol. III, No. 2, (Fall 1960).

† New York University.

I. THE THREAT OF NATIONALISM

Through much of the world, especially in the less developed areas, the environment for U.S. business is dominated by two forces:

1. The powerful emotion of nationalism combining patriotic pride and a thrust for independence with negative reactions against racism, colonialism, economic dependence and in general to being "second-class" citizens of the world society.
2. A substantial measure of dependence for rapid economic progress upon the capital and industrial know-how of the economically more advanced nations, especially the United States.

These forces are fundamentally in opposition, and it has only been the overriding political and economic importance of the second which has held the first in check. But the balance between the two is by no means static, it is in every sense dynamic and one of the major keys to future planning is recognition that the second, dependence on what U.S. business has to offer, is declining steadily while nationalism shows little signs of abating.

What this means for U.S. business has been spelled out recently from two quite different viewpoints with conclusions, which though different in fact are very similar in implication. Speaking from the perspective of their global study of industrial conditions, Professors Harbison and Myers observe:

> Eventually the firm is forced to recognize that, in the opinion of the effective political leaders, foreign management and foreign financial control are only temporary instruments for industrial development. In a very real sense, therefore, expatriate managers are expendable, and their power and influence in any rapidly industrializing country will inevitably shrink. Like patrimonial management in the advanced countries, expatriate management too will become an anachronism in modern society. . . . We feel that the wholly owned foreign firm has a limited role to play in the industrializing countries. The future is likely to see an expansion of locally controlled companies which have an affiliation, through licensing, marketing, or consulting arrangements, with large business organizations in the United States, England, and Europe.[1]

Approaching the situation with the eyes of a practicing executive, Harold Solmssen of Schering Corporation perceives the same sort of trend.

> As far as we can remember, ours was the most progressive economy and, as a result, we are the leading economic power today. The rest of the world had to adapt itself to our methods if they wanted our money and our products.

[1] Frederick Harbison and Charles A. Myers, *Management in the Industrial World* (McGraw-Hill Book Company, New York, 1959), p. 391.

But this may not always be so and we should guard against considering our views right and those of the others "unfair" or "wrong."[2]

Thus there is a pressing need for U.S. international operations to set their policies so that they will be welcome in countries abroad when the need for our capital and know-how has largely passed. What does this require?

The answer lies essentially in policies that satisfy the major aspirations in the host country falling within the province of the U.S. operations. While the importance of these will vary among countries, we may define at least four such aspirations:

1. The quest of individuals, especially at the managerial level, for personal opportunity and advancement;
2. The urge of the individual with entrepreneurial instincts to realize them in the creative and financial satisfactions of developing a business venture;
3. The desire of local government and financial circles to retain within their borders a full share of the financial returns of industrial operations; and
4. The drive of governments for economic progress directed in large measure by their plans and conceptions of what is in the best national interest.

"Yankee Firm, Go Home!"

So there is a solid nucleus in frustration of objectives around which the forces of nationalism may be aroused against U.S. foreign operations. One solution of course is to accept the eventual withdrawal of U.S. companies from abroad. Rejecting this as a defeatist approach, the challenge lies in the conception of policies which give sufficient scope to national aspirations so that U.S. business remains, if not loved, at least accepted as a useful industrial citizen abroad.

Much of the thinking of affected national groups on this subject has coalesced around the concept of the "joint venture." The jointly financed enterprise, especially one in which U.S. interests have a minority position, is seen by government officials, local industrialists and others as the ideal for utilizing United States capital and especially a continuing flow of know-how while still giving full scope to national aspirations. In some instances by legal requirements, but more commonly by administrative pressure and persuasion, new United States ventures are encouraged to move in this direction in many countries.

Reflecting this influence, a research project on joint ventures directed by Professor Wolfgang Friedman at Columbia University, to be published

[2] "Organization Planning for International Operations," *The International Executive*, Winter, 1960, p. 5, summarized from a paper delivered at the American Management Association.

later this year, reveals that there has been a significant increase in interest in joint ventures in the post World War II era. As a percentage of new investments, however, joint ventures still remain a minority, and few established investments have been changed from 100% United States ownership to a joint ownership status.

According to the latest census of overseas investments only 26% of subsidiaries had as much as 5% ownership by local capital.[3] United States international managements have not as yet therefore, made any broad shift in policies in the direction of joint venturing. Should they? Or can the pressures of national aspirations be contained without such a policy shift?

Guide to Basic Policy

In answer to these questions I propose three basic guides in policy making. Individual situations will vary greatly from company to company and country to country defying universal recommendations. But a general adherence to these guide lines will, I believe, result in enduring policy decisions.

1. A joint venture which contemplates a substantial sharing of management control is fundamentally undesirable and to be avoided except in unusual circumstances.
2. A major portion of foreign national aspirations can and should be met by statesmanlike management policies independent of the ownership question.
3. Some sharing with local nationals of financial participation in foreign ventures without relinquishing of management control is desirable.

The first point is the most important for it strikes to the heart of joint venturing as many people conceive it. Their idea is that an existing or budding local entrepreneur joins forces with the management of a U.S. firm and, pooling their assets, they form a far stronger enterprise than either could present alone. The local entrepreneur knows his country, he has government contacts and, by giving the venture a strong local flavor, he contributes to the morale of the personnel and the public image of the company. The United States management brings its skills in management and technology and a continuing flow of new know-how from research. . . .

It can be shown quite readily that in the early stages of a joint venture the marriage of assets is of great value. The United States company new to a foreign country profits greatly from the local know-how of its partner, and the local partner derives great benefits from American products and technology not otherwise available to him. But these immediate benefits diminish in importance fairly rapidly and then the strengths of the joint

[3] U.S. Department of Commerce, *Foreign Investment of the United States*, Washington, 1953, p. 23.

venture as with any enterprise begin to depend upon the ability of its management to conceive and execute policies with a unified and persevering direction.

Joint Ventures

If the marriage has in fact been between two competent entrepreneurial managements (and that is assumed to be one of the key objectives of joint ventures) then, as market conditions change, political forces shift, product changes evolve, etc., it is almost certain that there will be significant differences of opinion between the management groups. It is possible that they may work them out and the advantages of the marriage will support effective union. It seems more likely, however, that the venture will either suffer from vacillation and inability to develop effective unified policy or that out of conflict will emerge one dominant management, so that the other loses an effective vehicle for achieving its objectives in the union. Either the entrepreneurial aspirations of the local national are frustrated or the United States company loses effective control over the policies of its foreign unit.

This negative conclusion leads to reexamination of the proposition put forward by many local nationals that joint ventures should be adopted as a means of satisfying the varied national aspirations listed on page 602. The position of the local nationals is justified today, but primarily for one major reason which need not exist.

If a major share of ownership were in local hands, they could readily force changes in those policies of many United States subsidiaries which currently frustrate national aspirations. For example, they could require the removal of U.S. executives and promotion of local personnel to top positions. However, it is certainly not essential that ownership be shared for such a change to be made.

The success of our most enlightened United States international companies in utilizing local executives, in blending company policies with those of government economic plans, in developing local suppliers, etc., is ample proof that a large portion of the local aspirations can be met without sharing management control.

The critical significance of the strong support of joint venturing from overseas, therefore, lies not so much in a yes or no response as in imaginative and persevering execution of policies which relieve the pressures for sharing management control by undertaking independently those actions which local nationals would foster if they gained control. This objective, we must grant, cannot be fully achieved for much the same reasons that even the most enlightened paternalism is never fully successful. There will always be a residual desire for full control which United States ownership frustrates. But, given a continuance of respect for private property, there seems every reason to assume that United States companies which make a concerted effort to give scope for national aspirations will be able to continue overseas operations indefinitely.

Profit Sharing

The third suggested guideline, sharing financial participation with foreign nationals, is essentially part of this approach, but it is treated separately because it is a more difficult area of execution than, for example, promotion of local executives. The rates of return on investment earned by American overseas operations are generally no greater than those of local capitalists, and the dollars allocated for remission of profits can almost always be justified on sound economic grounds as less than would be required for importation of products made locally as a result of the investment or gains from exports of the products of the U.S. operations. . . .

Summary

To summarize then, in this first area of policy planning we are confronted with the necessity of satisfying the aspirations which underlie nationalistic drives. Despite pressures to resolve all of these through acceptance of minority positions in joint ventures, United States managements will be wise to adhere to full operating control of overseas ventures seeking to satisfy local national aspirations through statesmanlike operating policies including sharing of some degree of financial ownership through broad sale of company stock.

II. DEVELOPMENT OF LOCAL NATIONAL EXECUTIVES

Today, as Dr. Shearer's study has noted, most of the key executive assignments in the overseas units of most companies are handled by United States executives. But the forces of economics and politics are set against this practice and in favor of the eventual transfer of all management jobs abroad to local nationals. The relatively higher salaries paid to United States executives and the travel and living allowances they require make it appreciably less expensive to employ local nationals in virtually any situation.

Equally important are the pressures of government officials and public opinion in favor of turning management over to local nationals. In some countries these pressures are felt tangibly in the form of laws requiring employment of nationals or refusing entry papers for American executives on the grounds that local personnel are adequate for the work. Such restrictions are not common in the case of senior executives, United States companies generally being legally allowed today to bring in men for top positions.

However, there is strong pressure from government and national opinion directed against those companies which are slow in turning over management to nationals and, conversely, in favor of those who do give responsibility to local executives. These pressures may be expected to grow as the number and capabilities of local executives increase.

Thus a sensible management must adopt a policy of turning over progressively greater management responsibility to local nationals and it must prepare for the day when the senior position in one country after another will be entrusted to a local executive. This thought may be disturbing to some, but it need not be. Some companies have already gone a long way down this road—National Cash Register, for example, has only some half dozen U.S. executives throughout its large and highly effective international organization. But the transition will be effective only if the national executives have been adequately prepared. There have been in recent years cases where management of a foreign unit was turned over to local executives who were not ready and who had subsequently to be replaced by U.S. executives with most unfortunate public relations and organizational repercussions. Thus, it is imperative that a thoughtful plan be evolved for the development of overseas executives.

What are the requisites of such a plan? First, it must be directed to the levels of managerial characteristics at which development is needed. Second, it must foster specific qualities essential for men in senior positions. And third, it must provide experiences which will have a permanent developmental effect. These are fundamentals applicable to all executive development. Our concern here is with the special considerations which enter into their application to overseas executives. . . .

III. INTERNATIONALIZING MANAGEMENT

There is little doubt that the international operations of most companies will grow in coming years both in absolute terms and in proportion to domestic business. This has been generally true for the past decade, and the higher rates of growth of foreign economies suggest a continuation of the trend. Inevitably the pattern of management will shift to accommodate this change in the nature of corporate business, but the manner in which the pattern evolves will require careful thought based on a realistic view of each company's situation.

The general thrust of the change of corporate management has been described in essentially similar terms by several authors in the past year.[4] It starts from the traditionally segregated status of export departments and international divisions which operate with a large measure of autonomy,

---

[4] For example, John J. Beauvois, "Internationalism: A New Concept for U.S. Business," *California Management Review*, Winter, 1960, pp. 28–37; and Gilbert H. Clee and Alfred di Scipio, "Creating a World Enterprise," *Harvard Business Review*, Nov.–Dec., 1959, pp. 77–89.

too often accompanied by ignorance and lack of interest on the part of senior company management and domestic associates. The international side of business draws products, know-how and capital from the rest of the company but structurally its operations are largely independent of the main body of domestic parent company functions. By contrast the emerging new patterns of management involve a high degree of integration between international activities and the rest of the company.

As a general trend this thesis is incontrovertible. It can readily be observed in various stages in many companies today, and the growing importance of international business argues for its continuation. The problem of planning lies not, therefore, in establishing the basic direction of change but rather in determining the character it should assume for a specific company. In all probability the result both in operating policies and organizational structure will show many characteristics of the ideal integrated world enterprise, but will retain some of the features of the segregated organizations which are still the dominant pattern today. . . .

This article has outlined three major areas in which major policy and organization changes are required for satisfactory international operations in the next few years: (1) meeting the threat of nationalism, (2) developing local national executives, and (3) internationalizing management. In each, the general direction of the future is quite clear. The problems lie therefore in the formulation of realistic and effective plans. This will be no small task.

In each area there are conflicting factors to consider and there are, as always, elements of inertia and ignorance to overcome. The hard facts of the tremendous potential of expanding world markets and the increasing competition to capture them should, however, provide ample incentive for U.S. managements to tackle the task realistically and energetically.

The emergence of the EEC has had a major impact on firms engaged in international marketing operations. Conclusions drawn from a study of marketing development in the European Economic Community are presented. Tendencies toward product rather than market orientation and fragmented marketing functions were observed in the international marketing operations of EEC members.

67. FINDINGS AND CONCLUSIONS*

Bertil Liander†

The establishment of the EEC is one of the outstanding events of this century. Its significance is reflected in the flood of arguments and controversies concerning future developments in international marketing.

The findings and conclusions drawn from this study represent an attempt to explore the path of future events by considering the following questions: What is the current status of marketing in the EEC, and what is the current role of marketing in the firm? What are the problems involved in establishing a common market? What are the major aspects of the marketing adjustment to the EEC? What are the attitudes of businessmen toward the EEC?

THE STATUS AND ROLE OF MARKETING

1. It is generally accepted in the United States that marketing development has lagged behind manufacturing development. The gap in the EEC seems much wider. Vast technological achievements have had little or no parallel in marketing. With the switch to a buyer's market and the advent of new competitive forces, many EEC firms are becoming increasingly concerned about their marketing operations.

2. Marketing is conceived by the respondent firms in a variety of contexts; e.g., the art of selling, the service of researching the market, and the system of planning and research. Few firms recognize marketing as a total system of interacting business activities.

---

* From *Marketing Development in the European Economic Community* by B. Liander. Copyright © 1964 by Marketing Science Institute. McGraw-Hill Book Company. Used by permission.

† Marketing Science Institute.

3. Most of the respondent firms are product rather than customer oriented; the center of their marketing philosophy rests on making the customer do what suits the interest of the producer. The producer tends to determine what he feels to be the most important product attributes and frequently emphasizes technical innovations that may not be judged significant by the consumer.

4. In many respondent firms, marketing tends to be a fragmented assortment of separate functions which lack coordination and synthesis. Frequently, certain important marketing functions are not under the control of the marketing executive. Also, top management is usually reluctant to delegate authority for basic price and product decisions.

5. In most respondent firms marketing planning represents the first stage of budgeting; in these firms, planning is both a prerequisite and a by-product of budgeting. In other respondent firms, planning is associated largely with investment decisions. Market studies and plans serve as a platform for decisions involving long-term financial commitments. There is a striking lack of that type of planning which is designed to meet anticipated changes in the firm's marketing opportunities.

6. In attempting to achieve a satisfactory level of demand, many manufacturers are prone to minimize rather than emphasize the differences in consumer demand. Subsequently, very little use is made of the strategy of market segmentation.

7. Product research and development play a different role from that observed in many American companies. For example, it is not usually built into the marketing strategy of many respondent firms; it is generally regarded as a technical question concerned more with manufacturing and production problems, and less with product and marketing innovations. Unlike the practice followed especially by many large firms in the United States, product research and development is seldom used as a competitive tool.

8. Marketing research can be said to be emergent; however, its scope is often limited to the solution of urgent current problems, and on other occasions to the obtaining and dispensing of marketing intelligence. Only a few respondent firms conceive of marketing research as a process involving the gathering of information for the purpose of planning, controlling, and evaluating marketing operations.

9. Pricing and promotional decisions do not seem to be critical elements in the respondent firm's marketing strategy. (Obviously, there are variations in degree depending on products produced, etc.) Inter-industry and inter-firm price and market agreements have usually limited the pricing alternatives available to the firm. Management skepticism about the price and promotional elasticities of demand has also limited use of pricing and promotion as effective tools of competition.

10. Many firms in the study hold an unfavorable attitude toward wholesale intermediaries. Consequently, they prefer to use direct channels

whenever possible. This is even true of firms manufacturing consumer nondurable goods.

PROBLEMS OF ESTABLISHING A COMMON MARKET

1. The EEC has made great progress in reducing internal tariff barriers and about half of the respondent firms found that tariffs were no longer an important hindrance to their exports. This was partly a result of rising demand in the EEC. On the other hand, about the same number of firms still considered tariffs to be an obstacle. This varied according to the Member Country's previous protection level and the individual firm's involvement in EEC trade.

2. Differing indirect tax systems in the Member Countries were frequently mentioned as a barrier as important as tariffs, or even as replacing tariffs as an obstacle. The EEC Commission proposal to harmonize these systems has caused little reaction from the manufacturing firms in the survey. ("Harmonization" is the term frequently used to describe the gradual reduction of differences and conflicts among EEC countries with reference to factors affecting markets and marketing.) The firms which spoke out on the proposal were divided primarily along national lines, with the French opposing and the others generally in favor.

3. The market divisions caused by diversity of national legislation and product regulations are still prevalent in the Common Market. Particularly respondent firms in the food, beverage, and packaging industries found the differences in legislation to be a major complication in exporting. Respondents did not believe that these regulations would be harmonized very soon.

4. There was little impact or awareness of the EEC Commission's program to harmonize social legislation. Although the principle of equal wages for men and women was supposed to be recognized by the EEC by the end of 1961, there is no consistent application. Feeling on this aspect of harmonization also follows national lines with the French favoring while the others oppose.

5. The Rome Treaty's provisions for increasing the mobility of labor in the Community have already had an effect, although this varies from country to country. The West German firms have felt the greatest impact but there were also firms in other countries which either had benefited or expected to benefit.

6. The Rules of Competition in the Rome Treaty and the competitive philosophy of the Commission are the cause of an increased wariness by manufacturers in their business practices. However, except for a dampening effect on the use of exclusive franchises, there has been no spectacular change in competitive behavior. Price agreements are still practiced and collaboration continues. The language of the Treaty and the Commission favors increased competition, but there are constraints on the EEC Com-

mission's power and staffing abilities. The prospect is for gradual change rather than revolution in competitive practices in the Common Market.

MARKETING ADJUSTMENTS TO THE EEC

Changes in Business Environment

1. Adjustments in companies' behavior have been caused more by anticipation and psychological factors than by an actual liberalization of trade.

2. The number of new companies becoming established in the different domestic markets does not seem to have increased as much as expected; although competition from United States firms having established operations in the EEC since 1958 has been an important influence.

3. Even if there is little obvious change so far in competitive behavior, there is already a marked awareness of increased competition in all countries and price is becoming a primary competitive factor. Service and quality are also important as bases for competition, but they are much less apparent than price.

Reactions by the Firm

1. An examination of the mergers in which companies in this survey had participated reveals that relatively few could be directly attributed to the EEC. This might be explained by the fact that a more obvious "harmonization" of market conditions must precede international mergers.

2. Differences between Member Countries of tastes, norms, and other sociological factors are many and do affect trade. One method frequently practiced to meet differing national demands is offering different combinations of merchandise to different national markets. However, there has not been a high degree of product adaptation in manufacturing. Producers still tend to expect a change in consumers' habits and attitudes, hence, feel little need to change their policies to suit the consumers.

3. The psychological impact of the EEC has increased contacts and communications between the Member Countries and thus tended to modify geographical variations in sales.

4. The EEC has resulted in two different, and almost equally popular, policies of production location: immediate establishment of production in a now national market, or a decision to "stay at home" and enjoy the benefits of large-scale production.

5. One-fourth of the firms in the survey have started new plants in other Member Countries since 1958. These were primarily firms with high export activity.

6. The creation of the EEC has led firms to a reappraisal of their general organization for marketing with an increased emphasis on marketing research.

7. Initial marketing research activities have in many cases been devoted to problems of an emergency nature, and are not yet integrated into overall marketing operations.

8. Export activities involving other EEC countries have frequently been administratively separated from other export activities.

9. More than half the respondent companies expect to increase their volume of intra-EEC trade and are preparing for such a change organizationally. No company expects to experience a decrease in its exports.

10. Almost half of the companies included in the sample had been motivated by the EEC to open one or more new sales offices in other Member Countries.

11. The organization and size of sales districts have not yet been affected by the wider market, although changes are being planned.

12. Respondents in about half of the companies claim that their firms have been forced to modify their distribution channel strategy since 1958.

13. Increased trade and communications between the Member Countries have thus far had little or no effect on the means of transportation employed to distribute manufacturers' products.

14. Profits per unit have been reduced both for manufacturers and distributors since 1958. Increased sales volume has, however, tended to more than offset the decline in unit profit and to cause total earnings to increase.

15. Much more attention has been paid to long-range planning since the Treaty of Rome. One reason for this is the increased confidence that has resulted from the minimizing of risks of unpredictable changes in national trade policies.

16. The changing market has had an impact on products. The flow of ideas and suggestions for new products has increased sharply since 1958. The life span of existing products has decreased and the number of new products appearing annually in the market is higher than before. Technical and other differences between products have been reduced. Still, this has not led to a decrease in the number or assortment of items produced by each individual manufacturer. Many expected that the initial impact of the EEC upon the breadth of most companies' product lines would be that of causing them to narrow as a result of the loss of tariff protection in home country markets. This would involve elimination of items not able to compete at home or abroad on a price or quality basis with the products of other EEC countries. This development has, however, been overshadowed by a current trend in the opposite direction as companies develop new products or revise old ones in response to the market opportunities now available in other EEC countries.

17. Consumer packages are tending to become more international

with respect to shape, size, illustration, and brand identification. Multilingual packages are becoming more common.

18. Until the harmonization regulations provided for in the Rome Treaty become effective, the price policies adopted by individual companies for various national markets will continue to be flexible and subject to variation.

19. Advertising expenditures relative to sales have increased in more than half of the responding companies. The increased expenditures do not, however, reflect any substantial changes in management's conservative attitude toward the use of modern advertising methods and advertising's role in the company's marketing program. There are also legal restrictions on the use of certain advertising media in several EEC countries.

Business Attitudes toward the EEC

1. The great majority of respondents thought the EEC would favor their own success. A few worried about the new competition they had to face, while some felt their success was independent of the EEC. The consensus was that the Common Market represented an improvement in the environment in which they operated. This was true for firms in all five countries, although there were national variations in response. The positive attitude toward the EEC also varied according to the extent of respondent firm involvement in the EEC market.

2. The attitude toward admission of new members to the EEC varied according to the respondent's evaluation of new members' probable effect on his own operations. The French firms were the most dubious about the desirability of admission of new members, although there were firms in each country which were also concerned about the new competition an expansion of the EEC would create. A third of the firms saw the admission of new members as questionable or harmful to them, while a larger number felt it would have no effect on them. About one-fifth believed an expansion of EEC would be beneficial.

3. Respondent firms were almost equally divided between those which felt that a collapse of the Common Market would hurt them and those which felt that such a collapse would have little impact on their own operations. Those who felt that its failure would not hurt them do not anticipate such an eventuality. These respondents appeared to ignore any dynamic effects of the Common Market in raising incomes and demand. Those who were more disturbed about the consequences of a collapse varied in the intensity of their concern.

B. Marketing and Economic Development

Marketing holds a key position as one of the most effective engines of economic development in underdeveloped countries. Frequently, in underdeveloped countries manufacturing and construction are stressed, while marketing is neglected. The development of marketing in such countries facilitates economic integration and optimum utilization of the economy's assets and productive capacity. Particularly valuable is marketing's ability to develop managers and entrepreneurs.

68. MARKETING AND ECONOMIC DEVELOPMENT*

Peter F. Drucker†

MARKETING AS A BUSINESS DISCIPLINE

The distinguished pioneer of marketing, Charles Coolidge Parlin, whose memory we honor today, was largely instrumental in developing marketing as a systematic business discipline:

In teaching us how to go about, in an orderly, purposeful and planned way to find and create customers;

* Reprinted from "Marketing and Economic Development," *Journal of Marketing*, Vol. XXII, No. 3 (January, 1958), pp. 252–59. This paper was first presented as a lecture given in memory of Charles Coolidge Parlin who is frequently identified as the founder of modern marketing research. This paper was one of the earliest and is still one of the most significant statements on marketing and economic growth.

† New York University.

To identify and define markets; to create new ones and promote them;

To integrate customers' needs, wants, and preferences, and the intellectual and creative capacity and skills of an industrial society, toward the design of new and better products and of new distributive concepts and processes.

On this contribution and similar ones of other Founding Fathers of marketing during the last half century rests the rapid emergence of marketing as perhaps the most advanced, certainly the most "scientific" of all functional business disciplines.

But Charles Coolidge Parlin also contributed as a Founding Father toward the development of marketing as a *social discipline*. He helped give us the awareness, the concepts, and the tools that make us understand marketing as a dynamic process of society through which business enterprise is integrated productively with society's purposes and human values. It is in marketing, as we now understand it, that we satisfy individual and social values, needs, and wants—be it through producing goods, supplying services, fostering innovation, or creating satisfaction. Marketing, as we have come to understand it, has its focus on the customer, that is, on the individual making decisions within a social structure and within a personal and social value system. Marketing is thus the process through which economy is integrated into society to serve human needs.

I am not competent to speak about marketing in the first sense, marketing as a functional discipline of business. I am indeed greatly concerned with marketing in this meaning. One could not be concerned, as I am, with the basic institutions of industrial society in general and with the management of business enterprise in particular, without a deep and direct concern with marketing. But in this field I am a consumer of marketing alone—albeit a heavy one. I am not capable of making a contribution. I would indeed be able to talk about the wants and needs I have which I, as a consumer of marketing, hope that you, the men of marketing, will soon supply:—a theory of pricing, for instance, that can serve, as true theories should, as the foundation for actual pricing decisions and for an understanding of price behavior; or a consumer-focused concept and theory of competition. But I could not produce any of these "new products" of marketing which we want. I cannot contribute myself. To use marketing language, I am not even "effective demand," in these fields as yet.

THE ROLE OF MARKETING

I shall today in my remarks confine myself to the second meaning in which marketing has become a discipline: The role of marketing in economy and society. And I shall single out as my focus the role of marketing in the economic development, especially of under-developed "growth" countries.

My thesis is very briefly as follows. Marketing occupies a critical role in respect to the development of such "growth" areas. Indeed marketing is the most important "multiplier" of such development. It is in itself in every one of these areas the least developed, the most backward part of the economic system. Its development, above all others, makes possible economic integration and the fullest utilization of whatever assets and productive capacity an economy already possesses. It mobilizes latent economic energy. It contributes to the greatest needs: that for the rapid development of entrepreneurs and managers, and at the same time it may be the easiest area of managerial work to get going. The reason is that, thanks to men like Charles Coolidge Parlin, it is the most systematized and, therefore, the most learnable and the most teachable of all areas of business management and entrepreneurship.

INTERNATIONAL AND INTERRACIAL INEQUALITY

Looking at this world of ours, we see some essentially new facts.

For the first time in man's history the whole world is united and unified. This may seem a strange statement in view of the conflicts and threats of suicidal wars that scream at us from every headline. But conflict has always been with us. What is new is that today all of mankind shares the same vision, the same objective, the same goal, the same hope, and believes in the same tools. This vision might, in gross over-simplification, be called "industrialization."

It is the belief that it is possible for man to improve his economic lot through systematic, purposeful, and directed effort—individually as well as for an entire society. It is the belief that we have the tools at our disposal—the technological, the conceptual, and the social tools—to enable man to raise himself, through his own efforts, at least to a level that we in this country would consider poverty, but which for most of our world would be almost unbelievable luxury.

And this is an irreversible new fact. It has been made so by these true agents of revolution in our times: the new tools of communication—the dirt road, the truck, and the radio, which have penetrated even the furthest, most isolated and most primitive community.

This is new, and cannot be emphasized too much and too often. It is both a tremendous vision and a tremendous danger in that catastrophe must result if it cannot be satisfied, at least to a modest degree.

But at the same time we have a new, unprecedented danger, that of international and interracial inequality. We on the North American continent are a mere tenth of the world population, including our Canadian friends and neighbors. But we have at least 75 per cent of the world income. And the 75 per cent of the world population whose income is below $100 per capita a year receive together perhaps no more than 10 per cent of the world's income. This is inequality of income, as great as anything the world has ever seen. It is accompanied by very high equality of income in the developed countries, especially in ours where we are in the process of proving that an industrial society does not have to live in extreme tension between the few very rich and the many very poor as lived all earlier societies of man. But what used to be national inequality and economic tension is now rapidly becoming international (and unfortunately also interracial) inequality and tension.

This is also brand new. In the past there were tremendous differences between societies and cultures: in their beliefs, their concepts, their ways of life, and their knowledge. The Frankish knight who went on Crusade was an ignorant and illiterate boor, according to the standards of the polished courtiers of Constantinople or of his Moslem enemies. But economically his society and theirs were exactly alike. They had the same sources of income, the same productivity of labor, the same forms and channels of investment, the same economic institutions, and the same distribution of income and wealth. Economically the Frankish knight, however much a barbarian he appeared, was at home in the societies of the East; and so was his serf. Both fitted in immediately and without any difficulty.

And this has been the case of all societies that went above the level of purely primitive tribe.

The inequality in our world today, however, between nations and races, is therefore a new—and a tremendously dangerous—phenomenon.

What we are engaged in today is essentially a race between the promise of economic development and the threat of international world-wide class war. The economic development is the opportunity of this age. The class war is the danger. Both are new. Both are indeed so new that most of us do not even see them as yet. But they are the essential economic realities of this industrial age of ours. And whether we shall realize the opportunity or succumb to danger will largely decide not only the economic future of this world—it may largely decide its spiritual, its intellectual, its political, and its social future.

SIGNIFICANCE OF MARKETING

Marketing is central in this new situation. For marketing is one of our most potent levers to convert the danger into the opportunity.

To understand this we must ask: What do we mean by "underdeveloped"?

The first answer is, of course, that we mean areas of very low income. But income is, after all, a result. It is a result first of extreme agricultural over-population in which the great bulk of the people have to find a living on the land which, as a result, cannot even produce enough food to feed them, let alone produce a surplus. It is certainly a result of low productivity. And both, in a vicious circle, mean that there is not enough capital for investment, and very low productivity of what is being invested—owing largely to misdirection of investment into unessential and unproductive channels.

All this we know today and understand. Indeed we have learned during the last few years a very great deal both about the structure of an under-developed economy and about the theory and dynamics of economic development.

What we tend to forget, however, is that the essential aspect of an "under-developed" economy and the factor the absence of which keeps it "under-developed," is the inability to organize economic efforts and energies, to bring together resources, wants, and capacities, and so to convert a self-limiting static system into creative, self-generating organic growth.

And this is where marketing comes in.

Lack of Development in "Under-developed" Countries

(1) First, in every "under-developed" country I know of, marketing is the most under-developed—or the least developed—part of the economy, if only because of the strong, pervasive prejudice against the "middleman."

As a result, these countries are stunted by inability to make effective use of the little they have. Marketing might by itself go far toward changing the entire economic tone of the existing system—without any change in methods of production, distribution of population, or of income.

It would make the producers capable of producing marketable products by providing them with standards, with quality demands, and with specifications for their product. It would make the product capable of being brought to markets instead of perishing on the way. And it would make the consumer capable of discrimination, that is, of obtaining the greatest value for his very limited purchasing power.

In every one of these countries, marketing profits are characteristically low. Indeed the people engaged in marketing barely eke out a subsistence living. And "mark-ups" are minute by our standards. But marketing costs are outrageously high. The waste in distribution and marketing, if only from spoilage or from the accumulation of unsalable inventories that clog the shelves for years, has to be seen to be believed. And marketing service is by and large all but non-existent.

What is needed in any "growth" country to make economic development realistic, and at the same time produce a vivid demonstration of what economic development can produce, is a marketing system:

A system of physical distribution;

A financial system to make possible the distribution of goods; and

Finally actual marketing, that is, an actual system of integrating wants, needs, and purchasing power of the consumer with capacity and resources of production.

This need is largely masked today because marketing is so often confused with the traditional "trader and merchant" of which every one of these countries has more than enough. It would be one of our most important contributions to the development of "under-developed" countries to get across the fact that marketing is something quite different.

It would be basic to get across the triple function of marketing:

The function of crystallizing and directing demand for maximum productive effectiveness and efficiency;

The function of guiding production purposefully toward maximum consumer satisfaction and consumer value;

The function of creating discrimination that then gives rewards to those who really contribute excellence, and that then also penalize the monopolist, the slothful, or those who only want to take but do not want to contribute or to risk.

Utilization by the Entrepreneur

(2) Marketing is also the most easily accessible "multiplier" of managers and entrepreneurs in an "under-developed" growth area. And managers and entrepreneurs are the foremost need of these countries. In the first place, "economic development" is not a force of nature. It is the result of the action, the purposeful, responsible, risk-taking action, of men as entrepreneurs and managers.

Certainly it is the entrepreneur and manager who alone can convey to the people of these countries an understanding of what economic development means and how it can be achieved.

Marketing can convert latent demand into effective demand. It cannot, by itself, create purchasing power. But it can uncover and channel all purchasing power that exists. It can, therefore, create rapidly the conditions for a much higher level of economic activity than existed before, can create the opportunities for the entrepreneur.

It then can create the stimulus for the development of modern, responsible, professional management by creating opportunity for the producer who knows how to plan, how to organize, how to lead people, how to innovate.

In most of these countries markets are of necessity very small. They are too small to make it possible to organize distribution for a single-product line in any effective manner. As a result, without a marketing organization, many products for which there is an adequate demand at a reasonable price cannot be distributed; or worse, they can be produced and distributed only under monopoly conditions. A marketing system is needed which serves as the joint and common channel for many producers if any of them is to be able to come into existence and to stay in existence.

This means in effect that a marketing system in the "under-developed" countries is the *creator of small business*, is the only way in which a man of vision and daring can become a businessman and an entrepreneur himself. This is thereby also the only way in which a true middle class can develop in the countries in which the habit of investment in productive enterprise has still to be created.

Developer of Standards

(3) Marketing in an "under-developed" country is the developer of standards—of standards for product and service as well as of standards of conduct, of integrity, of reliability, of foresight, and of concern for the basic long-range impact of decisions on the customer, the supplier, the economy, and the society.

Rather than go on making theoretical statements let me point to one illustration: The impact Sears Roebuck has had on several countries of Latin America. To be sure, the countries of Latin America in which Sears operates—Mexico, Brazil, Cuba, Venezuela, Colombia, and Peru—are not "under-developed" in the same sense in which Indonesia or the Congo are "under-developed." Their average income, although very low by our standards, is at least two times, perhaps as much as four or five times, that of the truly "under-developed" countries in which the bulk of mankind still live. Still in every respect except income level these Latin American countries are at best "developing." And they have all the problems of economic development—perhaps even in more acute form than the countries of Asia and Africa, precisely because their development has been so fast during the last ten years.

It is also true that Sears in these countries is not a "low-price" merchandiser. It caters to the middle class in the richer of these countries, and to the upper middle class in the poorest of these countries. Incidentally, the income level of these groups is still lower than that of the worker in the industrial sector of our economy.

Still Sears is a mass-marketer even in Colombia or Peru. What is perhaps even more important, it is applying in these "under-developed" countries exactly the same policies and principles it applies in this country, carries substantially the same merchandise (although most of it produced in the countries themselves), and applies the same concepts of marketing it uses in Indianapolis or Philadelphia. Its impact and experience are, therefore, a fair test of what marketing principles, marketing knowledge, and marketing techniques can achieve.

The impact of this one American business which does not have more than a mere handful of stores in these countries and handles no more than a small fraction of the total retail business of these countries is truly amazing. In the first place, Sears' latent purchasing power has fast become actual purchasing power. Or, to put it less theoretically, people have begun to organize their buying and to go out for value in what they do buy.

Secondly, by the very fact that it builds one store in one city, Sears forces a revolution in retailing throughout the whole surrounding area. It forces store modernization. It forces consumer credit. It forces a different attitude toward the customer, toward the store clerk, toward the supplier, and toward the merchandise itself. It forces other retailers to adopt modern methods of pricing, of inventory control, of training, of window display, and what have you.

The greatest impact Sears has had, however, is in the multiplication of new industrial business for which Sears creates a marketing channel. Because it has had to sell goods manufactured in these countries rather than import them (if only because of foreign exchange restrictions), Sears has been instrumental in getting established literally hundreds of new manufacturers making goods which, a few years ago, could not be made in the country, let alone be sold in adequate quantity. Simply to satisfy its own marketing needs, Sears has had to insist on standards of workmanship, quality, and delivery—that is, on standards of production management, of technical management, and above all of the management of people—which, in a few short years, have advanced the art and science of management in these countries by at least a generation.

I hardly need to add that Sears is not in Latin America for reasons of philanthropy, but because it is good and profitable business with extraordinary growth potential. In other words, Sears is in Latin America because marketing is the major opportunity in a "growth economy" —precisely because its absence is a major economic gap and the greatest need.

The Discipline of Marketing

(4) Finally, marketing is critical in economic development because marketing has become so largely systematized, so largely both learnable and teachable. It is the discipline among all our business disciplines that has advanced the furthest.

I do not forget for a moment how much we still have to learn in marketing. But we should also not forget that most of what we have learned so far we have learned in a form in which we can express it in general concepts, in valid principles and, to a substantial degree, in quantifiable measurements. This, above all others, was the achievement of that generation to whom Charles Coolidge Parlin was leader and inspiration.

A critical factor in this world of ours is the learnability and teachability of what it means to be an entrepreneur and manager. For it is the entrepreneur and the manager who alone can cause economic development to happen. The world needs them, therefore, in very large numbers; and it needs them fast.

Obviously this need cannot be supplied by our supplying entrepreneurs and managers, quite apart from the fact that we hardly have the surplus. Money we can supply. Technical assistance we can supply, and should supply more. But the supply of men we can offer to the people in the "under-developed" countries is of necessity a very small one.

The demand is also much too urgent for it to be supplied by slow evolution through experience, or through dependence on the emergence of "naturals." The danger that lies in the inequality today between the few countries that have and the great many countries that have not is much too great to permit a wait of centuries. Yet it takes centuries if we depend on experience and slow evolution for the supply of entrepreneurs and managers adequate to the needs of a modern society.

There is only one way in which man has ever been able to short-cut experience, to telescope development, in other words, to *learn something*. That way is to have available the distillate of experience and skill in the form of knowledge, of concepts, of generalization, of measurement—in the form of *discipline*, in other words.

THE DISCIPLINE OF ENTREPRENEURSHIP

Many of us today are working on the fashioning of such a discipline of entrepreneurship and management. Maybe we are further along than most of us realize.

Certainly in what has come to be called "Operation Research and Synthesis" we have the first beginnings of a systematic approach to the entrepreneurial task of purposeful risk-taking and innovation—so far only an approach, but a most promising one, unless indeed we become so enamored with the gadgets and techniques as to forget purpose and aim.

We are at the beginning perhaps also of an understanding of the basic problems of organizing people of diversified and highly advanced skill and judgment together in one effective organization, although again no one so far would, I am convinced, claim more for us than that we have begun at last to ask intelligent questions.

But marketing, although it only covers one functional area in the field, has something that can be called a discipline. It has developed general concepts, that is, theories that explain a multitude of phenomena in simple statements. It even has measurements that record "facts" rather than opinions. In marketing, therefore, we already possess a learnable and teachable approach to this basic and central problem not only of the "under-developed" countries but of all countries. All of us have today the same survival stake in economic development. The risk and danger of international and interracial inequality are simply too great.

Marketing is obviously not a cure-all, not a paradox. It is only one thing we need. But it answers a critical need. At the same time marketing is most highly developed.

Indeed without marketing as the hinge on which to turn, economic development will almost have to take the totalitarian form. A totalitarian system can be defined economically as one in which economic development is being attempted without marketing, indeed as one in which marketing is suppressed. Precisely because it first looks at the values and wants of the individual, and because it then develops people to act purposefully and responsibly—that is, because of its effectiveness in developing a free economy—marketing is suppressed in a totalitarian system. If we want economic development in freedom and responsibility, we have to build it on the development of marketing.

In the new and unprecedented world we live in, a world which knows both a new unity of vision and growth and a new and most dangerous cleavage, marketing has a special and central role to play. This role goes:

Beyond "getting the stuff out the back door";
Beyond "getting the most sales with the least cost";
Beyond "the optimal integration of our values and wants as customers, citizens, and persons, with our productive resources and intellectual achievements"—the role marketing plays in a developed society.

In a developing economy, marketing is, of course, all of this. But in addition, in an economy that is striving to break the age-old bondage of man to misery, want, and destitution, marketing is also the catalyst for the transmutation of latent resources into actual resources, of desires into accomplishments, and the development of responsible economic leaders and informed economic citizens.

Imaginative marketing is the key to the attainment of modern, industrial economies in newly emergent countries. Similarly, older nations faced with the need to change certain social or economic orientations will find that modern marketing practices can solve many of their immediate and most difficult problems. Systematic diffusion of technological and marketing skills will modernize and strengthen the agricultural and consumer goods sectors of an economy. The resulting widened domestic markets and diversified export offerings will provide the foundation, depth, and structural balance required in a modern industrial society.

69. THE CONCEPT OF A NATIONAL MARKET AND ITS ECONOMICS GROWTH IMPLICATIONS*

Walt W. Rostow†

I

I can tell you—without flattery—that I believe the skills this organization (American Marketing Association) commands and represents are going to prove critical in the generation ahead to the development of countries and regions which contain a clear majority of the world's population. I have in mind the developing countries of Asia, the Middle East, Africa, and Latin America. I also have in mind the Soviet Union and the countries of Eastern Europe. I would add, parenthetically, that should Communist China come, in time, to formulate a rational and effective development strategy—which it now lacks—marketing in all its dimensions must play there, too, a new and significant role.

II

To understand why this proposition is valid, one must look at the development theories and policies which have been applied to these re-

* Reprinted from "The Concept of a National Market and Its Economics Growth Implications," *Proceedings of the Fall Conference of the American Marketing Association*, 1965, pp. 11–20

† Special Assistant to the President of the United States.

gions over the past generation, examine where they now stand and where they must go as they move forward in their stages of development.

With a few exceptions, the developing nations of Asia, the Middle East, Africa, and Latin America began their first purposeful stage of modernization by concentrating their efforts in two areas: the production of manufactured goods in substitution for consumer goods imports and the creation of basic infrastructure; that is, roads, electric power, ports, education, etc. Agriculture and the modernization of rural life were systematically neglected, yielding now a dangerous decline in per capita food production in some major regions.

There was a certain legitimacy in these initial priorities. The development of an economy, at its core, consists in the progressive diffusion of the fruits of modern science and technology. Industry is the most dramatic form which modern science and technology assumes; and basic infrastructure is directly required for industrialization.

But there was also an element of irrationality. Agriculture was associated with the period of colonialism and/or with excessive dependence on export markets in industrial countries. It appeared to be second order—and, even, faintly humiliating business, as compared to industrialization.

The combination of these two factors—rational and irrational—has led to a phase of development concentrated largely in a few cities, centered around a few industries, and, as I say, to a systematic neglect of what agriculture could and must contribute by way of food, industrial raw materials, foreign exchange, and enlarged domestic markets.

The start of industrialization varied in time as among the developing countries of the contemporary world. The Latin American countries generally began just before or during the Second World War, while many others began seriously only in the years after 1945. Some, indeed, have not yet launched their first phase of sustained industrialization. Nevertheless, it is broadly true that we have come to the end or are coming to the end of the phase when the initial, narrow postwar strategy for development can be regarded as viable.

In one developing country after another the perception is spreading that the next phase of development must be based on a systematic diffusion of the modern skills, now largely concentrated in urban areas, out into the countryside; on the making of efficient national markets; and, from this widened basis, on the generation of new lines of diversified exports which alone promise to earn the foreign exchange which the developing countries will need in the years ahead. Only this pattern of widened domestic markets and diversified exports promises to provide the foundation for that deepening of the industrial structure (from consumers goods down to capital goods and the heavy industry sectors) which a modern industrial society requires.

If I may be permitted to use a somewhat private vocabulary,[1] it can be said that during the past generation we have had in many parts of the world a take-off in which the leading sectors have been import-substitution industries in consumer goods fields; and for these nations to move on into the drive to industrial maturity requires that they convert their somewhat isolated urban industrial concentrations into active, dynamic centers which purposefully diffuse the process of modernization out across the nation, while they generate the capacity, on this wider market foundation, to pay their way as they move to full industrialization of their societies.

This is a shorthand approximation of the task for the next generation that lies before the nations within the Free World, which contain most of the population of Asia, the Middle East, Africa, and Latin America; and it is also the problem which must be solved if a modern industrialized China is really going to emerge.

III

The problem in the Soviet Union and much of Eastern Europe is, of course, somewhat different. There the origins of industrialization generally reach back to the last quarter of the nineteenth century—in some regions even earlier. These nations (with certain exceptions) have moved forward in the postwar generation to complete the drive to industrial maturity. They did so under doctrines which made the expansion of heavy industry virtually an object in itself; that is, heavy industry was built either to supply military forces or to build more heavy industry. But they have now come to a stage in their development where Khrushchev was quite right in attacking what he called the "steel eaters." He asked, you may remember, 'What do you want us to do with more steel, eat it?' It is the inevitable—and predicted—slowing down in the heavy industry sectors which mainly accounts for the over-all sluggishness of these economies. They have exhausted the capacity of the heavy industry sectors to lead in the growth process.

Along this way, like the developing countries, the Soviet Union and the countries of Eastern Europe have neglected agriculture. In addition, they have kept it under forms of collective organization which were grossly inefficient in their use of capital and manpower, although collective arrangements are being diluted in parts of Eastern Europe in an effort to provide effective incentives to the farmer.

The next stage of development in the Soviet Union and Eastern Europe must, evidently, be based not merely on a correction of agricultural inefficiency but upon the turning of their relatively mature industrial

[1] Dr. Rostow refers here to his book, *The Stages of Economic Growth: A Non-Communist Manifesto,* Cambridge University Press, 1960.

complexes to supply the things which people want when average income levels reach the point at which they now stand in these countries.

If high rates of growth are to be resumed in the Soviet Union and in Eastern Europe, they will come about by some version of the economic and social revolution which we in the United States began in the 1920's and which began to grip Western Europe and Japan in the 1950's; that is, the revolution centered about the rapid diffusion of the automobile, durable consumers goods, suburban housing, and all the rest of the now familiar package.

I may say in passing that this revolution is not to be understood simply in terms of industrial gadgetry. Behind the desire for a private automobile, a television set, a suburban house with a little grass and a fence, are two profound human desires which, from all we can thus far observe, are universal; namely, a desire for mobility—for getting over the horizon—and a desire for privacy. The gadgets we command represent, simply, the ways modern industry has found to satisfy these deep, legitimate, and decent human desires.

Again, reverting to my own terms, I would say that, just as most of the developing world is in a process of adjustment from take-off to the drive to technological maturity, the Soviet Union and Eastern Europe are in a process of adjustment from their own version of the drive to technological maturity to the age of high-mass consumption.

IV

And here, of course, is where marketing comes in.

The modernization of the countryside in the developing countries evidently has many dimensions. We now know enough from practical experience to be able to say that, assuming roads and minimum basic education and assuming, also a certain backlog of relevant agricultural science, there are four necessary and sufficient conditions for an agricultural revolution.

First, the farmer must receive a reliable and fair price for his product.

Second, credit must be available at reasonable rates for him to make the change in the character of his output or the shift in productivity desired.

Third, there must be available on the spot technical assistance that is relevant to his soil, his weather conditions, and his change in either output or in productivity.

Finally, there must be available at reasonable rates two types of industrial products: inputs such as chemical fertilizers, insecticides, and farm tools; and incentive goods—that is, the consumer goods of good quality he and his family would purchase in greater quantity or work harder to get if they were cheaper or if his income were higher.

These four conditions can be satisfied in a good many ways. As I have wandered about the developing areas and studied the evidence available, I have been struck by the variety of institutional forms in which agricultural success stories appear—producers' cooperatives, food processing firms, large commercial farms, etc.; but they all have the characteristic of organizing around the farmer these four necessary and sufficient conditions.

You will note that marketing enters directly into these conditions both ways; that is, marketing from the farm to the city and from the city to the farm.

If the farmer is to receive a fair price for his product without a rise of food prices in the cities, there must be a modernization of marketing arrangements which permits this to happen. No aspect of the developing world troubles me more than the widespread situation where the farmer gets 15 or 20 percent of the selling price of his product—with the selling price in the city high and great wastage occurring along the way.

It is sometimes argued that the fragmented and expensive marketing arrangements which exist for many commodities in developing countries are, simply, an aspect of underdevelopment which will pass away with time and the progress of modernization as a whole. Specifically, it is sometimes pointed out that the modernization of marketing might remove from employment people who are now engaged, even at a low level of productivity.

Three considerations argue against this more complacent line of thought.

First, in many cases the marketing arrangements which confront a farmer in a developing country are what economists call monopsonistic; that is, the individual farmer is confronted with a situation where there is only one intermediary to whom he can sell his product. At the critical point of the harvest season the farmer is at the mercy of such intermediaries. That inequitable bargaining circumstance is often made worse because the purchaser of the farmer's products is often also the only available source of credit to the farmer. In short, traditional marketing arrangements are not only inefficient, they often do not have the competitive characteristics economists implicitly assume.

Second, the gap between prices on the farm and prices to the urban consumer constitutes a quite special barrier between the cities and the countryside, the effects of which must be measured not merely in terms of the alternative employment of labor but in terms of the whole urban–rural relationship. Specifically, archaic marketing arrangements make it unprofitable for the farmer to engage in higher productivity agricultural production; and they thereby reduce not only agricultural output but also the size of the market for manufactured goods. In modernizing marketing relations, we must take into account not merely the possible displacement of labor in the present marketing chains but the total effects on output and markets of what one Latin American president has called the Chinese wall they constitute between the city and the countryside.

Third, quite pragmatically, where modern marketing arrangements have been introduced (through producers' cooperatives, food processing firms, commercial farming, or other arrangements), the process of adjustment in employment in the marketing sector has not, in practice, proved difficult.

In short, I am confident that the modernization of marketing arrangements from the farm to the city is a crusade we can enter with a conviction that the benefits will far outweigh the costs in readjustment.

Looked at from the other side, that is, from the city to the countryside, the modernization of rural life demands new and effective ways of getting to the farmer both the things he needs to increase productivity and incentive goods.

With respect to chemical fertilizers, insecticides, seeds, and farm machinery, there is a role, beyond conventional marketing, to be undertaken by the salesman. It may be regarded as sacrilege by some, but it has generally proved true that the most powerful agent in the diffusion of new agricultural technology has been the commercial firm rather than public institutions set up for technical assistance purposes. I would not for a moment denigrate the role in the United States of the county agent nor of those who have followed in his tradition in the developing areas; but it is simply a fact that there are not enough county agents out working in the villages to do the job in contemporary developing areas. Among other reasons, too many trained agricultural technologists are to be found working in government offices in the capital city rather than in grass roots jobs. A good, pragmatic performance in the diffusion of technical knowledge can be and is being done in many parts of the world by those who have a straight commercial interest in selling their products. The salesman knows he must spend his time with potential customers.

With respect to incentive goods, we must begin by accepting the fact that people in the rural areas of the developing world are poor. Until their income rises, they may not be able to buy a great deal more than they are buying. On the other hand, it is also true that what they can buy in their villages by way of manufactured goods is often shoddy and expensive. We know from the history of rural areas in the United States—even the quite recent experience of the Tennessee Valley area—that the availability of attractive and inexpensive consumer goods can be an important stimulus to production and productivity. Lower prices can yield more purchases in the short run; lower prices and the availability of incentive goods of good quality can yield more output, income, and purchases in the longer run. The same lesson can be observed in Mexico and other developing areas where efforts to increase productivity on the supply side are combined with such incentives.

The technical marketing problem from the city to the countryside consists in finding ways to lower the unit cost of distribution under circumstances where rural markets are scattered and the volume of any one commodity to be sold at any one point is low. The most successful solution in developing countries is, of course, the marketing of beer and soft drinks. The volume of sales, however, is sufficient in this case to support regular truck deliveries even at low levels of rural income. What appears to be required is the development of unified marketing arrangements for a wide range of consumer goods so that the overhead distribution costs for each commodity are reduced.

As I have seen soft drink trucks roll into distant villages, I have often wished they had a trailer attached containing textiles, shoes, household equipment, flashlights, transistor radios, books and the other things the villagers would buy if prices were lower.

Producers' cooperatives, food processing plants, and other substantial institutions in rural areas can often serve as centers for the efficient assembly and distribution of such incentive goods, as well as the fertilizers, insecticides, etc., needed to increase productivity.

V

I have tried to indicate concretely the kind of marketing operations required if those engaged in distribution are to play their part in breaking down the Chinese wall between urban and rural life in developing countries and in assisting in the creation of national markets. The modernization of rural life, which lies at the heart of this structural problem, evidently involves elements which go beyond distribution itself. . . .

Nevertheless, it is clear that there is a ferment in the Soviet Union and in Eastern Europe centered on the lack of incentives to productivity in agriculture and on methods for making the distribution system more responsive to the interests and tastes of the consumer. There is a growing awareness of the inner contradiction between the modes of organization which have been created in the past out of their ideological commitments and the imperatives of progress. No one can predict the outcome of these debates and the changes in policy that will ensue; but they constitute an interesting and important element for change on the world scene, which is essentially hopeful.

VI

The making of national markets through the more effective linking of urban and rural areas bears directly on the other great task of the developing countries in the years ahead; namely, their need to generate diversified exports. A whole range of special skills and special efforts is needed to market new products abroad. Potential markets must be studied with careful attention to local tastes; distribution channels must be established; regular and reliable flows of supplies must be moved and financed; quality controls must be built up; and efficient production must be generated if the exports are to be competitive. For countries whose first phase of industrialization has taken place internally, behind high tariff barriers which protected the local market, a quite revolutionary shift in mentality is required before business can generate the efficiency to face the winds of international competition. That shift is only beginning to take place in a few Latin American countries at the present time; although, in Asia, Taiwan has made the transition to diversified manufactured exports in good style, and South Korea is well on its way. In highly competitive international markets it does not take many cases of supplies that fail to arrive on time or of uncertain quality for the export effort to be set back.

That branch of the art of distribution concerned with the export trade will evidently be increasingly important in the developing areas in the years ahead.

But there is a further connection worth noting. Historically the export of manufactured goods has usually followed or paralleled the development of a national market. The classic case was that of cotton textiles. Starting with Great Britain, one country after another entered the textile export trade as a kind of reflex to learning how to produce and distribute efficiently within its own national market; for cotton textiles are the first modern manufactured product likely to develop a mass market in a relatively poor country. Other manufactured goods, in turn, have flowed into international channels as they took hold in domestic markets—right down to Japan's booming export of transistor radios. In concentrating in the years ahead on the development of national markets, therefore, the developing countries will also be laying the foundations for the export of those diversified manufactures on which their future foreign exchange earning capacity will substantially rest.

VII

The argument I have tried to lay before you today has a particular significance for the development of economic thought as well as for public policy. Whether we are conscious of it or not, our ways of thinking about the economy are still colored by ideas that go back to the classical economists of the nineteenth century and, indeed, back to the eighteenth century world of the physiocrats. They began to organize their thoughts by focusing on the physical factors of production, notably land and labor. The concept of the widening of the market was introduced and effectively dramatized, of course, by Adam Smith. But what it took to widen the market, beyond physical means of transport, was not generally taken seriously by the founding fathers of modern economic thought. In fact, distribution (and services generally) tended to be ignored or regarded, somehow, as an inferior kind of economic activity.

Down to the present day it is difficult to get development economists and policy makers to accord to problems of efficiency in distribution the same attention they give automatically to problems of production, investment, and finance.

For Communists the problem is compounded by the nature of Marxist economics. Karl Marx was, as an economist, rooted in the classical tradition. His propositions perpetuated in a particularly strong form the tendency to denigrate distribution—so much so that it is formally excluded from Communist concepts of national income.

Thus in facing now the tasks of widening the market, both in the developing areas and in the Soviet Union and in Eastern Europe, governments must overcome that most insidious of pressures; that is, the pressures created by the sometimes unconscious acceptance of ideas from the past that obscure the character and priority of current problems.

If I am correct that men must, in the generation ahead, diffuse the process of modernization out over long neglected rural regions, creating new efficient networks of distribution, we shall see not merely new and challenging tasks for those who command the skills of distribution but a new theoretical respect and appreciation for the art of that widening of the market which, for so long, was taken for granted.

Serious problems in planning new industrial projects and the implementation of manufacturing processes have resulted when insufficient attention was paid to marketing considerations. A strategic role can be played by marketing in optimizing the use of capital resources in most developing countries.

70. MARKETING IN THE INDUSTRIALIZATION OF UNDERDEVELOPED COUNTRIES*

A. A. Sherbini†

Industrialization is occupying an increasingly prominent position in the development programs of many underdeveloped countries. Its appeal

* Reprinted from "Marketing in the Industrialization of Underdeveloped Countries," *Journal of Marketing*, Vol. XXIX, No. 1 (January, 1965), pp. 28–32.

† Marketing Science Institute.

stems from many sources—for example, enhancement of the country's prestige and power, achievement of a higher degree of economic self-sufficiency, and realization of more favorable terms of trade.

However, industrialization has been a painful process in many developing countries. The literature on economic development is indeed flooded with examples of shortcomings that have undermined the efficient functioning of new industrial ventures in these countries. A typical list of pitfalls includes absence of a vigorous growth mentality, difficulties in administration and management, lack of advance planning, poor maintenance, and inadequate financial controls.[1]

Yet, the recent experiences of many underdeveloped countries have shown that marketing problems can be more obstructive than many other deterrents to the process of industrialization. A higher rate of capital formation and relatively large doses of investments in manufacturing have frequently failed to generate the anticipated increase in national income. Poor marketing bears a significant part of the responsibility for this failure.

THE PLANNING PHASE

Industrialization is usually incorporated in a national economic development plan. The benchmark for such a plan is invariably a "macro-economic" program that projects the development of such aggregates as national income and outlay, imports, and exports. This is then refined in a "micro-economic" program that fills in the framework with figures for individual industries, regions, or even some important plants.

What types of goods will have to be produced? This is usually the first question in micro-planning. For the most part, imports provide the shopping list from which new industrial ventures are selected. Thus, few economic planners show due concern about the determination of consumers' generic wants and needs to be served, and the alternative ways of satisfying these generic wants.

Furthermore, the lure of import-substitution often precludes a consideration of other important want-satisfying projects. For instance, certain products have distinct physical characteristics, such as high perishability, which limit their participation in international trade. Also, historically the interests of trade intermediaries and other institutions may have curbed the importation of low-margin, but significant, want-satisfying goods.

Another problem in micro-planning concerns decisions on productive capacity for individual projects. Blind reliance on import statistics has frequently led to grave miscalculations in estimating domestic market requirements.

[1] Albert O. Hirschman, *The Strategy of Economic Development* (New Haven: Yale University Press, 1958), p. 136.

Likewise, the tendency to overlook marketing considerations has often given rise to the acquisition of improper equipment and other physical facilities. For example: An important section in a bicycle factory was provided for the automatic assembly of bicycle parts. However, it turned out that for several reasons trade channels preferred to receive their shipments unassembled. The assembly section is now operating much below standard capacity.

But the primacy of marketing considerations is not restricted to the micro-planning phase. All too often, marketing is the basic determinant of the destiny of new manufacturing enterprises from the moment they are launched. The remainder of this paper focuses on the role of marketing in the operating phase.

THE OPERATING PHASE

Generally speaking, the tendency in the early life of new manufacturing concerns is to place primary emphasis on staffing the production, financial, and general administrative departments of the firm. All thinking about sales is generally deferred to the point of actual production. The presence of a ready market and the availability of experienced trade channels minimize executive anxiety. The general assumption is simply that the new firm will inherit the entire assets of the import market; but experience has shown that it also takes over the liabilities.

Product and Production Decisions

In approaching the operating phase, the management of the firm is confronted with critical product decisions. A first decision concerns the selection of proper *product attributes* upon which a satisfactory volume of demand may converge. This may be a difficult task, as imports often tend to segment the domestic market. The multiplicity of foreign sources of supply brings to the domestic market an array of products with varying attributes. Thus, the aggregate demand for a given "product" often consists of many thin and heterogeneous demand schedules that are not additive.

The demand for even a simple product such as imported sardines sometimes reflects a high degree of consumer attachment to certain product attributes—for example, shape and type of tin, sauce-packed or oil-packed, flavor, and price. Foreign exporters who sell in world-wide markets generally find it economically possible and feasible to cater to thin domestic market segments in underdeveloped countries. But domestic manufacturing obviously cannot economically serve all thin market segments.

A refrigerator manufacturer may decide to make only electric refrigerators and forego the needs of other market segments for refrigerators powered by kerosene or butane. The next question concerns the sizes, shapes, and colors to be manufactured. This is essentially a decision on *assortment* size and varieties. Yet, again, imports condition the market to varieties and assortments not economically feasible for domestic manufacturing.

A third decision pertains to the extent of the *product line*. In general, the advantages of a full product line are not well conceived by the management of the new firm. The major determinants of line composition are such factors as common raw materials, technical know-how, and common production facilities. Interrelationships of demand characteristics are usually of minor concern.

This tendency has given rise to many problems. First, a high degree of unnecessary and misdirected diversification has compounded the distribution problem of many new firms. Many firms begin their operations by manufacturing many different and unrelated products that sell in distinct markets and utilize diverse trade channels. A second result is that trade intermediaries in general, and retailers in particular, tend to supplement their incomplete and domestically-based product lines with imported products. Thus, an appliance dealer may carry a refrigerator and washing machine of a domestic base, together with other household applicances of a foreign base. The higher margins on imported articles have frequently deprived domestic manufacturers of adequate dealer support.

A fourth area in which marketing problems have led to grave consequences is that of *production planning and control*. One immediate problem concerns the decision on the proper or optimum *product mix*. How much should be manufactured of the different sizes and shapes of screws, bolts, and nuts? How much should be produced of the diverse types, accessories, and colors of chinaware or other dinnerware? These typical perplexing questions are encountered by new firms, Secondary sources of statistics throw little or no light on these knotty points. For many firms, trial and error, regardless of its extremely high cost, is the only answer to the product mix riddle.

Production scheduling can also be a formidable problem, particularly for multiple product firms serving the needs of many divergent end users. For example:

> A canvas and netting firm is equipped to manufacture such diverse products as canvas, heavy cloth, nets, and filters. These products may be sold to manufacturers of many different articles—footwear, luggage, sails, tents, furniture, sportsgoods, and fishing nets. Lacking adequate market information, the manufacturer operates on a job-order basis rather than engage in mass production in anticipation of demand. The result has been very high setup costs and very short production runs. Furthermore, the linkage effect expected from this new industry has been seriously undermined; for instance, cloth filters continued to be imported simply because the importing firm did not know that this item could be manufactured locally.

The lack of crucial feedback concerning inventory fluctuations and rate of sale at different intermediary levels has often given rise to sporadic gluts followed by periods of acute shortages. For instance:

A manufacturer of bakery products contracted to sell its entire line through a sole distributor. One item in the line, a specialty product that the distributor had not previously sold, was forced on him under a tie-in arrangement. The news of a serious drop in retail sales during the summer took a long time in being transmitted to the manufacturer. Because of dilapidation, large quantities of the specialty product were destroyed, and many problems ensued at the consumer and retail levels.

Price Decisions

Domestic manufacturers in developing countries often face a dual problem in setting their basic prices. First, imports frequently impose an upper ceiling on prices, regardless of the adopted policy toward imports. Secondly, prices become rigid once they are set. Price controls and the need for government approval put firm limits on price flexibility.

A mistake in pricing, however trifling, is therefore of grave consequence for the new manufacturer. For instance:

The prices of imported nine-ounce cans of luncheon meat were all "odd" prices. A domestic manufacturer decided to round the price of his product in order to simplify his accounting task. When his sales were not moving as anticipated, a market study was undertaken. It was found that retailers were pushing the competing imports because many customers did not ask for the small change. It took this manufacturer almost six months to obtain permission to change his retail price so as to conform to prices of other competing products.

A major pitfall that has caused many problems for new firms is the tendency to ignore the whole gamut of price differentials and discount structures. Many firms start operations with no specific plans concerning trade margins. Thus, the spread between retail price and factory price is often unplanned and occasionally fails to accommodate the necessary trade margins. To resolve this problem, many manufacturers resort to trade channels that can be accommodated by the given spread; channels that may not be the most desirable for the product in question.

Terms of sale and discount structures also receive little attention. Some firms make no distinction between cash and credit sales in pricing their products, which boosts credit sales and undermines net factory price, since the cost of discounting credit notes is not taken into account. Other firms insist on cash sales and, thereby, do not attain desirable sales goals. The problems of financing, price differentials, and discount structures are often compounded as a result of the need to devise new systems and procedures, which follows the shift from an import-based to a domestic-based source of supply.

Channels of Distribution

Can existing import-oriented channels be effectively used in the distribution of domestic manufactures? How can existing channels be adapted to local manufacturing? These difficult questions confront new firms in many developing countries. Ironically, the new firm has often adapted to the practices and operations of existing channels, in spite of special features that make these channels unsuitable for domestic manufacturing.

The conflicts between import-oriented channels and the needs of domestic manufacturing can be outlined in the following points:

1. Imports not only *segment* the domestic market, they may also *fragment* that market. Large import wholesalers are not prone to create a national market; their businesses tend to cluster in big cities where margins are high and sales are not too costly. Thus, existing channels may not serve the needs of a domestic manufacturer who is contemplating nationwide distribution.

2. Import-oriented channels are generally characterized by a lack of functional specialization. The concept of a channel as a chain of intermediaries directly linked to each other is hardly applicable to this model. Intermediaries may simultaneously assume such different functions as importing, wholesaling, semi-wholesaling, and retailing; their general operating rule is to be present in any capacity when a chance to sell appears. Thus, an intermediary does not sell to a specific link in the channel, but to a *range* of other intermediaries. A domestic manufacturer, on the other hand, would be interested in a "chain-type" of channel in which specific tasks can be assigned and responsibilities affixed.

3. Lack of functional specialization is coupled with a high degree of division of labor. Such tasks as financing, storage and warehousing, trucking, shipping and packing, bulking and sorting, grading and packaging, are often performed by separate agencies and intermediaries. Lack of adequate capital and the need sometimes for the simultaneous performance of different tasks account for this. But domestic manufacturing requires a greater integration of these tasks; the manufacturer may assume some of them.

4. An import-oriented channel usually works backward; consumers, retailers, and other intermediaries are always seeking goods. This results from the tendency of importers to throttle the flow of goods and from the sporadic and uneven flow of imports. Inventory hoarding as a means of choking the market can be achieved at relatively low cost and is obviously justified because of its lucrative speculative yields.[2] In contrast,

[2] Harper W. Boyd, Jr., and A. A. Sherbini, "Wholesaling in Egypt," in Robert Bartels (editor), *Comparative Marketing: Wholesaling in Fifteen Countries* (Homewood, Illinois: Richard D. Irwin, Inc., 1963), p. 100.

domestic manufacturing ensures a steady stream of merchandise, requiring a smooth flow free from obstructions and stockpiles.

5. The variations in product specifications, resulting from different foreign origins, and in available supplies, lead to certain practices unfavorable for domestic manufacturing. For instance bargaining becomes a standard practice since it makes possible rapid adjustments to any changes in the situation. Profits, in a sense, are not conceived as compensation for the performance of certain tasks; they simply reflect the trader's ability to take advantage of the situation.

6. The credit system utilized in the import-oriented channel may differ considerably from that required by domestic manufacturing. In practice, a commercial bank furnishes the importer with the necessary documentary credit. Upon arrival, the merchandise is stored in the Customs under a Custom bond. The importer need pay the bank only for the specific quantities withdrawn from the Customs. Since these are often sold prior to withdrawal, the importer's business is, in effect, self-financing. But this arrangement is very difficult to duplicate for domestic manufacturing.

Credit also plays a primary role in sustaining and regulating the flow of imports into the domestic market. The marketing channel may be viewed as "a sort of hydraulic system in which the balance of credit pressures at hundreds of larger and smaller couplings determines the speed, direction, and volume of the flow of goods through the system. Most of everyone's time is consumed in pursuing debtors and dunning them, or in trying to wheedle a little more credit from one's creditors.[3] Obviously, this system is not tailored to the needs of modern manufacturing; the latter requires a faster and more direct flow of goods.

7. Because of the above inherent conflicts, some new firms have tried to develop new channels of distribution to serve more adequately the needs of domestic manufacturing. This has often given rise to bitter struggles with existing marketing channels. The existence of strong corporate groups, often based on kinship ties, among larger importers and wholesalers frequently puts the new firm at a disadvantage. Again and again, these middlemen may use diverse means to undermine the position of the new firm—price cutting, coercion, bankrupting other intermediaries who cooperate with the new firm, and spreading devastating rumors about quality and performance of the domestic product.

Promotional Decisions

Of what significance are promotional decisions for the new firm? What is the extent of the monopolistic powers of import-substituting firms? In answering these questions, the following points may be made:

[3] E. E. Hagen, *On the Theory of Social Change* (Homewood, Illinois: The Dorsey Press, Inc., 1962), p. 392.

1. A new firm of the import-substituting type is often pictured as a monopolist with no promotional problems. However, imports are frequently needed to supplement domestic manufacturing, and may thereby represent a challenging competitive force.

2. Even when domestic manufacturing is planned to replace imports *in toto*, imports may still continue to flow. Often enough, there seems to be a lack of coordination among government agencies, which results in issuing import licenses for goods that are also produced locally.

3. In many developing countries interindustry competition may be of great concern to the domestic manufacturer. For instance, the advent of television in Egypt has shown remarkable effects on the sales of other consumer durables. Thus, the stimulation of primary demand may carry greater weight than the emphasis put on selective demand.

4. The new firm often encounters the knotty problem of "domophobia," that is, the mistrust and disbelief in the quality of domestic products. Sometimes, considerable effort is required to establish an acceptable image for domestic manufactures.

5. Dealer cooperation in promoting the domestic product is usually a problem for the new firm. In an import-based system, the costs of distribution are essentially buying costs rather than selling costs; creating an atmosphere of shortages is the classic technique for rapid disposition of merchandise. Domestic manufacturing requires a new philosophy and different behavioral patterns.

IN CONCLUSION

Marketing problems have recently surprised many development planners. The lack of attention given to marketing considerations has resulted in serious flaws in planning and implementing new industrial projects. These concern such things as improper productive equipment, excess or sometimes inadequate plant capacity, and uneconomical plant location.

But marketing problems are not restricted to the planning phase of new manufacturing projects; they remain much at work once the manufacturing process has started. They often turn into obstructive forces leading to the stagnation and decay of ventures that looked hopeful at first.

Marketing is, therefore, a key factor in the success or failure of industrialization programs. Viewed in proper perspective, marketing can play a strategic role in optimizing the utilization of capital resources that are in scarce supply in most developing countries.

Bibliography—Chapter VII

BARTELS, ROBERT (ed.). *Comparative Marketing: Wholesaling in Fifteen Countries.* Homewood, Ill.: Richard D. Irwin, Inc., 1963.

FAYERWEATHER, JOHN. *International Marketing.* Englewood Cliffs, N.J.: Prentice-Hall, Inc., 1965.

GOLDMAN, MARSHALL I. *Soviet Marketing: Distribution in a Controlled Economy.* New York: Free Press of Glencoe, 1963.

KENEN, PETER B. *International Economics.* Englewood Cliffs, N.J.: Prentice-Hall, Inc., 1964.

KRAMER, ROLAND. *International Marketing.* Cincinnati: South-Western Publishing Co., 1959.

LEIGHTON, DAVID S. R. *International Marketing: Text and Cases.* New York: McGraw-Hill Book Co., Inc., 1966.

LIANDER, BERTIL. *Marketing Development in the European Economic Community.* New York: McGraw-Hill Book Co., Inc., 1964.

NORTON-TAYLOR, DUNCAN. "What the U.S. Can Do About World Hunger," *Fortune,* Vol. LXXIII, No. 6 (June, 1966), pp. 110ff.

QUINN, JAMES BRIAN. "Technological Competition: Europe vs. U.S.," *Harvard Business Review,* Vol. XLIV, No. 4 (July–August, 1966), pp. 113–30.

SOMERS, J. C. "Impact of Technology on International Trade," *The American Journal of Economics and Sociology,* Vol. XXI, No. 1 (January, 1962), pp. 69 ff.

VIII. SOCIETAL AND DISCIPLINARY ASPECTS: THE BROADER ISSUES

What is the domain of marketing? What are the boundaries of marketing as a field of study and an area of business practice? What is marketing's role in modern society? Marketing ethics, values, responsibilities, and marketing-government relationships are involved in discussions of these questions. Societal considerations also underlie more specific questions related to marketing's broader role:

Can or should marketing, as a function of business, possess a social role distinct from the personal social roles of individuals charged with marketing responsibility?

Does the business, as a legal entity or structural framework, possess a personality and a conscience greater than the sum of these characteristics in its individual managers and owners?

Can it be assumed that the orientation of a business toward marketing's societal role reflects a consensus of management? Or, should each member of management be held personally accountable for social acts committed or omitted in the name of the business?

Answers to such questions change over time, but the trend has been toward an expanding definition of marketing responsibility. In Chapter II, the thesis was advanced that the metamarketing approach—integrating scientific, social, ethical, and managerial experience—could be added to the traditional approaches to marketing.[1] *Selections included in this chapter go*

[1] Metamarketing (beyond marketing) designates an approach that is concerned with critical analysis of marketing as a social process and as a field of study whether the field be defined in managerial or other terms. The concern of metamarketing is to focus all scientific, social, ethical, and managerial experience on problems and issues related to marketing. See Eugene J. Kelley, *Marketing Strategy and Functions.* Englewood Cliffs, N.J.: Prentice-Hall, Inc., 1965, p. 13.

beyond managerial marketing to broader societal and disciplinary aspects of marketing.

Many of the preceding questions converge in the marketing and public policy area. Grether has suggested that one of the most significant external environmental forces affecting the performance of the marketing system is intervention of government, especially the federal government. He notes that markets are both means and ends in a society that chooses to maintain a private enterprise base, and that, historically, market systems have regulated while being regulated. In a market economy in which maintenance of the rule of competition is deemed in the national interest, maintenance of a competitive general market system as a means of coordination, organization, regulation, and enforcement of market discipline is the alternative to governmental or cartel regulation. In an economy not commited to competition the "command economy" role of governments becomes even more important. In any case, the character and capacities of the market system must be conceptualized in terms of the historical background and drift, traditions, legal system, and social and political goals of a nation. Since national and societal goals are characterized by change, views on what constitutes individual and group responsibility and areas of societal responsibility are also changing. The trend is toward a broader view of individual and business responsibility to society.

Today few marketing practitioners or academicians disagree with the concept that marketing has important socioeconomic dimensions and can be viewed as a social instrument in an industrialized society. However, disagreements exist on the relative importance of marketing's social and economic dimensions as compared to the managerial or technical aspects of the field.

The traditional view has been that marketing management fulfills the greater part of its responsibility by profitably and efficiently providing products and services that satisfy consumer needs. As a natural result of this efficiency, the firm prospers, customers are satisfied and the well-being of society follows. It is feared that the acceptance of any other additional responsibilities by management and by students of the marketing process would threaten the foundation of a system based largely on the incentive motivation of profits. In addition, those skeptical of the possibilities of identifying social or noneconomic responsibilities of marketing, point to the problems of determining who will establish guidelines and sanction departures from these guidelines.

The newer dissenting view does not take issue with the ends of consumer satisfaction and economic growth. The premise of this view is that the task of marketing and its concurrent responsibilities are much wider in scope than purely economic concerns. This newer view is based on the concept that the market process has evolved into one of the controlling elements of the world's socioeconomic growth. It has been said that war is too important to leave to generals; so too, marketing may involve more than optimization of profits and customer satisfaction. Marketing is a social instrument through which a standard of living is transmitted to a society; it is a social discipline and involves social responsibilities.

A tangible indication of the importance of marketing in the United States is that over half of the nation's labor force derives its income from the marketing system. Almost all people depend on marketing to deliver a standard of living. Further, the transactional sphere where people judge, compare, and exchange relative values is perceived as the open manifestation of the beliefs, hopes, and ethics of the community. Nowhere, it is held, is the inner self of the populace more openly demonstrated than in the marketplace. It is an area where actions are the proof of the words, and transactions are the illustrations of both physical and moral values. Within this context, it is contended that marketing's social responsibility is only partially fulfilled through the economic process, that it has a greater responsibility to people and to the human dignity that is vital to the marketplace.[2]

Normative economic and social roles of marketing are discussed in the first half of this chapter. The views and questions presented are matters of concern for all informed individuals. They hold special significance for those persons concerned with marketing as a profession or discipline. Marketing as a discipline is the subject of the concluding section of this chapter. Today, the field of marketing is a recognized area of academic study and investigation. As background for this section, it should be recalled that marketing as a distinct and established discipline is a product of the 20th century. The greatest part of the massive collection of marketing information has been compiled, classified, and analyzed in the last 30 years. This body of marketing information serves as a base for important theoretical work in marketing and reflects the increasing maturity and growing rigor of the discipline. The use of theory in marketing is still in the pioneering stages. But enough significant work has been done to indicate that the extension of marketing thought and the stature of marketing as a science will be further enhanced through continuing theoretical exploration and analysis.

The development of marketing theory and advancement of the discipline are perhaps more difficult and demanding tasks than is theory building in engineering, mathematics, or the physical sciences. One reason is that marketing theorists must consider many intangibles, such as the complexities of consumer behavior. Since change is the rule in marketing, the dynamic aspects of marketing are nearly always a primary consideration. The interrelationships existing among marketing factors are quite involved. As noted earlier in the book, marketing systems are complex and broad in scope. Although practitioners can usually acquire sufficient data about the

[2] From Warren A. French, "The Social Process of Marketing," an unpublished paper prepared at The Pennsylvania State University in 1967. Mr. French contributed significantly to the development of this chapter introduction.

operation of marketing systems, there is a lack of formal and conceptual procedures for investigation, organization, and analysis of this information.

Specifically, several dimensions of marketing thought, the interdisciplinary approach, and the role of theory are discussed in this last chapter. Through integration of knowledge from such disciplines as mathematics, sociology, psychology, and philosophy the interdisciplinary approach to the study of marketing can help to develop and improve marketing judgment, comprehension, and practice.

In the future, more attention should be focused on the development of marketing knowledge that will aid in explaining relationships and strengthen the foundation of marketing as a discipline. The development of marketing knowledge is not a simple process. The problem is one of achieving an understanding of relationships, structures, and patterns suggested by new information. This process is crucial to extending marketing thought, developing marketing as a science, and the fulfillment of marketing's broader roles.

A. Societal Dimensions of Marketing

The marketing system is a creation and reflection of our society, used to accomplish social as well as economic goals. Comparative marketing gains significance through recognition of its social and political aspects. Before a society can use marketing as a social tool, that society must undergo a transformation in which marketing evolves as a key institution.

71. MARKETING AS A SOCIAL AND POLITICAL TOOL*

Robert Bartels†

That marketing is a tool has never been questioned. Whether it is a social and political tool, however, is a more profound proposition, particularly when this topic is related at the same time to "Ethical Considerations in Marketing" and to "Marketing: A Maturing Discipline." The implication is that because ethics is a consideration of the interrelated responsibili-

* Reprinted from "Marketing as a Social and Political Tool," *Proceedings of the Summer Conference of the American Marketing Association*, 1962, pp. 210–16. For related discussions in this topic area, see: Eugene J. Kelley, "Marketing and Moral Values in an Acquisitive Society," *Proceedings of the Winter Conference of the American Marketing Association,* 1961, pp. 195–203; Richard Eells, "The Climate Nurturing Social Responsibility," *The Meaning of Modern Business* (New York: Columbia University Press, 1960), pp. 72–94; and Thomas H. Huxley, "Ethics For an Atomic Age" [excerpted from *Evolution and Ethics,* (1893)], *Saturday Review,* Vol. 28, No. 35 (September 1, 1945), p. 18.

† Ohio State University.

ties of business and society, attention should be directed to the manner in which marketing is being used, as a tool, in fulfillment of its social responsibility. The extent of its attainment along this line is a measure of its maturity in the development from social irresponsibility toward social responsibility. That the discipline of marketing is maturing is evident even in the consideration of this topic, for twenty years ago it would not have been considered, and forty years ago there was even less concern with the social responsibility of marketing.

The question of whether marketing is a social and political tool appears on the surface to be a conclusive question, for which there may be a definite "yes" or "no" answer. Even a little consideration of it, however, suggests that it is a rhetorical or didactic question, one which serves better to evoke discussion than to make a definitive point. This is so because the question involves three or four concepts, all of which are still debatable and in the process of definition. Specifically, what is less finally defined than the terms of the title: "Marketing," "social," "tool." If this discussion can clarify these concepts, it will have made some contribution toward answering the question in issue.

WHAT IS MARKETING?

Although marketing has now been studied for fifty or sixty years, students of the subject are more tentative in their definition of the term now than in the past. Originally, it was simply a practice, known as trade. Then it became a complex of considerations underlying the trading practice. Next it was viewed as the aggregate of functions or activities which serve as the means to an end. Thus, over the years, the concepts of marketing have been multiplied, diversified, and broadened, so that it is no longer merely the *business* tool, as originally conceived, but is, as implied by our topic, a *social* tool. Certainly that which was conceived as marketing when defined as a business tool could not be the object in thought when it is referred to as a social tool.

The maturing conception of marketing is a broadening one. Today it is regarded as a social institution, rather than merely a business institution, or even primarily an economic institution. It is a comparative cultural means for society's attainment of some of its goals. That is to say that "marketing" designates in one society a means or institution which may be non-existent in another society, because either the latter's ends or means are different. Marketing is a particular type of societies' means of supplying the physical needs of its members. More precisely and elaborately stated, this concept implies that marketing is the means whereby society supplies its physical needs by the recognition and analysis of markets, the conception and promotion of marketable products, the physical distribution of them, and the transfer of their titles.

WHAT IS "SOCIAL"?

Returning to our original question, is marketing, so conceived, a *social* and *political* tool? From the sociological viewpoint, society is "an enduring, cooperative social group so functioning as to maintain itself and perpetuate the species." Society, therefore, embraces its institutions—including its political institution—through which it functions for the achievement of its goals. Thus society embraces and includes the economy, which serves but a particular type of social ends; it includes the market, which may dominate and characterize the economy; it includes marketing, which is a more specialized institution within the market. In this sense, marketing is a social institution, a concept and creation of society, a medium sanctioned and ratified by society. From this viewpoint, society must be held to embrace marketing, not marketing to embrace society.

WHAT IS A "TOOL"?

The concept of a tool, in the sense of marketing as a tool, implies that it is an instrument or instrumentality employed for the achievement of certain effects. As such, it would be a means to an end. Can it be said that society *uses* as tools its institutions, such as marriage, religion, business, private property, credit, free enterprise, and the like?

Two views of this question are held. One is that society *consists* of its institutions and is not said to "use" them. Society is distinguished and characterized by its institutions, which are themselves the end manifestation of the values, ideals, and objectives of the society. The other is that society spawns and maintains its institutions not as manifestations of, but rather as means of achieving, its social values. In this sense, the marketing institution may be regarded as a tool used for the realization of such social ends as the following:

Physical survival through the acquisition of the necessities of livelihood
Equality of opportunity to consume
Employment of specialized talents in specialized occupations
Full utilization of extensive production capacity
Freedom to negotiate
Freedom to communicate, educate, and propagandize

"Marketing" is the term identifying the system by which our present society attempts to obtain these and other similar goals. Thus, broadly conceived, marketing is a social, including political, tool.

Simply to conclude that marketing is a social tool, however, does not warrant the inference that it is universally so used, or that where used it inevitably achieves desirable social results. With some justification, marketing may be regarded as a mature social phenomenon or, perhaps better, as a phenomenon of a mature society. Moreover, the ethical implications of marketing are inseparable from the ethics of society. To enlarge upon these points, let us consider some of the comparative, historical, and contemporary aspects of marketing.

COMPARATIVE MARKETING

When it is recognized that marketing is a social institution, it will be acknowledged that the institution may vary in different societies. In some, which have not evolved the marketing concept, it may be non-existent. The potentiality of marketing as a social tool, therefore, is dependent upon the state or stage of development of the society in which it appears. The study of marketing as an institution relative to its social orientation is today known as Comparative Marketing, a subject of growing interest to students of marketing.

Even a glance beyond the borders of the United States, the home of the original conception and development of marketing, shows the prevalence of marketing throughout the world to coincide with the influence of Western business and, to some extent, with European colonization. Nations of so-called Western cultures have achieved the most advanced market economies and are making the most use of marketing as a social instrument, or tool, today. The underdeveloped countries—being not only underdeveloped in economic progress but culturally dissimilar from Western society—make little use of marketing either as a social, economic, or business tool. Those societies have not evolved in thought and practice the concept and institution of marketing.

One of the significant discoveries concerning marketing during the last decade relating to this is the realization that marketing is not such a tool as can be imposed upon a society like a decree or mandate. Somewhat over-zealous governmental agents and American businessmen abroad have experienced the failure of the American marketing institution in countries to which it is unoriented. Similarly, some foreign aspirants to the achievements which our society has attained through the use of marketing have failed, for they have seen it only as a business tool and not as a social tool.

Before a society can use marketing—before this tool can be the instrument of ethical or social responsibility to society—that society must undergo a transformation which evolves the institution of marketing. The following are some of the developments which must take place:

1. Consumer orientation of production and product planning. Although the market economy historically developed with production surpluses, until the viewpoint of production *for the market* is attained, the real significance of marketing is not recognized.

2. The conception of markets not as created by supply but as capable of

expansion through demand creation. The effect of following tradition rather than promoting innovation in the market has produced unimaginativeness and hopelessness for gaining a higher standard of living. Even economists, blinded by technological traditionalism, have under-estimated demand potentialities and limited their predictions of maximum markets. Holding a different view of this opens the way for marketing technology and an evolving marketing institution.

3. Profit motivation counteracting inertial indifference. Modern marketing cannot evolve where a business society prefers the leisure of low-volume turnover with high markups to higher profits resulting from low markup and large volume.

4. Willingness to accept standardization and uniformity. The notion of real or fancied individualism in the market, held by both distributors and consumers, prevents the use of techniques based upon concepts of mass consumption, mass distribution, and mass production, which are inherent in the modern marketing institution.

In other words, as society adopts attitudes and habits conducive to the development of marketing, it then finds contemporary marketing practices a tool for achieving social ends, in line with the adopted objectives.

THE TOOL IN CONTEMPORARY AMERICAN SOCIETY

The role which marketing has played and is playing in our contemporary society is inestimable. It has long been acknowledged as a business tool, an element in the management mix, a force for achieving corporate objectives, a means of imposing business standards upon the market. It is also an acknowledged economic tool—a solution for the disposition of production surpluses, an accelerating and a dynamic factor in the economy, a productive form of economic specialization. More than this, it is a social tool and is being used as such. Our marketing system is a social institution, a creation and reflection of our society, a highly complex and intricate mechanism or means used by society for the accomplishment not only of economic goals but also social objectives. The following are some of the ends attained by our society through the use of marketing:

1. The supplying of men's physical needs. Sociologists say that men have never lived self-sufficient unto themselves individually, but in all social systems either collective production, by such as the family or tribal group, or exchange has provided for the physical needs of men. We, today, are achieving this by the market economy and particularly by marketing.

2. Providing for a high degree of specialization of labor in society. Social and economic theorists have long held that specialization or division of labor is conducive to efficiency of performance. We today are dedicated to efficiency as perhaps no other society has been. In consonance with this, although a great number of people are employed in marketing activity, this total institution provides for not only regional and seasonal specialization in production, but also for specialized use of widely diversified talents in market activity.

3. Achieving a great diversity of products available for consumption. A criterion of status, standard of living, and self preservation in our society is the diversity of products consumed. Marketing spreads at every doorstep a cornucopia of the world's luxuries, as well as the uncounted gadgets of a machine age. It is recognized, of course, that neither efficiency nor a plethora of things represents the social objective of some people. For them, marketing is a less essential tool than for us.

4. Accelerating the rate of acquisition. Ours is an impatient society, whose market behavior seems to enact the philosophy that "it's later than you think." What might be acquired in the near or distant future is wanted today. Marketing, particularly through the instrument of credit, is used to make this possible.

5. Defining of a concept of fairness in society. Every society has its ethics, its codes of relationships, obligations, and values, and by custom or law these standards are spelled out. Our own ethical judgments have evolved with the growth of our society; and these principles have found expression, in part, in many regulations of marketing practice, thereby using the institution of marketing for the preservation of social values.

6. Shifting responsibilities for consumer decision-making to technical specialists. With economic specialization, consumption has taken on a distinct character. The function of planning the products to be used has been shifted to producers. The maintenance of supplies available for consumption has been shifted to retailers and wholesalers. By our policies relating to returns, adjustments, and guarantees, purchasing is not completed at the time of transaction but at an indefinite later time, as through the tool of marketing society achieves an objective of shifted responsibility.

7. Creating uniformity of living standards. Through marketing, by which almost all types of products are made available and accessible at many locations, a great mass market has been created, and an economic manifestation of our social concept of equality among men has been achieved. Our society's praise of democratic and religious equalization has found expression through the tool of marketing.

8. Achieving cultural integration among nations as the institution of marketing is introduced. Notwithstanding the fact that marketing is an institution which societies evolve, in this era marketing is also used as a means by which its underlying social values are taught to peoples with differing social structures, values, and customs. Whereas in times past colonizers and economic frontiersmen introduced corn seed, tobacco, or cattle stock for the development of a primitive economy, now cultural hybridation is undertaken by the introduction of marketing concepts and techniques. For example, the Swiss Migros chain of food stores has recently authorized the use of its name, trademarked merchandise, and operating methods in Spain, to aid the development of voluntary chains there and to extend consumer protection. Likewise, the opening of American type consumer loan companies in Latin American and European cities will also teach the commercialization of confidence, the impersonalization of borrowing, and the superiority of legal commercial practices to unregulated and illegal forms of lending.

9. Expressing society's changing sense of values. In a time of world uncertainty, our society is not credited with possessing the most stable set of values. Having elevated materialism somewhat, while at the same time, be-

cause of affluence, having directed desires from tangible to intangible objects, we have through the medium of marketing emphasized appeals which the world regards as superficial, wasteful, and decadent.

In summary, as Shakespeare admonished the players in Hamlet, "To hold, as 'twere, the mirror up to nature; to show virtue her own feature, scorn her own image, and the very age and body of the time his form and pressure," so marketing mirrors the society in which it has evolved and is practiced. It is a social tool, and, as such, it is as laudable as the society which employs it is good.

Marketing knowledge and capabilities can provide a significant contribution to the improvement of living standards in emerging nations. The development of a broad range of readily available products and an equitable return for the investor are complementary objectives. Few things are as likely to contribute to lasting world peace as a free exchange of marketing information, ideas, and opportunities.

72. SCIENCE, TECHNOLOGY, MARKET AFFAIRS AND WORLD PEACE*

James M. Gavin†

As men are not born equal, neither are nations. And many nations are now being born. Some nations are born with an abundance of resources; other nations are born with few and so at birth are dependent on others. Not long ago nations and individuals could experience a lifetime of struggle for survival, seeking to improve their lot but finding neither satisfaction nor a good relationship in the larger community of people and nations.

This is no longer true. Today people and nations are brought together through political, cultural, and economic associations that are unavoidable

* Reprinted from "Science, Technology, Market Affairs and World Peace," *Proceedings of the Fall Conference of the American Marketing Association*, 1965, pp. 21–29. For additional views of the socio-economic aspects of marketing, see Laurence P. Dowd, "Social Responsibilities in Distribution—An Integral Part of Marketing Education?" *Proceedings of the Winter Conference of the American Marketing Association*, 1960, pp. 204–9; and Neil H. Jacoby, "World and U.S.A. Social Progress," *Commercial and Financial Chronicle*, Vol. 186, No. 5674 (September, 1957), pp. 1226–36.

† Arthur D. Little, Inc.

on this small planet. And what I have said so far about the individual's opportunity for achievement applies to nations. They are not born equal, but they should have an equal chance to achieve what is worthwhile for their people; to enjoy the highest standard of living possible through their endeavors, recognizing, but hopefully not being thwarted by, the limitations imposed upon them by their natural resources. . . .

We are much aware of the rapidly shrinking barriers to travel and communication; we know, too, that in spite of these technological achievements, local customs, cultural views, and business practices have changed but little. Therefore, while marketing grows tremendously in the geographic sense, the problems encountered by those associated with marketing are as great as they have ever been in the past and, in many respects, they are greater. There is no other business function that encompasses so many different people, of such diverse backgrounds, skills, interests, and intellectual disciplines. Marketing properly conducted with awareness of all these things can extend understanding among nations, and it can create good will. It can stimulate trade and thus encourage people to share common interests. It can serve people in many parts of the world and provide them with educational opportunities.

Marketing is no longer a device for figuratively selling wooden nutmegs to an unwary buyer, as my Yankee ancestors have been accused of doing.

Recently a group of Nigerian government officials completed a year's training program at Arthur D. Little to prepare them to plan, administer, and implement the industrial development program in their own country. On the occasion of ceremonies marking the end of this program, the Nigerian Ambassador to the United Nations, Chief S. O. Adebo, commented on Nigeria's relations with other nations. His is one of the most promising new African nations; I believe his observations deserve to be noted with care. Speaking of outside assistance, he said,

> I do not think that receiving some assistance from your friends anywhere in the world is a crime, and we in Nigeria believe in and welcome any such assistance. But such assistance to be useful has to be genuine, it has to be given in the spirit of brotherhood, it has to be given in the spirit of mutual regard for one another, it must not be exploitative, it must help to do the things that the recipients want to do. We want assistance and we are prepared to show gratitude for it, but we want clean, honest assistance, assistance which will do us good and which will do the donor good.

Expressing the hope that businessmen would come to Nigeria to establish business and develop markets, Chief Adebo added,

> We pledge ourselves not to steal other people's money. But we don't want people to come and exploit us. We don't want people to come and steal the resources that we have. We want a partnership that is clean and honest.

I believe that in our marketing endeavors we should always keep in mind the need for assisting the countries in which we do business to improve their standard of living. We have a greater responsibility than mere selling. We have a responsibility to improve conditions where we market, not for our own benefit but for the benefit of others—to help them help themselves in achieving their goals.

And, indeed, the benefits of the best marketing techniques and attitudes—which imply service and the understanding of people and markets—can be mutual. Let us consider for a moment the developing countries.

What are the needs and wants of the people in these countries which offer potential new markets? Food and its distribution are problems in many nations; food may be plentiful in some areas but scarce in others. Professional marketing help can show the way to link supply and need, by establishing organization and distribution systems. Careful analysis of people's buying capacity as well as of their needs can direct marketing efforts toward useful products which will be bought because they are needed and economic and which will yield the investor an economic return. The knowledge of what people eat, for example, and how they cook are vital to the choice of food and related products for a given market; marketing may expand the options—for instance, by introducing new foods—but should not in so doing offer less useful products to the consumer with limited income. Properly located, after consideration of such factors, packaging and processing plants will not only be in the best position to satisfy consumer needs; they will benefit the local economy through employment of population as well as agricultural and natural resources.

This, in turn will stimulate the health of the local economy. As these young nations gain economic strength, so will their people enjoy improved health, and living, and working conditions. Each of these nations can then live peacefully in the entire community of nations, with the self-respect that comes from the knowledge of its capabilities and of its achievements. . . .

The expansion of trade between East and West offers another unique challenge to the marketing community. Surely if science and technology can give us the miracles of bridges and dams, of electrical and atomic energy, and of life-saving medicines, marketing can find areas of negotiation with nations of conflicting ideologies for mutual benefit, including a lessening of world tensions. Marketing efforts thus undertaken can help to alleviate and perhaps eliminate internal problems in the East European countries—for example, by offering new manufacturing opportunities in Poland to help absorb that country's excessive labor supply; or by helping to increase manufacturing efficiency and expand the industrial base in Czechoslovakia and Hungary to compensate for a labor shortage. What better way to afford skeptics evidence of the advantages of our marketing and manufacturing methods than through plants in which they can work and learn and whose output will benefit them and their people?

Recently, a major American firm reversed its decision to establish a plant in one of these countries, because of adverse publicity by one of its competitors. Thus was lost an opportunity to accomplish the things I have just been speaking of—to extend American marketing influence—for mutual benefit—into areas of economic need and conflicting ideologies.

Marketing in this country has developed the most advanced tools and research techniques that can be of great benefit to these East European countries. Simulation studies through mathematical models, for example, have aided business, industry, and government in this country. Such sophisticated methods should be increasingly useful in the new markets of the East European nations.

A healthy economy and self-realization are essential to any nation if it is to live in peace. Not long ago, it was believed by many people that businessmen were motivated by avarice and greed alone, that they would fight each other to their economic death for markets and marketing opportunities, that if necessary they would encourage their countries to support their efforts even to the point of international war. Now we know that men will cooperate for the common good, even to the detriment of their own interest or perhaps to that of their country. Within the free world many businessmen inspired by the need to serve this common good are striving to help mankind wherever their skills may be applied and wherever markets may be found. Many people here today exemplify this effort.

Much has been accomplished in our time through cultural exchanges with the Iron Curtain countries. I think now that the extension of trade to such areas where it now may be possible, and the expansion of this trade as rapidly as possible in other areas, is much overdue. Few things are as likely to contribute to lasting world peace as a free exchange of not only cultural interests, but merchandising, management ideas, and business opportunities among all people of the world. The long road from the discovery of the first truth about our environment to the growing prospect of peace has been a troubled one beset with wars and attendant great loss of life. Yet, it is one which we have traveled and along which we have learned many things, perhaps the most important being the need of men to trade and live together as a family if they are to prosper and achieve worthwhile goals. . . .

Concurrent with maintaining adequate defense posture—and I emphasize the importance of research in our defense—our own strategy must recognize the importance of economic growth and development. We should pursue the development of worldwide markets, encourage an exchange of information and goods, keeping in mind the need to bring together men from all corners of the earth. Threats will arise and they must be met; but they must always be met with restraint, for as we have learned, there is nothing to be gained by forcing a nation to the brink of total nuclear war. There is much to be gained by finding ways of living together and working together so that men everywhere, and the nations that they establish, may achieve the highest possible standard of living, opportunity, and education, and achieve also their goals of spiritual satisfaction.

Men who are interested in marketing have in their ranks scientists, technologists, and salesmen. They are involved in that world where a vast exchange of knowledge, ideas, and products is always ocurring. Their impact on the prospects for peace is perhaps greater than that of any other segment of our society. Their responsibility in contributing to international good will, and ultimately to world peace is equally as great, and it cannot be given to anyone else. Let us, therefore, take this responsibility to heart, keeping in mind our ultimate goal, that of a better world for men everywhere, a world in which people and nations can go as far as their resources will allow them, limited only by their respect for others and their institutions.

An opportunity and need exists for a reexamination of the nature and purpose of marketing in internationalized culture patterns. Marketing must be viewed more as a formative factor and less as an adaptive aspect of our culture. A parallel is drawn between the fundamental characteristics of the Renaissance period and the current need for a critical reappraisal of marketing's status. Several possible approaches to this reappraisal are presented in the form of questions.

73. MARKETING RENAISSANCE*

William R. Davidson†

Renaissance with a small "r" is a word the literal meaning of which is rebirth. It has been used to denote a wide range of phenomena, from outstanding events or turning points in the lives of individuals, to changes

* From "Marketing Renaissance," *Proceedings of the Winter Conference of the American Marketing Association*, 1963, pp. 3–14. Also see: Neil H. Jacoby, "World and U.S.A. Social Progress," *Commercial and Financial Chronicle*, Vol. 186, No. 5674 (September 19, 1957), pp. 1226–30; Raphael Demos, "Business and the Good Society," *Harvard Business Review*, Vol. 33, No. 4 (July–August, 1955), pp. 33–44; Richard H. Buskirk, "Importance of Marketing," *Principles of Marketing: The Management View* (New York: Holt, Rinehart & Winston, Inc., 1961), pp. 6–10; and Gabriel Hauge, "Accent on the Individual," *Saturday Review*, January 11, 1964, p. 48.

† Ohio State University.

in the whole culture. Mostly, however, and especially as a proper noun, Renaissance is applied to the civilization of Europe in the period from the 14th through the 16th centuries. Such a characterization of this era implies a cultural outburst of an outstanding nature—a decisive turn in historical evolution.

There are several things about the *R*enaissance that I find of special interest when contemplating the potentiality of a *r*enaissance in marketing today.

The Renaissance arose out of confrontation with other cultures, as those from Europe going out on the Crusades were exposed to the heritage of the Greeks, the Romans, and Islam.

The stimulus for the Renaissance was in the universities, which were the centers of thought and culture for the times.

There was a more honest address to fundamentals, with the elimination of frills, facades, and artificialities of the Middle Ages.

There was a new emphasis on humanism and the realities of human values, as opposed to supernaturalism and mysticism.

The best of the classical old was preserved in the rebirth.

I suggest that there is some parallel today in marketing, as educators and other professionals in marketing are confronted with the opportunity and need for re-examining the nature and purpose of marketing in internationalized culture patterns, where many of the frills and fancies of competitive selling will not be adequate to cope with the emerging realities of a new world.

PHILOSOPHY OF MARKETING

Whether it will be agreed that such a parallel exists no doubt depends upon one's concept of or philosophy about marketing. Certainly many divergent views are a matter of definition rather than of substance, as illustrated by the fact that marketing has been described by one person or another as a business activity; as a group of related business activities; as a trade phenomenon; as a frame of mind; as a coordinative, integrative function in policy making; as a sense of business purpose; as an economic process; as a structure of institutions; as the task of getting goods from production to consumption; as a process of exchanging or transferring ownership of products; as a process of concentration, equalization, and dispersion; as the creation of time, place, and possession utilities; as a process of demand and supply adjustment; and as so many other things.[1] Each of these concepts may be appropriate for a given person, at a given time, when examining marketing problems from a given point of view. For purposes of marketing education, which to me involves striving for

[1] See Robert Bartels, *The Development of Marketing Thought,* Homewood, Ill.: Richard D. Irwin, Inc., 1962, Chaps. 2, 3, and 12, for a discussion of various concepts of marketing.

higher levels of sophistication in knowledge as well as facilitating socially useful and self-fulfilling careers for marketing students, some stated philosophy is needed. This has been a matter of considerable recent discussion at The Ohio State University as, I am sure, has also been the case at many other schools.

In a rough statement which was one of several prepared for discussion among my colleagues at home, I have described a philosophy of marketing education—

> as a system of thought that sets forth our goals and indicates the direction to move in order to achieve them. It provides a sense of purpose, a means of unifying individual efforts, a tool for achieving internal consistency among the components of the curriculum, a guideline for maintaining a charted course, and a statement to clarify our views to others.

In order for universities to exercise more conspicuous leadership in some potential marketing renaissance, more clear-cut philosophies of marketing education will be needed. They must be founded upon a concept of and a philosophy about marketing itself. For the efforts of universities to be desirably cumulative for maximum total force, there must be more unanimity about the nature and purpose of marketing.

I believe that the trend is rather clearly in this direction. As a result of the rather widespread acceptance of the so-called marketing concept in the 1950's, marketing has been regarded as more of a consumer-oriented, more of a value producing, and more of an integrative function in business than was formerly the case. When accompanied by general economic and social trends that have focused emphasis upon the interdependence of institutions, the marketing concept has given marketing added emphasis as a social process.

Marketing as a Social Process

To an increasing extent, marketing is conceived as a social process, the purpose of which is the identification and the satisfaction of the wants of customers. When so viewed as a social process concerned with want satisfaction, marketing is readily identified as a subject of much broader scope than the compilation of functions or activities commonly identified as marketing responsibilities in individual companies.

Most here present will accept this view, but nevertheless there are many teachers in the room who very recently were using textbooks, or were relying upon the AMA glossary of terms, that defined marketing as "the performance of business activities that direct the flow of goods and services from producer to consumer or user."[2]

Recognition that marketing is indeed a social process that extends far

[2] Committee on Definitions, *Marketing Definitions*, Chicago: American Marketing Association, 1960, p. 15.

beyond the business activities of individual participants operating within the process is indeed a considerable advance. It gives to marketing a dynamic quality and a sense of purpose that was more often lacking under the common concept of getting goods from production to consumption.

Consumer Orientation Exaggerated

Yet, whether we be educators or practitioners, in espousing marketing as a social process concerned with the want satisfaction of consumers, we may have inadvertently exaggerated the consumer-oriented nature of marketing. From much of the recent literature, including some of my own, one might well get the impression that marketing consists mostly of business firms finding nice things to do for people. However, much of what actually goes on under the guise of marketing in our present social system has nothing to do with the wants of people, except in the most broad and general sense if even then we can attribute decisions of politicians and government administrators to a reflection of the will of the people. To do so is certainly tenuous, for who can say that consumers can even comprehend, yet alone desire, the presumed values of being first on the moon, of having concrete rather than asphalt highways, of rushing to provide more facilities for higher education, of rebuilding the core of cities through urban renewal programs, or of having planes built by General Dynamics rather than by Boeing. Similarly, a decision on the part of a public electric utility to construct a large new power plant rather than to purchase energy from others for distribution may have substantial marketing impact in industry, although changing in no appreciable way the values sought or received by consumers, as may also be the case when aluminum rather than stainless steel is specified to sheath the frame of a new office building.

There is another defect in the concept of marketing as a social process concerned with the identification and satisfaction of customer wants. The concept as commonly stated assumes that marketing is an adaptive process in our culture. In accordance with this view, it is generally assumed or stated that the firm is adjusting its product offer to market requirements which it has discovered by marketing research approaches. While this may well be true, when viewed from the standpoint of any one manufacturer of perfume, coffee, or cigarettes, the aggregate social impact of all marketing activity is, in my judgment, commonly underestimated, especially by those in the marketing field.

A relatively strong case can be made for the point that marketing is more of a formative factor and less of an adaptive aspect of our culture than it once was. This may be supported by the wave of mergers and consolidations in recent years which have increased the marketing capabilities of many firms. It may be partially established by the influence that advertisers and the advertising industry have over media of mass communications. It may be attested to by concentration on buying power among a smaller number of purchasing influencers in general merchandise retailing. It may be argued on the basis of the claimed efficiency of mathematical models used to predict new product sales behavior or to allocate advertising effort by media. It may be inferred from so many directions that few indeed will deny marketing a position of at least some importance in shaping a culture often characterized as the consumption of abundance.

The concept of marketing that underlies the so-called modern marketing concept has well served many firms engaged in the marketing of consumer goods and services. Such a consumer-oriented view is also consistent with a social process view of marketing as concerned with want fulfillment. But, it appears that popular concepts of marketing fall short of reflecting the reality of *all* marketing effort.

If universities are to stride forward in a renaissance of marketing, perhaps a first requirement will be a more realistic and a more comprehensive philosophy of marketing, upon which can be built a desirable philosophy of marketing education for the future. Such a philosophy, it seems to me, must be an improvement over what we now have in at least two respects: first, that it give proper cognizance to influencers and interests other than consumers, as in the case of government, defense, space age, and industrial marketing; and, second, that it recognize properly the marketing process as a formative as well as an adaptive aspect of our culture. . . .

New Questions

In this era, when our private enterprise system is confronted by rivalries with other cultural patterns throughout the world, when change in our own culture is rushing past us at unprecedented rates, and when marketing itself is one of the factors contributing to cultural change, *will the present status of marketing suffice?* Or, do those of us who are professionally interested in marketing have an obligation to raise some serious questions, which require deeper insight than those commonly investigated by marketing practitioners? Some such questions are matters more likely to be discussed by critics of contemporary marketing. I am suggesting, however, that professional marketing people can well afford to be their own constructive critics rather than self-righteous defenders against the criticism of others, and indeed they may well have to be, if there is to be a renaissance in marketing which will advance our competence to meet new and radically different situations.

As professional people, as members of an association dedicated to advancement of science in our field, as witnesses to the internationalism of culture and trade, as educators influencing the youth of marketing who will help to shape the culture in which they will live, are we not at the point of raising some higher level questions of research, of perhaps getting at some totally new jobs, rather than merely finding new ways to do old jobs better? At this point, we can only list some possible questions or topics with the hope that they may spark some interest, and set the stage for new areas of research activity.

Among the questions I would pose for your thoughtful consideration are the following:

1. *What Is Actually Being Done and What More Should Be Done to Spread Knowledge about International Marketing?* At a recent conference on international business programs at Indiana University, there seemed to be substantial agreement that businesses are increasingly international. Yet we have little knowledge about the educational requirements for international marketing now or in the future.

2. *What Is the Social Cost of New Product Development?* Given the tremendous number of new products, the high cost of introducing one to the market, and the high mortality rate, have marketing people burdened our domestic economy with a tremendous social cost of "innovation?" Should we not study this matter objectively, rather than merely extol the virtues of workable competition under a private enterprise economy while answering the criticism of others on this score?

3. *What Is the Social Cost of Competitive Product or Service Strategies?* For example, on highly competitive airline routes between a number of major cities, each major carrier has more flights daily than warranted by traffic volume. This is done so as to be competitive on the basis of promoting destination service. The result is a sky full of near empty jets on such routes on many days. As our whole private enterprise system becomes more challenged by other economies, can we afford the dissipation of economic resources on such competitive strategies, when little if anything is added to the total stock of consumable values?

4. *What Adjustments Will Marketing Have to Make in a Changing Culture in Which the Fastest Growing Occupation Is Nonwork?* Looking beyond the short term, with which most marketing research is now concerned, how will marketing have to respond to a system in which increasing proportions of the gross national product are to be distributed on some basis other than income earned from current work? How will this affect our cultural values, the importance of broad categories of consumption expenditures, the demand for specific classes of products?

5. *What Contribution Is Marketing Making to Other Disciplines?* In this contemporary era of interdisciplinary approaches, it has been popular to seek out the contributions that can be made to marketing by economics, sociology, anthropology, cultural ecology, demography, political science, history, and so on. Marketing is often portrayed as the parasite, feeding upon the other disciplines mentioned, as well as others. Now, recognizing that marketing is a formative aspect of our culture, should we as marketing people be inquiring about the impact of modern marketing upon sociology, upon demography, upon history, and so on?

These are merely illustrative of questions of broader and deeper significance that come to my mind. Still others, and probably better ones, will occur to you, as you think more about the impact of marketing on our changing times. None of the questions I have suggested is a common matter of activity in marketing research departments. If they are to be dealt with, it will likely be by independent scholars working in universities, foundations, institutes, or associations. . . .

Defining marketing as "behavior in relationships" will facilitate the integration of marketing thought. The technical, behavioral, and social process definitions of marketing are discussed and synthesized into a single working definition. The contents and tasks of marketing technology are enumerated.

74. MARKETING TECHNOLOGY, TASKS, AND RELATIONSHIPS*

Robert Bartels†

Is marketing a *technology* which is applicable to a process, or is it a *process* in which marketing technology is one of several guides to action?

This is not a semantical question. It is a proposition with significance for marketing practitioners and theoreticians alike.

Stated otherwise: Is marketing the knowledge and practice of technical laws and precepts, the actions of individuals, a microphenomenon in a world of business? Or is it a process more broadly conceived, involving a variety of actions, one guide to which is knowledge of market and marketing behavior?

Evidence of such a divergence of viewpoints appeared as early as the 1930s both in marketing theory—with integrative expositions differing from traditional functional-institutional analyses—and in marketing practice—with traditional profit factors as a sole guide to marketing action being supplemented by reciprocal interests in the seller-buyer and seller-public dyads.

So marked have these differences become in recent years that academicians and their programs have been identified with one or the other

* Reprinted from "Marketing Technology, Tasks, and Relationships," *Journal of Marketing*, Vol. XXIX, No. 1 (January, 1965), pp. 45–48.

† Ohio State University.

concept; and business concerns have been characterized by the extent to which they rejected or accepted consumer-orientation, social responsibility, and interactional behavior.

While divergent viewpoints are wholesome in a growing discipline, sooner or later the integration of them in a unified statement is desirable. Seldom is this the work of any one individual but more often a gradual clarification of concepts and issues.

HISTORICAL PERSPECTIVE

Appraisal of the current status of marketing must be made in terms of its history. Thus, one looks to evolution in social change as the nutriment of change in marketing practice and theory. Successive tasks imputed to marketing impelled the emergence of the traditional functional-institutional approach to marketing, the managerial decision-making approach, the behavioristic or inter-disciplinary approach, and the quantitative statement of marketing variables.

The formulation of this branch of knowledge is for purposes of action in business situations—particularly for the making of administrative decisions by individuals engaged in marketing. While this is often termed "marketing management" or "managerial decision-making," neither formerly nor currently have all marketing decisions been made on the "managerial" level in business. Some have been made below that level, some above.

Moreover, many marketing decisions are made outside the formal organization for management in the business establishment—such as those made by consumers, by governmental agencies, by the general public, and by informal organizations of business entrepreneurs.

The real issue is: What kinds of knowledge for what kinds of action?

MARKETING TECHNOLOGY

The sum of marketing knowledge has been variously designated—as a "science," an "art," and a "discipline." There is justification for considering also another term in connection with marketing, namely, *technology*—marketing technology.

The concept of marketing knowledge as a technology has some useful implications. Marketing practice developed as a technique; marketing thought developed as a technology.

Technique was the preoccupation of practitioners. Technology was the concern of marketing scholars, who in addition to the description, conceptualization, and synthesis of prevailing techniques undertook also to rationalize, interpret, account for, and appraise them.

All of the circumstances which gave rise to marketing called for a technology. At the turn of this century there was practically no systematic knowledge of the processes of business in the marketplace.

Economic theory provided no guidance for individual behavior in distribution; it has been conceived as general economic analysis rather than as working technology. Moreover, even if it had, the changing circumstances of production, distribution, consumption, and changes in the state of the arts, social values, attitudes, and practices at that time called for new actions and new guides to action.

Prominent among the problems of that day were the stimulation of consumption in a growing buyers' market, the pricing of products in new multichannel systems of distribution, the appraising of credit applicants in an evolving credit economy, and the like.

The outcome of this need was a melange of ideas which became known as "marketing"—a combination of borrowings from economics, psychology, management theory, and original findings. "Marketing" came to designate *both* technique and technology.

Throughout ensuing years the questions have been even more significant: Is marketing the core of concepts which are uniquely characteristic of this area of inquiry and behavior—the marketing technology? Or is it the broad inclusion of all types of concepts and findings, drawn from a variety of disciplines? And if it is the latter, where is the line to differentiate marketing from other areas of thought?

Closer scrutiny of marketing thought discloses that it has generally dealt either with *nonhuman* aspects of human behavior in distribution, or with *individual* behavior in the process of distribution. It scarcely need be said that *people* use marketing techniques, and that marketing technology describes the techniques of an *interpersonal process.*

However, the contents of marketing traditionally have been concerned primarily with the nonhuman and impersonal:

Nonhuman:
- Economic concepts—
  - Price, costs, profits, margins, turnover
- Space-time elements—
  - Location, layout
- Processes—
  - Selling, buying, financing
- Intangibles—
  - Brands, images, policies
- Objects—
  - Product classes, consumer types

Impersonal:
- Institutions—
  - Wholesalers, retailers, producers, government
- Collectivities—
  - Markets, credit risks, competitors

The circumstances which evoked this technology called for guides to action in marketing relationships; but the actual behavior of individuals in these relationships was little considered.

There were several reasons. Human behavior was taken to be what, in classical economic concepts of man, it was assumed to be. Market behavior was assumed to conform to patterns of the economic man and the regulatory government. Business was synonymous with management; and one viewpoint, a managerial viewpoint, was paramount. Management was dominant. Success varied with the application of techniques, the flow of influence being outward and unidirectional from management. Moreover, the mechanics of the firm subordinated individual identities within it.

There are several advantages to regarding marketing thought as a technology. It assists in differentiating the technology of marketing from other business technologies—such as those of manufacturing, agriculture, finance, accounting, and law. It differentiates marketing also from other social disciplines which are not business technology, but which have contributed to business and marketing thought—economic theory, sociology, anthropology, psychology, political theory, etc. It identifies that segment of thought in which marketing specialists are presumed to be responsible for original and creative thinking—that segment of thought which is essential in a marketing curriculum.

CONTENTS OF MARKETING TECHNOLOGY

The technology itself consists mainly of concepts and of relationships among variables. The main categories of thought are derivations of a concept of the marketing task or process, of which there are several—distributing products, performing functions, managing institutions or organizations involved in distribution, serving markets to be supplied.

Its categories reflect, too, several concepts from the economics of the firm—profit motivation, specialization and integration; economies of scale or operation; and variability of costs. They represent marketing as a technical, mechanistic process in a nontechnical, social environment, in which consumer and government behavior are recognized at least to be affected by many noneconomic factors.

Thus, the framework of marketing typically has consisted of the concepts and principles implicit in the process of distributing goods and transferring title to them, as marketing has generally been defined. Its principal structural elements have been these:

Market research, delimitation, segmentation
Product conception, adaptation, identification, diversification
Functional performance, including demand creation
Institutional specialization and channel composition
Price-cost-profit relationships in internal and external management decisions
Market and marketing finance
Social regulation of marketing

Throughout its history the technology of marketing thought has provided a guide for action on several management and operational levels. But this technology has been generally used as though action were simply an *act*, rather than an *interaction*—as though it were a guide mainly for the achievement of self-determined corporate goals, rather than of the interrelated expectations of a number of participants in the marketing process.

UNORTHODOXY IN MARKETING THOUGHT

The unorthodox interpretations of marketing represented views which are in some way broader than the concept of marketing found in traditional marketing thought. They emphasize several things not explicit in the usual technology:

1. *Economic theory descriptive of conditions antedating those which gave rise to the new marketing technology.* Moriarity, for example, differed with some marketing technology of the 1920s because of his emphasis of classical economic concepts.
2. *Relationships among components of the marketing channel,* through which "flow" information, orders, credit, payment, etc. Thus, the interstices rather than the institutions were emphasized by Breyer, Cox, and Revzan.
3. *The entirety of the marketing process* (a holistic view), by which not merely units nor sets but rather systems of behavior were considered collectively and entirely. Vaile, Grether, and Cox have propounded this view.
4. *Managerial decision-making,* whereby marketing technology is integrated with other technologies in achievement of overall corporate objectives, as developed by Howard, Davis, McCarthy, and Mauser.
5. *Models, simulation, and quantification,* whereby relationships of numerous factors, internal and external, are dealt with systematically. Bass and others have written in this area.
6. *Interdisciplinary aspects of marketing,* complementing rather than supplementing the usual technology. Alderson is associated with this type of thought.

These innovations in marketing thought have in recent years overshadowed the traditional technology. They have improved some processes long-guided by traditional marketing thought; yet they alone, without the technology, do not offer complete solutions to marketing problems.

The cause of their appearance is that new views of the marketing task and processes have opened up, views which depict marketing as a social process, a process of social interaction, as systems of role relationship, and as a type of management responsibility.

MARKETING AS A SOCIAL PROCESS

It is generally conceded that marketing is a process, but there often is disagreement as to what kind of a process it is. Traditionally it has been regarded as a *managerial process* and as an *economic process*. The former embodies the application of a marketing technology: the latter assumes economic behaviorism.

Cross-cultural and comparative marketing studies, however, along with increasing pollination of marketing thought with sociological concepts, have shown marketing to be also a *social process*. That phrase has meant to some marketing teachers and practitioners only that social circumstances of consumers, other than those that are economic, must be taken into consideration in planning marketing strategy.

More broadly considered, the process of marketing is *social*, in that it is a process whereby society is fulfilling the personal and institutional needs of the society for physical or consumption goods and services. Every society is supplying this common need of its members through means that are similar or dissimilar—depending on the character, organization, objectives, and technologies of the particular society.

MARKETING AS SOCIAL INTERACTION

Marketing is a process not merely of *action* but of *interaction*. It is not merely what is done *by* wholesalers, retailers, producers, and others as separate and discrete economic or social entities.

Rather, it is the action and interaction of *people* (not as wholesalers, but as people) in the broad process of economic want-fulfillment.

Although a wholesale establishment is a technical or mechanistic specialist performing assembly and redistribution and operating under the technology of the economics of the firm, it is, socially viewed, some individual acting in the role of management.

From the standpoint of his retail customer, he is acting in the role of resource or supplier; from the standpoint of the original producer, he is acting in the role of an intermediate customer. The person acting as a wholesaler does not act wholly as an economic man; and therefore the traditional technology, based upon the assumption that he does, cannot fully explain or provide a guide for his actions.

MARKETING TASKS AND ROLES

As a social process, *marketing in its entirety constitutes the sets of relationships which arise in the performance of the process of economic want-satisfaction.* In our consumer-oriented, profit-motivated, market-guided, enterpreneur-initiated, government-regulated society, ten participating business role positions are identifiable:

manager	intermediate customer
employee	resource
owner	competitor
other investor	government
consumer	community

Marketing is the process of interaction among these sets or systems of relationships.

Of course, marketing has not always consisted of this full range of roles, nor have their relative positions always been the same. Throughout the 19th century and during the early formative years of the study of marketing in this century, the owner and manager roles (sometimes combined, and sometimes separated) constituted the sole or principal relationship. Management assumed no other responsibilities, as is evidenced by such concepts as "laissez faire," "caveat emptor," and "Social Darwinism." Guides to behavior were mainly profit guides; and the task of marketing was to make a profit.

When in 1890 a new dimension was given to management in the Sherman Act, and thereafter in subsequent marketing legislation, the role of the *competitor* became more of a factor in management. With labor legislation in the 1920s, the relations of management to *employees* became more prominent.

Similarly, with the "consumer movement" the role of the *consumer* was emphasized.

In subsequent years the roles of *government*, *investors*, and the *community* became more prominent; and with each successive addition the task of management in the marketing process has become increasingly complex.

MARKETING MANAGEMENT

The task of marketing management today is not merely to run the mechanism of a marketing establishment, but also to coordinate and to balance the expectations of individuals in their various roles. In performing this function as a social-role participant, management today has a different and vastly more complex obligation than some years ago. Prominent among the guides to action is the whole body of marketing technology to which we have been referring.

However, the important distinction between marketing past and marketing to come is the fact that hereafter one will be less likely to confine his competence simply to a knowledge of "marketing"—marketing technology—as though solitary action within this framework were the attainment of the ultimate.

Rather, the marketing manager of tomorrow—recognizing his position as a social role in a social process wherein he and all whom he contacts are presumed to be *social rather than mere economic or technical entities*—will regard marketing technology simply as one of several tools to guide him as to what is "right" and "wrong" to do in the marketing process.

This accentuates rather than diminishes the imperative for him to know marketing technology. Similarly such a viewpoint adopted by marketing academicians should increase their concern for how the marketing process is accomplished in society, rather than merely with marketing technology per se.

IMPLICATIONS

To define marketing as a *technical*, mechanistic, or managerial process emphasizes technology, economic behavior, and conventional marketing "principles." To define it as a *behavioral* process emphasizes noneconomic, nonbusiness motivations, and human behavior patterns. To define it as a *social* process emphasizes the cultural orientation of business in relation to other social institutions, organizations, and values.

The concept of marketing as *behavior in relationships* holds a promise of integrating marketing thought of yesterday, today, and tomorrow.

B. Marketing as a Discipline

Marketing practitioners and academicians can expect to increase their professional competence and levels of achievement as they succeed in integrating the contributions of related disciplines with marketing. Findings from the social, behavioral, and physical sciences and from the functional areas of business have had a limited impact on the development of marketing insights, concepts, and techniques. This article presents evidence that the interdisciplinary approach may become the preferred method of solving marketing problems.

75. INTERDISCIPLINARY CONTRIBUTIONS TO MARKETING MANAGEMENT*

William Lazer† and Eugene J. Kelley‡

I. INTRODUCTION

This article surveys and analyzes the contributions of the interdisciplinary approach to marketing management. It investigates the scope, nature, and merits of behavioral science findings and quantitative measurement

* Reprinted from Marketing and Transportation Paper No. 5, Bureau of Business & Economic Research, College of Business and Public Service, Michigan State University, 1959. See also "Interdisciplinary Horizons in Marketing" by William Lazer and Eugene J. Kelley, *Journal of Marketing*, Vol. 25, No. 2 (October, 1960), pp. 24–30.

† Michigan State University.

‡ Pennsylvania State University.

methods. The recognized body of marketing knowledge which has been developed within the last fifty years is the point of departure for the study. During this period an academic discipline and a body of marketing research methodologies have emerged. The result has been a deeper understanding of business action and continued progress toward a more rigorous, penetrating, and multi-dimensional discipline of marketing.

Marketing has reached a stage in its development where it can profit through critical evaluation and incorporation of fruitful research findings and theories from other fields. A vast body of material which is potentially useful to marketing management exists in other disciplines. Contributions from these disciplines may add perspectives to the recognized field of marketing by extending concepts, improving analytical tools, and increasing the effectiveness of decision making in marketing. However, caution and empirical evaluation are necessary before accepting the value of particular findings and techniques to marketing.

This article does not treat in depth specific contributions from other disciplines. The ideas are presented to stimulate further research and thinking. More questions are raised about the merits of the interdisciplinary approach than answers given. Such questions concern the relationship of findings within the functional areas of business administration, the managerial and educational implications of the probable extension of interdisciplinary activity, and the contributions of an interdisciplinary approach to systems thinking in marketing management. It is hoped that the discussion will stimulate marketers to examine critically the promising areas of related activity and to select the most productive concepts and tools for the study of particular marketing problems. When this is done, valuable ideas will be gleaned from the interdisciplinary focus. As a result, executives will be better able to cope with the increasingly dynamic and intellectually demanding tasks of managing marketing resources.

Interdisciplinary Approach: Definition

The interdisciplinary approach is often considered as including only findings of non-business administration areas. From this narrow and restricted point of view the approach consists largely of the application of social and behavioral science findings to marketing. Such a limited definition, however, results in a misconception.

The interdisciplinary orientation in its broader dimensions includes not only social and behavioral science contributions but also those of the physical sciences and, most important, those of various business administration areas. The contributions of the functional fields of business administration should be regarded as integral components of the interdisciplinary approach. Findings of such subjects as management, cost accounting, production, human relations, purchasing, and financial administration are significant stimuli to the development of marketing practice and knowledge. Business administration contributions, while not logically separable from those of the behavioral sciences, are currently more important for marketing management than the latter.

The interdisciplinary approach properly includes the application and integration of all findings pertinent to marketing. It embodies a holistic, dynamic approach to marketing thought, concepts, information, and techniques. The strength of this approach lies in adding more meaningful perspectives and new dimensions to various marketing concepts, developing improved techniques for solving marketing problems, integrating findings and theories with marketing practice, and developing a more widely applicable and generally useful body of knowledge. The results of its application should be a more comprehensive, logically consistent, and useful discipline of marketing.

Interdisciplinary Approach: The Potential

The interdisciplinary approach and its contributions are not new in many behavioral sciences. Boulding has stated with reference to economics that:

> Something which might be called an interdisciplinary movement has been abroad for some time. The first signs of this are usually the development of hybrid disciplines. . . . In the social sciences, social anthropology is fairly well established. Economic psychology and economic sociology are just beginning.[1]

In recent years there has been an added impetus, according to Boulding, of the development of "multi-sexual" disciplines. Included among such disciplines are cybernetics, information theory, and organization theory. Cybernetics evolved out of electrical engineering, neurophysiology, physics, biology, and economics; information theory originated in communications engineering and has applications in many fields stretching from biology to social sciences; organization theory developed out of economics, sociology, engineering, physiology, and management science. These hybrid disciplines and behavioral science developments are forcing a re-examination of the potential contributions of the interdisciplinary approach.

The potential promise of an interdisciplinary approach to the development of marketing theory was discussed by Wroe Alderson and Reavis Cox a decade ago. They wrote then:

> . . . here and there in the literature of several intellectual disciplines are appearing the elements from which an adequate theory of marketing will be constructed.[2]

---

[1] Kenneth E. Boulding, "General Systems Theory—The Skeleton of Science," *Management Science*, April, 1956, p. 199.

[2] Wroe Alderson and Reavis Cox, "Toward a Theory of Marketing," *Journal of Marketing*, October, 1948, p. 142.

To date most of these elements are still just vague ideas and suggestions and they have not been refined and developed into effective marketing concepts and techniques. However,

The accumulating elements for at least a rudimentary theory of marketing are scattered throughout the literature of the social sciences. Many of them are isolated ideas, often little more than flashes of inspiration to be found in longer discussions of entirely different matters. Some of them are indirect suggestions concerning concepts and methodology that can be derived from the efforts of workers in economic fields other than marketing.[3]

Interdisciplinary Approach: Present Status

There has not yet been any great acceptance of a truly interdisciplinary approach to marketing knowledge.[4] Hybrid disciplines involving the study of marketing have not appeared. A step in this direction may be noted in the development of such courses as psychology of advertising and selling, the economics of advertising, and marketing management. Yet these are far from the stage of mature hybrid disciplines.

Marketing's use of other disciplines to date may best be characterized as multi-disciplinary. Individual marketers have brought specific problems to psychologists, sociologists, anthropologists, social psychologists, and other behavioral scientists who in many instances were able to find solutions. These specialists, however, study marketing activities from the perspectives of their particular subject-matter areas. One result has been that the needed cross-fertilization of ideas and the integration necessary to obtain more widely applicable generalizations and marketing concepts has not occurred on any large scale.

Two developments may become part of the next breakthrough in the development of marketing science: a blending of various useful disciplines which would result in a truly interdisciplinary focus, and the emergence of hybrid marketing disciplines. These developments will contribute to a more rigorous discipline of marketing. The multidisciplinary practice of using social and behavioral science findings in marketing, now in vogue, can be the first stage in the adoption of an integrated interdisciplinary orientation.

The interdisciplinary approach will be judged largely on the basis of its value to marketing managers. The soul-searching and ferment among marketing men concerning the merits of the interdisciplinary orientation indicate the general interest in the development of a discipline of marketing management:

---

[3] *Ibid.*

[4] The findings of social and behavioral scientists are being used increasingly in industry. Leading companies are adding social scientists to their research staffs and sponsoring behavioral science research. Among these are American Telephone and Telegraph, General Electric, Standard Oil, General Foods, Eastman Kodak, and Dow Chemical. See *The Wall Street Journal*, February 11, 1959, p. 1.

Marketing management involves the planning, organizing, actuating, and controlling of marketing factors to achieve clearly defined market and corporate objectives. It is characterized by the application of creative executive leadership and effective management to the solution of market-related problems.[5]

Prime values of the interdisciplinary approach to marketing management are the insights and perspectives which it furnishes about the fundamental elements of marketing problems. It can be useful in helping to understand market change. The comprehension of the dynamics of marketing action and consumer behavior is essential for more effective decision making by marketing management.

Perhaps the one constant that marketing managers can be certain of during the future is change. A useful perspective on the future rate of change has been presented by Edwin Teller. Teller stated recently that in each century since 1650 man has roughly doubled his knowledge of the world and of mankind in this world.[6] While any such observation is only an approximation, it is suggestive of the enormous accumulation of knowledge that has taken place over the last three hundred years. What interests marketing executives, of course, is the likelihood that this rate of change will accelerate. For instance, scholars in several fields have predicted that they will learn as much in their particular fields in the next century as they have in literally hundreds of years or, in some cases, in all previous history. If this accumulation of knowledge occurs, the sources and quality of potential interdisciplinary contributions to marketing will be enhanced greatly. The rate of acceleration of marketing knowledge confronting marketing managers over the next 25 years could then be nearly as great as that of the past century. This would have a tremendous impact upon marketing practice.

New Concepts: A Marketing Need

Managing marketing effort under conditions of increasing change will require new concepts and more creative ways of thinking about marketing management problems. New concepts can facilitate the development of marketing and add creative approaches to problem solving. A basic value of integrating behavioral and social science findings in marketing is that of developing more comprehensive and meaningful bases for understanding marketing activities.

Firms often have difficulty in clarifying their marketing concepts. For instance, basic considerations such as what a product really is and does for consumers is often unclear. In many cases, the product perspective of the firm is significantly different from that of the consumer. Firms often tend

[5] Fugene J. Kelley and William Lazer (eds.), *Managerial Marketing: Perspectives and Viewpoints*. Homewood, Illinois: Richard D. Irwin, Inc., 1958, p. 478.

[6] G. L. Bach, "Some Observations on the Business School of Tomorrow," *Management Science*, July, 1958, pp. 351–52.

to conceptualize their products in terms of technical, physical and manufacturing considerations. The more crucial considerations for company operations may be those of consumer perceptions of the want-satisfying characteristics of the product. Marketing management must be concerned with such problems as consumer-product expectations, channel and brand image conveyed and the biological and psychological needs satisfied.

These are not simple problems. Many consumer reactions stem from subconscious motives. Therefore, it is necessary to probe beneath the surface to obtain meaningful information about them. The behavioral sciences may be able to provide keys to some of the answers. They may stimulate the development of more meaningful information.

Many of the topics studied by other disciplines have marketing connotations. Included among the disciplines investigating subjects which can be used to increase the effectiveness of decision making in marketing are: 1) sociology, with its studies of group behavior, social class, use of leisure time, symbols and images, group characteristics and their influences in consumption; 2) social psychology, as it is concerned with mass communications, attitude measurements, and public opinion; 3) psychology, which deals with motives, product symbols, projective techniques, images, acceptance of new products, advertising appeals and effects of color; 4) ecology, which has as one of its centers of study the growth and development of cities and suburbs; 5) social anthropology, which investigates social status and social systems; and 6) demography, which is concerned with population trends, predictions and shifts.

Some of the contributions made to marketing theory and practice by psychology and sociology are quite widely recognized. The potential contributions of many other disciplines are generally not as well known. It will be profitable for students of marketing to pursue a broader-gauged and deeper investigation of related subjects than has been conducted thus far. If this is done, areas worthy of further investigation will be delineated, key concepts identified, and interdisciplinary progress will be made at a more rapid rate.

The point of departure and the focus of study differ among the disciplines. Sociologists, anthropologists, or psychologists studying consumers and consumer behavior use different approaches than marketing scholars. However, there are frequently great similarities between marketing and other disciplines in both methodology and content. Marketing progress can be furthered by studying the similarities among disciplines rather than by emphasizing the differences. Actually, the overlapping of concepts and techniques among various subject-matter areas is an important aspect of the interdisciplinary approach to the study of marketing.

Students and practitioners who adopt the interdisciplinary approach should gain added insights into the nature and scope of marketing activity. A person's concept of marketing is shaped by the knowledge he gains through his own or vicarious experiences. The interdisciplinary orientation adds valuable dimensions to one's marketing experiences. Marketing horizons may be broadened with an increased understanding of related subject-matter areas. An executive sympathetic to the interdisciplinary approach is not likely to view his problems in strictly functional terms or in terms of only one perspective. He will tend to see more clearly the many dimensions of business problems. The interdisciplinary approach, therefore, can foster the development of a wider purview and contribute to the increased professionalization of marketing.

Reciprocal Relationship

The relationship between marketing and other disciplines can be a reciprocal one. Marketing is concerned with the study of human action in the market place, the study of the process of exchange and economic transaction and of the interacting efforts and responses of buyers and sellers in the market. This sphere of human action is essential to our economic system and is growing in importance. The field of marketing provides a testing ground on which to verify, modify, and extend the hypotheses which have been described by various behavioral sciences.

In the future, marketing may be a discipline in which an integration occurs between the research findings of social and behavioral scientists and business practice. In this process marketing may become a basic source of concepts, hypotheses, and methodologies to be used by other disciplines. If it does so, marketing may aid in developing a general theory of social behavior and add to the fund of knowledge about man in his environment.

II. MARKETING MANAGEMENT: BEHAVIORAL SCIENCE CONTRIBUTIONS

Table 1 relates specific behavioral science concepts to particular problems being faced by marketing management. It illustrates the value of the interdisciplinary approach in extending the frontiers of marketing knowledge and in helping to solve marketing problems. For example, such ideas as communication and information, motivations and behavior, creativity, problem solving, and decision making have significant implications for effective marketing management. They are being investigated from different vantage points by such disciplines as psychology, sociology, social psychology, anthropology, and political science.

Behavioral Sciences and the Marketing Mix

In Table 1, several topics of interest to marketing management are grouped according to four major marketing problem areas. These areas are marketing administration and the three marketing mixes that comprise the total marketing mix. The three mixes are: 1) *the goods and services mix*, which includes product and service policies and pricing tactics; 2) *the communications mix*, which includes the functional areas of advertis-

TABLE 1

BEHAVIORAL SCIENCE CONTRIBUTIONS TO SELECTED MARKETING MANAGEMENT PROBLEMS

	Psychology	Sociology	Social Psychology	Anthropology	Political Science
Marketing Administration					
Creativity, Problem Solving & Decision Making	Considerable	Some	Some	Some	Little
Leadership and Administration	Considerable	Considerable	Considerable	Little	Some
Organization	Some	Considerable	Considerable	Some	Some
Systems--Survival and Growth	Little	Considerable	Some	Considerable	Some
Goods and Services Mix					
Adjustment and Change	Considerable	Some	Considerable	Some	Little
Consumers and Consumption	Considerable	Considerable	Some	Little	Little
Innovation	Some	Some	Some	Some	Some
Products, Packages, Brands & Images	Considerable	Some	Some	Little	Little
Role, Status, and Symbol	Some	Considerable	Considerable	Some	Some
Communications Mix					
Attitudes and Opinions	Considerable	Considerable	Considerable	Some	Some
Communications and Information	Some	Some	Considerable	Some	Some
Individuals and Group Relations	Considerable	Considerable	Considerable	Some	Some
Motivations and Behavior	Considerable	Some	Considerable	Some	Some
Persuasion and Influence	Some	Some	Considerable	Little	Some
Distribution Complex: Channels & Physical					
Centralization, Decentralization & Integration	Little	Considerable	Little	Some	Some
Institutional Structure	Little	Considerable	Some	Considerable	Considerable
Wealth and Income	Little	Little	Little	Some	Some
Wants, Needs, and Goals	Considerable	Some	Considerable	Some	Little

Key
- (black) Considerable significance
- (gray) Some significance
- (white) Little significance

ing, sales promotion, and personal selling; and 3) *the distribution mix*, which is comprised of channels of distribution and physical distribution policies.

The table illustrates the significance of the findings of several behavioral sciences to marketing management in solving specific problems within each of the mixes. Those contributions that are of considerable significance are indicated by black, those of some significance by gray, while those of little significance at the present time are represented by white. For example, in determining the goods and services mix, marketing management is concerned with consumers and consumption. For these problems the findings of psychology and sociology are of considerable significance, those of social psychology are of some significance, and the contributions of political science and anthropology are less significant.

These rankings are an attempt to indicate in broad terms the degree of significance for marketing of the concepts, information, and research findings from various behavioral disciplines. The ordering was arrived at after an investigation of the literature and consultation with specialists in psychology, sociology, social psychology, anthropology, and business administration areas. The rankings, by nature subjective, are open to controversy. They may be criticized, modified, or even refuted by the findings of other research.

Marketing Management: Behavioral Areas and Concepts

Table 2 amplifies the information contained in Table 1. It includes over 250 topics of interest to marketing management classified by contributing disciplines. It presents in greater detail selected concepts from various disciplines that have marketing implications and portrays something of the nature, scope, and variety of interdisciplinary contributions to marketing management.

It is evident that several important areas have been omitted from these tables as, for example, economics. Since marketing as a discipline is essentially economic in character, economics has been one of the major contributors to its development. It is interesting to note that economics is itself becoming more interdisciplinary in its orientation. Boulding refers to this significant development and its impact:

> Thus the economist who realizes the strong formal similarity between utility theory and economics and field theory and physics is probably in a better position to learn from the physicist than one who does not. Similarly, a specialist who works with the growth concept—whether the crystallographer, the virologist, the sitologist, the physiologist, the sociologist, or the economist—will be more sensitive to the contributions of other fields if he is aware of the many similarities of the growth process in widely differing empirical fields.[7]

Many of the functional areas of business administration vital to the development of marketing knowledge have also been omitted from the tables. Students of marketing should be well aware of the significant contributions of management, cost accounting, finance, production, human relations, and other business administration subject areas. They should be able to recognize the interdisciplinary activity taking place among business administration subjects. Integrated studies of administration, organization, and business research are being pursued by scholars who are incorporating the relevant findings of many business administration subject areas.

[7] Boulding, *op. cit.*, p. 199.

TABLE 2

Marketing-Related Topics Classified by Selected Disciplines

Psychology

- acceptance
- adjustment
- analysis
- apperception
- aptitudes
- assumptions
- association of ideas
- association of words
- attention
- attitudes
- beliefs
- behaviorism
- character
- clinical study
- cognition
- compensation
- conception
  - (abstract
  - (concrete
- consciousness
  - (ego
  - (super-ego
- control
- conditioned responses
- differences
- emotions
  - (conflict
  - (frustration
  - (energy
  - (integration
  - (stimuli
- empathy
- empiricism
- enthusiasm
- experiences
- experimentation
- Gestalt
- habit
- human dynamics
  - (appeals
  - (demands
  - (desires
  - (interests
  - (needs
  - (urges
  - (wants
- human engineering
- ideation
  - (association
  - (memory
  - (discrimination
  - (imagination
- identification
- imagination
- imitation
- impulse
- individuality
- induction & deduction
- inhibitions
- instincts
- intellectual orientation
  - (appraisals
  - (empiricism
  - (forecasting
  - (interpretations
  - (measurement
  - (methodology
  - (procedures
  - (techniques
- interests
- interpersonal relations
- intuition & judgment
- imagery
- interviewing
  - (depth
  - (focused
  - (non-directive
- learning
- leadership
- logic
- mind
- morale
- memory
- motivations
  - (activity
  - (compensation
  - (direction
  - (identification
  - (projection
  - (rationalization
  - (regressions
  - (symbolism
- negotiations
- observation
- perception
- personality
- projection
- psychometrics
- propaganda
- reasoning
- scaling
- senses & sensations
- subconscious
- sublimation
- testing
  - (intelligence
  - (interviewing
  - (questionnaire
  - (stimuli-response
- theory of opposition
- transference

Social Psychology

- attitude measurement
- empathy
- experimentation
- identity
- interviewing
- interpersonal relations
- man & environment
- mass communication
- mass psychology
- morale
- motivations
- power structure
- prestige
- public opinion
- role & status
- situational behavior
- social adjustment
- social conflict
- social interaction
- social pressure
- social surveys
- sociometry
- statics & dynamics
- stereotype

Sociology

- analytic processes
- appraisals
- cities & towns
- civilization
- class behavioral patterns
- class distinction
- class status
  - (fluidity
  - (rigidity
- class stimuli
- class controls
- communication
- community life
- cost & standard of living
- cultural change
- culture diffusion
- culture evolution
- customs & mores
- deductive processes
- differentiation
- empiricism
- environment
- family
- fashion
- forecasting
- group dynamics
- group orientation
- group surveys
- group testing
  - (analyses—quantitative & qualitative
  - (experimentation
  - (impact
  - (recall
  - (recognition
- individualism
- innovation & change
- institutions
- leadership
- leisure & recreation
- life cycle
- mass behavior
- measurement
- populations
- power
- procedure
- propaganda
- public opinion
- social adjustment
- social change
- social class
- social ethics
- social groups
- social interaction
- social mobility
  - (horizontal
  - (vertical
- social nature
- social pressures
- social values
- status
- structure
- systems
- techniques
- technology & civilization

TABLE 2 (*continued*)

Political Science
- administrative law
- administration theory
- authoritarianism
- comparative marketing systems
- ethics
- marketing regulations
- marketing theory
- organization theory
- power pressure groups
- propaganda
- public opinion
- tariffs
- trade regulations & practices

Anthropology
- anthropometry design
- assimilation
- attitudes
- civilization
- consumption
- cultural dynamics
- cultural lag
- cultural processes
  - (coherent synthesis
  - (derivation
  - (evolution
  - (integration
  - (interpretation
- family
- human culture
- innovation
- modes of living
- national characteristics
- rituals
- social change
- social systems
- standards of living
- status
- status symbols

Demography, Geography, Ecology
- anthropogeography
- dispersion
- fertility
- functional allocation
- geopolitics
- group behavioral systems
- growth
- man-influence of climate
- man-influence of environment
- megalopolis
- migrations
- nucleation
- population-forecasting
- regionalism
- resources
- spatial distributions
- spatial forces
- symbiosis
- temporal forces
- trade routes
- urbanism
- vital statistics

Philosophy is another subject not included in Tables 1 and 2. Yet marketing theorists and practitioners should be cognizant of the findings and concepts of philosophy that can foster the development of marketing thought. Philosophy includes the study of such topics as theory construction, ethics, values, judgment, scientific methodology, including problem definition and the testing of hypotheses, decision making, aesthetics, probability, measurement, belief, creativity, induction and deduction, concept formation, thought, senses, semantics, and the concept of time and space. All of these have significant implications for the development of a discipline of marketing.

Tables 1 and 2 portray some of the potential contributions of several disciplines to marketing knowledge. Such a presentation has certain obvious limitations. The tables are neither complete nor comprehensive. They may be characterized as tentative or preliminary presentations to be developed more fully as research progresses. The disciplines selected are not necessarily the most significant ones for the development of particular areas of marketing thought. Moreover, many concepts cannot be conveniently classified as belonging to only one discipline. As intensive investigations are conducted into specific topics from an interdisciplinary perspective, such tables will become more inadequate and various concepts will appear to be more multi-dimensional. The situation represented may be artificial. It can suggest some of the aims and benefits of an interdisciplinary approach to the study of marketing. The tables indicate some of the contributions which might be made in solving specific marketing problems. Table 1 ranks the disciplines on the basis of their potential contributions to marketing.

Multiple Approaches of Behavioral Disciplines

A word of caution concerning the integration of the findings of other disciplines with the findings of marketing might be injected profitably at this juncture. Psychologists, sociologists, anthropologists, and other social and behavioral scientists are not necessarily any more unified in the concepts they hold of their disciplines than are marketers. Complete agreement does not exist among these scientists as to the most promising lines of development for particular aspects of their subject matter areas. For example, consider the important marketing subject area of motivation. Motivation has been studied at considerable length by psychologists and other behavioral scientists. However, rather than any one unified approach emerging, there are at least three major directions followed by psychologists pursuing motivation studies. A number of different approaches may even be suggested by other behavioral scientists.

First, there is the approach of laboratory, or "rat," psychologists, who have tended to focus upon the physiology of psychology. Then there are clinical psychologists who have centered on the role of certain psychological factors in motivation. This group tends to minimize the biological drives as influencing human motivation and behavior. The third psychological approach is represented by the Gestalt psychologists, particularly Kurt Lewin and his followers. Of the three, this latter approach may have the greatest significance for marketing people in studying human motives and other related questions.[8]

This Gestalt approach is essentially socio-psychological in nature. It stresses the thesis that people do react to environmental factors. From the Gestalt viewpoint motivations and behavior are analyzed as a function of the particular person, his inherent drives, and of the immediate environment of which he is a part.

These three different psychological approaches are cited to indicate that in any one discipline a variety of theories and avenues to the understanding of human behavior may exist. A problem in trying to integrate and utilize behavioral science concepts in marketing management is evaluating and reconciling various theoretical explanations and research results relating to a subject. As a result, the attempt to integrate numerous and often conflicting explanations of behavioral scientists into a practicable solution can become a highly perplexing experience.

Discovery and Application Disciplines

The behavioral sciences do not as yet offer useful concepts or methods for many problems facing marketing management. Bach has stated:

[8] Herta Herzog, "Behavioral Science Concepts for Analyzing the Consumer," paper given at the Conference of Marketing Teachers from Pacific Coast States held at the University of California, Berkeley, September 9, 1958.

The behavioral sciences as they now stand do not provide a large reservoir of immediately useful analytical concepts and models.[9]

In the study of certain concepts, marketing knowledge may be more fully developed than other disciplines. For example, consider the study of pricing, consumer reactions in the market place, the process of exchange, and the analysis of various institutions by marketing. However, it is the promise of help from other disciplines in the development of marketing thought, as suggested in the tables, that concerns us in the long run. It would be sheer folly for marketing management to ignore the potential contributions from the application of an interdisciplinary approach merely because this movement is in its primary stages of development.

With regard to the future development of the social sciences themselves, it has been suggested that by 1975 the social sciences will have a considerably enhanced power of accomplishment, and that these sciences will take on the characteristics of a dual grouping of discovery disciplines and application disciplines.

The discovery disciplines will derive their orientation from special or specific subjects of study, and they will strive for the discovery of facts and of regularities in the flux of social events. The application disciplines, in contrast, will derive their orientation from specific problems. They will strive for techniques of solving particular classes of such problems.[10]

It is likely then that marketing people will be particularly interested in applying some of the important findings of the related discovery and application disciplines. It may be that the findings of other discovery disciplines will be adapted, modified, applied, and tested through the methods and techniques used in solving marketing problems. As an application discipline, marketing may then develop and refine various techniques suggested by other application disciplines. Thereby marketing thought and practice will be enhanced and the total knowledge of human behavior and the development of measurement techniques advanced at an accelerated rate.

III. MEASUREMENT AND THE MARKETING SYSTEM

In addition to the interdisciplinary information listed in Tables 1 and 2, marketing practitioners and teachers are aware of the numerous measurement methods that have been developed by various subject-matter areas. Some of these are being applied effectively to solve marketing problems. Included among these measuring devices are tools such as scaling and ranking techniques, personnel tests, various projective techniques, interviewing and questionnaire methods, statistical sampling and measurements, and mathematical models and programming.

---

[9] Bach, *op. cit.*, pp. 354–55.

[10] Sidney Schoeffler, "The Social Sciences," *Challenge*, August–September, 1957, pp. 13–17.

Marketing Measurement

Chart I shows some of the more promising contributions to measurement in marketing of five related disciplines: sociology, psychology, social psychology, statistics, and operations research. It lists specific measurement techniques from each discipline which have been, or may be, profitably applied to marketing research. These techniques may be useful in solving problems in such marketing areas as advertising, product and price analysis, sales forecasting, and market potentials. They contribute to

CHART I

Measurement in Marketing

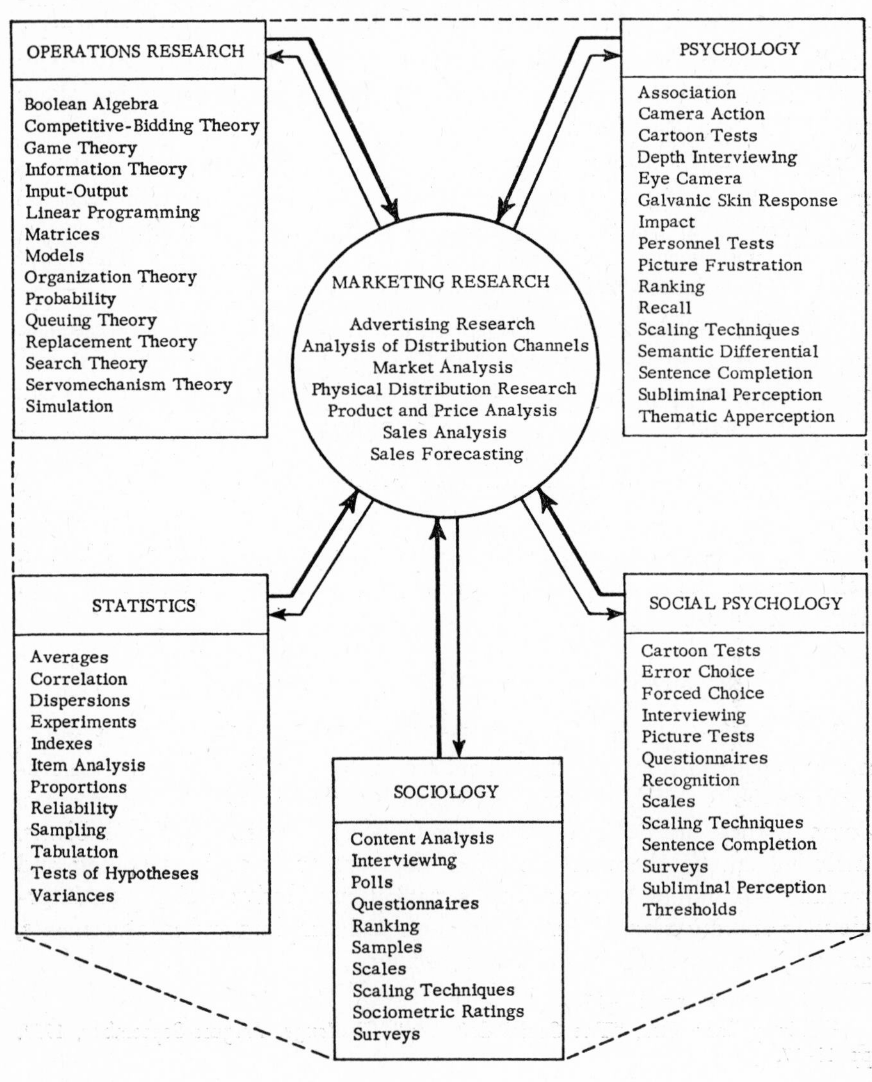

more precise cardinal and ordinal measurements in marketing and facilitate the planning and control of marketing operations.

In many instances the particular tools borrowed from behavioral sciences are adapted and modified by marketing researchers. Through refinements in application, the basic measurement techniques themselves are improved and marketing research thereby contributes to other disciplines.

This classification of measurement techniques is not comprehensive nor are the categories mutually exclusive. There are a number of other important contributing subject areas. Many of the techniques could be classified under several of the disciplines cited. In the chart this has been done only in a limited number of cases to avoid much duplication and still indicate the interdisciplinary overlapping of many of the methods of measuring specific aspects of human behavior.

Marketing Systems

Marketing administrators may be on the verge of a new level of sophistication in understanding marketing's role in the total system of business action. Business managers generally are becoming increasingly interested in the interaction between the components of business enterprise. Forrester has pointed out that business achievement depends on the successful interaction among the flows of information, materials, money, manpower, and capital equipment within the firm.[11] These five subsystems interlock to amplify one another within the total business complex. Thinking in limited functional terms may not be adequate for an understanding of the effects of these interactions. It does not allow for anticipated impacts on decisions, policies, organizational forms, and investment choices within the firm.

In many companies the basic problem involves the integration of the functional fields within the field of business administration itself rather than the integration with such disciplines as sociology or psychology. The problem is one of viewing business as an operating system—a whole. The impact of marketing, finance, production, or human relations decisions on other aspects of company operations and on the business as a whole must be considered.

Chart II portrays such relationships. The disciplines indicated in the area bordering the external non-controllable forces can be useful in providing information and insights about marketing. Consumers are at the core; they are the focal point of the entire system of business action. They are separated from firms attempting to serve them in space, time, ownership, valuation, and knowledge. These separations tend to increase in complex socio-economic systems. Sellers attempt to overcome the frictions of space and time by communicating to the consumer the want-

[11] J. W. Forrester, "Industrial Dynamics, a Major Breakthrough for Decision Makers," *Harvard Business Review*, July–August, 1958, pp. 37–66.

CHART II

A Systems Overview of Marketing Management

BUSINESS ADMINISTRATION
ECONOMICS
OPERATIONS RESEARCH
STATISTICS
ENGINEERING
MATHEMATICS
HISTORY
PHILOSOPHY
EXTERNAL NON-CONTROLLABLE FORCES
GOVERNMENTAL
LEGAL
INTERNATIONAL
ETHICAL
SOCIAL
CULTURAL
COMPETITIVE
ECONOMIC
NATURAL
RESOURCES
CORPORATE OBJECTIVES
HUMAN FINANCIAL & PHYSICAL RESOURCES
DISTRIBUTION STRUCTURE
COMMUNICATIONS MIX
GOODS AND SERVICES MIX
DISTRIBUTION MIX
THE CONSUMER
MARKETING PROGRAMMING
PSYCHOLOGY
SOCIAL PSYCHOLOGY
SOCIOLOGY
ANTHROPOLOGY
DEMOGRAPHY
GEOGRAPHY
POLITICAL SCIENCE
ECOLOGY

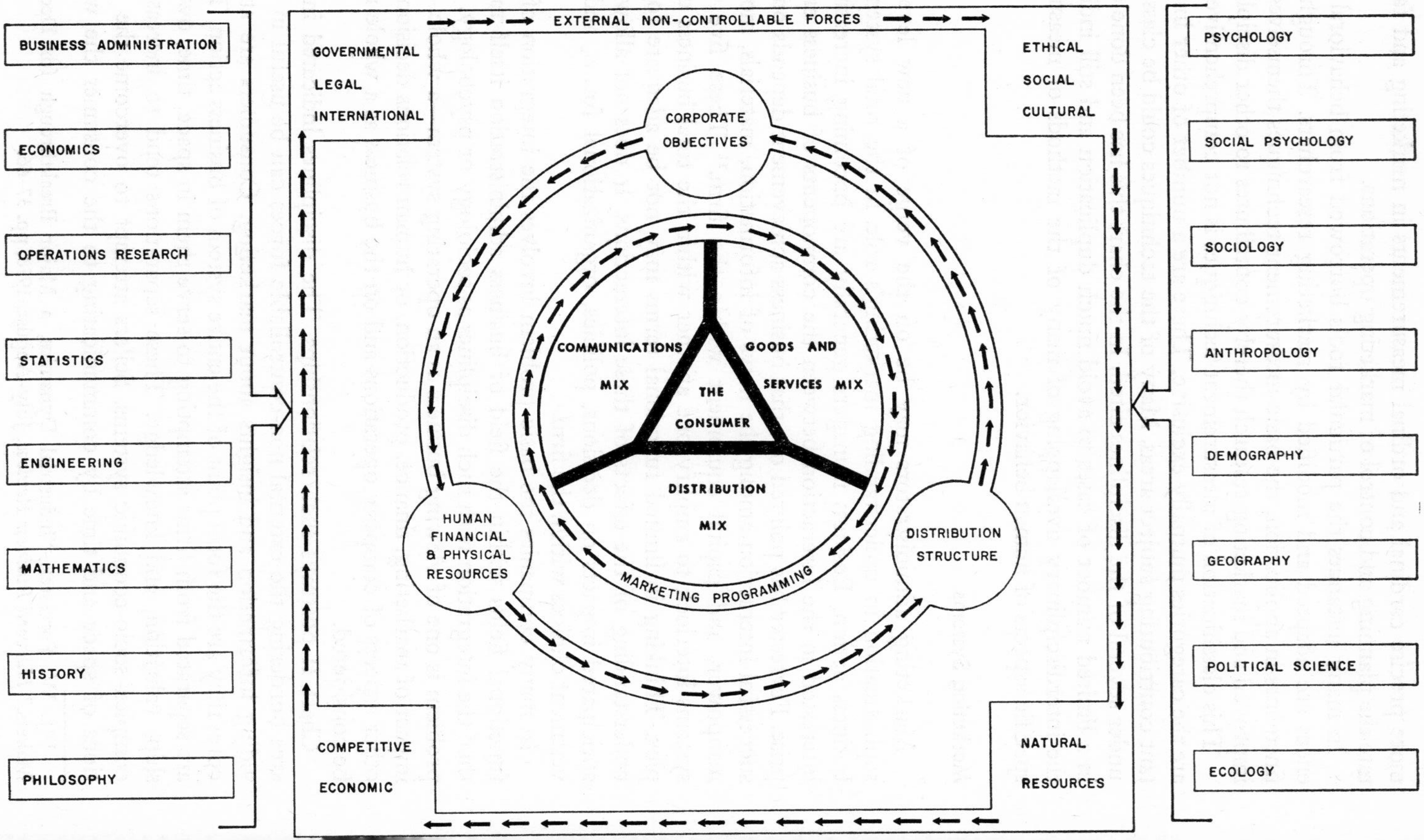

satisfying characteristics of the products offered through the marketing program. Management is constantly striving to find the optimal blend of the three program mixes: *goods and services*, which is concerned with product and price policies; *communications*, involving the blend between advertising, selling, and sales promotion; and the *distribution mix* of channel selection, location and physical distribution decisions. The chart is designed to indicate the interaction and interdependence of the elements of the marketing mix.

The marketing program is but one significant element in the total business system. Marketing decisions are made in terms of their impact on the company as a whole and their contributions to overall objectives. The human, financial, and physical resources of the firm are factors in marketing decision making just as the marketing program affects these factors.

This corporate complex also includes the interrelationships and coordination of the activities of the manufacturing firm with distributors and dealers as part of their joint effort to serve the consumer. The interdisciplinary concepts and ideas in Table 1 and 2 are numerous enough and suggestive enough to be conceived of as being potentially useful in marketing decision making.

Marketing and corporate decisions are influenced—perhaps determined—by various forces which are largely beyond the control of the management of an individual enterprise. These include competitive, social, political, legal, ethical, and international forces. The interdisciplinary approach can be useful in understanding and even predicting the influence of these external forces on marketing decisions. The arrows represent change. As business systems become more complex, the rate of change tends to increase with corresponding increases in stress in individuals and organizations.

The systems approach to business action is particularly important to marketing executives and educators. They have a unique opportunity to integrate business management functions into a meaningful whole and to take leadership in advancing systems thinking in business administration. This opportunity stems from two related developments: 1) businesses in the future will become more market oriented and 2) the total marketing concept will be adopted in which marketing will be viewed as an integral sub-system within the total system of business action.

IV. CONCLUDING OBSERVATIONS

The greatest long-run contribution of the interdisciplinary approach to the study of managerial marketing may be its influence upon the ways of thinking about marketing and business problems, rather than its production of new marketing information. Marketing students and practitioners using the interdisciplinary approach should gain insights into the nature and scope of marketing management activities. This is because a person's concept of marketing management, or any other subject, depends largely upon the knowledge of the area gained through his own and vicarious experiences.

Not all of the hypotheses, theories, findings, or facts that behavioral sciences have uncovered need be reflected in the interdisciplinary concept of marketing management. Many areas of psychology, sociology, social psychology, and anthropology have only a limited relevance for marketing. There are many highly speculative formulations in the newer behavioral sciences which are not applicable at present. Marketing management cannot and need not take into account all the information and refinements of other disciplines. It should separate and assimilate those findings and concepts which have a direct bearing on central marketing problems. By integrating those ideas which are relevant to marketing management, a more insightful approach and holistic perspective will be developed.

The interdisciplinary orientation does not imply that marketing executives and academicians are interested in becoming marketing psychologists or sociologists. Such is not the case. Neither are behavioral scientists willing to give up their professional identification and become marketing men. However, both groups are, or should be, interested in the relevant concepts and perspectives developed by other disciplines. Marketers should be sensitive to the development of improved ways of thinking about the relationship of academic research to business problems. Some marketing men may be wearing an interdisciplinary halo. They may be too prone to believe that social and behavioral sciences have most of the answers to marketing problems. The assumption is that these sciences are developed well beyond the stage of maturity reached by marketing. However, other disciplines do not have ready-made answers to marketing problems. These disciplines are also developing their cores of information and generalized theories and seeking solutions to problems concerning human behavior.

The immediate results of the interdisciplinary approach to marketing will probably not be startling. The findings which are incorporated and integrated into marketing knowledge from other disciplines are more likely to prove to be evolutionary rather than revolutionary. Today the interdisciplinary approach is in vogue. Business administration people generally accept and endorse it. But if marketers wear the interdisciplinary halo too tightly, severe academic and practical headaches may result.

The challenge facing marketers is to develop in detail specific applications of the interdisciplinary approach. This can only be done if the theories, findings, and concepts which appear in other disciplines are investigated thoroughly and integrated into marketing thought.

Instead of merely endorsing the interdisciplinary approach and speaking in vague and obscure language about its benefits, marketers must deal more with the specifics and facts. They should consider concrete applications and values of this approach to the functional fields of business and to particular problems in the fields. One purpose of this monograph is to suggest some of these values and applications.

The interdisciplinary approach does not offer marketing a large number of ready-made pertinent facts, principles, and theories which can be applied directly to solve marketing problems or to immediately advance marketing knowledge. A search of the literature of the behavioral sciences and related areas has revealed a paucity of specific marketing materials. But much information with marketing overtones and implications is available. This information has to be further researched, developed, refined, tested, and adapted from a marketing viewpoint.

This situation is not surprising. Behavioral and social scientists do not have the same interests in marketing problems that marketers do. They are not going to perform the fundamental research in marketing or the basic integration which is necessary to utilize the interdisciplinary approach to marketing effectively. This is a challenge which confronts marketing people. It cannot be relegated to the areas of responsibility of other disciplines.

Like other disciplines, marketing is going through several distinct developmental stages. These stages include: (a) the evolution of a body of marketing information based on observations, empirical findings, and philosophic speculation; (b) the formulation of currently useful generalization; (c) the delineation of likely hypotheses which can be tested by various disciplines; (d) the division of marketing into specialized subject-matter areas; (e) the specialization of marketing personnel, both practitioners and academicians; and (f) the development and refinement of research methods and techniques.

Like many other disciplines, marketing has reached a stage in its development where significant benefits may accrue from the application of the interdisciplinary approach. It is at a point where problems of interest to it may be profitably investigated and researched in the light of cooperative findings. If this is done, the effect will be that marketing theory and practice and the research findings from other disciplines will be integrated and will give rise to more general and useful knowledge of marketing behavior.

It is possible that the interdisciplinary movement can influence substantially the type of education offered students to help prepare them for marketing management responsibility. Educators are concerned with preparing men for positions of responsibility in the next ten, twenty, and thirty years. A fundamental problem facing educators is that of coping with the rate of change and its impact on marketing knowledge in the future. Educators may have to ask some tough questions about the impact of change on curricula, methods, and educational objectives. This will be especially true if the interdisciplinary orientation does make major advances in understanding change and developing marketing thought and particularly if it meets the profit criteria of business practice.

Marketing problems may be viewed as problems arising from the gratification of human wants and needs. As such, particular marketing activities become a part of the more general problem of raising the standard of living through satisfying the needs of human beings. Thus the discipline of marketing in this perspective is seen as an integral component of a broader science which encompasses man and his culture. If marketing men accept this fundamental proposition, then the task of the interdisciplinary approach becomes clearer. It becomes one of relating the findings of marketing theory and practice to the concept of man and his culture as it emerges from the integrated findings of the behavioral and social sciences. However, in accepting such a multi-dimensional approach, we must guard against the possible error of viewing human conduct as merely a passive adaptation to environmental conditions. It may be well to recall that from a management point of view, the job of the marketer is to stimulate the consumer to an action response compatible with marketing and corporate goals.

Marketing knowledge has been significantly advanced through management findings and through the materials of cost accounting, human relations, financial administration, and other business administration areas. It is likely that in the future these business administration areas will continue to be among the principal contributors to the interdisciplinary approach to marketing knowledge; yet their contributions in adding to marketing thought have been underplayed and possibly the role of nonbusiness disciplines overstated.

The treatment given to various subjects in an interdisciplinary consideration of marketing is uneven. The contributions and potential contributions of certain social science disciplines have often been ignored while those of other areas may have been over-emphasized. For example, recently much attention has been given to psychology through the application of motivation research, the use of various depth interviewing and projective techniques, and the development of the image concept. These psychological findings have made important contributions to the field of marketing. The point is that marketers may be overlooking other fertile areas, for example information theory, persuasion theory, communications, the contributions of demography, ecology, ethics, and spatial planning. It may well be that by directing attention to areas other than just psychology and sociology, greater contributions to marketing knowledge will accrue.

Marketers should remember that the interdisciplinary approach is a two-way street. Marketing is often considered only as a beneficiary of benefits heaped upon it by other sciences. Other sciences are viewed as discovery disciplines and marketing merely becomes an application discipline. But marketing can also be a discovery discipline. It can be a contributor to the interdisciplinary study of human behavior. Marketing can test and add to the theories and hypotheses of other sciences, thereby extending the dimensions and frontiers of knowledge. Similarly the interdisciplinary approach can add valuable perspectives and viewpoints to marketing knowledge. A more complete understanding of marketing behavior will be possible as this two-way approach is developed. What is required is an interdisciplinary approach to the study of marketing management rather than an interdisciplinary approach in lieu of marketing management.

In the last analysis, it is likely to be marketing men rather than pure behavioral scientists who will contribute most to the solution of tough marketing problems and the development of marketing thought. In the future, as in the past, the major advances in marketing knowledge probably will come from people who have a marketing background, who are immersed in the discipline, who have a marketing orientation, and who possess an intense professional interest in advancing science in marketing.

A current assessment of interdisciplinary contributions to marketing is offered. Indications are that advances in mathematics, statistics, computer science, systems engineering, and some functional areas of business administration have helped accelerate the interdisciplinary process. Not only is this process making a positive contribution to the advancement of science in marketing, but it is also becoming a reciprocal exercise in which marketing is making its own contributions to allied disciplines. Some problems inherent in the interdisciplinary approach are presented.

76. THE INTERDISCIPLINARY APPROACH TO MARKETING: A MANAGEMENT OVERVIEW*

William Lazer†

THE INTERDISCIPLINARY CONCEPT

To discuss the interdisciplinary approach with clarity, several related concepts should be examined, particularly transdisciplinary, multidisciplinary, and interdisciplinary. Transdisciplinary is the broadest concept. It

* An adaptation of a manuscript being published in a forthcoming book by Frank M. Bass, Charles W. King, and Edgar Pessemier, *Application of the Sciences in Marketing Management* (New York: John Wiley & Sons, Inc., 1967).

† Michigan State University.

refers to the crossing of discipline boundaries. Both the multidisciplinary and interdisciplinary approaches, by definition, therefore, are transdisciplinary. There is, however, considerable difference between their respective approaches.

The multidisciplinary approach uses stores of knowledge and viewpoints from many disciplines. It borrows concepts and techniques. It expands a discipline and provides greater understanding and problem-solving capability. But it tends to leave the general discipline boundaries more or less intact.

The interdisciplinary approach integrates concepts and ideas, restructures fields, changes subject-matter boundaries, and bridges theoretical gaps. It tends to develop more coherent and logical structure, more adequate theories, and leads to new concepts, techniques, and even subjects. It synthesizes concepts, findings, and ideas. Sometimes it even results in new disciplines. Often the interdisciplinary approach follows the multidisciplinary.

Since marketing problems have been studied by subject-matter specialists external to marketing—for example, psychologists and sociologists—marketing has long felt the impact of a multidisciplinary approach. Specialists, however, investigate marketing problems from the perspectives of their own particular disciplines. A useful overflow from one area to another often occurs, and disciplines are given new vitality, but they are not transmuted. Yet this very transfer of knowledge can challenge old categories and strain discipline boundaries.[1]

Marketing has borrowed from both the social and behavioral sciences. Initially, major contributions from the social sciences resulted in a heavy macroperspective. Later multidisciplinary contributions emphasized the behavioral sciences and a microemphasis. This is to be expected since "the twentieth century marks the coming-of-age of the behavioral sciences."[2]

The interdisciplinary approach requires a true federation of disciplines. It is not just a matter of borrowing among disciplines. It is concerned with the combination and integration of the endeavor of several specialized fields of study for the purpose of gaining marketing knowledge and solving marketing problems. The interdisciplinary approach offers tentative concepts, findings, postulates, working hypotheses, and methodology for the direction and organization of inquiry in marketing. It abandons reified categories of disciplines and tends to unify scientific inquiry.

The interdisciplinary approach, however, is not one unified ap-

---

[1] See William H. Ittelson, Martin Landow, and Harold Proshansky, "The Interdisciplinary Approach and the Concept of Behavioral Science," in Norman Washburne (ed.), *Decisions, Values, and Groups* (Interdisciplinary Research Conference, University of New Mexico, 1950), Vol. II, pp. 7–24.

[2] Bernard Berelson and Gary A. Steiner, *Human Behavior, an Inventory of Scientific Findings* (New York: Harcourt, Brace, and World, Inc., 1964), p. 11.

proach—rather it is many approaches. It is a loose coalition of perspectives, findings, and avenues. It can sometimes be a maze of conflicting hypotheses, findings, and ideas. This conflict, of course, can be challenging and desirable, and can lead to imaginative research.

In relating to other disciplines, marketing has drawn from four discipline groups.

1. Those that are directly allied to marketing. This includes microeconomics, management, organization theory, finance, and accounting. These disciplines investigate many marketing problems and subjects as part of their normal approach.
2. Those that study behavior, particularly human behavior such as psychology, sociology, and cultural anthropology.
3. Those that focus on broader societal issues and problems such as philosophy, political science, and macroeconomics.
4. Those that concentrate on tools and techniques. This includes mathematics, statistics, systems engineering, and computer science.

It is worth noting that an intradisciplinary approach has also been felt in marketing. It leads to the integration and blending of concepts, ideas, and findings within the marketing discipline itself. It is being spurred by the acceptance of a systems approach to marketing. For example, physical distribution, the result of a systems approach, integrates transportation, storing, warehousing, distribution, handling, sorting, and moving. Marketing intelligence results from an amalgamation of various subjects dealing with gathering, analyzing, interpreting, and using data. Marketing promotion refers to the coordination of all promotional aspects—advertising, personal selling, and publicity.

KINDS OF INTERDISCIPLINARY CONTRIBUTIONS

The interdisciplinary approach to marketing results in three kinds of contributions: those that are direct and immediate, those that are direct but potential, and the indirect and potential contributions.

Direct and immediate contributions refer to those concepts, ideas, and findings that can be applied directly by marketing. Included are various techniques of measurement, concepts such as life cycle, social stratification, and data including income and demographic data. They result in an immediate infusion of knowledge. We shall consider such contributions later.

Direct but potential contributions are those that seem to have direct carryover but require further research, development, or refinement. They constitute the bulk of the interdisciplinary contributions. For example, research on farm product innovations reveals that innovators and early adopters are more means-oriented, tend to be more secure as individuals, and have greater ability to deal with abstractions. Is this true for other product categories? Similarly, the following changes in values have been ascribed to our society:[3]

1. Less emphasis on personal values and more on group standards and welfare.
2. Increased positive evaluation of psychological criteria.
3. Receding of value on future success in favor of respectable and stable security.
4. Rise in value of aesthetic considerations.
5. Greater value placed on explicit values.

These changes seem to hold implications for marketing, but further research is required before the implications are fully understood.

Indirect potential contributions are those which are somewhat tangential but contain a glimmer of an idea, a concept, or suggest hypotheses that, with considerable work, may be useful. Resemblances, analogies, and identities often fall into this category. For instance, reasoning that marketing might be analyzed as a system, or seeking what correspondence the concepts of homeostasis, transaction, and transvection have in marketing, while indirect, at least initially, and requiring development, often proves useful. Hart's two laws of social change: (1) the Law of Cultural Acceleration, which states that the means for accomplishing purposes have increased at an accelerating rate; and (2) the Law of Logistic Surges, which explains that the logistics curve describes specific instances of cultural accumulation, are examples of indirect potential contributions. They are suggestive in developing and understanding product innovation and acceptance.[4] Similarly, diagramatic representation of ten theories of the direction of change have been offered. They seem to hold potential for developing marketing thought.[5]

CURRENT STATUS

What is the present status of the use of other disciplines in marketing? Marketing's use of other disciplines to date may best be characterized as multidisciplinary rather than interdisciplinary. Yet, marketing as an area of study is moving from the multidisciplinary to the interdisciplinary stage. This current multidisciplinary emphasis is the prelude to the adoption of a more integrated interdisciplinary orientation. As a result of the

[3] Clyde Kluckhohn, "Have There Been Discernible Shifts in American Values during the Past Generation?" in Elting E. Morrison (ed.), *The American Style* (New York: Harper & Bros., 1958), p. 204.

[4] Hornell Hart, "Social Theory and Social Change," in Llewellyn Gross (ed.), *Symposium on Sociological Theory* (Evanston, Ill.: Row-Peterson, 1959), p. 202.

[5] Wilbert E. Moore, *Social Change* (Englewood Cliffs, N.J.: Prentice-Hall, Inc., 1963), p. 38.

current stage of progress, throughout the rest of the paper I shall not distinguish the multidisciplinary from the interdisciplinary.

Cronbach's statement about the lack of integration of various psychological approaches is very appropriate for marketing. He states that if approaches are "kept independent, they can give only wrong answers or no answers at all regarding certain important problems."[6] For example, we cannot argue that marketing will deal with market forces and consumer behavior, while psychology will formulate the laws of motivation or change.

But the aim of the interdisciplinary approach should not be the cross-fertilization of ideas to unify the disciplines. Rather it should be the use of various tools and concepts to come to grips with marketing problems. It should offer a joint attack on common problems in marketing, using the contributions of various disciplines, rather than promise unification of all disciplines.

The lines of disciplines are blurring, and an integration and federation of some of them is occurring. It is becoming more difficult to differentiate parts of psychology and sociology from marketing, and vice versa. Will the disciplines be united into fewer and fewer subject-matter areas? Will the marketing boundaries vanish? The answer, I believe, is no. Several forces will hold the marketing discipline intact. Its problems, theories, and methods; its instructional involvement; its identification with functions that are most significant to business; and its meaning for competition and international development will insure that marketing will continue as a unit for teaching, research, and problem solving.

But the gaps among marketing and other areas will narrow. The tools will become similar. The concepts and ideas of many disciplines will continue to converge on marketing problems. More hybrid disciplines will emerge, and common concepts will evolve. Conceptual bridges between marketing and neighboring subject-matter areas will emerge. Marketing's relationship with other disciplines will change. It will become more reciprocal in nature.

Currently, there are shifts in environmental factors encouraging the convergence of the research effort from many disciplines on marketing factors. Psychology, for example, is now feeling the impact of automation and abundance, and the "area of psychological research interest tends to shift from the producer to the consumer . . . what is needed is an understanding of consumer behavior."[7] Such influences will buttress the interdisciplinary approach to marketing.

---

[6] Lee J. Cronbach, "The Two Disciplines of Scientific Psychology," *The American Psychologist*, Vol. 12, No. 11 (November, 1957), p. 673.

[7] Mason Haire, "Psychology and the Study of Business: Joint Behavioral Sciences," in Robert A. Dahl, Mason Haire, and Paul F. Lazarsfeld, *Social Science Research on Business Product and Potential* (New York: Columbia University Press, 1959), p. 54.

Interdisciplinary emphasis is affecting the development of marketing in yet another way. As the marketing discipline built on concepts from other disciplines, and as the field of marketing became established, specialization spread. Marketing as a discipline turned inward and became fractionalized. With the interdisciplinary approach, marketing has turned outward, and the result is more meaningful perspectives, new concepts and theories, improved techniques, and a more userul body of knowledge.

An investigation of marketing management practice and marketing thought reveals that a more rigorous and penetrating analysis of marketing and business has resulted from multidimensional approaches to the study of marketing. Consider the use of economic theory. Demand, a core marketing concept, is now analyzed in terms of dimensions that extend well beyond those of the initial economic boundaries. It is viewed in terms of motivation, perception, status, imagery, symbolism, communications networks, conformity, resistance to change, levels of aspiration, life cycle, life style, mobility, search and expectations. New questions are asked and new answers sought. Realistic involvement of many disciplines results. "A vast body of material which is potentially useful to marketing management exists in other disciplines."[8]

Kapp has noted that "the essential characteristics of society are those of structural interdependence. Social structure is primary, and from it all social inquiry must derive its basic scientific strategy."[9] In fact, some disciplines have been referred to as integrating disciplines. "For example, both anthropology and sociology are claimed to be 'integrating sciences,' the one taking 'culture' as the basic and integrating idea, and the other, 'social group or society.' "[10] Viewed from this perspective, marketing is an integrating discipline. Markets are among the core institutions of our society. Marketing is characteristically American and exerts basic influences on our life style, culture, wealth, production, and values.

Marketing provides a common conceptual framework for studying many problems that cross disciplinary lines. The very scope and dimension of marketing problems carry theorists and practitioners over discipline boundaries. Although the "point of departure and the focus of study differ among the disciplines . . . there are frequently great similarities between marketing and other disciplines in both methodology and content."[11]

The interdisciplinary approach confronts the empirical findings of marketing with the conceptual and theoretical formulations of other

[8] William Lazer and Eugene Kelley, "Interdisciplinary Contributions to Marketing Management," MTA Paper No. 5 (East Lansing: Michigan State University Bureau of Business and Economic Research, 1959), p. 1.

[9] K. W. Kapp, *Toward a Science of Man in Society* (Netherlands: Nijhoff, Heinman Imported Books, 1961), p. 203.

[10] Rollo Handy and Paul Kurtz, "A Current Appraisal of the Behavioral Sciences," (Great Barrington, Mass.: Behavioral Research Council, 1963), sec. 1, p. 9.

[11] Lazer and Kelley, MTA Paper No. 5, *op. cit.*, p. 6.

disciplines and vice versa. The result is that all confronted disciplines benefit. Marketing's direct and significant ties with economics and sociology are examples.

It seems that the most rapid period of progressive change in marketing is associated not with discoveries within the field but with the importation, borrowing, and diffusion of contributions outside marketing. In turn, however, these borrowed elements are changed in the assimilation process which results in new ideas and concepts.

In reality, marketing and its research are brought into existence to serve a purpose—a specific area of study. Yet as soon as marketing discovers ideas and information, it also serves other purposes and works with other subjects. As it does, it adds valuable dimensions and a wider purview to one's understanding of both marketing and related areas. Marketing problems are seen in many dimensions.

DISCIPLINE CONTRIBUTIONS EVALUATED

It is difficult to evaluate contributions of other disciplines to marketing. First, it is often impossible to classify contributions by disciplines because of the cross-fertilization that has taken place. People trained in one discipline work in another, and there is a tendency to select concepts, tools, and techniques from any discipline and modify and adapt them to solve marketing problems. Second, it is impossible to develop a rating scheme to evaluate objectively the overall contributions of various disciplines to marketing.

Yet, Table 1 presents an assessment about the nature of discipline contributions.

Disciplines are rated on the basis of whether they seem to have very limited application or perhaps undeveloped potential; whether they are useful in suggesting general approaches, or as framework knowledge; whether they provide useful tools, theories, or concepts; or whether they are being actively applied and shape marketing. These categories are imprecise and are not mutually exclusive nor collectively exhaustive. Ratings are subjective and represent one opinion at this point in time, but the general meaning of the ratings will be clear. Other researchers will have different opinions, and an interchange of ideas should be useful.

SPECIFIC USE OF RELATED DISCIPLINES

Table 2 is illustrative of the direct and specific use of various concepts or tools from other disciplines in marketing. It lists various marketing sectors, the specific decision area in which interdisciplinary concepts are used, the related discipline, and the concept or tool. Each of these contributions is keyed to a literature reference. The table is designed to be illustrative rather than comprehensive or definitive.

TABLE 1

AN EVALUATION OF INTERDISCIPLINARY ASSOCIATIONS AMONG NON-BUSINESS ADMINISTRATION DISCIPLINES AND MARKETING*

Area or Discipline	*Rating*						
	Limited or Undeveloped Potential		*Useful Perspectives and Approaches*		*Useful Techniques, Concepts, and Theories*		*Significant Applications*
Anthropology—social and cultural				***			
Anthropology—physical	***						
Biology		***					
Computer technology							***
Communications							***
Demography							***
Ecology					***		
Economics—international				***			
Economics—macro				***			
Economics—micro						***	
Econometrics				***			
Engineering—electrical			***				
Engineering—human				***			
Engineering—systems						***	
Esthetics			***				
Ethics				***			
Genetics		***					
Geography—economic				***			
History	***						
International relations			***				
Land economics			***				
Law					***		
Linguistics	***						
Mathematics						***	
Natural resources		***					
Operations research						***	
Philosophy of science				***			
Political science				***			
Psychiatry				***			
Psychology—behavioral							***
Psychology—clinical						***	
Psychology—Gestalt						***	
Psychology—personality					***		
Social psychology						***	
Sociology							***
Sociology—rural						***	
Statistics							***
Urban planning	***						

* It is extremely difficult to rate the overall contributions of disciplines to marketing. Moreover, the categories used are not mutually exclusive, and different researchers will arrive at different assessments. Yet some trends are evident from such ratings.

TABLE 2

SPECIFIC USE OF RELATED DISCIPLINES IN MARKETING MANAGEMENT

Marketing Sector	*Decision Area*	*Discipline*	*Concept or Tool*	*Literature Reference**
Market communication......	Personal influence, mass communication and adoption of innovation	Sociology	Two-step flow of communication, opinion leaders	1
	Communication and acceptance of innovation	Sociology	Trickle effect	2
	Communication of fashions	Sociology, statistics	Innovators, adoption theory, communication behavior	3
Retailing......	Choice of retail stores	Mathematics	Product-patronage matrix	4
	Store loyalty and promotional strategy	Psychology	Consumer panel	5
	Measurement of retail market position	Mathematics	Isolines	6
Pricing.......	Determining a pricing strategy	Statistics	Bayesian statistics	7
	Pricing	Psychology, economics	Sensitivity analysis	8
Branding......	Adjusting mature brands to changing markets	Sociology	Market segmentation and sequential purchasing behavior	9
	Brand and styles acceptance	Psychology	Tastes	10
Consumers and consumer behavior....	Advertising strategy and consumer behavior	Psychology	Dissonance and consumers	11
	Understanding consumer behavior	Psychology	Cognitive dissonance	12
	Consumer decisions	Psychology and social psychology	Risk taking and confidence	13
	Purchase influences	Sociology	Reference groups	14
	Determination of buying patterns	Sociology, economics	Life cycle	15
	Understanding consumer behavior	Sociology, economics	Life cycle, patterns, and elasticity of demand	16
	Status and consumer behavior	Psychology, sociology	Status	17
Allocating marketing effort.......	Determination of marketing strategies		Marketing mix	18
	Proper allocation of marketing resources	Accounting, management	Integrated information system	19
	Pretest and determination of market strategies	Mathematics, electrical engineering	Computer simulation	20

TABLE 2 (*continued*)

Marketing Sector	*Decision Area*	*Discipline*	*Concept or Tool*	*Literature Reference**
Allocating marketing effort.......	Determination of value of alternative plans	Operations research	Markov process	21
Market segmentation........	Expenditures by social class	Sociology	Social class position and mobility	22
	Tastes and purchase decisions	Sociology	High-, middle-, low-brow culture stratification of markets	23
	Segmentation of markets	Sociology, psychology	Segmentation analysis	24
	Consumption and social strata	Sociology	Social class stratification	25
	Market penetration and market segments	Sociology, psychology	Consumption systems	26
Sales effort....	Selling effort and purchase behavior	Psychology	Communication systems	27
	Selection of salesmen	Psychology	Empathy and ego drive	28
	Measuring sales effectiveness	Accounting, finance	Return on investment	29
Research and forecasting..	Predicting consumer attitudes	Economics	Habits, motives, expectations	30
	Determining expenditure for marketing research	Statistics	Bayesian statistics	31
	Allocations of R&D resources	Mathematics, computers	Simulation	32
	Predicting sales for new products	Mathematics	Markov process	33
	Forecasting sales	Statistics	Time series analysis	34
New product acceptance..	Market acceptance of new products	Sociology	Innovators, early and late adopters	35
	Determining acceptance of new products	Sociology	Mobility scales	36
	Encouraging product adoption	Law	Patents	37
Product line...	Adjusting product to consumer behavior	Anthropology	National character, subcultures, themes	38
	Elimination of weak products	Mathematics, electrical engineering	Product retention index, computer program	39
	Selection of new products	Accounting	Return on investment	40
	Use of information in product planning	Operations research	Sales information	41
Advertising strategy....	Pretest of advertising strategies	Communication, persuasion research	Differential attitude technique	42
	Effects of advertising and selling	Psychology	Subliminal impact	43
	Measuring cumulative advertising effects	Economics, statistics	Econometric model	44

TABLE 2 (*continued*)

Marketing Sector	*Decision Area*	*Discipline*	*Concept or Tool*	*Literature Reference**
Advertising strategy....	Selecting advertising strategies	Mathematics, psychology	Computer simulation	45
	Measuring advertising effectiveness	Mathematics	Probability transition matrix	46
	Selection of media decisions	Computer technology	Data breeder model	47
	Identifying advertising audiences	Sociology	Roster-reconstruction model	48

* See the corresponding numbered list of references which follows this table.

REFERENCES

1. "The Two-Step Flow of Communication: An Up-to-Date Report on an Hypothesis," Elihu Katz, *Public Opinion Quarterly*, Spring, 1957, pp. 61–78.

2. "A Note on the Trickle Effect," Lloyd A. Fallers, *Public Opinion Quarterly*, Fall, 1954, pp. 314–21.

3. "Communicating with the Innovator in the Fashion Adoption Process," Charles W. King in *Marketing and Economic Development*, ed. Peter D. Bennett (Washington, D.C.: Proceedings of the Fall Conference of the American Marketing Association, 1965), pp. 425–39.

4. "Retail Strategy and the Classification of Consumer Goods," Louis P. Bucklin, *Journal of Marketing*, January, 1963, p. 50.

5. "Store Loyalty as a Measure of Promotional Effectiveness of Supermarkets," Stanley J. Shapiro and Robert J. Colonna, *Business Horizons*, Vol. 7, No. 3 (1964), p. 67.

6. "Measuring Retail Market Penetration for a Discount Food Supermarket—A Case Study," William Applebaum, *Journal of Retailing*, Summer, 1965, p. 1.

7. "Bayesian Decision Theory in Pricing Strategy," Paul E. Green, *Journal of Marketing*, January, 1963, p. 5.

8. "Sense and Sensitivity in Pricing," Richard T. Sampson, *Harvard Business Review*, November, 1964, p. 99.

9. "Markets in Motion," Robert Mainer and Charles C. Slater, *Harvard Business Review*, March 1964, p. 64.

10. "The Learning of Tastes," Herbert E. Krugman and Eugene L. Hartley, *Public Opinion Quarterly*, Winter 1960.

11. "Are Automobile Purchasers Dissonant Consumers?" James F. Engle, *Journal of Marketing*, April, 1963, p. 55.

12. "Cognitive Dissonance and Consumer Behavior," Harold H. Kassarjian and Joel B. Cohen, *California Management Review*, Fall 1965, p. 55.

13. "Consumer Behavior on Risk Taking," Raymond A. Bauer, *Proceedings of the 43rd National Conference of the American Marketing Association*, ed. Robert S. Hanock (June 15–17, 1960), pp. 389–98.

14. "Group Influences in Marketing and Public Relations," Francis S.

Bourne in *Some Applications of Behavior Science Research*, ed. Rensis Likert and Samuel P. Hayes, Jr. (Paris: UNESCO, 1957), pp. 217–24.

15. "The Life Cycle and Buying Patterns," S. G. Barton in *Consumer Behavior*, ed. Lincoln H. Clark (New York University Press, 1955), Vol. II, p. 28.

16. "Life Cycle Analysis in Research on Consumer Behavior," Janet A. Fisher in *Consumer Behavior*, ed. Lincoln H. Clark (New York University Press, 1955), Vol. II, p. 28.

17. "Social Status and Consumer Behavior," Burleigh B. Gardner in *Consumer Behavior*, ed. Lincoln H. Clark (New York University Press, 1955), Vol. II, p. 53.

18. "Product Characteristics and Marketing Strategy," Gordon E. Miracle, *Journal of Marketing*, January, 1965, p. 18.

19. "How to Measure Marketing Performance," Richard A. Feder, *Harvard Business Review*, May, 1965, p. 132.

20. "Computer Simulation of Consumer Behavior," William D. Wells, *Harvard Business Review*, May, 1963, p. 93.

21. "Customer Behavior as a Markov Process," Jerome D. Herniter and John F. Magee, *Journal of Operations Research*, January–February, 1961, p. 105.

22. "Social Classes and Spending Behavior," Pierre Martineau, *Journal of Marketing*, October, 1958, p. 121.

23. *The Tastemakers*, Russell Lynes (New York: Harper & Bros., 1957).

24. "New Criteria for Market Segmentation," Daniel Yankelovich, *Harvard Business Review*, March, 1964, p. 83.

25. "The Significance of Social Stratification in Selling," Richard P. Coleman, *Proceedings of the 43rd National Conference of the American Marketing Association*, ed. Martin L. Bell (December, 1960), pp. 171–84.

26. "New Dimension in Consumer Analysis," Harper W. Boyd, Jr. and Sidney J. Levy, *Harvard Business Review*, November, 1963, p. 129.

27. "Relating the Selling Effort to Patterns of Purchase Behavior," Robert C. Brooks, Jr., *Business Topics*, Winter 1963, p. 73.

28. "What Makes a Good Salesman," David Mayer and Herbert M. Greensborg, *Harvard Business Review*, July, 1964, p. 119.

29. "The Use of ROI in Sales Management," Michael Schiff, *Journal of Marketing*, July, 1963, p. 70.

30. "The Predictive Value of Data on Consumer Attitudes," George Katona, *Consumer Behavior*, ed. Lincoln H. Clark (New York University Press, 1955), Vol. II, p. 66.

31. "Marketing Research Expenditures—A Decision Model," Frank M. Bass, *Journal of Business*, January, 1963, p. 77.

32. "A Probability Model for Early Prediction of New Product Market Success," William D. Barclay, *Journal of Marketing*, January, 1963, p. 63.

33. "Directing R&D for Profitable New-Product Development," Edgar A. Pessemier, pp. 279–87; and "Communicating with the Innovator in the Fashion Adoption Process," Charles W. King, pp. 425–39; both in *Marketing and Economic Development*, ed. Peter D. Bennett (Washington, D.C.: Proceedings of the Fall Conference of the American Marketing Association, 1965).

34. "The Breakthrough in Sales Forecasting," Robert L. McLoughlin, *Journal of Marketing*, April, 1963, p. 46.

35. "The Communications Process and Innovation," William Lazer and William E. Bell, *Journal of Advertising Research*, forthcoming issue.

36. "Behavioral Science Offers Fresh Insights on New Product Acceptance," Steven J. Shaw, *Journal of Marketing*, January, 1965, p. 9.

37. "Get Inventions Off the Shelf," Carl E. Barnes, *Harvard Business Review*, January, 1966, p. 138.

38. "Anthropology's Contributions to Marketing," Charles Winick, *Journal of Marketing*, July, 1961, p. 53.

39. "Phasing Out Weak Products," Philip Kotler, *Harvard Business Review*, 1965, p. 107.

40. "ROI for New-Product Policy," Philip A. Scheuble, Jr., *Harvard Business Review*, November, 1964, p. 110.

41. "An Operations Research Evaluation Technique of the Use of Sales-Research Information," George H. Chacko, *Journal of Operations Research*, May–June, 1959, p. 313.

42. "Pretesting Advertising with the Differential Attitude Technique," Harvey W. O'Neill, *Journal of Marketing*, January, 1963, p. 20.

43. "Motivation Research and Subliminal Advertising," Alvin W. Rose, *Social Research*, Autumn, 1958, pp. 271–84.

44. "The Measurement of Cumulative Advertising Effects," Kristian S. Palda, *Journal of Business*, April, 1965, p. 162.

45. "Mating Behavioral Science and Simulation," Raymond A. Bauer and Robert D. Buzzell, *Harvard Business Review*, September, 1964, p. 116.

46. "Measuring Advertising Effectiveness: Use of PTM," Irvin M. Grossack and Robert F. Kelly, *Business Horizons*, Vol. 6, No. 3 (1963), p. 83.

47. "Practical Media Decisions and the Computer," William T. Morgan, *Journal of Marketing*, July, 1963, p. 26.

48. "A Low-Cost Method for Identifying TV Audiences," Laurence Roslow and Sidney Roslow, *Journal of Marketing*, April, 1963, p. 13.

PROBLEMS IN USING THE INTERDISCIPLINARY APPROACH

The interdisciplinary approach could result in the misguided direction of research and problem-solving activities in marketing. First, attempts to manipulate the concepts, ideas, and findings of other disciplines to achieve unifying research results can lead to a neglect of marketing and its particular needs. Marketing activities may be shaped and structured to meet the dimensions, requirements, and constraints of other disciplines.

Second, although the problems, concepts, and findings of many disciplines have marketing relevance, the details, assumptions, and perspectives often vary. Researchers from other disciplines bring a different point of view, different training, and experience to a problem. Researchers and discipline specialists often make marketing and marketing problems correspond to their own background and interests rather than the reverse. In reality, common concepts have different operational meanings to each specialist.

Third, controversies exist within and between the disciplines, and they are hard to resolve. Behavioral and social scientists are not unified in their approaches, concepts, and findings; and bewilderment and confusion result. "For example, consider the important marketing subject area of motivation . . . rather than any one unified approach emerging, there are at least three major directions followed by psychologists pursuing motivation studies."[12] The integration of numerous conflicting explanations into practical solutions for marketing is a most perplexing task.

Fourth, marketers generally have tended to overstate the value of contributions of other areas. They have not evaluated situations realistically. The limitations of other areas are skirted or ignored. Consider, for example, the early reactions to motivation research or operations research. Marketing failed to examine and adjust the theories, concepts, and findings of other disciplines, and modify them in light of its own knowledge and intellectual insights. Marketing has failed in its search to sort the contributions, to order the directly useful, adjust and adapt the relevant, and discard the irrelevant.

Fifth, it is possible for the interdisciplinary approach to delay and even deter marketing developments. For instance, the uncritical application of stimulus–response theory, psychoanalytic tools, findings of "rat psychologists," or hypothetical economic models to marketing problems can lead to intellectual barrenness in various marketing areas. The concept of equilibrium, for instance, with its analog in the mechanical concept of forces and counterforces that reach a point of stability, has severe limitations when applied to energy and matter, or to the dynamic aspects of marketing.

Sixth, the results of an interdisciplinary approach are often qualified and indecisive. Sometimes they are theoretical and cannot stand up to the pragmatic demands of problem solving. The assumptions made by other disciplines are often unreal or too limiting. Many times the kinds of problems that can be handled best are often those that are not critical or which can be dealt with adequately at present.

Seventh, discipline specialists can only make a great contribution to marketing to the extent that we are able to communicate with and question them, and evaluate what they offer. Despite contiguous borders among disciplines, adequate communications are lacking. Jargon and terminology vary, and attempts to relate findings, theories, and constructs are usually very frustrating and ineffective. As specialization and compartmentalization increase and new hybrid disciplines evolve, communication tends to decrease.

Eighth, there are also a number of problems associated with getting

---

[12] Herta Herzog, "Behavioral Science Concepts for Analyzing the Consumer," paper given at the Conference of Marketing Teachers from Pacific Coast States (Berkeley: University of California, September 9, 1958).

people from other disciplines to concentrate on marketing. Included are the problems of loss of identification and stature in one's discipline and the loss of security inherent in tackling new concepts and ideas.

CONCLUDING OBSERVATIONS

The following are several statements about the interdisciplinary approach to marketing.

1. The development of marketing science is closely tied to the amenity of marketing to the methods and findings of other disciplines, particularly mathematics, statistics, and the behavioral sciences.
2. Marketing is now, and will continue to be, one of the major environmental factors influencing man in society. Since the consideration of man in his enviroment is one of the tasks that pervades social and behavioral sciences, marketing is a natural area of interdisciplinary convergence for understanding human relationships, and its interdisciplinary role will become increasingly important. It will become one of the sciences of society.
3. The interdisciplinary approach has had a profound effect in shaping marketing thought, ideas, and research effort. As a result of the interdisciplinary approach, curricula have been restructured, courses revised, and new marketing subject-matter areas developed. It has had a more modest but still important impact on marketing action.
4. The greatest and most lasting contribution of the interdisciplinary approach may be its influence on ways of conceptualizing, formulating, and thinking about marketing problems rather than providing marketing information and solutions for problems. The systems approach and functionalism are examples.
5. Most of the concepts, theories, hypotheses, and facts of other disciplines have only limited relevance for marketing. Marketing has failed to sift and sort in a systematic fashion the findings and concepts from other disciplines and to identify those that have direct importance for marketing. The result is that the interdisciplinary approach has not made the impact it could.
6. The successful injection of subject-matter specialists from other areas into marketing requires a rather unique individual. Competence in a behavioral, social, or quantitative discipline is not enough. People rooted in the marketing discipline, rather than behavioral or social scientists, or quantitative specialists, will contribute most to the future development of the marketing discipline.[13]
7. It is easier to use the concepts and approaches of other disciplines in a general way than it is to apply theories and findings to solve specific problems or to use specific data.
8. Much of the contribution of the interdisciplinary approach lies in

[13] Lazer and Kelley, MTA Paper No. 5, *op. cit.*, p. 31.

data, concepts, and theories that have marketing overtones but which must be developed further. The direct transference of concepts or findings from other disciplines to marketing is often not practicable. Adaptation and adjustment is required to integrate them into marketing thought. Marketing faces the challenge of determining the concepts, models, and theories required to solve its problems, which are not available in other disciplines, and developing them itself. Such contributions can in turn shape the related disciplines.

9. Marketing is an integrative subject-matter area. Marketing problems may be viewed from social, behavioral, and measuremental perspectives. Marketing is a fundamental economic activity. The result is that marketing can contribute actively to the development of other disciplines.

10. Among the most direct and significant contributions to marketing thought are those from other business administration areas.

11. As an economy matures, the marketing problems come to the forefront and their sociological and psychological dimensions become more important. The tools of economics, then, must be bolstered by those of other behavioral and social disciplines. Theory, adequate to the demands of marketing tasks, must be concerned with the political, economic, sociological, cultural, and psychological dimensions. The multidisciplinary and interdisciplinary movement is a natural development.

12. As a direct result of transdisciplinary efforts, some of the findings and theories of a variety of disciplines will eventually be integrated into theories of market action that will parallel those of social action.

The purpose of marketing theory is to order facts so that they facilitate the explanation, comprehension, and prediction of marketing phenomena. The development of marketing theory is shifting from descriptive factualism and classical behavioralism toward generalism and functionalism. Marketing theory and marketing science are inextricably intertwined. For marketing science to grow, major attention must be directed to constructing marketing theory. There is a need for marketing philosophers as well as for problem solvers, technicians, and empiricists.

77. SOME OBSERVATIONS ON THE 'STATE OF THE ART' OF MARKETING THEORY*

William Lazer†

Assessing the "state of the art" of marketing theory is at best a difficult task. Marketing theory is not a well-categorized and orderly collection of substantive ideas, concepts, hypotheses, and generalizations. It has not

* Reprinted from "Some Observations on the 'State of the Art' of Marketing Theory," *University of Washington Business Review*, Vol. XXIV, No. 3 (February, 1965), pp. 11–20. A partial theory relating to the movement of goods and information through the marketing system is presented in Wroe Alderson and Miles W. Martin, "Toward a Formal Theory of Transactions and Transvections," *Journal of Marketing Research*, Vol. II, No. 2 (May, 1965), pp. 117–27.

† Michigan State University.

EDITORS' NOTE: The question of whether marketing is an art or a science has been explored in several articles besides those in this book. These articles, arranged chronologically, include: Paul D. Converse, "The Development of the Science of Marketing —An Exploratory Survey," *Journal of Marketing*, Vol. X, No. 1 (July, 1945), pp. 14–23; Lyndon O. Brown, "Toward a Profession of Marketing," *Journal of Marketing*, Vol. XIII, No. 1 (July, 1948), pp. 27–31; Wroe Alderson and Reavis Cox, "Toward a Theory of Marketing," *Journal of Marketing*, Vol. XIII, No. 2 (October, 1948), pp. 137–52; Roland S. Vaile, "Toward a Theory of Marketing—A Comment," *Journal of Marketing*, Vol. XIII, No. 4 (April, 1949), pp. 520–22; Robert Bartels, "Can Marketing Be a Science?" *Journal of Marketing*, Vol. XV, No. 3 (January, 1951), pp. 319–28; Kenneth D. Hutchinson, "Marketing As a Science: An Appraisal," *Journal of Marketing*, Vol. XVI, No. 3 (January, 1952), pp. 286–93; W. J. Baumol, "On the Role of Marketing Theory," *Journal of Marketing*, Vol. XXI, No. 4 (April, 1957), pp.

resulted from orderly inquiry and development, nor has it provided a cumulative summation and framework of marketing knowledge. Rather, marketing theory is comprised of a haphazard array of research findings, published and unpublished manuscripts, philosophical constructs and speculations, and untested hypotheses from a wide variety of sources concerning a broad and complex spectrum of topics related to marketing.

Marketing theory has often been used by those interested in the more practical aspects of marketing to mean the opposite of factual, useful, or practical. Sometimes it is used to connote the lack of evidence, or unverified hypothetical speculation. ("That's all right in theory.") But marketing theory is not "pure" theory in the sense of being only hypothetical and philosophic. Rather it is applied theory.[1] It is concerned with reality, problem solving, policies, gaining factual information, and developing useful principles and bodies of knowledge. Marketing theory must have an empirical footing and be tested on a pragmatic basis.

The masterworks of marketing theory are not to be found in marketing textbooks. They are still to be developed. Marketing theory is not a heritage all laid out; it is a vital, viable, emerging area.

A good proportion of marketing literature is descriptive. The description of marketing activities and accumulation of observations, however, is important to marketing theory. It is only through the progress of specialized research, and the assembly of marketing facts and information, that marketing becomes recognized as a self-supporting subject matter entity, and marketing thought develops.[2]

Marketing thought, nevertheless, cannot proceed merely by the accumulation of observations unregulated by theory. Fruitful observations cannot be made, nor their results ordered and correlated, without the use

---

413–18; Joseph W. Newman, "New Insight, New Progress for Marketing," *Harvard Business Review*, Vol. XXXV, No. 6 (November–December, 1957), pp. 95–102; Alfred R. Oxenfeldt, "Scientific Marketing: Ideal and Ordeal," *Harvard Business Review*, Vol. XXXIX, No. 2 (March–April, 1961), pp. 51–64; Harlan D. Mills, "Marketing As a Science," *Harvard Business Review*, Vol. XXXIX, No. 5 (September–October, 1961), pp. 137–42; E. B. Weiss, "Will Marketing Ever Become a Science?" *Advertising Age*, Vol. XXXIII, No. 34 (August 20, 1962), pp. 64–65; Theodore N. Beckman, "A Challenge For a Reappraisal of the Basic Nature and Scope of Marketing," in William S. Decker (ed.), *Emerging Concepts in Marketing* (Proceedings, American Marketing Association, December, 1962), pp. 3–15; Robert D. Buzzell, "Is Marketing a Science?" *Harvard Business Review*, Vol. XLI, No. 1 (January–February, 1963), pp. 32ff; Charles E. Lee, "Measurement and the Development of Science and Marketing," *Journal of Marketing Research*, Vol. II, No. 1 (February, 1965), pp. 20–25; Weldon J. Taylor, "'Is Marketing a Science?' Revisited," *Journal of Marketing*, Vol. XXIX, No. 3 (July, 1965), pp. 49–53.

[1] E. T. Grether, "A Theoretical Approach to the Analysis of Marketing," *Theory in Marketing*, ed., Reavis Cox and Wroe Alderson (Homewood, Ill.: Richard D. Irwin, Inc., 1950), pp. 113–123 at p. 114.

[2] William Lazer, "Philosophic Aspects of the Marketing Discipline," *Managerial Marketing: Perspectives and Viewpoints*, William Lazer and Eugene J. Kelley, eds. (revised edition, August, 1962), pp. 606–612 at p. 610.

of hypotheses which go beyond the existing state of knowledge. The development of marketing theory does not merely require stockpiling of facts upon facts. Yet much of the current literature consists of isolated facts and findings, which relate to restricted areas of interest, changing subjects, and limited spans of time. The problem of deriving generalizations from the facts, and relating generalizations by higher-order conceptual schemes is a critical one for marketing theory.

I. PURPOSE AND REQUISITES OF MARKETING THEORY

Purpose

The major purpose of marketing theory is to order facts so they facilitate the explanation, comprehension, and prediction of marketing phenomena. Marketing theory is concerned with generating postulates and theorems from which implications can be derived; establishing laws and principles which summarize empirical investigations and explain facts; and developing general theories which formulate propositions about universals.

The development of marketing theory will require the organization and unification of findings, the synthesis of theoretical and practical constructs, and an emphasis on the value of a theoretical perspective. Marketing theory should summate findings and hypotheses in such related areas as consumer behavior, distribution channels, physical distribution, marketing planning, and the measurement of advertising effectiveness. It should systematize, integrate and relate marketing knowledge, and help provide a framework for analyzing and solving problems.

Practitioners in approaching marketing theory often expect to find direct answers to current problems—particularly research problems. When answers are not found, marketing theory is rejected as useless. However, the total purpose of marketing theory is not problem solving. A major function of marketing theory is to stimulate thought, and generate insight, understanding, hypotheses, and new theories.

The achievement of solutions, and the generation of information alone, are not enough to develop marketing science and to advance the marketing discipline. Abstractions as well as facts become important in explaining marketing phenomena.

Requisites

Two requisites for an adequate body of marketing theory are:

(1) The existence of an adequate and unified conceptual framework within which meaningful statements about marketing phenomena can be formulated. This refers to the synthesis of facts, the search for universals,

principles, laws and hypotheses, and the development of theories related to broad categories of marketing activity.

(2) The usefulness of these theoretical statements in explaining, interpreting and predicting marketing phenomena. This emphasizes the role of theory in understanding and solving marketing problems.

In general these criteria are not met, partly because marketing phenomena are intangible, vague and imperfectly observable. Much of the theoretical literature in marketing takes the form of descriptive, verbalistic essays, which lack clarity, precision, operational meaning, and verification, and which appeal to common sense intuitive understanding. Marketing is lacking in neat uniform theories derived from fundamental axioms, basic concepts, definitions, and theorems.

General Theories

General theories in marketing cannot be expected to provide theorems or principles that correspond exactly to specific research tasks. Marketing theory, however, should be expected to provide guides and directives for research and problem solving. It should serve as a point of reference for evaluating the significance and meaning of empirical evidence. It is not the province of marketing theory to state precisely what the impact of competitor A's ads will be when interacting with competitor B's ads. Rather, theory must focus on general questions, problems, and basic interpretations involving universals.

Questions have been raised in the literature about the necessity and possibility of developing a general theory of marketing. Many theorists seem to hold little promise for the development of a useful general theory of marketing. They seem to feel that because of the diversity and complexity of the subject matter, the large number of variables, and the dynamic nature of marketing phenomena, that rather than a general theory of marketing, a number of theories about specific aspects of marketing probably will be developed.

To date, we are a long way from a general system, or systems, of marketing theory. Much of the literature on marketing theory is comprised of imprecise, inoperable verbages. It is not comprised of axiomatic systems, hypothetical laws, principles, or theorems that can be tested. Many of the theoretical generalizations contained in the marketing literature seem to fall into the following categories:

(1) Tautologies, truisms, or overly general statements that are of very limited use in developing marketing science;
(2) Specific statements that apply to a particular or unique case only;
(3) Statements which are directly in the realm of another discipline tangential or contiguous to marketing, such as psychology, sociology, or anthropology.

II. CHANGING FOCUS OF MARKETING THEORY

Marketing theory is now in a period of transition. It is reflecting the legitimization of the marketing discipline which is progressing rapidly. The process of legitimization is evident in the increasing attention being directed to the societal aspects of marketing (marketing as the means of satisfying consumer wants and needs); the scientific methods of investigation that are being utilized; the basic models and paradigms that are being developed; and the concepts and theoretical findings from other disciplines that are being introduced.

Important Changes

Among the important changes occurring in the marketing discipline from the point of view of marketing theory are:

(1) Less reliance on the speculative, intuitive approach to marketing;
(2) The recognition and emancipation marketing is seeking as a science;
(3) The expansion of the concept of marketing from one of sales, or of institutions, to include marketing as a pervasive force in the firm as a whole, in our economic system and competitive environment, in our society, and in world affairs and markets;
(4) The de-emphasis of the introspective concern with description and classification;
(5) Concentration on marketing decision making, marketing planning, and marketing systems;
(6) Placement of marketing under the same rigorous methods as other scientific disciplines such as physics, chemistry, sociology, and psychology.

The decade of the 1920's has been labeled the "golden decade" in the development of marketing because of the integration, classification, refinement, and development of marketing thought, as well as the publication of principles textbooks.[3] For the development of marketing theory, however, the period since 1941, particularly the postwar years, have the greatest significance and the most relevance. Most of the major articles, books, and doctoral dissertations in the theory area have appeared since that time.

Two Extremes

Two extremes in the development of marketing theory seem to be suggested: descriptive factualism and generalism. Marketing theory seems to be moving away from the extreme end of descriptive factualism toward

[3] Robert Bartels, *The Development of Marketing Thought* (Homewood, Illinois: Richard D. Irwin, Inc., 1962), p. 174.

the development of general principles and theories. It also seems to be progressing from classical behavioralism which emphasized descriptive accounts of institutional behavior toward functionalism. The latter emphasizes the adjustive and adaptive aspects of behavior, the interaction and adjustment of the business with the external environment, and the linkage of marketing and corporate success with consumer behavior.

To a considerable extent, marketing theory has been rooted in descriptive empiricism and factualism, that in general seem to approach Bacon's process of simple enumeration. Facts have been stressed more than generalizations, principles or laws. Generalizations and theories are challenged on the basis of lack of correspondence with particular events in reality—the practical. Static descriptions, definitions, and categorization seem to be especially characteristic of the theoretical material prior to the war. Dynamic theories, quantitative models, and probabilistic reasoning have been introduced in the theoretical writings after the war.

Shift in Approach and Method

Marketing theory has witnessed a shift in both approach and method. There has been a shift from subjective intuitive approaches to objective, more formalized approaches to theory (models, mathematics, statistics); from the qualitative to the quantitative, even in "unlikely" areas, of attitudes, opinions, and motivations (scaling and projective techniques); from rigorous classifications to gradations and refinements; from classification to causation; from static to dynamic theories; from disjointed facts and descriptions to a search for generalizations, principles, theories, and laws; from surface analysis to depth investigations; from sheer speculation (which is necessary) to realism and more directly applicable concepts and theories.

III. MARKETING THEORY, MARKETING SCIENCE, AND MARKETING TECHNOLOGY

Marketing scientists and marketing technologists or clinicians differ in their emphasis. Theory building is one of the primary focuses of marketing scientists.[4] Problem solving is the major concern of the technologist or clinician. Yet, the domain of each is overlapping.

Marketing theory and marketing science are linked inextricably. Like marketing theory, marketing science is concerned with classified and systematized bodies of marketing knowledge that are organized around central theories, laws, principles, and concepts, which permit prediction (and sometimes control), and which often may be expressed in quantitative terms.

Marketing theory is the handmaiden of marketing science. It also is one

[4] For a discussion of marketing as a science see Robert Bartels, "Can Marketing Be a Science," *Journal of Marketing*, Vol. XV (January, 1951), pp. 319–328.

of the goals of marketing science. It is the goal of marketing science, since science tries to explain as much of reality as possible in the form of generalizations that permit prediction. Marketing theory, in fact, is validated by its capacity to predict marketing behavior and consequences under specified conditions. Its foundation is controlled observation of the real world and verifiable hypothetical speculations.

Marketing theorists and marketing technologists or clinicians have common tasks and concerns. As a result of technologists' research and problem solving activities, masses of facts have been accumulated about various aspects of marketing for specific companies, products, industries, and techniques. The marketing theorist needs more practical facts and knowledge upon which to base generalizations and test hypotheses and theories. The practitioner requires more orderly knowledge about marketing phenomena as guides to action and aids in prediction. This is not necessarily the case in other social or behavioral sciences.

For instance, in the field of learning theory, or perception, the psychologist tends to rely almost exclusively upon his experiments rather than checking the predictable consequences of conclusions by happenings in the real world. In marketing, however, it appears that experience and factual observations provide the major opportunities for theory construction. Marketing theory seems to be experientially, rather than experimentially based. Currently, some tendency toward the experimental may be noted.

Perhaps it is meaningful and helpful to distinguish two kinds of theory in marketing: scientific theory and clinical or technical theory. Scientific theories are concerned with the development of generalizations that link together unique and distinct theoretical formulations about marketing into more general theoretical constructs. Clinical or technical theories are those marketing theories that have prescription, or problem solving, as their major emphasis.

The distinction drawn is not absolute. However, it points up the direct linkage in marketing between the theoretical and the pragmatic. Both are necessary for a better understanding of marketing and the development of marketing theory and marketing science.

IV. LACK OF THEORETICAL EMPHASIS

Theory has been a neglected area of marketing. It has been neglected by both the academicians and practitioners. Facts and descriptions have been stressed. Emphasis has been given to what is, rather than to theoretical foundations of what is.

Lack of Theorists

Marketing unfortunately has never had theorists as have the fields of physics, mathematics, statistics, economics, and sociology. The latter disciplines accord the highest rating and stature to theoreticians. Theorists are usually recognized as masters of their professions—they are valued and esteemed. This is not the case in marketing. The practitioner, the technician, the researcher, and problem-solver, who implement techniques and concepts in practical situations, seem to receive the greatest acclaim in marketing. Theory tends to be skirted and ignored.

Institutions Neglect Theory Courses

The lack of theoretical emphasis in marketing, even in academic institutions, is readily evidenced. The Marketing Science Institute recently conducted a survey of marketing theory courses offered at the graduate level in schools of business. A survey was taken by mail of 181 graduate schools offering courses in marketing. They were asked about "marketing theory courses" offered and the books and periodicals used in the course. Of 153 responses received, only 24 course offerings in either marketing theory or the development of marketing thought were reported. Another 28 schools reported that they offered "some theory in their seminars and courses."

From the results of the survey it would appear that the desirability of offering "marketing theory courses" is recognized by graduate schools of business. The actual courses, however, have been neglected. Many of the answers received revealed a rather defensive attitude toward the lack of theory courses. A large proportion of the answers expressed the thought that, "while we don't have a course in marketing theory specifically, we cover theory in our courses on . . ."

The list of material used in courses described as "theory courses" ranged from basic textbooks and case books (hardly theoretical sources), to books on inventory control and readings in journals of related disciplines.

It is reasonable to expect that marketing as a discipline taught at the graduate level should emphasize theoretical content. A common core of concepts, generalizations, and areas of study might be anticipated. This, however, is not the case. Current perceptions of theoretical material are extremely varied. Common theoretical denominators for marketing theory courses seem to be lacking.

Interest in Theory Increases

Despite the lack of theoretical accomplishment in marketing, interest in theory seems to be increasing. Since 1950 greater emphasis has been given to books, monographs, and articles relating to marketing theory. Several doctoral dissertations have been written on the general subject of marketing theory. The informal, invitational Marketing Theory Seminar has recently received more than passing attention by marketing scholars. It appears that the long overdue recognition of the importance and necessity of developing marketing theory is at last emerging.

To date, however, the most theoretical aspects of marketing seem to be those areas most closely and directly related to economic theory. The constructs associated with demand analysis and pricing under various market conditions are examples. This is not unexpected since economics is the parent discipline of marketing. Marketing emerged at a time when the institutional approach to economics was developing and the fundamental and direct theoretical contributions of economics are still underscored. Increasingly, however, emphasis is being given to the contributions of disciplines other than economics to the development of marketing theory. They will become more significant in the future.

V. APPROACHES TO MARKETING THEORY

Marketing theory has no schools of thought to parallel those existing in other disciplines. For example, the marketing equivalent of Gestalt, Behavioral, or Clinical schools of psychology does not exist. The marketing literature contains no burning debates about the superiority of one approach, emphasis, or group of concepts to others. The closest approach to a school of thought in marketing is functionalism as developed by Alderson, which examines the way in which organized marketing groups function in the continuous adjustment to an operating environment.[5]

Interdisciplinary Approach

The interdisciplinary approach to marketing is receiving increasing attention and is shaping theoretical contributions.[6] It recognizes the theoretical and conceptual contributions of other disciplines in addition to economics. Both behavioral science and quantitative concepts are proving to be helpful in extending marketing theory. Concepts of social class, status, symbols, images, systems, and such quantitative models as linear programming, Markov process, and exponential smoothing are examples.

The interdisciplinary perspective broadens the theoretical horizons of marketing. It can offer classification and interchange of information and viewpoints, terms, concepts, findings, and hypotheses. By searching out and sifting common areas, findings are being fused, evidence accumulated, insights gained, and theoretical boundaries extended.

As the frontiers of marketing theory are pushed out they will permit

[5] Wroe Alderson, *Marketing Behavior and Executive Action* (Homewood, Illinois: Richard D. Irwin, Inc., 1957; and William J. Baumol, "On the Role of Marketing Theory," *Journal of Marketing*, Vol. XXI (April, 1957), pp. 413–418.

[6] For a discussion of the interdisciplinary approach to marketing see William Lazer and Eugene J. Kelley, "Interdisciplinary Contributions to Marketing Management," *Marketing and Transportation Paper No. 5,* Bureau of Business and Economic Research, Michigan State University, 1959.

increasing unification of marketing theory with other areas of theory. However, this will not result in a merging of disciplines at the conceptual level. Rather it is a matter of using the data and findings of disciplines for marketing insights. Marketing theory is supplemented by, but different from, sociological, psychological, and anthropological theory. Marketing has its own viewpoint and set of problems which circumscribe the parameters of marketing theory.

EARLY APPROACHES

Most of the early approaches to marketing theory were rather mechanistic in nature. Machine-type concepts and models that seem to parallel the concepts of classical mechanics were used. Various models of wholesale and retail institutions, selling formulas, pricing strategies, and advertising guides are examples. Recently, however, dynamic probabilistic concepts and techniques have been employed. The use of simulation, Markov models, game theory concepts, and Bayesian statistics are manifestations of a trend away from mechanistic approaches. Acceptance of probability concepts and approaches helps overcome criticism of the lack of exactness and the demand for complete correspondence between marketing theory and the real marketing world.

Quantitative and Behavioral Approaches

Quantitative and behavioral approaches seem to be accepted as superior to the more traditional or classical approaches in constructing marketing theory. All marketing activity, however, is not quantifiable, nor does it fit the present molds of behavioral science concepts and theories. Even the tautological generalizations and truisms, which make up a good portion of the theory literature in marketing references, are useful. Description and classification of marketing activities along classical lines is both necessary and valuable. The traditional marketing approaches should not be cast aside because they are classical; rather the framework presented should be enriched.

VI. CONCLUDING STATEMENTS

The exciting age in marketing theory is still to come. Marketing theorists are presently concerned with clarification, language, concepts, consolidation, and synthesis which may be a preview to a major attack on marketing theory. Unlike economics, psychology, and sociology, marketing has not felt the theoretical impact of a Keynes, Freud, or Parsons. However, a feeling of greater intellectual excitement about theoretical aspects of various areas of marketing seems to exist.

Marketing is a long way from the development of a general theory of marketing, or systems of general marketing theories. Theoretical frameworks for marketing findings are lacking and the emphasis has been on the pragmatic, action and factual areas. However, the need for marketing theory is more widely recognized and its importance to the marketing discipline and marketing science is better understood. The universals of marketing theory are not yet clearly identified. For marketing science to blossom, major attention must be directed at constructing marketing theory. The two are inextricably intertwined.

While definite schools of marketing thought do not exist, differences are evident in approaches and interpretations of marketing. The economic approach, the managerial approach, and the functional, institutional, and commodity approaches are examples. Relatively little controversy concerning approaches to marketing, assumptions, models, theoretical constructs, and analysis appears in the literature.

The marketing areas that seem to have the most substantial proportion of theoretical references, and cores of theoretical statements, are consumption and consumer behavior, and advertising. The former contains some of the most valuable theoretical marketing statements and insights. Research designed to develop more general theories about consumption and consumer behavior should prove to be fruitful.

The trend to the specialization of marketing activities and subject matter leads to two opposite theory forces. On the one hand, additional facts and insights are being gained about narrow spectra of the marketing domain which may prove useful for theory. On the other, advances in marketing theory require the perspective of the generalist—the development of higher-order generalizations and conceptual schemes.

Marketing theory has gone through a period of considerable concern with the use of scientific methodology in gathering factual evidence. A reaction may set in to assure increasing emphasis on hypothetical speculation and philosophic perspectives. The need for marketing philosophers as well as problem solvers, technicians, and empiricists is evident.

Marketing should be recognized as an inexact science with the associated problems of arriving at principles, theories, and laws. Marketing theories cannot be expected to provide theorems that fit specific research tasks exactly and provide optimal answers to specific problems. Rather, marketing theories should serve as guides and points of reference. The province of marketing theory is not problem solving alone. Marketing theory must stimulate thought, generate insights and ideas, and foster higher levels of conceptualization.

The interdisciplinary approach to the study of marketing centers mainly on the behavioral sciences, such as psychology and sociology. However, philosophy also can contribute significantly to the development of marketing theory. Philosophy can serve as a foundation and unifying force in the integration of marketing knowledge with other disciplines. It can also provide a frame of reference for evaluating the concepts and assumptions that underlie marketing thought.

78. PHILOSOPHIC ASPECTS OF THE MARKETING DISCIPLINE*

William Lazer†

"What one thinks about marketing depends largely upon the knowledge of it he has gained from first- and second-hand observation. How he thinks of it, on the other hand, depends also upon the understanding he has of other subjects."[1] A knowledge of related fields offers useful bases for the analysis of various aspects of marketing activity. Ideally a student of marketing should become a specialist in the area of marketing and a generalist in the subject-matter areas which are adjacent or tangential to marketing but promote a better understanding of marketing processes and market behavior. This is reflected in the interdisciplinary approach to the study of marketing activity.

We are on the verge of an explosion of useful knowledge. It has been estimated that during the next twenty-five years more additions will be made to knowledge than have been made in any previous century. Even at present the information accumulated about human action and the real world is far more extensive than marketing theory and practice reflect. As a result marketing faces and will continue to face a great challenge in

---

* Not previously published. For related discussions, see John W. Gardner, "The Ever-Renewing Society," *Saturday Review* (January 5, 1963), pp. 92–95; and Julian Huxley, "The Future of Man," *Bulletin of the Atomic Scientists* (December, 1959), pp. 402–4, 409.

† Michigan State University.

[1] Bartels, R. D. W., *Marketing Literature—Development and Appraisal,* Unpublished Doctoral Dissertation, The Ohio State University, Columbus, Ohio, 1941, p. 134.

trying to incorporate useful concepts, ideas, techniques, and information developed in related disciplines.

On the whole, marketing has scarcely utilized the rich sources of concepts available in other subject-matter areas. Yet experience has indicated that findings from related fields may be applied profitably. The results of an interdisciplinary approach to marketing have been a better understanding of human behavior in the market place and a more effective formulation and implementation of marketing decisions. Some contributions from related disciplines which have proven beneficial to policy makers are:[2]

a) Mathematics: effectiveness of advertising, efficient inventory control, location of warehouses and retail stores, forecasting sales.

b) Economic geography: store location, population projections, resource analysis, international trade.

c) Sociology: group behavior, shopping habits, use of leisure time, group characteristics and their influences on consumption.

d) Social psychology: mass communications, group influences, attitude measurement, dissemination of ideas, public opinion.

e) Psychology: motives, projective techniques, product symbols and images, resistance to change, acceptance of new products, creativity, advertising appeals, effects of color.

f) Ecology: adjustments by systems, growth and developments of suburbs and exurbs.

g) Social anthropology: social status and social systems.

h) Demography: population trends, predictions and shifts.

This paper is concerned with the possible usefulness of another field of study to marketing, the subject of philosophy, sometimes referred to as the science of the sciences.[3] Can a philosophic emphasis result in significant contributions which will aid in the development of the science of marketing? What has been or may be its function in the growth of marketing theory? It is with this general aspect of the interrelationship and possible usefulness of a philosophic approach that this paper is concerned.

---

[2] This is not intended as a complete list of either the related sciences or the respective findings. Moreover, there is no universal acceptance of clear-cut boundaries which denote unambiguously the subject matter content of the various sciences listed. Hence, it can be argued that the findings attributed by the author to one discipline are actually the province of another or that a broad science such as sociology embraces some of the other fields listed. This should not detract from the validity of the major point that various disciplines can contribute to marketing knowledge.

[3] While a universally accepted and unchanging definition of philosophy does not exist, in this paper the term is used in its widest and broadest sense of "a reflective and reasoned attempt to infer the character and content of the universe, taken in its entirety as a single whole for the observation and study of the data presented by all its aspects." See B. A. G. Fuller, *A History of Philosophy* (New York: Henry Holt and Co., 1945), p. 1.

CHANGES IN EMPHASIS OF PHILOSOPHIC STUDY

Philosophy is usually accorded a rather broad and encompassing province of knowledge. The concept of philosophy as the pursuit of knowledge, love of wisdom, or all-inclusive subject occupied with any and every department of knowledge rather than any specific aspect of it reflects philosophy's pervasiveness. The broad spectrum of knowledge encompassed results directly in a continuous change in the emphasis of philosophic study through time. "The changes of philosophy are all inherently bound up with problems that arise when new emphasis and new redistributions in the significance of values takes place."[4]

Some parallels exist between current developments in philosophic and marketing thought which suggest certain similarities of interest. At present, social science literature reflects the great interest of our times in science and scientific method. The scientific emphasis is evidenced both in marketing and in marketing practice. The growth and impact of marketing research courses, techniques and departments, and the utilization of the operations research techniques to solve marketing problems, all reflect the scientific approach. Likewise, a corresponding emphasis may be noted in contemporary philosophic study in which the philosophy of science occupies a prominent position. The journal, *Philosophy of Science*, often presents articles of interest to marketing theorists.

Currently, our society is concerned with the strategic functions of business executives and the impact and consequences of their decisions on society. Much attention is being directed to business decision making, and the social and ethical dimensions of business action rather than the purely economic. A similar development is occurring in the subject matter being investigated by modern philosophers. Some philosophers have now turned to a consideration of business problems. "In the insurance field, philosophers have been utilized to screen complex policies to see that the firm does not contradict itself. One of the major problems in industry, research, and government is the making of policy decisions . . . the philosopher in the special field of ethics . . . is able to explicitly identify goals and values and can help assess the available means for attaining those goals."[5]

Marketing executives are increasingly becoming interested in the use of computers and mathematical models and techniques as aids in making better marketing decisions. Philosophers, especially those trained as logicians, have been engaged in applying such operations research tools as simulations and waiting-line theory to solve business problems. Several principles of organization have been developed by a philosopher through

[4] John Dewey, *Encyclopaedia of the Social Sciences*, Vol. XII (New York: Macmillan Co., 1934), p. 121.

[5] Richard S. Rudner, as quoted in *Business Week*, September 7, 1957, p. 86.

the application of Boolean Algebra.[6] Philosophers have been employed in designing electronic computers and in programming instructions for these "brains," thereby extending management planning and control through more rapid and effective handling of information.

One of the major challenges facing our society in the immediate future will be that of solving our economic problems. The achievement of efficient marketing has been designated as the crux of these problems.[7] Thus, it is likely that one of the new emphases of philosophic study will be that of a more intensive examination of marketing thought and data in its various aspects.

Marketing academicians and practitioners may well ask what possible contributions philosophic thought has made, or may make, to the particular subject matter area of marketing. A philosophic approach can enhance marketing knowledge in four major ways:

1) It can provide the basis for a foundation and unifying force for marketing knowledge, thereby fostering the establishment and advancement of an independent science of marketing.

2) It can synthesize marketing and non-marketing information which will result in a more complete analysis and understanding of marketing activity.

3) It can evaluate the concepts and hypotheses underlying marketing thought, revealing inconsistencies, and creating a logical foundation for the promotion of sound marketing knowledge.

4) It can encourage and guide the development of theory in marketing and add new dimensions and directions to existing marketing thought.

A PHILOSOPHIC BASE FOR MARKETING

Philosophy has been considered as the ultimate science which deals with reality as a whole. In this role, philosophy may be viewed as one of the original and continuing sources of speculation about marketing reality. "There is, of course, nothing new or remarkable about philosophers speculating about matters of fact. Abhorring a vacuum, philosophers rush in where scientists fear to tread."[8] Philosophic study, then, serves as an important foundation for the development of a separate body of marketing knowledge and a formal marketing discipline. By concerning itself with the general facts and principles of reality, the study of philosophy

[6] R. S. Rudner, and R. J. Wolfson, "Constructional Framework For A Theory Of Organizational Decision Making," in *Values, Decisions, and Groups*, Norman Washburne, editor (London: Pergamon Press, 1962).

[7] Peter Drucker, *Automation—Forerunner of a Marketing Revolution?*, Proceedings of the Thirty-Seventh National Conference of the American Marketing Association (December, 1955), p. 38: "The great job is the development of a marketing system adequate to the mass market that has been created. I think that is probably the greatest, the most important and the most difficult of the new channels of our dynamic economy."

[8] May Broadbeck, "On the Philosophy of the Social Sciences," *Philosophy of Science*, Vol. 21, No. 2 (April, 1954), p. 141.

can foster and nurture the growth of marketing concepts and information.

It is only through the progress of specialized research and the assembly of marketing facts and information, however, that marketing becomes recognized as a self-supporting subject matter entity. Only recently has research into the specialized activities and institutions of marketing been conducted on a broad scale, and the subject of marketing clearly delineated from the realm of philosophical inquiry. Major advances have been made in achieving the stature of a particular science. As yet, however, the subject of marketing is still intertwined with philosophic speculation. Marketing has not attained the position of a totally independent science.

In the future, as the body of marketing thought and knowledge is advanced, marketing will furnish scientific data which may become the basis for further philosophic meditation. The province of philosophy will be extended by the particular science or discipline of marketing thereby reflecting the inherent marketing problems and climate and emphasis of the times. By analyzing, evaluating, and combining the marketing information received; identifying and alleviating logical contradictions and inconsistencies; and supplying new information, a philosophic approach can bring a wholeness and unity to marketing thought. As a foundation and unifying force, philosophy can spur the advancement of science in marketing.

INTEGRATING MARKETING FINDINGS

As independent sciences develop, investigation of the nature of the real world is parceled out to various separate subject matter areas, such as psychology, sociology, economics, and marketing. Then, a philosophical consideration of the character of the whole universe and a synthesis of the findings of specialized subject matter areas becomes a major force in furthering the thrust of marketing knowledge. It is well to remember that the value of the whole is often greater than the mere sum of its separate parts. So it is with the results of synthesizing the detailed knowledge of various specialized sciences with marketing or an interdisciplinary approach. The integrated whole is often of greater value than the knowledge of the separate independent sciences gained by specialists. Calder writes that, "Scientists are becoming intellectual cripples. By the excess of specialization forced upon them . . . they are so busy synthesizing nature they have no time to synthesize their own science. Science . . . has foresaken natural philosophy."[9]

Philosophic study, by coordinating the information and findings of other subject matter areas with those of marketing, can achieve a more comprehensive viewpoint and more complete body of marketing thought.

---

[9] Ritchie Calder, "The Fragmentation of Science," *The Advancement of Science* (December, 1955), p. 137.

Likewise, the relationships between marketing facts and the location of such facts in a broader interrelated context, supply a basis for the future development and direction of knowledge and theory.

EVALUATION OF BASIC MARKETING ASSUMPTIONS

Marketing, like other disciplines, is based on certain assumptions or pre-suppositions which form its framework or working hypotheses. Often these are not stated succinctly or precisely. A valuable service which can be performed by philosophic study is to submit these working concepts to a critical and rigorous analysis, and to evaluate their logical consistency and truth. Thus, areas of conflict can be indicated and the need for their revision advanced.

It is in this context of the relationship of marketing facts to the universe as a whole, rather than the considerations of facts themselves, that a contribution is rendered to the progress of marketing science. It is obvious that it is impossible to know the true nature of any marketing fact unless its relationship to the total system is known. "If science is not to degenerate into a medley of ad hoc hypotheses, it must become philosophical and must enter upon a thorough criticism of its own foundations."[10]

STIMULUS TO MARKETING THEORY

Marketing thought should not proceed merely by the accumulation of observations which are unregulated by theory. It is generally accepted that fruitful observations cannot be made, nor their results arranged and correlated, without the use of hypotheses which go beyond the existing state of knowledge. In extending and guiding the frontiers of marketing thought, there is a necessity for new comprehensive ideas and observations to replace those of the past. Important generative ideas of future scientific marketing import may first take shape in the speculative or philosophic form. Once these directive hypotheses are verified, they become a part of the accepted body of marketing beliefs.

A somewhat related contribution may be rendered to marketing by philosophic considerations which break from current orthodox concepts. It is conceivable that once scientific investigations in marketing become launched in a certain direction, they may take the accepted path and keep on moving in the same direction even though the results are not particularly fruitful. For the sake of progress, therefore, it is necessary that philosophic speculations be provided, which, though unorthodox, may channel thoughts to more profitable areas of inquiry.

Since a philosophic approach is not rooted in the details of the marketing process and is not limited by restrictive, specialized boundaries, it may

[10] A. N. Whitehead, *Science and the Modern World* (New York: The New American Library of World Literature, Inc., 1954), p. 18.

actually further the advancement of marketing thought. By freeing the imagination from a limited scope, it may bring new ideas and new directions to the attention of marketing specialists; hence, philosophic study may become a matrix within which marketing concepts are originated and developed. In this respect, the function and contributions of a philosophic emphasis, in the present and future development of marketing, assume important dimensions.

By acting as a foundation and unifying force, synthesizing marketing information with that of other disciplines, evaluating the basic assumptions of marketing, and fostering the development of marketing theory, philosophic study can play a significant part in furthering the development of science and thought in marketing. Since the status of any science depends on the nature of its generalizations and its method of investigation, as well as the subject matter, the potential contributions of a philosophic approach are basic ones. As John Dewey wrote, "There is an obvious reason why the affiliation of philosophy is more intimate in the case of the social sciences [and, hence, in marketing] rather than in that of the physical sciences, because the social sciences are more directly connected with the problems of policy which involve ends and purposes and thus value judgments."[11]

---

[11] John Dewey, *op. cit.*, p. 127.

Bibliography—Chapter VIII

ALDERSON, WROE. *Market Behavior and Executive Action.* Homewood, Ill.: Richard D. Irwin, Inc., 1957.

BARKER, CLARE WRIGHT, AND ANSHEN, MELVIN. *Modern Marketing.* New York: McGraw-Hill Book Co., Inc., 1939, pp. 10–11.

BARTELS, ROBERT. *The Development of Marketing Thought.* Homewood, Ill.: Richard D. Irwin, Inc., 1962.

BOWEN, HOWARD R. *Social Responsibilities of the Businessman.* New York: Harper & Bros., 1953, pp. 38–41, 228–29.

BUSKIRK, RICHARD H. *Principles of Marketing: The Management View.* New York: Holt, Rinehart & Winston, 1961, pp. 6–11, 592–93.

DEMOS, RAPHAEL. "Business and the Good Society," *Harvard Business Review,* Vol. XXXIII, No. 4 (July–August, 1955), pp. 33–43.

DOWD, LAURENCE P. "Social Responsibilities in Distribution," *Proceedings of the Winter Conference of the American Marketing Association,* 1961, pp. 204–9.

EELLS, RICHARD. *The Meaning of Modern Business.* New York: Columbia University Press, 1960, pp. 72–94.

———. "Social Responsibility—Can Business Survive the Challenge?," *Business Horizons,* Vol. II, No. 4 (Winter, 1959), pp. 33–41.

HALBERT, MICHAEL H. *The Meaning and Sources of Marketing Theory.* New York: McGraw-Hill Book Co., Inc., 1965.

HOWARD, JOHN A. *Marketing: Executive and Buyer Behavior.* New York: Columbia University Press, 1963.

SCHWARTZ, G. (ed.). *Science in Marketing.* New York: John Wiley & Sons, Inc., 1965.

TAYLOR, JOHN F. A. "Is the Corporation above the Law?" *Harvard Business Review,* Vol. XLIII, No. 2 (March–April, 1965), pp. 119–30.

Editorial Postscript: Horizons of Marketing Management and Education

The goals of higher education in marketing include the development of a disciplined approach to dynamic marketing problems, a capacity for analysis, and, most important, the motivation and ability for continuing intellectual growth in marketing and related fields. To assist readers in the achievement of these goals, a conceptual framework for the analysis of marketing management problems and of the major outlines of marketing management has been presented in this book. This analytical framework and the future orientation of the articles are designed to stimulate readers to think independently and creatively about current and emerging marketing problems and developments.

Two ideas which underlie the need for continuing professional development by all who aspire to understand marketing are emphasized: (1) the accelerating rate of knowledge accumulation; and (2) the interdisciplinary approach to the solution of marketing problems. Several selections in this book emphasize that marketing managers and scholars are confronted by rapidly changing environmental forces and an explosive development of usable knowledge. These forces and others—such as changing business needs and goals, the growing complexities of business, more rigorous competition, and increasing emphasis on research and innovation —influence both the practice and study of marketing.

The rate of knowledge accumulation in business administration, marketing, and the supporting fields will accelerate. Some believe that meeting the challenge of this change involves the solution of intellectual problems comparable in difficulty to those confronting education in the pure and applied sciences. Explanations for the current knowledge accumulation and its likely continuance are found in such frequently cited statements as: (1) we are spending more on research and development in the 60's than in all previous history; (2) in the next fifteen years scientists in all fields—including marketing—are likely to learn as much as they have in all previous history; and (3) we are currently increasing the world's fund of knowledge at the rate of 24 million published items a year.

Closer ties will develop between marketing and some nonmarketing subjects, as well as among the functional fields of business administration. Marketing managers will find it increasingly difficult to clearly distinguish between marketing and nonmarketing, between business and nonbusiness activities. The result of this interdisciplinary focus will be a better understanding of societal environments. The very foundations of business strategy are shaped by the environmental forces discussed in this book. The systems approach—with its emphasis on adjustment, survival, and growth—and the study of marketing as an input-output system reinforce the environmental perspective.

The accelerating rate of change means that it is easy for well-educated marketing students to become professionally obsolete in a few short years. The best insurance against obsolescence is individual commitment to the need for continuing study and professional growth. Indeed, to a greater degree than ever before, this commitment will be a prerequisite for success in the dynamic marketing environment of the future.

Any marketing curriculum provides only the foundation from which to continue self-education and development. Tomorrow's manager must continue to educate himself, and those with whom he works, if capabilities are to keep pace with the demands and opportunities of marketing.

The basic thrust of this book is influenced by systems theory. The systems approach is presented as an organizational orientation—as a way of studying marketing management problems. Systems analysis will continue to affect the development of the marketing management philosophy and the marketing concept. Both are, in fact, systems concepts. They emphasize the coordination and linkage of marketing elements to achieve a total system of business action.

Several of the concepts and ideas presented in this book have been restated and extended in summary form in this last chapter. The student or manager who has leadership as a goal must continue to study these themes and seek their integration. Each serious marketing student should develop an operational framework within which he can appraise and place marketing developments and opportunities as they relate to his special sphere of interests.

The Environmental System and Customer Orientation

Societies and markets of the world are in motion. Technological advances, increasing affluence, the population explosion and other forces are creating both the opportunity and necessity for innovation. Market and competitive pressures make the customer orientation vital to the survival and growth of a firm. Therefore, marketing managers must be environmentalists, anticipators of change, and creative innovators in order to meet market opportunities or threats.

It is easy to pay lip service to the "customer orientation" concept, but it is very difficult to achieve this orientation in practice. There is a subtle distinction between being "marketing oriented" and being "customer oriented." Customer orientation means the problem-solving focus is on customer needs and satisfactions first, then on marketing mix elements and the broader aspects of marketing policy. Customer orientation also means that the firm's research is not product or market bound but customer directed. It takes account of the fact that consumers throughout the world are in the midst of a life style-life space revolution. In the United States, for example, increased discretionary time, income and mobility are significantly changing not only life styles but also value systems. Time is becoming a critical consumption factor, and use utility is superseding the desire for ownership in many cases. Consumers are moving to new, higher levels on the hierarchy of needs. Leisure time activities and the "market of the mind" have become frontiers of market opportunity. Life style analysis provides a means of focusing on the values, consumption patterns and life space factors which must be considered in the formulation of market strategies.

The interdisciplinary approach to marketing provides a key to better identification and understanding of consumer characteristics, thus facilitating market segmentation and the development of product differentation. It has led to substantial advances in the development of quantitative and qualitative models of consumer behavior. Mathematical models, computer technology, simulation techniques and heuristic programming are improving the predictive ability of consumer behavior models. Increased emphasis upon the interdisciplinary approach to consumer understanding is expected to result in improved models for explaining and predicting consumer behavior.

Decision-Making Developments

Marketing decisions can be no better than the information, analytical techniques, and planning on which they are based. The generation of marketing managers now moving into positions of responsibility bring with them quantitative and behavioral backgrounds which promise improved problem-solving and predictive capabilities. The new decision technology offers possibilities of transforming data processing systems into marketing intelligence systems. As computerized real-time data processing systems and on-site input-output units grow in number and sophistication, decision information will improve greatly in quality and quantity. Computers will be assigned larger roles in processing marketing information and will contribute to improved quality in future marketing decisions.

Computers will not replace marketing managers, but properly used they will greatly increase productivity. At present, computer usage is typically at the routine data processing level in marketing. This stage is a prelude to a future when computer usage will center on extending the effectiveness of corporate decision making in nonroutine areas.

The increasing rate and magnitude of technological, economic, social and demographic change places new demands on the information and decision-making systems of the marketing organization. The revolution in information technology is providing marketing decision makers with new tools for diagnosis as well as prognosis. New tools and a firm's information system are ultimately evaluated in a business setting by their effectiveness and efficiency in contributing to better decisions.

Organizational Structure and the Marketing Mix

The term "ecosystem" describes an organization functionally linked to its environment through a pattern of dynamic interactions. The exchange process constitutes the dynamic interactions in a marketing ecosystem and is the core of the marketing concept. This ecosystem must permit adjustment to changing opportunities. In essence the most important managerial activity becomes the management of change. Marketing organizations must be developed which sense changing environmental opportunities and interpret them in terms of profitable corporate goals. As special knowledge is recognized as the key corporate resource, management of most organizations will bear an increasing resemblance to the management of a research and development activity. Since an expanding market does not insure corporate growth, greater attention will be given to programmed innovation to meet new needs and wants in the market place.

Marketing minded firms recognize that they are the creators and satisfiers of consumers, not producers of goods and services. They must change their marketing mixes to meet market opportunities. Consequently, the organization must become market oriented rather than production oriented. The result is that management of the marketing mix and its three submixes—the product and services mix, communications mix and distribution mix—is increasing in complexity. Environmental changes are forcing marketing managers to reevaluate old concepts and strategies in order to remain abreast of their competitors and technological developments. As values and life styles change, new external and internal organizational structures are formed which provide more effective linkage of companies with their environments.

International Marketing

The international perspective of marketing management is becoming commonplace; distinctions between domestic and international business are blurring. In the future many marketing managers will routinely assess market opportunities and perform other managerial functions across national and international boundaries.

The importance of international marketing will continue to increase as the forces which contribute to global economic development grow stronger. These forces include the emergence of world trading blocs such as the European Economic Community, the industrialization and increasing wealth of the "emerging" nations, the world-wide revolution of rising expectations and aspiration levels, growing world population, and significant technological advances in transportation. To the extent that countries recognize the economic necessity for lowering political barriers to world trade, marketing can and will become internationalized.

Marketing occupies a key position as one of the most effective "engines" of economic development. Viewed as a social process, international marketing emerges as a critical factor in satisfying the needs and wants of the world's societies and as a major formative force in both emerging and mature nations.

The difference between international marketing and domestic marketing lies not in techniques and tools but rather in perspectives and in the environments encountered. Divergent economic, political and social systems require new evaluations and new interpretations of marketing variables. The interdisciplinary approach can provide a comprehensive framework for the formulation of international marketing objectives, mixes and organizations.

Societal Aspects of Marketing

The evolution of the market process has been governed by the dictates of consumer satisfaction, profit optimization, and governmental control. During this evolution the market process has developed into one of the controlling factors of socioeconomic growth, a social instrument through which a standard of living is transmitted to society, and an area of increasing concern to public policy makers.

In recent years a broader view of the social responsibility of the firm has arisen. There is increasing concern with values, ethical issues and the societal dimensions of marketing. Marketing is being viewed not only as a business function or as a philosophy of business operation, but also as a social process. In the future, more attention will be given to marketing's fundamental role in understanding and influencing demand, competition and innovation.

The market process as a formative force in our culture carries a concomitant social responsibility. It has dimensions that extend beyond the profit motive. Marketing must be committed to consumer protection as well as consumer satisfaction, to value optimization by society as well as profit optimization by the firm. The acceptance of these social responsibilities by the firm will become an increasingly significant factor in the preservation of our market system.

Education for Marketing

The area of marketing education should be considered in any future-oriented discussion of marketing.[1] Marketing as a discipline involves intellectual problems of a high order of educational and social importance. Because of its social significance, marketing is an area of major importance in the modern institution of higher learning. University courses and curricula should reflect and lend direction to the changing needs of society. The modern university is the laboratory of society, and modern education should have its focus in the world of reality. Students in all areas of specialization should be familiar with marketing as a social process. Graduates of professional schools are concerned with intellect, values, ethics, esthetics, and important ideas of the times. Business administration courses, including those in the marketing sector, can be as broadly intellectual, educational, and challenging as those of any other discipline.

Our society is not faced with the question of whether there should or should not be university education in marketing. Such a question evades the realistic issues. We shall have marketing education on both the undergraduate and graduate levels. Moreover, the numbers educated will continue to expand. The real questions confronting executives and teachers are what forms marketing education of the future should take and what forms it will take.

Marketing's role in society, as it has been portrayed in this book, is a more formative factor than university curricula now reflect. Marketing is a dynamic social process of direct relevance to many other university curricula. It is a major and distinguishing characteristic of American business. Marketing knowledge and technology are being studied and adapted on a global basis within the context of various economic systems. An understanding of marketing is, in fact, essential to develop a thorough comprehension of our economic system, our way of business life, and indeed our very life style.

The marketing discipline itself is in a state of flux. It is not a mature discipline with a well-established body of information, theories, and principles that have been shaped and structured and institutionalized through centuries of university affiliation. Rather, marketing is a discipline and

---

[1] William Lazer, "Changing Trends in the Body of Knowledge in Marketing," *Proceedings of the 47th Annual Meeting of The American Association of Collegiate Schools of Business*, 1965, pp. 67–79. This last section is based on this address.

For a discussion of some implications of the growing rate of knowledge accumulation for marketing educators, see William Lazer, "Education for Marketing in the 1970's," *Journal of Marketing*, Vol. 30, No. 3 (July, 1966), pp. 33–37; Eugene J. Kelley, "Planning Curriculum Changes for a Maturing Marketing Discipline," *Proceedings of the Winter Conference of the American Marketing Association*, 1960, pp. 251–58; and Eugene J. Kelley, "Business Subjects in the Doctoral Program," *Proceedings of the Winter Conference of the American Marketing Association*, 1961, pp. 347–56.

phenomenon of our century and of the American culture. As a field of study it is very young.

The marketing curriculum or approach of any one school either now or in the future will not be superior to all others. Although desirable goals in marketing education have been identified rather clearly, the means of achieving them will vary. It is unrealistic to expect all business schools to offer the same marketing curriculum. No one superior model exists, and educational strength is rooted in diversity.

Marketing education need not produce narrow, specialized, uneducated graduates. True professionalism requires both specialization and breadth in education. Marketing as a professional area must have educational objectives that are broader than job requirements. This requires striking a delicate and rather difficult balance between general education and professional competence, between broad preparation for life and more specialized professional education. Knowledge gained from the liberal arts and the sciences is valuable for marketing students. Yet it is not a substitute for education in marketing. General education furnishes a broad base on which marketing can build. However, the converse is also true. Knowledge of marketing is of great value to students in various scientific areas. This is not widely recognized nor accepted yet.

The discipline of marketing may be entering a new stage of development. There is a clear trend away from the study of current practice to emphasis on the sciences underlying marketing, away from primary concern with immediate considerations to greater attention to the scientific, theoretical, intellectual and social content of marketing. This trend is likely to continue and will probably result in new incentives and opportunity for the extension of marketing's frontiers and for the relating of marketing to other disciplines. It now seems likely that marketing is on the verge of significant breakthroughs along a number of fronts. It is also likely that advances in marketing education and practice will add significant knowledge to other disciplines.

INDEXES

NAME INDEX

SUBJECT INDEX

J

L

P

This book has been set on the linotype in 10 and 9 point Janson, leaded 2 points. Chapter numbers are in 48 point Lydian and chapter titles, 24 point Lydian. The size of the type page is 27 by 47 picas.